Lawrenceville Press

A Guide to Microsoft® Office XP Professional

for Windows®

Bruce Presley
Beth Brown
Elaine Malfas
Jan Marrelli

All orders including educational, Canadian, foreign, FPO, and APO may be placed by contacting:

Lawrenceville Press, Inc.
P.O. Box 704
Pennington, NJ 08534-0704
(609) 737-1148
(609) 737-8564 fax

This text is available in hardcover and softcover editions.

16 15 14 13 12 11 10 9 8 7 6 5 4 3 2 1

W̲e believe the best way to introduce students to computing is with an applications course that gives them considerable "hands-on" computer experience. This objective is best accomplished with an applications suite such as Microsoft Office, which has features for integrating data between the word processor, spreadsheet, database, and presentation applications. A well-rounded applications course should include discussions on e-mail, the Internet, personal management applications such as Outlook, the roles computers play in modern society, and a brief history of computers. Learning the vocabulary of computing is also important. These goals are accomplished by this text. The emphasis of this text is on the concepts of computing and problem-solving so that students learn how computer applications can be applied to a wide range of problems. The text is written to be used either in a one or two term course by students with little or no previous computer experience.

A Guide to Microsoft Office XP Professional

Our applications texts have established Lawrenceville Press as a leader in the field of educational textbook publishing, with more than two million students having been introduced to computing using our "hands-on" approach. With this text, we have made significant improvements to our approach based on the many comments we received, a survey of instructors, and our own classroom experiences.

This text presents Outlook, Word, Excel, Access, and PowerPoint, written in a style appropriate for students at a variety of levels. The integration of data between applications is covered in two chapters. Outlook is discussed in two chapters as well. Other chapters introduce PowerPoint, history of computers, networks and the Internet, telecommunications, and computer careers.

A Guide to Microsoft Office XP Professional is available in hardcover and softcover editions. The softcover edition has a sewn lay-flat binding, which keeps the text open at any page and gives the book additional strength.

Design and Features

Format   Each chapter contains numerous examples and screen captures to help students visualize new concepts. Commands are listed on the first page of each chapter. Menus and buttons are displayed in the margins for easy reference.

Expectations   An outline of the significant topics that will be covered is presented at the beginning of each chapter.

Sidebars   Additional topics that complement the text are in boxes in the margin.

Hands-on Practices   Concepts are presented, discussed, and then followed by a "hands-on" practice that requires the student to test newly learned skills using the computer. The practices also serve as excellent reference guides to review commands. Answers to all the practices are included in the *Teacher's Resource Package*.

Chapter Summaries   Each chapter concludes with a summary that briefly discusses the concepts covered in the chapter.

Vocabulary Sections   At the end of each chapter is a list of new terms and definitions and a list of Office commands and buttons.

Review Questions   Numerous review questions are keyed to each section of a chapter, providing immediate reinforcement of new concepts. Answers to all review questions are included in the *Teacher's Resource Package*.

Exercises   Chapters 2 through 17 each include a set of exercises of varying difficulty, making it appropriate for students with a wide range of abilities. Answers to all exercises are included in the *Teacher's Resource Package*.

Networks, the Internet, and Computer History   Chapter 1 includes a brief history of computers, computer network concepts, an introduction to the Internet, and telecommuting. Netiquette is also discussed.

Outlook   Chapter 2 introduces Outlook for personal time management. Chapter 3 explains the features of Outlook related to e-mail. E-mail etiquette is also discussed.

Computer-Related Careers   It is hoped that many students will become interested in knowing more about computer careers based upon their experience in this course. Chapter 1 outlines careers related to different aspects of computer use.

Appendices   Using Microsoft Office help, Office keyboard shortcuts, functions, and creating and editing forms and reports in Design view are presented in appendices at the end of the text.

Teacher's Resource Package

When used with this text, the Lawrenceville Press *Teacher's Resource Package* provides all the additional material required to offer students an excellent introductory computer applications course. These materials place a strong emphasis on developing the student's problem-solving skills. The Package contains the following features that correspond to each of the chapters in the text:

- **Assignments** Suggested reading and problem assignments.

- **Teaching Notes** Helpful information that we and our reviewers have learned from classroom experience.

- **Discussion Topics** Additional material that supplements the text and can be used in leading classroom discussions.

- **Worksheets** Problems that supplement the exercises in the text by providing additional reinforcement of concepts.

- **Critical Thinking Worksheets** Thought-provoking written-response questions keyed to concepts practiced in the text.

- **Quizzes** A short quiz that tests recently learned skills.

- **Tests** A test for each chapter as well as a midterm and final examination. Each test consists of completion, multiple choice, and true/false questions and "hands-on" problems that are solved using the computer. Additional tests can be created using the **Exam***View*® test generator program included on CD.

- **Review Question answers** Printed answers for the review questions presented in the text.

CDs included with the Package contain the following:

- **Data files** All files the student needs to complete the practices and exercises in the text, as well as the files needed to complete the worksheets, quizzes, and tests in the Package.

- **Exam***View*® **Test Generator Program** Test question banks and the popular **Exam***View*® software are included so that multiple tests can be created for each chapter.

- **Answer files** Answers to the practices, exercises, worksheets, quizzes, and tests.

Student data diskettes that contain the files needed to complete the practices and exercises can easily be made by following the directions in the Teacher's Resource Package Introduction. Student CDs are also available for purchase in packs of 10.

As an added feature, the Package is contained in a 3-ring binder. This not only enables pages to be removed for duplication, but also allows the instructor to keep notes in the Package.

Acknowledgments

The authors are especially grateful to the many instructors and their students who classroom test our texts as they are being written. Their comments and suggestions have been invaluable.

The success of this and many of our other texts is due to the efforts of Heidi Crane, Vice President of Marketing at Lawrenceville Press. She has developed the promotional material which has been so well received by instructors around the world, and coordinated the comprehensive customer survey which led to many of the features in this edition. Joseph

DuPree and Christina Albanesius run our Customer Relations Department and handle the thousands of orders we receive in a friendly and efficient manner. Richard Guarascio and Michael Porter are responsible for the excellent service Lawrenceville Press offers in shipping orders.

We thank John Olivari of Courier Book Companies, Inc. who supervised the printing of this text. The line drawings were created by John Gandour.

We also thank Nanette Hert, computer science teacher at Saint Andrew's School, for all her input on this text. She has edited the text for accuracy and contributed to other aspects of development.

Finally, we would like to thank our students, for whom and with whom this text was written. Their candid evaluation of each lesson and their refusal to accept anything less than perfect clarity in explanation have been the driving force behind the creation of *A Guide to Microsoft Office XP Professional*.

About the Authors

Bruce W. Presley, a graduate of Yale University, taught computer science and physics at The Lawrenceville School in Lawrenceville, New Jersey for twenty-four years where he served as the director of the Karl Corby Computer and Mathematics Center. Mr. Presley was a member of the founding committee of the Advanced Placement Computer Science examination and served as a consultant to the College Entrance Examination Board. Author of more than thirty computer texts, Mr. Presley is president of Lawrenceville Press.

Beth A. Brown, a Computer Science graduate of Florida Atlantic University, is director of development at Lawrenceville Press where she has coauthored a number of applications and programming texts and their accompanying Teacher's Resource Packages. She has taught computer applications and programming at the high school level.

Elaine Malfas is a graduate of Hartwick College and earned her M.S. degree in Technical Communication from Rensselaer Polytechnic Institute. Ms. Malfas has coauthored several computer texts and their accompanying Teacher's Resource Packages. She has taught computer applications and desktop publishing at the high school level.

Jan Marrelli has a Bachelor of Science in Business Administration from Lake Superior State University and a Bachelor of Education from the University of Western Ontario. She has been a Business Coordinator and taught computer applications and programming for the Algoma District School Board as well as participating in curriculum development and assessment projects for the Ontario Ministry of Education.

Table of Contents

Chapter 1
Introducing the Computer

Chapter 2
Introducing Outlook

Chapter 3
Advanced Outlook Features and E-mail

Chapter 4
Introducing the Word Processor

Chapter 5
Formatting Documents

Chapter 6
Word Processor Features

Chapter 7
Advanced Word Processor Features

Chapter 8
Introducing the Spreadsheet

Chapter 9
Spreadsheet Techniques

Chapter 10
Worksheets and Charts

Chapter 11
Advanced Spreadsheet Techniques

Chapter 12
Integrating Data Between Word and Excel

Chapter 13
Introducing the Relational Database

Chapter 14
Relational Database Techniques

Chapter 15
Relational Database Reports and Advanced Database Techniques

Chapter 16
Integrating Data Between Access, Word, and Excel

Chapter 17
PowerPoint Presentations

Appendix A
Using Microsoft Office Help

Appendix B
Functions and Keyboard Shortcuts

Appendix C
Creating Customized Forms and Reports

Introducing the Computer

Chapter 1 Expectations

After completing this chapter you will be able to:

1. Discuss the history of computers.
2. Differentiate between the four generations of computers.
3. Describe the components of a personal computer.
4. Understand how computers work.
5. Define hardware and software.
6. Describe common storage and peripheral devices.
7. Describe network classifications and LAN topologies.
8. Differentiate between various types of transmission media.
9. Apply netiquette when using a network.
10. Describe the Internet and Internet services including the World Wide Web.
11. Understand telecommunications.
12. Discuss ethical issues associated with computers.
13. Identify computer-related careers.

This chapter discusses the history of computers and how computers process and store data. Networks and important social and ethical issues relating to computers are also discussed.

1.1 Mechanical Devices

Pascaline

One of the earliest mechanical calculating devices was the *Pascaline*, invented in 1642 by the French philosopher and mathematician Blaise Pascal. The Pascaline was a complicated set of gears that operated similarly to a clock. It was designed to only perform addition. Unfortunately, due to manufacturing problems, Pascal never got the device to work properly.

Blaise Pascal
1623 – 1662

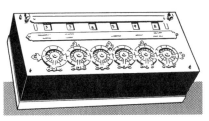

The Pascaline was a mechanical calculating device invented by Blaise Pascal in 1642

Stepped Reckoner

Later in the 17th century Gottfried Wilhelm von Leibniz, a famous mathematician, invented a device that was supposed to be able to add and subtract, as well as multiply, divide, and calculate square roots. His device, the *Stepped Reckoner*, included a cylindrical wheel called the *Leibniz wheel* and a moveable carriage that was used to enter the number of digits in the multiplicand. However, because of mechanically unreliable parts, the device tended to jam and malfunction.

Gottfried Wilhelm von Leibniz
1646 – 1716

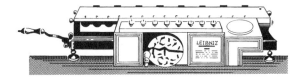

The Stepped Reckoner was another early attempt at creating a mechanical calculating device

Difference Engine

In 1822 Charles Babbage began work on the *Difference Engine*. His hope was that this device would calculate numbers to the 20ᵗʰ place and then print them at 44 digits per minute. The original purpose of this machine was to produce tables of numbers that would be used by ships' navigators. At the time, navigation tables were often highly inaccurate due to calculation errors. In fact, a number of ships were known to have been lost at sea because of these errors. Although never built, the ideas for the Difference Engine led to the design of Babbage's Analytical Engine.

Analytical Engine

The *Analytical Engine*, designed around 1833, was supposed to perform a variety of calculations by following a set of instructions, or program, stored on punched cards. During processing, the Analytical Engine was planned to store information in a memory unit that would allow it to make decisions and then carry out instructions based on those decisions. For example, when comparing two numbers, it could be programmed to determine which was larger and then follow an appropriate set of instructions. The Analytical Engine was also never built, but its design served as a model for the modern computer.

The History of Punched Cards

Punched cards were originally used to provide instructions for weaving looms. In 1810 Joseph Jacquard, a French weaver, placed punched cards in his looms so that as the cards passed through the loom in sequence, needles passed through the holes and picked up threads of the correct color or texture.

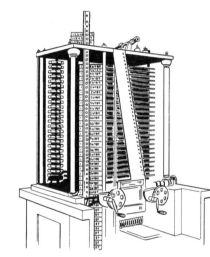

Babbage's Analytical Engine was designed as a calculating machine that used punched cards to store information

*Charles Babbage
1792 – 1871*

Babbage's chief collaborator on the Analytical Engine was Ada Byron, Countess of Lovelace, the daughter of Lord Byron. Interested in mathematics, Lady Byron was a sponsor of the Analytical Engine and one of the first people to realize its power and significance. She also wrote of its achievements in order to gain support for it. Ada Byron is often called the first programmer because she wrote a program based on the design of the Analytical Engine.

Babbage had hoped that the Analytical Engine would be able to think. Ada Byron, however, said that the Engine could never "originate anything," meaning that she did not believe that a machine, no matter how powerful, could think. To this day her statement about computing machines remains true.

*Ada Byron
1815 – 1852*

1.2 Electro-Mechanical Devices

By the end of the 19th century, U.S. Census officials were concerned about the time it took to tabulate the continuously increasing number of Americans. This counting was done every 10 years, as required by the Constitution. However, the Census of 1880 took nine years to compile which made the figures out of date by the time they were published.

Hollerith's tabulating machine

In response to a contest sponsored by the U.S. Census Bureau, Herman Hollerith invented a tabulating machine that used electricity rather than mechanical gears. Holes representing information to be tabulated were punched in cards, with the location of each hole representing a specific piece of information (male, female, age, etc.). The cards were then inserted into the machine and metal pins used to open and close electrical circuits. If a circuit was closed, a counter was increased by one.

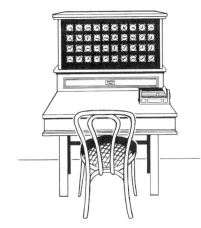

Herman Hollerith's tabulating machine, invented for the Census of 1890, used electricity instead of gears to perform calculations

Herman Hollerith
1860 – 1929

Based on the success of his tabulating machine, Herman Hollerith started the Tabulating Machine Company in 1896. In 1924, the company was taken over by International Business Machines (IBM).

Hollerith's machine was immensely successful. The general count of the population, then 63 million, took only six weeks to calculate. Although the full statistical analysis took seven years, it was still an improvement over the nine years it took to compile the previous census.

Mark I

In 1944, the *Mark I* was completed by a team from International Business Machines (IBM) and Harvard University under the leadership of Howard Aiken. The Mark I used mechanical telephone relay switches to store information and accepted data on punched cards. Because it could not make decisions about the data it processed, the Mark I was not a computer but instead a highly sophisticated calculator. Nevertheless, it was impressive in size, measuring over 51 feet in length and weighing 5 tons. It also had over 750,000 parts, many of them moving mechanical parts which made the Mark I not only huge but unreliable.

Howard Aiken
1900 – 1973

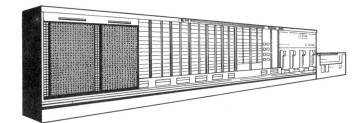

The Mark 1 was over 51 feet long and weighed over 5 tons

Atanasoff-Berry Computer

John Atanasoff
1903 – 1995

Clifford Berry
1918 – 1963

The first electronic computer was built between 1939 and 1942 at Iowa State University by John Atanasoff, a math and physics professor, and Clifford Berry, a graduate student. The *Atanasoff-Berry Computer* (ABC) used the binary number system of 1s and 0s that is still used in computers today. It contained hundreds of vacuum tubes and stored numbers for calculations by electronically burning holes in sheets of paper. The output of calculations was displayed on an odometer type of device.

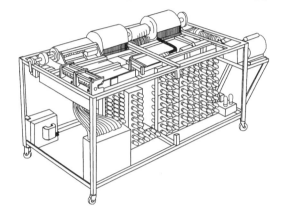

The Atanasoff-Berry Computer used the binary number system used in computers today

The patent application for the ABC was not handled properly, and it was not until almost 50 years later that Atanasoff received full credit for his invention. In 1990, he was awarded the Presidential Medal of Technology for his pioneering work. A working replica of the ABC was unveiled at the Smithsonian in Washington, D.C. on October 9, 1997.

ENIAC

John Mauchly
1907 – 1980

J. Presper Eckert
1919 – 1995

In June 1943, John Mauchly and J. Presper Eckert began work on the *ENIAC* (Electronic Numerical Integration and Calculator). It was originally a secret military project which began during World War II to calculate the trajectory of artillery shells. Built at the University of Pennsylvania, it was not finished until 1946, after the war had ended. But the great effort put into the ENIAC was not wasted. In one of its first demonstrations, ENIAC was given a problem that would have taken a team of mathematicians three days to solve. It solved the problem in twenty seconds.

The ENIAC was originally a secret military project

The ENIAC weighed 30 tons and occupied 1500 square feet, the same area taken up by the average three bedroom house. It contained over 17,000 vacuum tubes, which consumed huge amounts of electricity and produced a tremendous amount of heat requiring special fans to cool the room.

computer

The ABC and the ENIAC are first generation computers because they mark the beginning of the computer era. A *computer* is an electronic machine that accepts data, processes it according to instructions, and provides the results as new data. Most importantly, a computer can make simple decisions and comparisons.

1.4 The Stored Program Computer

The ABC and ENIAC required wire pulling, replugging, and switch flipping to change their instructions. A breakthrough in the architectural design of first generation computers came as a result of separate publications by Alan Turing and John von Neumann, both mathematicians with the idea of the stored program.

Alan Turing
1912 – 1954

program

In the late 30s and 40s, Alan Turing developed the idea of a "universal machine." He envisioned a computer that could perform many different tasks by simply changing a program rather than by changing electronic components. A *program* is a list of instructions written in a special language that the computer understands.

CPU

In 1945, John von Neumann presented his idea of the stored program concept. The stored program computer would store computer instructions in a *CPU* (Central Processing Unit). The CPU consisted of different elements used to control all the functions of the computer electronically so that it would not be necessary to flip switches or pull wires to change instructions.

John
von Neumann
1903 – 1957

EDVAC
EDSAC

machine language

Together with Mauchly and Eckert, von Neumann designed and built the *EDVAC* (Electronic Discrete Variable Automatic Computer) and the *EDSAC* (Electronic Delay Storage Automatic Computer). These computers were designed to solve many different problems by simply entering new instructions that were stored on paper tape. The instructions were in *machine language*, which consists of 0s and 1s to represent the status of a switch (0 for off and 1 for on).

UNIVAC
C-10

The third computer to employ the stored program concept was the *UNIVAC* (UNIVersal Automatic Computer) built by Mauchly and Eckert. With the UNIVAC came the first computer language called *C-10*, which was developed by Betty Holberton. Holberton also designed the first computer keyboard and numeric keypad in an effort to make the computer more user-friendly. The first UNIVAC was sold to the U.S. Census Bureau in 1951.

Francis "Betty"
Holberton
1917 – 2001

These first generation computers continued to use many vacuum tubes which made them large and expensive. They were so expensive to purchase and run that only the largest corporations and the U.S. government could afford them. Their ability to perform up to 1,000 calculations per second, however, made them popular.

1.5 Second Generation Computers

transistor

In 1947, William Shockley, John Bardeen, and Walter Brittain of Bell Laboratories invented the *transistor*. The invention of the transistor made computers smaller and less expensive and increased calculating speeds to up to 10,000 calculations per second.

John Bardeen, William Shockley, and Walter Brittain

One transistor (on right) replaced many tubes, making computers smaller, less expensive, and more reliable

Model 650

In the early 1960s, IBM introduced the first medium-sized computer named the *Model 650*. It was expensive, but much smaller than first generation computers and still capable of handling the flood of paperwork produced by many government agencies and businesses. Such organizations provided a ready market for the 650, making it popular in spite of its cost.

Second generation computers also saw a change in the way data was stored. Punched cards were replaced by magnetic tape and high speed reel-to-reel tape machines. Using magnetic tape gave computers the ability to *read* (access) and *write* (store) data quickly and reliably.

read, write

1.6 High-Level Programming Languages

Second generation computers had more capabilities than first generation computers and were more widely used by businesses. This led to the need for *high-level programming languages* that had English-like instructions and were easier to use than machine language. In 1957, John Backus and a team of researchers completed *Fortran*, a programming language with intuitive commands such as READ and WRITE.

Grace Murray Hopper 1906 – 1992

Rear Admiral Dr. Grace Murray Hopper is also known for using the term "debug" for a programming error. A program running on the Mark II had to be "debugged" when a moth flew into the computer's circuitry causing an electrical short.

One of the most widely used high-level programming languages has been COBOL, designed by Grace Murray Hopper, a Commodore in the Navy at the time. *COBOL* (COmmon Business Oriented Language) was developed by the Department of Defense in 1959 to provide a common language for use on all computers. The Department of Defense (DOD) also developed Ada, a programming language named after Ada Byron.

Developed in the 1960s by John Kemeny and Thomas Kurtz at Dartmouth University, BASIC was another widely used programming language. *BASIC* (Beginner's All-Purpose Symbolic Instruction Code) has evolved to Visual Basic .NET, which is widely used today for Windows programming. Other languages used today include Java and C++.

A Guide to Microsoft Office XP Professional

1.7 Third Generation Computers

integrated circuits

The replacement of transistors by integrated circuits (IC) began the third generation of computers. In 1961, Jack Kilby and Robert Noyce, working independently, developed the IC, also called a *chip*. One IC could replace hundreds of transistors, giving computers tremendous speed to process information at a rate of millions of calculations per second.

ICs are silicon wafers with intricate circuits etched into their surfaces and then coated with a metallic oxide that fills in the etched circuit patterns. This enables the chips to conduct electricity along the many paths of their circuits. The silicon wafers are then housed in special plastic cases that have metal pins. The pins allow the chips to be plugged into circuit boards that have wiring printed on them.

A typical chip is about 1 cm wide by 2.5 cm long

In 1964, the IBM *System 360* was one of the first computers to use integrated circuits and was so popular with businesses that IBM had difficulty keeping up with the demand. Computers had come down in size and price to such a point that smaller organizations such as universities and hospitals could now afford them.

Robert Noyce
1927 – 1990

Noyce developed the integrated circuit while working for Fairchild Semiconductor. In 1968, he left Fairchild to form the company now known as Intel Corporation.

1.8 Mainframes

A *mainframe* is a large computer system that is usually used for multi-user applications. They are used by large corporations, banks, government agencies, and universities. Mainframes can calculate a large payroll, keep the records for a bank, handle the reservations for an airline, or store student information for a university—tasks that require the storage and processing of huge amounts of information. The IBM System 360 was one of the first mainframes available.

Jack S. Kilby
1923 –

Kilby, working for Texas Instruments, developed the first integrated circuit. To demonstrate this new technology, he invented the first electronic hand-held calculator. It was small enough to fit in a coat pocket, yet as powerful as the large desktop models of the time.

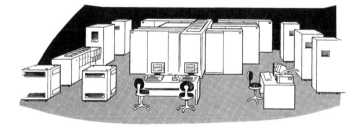

Mainframe computers are large and set up in their own rooms

terminals

Most people using mainframes communicate with them using *terminals*. A terminal consists of a keyboard for data input, and a monitor for viewing output. The terminal is connected by wires to the computer, which may be located on a different floor or a building a few blocks away. Some mainframes have hundreds of terminals attached.

1.9 Fourth Generation Computers

microprocessor

Marcian Hoff
1937 –

Stephen Wozniak
1950 –

Steve Jobs
1955 –

In 1970, Marcian Hoff, an engineer at Intel Corporation, invented the *microprocessor*, an entire CPU on a single chip. The replacement of several larger components by one microprocessor made possible the fourth generation of computers.

The small microprocessor made it possible to build a computer called a *microcomputer* that fits on a desktop. The first of these was the Altair built in 1975. In 1976, Stephen Wozniak and Steven Jobs designed and built the first Apple computer.

Advances in technology made microcomputers inexpensive and therefore available to many people. Because of these advances almost anyone could own a machine that had more computing power and was faster and more reliable than either the ENIAC or UNIVAC. As a comparison, if the cost of a sports car had dropped as quickly as that of a computer, a new Porsche would now cost about one dollar.

1.10 The Personal Computer

Microcomputers, often called *personal computers* or *PCs*, fit on a desktop. Modern PCs have the computing power and storage capacity that rival older mainframes.

A PC combines a keyboard, monitor, external drives, and a mouse in a desktop-sized package

Microcomputers contain four types of hardware components:

1. **Input Devices:** devices from which the computer can accept data. A keyboard, CD-ROM drive, disk drive, and a mouse are all examples of input devices.

2. **Memory:** ICs inside the base unit that store data electronically.

3. **CPU (Central Processing Unit):** an IC inside the base unit that processes data and controls the flow of data between the computer's other units. It is here that the computer makes decisions.

4. **Output Devices:** devices that display or store processed data. Monitors and printers are the most common visual output devices. The hard disk, which is inside the base unit, and the diskette and CD-ROM are the most common storage output devices.

The IBM–PC

In 1981, IBM introduced the IBM–PC. The computer was an instant success because of the availability of spreadsheet, accounting, and word processor software. Sales of the PC skyrocketed further when Lotus Development Corporation introduced their spreadsheet program Lotus 1-2-3.

The diagram below illustrates the direction that data flows between the separate components of a computer:

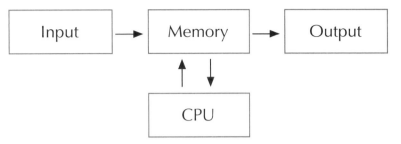

Notice that all information flows through the CPU. Because one of the tasks of the CPU is to control the order in which tasks are completed, it is often referred to as the "brain" of the computer. However, this comparison with the human brain has an important flaw. The CPU only executes tasks according to the instructions it has been given; it cannot think for itself.

software

Microcomputers also contain *software* that instruct the computer what to do. *Operating system software* is run automatically when the computer is turned on and enables the user to communicate with the computer by using input devices such as the mouse and keyboard. *Applications software* is written by programmers to perform a specific task, such as a word processor. Software is also called a program or an application.

1.11   Memory

Computers have two types of memory contained on chips, *ROM* and *RAM*. Read Only Memory, or ROM, contains the most basic operating instructions for the computer. The data in ROM is a permanent part of the computer and cannot be changed. The instructions in ROM enable the computer to complete simple jobs such as placing a character on the screen or checking the keyboard to see if any keys have been pressed.

ROM

RAM

Random Access Memory, or RAM, is temporary memory where data and instructions can be stored. Data stored here can be changed or erased. When the computer is first turned on, this part of memory is empty and, when turned off, any data it contains is lost. Because RAM storage is temporary, computers have auxiliary data storage devices. Before turning the computer off, the data in RAM can be saved to a floppy diskette or a hard disk so that it can be used again at a later time.

cache
SRAM

Personal computers also contain a type of memory called *cache* (pronounced "cash"). This memory is comprised of SRAM, or Static Random Access Memory. It is used to store data that is frequently used so that it can be quickly retrieved by an application.

1.12   The CPU

The CPU (Central Processing Unit) directs the processing of information throughout the computer. It can only follow instructions that it gets from ROM or from a program in RAM.

A CPU chip measures about 2 cm by 2 cm

Within the CPU is the *ALU* (Arithmetic Logic Unit), which can perform arithmetic and logic operations. The ALU is so fast that the time needed to carry out a single addition is measured in *nanoseconds* (billionths of a second). The ALU can also compare numbers to determine whether a number is greater than, less than, or equal to another number. This ability is the basis of the computer's decision-making power.

1.13   Bits and Bytes

binary

The electrical circuits on an IC have one of two states, off or on. Therefore, the *binary number system* (base 2), which uses only two digits (0 and 1), was adopted for use in computers. To represent numbers and letters, a code was developed with eight binary digits grouped together to represent a single number or letter. Each 0 or 1 in the binary code is called a *bit* (BInary digiT) and an 8-bit unit is called a *byte*.

bit, byte

ASCII

In order to allow computers to interchange information, the American Standard Code for Information Interchange, or *ASCII*, was developed. ASCII uses one byte to represent each letter of the alphabet, both uppercase and lowercase, and each symbol, digit, and special control function as an assigned a number. The ASCII representation of the letters in the name JIM are 74, 73, 77. Both the decimal and binary code representations of those numbers are shown below:

Letter	Decimal	Binary code
J	74	01001010
I	73	01001001
M	77	01001101

MB

GB

Computer memory, file sizes, and storage device capacities are measured in bytes. For example, a computer might have 128MB of RAM. In computers and electronics *MB* stands for *megabytes* where mega represents 2^{20} or 1,048,576 bytes and *GB* stands for *gigabytes*, which is 2^{30} or 1,073,741,820 bytes. Simple files, such as a text document, can be measured *kilobytes*, for example 256K. The *K* comes from the word *kilo* and represents 2^{10} or 1,024. Therefore, a 64K file uses 65,536 bytes (64×2^{10}) of storage.

K

1.14 Storage Devices

Computers include devices for long-term storage. The capacity of these storage devices is measured in bytes, just as memory, and ranges from 1.44 MB to many gigabytes. Most PCs have a *diskette drive*, a *CD/DVD drive*, and a *hard disk drive*. The diskette and CD/DVD drives are accessible from outside the base unit, and the hard disk is completely contained inside the base unit. Each drive uses a different kind of storage media:

diskette   CD/DVD   hard disk

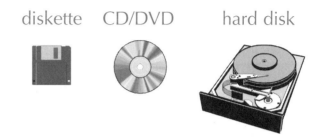

Data can be stored on diskette, CD/DVD, or hard disk (internal)

diskette

CD/DVD

hard disk

Sometimes called a floppy disk, *diskettes* are made of a Mylar (thin polyester film) disk that is coated with magnetic material and then loosely encased in hard plastic. Each diskette has a capacity of 1.44 MB. *CDs* and *DVDs* are made of a Mylar disk with a reflective coating that is sealed in clear, hard plastic. A CD can store over 650 MB of data. A DVD can store over 4 GB and is used for video and audio, and other media that require large file sizes. CD/DVD drives can be read-only or read-write. *Hard disks* are made of an aluminum disk coated with a magnetic material. Unlike diskette and CD/DVDs, hard disks are permanently installed inside a hard disk drive. Each hard drive may have multiple disks inside, and therefore have large storage capacities of many gigabytes.

Other storage devices, some of which are standard in PCs, are:

Storage Device	Capacity	Description
DVD-ROM drive	4.7–17 GB	Reads data, audio, and video from a digital versatile disc (similar to a CD). It can also read traditional CDs.
DVD-RAM drive	5.2 GB	Reads and writes data to a digital versatile disc.
Iomega Zip drive	250 MB	Reads and writes data to a disk almost as small as a diskette
Iomega Jaz drive	2 GB	Reads and writes data to a disk almost as small as a diskette
SuperDisk drive	120 MB	Reads and writes data to a disk similar to a floppy diskette. It can also read and write to floppy diskettes.
tape drive	7 GB	Stores data on magnetic tape sealed in a cartridge.
removable hard drive	1–160 GB	Reads and writes data to a disk constructed like diskettes but larger.

hard disk array   Completely external to the PC is the *hard disk array*. Enormous amounts of data can be made transportable using hard disk arrays. These are towers of several hard drives (not just large diskettes as in the removable hard drives) that combine to equal 72 GB or more. Each hard drive can be removed from the tower and transported to another array tower.

1.15   Peripheral Devices

A PC becomes much more versatile when other devices such as printers and scanners are used with it. Such devices are sometimes called *peripheral devices* because they are outside the computer base unit.

laser printer   Two commonly used types of printers are laser and inkjet. A *laser printer* uses a laser and toner to generate characters and graphics on paper. *Toner*
ink jet printer   is a fine powder that fuses to paper when heated. An *inkjet printer* uses an ink cartridge to place very small dots of ink onto paper to create characters and graphics. Inkjet printers are less expensive than laser printers and can be used to inexpensively generate full-color images and text. Laser printers, however, can generate images that are of higher resolution and quality than the images generated by an inkjet printer. Color laser printers are also available, but are relatively expensive.

scanner   Another common peripheral device is the scanner. A *scanner* uses a laser to create a digital image from artwork such as photos and drawings. The digitized image can then be incorporated into a document.

1.16   Networks

A *network* is a combination of software and hardware that works together to allow computers to exchange data and to share software and devices, such as printers. Networks are widely used by businesses, universities, and other organizations because a network:

- allows users to reliably share and exchange data
- can reduce costs by sharing devices such as printers
- can be set up to allow users access to only specific files
- simplifies the process of creating backup copies of files
- allows users to communicate with e-mail

Networks are classified by their size, architecture, and topology. One
LAN   common size classification is *LAN* (Local-Area Network), which is a network used to connect devices within a small area such as a building or a
WAN   campus. The *WAN* (Wide-Area Network) is used to connect computers over large geographical distances. A WAN can be one widespread network or it can be a number of LANs linked together.

network interface card   The computers and other devices in a LAN contain a circuit board called a *network interface card*:

A Guide to Microsoft Office XP Professional

network interface card

A cable plugs into the network interface card to connect one device to another to form the LAN.

network architecture

client/server

peer-to-peer

Network architecture includes the type of computers on the network and determines how network resources are handled. Two main types of network architecture are called client/server and peer-to-peer. A *client/server* network consists of a group of computers, called *clients*, connected to a server. A *server* is a powerful computer used to manage network functions such as communications and data sharing. A *peer-to-peer* network does not have a server. Each computer on the network is considered equal in terms of responsibilities and resource sharing.

topology

node

Topology is the logical arrangement of the nodes on a network. A *node* is a device, such as a computer or printer, that is connected to the network and is capable of communicating with other network devices.

bus topology

A popular LAN topology is the *bus topology* where each node is attached to a single shared communication cable that is often referred to as the bus:

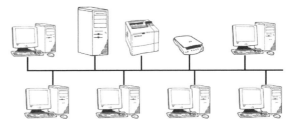

LAN using a bus topology

star topology

hub

In a *star topology*, each node is attached to a *hub*, which is a device that joins communication lines at a central location on the network:

Baseband and Broadband Technology

Most LANs use baseband technology which means the transmission media carries one signal at a time. Broadband technology allows for data transmission of more than one signal at a time. Broadband technology is found in WANs.

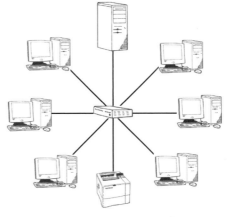

LAN using a star topology

ring topology

A *ring topology* connects each node to form a closed loop. Data travels in one direction and is sent from node to node, with each node examining the data and either accepting it or passing it on to the next node in the ring. A LAN with a ring topology can usually cover a greater distance than a bus or star topology:

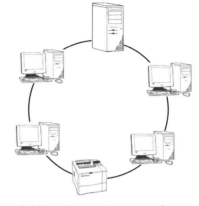

LAN using a ring topology

It is important to note that topology refers to the logical connection between the nodes and not the physical setup. For example, a ring topology may be set up in an arrangement other than a circle as long as the nodes form a closed loop.

1.17   Transmission Media

Computers must be connected in order to transmit data between the nodes. The type of connection used is called the *transmission media*. The amount of data and the speed at which the data can travel over the transmission media is called its *bandwidth* and is measured in bits per second (bps). Each type of transmission media has different length or range restrictions, data transmission rates, costs, and installation requirements:

transmission media

bandwidth

twisted-pair wiring

- *Twisted-pair wiring* consists of pairs of insulated strands of copper twisted around each other to form a cable. Twisted-pair cable is the least expensive transmission media. Older telephone systems use twisted-pair wiring.

coaxial cable

- *Coaxial cable* is made up of a central copper wire, a layer of insulation, a braided metal shield, and an outer shield. Coaxial cable provides a greater bandwidth than twisted-pair cable, but is more expensive. It is widely used in networks and is the type of wire used for cable television.

fiber optic cable

- *Fiber optic cable* is composed of a bundle of thin strands of glass or plastic fibers that transmits data modulated onto light waves. Fiber optic cable has a greater bandwidth than twisted-pair and coaxial cable, but it is expensive. Traditional phone lines are continually being replaced with fiber optic cable.

wireless networks

- *Wireless networks* do not use cables. Instead they use high frequency radio waves or infrared signals to transmit data. WLANs (wireless local-area networks) are becoming more common as the cost decreases and performance improves.

1.18   Using a Network

Network users are assigned a user name and password to log on to a network. This enables networks to identify who has permission to log on. Users are also given a level of access, again to maintain security and privacy. Network users should follow a certain etiquette referred to as *netiquette*:

netiquette

- Do not attempt to access the account of another user without authorization.

- Do not share your password, and change it periodically.

- Use appropriate subject matter and language, and be considerate of other people's beliefs and opinions. This is especially important when posting messages that will be sent to every user on the network.

Some networks run a *firewall*, which is a network security system that prevents unauthorized network access.

History of the Internet

The Internet evolved from ARPANET and the theory of open architecture networking, meaning internetworking different networks regardless of what type of network technology they used. ARPANET was created in the late 1960s by the Department of Defense's ARPA (Advanced Research Projects Agency.) ARPANET initally connected computers at the University of California Los Angeles and the Stanford Research Institute.

1.19   The Internet

The largest and most widely accessed network is the *Internet*, a worldwide network of computers that is not controlled by any one organization. The Internet has had an undeniable impact on modern society because it allows users worldwide to communicate in a matter of seconds.

The Internet is actually numerous networks all linked together through routers. *Routers* are devices that can connect different network technologies together. The networks connected to routers use *TCP/IP* (Transmission Control Protocol/Internet Protocol) software to communicate.

routers
TCP/IP

Computers on the Internet are either servers or clients. A *server* computer, often called an *Internet site*, provides information. A *client* computer accesses servers to request information. The client/server structure of the Internet is called *interactive* because the information accessed is a result of selections made. For example, when you connect to the Internet, your computer becomes a client on that network. You can then interact with the Internet by selecting the information you wish to receive.

Internet site

1.20   Internet Service Providers

Many organizations link their networks to the Internet. Individuals can get access to the Internet through telecommunications and an Internet service provider or an online service. An *ISP* (Internet Service Provider) offers access to the Internet for a fee. An *online service*, such as AOL, offers access to the Internet as well as other services for a fee.

ISP
online service

ISPs typically charge a monthly fee. They also provide the necessary software, a username, password, and dial-up number for a conventional modem.

1.21　Telecommunications

Telecommunications is the transmitting and receiving of data. Data can be in various forms including voice and video. Telecommunications can be wireless, but usually requires a modem or adapter and a line or cable. Numerous telecommunications options are available, which vary in speed and cost:

- A *conventional modem* uses analog phone lines. A conventional modem is a 56 Kbps modem, which means data is transmitted upstream at speeds of 28.8 and 36.6 Kbps, and received downstream at 56 Kbps. Many home computers use a conventional modem.

- A *DSL* (Digital Subscriber Line) modem uses an analog phone line called an ADSL (Asymmetric DSL) line that allows data to be transmitted upstream at speeds up to 640 Kbps and received downstream at 8 Mbps.

- A *cable modem* transmits data through a coaxial cable television network. A cable modem transmits data upstream at speeds from 2 Mbps to 10 Mbps and receives data downstream at speeds of 10 Mbps to 36 Mbps.

- *Leased/Dedicated lines* are being used by many businesses and schools for Internet access because they allow for a direct connection to the Internet. The cost of a leased line is usually a fixed monthly fee. A T-1 carrier is a type of leased line that transmits data at speeds up to 1.544 Mbps.

- *ISDN* (Integrated Services Digital Network) is a digital telephone network provided by a local phone company. ISDN eliminates the digital to analog conversion that is required with analog phone lines. ISDN is capable of transmitting and receiving data at speeds of up to 128 Kbps. ISDN requires the use of an ISDN terminal adapter instead of a modem.

telecommuting

Telecommuting is the use of telecommunications to work at home rather than in the office. For example, writers and news reporters can write their stories at home on a word processor and then transmit the documents to their office. As another example, financial consultants, accountants, and travel agents can easily access databases from home rather than driving to an office.

1.22　Internet Services

The most widely used Internet service is the World Wide Web (WWW), also called the Web. The *Web* allows you to search and access information available on the Internet. A *web browser* is software, such as Microsoft Internet Explorer, that is required to view information at a web site. Web sites cover a variety of topics with each *web site* made up of a series of related web pages. Web sites can provide, for example, valuable information when researching a topic for a term paper, updating stock values, or gathering data for a database.

Conventional Modem

A modem and communications software is required to send and receive data over analog phone lines.

A modem converts a computer's binary data into tones that can be transmitted over phone lines. To receive data, a modem converts the tones from the phone line into binary data. This process involves what is called signal modulation and demodulation, hence the name modem.

History of the Web

The Web came into existence in 1980 when Tim Berners-Lee, a consultant for CERN in Europe, wrote a program that allowed special links between arbitrary computers on the Internet. With the new program, data could be transmitted and received over the Internet in the form of text, graphics, and sound from locations called sites. The Web has now grown to include many millions of Internet sites.

---

e-mail   Another widely used Internet service is e-mail. *E-mail*, which means *electronic mail*, allows an individual with an e-mail account to send messages to another person with an e-mail account. E-mail can be received in a matter of seconds, even if the recipient is located half way around the world. E-mail is discussed in Chapter 3.

IRC   A popular service provided through the Internet and online service providers is called *Internet Relay Chat* (IRC), or just *chat*. IRC was developed in 1988 by Jarkko Oikarinen. Chatting is communicating with someone else who is also online by typing messages back and forth to each other. After one person writes something the other person receives the message and replies. There may be a short delay while the person responds, but the "conversation" is said to be in real time.

bulletin board   A *bulletin board service*, sometimes referred to as a *BBS*, allows a user to participate in a discussion group. There are thousands of bulletin board services with topics ranging from accounting to zoology. Businesses often maintain a bulletin board service for their employees only. Other bulletin board services allow any network user to join.

netnews   *Network News*, also referred to as *Netnews,* is a popular BBS available on the Internet. This system uses the term *newsgroup* to refer to an individual bulletin board, and *article* refers to a message posted to the newsgroup. Subscribers of a newsgroup can check for new articles and post (send) articles regarding the topic of discussion. *USENET* refers to the collection of all the servers that offer Netnews.

listserv   Internet users can also join a listserv. A *listserv* is a discussion group that uses e-mail to send messages. *LISTSERV* is a program that maintains the *mailing list*, a list of the e-mail addresses of the users who subscribe to the listserv. When a subscriber posts a message to a listserv, every subscriber receives a copy of the message.

1.23   Computer Use Privacy Issues

A serious ethical issue associated with computers is the invasion of privacy. Every time you use a credit card, make a phone call, withdraw money, reserve a flight, or register at school a computer records the transaction. These records can be used to learn a great deal about you—where you have been, when you were there, and how much money you spent. Should this information be available to everyone? To protect both the privacy of an individual and the accuracy of data stored about individuals, a number of laws have been passed.

The **Fair Credit Reporting Act of 1970** deals with data collected for use by credit, insurance, and employment agencies. The act gives individuals the right to see information maintained about them. If a person is denied credit they are allowed to see the files used to make the credit determination. If any of the information is incorrect, the person has the right to have it changed. The act also restricts who may access credit files to only those with a court order or the written permission of the individual whose credit is being checked.

The **Privacy Act of 1974** restricts the way in which personal data can be used by federal agencies. Individuals must be permitted access to information stored about them and may correct any information that is incorrect. Agencies must insure both the security and confidentiality of any sensitive information. Although this law applies only to federal agencies, many states have adopted similar laws.

The **Financial Privacy Act of 1978** requires that a government authority have a subpoena, summons, or search warrant to access an individual's financial records. When such records are released, the financial institution must notify the individual of who has had access to them.

The **Electronic Communications Privacy Act of 1986** (ECPA) makes it a crime to access electronic data without authorization. It also prohibits unauthorized release of such data.

The **Electronic Freedom of Information Act of 1996** requires federal government agencies to make certain agency information available for public inspection and is designed to improve public access to agency records.

The **Safety and Freedom through Encryption Act of 1999** (SAFE) gives Americans the freedom to use any type of encryption to protect their confidential information. It also prohibits the government from monitoring people's communications without their knowledge or consent.

1.24   Computers at Home

Personal computers are so inexpensive that many homes include at least one. Much of the software created in recent years has been specifically designed for the home user.

Internet

The fastest growing use of home computing is Internet access. With Internet access, home users can shop online, make travel arrangements, do research, and take educational courses, among many other things.

entertainment

A popular use for home computers is in the field of entertainment. For example, there are thousands of different types of computer games available. Educational software for children are often in the form of a game. The Internet has also become a form of entertainment, allowing users to chat online and play games with other people who are online.

fax/modem

A fax/modem is also standard in many home systems. A *fax/modem* can operate as both a modem for telecommunications and as a fax machine that can receive and send files.

productivity software

Home users often make use of productivity software. Commonly used packages include financial software for maintaining bank accounts and investments, desktop publishing software for creating newsletters, and specialized software packages for creating cards, banners, and family trees. For example, software is now available that edits home videos and produces graphics that can be added to the video. This allows the home user to produce professional-looking home videos that include titles and animation.

multimedia   *Multimedia* is the integration of computer animation, graphics, video, and audio. Commonly used multimedia applications are encyclopedias, games, and trip planners.

1.25   Computer-Related Careers

As computers have become more powerful they play an ever increasing role in the world we live in. Consequently many people, no matter what field they are employed in, use computers in some way. Following are computer-related careers and their typical educational requirements.

data processing   The area of computing that employs the largest number of people is data processing. *Data processing* involves the electronic entry, storage, manipulation, and retrieval of data. Almost any organization requires the management of large amounts of data and therefore need employees capable of data processing. Careers in data processing are usually divided into five categories: data-entry operator, system analyst, system developer (programmer), system manager, and computer scientist.

data-entry operator   A *data-entry operator* types data into a computer. Data-entry operators may work for banks entering cancelled checks, department stores entering inventory figures, or educational institutions entering student records. A data-entry operator should possess a high school diploma or associate degree and the ability to type quickly and accurately.

system analyst   Before a data processing system can be set up a *system analyst* must first analyze and design the system. The analyst must determine how an organization will use the computer system, what data will be stored, how it will be accessed, and how the system is expected to grow in the future. A system analyst should possess a comprehensive knowledge of data-processing methods, software, hardware, and programming languages. Most system analysts are college graduates who have majored in computer science or information systems or both.

programmer   After the system analyst has determined what type of system should be installed, the *programmer* creates the necessary software. A programmer should possess a detailed knowledge of the programming language or languages being used as well as an ability to reason analytically and pay close attention to details. Many businesses employ programmers who have graduated from a technical school or community college with a degree in programming. Large or specialized companies, which need highly sophisticated programming, usually require employees with a four-year college degree.

MIS manager   Companies with large data processing requirements usually employ a manager who is responsible for running the Management Information Systems department (MIS). The *MIS manager* must organize the computer and human resources of the department in order to best achieve the organization's goals. A system manager should possess a detailed understanding of data-processing methods, hardware, and software. A college degree in business administration with a concentration in information systems is usually required.

computer scientist

The study of computer science is a very broad field involving many disciplines including science, electronics, and mathematics. A *computer scientist* often works in research at a university or computer manufacturer developing new computer applications software and hardware. It is computer scientists who design and develop robots, natural language processors, and the many applications that we have mentioned. A computer scientist usually has both undergraduate and graduate degrees in computer science.

computer engineer

Computer engineers design and manufacture computers. This field is broad and includes engineers who develop new computer applications. Other engineers translate ideas produced by researchers into manufactured products. A computer engineer usually possesses both undergraduate and graduate degrees in engineering.

manufacturing worker

The people who help build computer systems need to possess the ability to work well with tools. *Manufacturing workers* usually have earned a high school diploma or community college degree. Good preparation for such a career includes taking courses in mechanical arts as well as science and mathematics.

technical support technician

Working mainly over the phone, *technical support technicians* assist customers of both hardware and software companies. Customers that have questions or problems with any aspect of the company's products, including installation and compatibility call the technical support phone number and speak with a technician who then identifies the problem and offers a solution. A technical support technician is usually a graduate of a technical school or community college.

sales representative

A large number of people sell computers either as representatives who travel and visit clients or as salespeople in computer stores. It is important that they possess a thorough knowledge of the computer equipment they sell and be able to explain how it may be used. The level of education required for this job will depend on the sophistication of the equipment being sold. Often a high school or community college degree is sufficient. To sell large computer systems, a sales representative may be required to have a four-year college degree.

computer teacher

Employees currently working in a computer-related field are often there because of *computer teachers*. In high schools and colleges, teachers and professors do research and teach all aspects of computing from computer science to ethics. For teaching at the high school level, a four-year college degree in a computer field is the minimum. At the college level, a graduate degree is the minimum requirement.

technology coordinator

At most educational institutions, it is the job of the *technology coordinator* to plan and oversee the acquisition, distribution, and utilization of computer technology. Schools require such a person to insure that they have working computer facilities and are keeping up with new advancements in technology. A graduate degree in a computer field is often required.

webmaster

With the rapid increase in the use of the World Wide Web, there is now a need for Webmasters. A *Webmaster* does everything from designing and creating web pages to creating graphics for the site to maintaining the site. A Webmaster possesses extensive Internet knowledge, including programming skills, as well as design experience.

Chapter Summary

The earliest computing devices were mechanical and were often unreliable. The advent of electricity brought about electromechanical machines, and later first generation computers that used vacuum tubes. The architectural design of computers changed with the idea of a machine that could perform many different tasks by simply changing its program. With the development of the transistor came second generation computers that were much smaller and faster. Programming languages were developed so programmers could write English-like instructions. Third generation computers used integrated circuits. Fourth generation computers, the modern microcomputers of today, include an entire CPU on a single chip.

All PCs have several hardware components: (1) input devices (keyboard, mouse, drives), (2) memory, (3) a central processing unit, and (4) output devices (monitor, printer, drives). PCs also have an operating system and applications software.

Memory is ICs that come in two forms, RAM, which can be erased and used over, and ROM, which is permanent. Because the contents of RAM are lost when the computer's power is turned off, storage devices such as diskettes, CD-ROMs, and hard disks are used to store data.

A CPU directs the processing of information throughout the computer. Within the CPU is the ALU, which is the basis of the computer's decision-making power.

Because the electrical circuits of an IC have one of two states, off or on, the binary number system is used to represent the two states: 0 for off and 1 for on. Each 0 or 1 in binary code is called a bit. The computer uses binary digits grouped into bytes to store information. ASCII is used to represent numbers, letters, and symbols in one byte. Memory, file size, and storage device capacities are measured in bytes, usually MB or GB.

Peripheral devices are devices such as scanners and printers that are outside a PC. Two commonly used types of printers are laser and inkjet. A scanner uses a laser to create a digital image from artwork.

Networks allow computers to exchange data and to share software and devices. Two common network technologies are LAN, used to connect devices within a building, and WAN, used to connect devices over a very long distance. Network architecture types include client/server and peer-to-peer. Topology is the arrangement of the nodes on a network. Popular topologies include bus, star, and ring. Network users should follow a certain etiquette called netiquette.

Transmission media is used to connect computers. Each type has different length restrictions, data transmission rates, costs, and installation requirements. Transmission media types include twisted-pair wiring, coaxial cable, fiber optic cable, and wireless.

The most widely accessed network is the Internet. Computers on the Internet communicate with TCP/IP software. Internet access is provided through an organization's network, or purchased through an Internet service provider or an online service. Internet services include the Web, e-mail, IRC, bulletin board services, network news, and listservs.

Telecommunications is the transmitting and receiving of data and requires a modem or adapter and a line or cable. Options include conventional modem, DSL, cable modem, leased/dedicated lines, and ISDN. Telecommuting is the use of telecommunications to work at home rather than in an office.

An ethical issue related to computer use is the possibility of invasion of privacy. Laws have been passed to protect us from the misuse of data stored in computers.

The use of personal computers in the home has become popular and will grow with the increased availability of telecommunications and networks. Home computers are often used to play games, entertain, and help users be more productive.

Computer related careers and the educational requirements needed to pursue them are discussed in this chapter. Careers which require only a high school education as well as those requiring a college education are presented.

Vocabulary

ALU (Arithmetic Logic Unit)   The part of the CPU that handles arithmetic and logic operations.

Applications software Commercially produced programs written to perform specific tasks.

Article   A message posted to a newsgroup.

ASCII (American Standard Code for Information Interchange)   The code used for representing characters in the computer.

Bandwidth   A unit of measurement in bits per second (bps) that reflects the amount of data and the speed at which the data can travel over a transmission media.

Base unit   Unit where the CPU, memory, and internal hard disk drive is housed.

BASIC   A high-level computer language developed by John Kemeny and Thomas Kurtz.

BBS (bulletin board service)   A network service that allows a user to participate in a discussion group.

Binary number system   Number system used by modern computers—uses only digits 0 and 1. Also called Base 2.

Bit (BInary digiT)   A single 0 or 1 in binary code.

Bits per second The rate at which data is transmitted.

Bus Topology   Connects each node of a network to a single shared communication cable called a bus.

Byte   A group of 8 bits.

Cable modem   Transmits data through a coaxial cable television network.

CD Disc made of Mylar with a reflective coating that is sealed in clear, hard plastic.

CD-ROM drive   Drive accessible from outside the base unit. Used to read the data on a CD.

CD-RW drive   Drive accessible from outside the base unit. Used to read and write data on a CD.

Chip   See Integrated circuit.

Client A computer accessing the Internet to request information.

Client/Server Network A group of computers, called clients, connected to a server.

Coaxial cable   Made up of a central copper wire, a layer of insulation, a braided metal shield, and an outer shield.

COBOL   A high-level programming language designed by Grace Murray Hopper.

Computer An electronic machine that accepts data, processes it according to instructions, and provides the results as new data.

CPU (Central Processing Unit)   An IC inside the base unit that processes data and controls the flow of data between the computer's other units.

Data Information either entered into or produced by the computer.

Diskette Sometimes called a floppy disk. Made of Mylar coated with a magnetic material and then loosely encased in hard plastic.

Diskette drive Drive accessible from outside the base unit. Used to read and write data to a diskette.

DSL (Digital Subscriber Line) Modem that uses an analog phone line called an ADSL (Asymmetric DSL) line to transmit data upstream at speeds up to 640 Kbps and receive data downstream at 8 Mbps.

DVD A digital versatile disc similar to a CD, that stores 4.7 to 5.2 GB of data. Used in a DVD-ROM or DVD-RAM drive.

DVD-RAM drive Drive accessible from outside the base unit. Used to read and write data to a DVD.

DVD-ROM drive Drive accessible from outside the base unit. Used to read data from a DVD.

E-mail (electronic mail) A message sent over a network to another user on the network.

fax/modem Both a modem for telecommunications and a fax machine that can receive and send files.

Fiber Optic Cable Composed of a bundle of thin strands of glass or plastic fibers that transmits data modulated onto light waves.

Firewall A network security system that prevents unauthorized access.

Fortran A high-level programming language developed by John Backus.

GB (gigabyte) 1,073,741,820 bytes.

Hard disk Made of aluminum coated with a magnetic material. Permanently installed inside the hard disk drive.

Hard disk array A tower of several hard drives where each drive can be removed and transported to another array.

Hard disk drive Drive completely enclosed in the base unit. Used to read and write to disks within the hard drive.

High-level programming language A programming language that uses English-like instructions.

HTTP (HyperText Transfer Protocol) The protocol used by web sites to transfer data over the Internet.

Inkjet printer A printer that uses an ink cartridge to place very small dots of ink onto paper to create characters and graphics.

Input Data used by the computer.

Internet Relay Chat (IRC) Also called chat. Communicating with someone else who is also online by typing messages back and forth to each other.

IC (Integrated Circuit) Also called a chip. A silicon wafer with intricate circuits etched into its surface and then coated with a metallic oxide that fills in the etched circuit patterns.

Interactive Where information received is a result of selections made.

Internet A worldwide computer network.

Internet service provider (ISP) A company that offers access to the Internet for a fee.

Internet site See server.

ISDN (Integrated Services Digital Network) A digital telephone network provided by a local phone company.

Jaz disk A disk, almost as small as a diskette, that stores 2 GB of data. Used in a Jaz drive.

Jaz drive Drive used to read and write data to a Jaz disk.

K (kilobyte) 1,024 bytes.

Laser printer A printer that uses a laser and toner to generate characters and graphics on paper.

Leased/Dedicated lines Allow for a direct connection to the Internet.

Listserv A discussion group that uses e-mail to send messages.

LISTSERV A program that maintains a list of the e-mail addresses of the users who subscribe to the listserv.

Local Area Network (LAN) A network that connects computers within a small area.

Machine language Instructions in binary code (0s and 1s).

Mailing list A list of e-mail addresses.

Mainframe Computer system that is usually used for multiuser applications.

MB (megabyte) 1,048,576 bytes.

Memory ICs in the base unit that store data electronically.

Microcomputer A computer that fits on a desktop and uses a microprocessor.

Microprocessor An entire CPU on a single chip.

Modem Device that converts binary data into tones and tones back into binary data so that computer data can be sent over telephone lines.

Monitor Used to display computer output.

Mouse An input device from which the computer can accept information.

Nanosecond One billionth of a second.

Netiquette Network etiquette.

Netnews See Network News.

Network Allows computers to exchange data and to share applications software and devices.

Network Architecture Includes the type of computers on the network and determines how network resources are handled.

Network interface card A circuit board in the base unit of a networked computer.

Network News A BBS available on the Internet.

Newsgroup An individual bulletin board.

Online service A company that offers access to the Internet as well as other services for a fee.

Operating system software Software that allows the user to communicate with the computer.

Output Data produced by a computer program.

PC (Personal Computer) A small computer employing a microprocessor. See also microcomputer.

Peer-to-Peer Network A group of computers that share responsibilities and resources equally without a server.

Peripheral device A device attached to a PC.

Printer An output device.

Program List of instructions written in a special language that the computer understands.

RAM (Random Access Memory) Temporary memory where data and instruction can be stored.

Read Accessing data from a storage medium.

Removable hard drive Drive used to read and write data to a removable disk.

Ring Topology Each node of a network is connected to form a closed loop.

ROM (Read Only Memory) Data that is a permanent part of the computer and cannot be changed.

Scanner Uses a laser to create a digital image from artwork.

Server A computer on the network of the Internet that provides information.

Software Instructions stored as electronic data that tells the computer what to do.

Star Topology Connects each node of a network to a hub, which is a device that joins communication lines at a central location on the network.

SuperDisk A disk, very similar to a floppy diskette, that stores 120 MB of data. Used in a SuperDisk drive.

SuperDisk drive Drive used to read and write data to a SuperDisk.

Tape drive Drive used to read and write data to a magnetic tape.

TCP/IP Communication software used for computers connected to routers.

Telecommunications Transmitting and receiving computer data over telephone lines.

Telecommuting Using telecommunications to work at home.

Terminal A keyboard and monitor used to communicate with a mainframe.

Toner A fine powder that fuses to paper when heated. Used in laser printers.

Topology The logical arrangement of the nodes on a network. A node is a device, such as a computer or printer that is connected to the network and is capable of communicating with other network devices.

Transistor An electronic device that replaced the vacuum tube making computers smaller and less expensive and increasing calculating speeds.

Transmission Media The type of connection used to connect computers.

Twisted-pair wiring Consists of pairs of insulated strands of copper twisted around each other to form a cable.

Uniform Resource Locator (URL) An address that tells a web browser which web site to access.

Web See World Wide Web.

Web browser Software that is required to view information at a web site..

Web page Information at a web site that can include graphics, text, and links to other web sites or pages.

Web site A location on the WWW where information is presented in web pages using graphics, text, and sound.

Wide Area Network (WAN) A network that connects computers over a long distance.

Wireless Networks Transmission media that uses high frequency radio waves or infrared signals to transmit data.

World Wide Web (WWW) Computers on the Internet that provide information in the form of text, graphics, and sound.

Write Storing data on a storage medium.

Zip disk A disk, almost as small as a diskette, that stores 250 MB of data. Used in a Zip drive.

Zip drive Drive used to read and write data to a Zip disk.

Review Questions

Sections 1.1 — 1.4

1. Briefly describe the Pascaline and explain what mathematical operations it was designed to perform.

2. a) What mathematical operations was the Stepped Reckoner supposed to perform?
   b) Why was it unreliable?

3. What did Ada Byron mean when she said that the Analytical Engine could never "originate anything"?

4. a) For what purpose did Herman Hollerith invent his tabulating machine?
   b) What were punched cards used for in the tabulating machine?

5. Why wasn't the Mark 1 considered a computer?

6. What number system did the Atanasoff-Berry Computer use?

7. For what purpose was the ENIAC originally designed?

8. What is a computer?

9. In what way did Alan Turning and John von Neumann improve upon the design of the ENIAC?

10. a) What is a program?
    b) What is machine language?
    c) List the first three computers designed to use a stored program.

Sections 1.5 — 1.9

11. Why was the invention of the transistor important to the development of computers?

12. How did the use of magnetic tape improve the performance of computers?

13. a) What is a high-level programming language?
    b) Who designed COBOL?
    c) List three high-level programming languages.

14. Explain what integrated circuits are and why they have been important in the development of computers.

15. a) What is a mainframe?
    b) What is the usual way for a person to communicate with a mainframe?

16. Why was the invention of the microprocessor important to the development of computers?

17. List some of the advantages of a microcomputer compared with the ENIAC or UNIVAC.

18. What are input and output devices used for?

19. Describe the flow of data between the components of a computer.

20. In what way was the design of Babbage's Analytical Engine similar to the modern computer?

21. a) What is the difference between ROM and RAM?
    b) How is each affected by turning off the computer?

22. Explain what a CPU does.

23. Why was the binary number system adopted for use in computers?

24. Explain what a bit and a byte are.

25. Why was ASCII developed?

26. a) How many bytes of data can 32 MB of RAM store?
    b) How many bytes of data can a 3 GB hard drive store?

27. a) Describe the diskette drive, CD-ROM drive, and hard disk drive and the storage media they use.
    b) List three other storage devices.

28. What is the difference between a laser printer and a ink jet printer?

Sections 1.16 — 1.22

29. What is a network?

30. List four benefits of using a network.

31. a) What are the two most common size classifications for networks?
    b) What size classification is used to connect devices over large geographical distances?

32. a) What does network architecture include?
    b) Describe clients and servers.

33. a) What is topology?
    b) What is a node?
    c) What topology uses a hub?
    d) What topology connects each node to form a closed loop?

34. List and describe four types of transmission media.

35. List three netiquette rules.

36. What is the largest and most widely accessed network?

37. What is a router?

38. a) On the Internet, what does a server computer do?
    b) Why is the client/server structure called interactive?

39. a) How can individuals get Internet access?
    b) Give an example of an online service.

40. a) What is telecommunications?
    b) List three options available for telecommunications.

41. a) If a business needed constant access to the Internet, what type of connection line would be a good choice?
    b) What does a cable modem use instead of analog phone lines?

42. What is telecommuting?

43. What is the most widely used Internet service?

44. What is e-mail?

45. a) What is chatting?
    b) What is meant by realtime?

46. What does a bulletin board service allow a user to participate in?

47. What is network news?

48. What is a listserv?

Sections 1.23 — 1.25

49. How can computers be used to invade one's privacy?

50. List and then explain three laws passed to protect an individual's privacy.

51. List two ways computers are used in the home.

52. List three careers in the computer field and describe them.

New All Day Event

Delete

Open

Exit

Mark Complete

Print Preview

Print

Chapter 2 Expectations

After completing this chapter you will be able to:

1. Explain how Outlook tools can be used to simplify the organization of personal and business activities.
2. Define link.
3. Describe the purpose of the Calendar tool.
4. Display Calendar in different views.
5. Add events and appointments to Calendar.
6. Minimize the Outlook window.
7. Quit Outlook.
8. Add tasks to the Taskpad.
9. Print a calendar.

This chapter introduces Microsoft Outlook. The Outlook Calendar tool will be used to organize events, appointments, and tasks.

2.1 What is Outlook?

Developing good organizational skills can help contribute to success in both school and work. Computer applications, such as Microsoft Outlook, can simplify the organization of personal and business activities. *Microsoft Outlook* is a personal management application that has tools for organizing appointments and listing tasks.

Outlook is started by selecting Microsoft Outlook from the Programs submenu in the Start menu, which displays Outlook Today:

title bar
menu bar
toolbar
address bar

Outlook bar

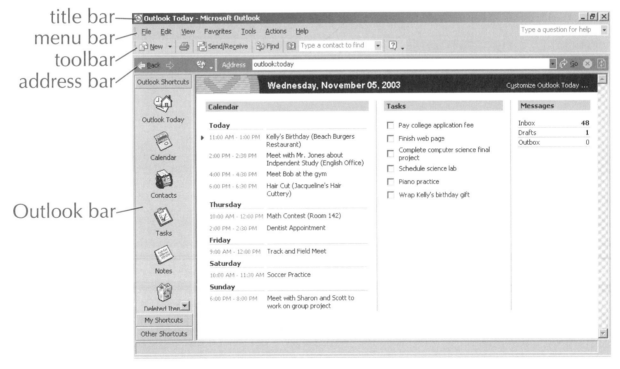

Outlook Today

link

Outlook Today displays the current date, a calendar summary for a number of days, tasks, and a summary of e-mail messages. The titles <u>Calendar</u>, <u>Tasks</u>, and <u>Messages</u> are links to those Outlook tools. A *link*, or *hyperlink*, is text that can be clicked to display a destination, such as an Outlook tool. For example, pointing to <u>Calendar</u> changes the pointer to a hand (🖑) which indicates a link:

Other Outlook features that are annotated on the previous page include:

- the **title bar**, which displays the Outlook tool name.
- the **menu bar**, which contains the names of drop-down menus that contain commands.
- the **toolbar**, which contains buttons that represent different actions.
- the **address bar**, which is used to display web pages without having to use a different web browser, such as Internet Explorer.
- the **Outlook bar**, which contains shortcuts to the Outlook tools.

In the example on the previous page, the information under the Calendar and Tasks headings was previously entered using the appropriate Outlook tool.

2.2 Calendar

Calendar is an Outlook tool that can be used to keep track of assignment due dates, create reminders about events, and schedule appointments and meetings. Clicking the Calendar shortcut on the Outlook bar or the Calendar link in Outlook Today displays Calendar:

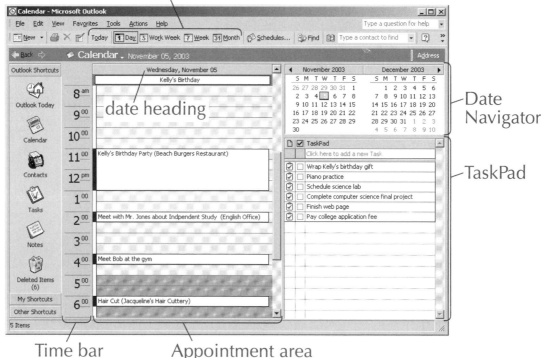

- The **View buttons** on the toolbar change the way Calendar is displayed. Day view is shown on the previous page.

- The **Date Navigator** displays a calendar for the current and next month.

- The **TaskPad** displays a list of current tasks.

- The **Appointment area** contains details and reminders of appointments. The **date heading** at the top of the Appointment area displays the date that the calendar is referring to.

- The **Time bar** displays a series of time intervals indicating the time of day.

2.3 Date Navigator

Date Navigator can be used as a calendar reference. For example, Date Navigator can be used to find out what day of the week November 21 falls on. It can also be used to display the appointments for a selected day by clicking that day. For example, clicking November 21 in Date Navigator displays the appointments for November 21:

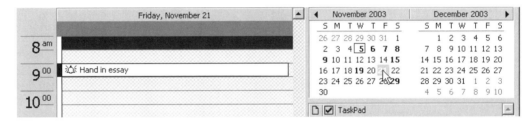

Clicking the arrow to the left or right of the displayed month displays the previous and next month, respectively:

Clicking the name of the month or the year displays a list where the past three months or the next three months can be selected:

Using the Mouse

Sliding the mouse to move the pointer on the screen is called *pointing*. An object on the screen can be selected by pointing to it and pressing the left mouse button and releasing it quickly. This type of selection is called *clicking*.

Double-clicking means to point to an object and press the left mouse button twice in rapid succession.

Right-clicking means to point to an object and press and release the right mouse button quickly.

2.4 Calendar Views

Calendar can be displayed in four different views using the View buttons on the toolbar. For example, Day view is shown in Section 2.2 and displayed by clicking the Day button (1 Day) on the toolbar. Clicking the Work Week button (5 Work Week) on the toolbar displays Monday through Friday of the current week:

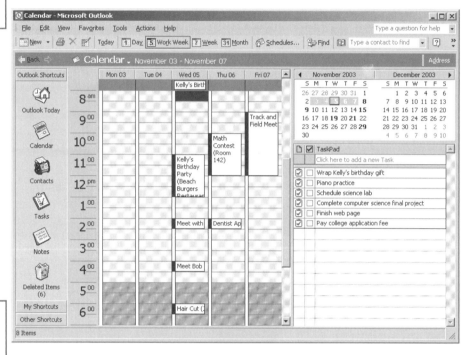

Clicking the Week button (7 Week) on the toolbar displays Monday through Sunday of the current week:

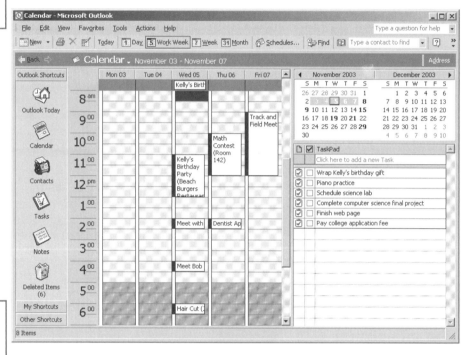

Using the Toolbar

Clicking a button on the toolbar executes a commonly performed action, such as changing calendar views.

Using Menus

Clicking a menu name displays the menu. Pointing to a command on the menu and then clicking selects the command. Clicking outside a displayed menu or pressing the Esc key removes the menu.

View Commands

The Day, Work Week, Week, and Month commands in the View menu can also be used to display the Calendar in different views.

Clicking the Month button () on the toolbar displays a scrollable calendar with one week per row:

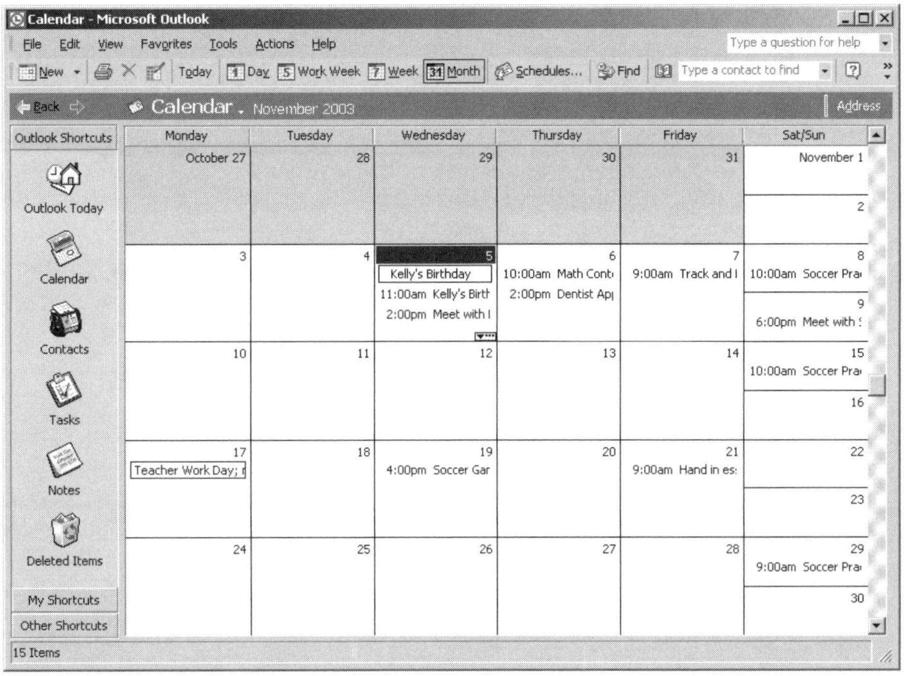

Scrolling

In Calendar, Week and Month views display scrollable calendars. This means that other calendar dates can be displayed in the window by clicking the down scroll arrow (▼) in the bottom-right corner of the window. Clicking once on the down scroll arrow moves the Calendar down by one week.

Today   Clicking the Today button (Today) on the toolbar selects and displays the current day in any view.

Practice 1

In this practice you will open Microsoft Outlook and display Calendar. Calendar will be displayed in different views and Date Navigator will be used.

① *START OUTLOOK*

On the Taskbar, click Start → Programs → Microsoft Outlook. Microsoft Outlook is started and Outlook Today is displayed.

② *OPEN THE CALENDAR*

a. In the Outlook bar, click the Calendar shortcut. Calendar is displayed.

b. On the toolbar, click the Day button ([1] Day) if it is not already selected. Calendar is displayed in Day view. Note the features of Calendar including Date Navigator, the View buttons, the Appointment area and TaskPad.

③ *CHANGE THE DATE NAVIGATOR DISPLAY*

a. In Date Navigator, click ◀ to the left of the current month. The previous month is displayed and the current month moves to the right side of Date Navigator.

b. In Date Navigator, click ▶ to the right of the current month. The current month is displayed on the left side of Date Navigator with the next month displayed on the right side.

c. In Date Navigator, click and hold the current month's name. A list is displayed that includes the past three months and the next three months.

d. In the list, select the month that is three months ahead of the current month. Date Navigator displays the selected month.

④ *DISPLAY THE CALENDAR FOR A DIFFERENT DAY*

    a. Note the date heading at the top of the Appointment area.

    b. In Date Navigator, click a different date. The selected date is displayed.

    c. On the toolbar, click the Today button (Today). The current day is displayed.

⑤ *DISPLAY THE CALENDAR IN DIFFERENT VIEWS*

    a. On the toolbar, click the Work Week button (5 Work Week). Monday through Friday of the current week is displayed.

    b. On the toolbar, click the Week button (7 Week). Monday through Sunday of the current week is displayed.

    c. On the toolbar, click the Month button (31 Month). A scrollable calendar with one week per row is displayed. Scroll beyond the current month.

    d. On the toolbar, click the Today button (Today). The calendar automatically scrolls to display the current date in Month view.

    e. On the toolbar, click the Day button (1 Day). Calendar is displayed in Day view.

2.5 Calendar Events

An *event* is an activity that is scheduled for a specific day, but is not assigned a start or an end time. Events are displayed in the Event banner at the top of the Appointment area. In the example below, Kelly's Birthday is displayed as an event on Wednesday, November 05:

date heading—
Event banner—

adding an event

An event is added to Calendar by first using Date Navigator to display the appropriate calendar day and then double-clicking the date heading or selecting New All Day Event from the Actions menu, which displays an Untitled Event window. Selecting the Appointment tab displays options for adding event information:

Color Coding Events

Events can be color coded to indicate the type of event by clicking the Label arrow in the Event dialog box, which displays a list of options:

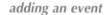

Label: None
- None
- Important
- Business
- Personal
- Vacation
- Must Attend
- Travel Required
- Needs Preparation
- Birthday
- Anniversary
- Phone Call

Selecting a type of event from the list displays the background of the Event banner in the corresponding color.

A Guide to Microsoft Office XP Professional

Insertion Point

Clicking a box, such as the Subject box in the Untitled Event window, places the insertion point. The *insertion point* is a blinking line that indicates where the next typed character will be placed.

The information to be displayed in the Event banner is typed in the Subject box. The All day event check box is automatically selected. If an event lasts longer than one day, clicking the End time arrow allows a different date to be selected:

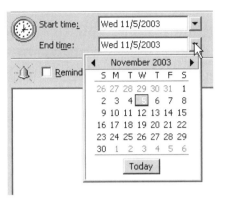

saving an event

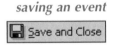

Clicking the Save and Close button (Save and Close) on the Event window toolbar removes the Event window and displays the event information in the Event banner.

deleting an event

An event can be removed from the Event banner by right-clicking the event and selecting Delete from the menu or by selecting the event and then clicking the Delete button (X)on the toolbar.

Practice 2

In this practice you will add an event to Calendar. Calendar should already be displayed.

① *USE DATE NAVIGATOR TO DISPLAY A DATE*

In Date Navigator, click the date three days from today. The calendar for the selected day is displayed.

② *ADD AN EVENT*

a. In the Appointment area, double-click the date heading. An Untitled Event window is displayed.

    1. Select the Appointment tab if those options are not already displayed.

    2. In the Subject box, type Jordan's Birthday.

    3. Select the All day event check box if it is not already selected.

    4. On the Event window toolbar, click the Save and Close button (Save and Close). The window is removed and the event is displayed on the Event banner.

③ *DISPLAY OUTLOOK TODAY*

a. On the Outlook bar, click the Outlook Today shortcut. Outlook Today is displayed. Note the event under Calendar.

b. On the Outlook bar, click the Calendar shortcut. Calendar is displayed for today.

2.6 Calendar Appointments

An *appointment*, just like an event, is an activity scheduled on a specific day. However, an appointment differs from an event in that it has a specific starting and ending time. For example, Kelly's Birthday was added as an event that occurs for the whole day. Kelly's Birthday Party, which occurs from 11:00 a.m. to 1:00 p.m., is an appointment because it has a starting and ending time.

An appointment is displayed in the Appointment area of Calendar in the appropriate time slot, with the time scheduled for the appointment outlined as a block:

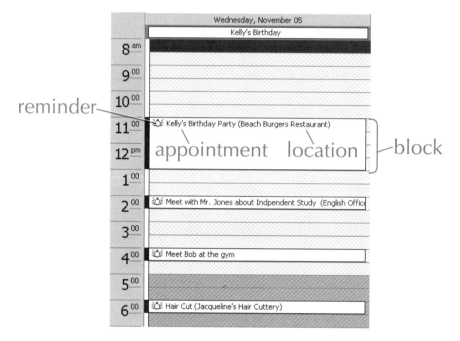

If an appointment location is specified, it is shown in parentheses next to the appointment information. In this example, Beach Burgers Restaurant is the location of the 11:00 appointment. The bell to the left of each appointment indicates a sound will play and a reminder about the appointment will be displayed at a set time.

adding an appointment

In any view, an appointment can be added by clicking the New button (New) on the toolbar, which displays an Untitled Appointment window. The Untitled Appointment window can also be displayed in Day view by double-clicking the row to the right of the start time interval in the Appointment area. For example, double-clicking the 11:00 a.m. slot displays an Untitled Appointment window:

Appointment information is typed in the Subject box. The location of the meeting can be typed in the Location box. The Start time lists contain a date and time that corresponds to the slot that was double-clicked. By default, the End time lists contains the same date and a time 30 minutes later than the Start time. Start time and End time lists can be changed by typing a time in the corresponding box or by clicking the corresponding arrow and selecting a time in the list:

Additional notes about the appointment can be typed in the notes area of the window:

notes area

adding a reminder

The Reminder check box can be selected so that a sound is played and the Reminder window is displayed 15 minutes before the appointment time. The amount of time before an appointment that the Reminder window is displayed can be changed by selecting or typing a time in the Reminder box. For example, the Reminder window with Kelly's Birthday Party looks similar to:

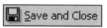

The Reminder window displays the appointment with the time left before the appointment starts (Due in). The Due in time is automatically updated. In the example above, the Reminder window was displayed 15 minutes before the appointment time and now indicates the party starts in 4 minutes. The Reminder window is removed by clicking Dismiss.

removing the Reminder window

Clicking the Save and Close button (![Save and Close]) on the Appointment window toolbar removes the Appointment window and displays the appointment in the appropriate row in the Appointment area.

modifying an appointment

An appointment can be modified by double-clicking it or by right-clicking it and selecting Open from the menu, which displays the Appointment window. Changes can then be made to the existing appointment information. Clicking the Save and Close button on the Appointment window toolbar saves any changes and removes the Appointment window.

deleting an appointment

An appointment can be deleted in any view by right-clicking the appointment and selecting Delete from the menu or by selecting the appointment and then clicking the Delete button (![X]) on the toolbar.

2.7 Minimizing and Quitting Outlook

Outlook should remain running, even when working in another application, so that the Reminder window will be displayed. Outlook can be *minimized* by clicking the Minimize button (![-]) in the upper-right corner of the Outlook window, which leaves it running but reduces it to a button on the Taskbar:

![Taskbar with Start button and Calendar - Microsoft Outl...]

Outlook can be displayed again when needed by clicking the Outlook button on the Taskbar.

The Maximize Button

The Maximize button (![□]) in the upper-right corner of the Outlook window can be used to expand the Outlook window to fill the entire screen.

quitting Outlook   When Outlook is no longer needed, it should be quit properly. *Quitting Outlook* means that its window is removed from the screen and the program is no longer in the computer's memory. Outlook is quit by selecting Exit from the File menu. Outlook can also be quit by clicking its Close button (⊠) in the upper-right corner of the Outlook window. Note that the Reminder window will only be displayed if Outlook is running.

Practice 3

In this practice you will add an appointment to Calendar and minimize Outlook. Calendar should already be displayed.

① USE DATE NAVIGATOR TO DISPLAY A DATE

In Date Navigator, click the date three days from today. The calendar for the selected day is displayed.

② ADD AN APPOINTMENT

a. Double-click the 4:00 p.m. slot. An Untitled Appointment window is displayed.

1. Select the Appointment tab if those options are not already displayed.
2. In the Subject box, type Band Practice.
3. In the Location box, type Alexandra's Garage.
4. Note that the End time currently displays 4:30 PM.
5. Click the End time arrow and select 6:00 PM from the list. The end time of the appointment is changed.
6. Select the Reminder check box if it is not already selected.
7. Click the Reminder arrow and select 30 minutes from the list. The reminder time is changed.
8. On the Appointment window toolbar, click the Save and Close button (🖫 Save and Close). The window is removed and the appointment is displayed in the Appointment area of Calendar.

③ MINIMIZE OUTLOOK

a. In the upper-right corner of Calendar, click the Minimize button (▁). Calendar is reduced to a button on the Taskbar.

b. On the Taskbar, click the Calendar button. Calendar is again displayed.

④ DISPLAY OUTLOOK TODAY

On the Outlook bar, click the Outlook Today shortcut. Outlook Today is displayed. Note that the appointment is displayed under Calendar.

2.8 Outlook Tasks

A *task* is a job, chore, or errand that needs to be completed. Tasks can be entered and tracked in the TaskPad area of Calendar:

☐	☑	TaskPad
		Click here to add a new Task
☑	☐	Wrap Kelly's birthday gift
☑	☐	Piano practice
☑	☐	Schedule science lab
☑	☐	Complete computer science final project
☑	☐	Finish web page
☑	☐	Pay college application fee

The Taskpad is displayed in all Calendar views except Month view.

adding a task

A task is added to the TaskPad by first clicking the Click here to add a new Task row in the TaskPad, which places the insertion point. Typing text and pressing Enter adds the task to the TaskPad.

Additional information about a task can be added by double-clicking the task in the TaskPad which displays the Task window. Options in the Task tab are used to add additional information about the task:

A due date for the task can be specified by selecting or typing a date in the Due date box. Additional notes about the task can be typed in the notes area of the window:

The Tasks Window

Tasks

Clicking the Tasks shortcut on the Outlook bar displays the Tasks window. The Tasks window displays a list of all tasks that have been added to the TaskPad and their due dates. The Tasks window can be used to organize, add, and modify tasks.

The New Button

A task can be added in any view by clicking the New button arrow (New) on the toolbar and selecting Task or by selecting Task (Ctrl+Shift+K) from the New submenu in the File menu.

Recurring Tasks

Tasks that occur on a regular basis, such as once a week, only have to be entered in the Task window once by clicking the Recurrence button (Recurrence...) on the toolbar, which displays the Task Recurrence dialog box.

Selecting a Recurrence pattern, such as Weekly, enters the task on the TaskPad according to the pattern.

Clicking the Save and Close button on the Task window toolbar closes the window. The task will also be automatically added to Outlook Today under the Tasks heading.

modifying a task

A task can be modified by double-clicking it or right-clicking it and selecting Open from the menu, which displays the Task window. Changes can then be made to the existing task information. Clicking the Save and Close button on the Task window toolbar saves any changes and removes the Task window.

completing a task

Once a task has been completed, selecting its check box or right-clicking the task and selecting Mark Complete from the menu displays the task as complete in the TaskPad:

A completed task remains in the TaskPad and is displayed with a line through it. A task is deleted by right-clicking the task and selecting Delete from the menu or clicking the task and then clicking the Delete button (✖) on the toolbar.

In Outlook Today, the tasks list is displayed under the Tasks heading. Clicking a task's check box marks it as complete.

2.9 Previewing and Printing the Calendar

A calendar can be printed so that the information can be used as a reference away from the computer. *Previewing* displays the calendar as it will appear when printed. Selecting a view and then selecting Print Preview from the File menu displays the calendar in the Print Preview window. For example, the following Calendar was displayed in Day view and then Print Preview was selected from the File menu:

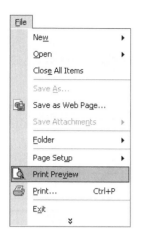

Actual Size button Displays the calendar in the size it will be printed.

Close button Removes the Print Preview window and displays Calendar.

Print button Displays the Print dialog box.

The calendar can be printed by clicking the Print button, which displays a Print dialog box similar to:

The Print dialog box varies depending on the printer

The Start and End lists in the Print range area can be used to print the calendar for more than one date by clicking the Start or End arrows and selecting a different date. Selecting the Hide details of private appointments check box prints the calendar without the appointment information. Selecting OK prints the calendar for the selected date(s).

A calendar can also be printed by selecting <u>P</u>rint (Ctrl+P) from the <u>F</u>ile menu or clicking the Print button () on the toolbar, which displays the Print dialog box. Selecting OK prints the calendar for the selected date(s).

Practice 4

In this practice you will add and modify tasks and print the calendar for a specific day. Outlook Today should already be displayed.

① *DISPLAY CALENDAR*

Display Calendar in Day view.

② *ADD TWO TASKS*

    a. Click the Click here to add a new Task row in the TaskPad. The insertion point appears.

    b. Type Pay student activity fee and press Enter. The task is added to the TaskPad.

    c. Type Update web page and press Enter. The new task is added to the top of the list in the TaskPad.

    d. Double-click the new task. The Update web page Task window is displayed.

    e. Click the Due date arrow. A calendar is displayed.

    f. Click the date that represents Monday of next week. The selected date is displayed in the Due date box.

    g. On the Task window toolbar, click the Save and Close button (☐ <u>S</u>ave and Close). The window is removed and the modified task is displayed on the TaskPad. Note that there is no difference in the way the task is displayed in the TaskPad.

    h. Switch to Outlook Today. Note the tasks in the Tasks list. The due date for the Update web page task is displayed in parentheses.

③ *MARK A TASK AS COMPLETE AND THEN REMOVE THE TASK FROM THE TASKPAD*

    a. Click the check box to the left of the Pay student activity fee task. The task is displayed as complete.

    b. Switch to Calendar. Note the completed task in the TaskPad.

    c. Right-click the Pay student activity fee task. A menu is displayed.

    d. Select Delete from the menu. The task is removed from the TaskPad.

④ *PREVIEW AND THEN PRINT THE CALENDAR*

    a. In Calendar, display the calendar for today's date in Day view if it is not already displayed.

    b. Select <u>F</u>ile → Print Pre<u>v</u>iew. Calendar is displayed as it will appear when printed.

    c. On the toolbar, click the Print button (🖨 Print...). The Print dialog box is displayed.

        1. Select OK. The dialog box is removed and the calendar for today's date is printed.

⑤ *QUIT OUTLOOK*

Select <u>F</u>ile → E<u>x</u>it. The application window is removed from the Desktop. Note that the Reminder window will not be displayed unless Outlook is running.

Microsoft Outlook is a personal management application that has tools for organizing appointments and listing tasks.

When Outlook is started, Outlook Today is displayed. Outlook Today shows the current date, a calendar summary for a number of days, existing tasks, and a summary of e-mail messages. The titles <u>Calendar</u>, <u>Tasks</u>, and <u>Messages</u> are links to those Outlook tools. A link, or hyperlink, is text that can be clicked to display a destination, such as an Outlook tool.

Calendar

Calendar is an organizational tool that can be used to keep track of assignment due dates, create reminders about events, and schedule appointments and meetings. Clicking the Calendar shortcut on the Outlook bar or clicking the Calendar link in Outlook Today displays Calendar. In Calendar, Date Navigator can be used as a calendar reference and also be used to display the calendar for a selected day.

Calendar can be displayed in Day, Work Week, Week, or Month view. In any view, the current day is displayed by clicking the Today button. The View buttons on the toolbar are used to change the way the calendar is displayed.

An event is an activity that is scheduled for a specific day, but is not assigned a start or an end time. Events are displayed in the Event banner at the top of the Appointment area. An event is added to Calendar by first using Date Navigator to display the appropriate calendar day and then double-clicking the date heading or selecting the New All Day Event command. An event can be removed from the Event banner by right-clicking the Event banner and selecting Delete from the menu or by selecting the event and then clicking the Delete button on the toolbar.

An appointment is an activity scheduled on a specific day that has a specific starting and ending time. An appointment is displayed in the Appointment area of Calendar in the appropriate time slot. In any view, an appointment can be added by clicking the New button on the Appointment window toolbar. An appointment can be deleted in any view by right-clicking the appointment and selecting Delete from the menu or by selecting the appointment and then clicking the Delete button on the toolbar.

The Reminder check box can be selected so that a sound is played and the Reminder window is displayed 15 minutes before the appointment time. The amount of time before an appointment that the Reminder window is displayed can be changed by selecting or typing a time in the Reminder box.

Outlook should remain running while working in another application, such as Microsoft Word, so that the Reminder window will be displayed. Outlook can be minimized by clicking the Minimize button ( ) in the upper-right corner of the Outlook window, which leaves it running but reduces it to a button on the Taskbar. Clicking the Outlook button on the Taskbar switches to the Outlook application. Outlook is quit by selecting the Exit command. Outlook can also be quit by clicking its Close button in the upper-right corner of the Outlook window. The Reminder window will only be displayed if Outlook is running.

A task is a job, chore, or errand that needs to be completed. Tasks can be entered and tracked in the TaskPad area of Calendar. A task is added to the TaskPad by first clicking the Click here to add a new Task row in the TaskPad. Additional information about a task can be added by double-clicking the task in the TaskPad. A task can be modified by double-clicking it or by right-clicking it and selecting Open from the menu. Once a task has been completed, selecting its check box or right-clicking the task and selecting Mark Complete from the menu displays the task as complete in the TaskPad.

A calendar can be printed so that the information can be used as a reference away from the computer. Previewing displays the calendar as it will appear when printed. In the Print Preview window, selecting the Print button prints the calendar. A calendar can also be printed by selecting the Print command or clicking the Print button on the toolbar.

Vocabulary

Appointment An activity scheduled on a specific day that has a specific starting and ending time.

Calendar An Outlook tool that can be used to keep track of assignment due dates, create reminders about events, and schedule appointments and meetings.

Date Navigator A calendar reference that can be used to display the appointments for a selected day.

Event An activity that is scheduled for a specific day, but is not assigned a start or an end time.

Hyperlink See Link.

Link Text that can be clicked to display a destination, such as an Outlook tool.

Microsoft Outlook A personal management application that has tools for organizing appointments and listing tasks.

Minimize Reduces a window to a button on the Taskbar.

Previewing Displays the calendar as it will appear when printed.

Quitting Outlook The process of removing the Outlook window from the screen and the program from the computer's memory.

Task A job, chore, or errand that needs to be completed.

Outlook Commands and Buttons

Day button Displays the calendar for the current day in Day view. Found on the toolbar.

Delete command Deletes an event, appointment, or task. Found in the menu displayed by right-clicking an event, appointment, or task. The Delete button on the toolbar can be used instead of the command.

Exit command Quits Outlook. Found in the File menu. The Close button in the upper-right corner of the application window can be used instead of the command.

Mark Complete **command** Displays a task as complete. Found in the menu displayed by right-clicking a task.

Minimize button Reduces the Outlook window to a button on the Taskbar. Found in the upper-right corner of the Outlook window.

Month button Displays a scrollable calendar with one week per row. Found on the toolbar.

New button Displays an Untitled Appointment window used to add a new appointment. Found on the Untitled Appointment window toolbar.

New All Day Event **command** Displays an Untitled Event window used to add an event to Calendar. Found in the Actions menu.

Open **command** Displays a window used to modify an appointment or task. Found in the menu displayed by right-clicking an appointment or a task.

Print **command** Displays a dialog box used to print a calendar. Found in the File menu. The Print button on the toolbar can be used instead of the command.

Print Preview **command** Displays the calendar as it will appear when printed. Found in the File menu.

Save and Close button Saves information typed in the Event, Appointment, and Task windows and removes the window. Found on the toolbar of the Event, Appointment, and Task windows.

Today button Selects and displays the calendar for the current day regardless of the view. Found on the toolbar.

Week button Displays the calendar for Monday through Sunday of the current week. Found on the toolbar.

Work Week button Displays the calendar for Monday through Friday of the current week. Found on the toolbar.

Review Questions

Sections 2.1 — 2.9

1. What is Microsoft Outlook?

2. a) List the steps required to start Outlook and display Outlook Today.
   b) What does Outlook Today display?
   c) What is a link?
   d) Give an example of a link found on the Outlook Today page.

3. What does the toolbar contain?

4. a) List three uses for the Outlook tool Calendar.
   b) List two ways to display Calendar from Outlook Today.

5. List two uses of Date Navigator.

6. List the steps required to change the Date Navigator to display the month two months ahead of the current month.

7. a) List the four views Calendar can be displayed in.
   b) List the step required to change Calendar from Day view to Month view.
   c) What view displays Monday through Sunday of the current week?
   d) List the step required to display the current day.

8. List the steps required to display the appointments for July 12, 2003.

9. a) What is an event?
   b) Where are events displayed?

10. List the steps required to add the event "Paula and Rick's 30th Anniversary" on April 4, 2003.

11. What is the difference between an appointment and an event?

12. a) Where is an appointment displayed?
    b) How is an appointment location displayed?
    c) What does a bell to the left of an appointment indicate?

13. In what view(s) can the New button be used to add an appointment?

14. a) List the steps required to add the appointment "Dentist" from 3:00 p.m. to 4:00 p.m. on January 21, 2003, from Day view.
    b) List the steps required to modify the appointment added in part (a) to include a reminder 30 minutes before the appointment time.
    c) List the steps required to delete the appointment added in part (a).

15. a) Why should Outlook remain running while working in other applications?
    b) What does minimizing Outlook do?

16. List two ways to quit Outlook.

17. a) What is a task?
    b) Where are tasks entered and tracked?
    c) What view does not display Taskpad?

18. a) List the steps required to add the task "Study for Java test" with a due date of November 17, 2003.
    b) List the steps required to modify the task in part (a) to include the note, "Test covers chapters 1 through 7."

19. a) List the steps required to mark a task as complete.
    b) How is a completed task displayed in the Taskpad?
    c) List the steps required to delete a completed task.

20. What is displayed when the calendar is previewed?

21. Is it possible to print the calendar without the appointment information?

Use the Outlook Calendar tool to complete the following steps:

a) Add relevant school events. These may include sports events, picture day, and school holidays.

b) Add appropriate personal events. These may include family birthdays, anniversaries, and trips.

c) Using the course syllabus for each of your courses, add relevant school appointments. These may include group work and study sessions, as well as assignment, project, test, and exam dates. Add reminders and notes as necessary.

d) Add appropriate personal appointments. These may include hair appointments, work-out schedule, and dates.

e) On the TaskPad, add school-related tasks that need to be completed. Add additional information as necessary. These may include returning a library book, paying an activity fee, and completing a project.

f) On the TaskPad, add appropriate personal tasks that need to be completed. These may include purchasing a birthday gift, practicing an instrument, and completing chores.

g) Print a copy of the current month's calendar to be used as a reference away from the computer.

h) Maintain the calendar throughout the school year. This includes modifying events and appointments and marking tasks as complete when appropriate.

Chapter 3
Advanced Outlook Features

Detailed Address Cards

Phone List

Mail Message

New Folder

Empty "Deleted Items" Folder

Options

Export to vCard file

Chapter 3 Expectations

After completing this chapter you will be able to:

1. Describe the purpose of the Contacts tool.
2. Add a contact.
3. Modify a contact.
4. Display the contacts list in different views.
5. Print the contacts list.
6. Use Outlook to send e-mail messages.
7. Display the Address Book.
8. Organize e-mail messages in the Folder List.
9. Add a signature to e-mail messages.
10. Create a vCard.
11. Send a meeting request.

This chapter introduces the Outlook Contacts tool and e-mail. E-mail etiquette is also discussed.

3.1 The Outlook Contacts Tool

Contacts is an Outlook tool that is used to create an electronic address book that stores information such as addresses and phone numbers of individuals and businesses. Contacts is also linked to the Address Book, an Outlook tool that contains e-mail addresses.

Contacts

Clicking the Contacts shortcut on the Outlook bar displays the contacts list:

The Contacts Index

The Contacts Index contains a series of buttons that can be clicked to display contacts whose name begin with a specific letter.

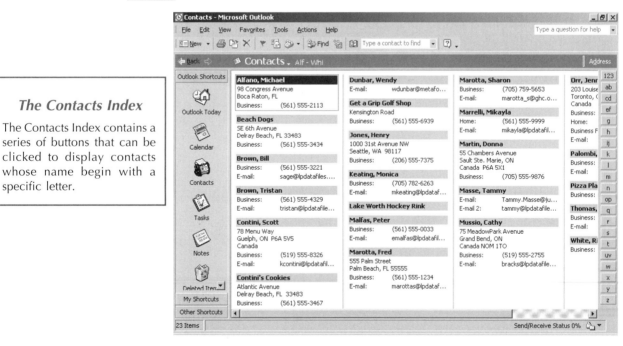

Address Cards view   The contacts list above is displayed in Address Cards view.

3.2 Adding a Contact

A new contact is added by clicking the New button (⬛ New ▾) on the toolbar or by double-clicking a blank area of Contacts, which displays an Untitled Contact window:

Displaying the Untitled Contact Window

The Untitled Contact window can also be displayed by selecting Contact (Ctrl+N) from the New submenu in the File menu.

The Details Tab

In the Contact window, selecting the Details tab displays additional fields, such as Birthday and Nickname fields.

field
moving through fields

Contact information is entered into a set of fields. A *field* is a single piece of information, such as an e-mail address. The insertion point is moved from field to field by pressing the Tab key. Pressing Shift+Tab moves the insertion point to the previous field. Information does not have to be entered for every field.

In the Full Name box, typing a name such as Jim Wilson and then pressing the Tab key or clicking another box automatically displays Jim Wilson on the title bar of the Contact window and changes Jim Wilson in the Full Name box to Wilson, Jim. Wilson, Jim is also automatically displayed in the File as box.

Full Name Box

Clicking Full Name displays the Check Full Name dialog box. The Check Full Name dialog box can be used to enter full name data in separate fields, including Title, Middle, and Suffix.

The Check Full Name dialog box is also displayed automatically if Outlook is unsure how to file the data typed in the Full Name box.

filing in the Contacts list

The File as box is used to determine the placement of the new contact in the contacts list.

If a company name is entered in the Company field and the Full Name box is left blank, Outlook files the contact by the company name as it is typed. For example, if Beach Dogs is entered in the Company field, the Company box and the File as box display Beach Dogs:

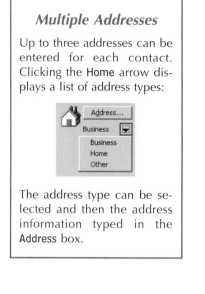
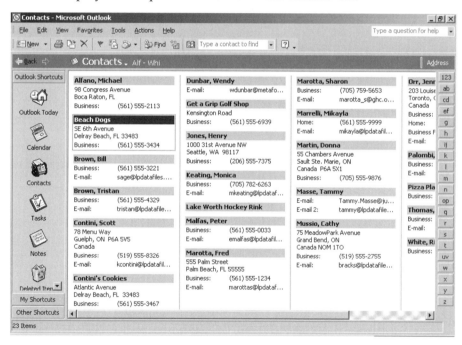

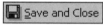

After all the information has been entered, clicking the Save and Close button () on the Contact window toolbar saves the contact and displays it in alphabetical order in the contacts list:

3.3 Modifying a Contact

In the Contacts list, double-clicking a contact displays a window with the contact's information. Editing the information and then clicking the Save and Close button on the Contact window toolbar saves the modified contact information. Clicking the Close button (X) in the upper-right corner of the window and selecting No if prompted to save removes the Contact window without saving any modifications.

deleting a contact A contact is deleted by right-clicking the contact and selecting Delete from the menu or by clicking the contact once to select it and then clicking the Delete button (☒) on the toolbar.

Practice 1

In this practice you will start Microsoft Outlook and add contacts, modify a contact, and delete a contact.

① *START OUTLOOK*

On the Taskbar, click Start → Programs → Microsoft Outlook. Microsoft Outlook is started and the Outlook Today window is displayed.

② *DISPLAY CONTACTS*

In the Outlook bar, click the Contacts shortcut. Contacts is displayed. Note the features of Contacts including the Contacts Index. A message may be displayed indicating there are no items to show in this view.

③ *ADD A CONTACT*

   a. On the toolbar, click the New button (New). An Untitled Contact window is displayed and the insertion point is in the Full Name box.
   b. In the Full Name box, type John Wells.
   c. Press the Tab key. The insertion point appears in the Job title box. Note that Wells, John is displayed in the File as box and the title bar displays John Wells – Contact.
   d. Press the Tab key. The insertion point appears in the Company box.
   e. Type ADSB Computers and then click the Business telephone box. The insertion point appears in the Business box.
   f. Type (561) 555-3871 and then click the Business Fax box. The insertion point appears in the Business Fax box.
   g. Type (561) 555-3875 and then click the E-mail box. The insertion point appears in the E-mail box.
   h. Type jwells@lpdatafiles.com.
   i. On the Contact window toolbar, click the Save and Close button (Save and Close). The window is removed and the contact is displayed alphabetically by the File as field in the contacts list.

④ *ADD A SECOND CONTACT*

   a. On the toolbar, click the New button (New). An Untitled Contact window is displayed and the insertion point is in the Full Name box.
   b. In the Company box, type Lake Worth Hockey Rink.
   c. Click the Business phone box. Note that Lake Worth Hockey Rink is displayed in the File as box and Lake Worth Hockey Rink – Contact is displayed in the title bar.
   d. Type (561) 555-3545.
   e. In the Web page address box, type www.lwhockeyrink.lpdatafiles.com.
   f. On the Contact window toolbar, click the Save and Close button (Save and Close). The window is removed and the contact is displayed alphabetically by the File as field in the contacts list.

⑤ **ADD A THIRD CONTACT**

    a. On the toolbar, click the New button (⊞ New ▾). An Untitled Contact window is displayed and the insertion point is in the Full Name box.

    b. In the Full Name box, type Cathy Mussio.

    c. In the Job title box, type Manager.

    d. In the Company box, type The Grand Bend Hotel.

    e. In the Business phone box, type (561) 555-8765.

    f. In the Home box, type (561) 555-0002.

    g. In the Business Fax box, type (561) 555-0006.

    h. In the Mobile box, type (561) 555-0004.

    i. In the E-mail box, type mussio@lpdatafiles.com.

    j. In the Web page address box, type www.thegrandbendhotel.lpdatafiles.com.

    k. On the Contact window toolbar, click the Save and Close button (⊞ Save and Close). The window is removed and the contact is displayed in the contacts list.

⑥ **ADD A FOURTH CONTACT**

    a. On the toolbar, click the New button (⊞ New ▾).

    b. In the Full Name box, type your name.

    c. In the Address box, type your address.

    d. In the E-mail box, type your e-mail address, if you have one.

    e. On the Contact window toolbar, click the Save and Close button (⊞ Save and Close). The window is removed and the contact is displayed in the contacts list.

⑦ **MODIFY CONTACT INFORMATION**

    a. Double-click the Cathy Mussio contact. The Cathy Mussio Contact window is displayed.

    c. Click the Business phone box and change the phone number to (561) 555-4343.

    d. On the Contact window toolbar, click the Save and Close button. The modified contact information is saved and the updated contacts list is displayed.

⑧ **DELETE A CONTACT**

    a. In Contacts, click the John Wells contact to select it.

    b. On the toolbar, click the Delete button (✕). The contact is deleted.

3.4 Contacts Views

The contacts list can be displayed in several different views. Commands in the View menu are used to change the way the contacts list is displayed. For example, Address Cards view is shown in Section 3.1. Address Cards view displays selected contact information and is a quick way to reference frequently used information, such as phone numbers and e-mail addresses.

Detailed Address Cards view

Selecting Detailed Address Cards from the Current Underline{V}iew submenu in the Underline{V}iew menu displays all the contact information in an expanded address card format:

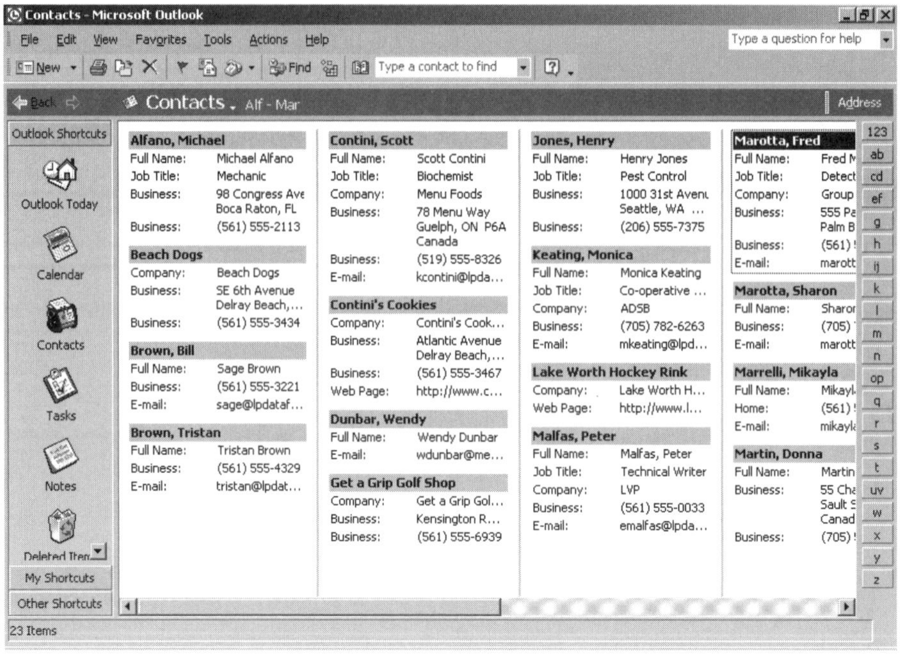

Phone List view

Selecting Phone List from the Current Underline{V}iew submenu in the Underline{V}iew menu displays phone and fax numbers:

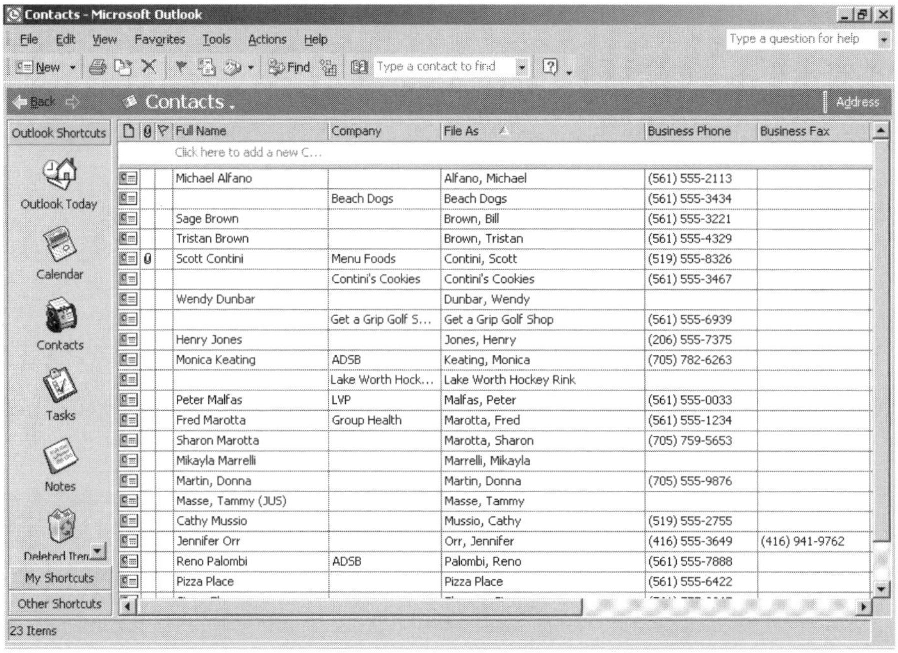

A Guide to Microsoft Office XP Professional

3.5 Printing Contacts

The contacts list can be printed so that the information can be used as a reference away from the computer. The contacts list is printed by first selecting the view to print and then selecting Print Preview from the File menu, which displays the contacts list as it will appear when printed:

status bar

footer

Outlook automatically adds a footer to the bottom of each printed page. The footer contains the user name, the page number, and the current date. The status bar displays a Page indicator. In the example above, Page 1 of 3 indicates page 1 is currently displayed and the contacts list will be printed on 3 pages. Other features of Print Preview include:

Page Up button   Displays the previous page.

Page Down button   Displays the next page.

Actual Size button   Displays the page in the size it will be printed.

Print... **Print button**   Displays the Print dialog box.

Close **Close button**   Removes the Print Preview window and returns to the Contacts window.

The calendar can be printed by clicking the Print button which displays a Print dialog box similar to:

Changing the Footer

The information in the footer can be changed in Print Preview by selecting the Page Setup button (Page Setup...), which displays the Page Setup dialog box. Selecting the Header/Footer tab displays those options.

The Print dialog box varies depending on the printer

Print Style

The view the Contacts list is displayed in determines the Print style, which is displayed in the Print dialog box. For example, Address Cards view is printed in Card Style and Phone List view is printed in Table Style.

Note that Card Style is selected as the Print style. Selecting OK prints the Contact list as displayed in the Print Preview window. The contacts list can also be printed as a booklet by selecting a different print style. For example, selecting Small Booklet Style prints the contacts list so that printed pages can be made into a booklet:

Printing on Both Sides of the Paper

A booklet can be printed on both sides of the paper only if the printer supports double-sided printing. If the printer does, the double-sided printing option must be selected in the Print dialog box.

Note that booklets can be printed on both sides of the paper. A warning box may appear when the Small Booklet Style option is selected:

Selecting Yes prints the booklet on one side of the paper. Selecting No cancels the print request and returns to the Contacts window.

Contacts can also be printed by selecting Print (Ctrl+P) from the File menu or clicking the Print button (🖨) on the toolbar, which displays the Print dialog box. Selecting OK prints the contacts in the selected view.

Practice 2

In this practice you will display Contacts in different views and modify the current contact information. Contacts should already be displayed.

① DISPLAY THE CONTACTS LIST IN ADDRESS CARDS VIEW

Select View → Current View → Address Cards if the contacts list is not already displayed in Address Cards view. Note how the information is displayed.

② CHANGE TO PHONE LIST VIEW

Select View → Current View → Phone List. Contacts is displayed in Phone List view. Note how the information is displayed.

③ CHANGE TO DETAILED ADDRESS CARDS VIEW

Select View → Current View → Detailed Address Cards. Contacts is displayed in Detailed Address Cards view. Note the additional information that is displayed, such as the web page address in the Lake Worth Hockey Rink contact.

④ PRINT PREVIEW AND PRINT

a. Select File → Print Preview. The Print Preview window is displayed.

b. Click the Actual Size button (🔍). The contacts list is displayed as it will appear when printed.

c. Click the Print button (🖨 Print...). A dialog box is displayed.

    1. In the Print dialog box, select Small Booklet Style.

    2. Select OK. A warning box may appear. If the warning box appears, select Yes. The dialog is removed and the contacts list is printed.

LAN

A network is a combination of software and hardware that work together to allow computers to exchange data and to share software and devices, such as printers. A LAN (Local Area Network) is a network used to connect devices within a small area.

ISP

An ISP (Internet Service Provider) offers access to the Internet for a fee. An online service, such as AOL, offers access to the Internet as well as other services for a fee.

3.6 What is E-mail?

E-mail, or electronic mail, is the sending and receiving of messages and computer files over a communications network such as a LAN (Local Area Network) or the Internet.

An e-mail address is required in order to send and receive e-mail messages. E-mail addresses are provided when registering with an ISP (Internet Service Provider) or an online service. A typical e-mail address is similar to:

christina@lpdatafiles.com

user name — host or domain name — top-level domain

E-mail software is also required for sending and receiving messages. Outlook includes e-mail software.

3.7 The Address Book

The Address Book is an Outlook tool that contains contact names and e-mail addresses. It is automatically updated when a contact that includes an e-mail address is added to the contacts list.

 The Address Book is displayed by clicking the Address Book button () on the toolbar:

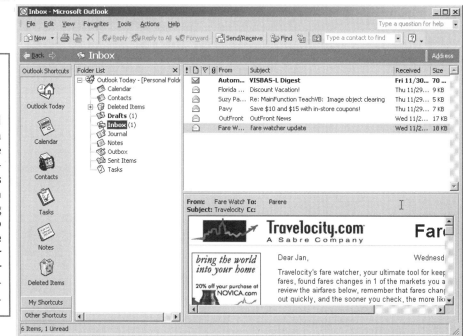

The Address Book

The Address Book can also be displayed by selecting **Address Book** (Ctrl+Shift+B) from the **Tools** menu.

closing the Address Book Clicking the Close button (☒) in the upper-right corner of the window closes the Address Book.

3.8 Using Outlook to Send E-mail

Outlook can be used to send and receive e-mail messages. Clicking Messages in Outlook Today displays the Inbox window:

Making Outlook the Default E-mail Program

If more than one e-mail application is installed on a computer, Outlook can be made the default e-mail program by selecting **Options** from the **Tools** menu, which displays the Options dialog box. Selecting the **Other** tab and then selecting the **Make Outlook the default program for E-mail, Contacts, and Calendar** check box and **OK** makes Outlook the default mail program.

The Folder List

If the Folder List is not displayed, Folder List can be selected from the View menu.

The Preview Pane

If the Preview pane is not displayed, Preview Pane can be selected from the View menu.

Microsoft Word

Outlook uses Microsoft Word as the default mail editor. Using Word as the e-mail editor allows the use of features such as AutoCorrect, the spelling checker, the grammar checker, and bulleted lists. Word is introduced in Chapter 4.

Inbox contains three panes. The pane on the left is the Folder List where e-mail messages are stored. The top pane lists the messages in the selected folder, and the Preview pane below it displays the selected message.

A new e-mail message is created by clicking the New button (New) on the toolbar or selecting Mail Message (Ctrl+N) from the New submenu in the File menu, which displays an Untitled Message window:

The e-mail address of the recipient is typed in the To box. An e-mail address can also be added by clicking the To button (To...), which displays the Select Names dialog box:

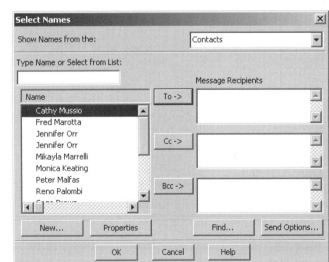

The Name list contains the names of individuals or businesses in the Address Book. Selecting a name and then clicking To -> displays the selected name and e-mail address in the Message Recipients box. Selecting OK adds the name and e-mail address to the To box in the Untitled Message window:

Cc The e-mail addresses of additional recipients are typed in the Cc box. Additional recipients can also be added by clicking the Cc button (Cc...), which displays the Select Names dialog box where recipients can be selected.

Subject A message title is typed in the Subject box and then the message is typed in the lower portion of the Untitled Message window.

attachment An e-mail can also include an attachment. An *attachment* is a file sent along with an e-mail message to the recipient. For example, a resume that is a Word document can be attached to an e-mail message. The recipient can read the message and then open the resume in Word. A file is attached to an e-mail message by clicking the Insert File button ( ) on the Untitled Message toolbar, which displays the Insert File dialog box:

E-mail Attachments

Outlook has security features that prevent many file types from being sent or received. For example, screen saver files (SCR), programs (EXE), and scripts.

The Look in list and contents box below it are to locate the file to be attached. Clicking a file name in the contents box and then selecting Insert attaches a copy of that file to the e-mail message. Clicking the Send button (Send) on the Untitled Message toolbar sends the message. It is important to review the message carefully before sending, because once a message is sent it cannot be retrieved.

POP3

The way sent messages are received varies from system to system. *POP3* (Post Office Protocol 3) is the most common protocol used to retrieve messages from an e-mail server.

When an e-mail message is sent, it resides in an electronic mailbox on a mail server until it is retrieved. The Send/Receive button (Send/Receive) on the Inbox window toolbar is clicked to receive messages from the e-mail server and place them in the Inbox folder.

Other commonly used e-mail features in Outlook include:

Reply button Displays an e-mail message window that includes the original message and the sender's e-mail address in the To box. The Reply button should be used to respond to an e-mail message so that the recipient can refer to the original message.

Forward button Sends a selected e-mail message to another e-mail address. A forwarded message includes the original e-mail message and the original sender's e-mail address. Additional information can be added above the original message.

Print button Prints the displayed e-mail message.

Find button Displays a dialog box that can be used to search for specific messages.

3.9 Organizing E-mail Messages

The Folder List can be used to organize e-mail messages:

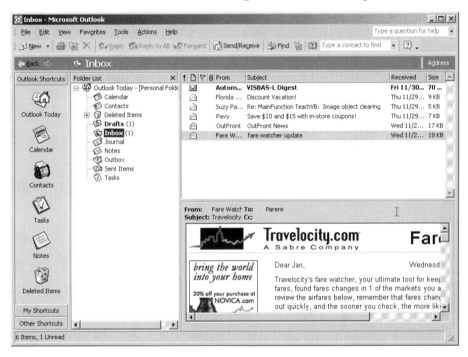

A new folder can be added to the Folder List to store related e-mail messages. For example, a folder named College Correspondence could be used to store all e-mail messages concerning college applications. This folder is created by right-clicking the Inbox folder in the Folder List and selecting New Folder from the menu, which displays the Create New Folder dialog box.

A new folder name is then typed in the Name box:

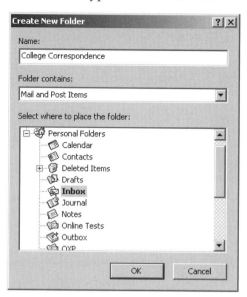

Selecting OK creates the new folder and displays the folder name in the Folder List:

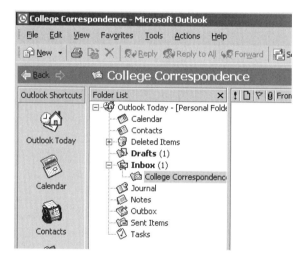

moving a message

A message is moved to a folder by dragging it from the top pane of Inbox to a folder in the Folder List. For example, an e-mail message about college applications is moved to the College Correspondence folder by clicking Inbox in the Folder List to display the message and then dragging the message from the Inbox top pane to the College Correspondence folder in the Folder List.

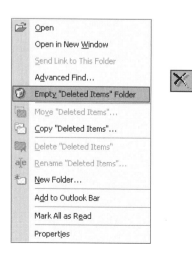

Clicking the Delete button (❌) on the toolbar moves a selected e-mail message to the Deleted Items folder. E-mail messages in the Deleted Items folder are permanently deleted by right-clicking the Deleted Items folder and selecting Empty "Deleted Items" Folder.

3.10 Adding a Signature to E-mail Messages

A *signature* is text that is added to an e-mail message. Named signatures can be created and stored in Outlook so that signature text does not have to be retyped over and over again. The steps for creating a named signature are:

1. **Display the Options dialog box**. Selecting Options from the Tools menu displays the Options dialog box. Selecting the Mail Format tab displays those options:

2. **Display the Create Signature dialog box.** Selecting Signatures displays the Create Signature dialog box:

3. **Name the Signature.** Selecting New displays the Create New Signature dialog box. Type a name in the Enter a name for your new signature box and select Start with a blank signature if it is not already selected:

4. **Create the Signature text.** Selecting Next displays the Edit Signature dialog box. Type the signature text in the Signature text box:

5. **Add the Signature to Outlook.** Selecting Finish adds the Signature to Outlook and displays the Create Signature dialog box:

6. **Display the signature.** Selecting OK twice removes the dialog boxes. The new signature becomes the default signature that is automatically added to every new e-mail message. For example, clicking the New button (📧 New ▾) on the Inbox toolbar displays a new Untitled Message window with a signature already inserted:

Practice 3

In this practice you will create a signature that can be added to e-mail messages. Contacts should already be displayed.

① CREATE A NAMED SIGNATURE

   a. Select Tools → Options. A dialog box is displayed.

     1. Select the Mail Format tab to display those options.
     2. Select Signatures. The Create Signature dialog box is displayed.
     3. Select New. The Create New Signature dialog box is displayed.
     4. In the Enter a name for your new signature box, type your first and last name.
     5. Select the Start with a blank signature option if it is not already selected.
     6. Select Next. The Edit Signature dialog box is displayed.
     7. In the Signature text box, type your first and last name.
     8. Select Finish. The signature is added to Outlook and displayed in the Preview box.
     9. Select OK twice. The dialog boxes are removed and the signature will automatically be added to any outgoing e-mail messages.

② QUIT OUTLOOK

3.11 Using Contacts to Create a vCard

A *vCard* is a standard for creating and sharing virtual business cards over the Internet. A vCard can be created in Contacts and then sent as an e-mail attachment.

A vCard is created by double-clicking a contact, which displays a window with the contact's information. Selecting Export to vCard file from the File menu displays the VCARD File dialog box:

Virtual

Virtual describes a device or element that is simulated by the computer so that it appears to exist to the user but does not actually physically exist.

The Save in list displays a location name, with the location contents displayed in the box below. Double-clicking a folder in the contents box places that folder name in the Save in list. The contents of that folder is then displayed in the contents box. When the Save in list displays the appropriate location for the file to be saved, selecting Save saves the vCard using the contact name as the file name. Outlook automatically adds the extension .vcf to the vCard file name.

Once a vCard is created, it can be sent with an e-mail message as an attachment. The attachment can be opened in any application that supports vCards. If Outlook is installed, opening the attachment file displays the vCard in a Contact window. The vCard can then be saved to the contacts list by clicking the Save and Close button on the Contact window toolbar.

3.12 E-mail Etiquette

E-mail messages are not private. An e-mail message goes through several mail servers before it reaches the recipient, making it easily accessible for others to read. Therefore, sending e-mail messages requires following a certain etiquette:

- Send messages through your account only.
- Use appropriate subject matter and language.
- Be considerate of other people's beliefs and opinions.

When sending e-mail at work or school, it is important to remember that employers and school administrators have the right to read any e-mail messages sent over the corporate or school network, as well as the right to track online activity.

The Love Bug Virus

In May 2000, the Love Bug virus spread around the world erasing data and shutting down electronic communications. This virus was in an attachment of what appeared to be a friendly e-mail message with the subject line I LOVE YOU. This virus infected many computers including those at the Pentagon, NASA, the House of Commons in London, and Ford Motor Corporation.

Worm

A worm is a type of virus that can reproduce itself and use the memory of a computer, but it cannot attach itself to a program.

3.13 E-mail Viruses

Many computer viruses have been associated with e-mail attachments. A *virus* is a program that is designed to reproduce itself by copying itself into other programs stored on a computer without the user's knowledge. Viruses have varying effects, such as displaying annoying messages, causing programs to run incorrectly, and erasing the contents of the hard drive. Precautions need to be taken to avoid getting a virus:

- Invest in antivirus software. Antivirus software will detect many types of viruses by scanning incoming e-mail messages before they are opened. If a virus is detected, the software will display a warning and try to remove the virus.
- Update the antivirus software frequently. New viruses are continually being created and new virus definitions must be downloaded on a regular basis in order for the antivirus software to be effective.
- Always save an attachment file and then virus-check the file before opening it. This precaution should be taken for all messages from known and unknown sources, since many viruses target address books and fool users into thinking the e-mail is from someone familiar.

In Outlook, e-mail can be used to send a meeting request. A meeting request can be used to set up a time for members of a club to meet, notify individuals of a project due date, or schedule a group project meeting. Recipients can add it to their calendar or decline the request. Note that the individual receiving the request needs to have Outlook installed if they want to add the request to their calendar.

A meeting request is created by first displaying Calendar and then adding meeting information the same way an appointment is added.

Clicking the New button (New) on the toolbar displays an Untitled Appointment window:

Meeting information is typed in the Subject box and the location of the meeting can be typed in the Location box. The Start time and End time can be specified, a Reminder can be added, and a note typed in the notes area:

Clicking the Invite Attendees button (Invite Attendees...) on the Untitled Appointment window toolbar displays the appropriate Meeting window:

![Project Meeting - Meeting window showing the Appointment tab with To, Subject (Project Meeting), Location (Room 242), Start time Mon 11/24/2003 9:00 AM, End time Mon 11/24/2003 11:00 AM, Reminder 15 minutes, Show time as Busy, and a message body reading "Please bring your research notes."]

E-mail addresses for recipients are typed in the To box separated by semi-colons (;). The To button (To...) can be used for selecting e-mail addresses from the Address Book. Clicking the Send button (Send) on the Meeting window toolbar sends the meeting request.

Each individual receiving the meeting request is able to accept, tentatively accept, decline, or propose a new meeting time by clicking the appropriate button at the top of the e-mail message:

![E-mail message showing buttons Accept, Tentative, Decline, Propose New Time. "No responses have been received for this meeting." Subject: Project Meeting, When: Monday, November 24, 2003 9:00 AM-11:00 AM., From: jan marrelli, Location: Room 242. When: Monday, November 24, 2003 9:00 AM-11:00 AM (GMT-05:00) Eastern T: Where: Room 242. Please bring your research notes.]

Clicking the Accept button (✔ Accept) automatically places the meeting request information on the individual's calendar:

![Calendar for Monday, November 24 showing time slots from 8am to 12pm, with "Project Meeting (Room 242)" scheduled in the 9:00 slot.]

The icon to the left of Project Meeting indicates that others have been invited to attend. When the Accept button is clicked, the e-mail message is removed from Inbox and a dialog box may be displayed:

Clicking OK automatically sends a response to the sender indicating the request has been accepted. Clicking Don't send a response and then OK removes the dialog box without sending a response.

Clicking the Decline button (✗ Decline) automatically sends a response to the sender indicating that the individual has declined the request. Clicking the Propose New Time button (↰ Propose New Time) sends a response that proposes a new time for the meeting.

The Tentative Button

Clicking the Tentative button (? Tentative) automatically places the meeting request information on the individual's Calendar with a notation indicating a Tentative acceptance.

✗ Decline

↰ Propose New Time

Chapter Summary

Contacts is an Outlook tool that is used to create an electronic address book that stores information such as addresses and phone numbers of individuals and businesses. Contacts is also linked to the Address Book, an Outlook tool that contains e-mail addresses.

Clicking the Contacts shortcut on the Outlook bar displays the contacts list. A new contact is created by clicking the New button on the toolbar or by double-clicking a blank area of Contacts. Contact information is entered into a set of fields. A field is a single piece of information. Clicking the Save and Close button on the Contact window toolbar saves the contact information and displays the contact in alphabetical order in the contacts list. Contact information is modified by double-clicking a contact and then editing the information. A contact can be deleted by clicking the contact once to select it and then clicking the Delete button.

Commands in the View menu are used to change the way the contacts list is displayed. The Detailed Address Cards command displays all the contact information entered in an address card format. The Phone List command displays phone and fax numbers.

The contacts list can be printed by selecting the Print Preview command, which displays the contacts list as it will appear when printed. The contacts list can also be printed as a booklet.

E-mail, or electronic mail, is the sending and receiving of messages and computer files over a communications network. An e-mail address and e-mail software are required in order to send and receive messages. Outlook includes e-mail software.

The Address Book is a tool that contains contact names and e-mail addresses. It is displayed by clicking the Address Book button on the toolbar. Clicking the Close button in the upper-right corner of the window closes the Address Book.

Clicking <u>Messages</u> in Outlook Today displays the Inbox where e-mail messages can be sent and received. A new e-mail message is created by clicking the New button on the toolbar or selecting the <u>M</u>ail Message command. When an e-mail message is sent, it resides in an electronic mailbox on a mail server until it is retrieved. The Send/Receive button on the toolbar is clicked to receive messages from the e-mail server and place them in the Inbox folder.

The Folder List can be used to organize e-mail messages. A new folder can be added to the Folder List by selecting the New Folder command. The Delete button on the toolbar is used to move selected e-mail message to the Deleted Items folder. E-mail messages in are permanently deleted by right-clicking the Deleted Items folder and selecting Empty "Deleted Items" Folder.

A signature is text that is added to an e-mail message. Named signatures can be created and stored in Outlook by selecting the <u>O</u>ptions command.

A vCard is a standard for creating and sharing virtual business cards over the Internet. A vCard can be created in Contacts and then sent as an e-mail attachment. A vCard is created by displaying Contacts, double-clicking a contact, and selecting the E<u>x</u>port to vCard file command.

E-mail is not private and E-mail etiquette should be used when sending electronic messages. Many computer viruses have been associated with e-mail attachments, so precautions need to be taken.

E-mail can be used to send meeting requests. A meeting request can be used to set up a time for members of a club to meet, notify individuals of a project due date, or schedule a group project meeting. The individual(s) receiving the request can add it to their Calendar or decline the request. A meeting request is created by adding meeting information the same way an appointment is added and then clicking the Invite Attendees button, which displays the appropriate Meeting window. E-mail addresses for attendees are typed in the To box, or the To button is used to select an e-mail address from the Address Book. Clicking the Send button on the toolbar sends the meeting request. The recipient is able to accept, tentatively accept, decline, or propose a new meeting time by clicking the appropriate button at the top of the e-mail message.

Vocabulary

Attachment A file sent along with an e-mail message to the recipient.

E-mail (electronic mail) The sending and receiving of messages and computer files over a network

Field A single piece of information, such as an e-mail address.

Signature Text that is added to an e-mail message.

vCard The Internet standard for creating and sharing business cards over the Internet.

Virus A program that is designed to reproduce itself by copying itself into other programs stored on a computer without the user's knowledge.

Address Book button   Displays the Address Book. Found on the toolbar.

Cc button   Displays the Address Book where additional recipients for the e-mail message can be selected. Found in the Untitled Message window.

Close button   Closes the Address Book window. Found in the upper-right corner of the window.

Delete command   Deletes a selected contact or an e-mail message. Found in the menu displayed by right-clicking a contact or e-mail message. The Delete button on the toolbar can be used instead of the command.

Detailed Address Cards command   Displays all the contact information entered in an expanded address card format. Found in the Current View submenu in the View menu.

Empty "Deleted Items" Folder command   Permanently deletes e-mail messages in the Deleted Items folder. Found in the menu displayed by right-clicking the Deleted Items folder.

Export to vCard file command   Displays a dialog box that is used to create a vCard. Found in the File menu.

Find button   Displays a dialog box that can be used to search for specific messages. Found in the Inbox window.

Forward button   Sends a selected e-mail message to another e-mail address. Found in the Inbox window.

Insert File button   Displays a dialog box that is used to send a file with an e-mail message. Found in the Untitled Message window.

Invite Attendees button   Displays a Meeting window. Found in the Appointment window.

Mail Message command   Used to create a new e-mail message. Found in the New submenu in the File menu. The New button on the Inbox window toolbar can be used instead of the command.

New button   Used to add a new appointment to the calendar. Found on the toolbar of the Calendar window.

New button   Used to add a new contact to the contacts list. Found on the toolbar of the Contacts window.

New Folder command   Used to add a new folder to the Folders list. Found in the menu displayed by right-clicking Inbox in the Folders List.

Options command   Displays a dialog box used to create a signature. Found in the Tools menu.

Phone List command   Displays the phone and fax numbers entered in the contacts list. Found in the Current View submenu in the View menu.

Print command   Displays a dialog box used to print a calendar or an e-mail message. Found in the File menu. The Print button on the toolbar can be used instead of the command.

Print Preview command   Displays the contacts list as it will appear when printed. Found in the File menu.

Reply button   Displays an e-mail message window that includes the original message and the sender's e-mail address in the To box. Found in the Inbox window.

Save and Close button   Saves entered contact information and closes the window. Found on the toolbar of the Contact window.

Send button   Used to send e-mail messages and meeting requests. Found in the Untitled Message window.

Send/Receive button   Sends and Receives messages from the e-mail server. Found in the Untitled Message window and Meeting window.

To button   Displays a dialog box used to select a name from the Address Book. Found in the Untitled Message window.

Review Questions

Sections 3.1 — 3.5

1. What is Contacts?

2. List the step required to display the contacts list.

3. a) What is a field?
   b) In a contact window, does information have to be entered for every field?

4. What does the information in the File as box determine?

5. a) List the steps required to add a new contact with the name Manuel Burgos, job title IT Systems Administrator, and business telephone number (954) 555-6230.
   b) List the steps required to modify the contact added in part (a) to include the e-mail address bugosm@it.lpdatafiles.com.
   c) List the steps required to delete the contact added in part (a).

6. a) List the three view that the contacts list can be displayed in.
   b) What information does Phone List view display?

7. a) List one reason why you would print the contacts list.
   b) What information does the footer that is automatically added to each printed contacts list page contain?
   c) List the steps required to display the contacts list in the size it will be printed.

Sections 3.6— 3.14

8. What is e-mail?

9. a) What is required in order to send and receive e-mail messages?
   b) Give an example of a typical e-mail address.

10. a) What is the Address Book?
    b) When is the Address Book automatically updated?

11. List the step required to display the Address Book.

12. a) How is the Inbox window displayed?
    b) What does the Preview pane display?

13. List the steps required to send an e-mail message to an individual in the Address Book.

14. a) What is an attachment?
    b) List the steps required to attach a file to an e-mail message.

15. When an e-mail message is sent, where does it reside?

16. a) List the steps required to reply to an e-mail message.
    b) List the steps required to forward an e-mail message.

17. a) What is the Folder List used for?
    b) List the steps required to add a new folder called Project to the Folder list.
    c) List the steps required to move an e-mail message from the Inbox folder to the Project folder created in part (b).

18. List the steps required to permanently delete an e-mail message.

19. a) What is a signature?
    b) Why would you created a named signature?
    c) List the steps required to create a signature named Susan Smith that automatically adds Susan Smith, Project Manager to every new e-mail message.

20. What is a vCard?

21. List the steps required to create a vCard.

22. List the steps required to send a vCard with an e-mail message.

23. List three examples of e-mail etiquette.

24. a) What is a virus?
    b) Give two examples of effects that viruses may have.
    c) List three precautions that should be taken to avoid getting a virus.

25. a) List three examples of when you might send a meeting request.
    b) List the steps required to send a meeting request.

Use the Outlook Contacts tool to complete the following steps:

a) In the Contacts window, add contact information for at least ten individuals or businesses. These may include friends, coaches, restaurants, and family members.

b) Display the contacts list in Detailed Address Card view and then print a copy in Small Booklet style.

c) Display the Address Book and note the information that has been automatically added from the contacts list.

d) Exchange e-mail messages with a classmate who is not in your contacts list. Update your contacts list to include this new information.

e) Check the Address Book and note that the new contact was automatically added.

f) Send an e-mail message to the classmate in part (d) with Contacts list completed as the subject and the message I am finished typing the information for my contacts list. Have you finished? Please reply using the Reply button.

g) Reply to the classmate's e-mail message using the Reply button. Note that you may have to click the Send/Receive button on the Inbox toolbar to receive the message from the e-mail server.

h) Organize your e-mail messages by creating two new folders, naming the folders appropriately, and then moving messages to the new folders.

i) Create a named signature for your e-mail messages using your first and last name.

j) Create a contact using your personal information and then create a vCard from your contact information.

k) Send the vCard created in part (i) to the classmate in part (d). Note the named signature at the bottom of the new e-mail message.

l) When you receive a classmate's vCard, save it to the contacts list.

m) Send a meeting request to the classmate in part (d). The subject of the meeting is Group Project. The meeting will occur three days from today and will last from 11 a.m. until 3 p.m. The meeting will be held in the library.

Introducing the Word Processor

New Office Document

<u>S</u>ave

Ignore All

Ignore Once

<u>C</u>lose

E<u>x</u>it

Remove this Smart Tag

Open Office Document

<u>O</u>pen

<u>P</u>rint

<u>P</u>rint Layout

<u>N</u>ormal

<u>Z</u>oom

Chapter 4 Expectations

After completing this chapter you will be able to:

1. Describe a word processor.
2. Explain why the word processor is ideal for producing a variety of different documents.
3. Create a new word processor document.
4. Identify the different parts of the document window.
5. Use the word processor to enter and modify text.
6. Display menus and select commands.
7. Save a document.
8. Understand automatic spelling and grammar checking.
9. Use the toolbars.
10. Display formatting marks and identify them.
11. Close a document and quit Word.
12. Open a file.
13. Print a document.
14. Change how a document is viewed.
15. Move a document in the window.

The History of the Word Processor

In 1964, the term *word processor* was invented by IBM as a way to market the Selectric typewriter which could record words on a magnetic tape. The recording capability meant that revisions could be made to text without having to retype the entire document. Wang Laboratories and others soon surpassed IBM with their own versions of a dedicated word processor which by this time included magnetic diskettes for storage and display screens for viewing the document before printing. With the development of the PC in the early 70s came the development of word processor application software. The first word processor application was EasyWriter developed by John Draper for the Apple II computer. When the IBM PC was introduced in 1981, a version of EasyWriter was written for it as well. Another popular word processor for the PC was WordStar, developed by Rob Barnaby and Seymour Rubenstein. The cost of the PC was much less than a stand-alone word processor making the word processor obsolete. Today there are many word processor applications available.

T his chapter introduces Microsoft Word, a powerful word processor used to create printed and online documents. Word will be used to create, edit, save, and print documents.

4.1 What is a Word Processor?

A *word processor* is a computer application that is used to produce easy to read, professional-looking documents such as letters, résumés, and reports. It is a powerful tool that can be used to modify the look of a document. A document can be saved and then recalled later to make additional changes or to print another copy.

4.2 Creating a New Word Document

Microsoft Word is the word processor application in Microsoft Office. Selecting New Office Document from the Start menu on the Windows Taskbar displays the New Office Document dialog box. Selecting the General tab displays icons:

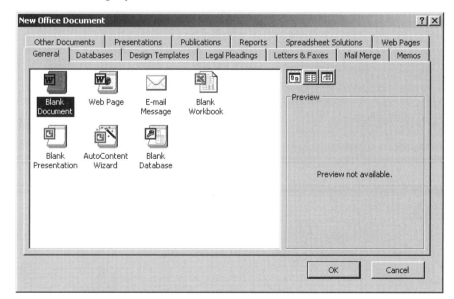

The Programs Menu

Another way to start an Office application is by selecting the application from the Programs submenu, found in the Start menu.

Clicking the Blank Document icon and then selecting OK starts Word and creates a new, empty word processor document:

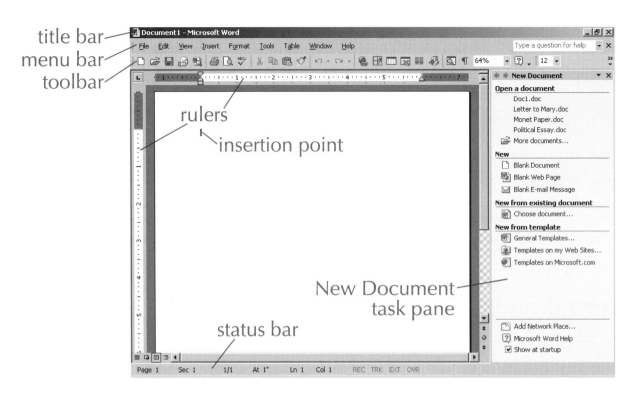

title bar
menu bar
toolbar
rulers
insertion point
New Document task pane
status bar

New Documents

If Word is already started, clicking the New Blank Document button (□) on the toolbar creates a new document.

Using the Mouse

Sliding the mouse to move the pointer on the screen is called *pointing.* An object on the screen can be selected by pointing to it and pressing the left mouse button and releasing it quickly. This type of selection is called *clicking.*

Double-clicking means to point to an object and press the left mouse button twice in rapid succession.

Right-clicking means to point to an object and press and release the right mouse button quickly.

Dragging means to press and hold the left mouse button while moving the mouse.

- The **title bar** displays the name and type of document. The name Document1 is used temporarily until it is given a name when saved.

- The **menu bar** contains the names of drop-down *menus* that contain commands.

- The **toolbar** contains buttons that represent different actions.

- The **rulers** are used for measuring and also contain markers used for formatting text.

- The **insertion point** is a blinking vertical line that indicates where the next character typed will be placed. In a new document the insertion point is in the upper-left corner.

- The **status bar** displays information about the document.

- The **New Document task pane** allows documents to be created and opened.

4.3 Using the Keyboard with Word

Keys on the keyboard are used to type text and perform actions, such as moving the insertion point or deleting text. A standard keyboard has a layout similar to:

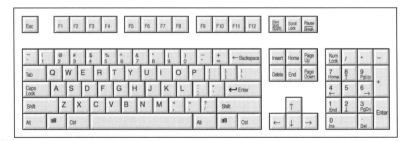

The keyboard

repeat key

The insertion point can be moved, without erasing or entering text, using the arrow keys. These keys can only be used to move the insertion point within existing text. Pressing an arrow key once moves the insertion point either up or down one line, or one character to the left or right. The arrow keys are repeat keys, meaning that the insertion point will continue to move as long as an arrow key is held down.

Ctrl

The Ctrl key (Control) can be used with the arrow keys to move the insertion point quickly in the document. Pressing the Ctrl key and the right arrow key moves the insertion point to the beginning of the word to its right.

Home **End**

Pressing the Home key or End key moves the insertion point to the beginning or end of the line of text, respectively.

Delete

The Delete key is used to erase the character directly to the right of the insertion point. When a character is deleted, the characters to its right are moved over to fill the gap.

← Backspace

The Backspace key is used to erase the character directly to the left of the insertion point. Characters to the right are moved over to fill the gap.

Esc

The Esc key (Escape) is used to cancel (escape from) the current operation. The specific effect that pressing the Esc key will have depends on the operation being performed.

← Enter

The Enter key is used to end a paragraph or to terminate a line of text. When Enter is pressed, the current paragraph is ended and a new one is created. Blank lines can be added in a document by pressing Enter, which creates a new, blank paragraph.

4.4 Editing Text in a Document

A document may be *edited*, or changed, as needed. For example, text can be added by using the arrow keys to move the insertion point to where new text is to appear, and then typing the new text. Existing text is automatically moved to the right to make room for the new text.

The mouse is used to place the insertion point. When the pointer is moved into a document, it changes from an arrow shape to the text pointer, or *I-beam pointer* (⌶). Clicking the I-beam pointer in text moves the insertion point to that position. This is a helpful technique when working with long documents.

4.5 Word Wrap

As text is typed, Word automatically determines if the next word will fit on the end of the current line or if it must go on the next line. This process is called *word wrap*.

The effects of word wrap can be seen when deleting or inserting text. When new text is added to a line, any words to the right are moved over, and those words that do not fit are moved to the next line. There may be a "domino" effect as words in the rest of the document move from one line to the next. Similarly, when text is deleted, words are moved up from the lines below.

One Space After a Period

The question often arises, "How many spaces are typed after a period?" The answer is *one* if you are using a word processor, and *two* if you are using a typewriter. Only one space is needed with a word processor because the distance between each character is adjusted proportionally, making it easy to read. On a typewriter, each character takes up the same amount of space, making it difficult to see blank spaces. An extra space is therefore needed at the end of a sentence.

Overtype mode means that as text is typed it replaces existing text, instead of inserting characters. Overtype mode in on if the OVR on the status bar is not dimmed:

REC TRK EXT **OVR**

Overtype mode can be turned off by double-clicking OVR on the status bar or by pressing the Insert key.

Toolbar Button Icons in Menus

An icon next to a command in a menu indicates that there is a button on the toolbar that can be used to select the command. For example, the 🖫 is next to Save in the File menu. The toolbar is discussed in Section 4.9.

The Assistant

When using Word, a small animated character called an Assistant may appear. The default Assistant is named Clippit and resembles a paper clip:

The Assistant may offer suggestions or tips. The Assistant can be removed by selecting **Hide the Office Assistant** from the **Help** menu. The Assistant can be displayed by selecting **Show the Office Assistant** from the **Help** menu or by clicking the Microsoft Word Help button (⬛) on the toolbar.

The Enter key should be used only to end a paragraph, because word wrap will wrap text to a new line. For example, a paragraph is ended and a new one created by pressing Enter.

4.6 Using Menus

At the top of the Word window is the menu bar. Each word on the bar is the name of a menu from which different commands can be selected. Clicking a menu name displays the menu. For example, clicking the word File displays the File menu:

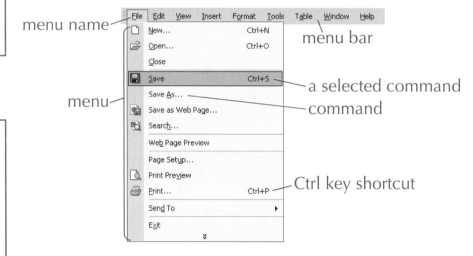

Pointing to a command on the menu changes its color, and clicking the command selects it. In the practices of this text, a ➔ symbol is used to denote selecting a command from a menu. For example, File ➔ Save indicates that Save should be selected from the File menu.

Clicking outside a displayed menu or pressing the Esc key closes the menu without selecting a command.

The arrows (⌄) at the bottom of a menu indicate that there are more commands available. Pointing to the arrows expands the menu to display more commands. Word remembers which commands have been selected and displays the most commonly used commands in the unexpanded menu.

Some commands may be dimmed, indicating that they cannot be selected at this time. Other commands may have an ellipsis (…) after the command name (New and Open are examples in the File menu). This means that a *dialog box* appears when the command is selected. A dialog box is used to supply the information needed to execute a command.

Menus may also be displayed using the keyboard. Note that one letter in each of the menu names is underlined. Pressing and holding the Alt key while pressing the underlined letter once displays that menu. For example, holding down the Alt key and pressing the F key once displays the File menu. In this text, we denote this sequence of keystrokes as Alt+F. Commands can be selected in a similar way. When the menu is displayed, pressing the key that corresponds to the command's underlined letter selects the command. For example, Save is selected from the File menu by first pressing Alt+F to display the menu, and then pressing the S key. This sequence is written as Alt+F S.

Some commands have a Ctrl key shortcut listed next to them in the menu. These shortcuts can be used to select a command without displaying a menu. For example, Ctrl+S is listed next to <u>S</u>ave in the <u>F</u>ile menu, which indicates that pressing and holding down the Ctrl key and pressing the S key once selects the <u>S</u>ave command.

Practice 1

In this practice you will create a new word processor document in Microsoft Word, enter text into the document and then edit the text.

If the Assistant appears during this practice, select <u>H</u>elp → Hide the <u>O</u>ffice Assistant to remove the assistant. The remaining practices in this text assume that the Assistant does not appear in the document window.

① *CREATE A NEW WORD PROCESSOR DOCUMENT*

    a. On the Taskbar, click Start. A menu is displayed.

    b. Select New Office Document. A dialog box is displayed.

        1. Select the General tab if those icons are not already displayed.

        2. Click the Blank Document icon and then select OK. Word starts and a new, empty word processor document is displayed. Note the menu bar, toolbar, and title bar.

② *TYPE A LINE OF TEXT INTO THE DOCUMENT*

    Type the following text, holding down the Shift key to produce the capital letter and the colon(:):

        Dear traveler:

    Do not press the Enter key.

③ *MOVE THE INSERTION POINT WITHOUT ERASING ANY TEXT*

    Move the insertion point to the right of the letter v by pressing the left-arrow key five times.

④ *DELETE THE LETTER "v"*

    Press the Backspace key once. Note how the text eler: has moved over to fill the area where the letter v appeared. The document now displays Dear traeler:.

⑤ *INSERT A CHARACTER*

    Press the V key. A v is inserted, and the text Dear traveler: is again displayed.

⑥ *MOVE THE INSERTION POINT AND CREATE NEW PARAGRAPHS*

    a. Press the right-arrow key until the insertion point is to the right of the colon. Press the right-arrow key again a few times. Word does not allow the insertion point to move beyond the text, and the assistant may offer a helpful tip. Ignore the Assistant for now.

    b. Press the Enter key twice. The Dear traveler: paragraph is ended, a blank line created, and a new paragraph is created. The Assistant may display a tip.

⑦ ENTER THE REST OF THE LETTER

Type the following text, pressing the Enter key as indicated (¶) and allowing the rest of the text to word wrap. Note that your word wrap may be slightly different than that shown below. Use the Delete key and arrow keys to correct any typing errors:

> Thank you for your recent request. Enclosed is our really good catalog of adventure gear and accessories, a pamphlet about our guided hiking trips, and a price list. Reservations are required for hiking trips. Please call us soon if you have any questions.¶
> ¶
> Sincerely,¶
> ¶
> ¶
> ¶
> Kevin Milford¶
> Gravel Pond Outfitters

Check – Your document should look similar to:

Dear traveler:

Thank you for your recent request. Enclosed is our really good catalog of adventure gear and accessories, a pamphlet about our guided hiking trips, and a price list. Reservations are required for hiking trips. Please call us soon if you have any questions.

Sincerely,

Kevin Milford
Gravel Pond Outfitters

⑧ MOVE THE INSERTION POINT AND DELETE TWO WORDS

a. Move the mouse so that the pointer is in the document. The I-beam pointer is now displayed.
b. Place the I-beam pointer on the word really in the second sentence of the letter.
c. Click the left mouse button. The insertion point is moved to the position of the I-beam pointer.
d. Press and hold the Ctrl key and press the right arrow key once. The insertion point is moved to the beginning of the word good.
e. Press Ctrl+right arrow again. The insertion point is moved to the beginning of the word catalog.
f. Press the Backspace key until the words really good are deleted. Be sure to leave only one space between our and catalog.

⑨ EDIT THE LETTER

Insert new text and use the Delete and arrow keys as necessary to make the following changes:

1. Change the word pamphlet to brochure
2. Insert a space and the words feel free to after the word Please
3. Remove the word soon and a space, leaving one space between us and if.

Check – Your document should look similar to:

Dear traveler:

Thank you for your recent request. Enclosed is our catalog of adventure gear and accessories, a brochure about our guided hiking trips, and a price list. Reservations are required for hiking trips. Please feel free to call us if you have any questions.

Sincerely,

Kevin Milford
Gravel Pond Outfitters

4.7 Saving a Document

A new document is stored in the computer's memory until it is saved. *Saving a document* creates a file of what is currently in the computer's memory. A *file* is a collection of related data stored on a lasting medium such as a hard disk, a CD, or a diskette. Once a document has been saved, it can be loaded into memory for further editing at a later time.

A file must be given a name to identify it. A *file name* is a unique name for a file stored on disk. File names can contain letters, numbers, spaces, and the underscore character (_). File names cannot contain colons (:), asterisks (*), question marks (?), and some other special characters. Word automatically adds the .doc extension to the file name. Examples of valid file names are Notes, CHAPTER 5, and 2nd Memo. A descriptive file name is helpful. For example, a file containing a letter to your friend Greta should be named Greta Letter or Letter to Greta rather than just Letter.

A document is saved by selecting Save (Ctrl+S) from the File menu. The Save As dialog box is displayed the first time a document is saved:

Why Save Often?

When working on a document, it should be saved often to prevent accidental loss. An interruption in power or a problem on a network can result in losing documents that were in the computer's memory. Saving before attempting to print is also important because a problem involving the printer could cause the most recent changes in a document to be lost.

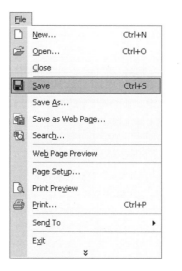

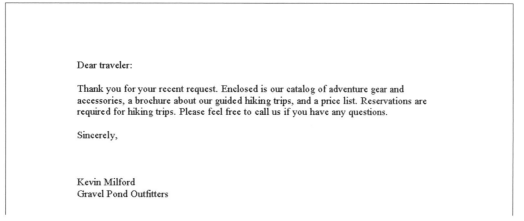

The Save in list displays a location name, with the location contents displayed in the box below. Double-clicking a folder in the contents box places that folder name in the Save in list. The contents of that folder is then displayed in the contents box. When the Save in list displays the appropriate location for the file to be saved, a descriptive file name should be typed in the File name box. Selecting Save copies the document to a file with the typed name.

Any changes made to a document after saving are not automatically stored in the file on disk. The file must be saved again, which *overwrites* the original file with the changed file.

4.8 Automatic Spelling and Grammar Checking

Word includes a spelling checker that automatically checks words as they are typed. Words typed in a document are compared to those in a dictionary file. If a word is spelled incorrectly or is not in the dictionary file, a red wavy line appears below it:

You do not need to bring a hair dryer to the campsite.

misspelled word

A misspelled word can be corrected by first right-clicking it to display suggested words, then clicking the correct spelling from the menu:

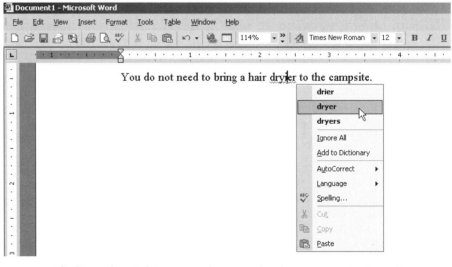

Clicking the right mouse button displays suggested spellings

Because the dictionary file does not contain every word in the English language, a red wavy line may appear below a correctly spelled word, such as a proper name. When this happens, the wavy line can be ignored. It will not appear on paper when the document is printed. However, the red wavy line can be removed from all occurrences of that word in the document by right-clicking the word and selecting Ignore All from the menu.

grammar checker Word also has a grammar checker that displays a green wavy line below a phrase or sentence when a possible grammatical error is detected:

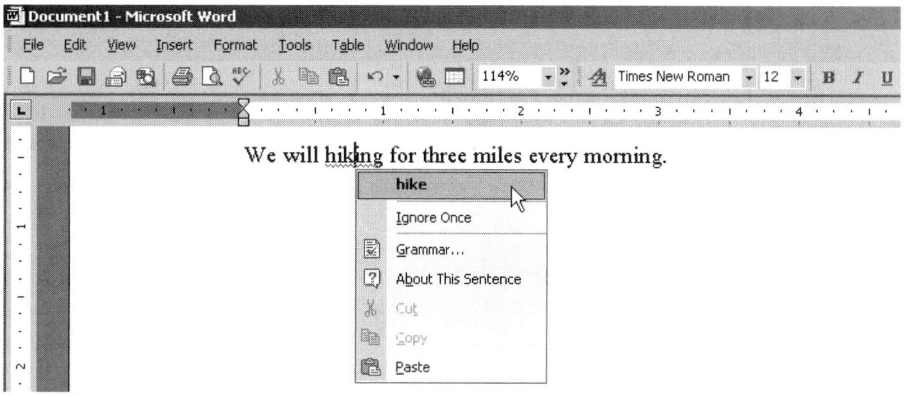

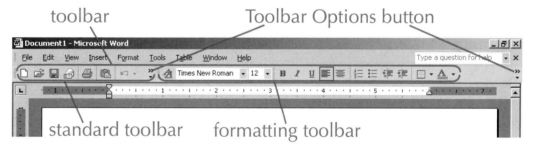

Right-clicking the green wavy line displays suggested corrections.

A green wavy line might appear below an acceptable sentence. When this happens, the wavy line can be ignored, or it can be removed from the document by selecting Ignore Once from the menu.

4.9 Using the Toolbar

The toolbar is usually displayed at the top of the Word window. The *toolbar* contains buttons that represent different actions, such as saving a document. The default toolbar in Word actually consists of two toolbars, the standard toolbar and the formatting toolbar:

Clicking the Toolbar Options button (⯯) at the far right of either toolbar displays more buttons:

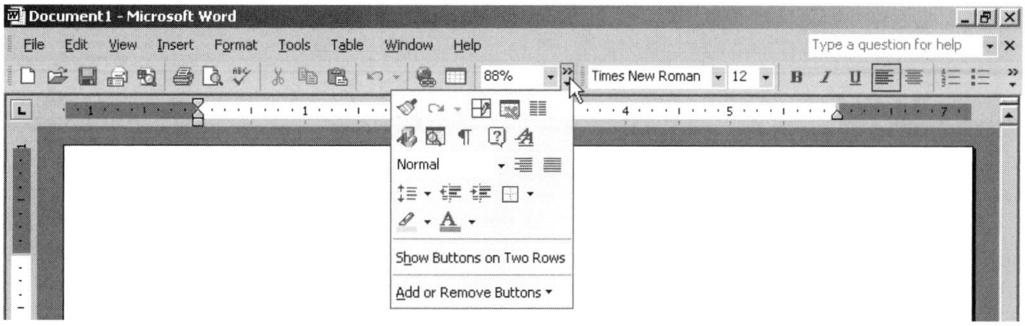

Toolbars may vary in appearance because Word remembers which buttons have been selected and displays the most frequently used buttons.

Clicking a button performs an action. Pointing to a button (not clicking) displays a *ScreenTip* which describes the action that button will perform:

ScreenTips describe the action performed by a button

Clicking the Save button (🖫) saves a document. If the document is new and has not yet been named, the Save As dialog box is displayed. Other buttons will be discussed when their corresponding actions are introduced.

Practice 2 ⟳

In this practice you will save the document created in Practice 1 using the name Catalog Reply, then edit the document and correct any misspellings. The document created in Practice 1 should be displayed.

① **SELECT SAVE FROM THE FILE MENU**

    a. Select File → Save. Since this is the first time the document is saved, Word displays a dialog box.

        1. The text in the File name box should already be selected. Type Catalog Reply to replace the existing text:

        2. Use the Save in list and the contents box below it to select the appropriate location for the file to be saved.

        3. Select Save. The file is saved in the selected location with the name Catalog Reply. Note that the file name is now displayed in the title bar of the document window.

② **EDIT THE DOCUMENT**

    a. Place the insertion point at the beginning of the word Dear at the top of the document.

    b. Type your first and last name and press Enter.

    c. Type 42 Thimble Roawd and press Enter. Note the red wavy line under Roawd, indicating that Word cannot find it in the dictionary.

d. Type Weston, MO 66018 and press Enter.

e. Press Enter again to create a blank line between the address and the greeting of the letter.

③ *CORRECT THE MISSPELLED WORD*

Point to Roawd and click the right mouse button. A menu is displayed with the word Road as one of the suggested spellings. Correct the spelling by clicking Road from the menu. Word makes the correction and the address now reads 42 Thimble Road.

Check – Your document should look similar to:

Your Name
42 Thimble Road
Weston, MO 66018

Dear traveler:

Thank you for your recent request. Enclosed is our catalog of adventure gear and accessories, a brochure about our guided hiking trips, and a price list. Reservations are required for hiking trips. Please feel free to call us if you have any questions.

Sincerely,

Kevin Milford
Gravel Pond Outfitters

④ *USE THE TOOLBAR TO SAVE THE MODIFIED CATALOG REPLY*

a. Point (do not click) to a button on the toolbar and hold the position for a few seconds. Note the ScreenTip describing the action of the button.

b. Point to the Save button (🖫) and then click. The modified Catalog Reply is saved on disk, overwriting the original file.

4.10   Displaying Formatting Marks

Why Display Formatting Marks?

Displaying formatting marks makes it easier to edit a document. For example, viewing spaces can help avoid problems such as having two spaces between words instead of one.

Spaces, tabs (discussed later in the text), and paragraphs are not normally displayed in a document, but can be displayed as special symbols. These symbols are called *formatting marks* and do not appear on paper when a document is printed:

tab mark   space mark

It·is·a·good·idea·to·show·formatting·marks,·so·that·you·can··find·mistakes··like·two·spaces·between·words.¶

paragraph mark (Enter)

It is much easier to edit a document when these marks are visible. Formatting marks are displayed by clicking the Show/Hide ¶ button (¶) on the toolbar. Clicking the Show/Hide ¶ button again hides the formatting marks.

¶

4.11 Closing a Document and Quitting Word

When you are finished working on a document, it should be saved and then closed. *Closing a document* means that its window is removed from the screen and the file is no longer in the computer's memory. A document is closed by selecting Close from the File menu. Attempting to close a document that has been edited but not saved displays a message:

> **Microsoft Word**
>
> ⚠ Do you want to save the changes to "Catalog Reply"?
>
> [Yes]   [No]   [Cancel]

Selecting Yes saves the edited file and then removes the document window. Selecting No removes the document window without saving the changes. Selecting Cancel removes the message and leaves the document open and displayed.

Another way to close a document is by clicking the Close button (⊠) in the upper-right corner of a document window.

When Word is no longer needed, it should be quit properly. *Quitting Word* means that its window is removed from the screen and the program is no longer in the computer's memory. Word is quit by selecting Exit from the File menu. Attempting to quit Word with an open document that has been edited but not saved displays the message dialog box shown above. Another way to quit Word is by clicking the Close button (⊠) in the upper-right corner of the application window.

4.12 Smart Tags

Word assesses the text in a document and determines if it is one of several types of data commonly used in other applications. Word then designates the text as a *smart tag* and a purple dotted underline called a *smart tag indicator* appears below it. For example, Word can recognize numbers and letters as a street address and designate it as a smart tag:

> Jade Boticelli
> 1137 Main Street ⟵ smart tag indicator
> Holyoke, NC 02401

Moving the pointer over the indicator displays the Smart Tag Actions button (ⓘ):

> ⓘe Boticelli
> 1137 Main Street
> Holyoke, NC 02401

Clicking the Smart Tag Actions button displays the type of data, the smart tag data, and a menu of actions:

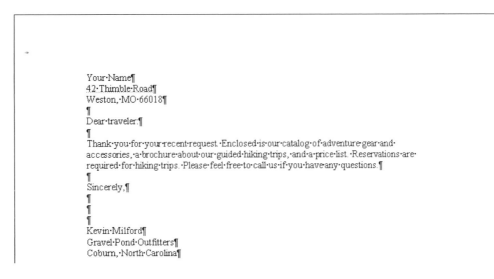

Selecting **Remove this Smart Tag** removes the purple dotted smart tag indicator from the text, and the data is no longer designated as a smart tag.

Practice 3

In this practice you will display formatting marks, edit Catalog Reply, save and close the document, and quit Word. The Catalog Reply document should be displayed from the last practice.

① SHOW FORMATTING MARKS

On the toolbar, click the Show/Hide ¶ button (¶) if formatting marks are not already displayed. You may need to click the Toolbar Options button (») at the far right of the standard toolbar to display the button. Note the formatting marks in the document.

② EDIT THE DOCUMENT

a. Place the insertion point at the end of the word Outfitters at the bottom of the document.

b. Press Enter. A new paragraph is created.

c. Type Coburn, North Carolina.

Check – Your document should look similar to:

> Your·Name¶
> 42·Thimble·Road¶
> Weston,·MO·66018¶
> ¶
> Dear·traveler:¶
> ¶
> Thank·you·for·your·recent·request.·Enclosed·is·our·catalog·of·adventure·gear·and·
> accessories,·a·brochure·about·our·guided·hiking·trips,·and·a·price·list.·Reservations·are·
> required·for·hiking·trips.·Please·feel·free·to·call·us·if·you·have·any·questions.¶
> ¶
> Sincerely,¶
> ¶
> ¶
> ¶
> Kevin·Milford¶
> Gravel·Pond·Outfitters¶
> Coburn,·North·Carolina¶

③ REMOVE THE SMART TAG

a. Point to the purple dotted underline below the 42 Thimble Road address at the top of the document. The Smart Tag Actions button (ⓘ) appears.

b. Click the Smart Tag Actions button (ⓘ▾). A menu is displayed.

c. Select **Remove this Smart Tag**. The menu and the smart tag indicator are removed.

④ **SAVE AND CLOSE THE DOCUMENT**

    a. Select File → Save. The document is saved.

    b. Select File → Close. The document no longer appears in the window. If a warning dialog box is displayed, select Yes to save the changes and close the document.

⑤ **QUIT WORD**

    Select File → Exit. The document window is removed from the screen.

4.13 Opening a File

Opening a file transfers a copy of the file contents to the computer's memory and then displays it in a document window. In Word, a file is opened by selecting Open Office Document from the Start menu, which displays the Open Office Document dialog box:

The file names of saved documents are displayed in the Open Office Document dialog box

The Look in list displays a location name, with the location contents displayed in the box below. Double-clicking a folder in the contents box places that folder name in the Look in list and displays its contents in the box below. When the contents box displays the appropriate file name, clicking that file name and then selecting Open starts Word, transfers a copy of the document to the computer's memory, and displays it in a document window.

If Word is running, an existing document can be opened by selecting Open (Ctrl+O) from the File menu or clicking the Open button (📂) on the toolbar, which displays the Open dialog box.

4.14 Printing a Document

A document is printed by selecting Print (Ctrl+P) from the File menu, which displays a Print dialog box similar to:

The Print dialog box varies depending on the printer

Selecting OK prints the document using the default settings. More than one copy of the document can be printed by typing a number in the Number of copies entry box and selecting OK.

The Print button (⊟) on the toolbar may also be used to print a document. However, clicking the Print button prints one copy of the document using the default settings without displaying the Print dialog box.

Practice 4

In this practice the Catalog Reply document will be opened, edited, saved, and then printed.

① OPEN CATALOG REPLY

    a. On the Taskbar, click Start. A menu is displayed.

    b. Select the Open Office Document command. A dialog box is displayed.

        1. Use the Look in list and the contents box below it to display the file name Catalog Reply, which was last modified in Practice 3.

        2. In the contents box, click Catalog Reply.

        3. Select Open. Word is started, a copy of Catalog Reply is transferred to the computer's memory, and the document is displayed in a window.

② EDIT THE DOCUMENT

    Change the greeting of the letter from Dear traveler: to Dear outdoor enthusiast:.

③ SAVE, PRINT, AND THEN CLOSE THE MODIFIED CATALOG REPLY

    a. Select File → Save. The document is saved.

b. Select File → Print. A dialog box is displayed.

1. Note that the Number of copies option is 1. Select OK to print one copy of Catalog Reply.

c. Select File → Close. Catalog Reply is removed from the window.

4.15   Changing Views

There are several different ways to view a document in its window. The view can be changed by selecting commands from the View menu. In *Print Layout* view, the document appears on separate pages, just as it will when printed:

Print Layout view

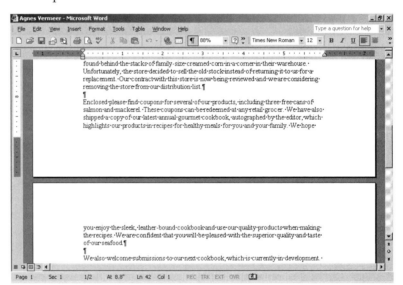

Normal view   In *Normal* view, the separation of pages in the document is represented with dotted lines:

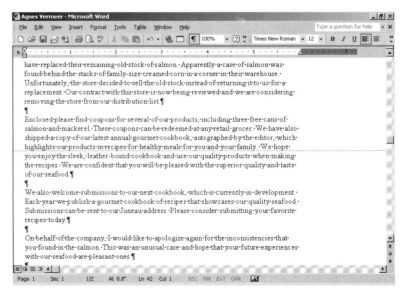

A Guide to Microsoft Office XP Professional

The magnification of a displayed document can also be changed. Selecting <u>Z</u>oom from the <u>V</u>iew menu displays the Zoom dialog box:

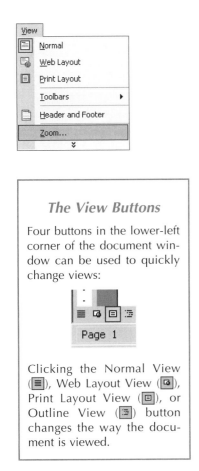

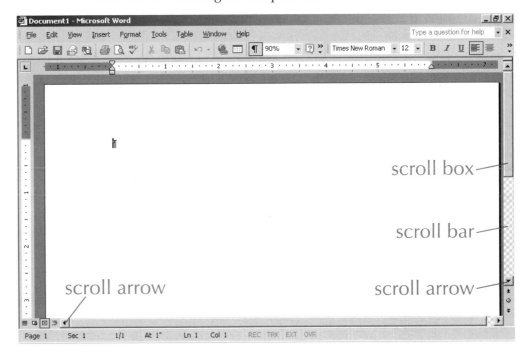

The Zoom to options affect how big or small the document appears in the document window.

The Zoom box (100% ▾) on the toolbar can be used to quickly change the magnification of a document.

4.16 Moving a Document in the Window

Long documents may not be entirely displayed in the window. Zoom magnification also affects how much of a document is displayed. The scroll bars on the right side and bottom of the window are used to move a document and bring hidden parts into view:

The View Buttons

Four buttons in the lower-left corner of the document window can be used to quickly change views:

Clicking the Normal View (▤), Web Layout View (⬛), Print Layout View (▣), or Outline View (▦) button changes the way the document is viewed.

- Clicking ▲ moves the document down one line, and clicking ▼ moves it up one line. At the bottom of the window, clicking ◄ or ► moves the document left or right, respectively.

- Dragging the *scroll box* moves the document in larger increments. For example, dragging the scroll box to the middle of the scroll bar displays the middle of the document.

- Clicking the *scroll bar* above or below the scroll box scrolls the document by one screen towards the top or bottom of the document, respectively.

Any text scrolled off the screen is not lost, it is just not displayed at that time. Note that the insertion point does not move within the document when the scroll bars are used.

The keyboard can be used to scroll a document by pressing the Page Up or Page Down keys. These keys scroll the document one window towards the top or bottom of the document, respectively. The insertion point can be moved quickly to the first character in a document by pressing Ctrl+Home, or to the last character by pressing Ctrl+End.

Practice 5

In this practice a document will be scrolled and the insertion point moved by using the mouse. A previously created Word document named SCROLL will be used. Each line in SCROLL is numbered to help demonstrate screen scroll. Start Word if it is not already running.

① *OPEN SCROLL*

Select File → Open. A dialog box is displayed.

1. Use the Look in list and the contents box below it to display the data files for this text.
2. In the contents box, click SCROLL.
3. Select Open. The SCROLL document is displayed.

② *CHANGE VIEWS AND MAGNIFICATION*

a. Display the View menu. Select Print Layout if it is not already selected.
b. Select View → Zoom. A dialog box is displayed.
   1. Select the Whole page option, and then select OK. The size of the displayed document is changed so that all of the edges of the page can be seen.
c. Select View → Normal. The document is now displayed in Normal view, without the page edges displayed.

③ *MOVE THE INSERTION POINT TO THE BOTTOM OF THE SCREEN*

Press the down-arrow key until the insertion point is on the last line of text currently displayed on the screen.

④ *SCROLL DOWN USING THE SCROLL ARROW*

a. At the bottom of the vertical scroll bar, click ▼ ten times. Note that each time the button is clicked, a line scrolls off the top of the screen and the next line in the document appears from the bottom.
b. Continue to click ▼ until a dotted line appears. The dotted line indicates the end of one page and beginning of the next page.

⑤ *PLACE THE INSERTION POINT IN THE LAST LINE IN THE DOCUMENT*

   a. In the vertical scroll bar, drag the scroll box to the bottom of the scroll bar and release the mouse button. The last line of the document, paragraph 70, is displayed.

   b. Move the I-beam pointer into the text of paragraph 70 and click the left mouse button to place the insertion point.

⑥ *SCROLL TO THE FIRST LINE IN THE DOCUMENT*

   a. In the vertical scroll bar, click and hold the ▲ button. The screen will scroll as long as the button is held down. Note how the scroll box moves in the bar as the screen scrolls. Also note that the insertion point does not move as the document is being scrolled.

   b. When paragraph 1 is displayed, release the mouse button.

⑦ *QUIT WORD*

   Select File → Exit. SCROLL is closed and the document window is removed from the screen.

Chapter Summary

This chapter introduced the word processor, which can be used to produce easy to read, professional-looking documents. Microsoft Word is the word processor application in Microsoft Office.

A new document is created by selecting New Office Document from the Start menu and selecting the Blank Document icon. The title bar, menu bar, toolbar, and rulers are displayed in the document window.

Keys on the keyboard are used to type text and perform actions. The insertion point can be moved using the arrow keys, Ctrl key, Home key, and End key. The Delete key erases the character to the right of the insertion point, and the Backspace key erases the character to the left of the insertion point. The Esc key is used to cancel the current operation. The Enter key is used to end a paragraph or to terminate a line of text.

When the pointer is moved into a document, it changes from an arrow shape to the text pointer, or I-beam pointer (I). Clicking the I-beam pointer in text moves the insertion point to that position.

Word automatically determines if the next word will fit on the end of the current line or the next line in a process called word wrap. The Enter key should be used only to end a paragraph.

Clicking a menu name in the menu bar displays the menu, and clicking a command selects it. The arrows (✨) at the bottom of a menu indicate that there are more commands available. Dimmed commands cannot be selected. Commands with an ellipsis (…) after the name display a dialog box when the command is selected. A dialog box is used to supply the information needed to execute a command.

Menus may also be displayed using the keyboard by pressing and holding the Alt key while pressing the underlined letter in a command name. Some commands have a Ctrl key shortcut listed next to them in the menu, which are used to select a command without displaying a menu.

Ctrl

A new document is stored in the computer's memory until it is saved. A document is saved by selecting the <u>S</u>ave command or the Save button. The file must be given a unique, descriptive name.

Word includes a spelling checker that automatically compares words in the document to those in a dictionary file. A red wavy line appears below a misspelled word, and right-clicking the red wavy line displays suggested spellings. Word also has a grammar checker that displays a green wavy line below a phrase when a grammatical error is detected.

The toolbar at the top of the Word window contains buttons that represent different actions. Clicking a button performs an action. Pointing to a button displays a ScreenTip which describes the action that button will perform.

 Spaces, tabs, and paragraphs can be displayed as special symbols called formatting marks which do not appear on paper when a document is printed. Formatting marks are displayed by clicking the Show/Hide ¶ button.

A document should be saved and then closed when it is not being worked on. A document is closed by selecting the <u>C</u>lose command or by clicking the Close button in the upper-right corner of the window.

When Word is no longer needed, it should be quit properly by selecting the E<u>x</u>it command or by clicking the Close button in the upper-right corner of the application window.

If text in a document is one of several types of data commonly used in other applications, Word designates the text as a smart tag. Moving the pointer over a smart tag indicator displays the Smart Tag Actions button, which displays a menu of actions when clicked.

In Word, a file is opened by selecting Open Office Document from the Start menu. If Word is running, a document can be opened by selecting the <u>O</u>pen command or by clicking the Open button. A document is printed by selecting the <u>P</u>rint command, or by selecting the Print button.

A document can be viewed in different views. In Print Layout view, the document appears on separate pages, just as it will when printed. In Normal view, the separation of pages in the document is represented with dotted lines. The magnification of a displayed document can be changed by selecting the <u>Z</u>oom command.

 The scroll bars and arrows at the ends of the scroll bars are used to bring hidden parts of a document into view. The Page Up or Page Down keys can also be used to scroll a document.

This chapter discussed the commands and procedures necessary to produce a word processor document:

1. Display the word processor document by either creating a new one or opening an existing document.
2. Type text or edit the document.
3. Save the document.
4. Print the document.
5. Close the document.
6. Quit Word properly.

Vocabulary

Closing a document   The process of removing a document from the computer's memory and from the screen.

Dialog box   A box that appears when a command is selected, and is used to supply the information needed to execute the command.

Edit   Change the contents of a document.

File   A collection of related data stored on a lasting medium such as a hard disk, a CD, or a diskette.

File name   A unique name for a file stored on disk.

Formatting marks   Symbols that do not appear on paper when a document is printed.

I-beam pointer   The shape of the pointer when it is moved into a document.

Insertion point   A blinking vertical line in a document that indicates where the next character typed will be placed.

Menu   A list of commands.

Menu bar   A horizontal bar below the title bar that contains the names of drop-down menus.

Microsoft Word   The word processor application in Microsoft Office.

Normal view   Displays a document with dotted lines representing where each page ends.

Print Layout view   Displays a document on separate pages, just as it will appear when printed.

Opening a file   The process of transferring a copy of the file contents to the computer's memory and then displaying it in a window.

Overwrite   Replacing the original file with the changed file.

Quitting Word   The process of removing the Word program from the computer's memory and from the screen.

Rulers   Located at the top and left side of the document window, and contain markers used for formatting text.

Saving a document   The process of creating a file of what is currently in the computer's memory.

ScreenTip   A description of the action that a button on the toolbar will perform.

Scroll bars   Used to scroll a document one screen up or down.

Scroll box   Used to move a document in large increments.

Smart tag   Text in a document with a purple dotted underline that has been assessed by Word to be one of several types of data commonly used in other applications.

Smart tag indicator   A purple dotted underline that appears under text that has been designated by Word as a smart tag.

Status bar   Displays information about a document.

Title bar   A horizontal bar that displays the name and type of document.

Toolbar   A horizontal bar that contains buttons that represent different actions.

Word processor   A computer application that is used to produce documents.

Word wrap   The process Word uses to determine if the next word will fit on the end of the current line or if it must go on the next line.

Word Commands and Buttons

☒ **Close command** Closes a document. Found in the File menu.

☒ **Exit command** Quits Word. Found in the File menu.

Ignore All command Removes the red wavy line from all occurrences of that word in the document. Found in the menu displayed by right-clicking a word that has a red wavy line.

Ignore Once command Removes the green wavy line from a sentence that contains a possible grammatical error. Found in the menu displayed by right-clicking a phrase or sentence that has a green wavy line.

New Office Document command Displays the New Office Document dialog box. Found in the Start menu.

Normal command Changes the view of a document to Normal view. Found in the View menu.

🗁 **Open command** Displays a dialog box used to open an existing document. Found in the File menu. The Open button on the toolbar can be used instead of the command.

Open Office Document command Displays a dialog box used to open an existing document. Found in the Start menu.

🖨 **Print command** Displays a dialog box used to print a document. Found in the File menu. The Print button on the toolbar can be used instead of the command.

Print Layout command Changes the view of a document to Print Layout view. Found in the View menu.

Remove this Smart Tag command Removes the purple dotted smart tag indicator from the text. Found in the menu displayed by clicking the Smart Tag Actions button.

🖫 **Save command** Saves a document. Found in the File menu. The Save button on the toolbar can be used instead of the command.

¶ **Show/Hide ¶ button** Displays formatting marks. Found on the toolbar.

ⓘ **Smart Tag Actions button** Displays the type of data, the smart tag data, and a menu of actions. Displayed by moving the pointer over a smart tag indicator.

» **Toolbar Options button** Displays more buttons in a toolbar. Found at the far right of each toolbar.

Zoom command Displays a dialog box with options that affect the magnification of the displayed document. Found in the View menu.

Sections 4.1 — 4.9

1. What is a word processor?

2. List the steps required to create a new Word document.

3. What is displayed in the title bar of the document window?

4. a) What is the insertion point?
   b) How may the insertion point be moved down 3 lines and then 10 places to the right without affecting text?

5. What are each of the following keys used for?
   a) Escape key
   b) Delete key
   c) Home key

6. a) What is the difference between pressing the Backspace key four times and the left-arrow key four times when the insertion point is located in the middle of a line of text?
   b) List the steps required to change the word sea to ocean in the sentence:

   Dolphins live in the sea.

7. What happens when the Enter key is pressed?

8. a) What is the shape of the pointer when it is in a document?
   b) How can the mouse be used to move the insertion point?

9. What is word wrap?

10. a) List two ways to display a menu.
    b) List two ways to close a menu without selecting a command.

11. a) What do the arrows at the bottom of a menu indicate?
    b) What does an ellipsis (...) after a command name indicate?
    c) What is a dialog box used for?
    d) What is a Ctrl key shortcut used for?

12. a) What does saving a file do?
    b) What is a file?
    c) What is a file name?
    d) What does Word automatically add to a file name when saving the file?

13. Which of the following file names are invalid?
    a) My Notes
    b) Science: Lab Report
    c) Issues?
    d) Letter 4 U

14. If changes are made to a previously saved file, will the changes be automatically made to the file on disk, or must the file be saved again?

15. a) What does it mean when a red wavy line appears under a word in a document?
    b) List the steps required to correct a misspelled word.
    c) What does it mean when a green wavy line appears under a sentence in a document?

16. a) How can buttons that are not on the toolbar be displayed?
    b) How can a document be saved without selecting Save from the File menu?

17. What is a ScreenTip?

Sections 4.10 — 4.16

18. a) What are formatting marks?
    b) How can formatting marks be displayed in a document?

19. a) What does closing a file do?
    b) What does quitting Word do?

20. a) What does it mean when a purple dotted line appears under text in the document?
    b) What is displayed when the Smart Tag Actions button is clicked?

21. What does opening a file do?

22. List the steps required to print the currently open document.

23. a) How does a document appear in Print Layout view?
    b) How does a document appear in Normal view?
    c) List the steps required to change the magnification of a document.

24. a) What are the screen bars used for?
    b) What does pressing the Page Down key do?
    c) What does pressing Ctrl+Home do?

Exercise 1 ——————————— Ceramics Info Request

You need a letter requesting that information be sent to your friend.

    a) In a new document create the following letter, allowing Word to wrap the text. Be sure there are five blank lines below the date and three blank lines below the closing word Sincerely.

September 22, 2003

Ms. Marcia Paloma
Periwinkle Ceramics
Big Pine Lane
Sunport, FL 33568

Dear Ms. Paloma:

I am excited about taking the introductory ceramics class. I look forward to making several projects this spring. My friend would also like to enroll in your ceramics program. Please send information to the following address:

Kaitlin Pruitt
44 Simple Lane
Plain City, FL 33101

Thank you very much.

Sincerely,

Kallie Gavrilos

    b) Check the document on screen for errors and misspellings and make any corrections.

    c) Save the document naming it Ceramics Info Request and print a copy.

    d) Make the following changes to the letter:

- Change the word introductory to advanced in the first sentence.
- Change the words enroll in to look into in the third sentence.
- Change Kallie Gavrilos to your name.

    e) Save the modified Ceramics Info Request and print a copy.

You have been asked to write a thank you letter to Mrs. Kristine LeBon for her donation.

a) In a new document create the following letter, allowing Word to wrap the text. Be sure there are five blank lines below the date and three blank lines below the closing word Sincerely.

January 21, 2003

Mrs. Kristine LeBon
17 North Main St.
Reedsburg, GA 04459

Dear Kristine:

I am writing to thank you for your very generous donation to the Sarah Bernstein Memorial Library. We are always appreciative of donations, both monetary and otherwise.

As you are well aware, our library has needed new carpeting for several years now. The old rugs were an ugly avocado color. The new carpeting not only looks beautiful, but will also help keep the environmental conditions good for books.

Thanks again from the gang at the Sarah Bernstein Memorial Library.

Sincerely,

Chris Warheit
Library Assistant

b) Check the document on screen for errors and misspellings and make any corrections.

c) Save the letter naming it Donation Thanks.

d) Make the following changes:

- Delete the word very in the first sentence.
- Add the following sentence to the end of the first paragraph in the body of the letter: Your donation was truly a welcome surprise.
- Delete the sentence The old rugs were an ugly avocado color. in the second paragraph in the body of the letter.
- Change good for books to favorable for printed materials at the end of the second paragraph in the body of the letter.
- Change the gang to all of us in the third paragraph in the body of the letter.
- Change Chris Warheit to your name.

e) Save the modified Donation Thanks and print a copy.

Exercise 3 ———————————————— Entertainment Review

The local newspaper has an opening for an entertainment critic. In a new document create a half-page review of the last movie, concert, play, art show, or similar event that you attended. Check the document on screen for errors and misspellings and make any corrections. Save the document naming it Entertainment Review and print a copy.

Exercise 4 ———————————————— Vacation

In a new document create a one-page description of your last vacation. Describe where you went, how you traveled, what you saw and what you did. Check the document on screen for errors and misspellings and make any corrections. Save the document naming it Vacation and print a copy.

Exercise 5 ———————————————— Geology Schedule

You have enrolled in an independent study of the geologic eras of the earth and your instructor wants a schedule of topics and due dates for your research papers.

a) In a new document create the following memorandum, substituting your name for Your Name and allowing Word to wrap the text:

MEMORANDUM

TO: Dr. Janet Sung, Geology Department
FROM: Your Name
DATE: January 15, 2003
SUBJECT: Geologic eras topics and due dates

The following schedule outlines the research paper topics and due dates for my independent study on the geologic eras of the earth:

Topic Due Date
Precambrian 1/29
Paleozoic 2/12
Mesozoic 2/26
Cenozoic 3/12

One week before each due date I will submit an outline containing a specific topic and a list of sources for each paper.

b) Check the document on screen for errors and misspellings and make any corrections.

c) Save the document naming it Geology Schedule and print a copy.

Exercise 6 ——————————————————————— Things To Do

In a new document create a list of eight things you want to do on the weekends. Include the title Things To Do at the top of the page. Make sure there is a blank line separating the title from the list. Check the document on screen for errors and misspellings and make any corrections. Save the document naming it Things To Do and print a copy.

Exercise 7 ————————————————————————— PROPOSAL

Dr. Ellie Peterson and Dr. Jeremy Prow are studying coral reefs off the coast of Florida. They have used the word processor to create a funding proposal for their coral research.

a) Open PROPOSAL and make the following changes:

- Change the heading so it reads A PROPOSAL FOR CORAL RESEARCH at the top of the page.
- Change the word effect to affect in the second sentence of the Summary paragraph.
- Change the word accomplish to complete in the last sentence of the Summary paragraph.
- Delete the phrase state of the art in the first sentence of the Purpose and Description paragraph.

b) Check the document on screen for errors and misspellings and make any corrections.

c) Save the modified PROPOSAL.

d) Use the following steps to print only page 1:

1. Select File → Print.
2. In the Pages entry box type 1.
3. Select OK to print only the first page of this multi-page document.

Exercise 8 ——————————————————————————— Journal

A word processor can be used to keep a journal. In a new document create a one-page journal entry describing what you did last week. Add your plans for the upcoming weekend. Check the document on screen for errors and misspellings and make any corrections. Save the document naming it Journal and print a copy.

Exercise 9 ———————————————————— Grand Opening

You have opened a retail store. Your store could sell jewelry, clothing, sporting goods, or anything else you wish.

a) In a new document create a flyer that will be sent to prospective customers announcing your grand opening. Be sure to include the name, address, and phone number of your store, as well as a list of some of the special items you will be selling. Also include the date and time of the grand opening.

b) Check the document on screen for errors and misspellings and make any corrections.

c) Save the document naming it Grand Opening.

d) Your promotions manager suggested having a special sale at the grand opening. At the very top of the flyer add the title 20% OFF EVERYTHING! Save the modified Grand Opening and print a copy.

Exercise 10 ———————————————————— Karate

The sports editor for your college newspaper would like you to write an essay on karate.

a) In a new document create the following essay, allowing Word to wrap the text:

Karate has become very popular among people of all ages. Karate is a form of martial arts that often improves overall physical and mental health. Learning self defense is one of the main reasons people study karate. It may also improve a person's self-esteem and teaches physical and mental discipline. Students often find that it helps them stay focused, and as a result improves their grades.

A typical karate class has four parts. Class begins with stretching and calisthenics. This is important because each person needs to be flexible and have stamina when doing karate. Next, drills on fundamental karate skills are performed. These drills are followed by a kata, which is a choreographed floor exercise. Classes are concluded with free sparring.

b) Check the document on screen for errors and misspellings and make any corrections.

c) Save the document naming it Karate.

d) Make the following changes:

- Delete the word overall in the second sentence of the first paragraph.
- Change the word performed to conducted in the fourth sentence of the second paragraph.
- Add the sentence Karate cannot only improve your physical and mental health but it is also fun to do. at the end of the second paragraph.

e) Save the modified Karate and print a copy.

Exercise 11 ——————————————————— Water Conservation

You have been asked to write an article for a newsletter about an environmental issue.

    a) In a new document create the following article, allowing Word to wrap the text:

Lawn Sprinklers

Fresh water is essential to survival. We need fresh water to cook meals, to drink, and to bathe. Many people do not realize that fresh water is a natural resource that needs to be used wisely. Although most of the earth is covered in water, only a very small percentage of that water is fresh water suitable for consumption.

One way you can help to conserve fresh water is to use lawn sprinklers efficiently. Lawn sprinklers should be set to run only during early morning and late evening hours when the sun is not hot. Running sprinklers in the middle of the day leads to much of the water evaporating and not being absorbed into the ground. Also, when nature's sprinklers (rain) are on, make sure your sprinklers are not.

If each of us does a little, we can do a lot to conserve our fresh water supply.

    b) Check the document on screen for errors and misspellings and make any corrections.

    c) Save the document naming it Water Conservation and print a copy.

Exercise 12 ——————————————————————— Ten Years

In a new document create a two or three paragraph essay on "What I will be doing 10 years from now." Check the document on screen for errors and misspellings and make any corrections. Save the document naming it Ten Years and print a copy.

Exercise 13 ———————————— Campsite Request

You need a letter to request camp sites for your club's annual camping trip.

a) In a new document create the following letter, allowing Word to wrap the text. Be sure there are five blank lines below the date and three blank lines below the closing word Sincerely.

Oliver Romanowska
1655 Jacaranda Blvd.
Plainfield, NC 28031
February 19, 2003

Ursula Verde
Birch Tree Campground
RR1
Clewiston, SC 02618

Dear Ursula:

I am writing to request a reservation for the annual Prairie Dog Wilderness Club camping trip. Last year we needed more room! Therefore, I would like to reserve eight tent sites in the remote camping area of your campgrounds. We will be arriving on June 7 and leaving on June 15. Enclosed is a check for $324 as a deposit. We look forward to camping!

Sincerely,

Oliver Romanowska

b) Check the document on screen for errors and misspellings and make any corrections.

c) Save the document naming it Campsite Request.

d) Make the following changes:

- Change the date to the current date.
- Change the words Oliver Romanowska to your name at the beginning and the end of the letter.
- Add another paragraph requesting brochures for the area attractions.

e) Save the modified Campsite Request and print a copy.

Chapter 5
Formatting Documents

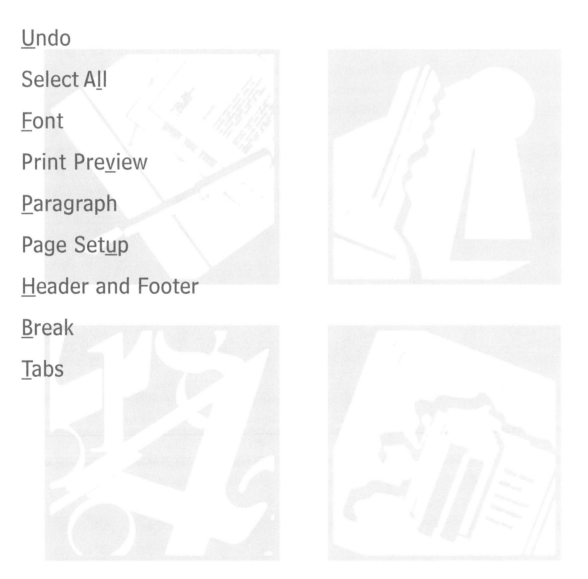

Undo

Select All

Font

Print Preview

Paragraph

Page Setup

Header and Footer

Break

Tabs

Chapter 5 Expectations

After completing this chapter you will be able to:

1. Explain the difference between character, paragraph, and page formats.
2. Reverse or repeat the effects of the last command using the Undo and Redo commands.
3. Demonstrate techniques for selecting text.
4. Delete selected text.
5. Apply character formats, such as different fonts and sizes.
6. Apply paragraph formats, such as alignment and line spacing.
7. Apply page formats, such as margins and headers and footers.
8. Print preview a document.
9. Insert page numbers into headers and footers.
10. Insert page breaks.
11. Position text using tabs and tab stops.

$\mathbf{T}$his chapter covers formatting options that improve the appearance and readability of documents. Using tabs and tab stops to format tables of data is also discussed, as well as previewing a document.

5.1 What is Formatting?

The way text appears on a page is called its *format*. There are three levels of formatting associated with a document: character, paragraph, and page. *Character formats* affect a character, a word, or several sentences of text. *Paragraph formats* affect an entire paragraph, and *page formats* affect the entire document. Note each of the formatting levels in the document below:

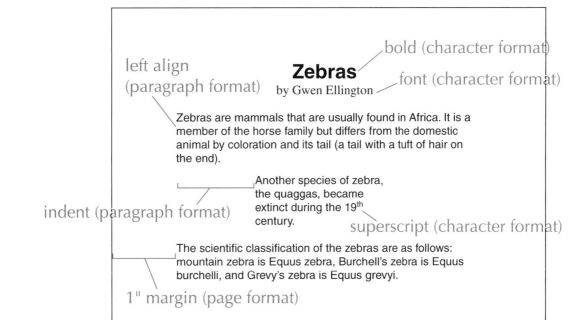

5.2 The Undo Command and the Repeat Command

There may be times when an action is performed by mistake. The effects of the last action are reversed by selecting Undo (Ctrl+Z) from the Edit menu. There are also some actions that cannot be reversed, such as selecting the Print button, because the document has already been printed.

The Edit menu is a *smart menu* that changes to reflect the current situation. For example, after typing text, the Edit menu contains the Undo Typing command. Selecting Undo Typing deletes all text entered since the last action performed.

There may also be times when a previous action needs to be repeated. The same action can be performed a second time by selecting Redo or Repeat (Ctrl+Y) from the Edit menu.

The Undo button () and the Redo button () on the toolbar can also be used to reverse or repeat actions. Clicking the Undo or Redo button arrow displays a list of the last actions performed. Selecting an option from the list will undo or redo that particular action. Note that saving a document clears the lists of any previous actions.

5.3 Selecting Text

Text needs to be selected to format it. Text is selected by dragging the pointer over any amount of text, from a single character to several pages. *Selected text* is shown highlighted on the screen:

> The·Lollipop·River·Troupe·will·perform·their·version·of·"Green·Grass·in·Ohio"·next· weekend.·Tickets·are·on·sale·at·the·box·office·and·are·priced·at·$5·for·adults,·$1·for· children·12·and·under.·The·box·office·is·open·from·2·p.m.·to·9·p.m.·every·Thursday· through·Sunday.¶

The second sentence is selected

Once text is selected, pressing a key replaces the text with the typed character, or pressing the Backspace key or Delete key removes the selected text. Clicking anywhere in the document or pressing an arrow key removes the selection without deleting the text.

In addition to dragging, there are several other methods for selecting text:

- Double-clicking a word selects it from the first character to the last and includes the space after the word.

- Holding down the Shift key and clicking anywhere in the document selects the text from the insertion point to the position where the pointer is clicked.

- Holding down the Shift key and pressing an arrow key selects in the direction of the arrow key. Holding down both the Ctrl and Shift keys and pressing an arrow key selects a larger amount of text in the direction of the arrow key.

- Holding down the Ctrl key and clicking a sentence selects the sentence.

- Moving the pointer to the left of the text (near the left edge of the page) changes the pointer to a right-pointing arrow (⇗). Clicking selects the line of text to the right of the pointer. Double-clicking selects the entire paragraph, and triple-clicking selects the entire document. Dragging up or down selects multiple lines of text.

- Select All (Ctrl+A) from the Edit menu selects all the text in the document.

Practice 1

In this practice you will select and delete text.

① OPEN WORKSHOP

> Open WORKSHOP, which is a data file for this text.

② SELECT TEXT BY DRAGGING

> a. Move the pointer into the paragraph at the top of the document that begins "Welcome!"
>
> b. Drag the pointer (hold down the left button and move the mouse) several words to the right. Each character the pointer passes over is selected.
>
> c. Release the mouse button. The selection remains.

③ REMOVE THE SELECTION

> Click anywhere in the document. The text is no longer selected.

④ SELECT A WORD

> a. Point to a word and double-click. The entire word and one space after it is selected.
>
> b. Press the up-arrow key. The word is no longer selected.

⑤ SELECT THE ENTIRE DOCUMENT

> a. Select Edit → Select All. All the text in the document is selected.
>
> b. Click anywhere in the document. The text is no longer selected.

⑥ SELECT A SENTENCE

> a. In the first paragraph of the introduction, point to the word "president" **but do not click**.
>
> b. Hold down the Ctrl key and click. The sentence that contains "president" is selected.

⑦ DELETE THE SELECTED TEXT

> Press the Delete key. The entire sentence is removed.

⑧ DELETE AND RESTORE THE NEXT PARAGRAPH

> a. Move the pointer to the left of the paragraph that begins "All Malfas Web…" until the right-pointing arrow (⤢) is displayed.
>
> b. Double-click. The entire paragraph is selected.
>
> c. Press the Delete key. The paragraph is removed.
>
> d. Select Edit → Undo Clear. The paragraph is restored.
>
> e. Click anywhere in the document. The text is no longer selected.

⑨ SAVE THE MODIFIED WORKSHOP

> Save the modified WORKSHOP. In future practices, any of these techniques may be used when selecting text.

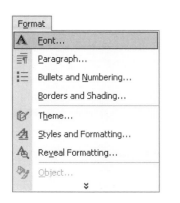

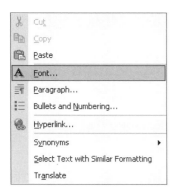

5.4 Character Formats - Fonts

A *font* or *typeface* refers to the shape of characters. The default font in Word is Times New Roman. There are also special fonts, such as Wingdings, that contain pictures called *dingbats*. Note how the characters are shaped differently:

Tahoma: ABCDEF abcdef 1234567890

Times New Roman: ABCDEF abcdef 1234567890

Georgia: ABCDEF abcdef 1234567890

Courier: ABCDEF abcdef 1234567890

Wingdings: ✋✌☝☞✌☞ 📁📄📑📰🖳📠🖰🖰📷📷

Text can be formatted in a different font by first selecting the text and then selecting Font from the Format menu, which displays the Font dialog box:

*Different fonts may be listed depending on
the installed fonts*

The Font list contains a list of fonts. Selecting a font displays a sample in the Preview area, and selecting OK applies the font to the selected text. The Font dialog box can also be displayed by right-clicking selected text and then selecting Font from the menu.

The Font box (Times New Roman ▾) on the toolbar can be used to change the font of selected text. Clicking the arrow displays a list of available fonts. Clicking a font in the list applies the font to any selected text.

Text can be displayed in different sizes. The size is measured in *points*, and there are 72 points to an inch. For example:

This is an example of 8 point Tahoma.
This is an example of 10 point Tahoma.
This is an example of 12 point Tahoma.
This is an example of 14 point Tahoma.
This is an example of 18 point Tahoma.

The Font Size box (12 ▾) on the toolbar can be used to change the size of selected text. Clicking the arrow displays a list of sizes to select from, and clicking a size applies the formatting to the selected text. A size can also be typed into the Font Size box, and Enter pressed to apply the formatting.

The Font dialog box discussed in Section 5.4 can also be used to change the size of text.

Practice 2

In this practice you will format text in a different font and size. Open WORKSHOP if it is not already displayed.

① CHANGE THE FONT OF THE ENTIRE TITLE

a. Select the entire title at the top of the document, "Web Graphics Workshop Malfas Web Design, Inc."

b. Select Format → Font. A dialog box is displayed.

  1. In the Font list, select Tahoma.

  2. Select OK. The selected text is formatted as Tahoma.

② INCREASE THE FONT SIZE OF THE ENTIRE TITLE

a. The title "Web Graphics Workshop Malfas Web Design, Inc." should still be selected.

b. On the toolbar, in the Font Size box select 18. The selected text is now 18 point.

c. Click anywhere in the document. The text is no longer selected.

Check – Your document should look similar to:

Web·Graphics·Workshop¶
Malfas·Web·Design,·Inc.¶
¶
Introduction¶
¶
Welcome!·All·of·us·at·Malfas·Web·Design·are·pleased·that·you·chose·us·for·your·web·graphics·training·needs.·We·look·forward·to·helping·you·become·proficient·and·up·to·date·in·the·world·of·web·graphics.·Our·staff·is·highly·qualified,·with·advanced·degrees·from·accredited·universities·and·every·certification·imaginable.·The·instructor·and·assistants·for·your·workshop·have·extensive·experience·in·the·field·of·web·graphics·and·can·pass·their·knowledge·on·to·you.¶

③ SAVE THE MODIFIED WORKSHOP

5.6 Character Formats - Style

The way in which a character is emphasized is called its *style*. The most common styles are bold, italic, and underline:

Bold text is printed darker so that words and phrases stand out on a page. It is often used for titles and headings.

Italic text is slanted and is mostly used for emphasis. It is sometimes used for headings.

<u>Underline text</u> has a line under it and is mostly used for emphasis. It is sometimes used for the title of a publication.

Regular text, sometimes called normal text, is the default style.

The Bold (**B**), Italic (*I*), and Underline (<u>U</u>) buttons on the toolbar can be used to apply or remove character styles from selected text. More than one button can be used on selected text to apply multiple styles.

The Font dialog box discussed in Section 5.4 can be used to format styles. Ctrl key shortcuts can also be used to apply styles to selected text:

SHORTCUT	STYLE
Ctrl+B	bold
Ctrl+I	italic
Ctrl+U	underline
Ctrl+spacebar	regular

5.7 Previewing a Document

A document can be previewed to see how it will appear when printed. Selecting Print Preview from the File menu or clicking the Print Preview button ( ) on the toolbar displays the Print Preview window:

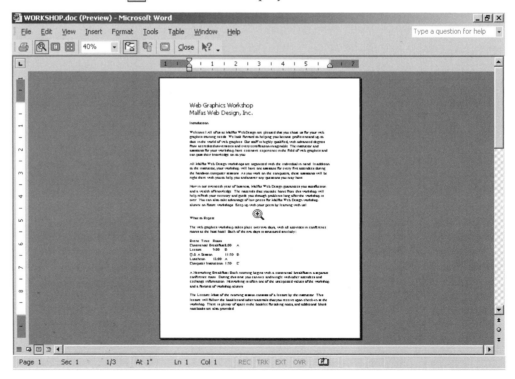

Once in print preview, the document can be viewed in different ways. For a multipage document, pressing the Page Up key or Page Down key displays the previous or next page, respectively. The previous or next page can also be displayed using the vertical scroll bar. When the pointer is moved onto the document, the pointer changes to a magnifying glass (⊕). Clicking the magnifying glass on the page zooms in to the portion of the page that was clicked, displaying the formatting in more detail. Clicking again displays the entire page.

Selecting the Print button (⬚) on the toolbar prints a copy of the document using the default printer settings. Selecting the Close button (Close) on the toolbar or pressing the Esc key returns to the document window.

Practice 3

In this practice you will format text in different styles, preview, and print a document. Open WORKSHOP if it is not already displayed.

① *BOLD THE ENTIRE TITLE*

    a. Select the entire title at the top of the document, "Web Graphics Workshop Malfas Web Design, Inc."

    b. Select Format → Font. A dialog box is displayed.

        1. In the Font style list, select Bold.

        2. Select OK. The dialog box is removed and the selected text is bold.

    c. Click anywhere to remove the selection.

② *FORMAT TEXT USING THE TOOLBAR AND THE KEYBOARD*

    a. Select the text in the next line, the "Introduction" title.

    b. On the toolbar, click the Italic button (*I*). The selected text is italic.

    c. Press Ctrl+B. Bold formatting is applied and the selected text is now both bold and italic.

    d. Click anywhere to remove the selection.

③ *FORMAT THE REST OF THE TITLES AS BOLD AND ITALIC*

    a. Scroll down page 1 until the "What to Expect" title is displayed, and select the title.

    b. Right-click the selected text. A menu is displayed.

    c. Select Font from the menu. A dialog box is displayed.

        1. In the Font style list, select Bold Italic.

        2. Select OK. The dialog box is removed and the selected text is bold and italic.

    d. Click anywhere to remove the selection.

    e. Scroll through the rest of the document and format the "What to Bring," "Our Computers," and "See You Soon!" titles as bold and italic.

④ *UNDERLINE A PHRASE IN THE INTRODUCTION*

    a. Scroll to the top of page 1.

    b. Select the words "We look forward to helping you become proficient" but do not select the rest of the sentence.

    c. On the toolbar, click the Underline button (U). The selected text is underlined.

    d. Click anywhere to remove the selection.

a. Place the insertion point just to the left of the "b" at the beginning of "become" in the underlined text.

b. Hold down the Shift key and then press the right-arrow key until "become proficient" is selected.

c. On the toolbar, click the Underline button. The selected text is no longer underlined.

d. Click anywhere to remove the selection. Only the first six words of the sentence are underlined.

Check – Your document should look similar to:

Web·Graphics·Workshop¶
Malfas·Web·Design,·Inc.¶
¶
Introduction¶
¶
Welcome!·All·of·us·at·Malfas·Web·Design·are·pleased·that·you·chose·us·for·your·web·graphics·training·needs.·We·look·forward·to·helping·you·become·proficient·and·up·to·date·in·the·world·of·web·graphics.·Our·staff·is·highly·qualified,·with·advanced·degrees·from·accredited·universities·and·every·certification·imaginable.·The·instructor·and·assistants·for·your·workshop·have·extensive·experience·in·the·field·of·web·graphics·and·can·pass·their·knowledge·on·to·you.¶

⑥ PREVIEW THE DOCUMENT

a. Save the modified document.

b. On the toolbar, click the Print Preview button (🔍). The first page of WORKSHOP is displayed in the Print Preview window.

c. Point to the middle of the page. The pointer changes to a magnifying glass (🔍).

d. Click in the middle of the page. The document is magnified.

e. Click again in the middle of the page. The entire page is displayed in the window.

f. Click ▼ in the vertical scroll bar. The second page of WORKSHOP is displayed.

g. Click the down scroll arrow again. The last page of WORKSHOP is displayed.

⑦ PRINT THE DOCUMENT

a. Press the Page Up key until page 1 of the document is displayed.

b. On the toolbar, click the Print button (🖨). The document is printed.

c. On the toolbar, click the Close button (Close). The Print Preview window is closed and the document window is displayed.

5.8 Character Formats - Superscripts and Subscripts

Superscript is a format that reduces the size of the text and raises it to the top of the current line. *Subscript* reduces the size of the text and lowers it to the bottom of the current line. For example:

In her 5th Avenue boutique, Dina Johannsen sold her designer perfume called "DJ's H$_2$O."

The "th" after the 5 is a superscript, and the "2" in H$_2$O is a subscript.

The Font dialog box discussed in Section 5.4 can be used to format superscripts and subscripts. Selecting Font from the Format menu displays the Font dialog box. The Effects area contains the Superscript and Subscript check boxes:

Clicking a check box and selecting OK applies the formatting to selected text.

Ctrl key shortcuts can also be used to apply superscript or subscript formatting to selected text:

SHORTCUT	STYLE
Ctrl+Shift+=(equal sign)	superscript
Ctrl+=(equal sign)	subscript

Practice 4

In this practice you will format text as superscript and subscript. Open WORKSHOP if it is not already displayed.

① FORMAT TEXT AS SUBSCRIPT

a. In the third paragraph of the introduction, select the word "low" in the sentence that reads "...take advantage of low prices...."

b. Select Format ➡ Font. A dialog box is displayed.

　1. In the Effects area, select the Subscript check box.

　2. Select OK. The selected text is smaller and at the bottom of the line of text.

② FORMAT TEXT AS SUPERSCRIPT

a. In the last sentence of the same paragraph, select the word "up."

b. Select Format ➡ Font. A dialog box is displayed.

　1. In the Effects area, select the Superscript check box.

　2. Select OK. The word "up" is smaller and at the top of the line of text.

Check – Your document should look similar to:

> help·refresh·your·memory·and·guide·you·through·problems·long·after·the·workshop·is·
> over.·You·can·also·take·advantage·of·low·prices·for·Malfas·Web·Design·workshop·alumni·
> on·future·workshops.·Keep·up·with·your·peers·by·learning·with·us!¶
> ¶

③ *SAVE THE MODIFIED WORKSHOP*

5.9 Paragraph Formats - Alignment

The *alignment* of text in a paragraph refers to its position relative to the sides of the page:

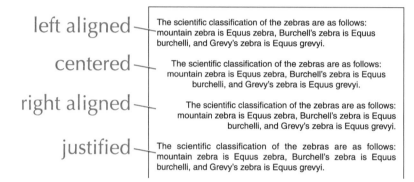

left aligned *Left aligned* is the default and means that the left edge of a paragraph is straight and the right edge of the paragraph is jagged. This format is most often used in letters and research papers. *Centered* means that the left and right edges of the paragraph are equally distant from the left and right sides of the page. Headings and titles are often centered. *Right aligned* means that the right edge of the paragraph is straight and the left edge is jagged. *Justified* alignment creates straight edges at both sides of a paragraph and is often used in newspapers and books.

centered

right aligned

justified

The alignment of a paragraph is changed by first placing the insertion point in the paragraph and then selecting Paragraph from the Format menu, which displays the Paragraph dialog box. Selecting the Indents and Spacing tab displays those options:

Paragraph [?][X]

Indents and Spacing | Line and Page Breaks

General

Alignment: [Left ▼]   Outline level: [Body text ▼]

Indentation

Left: [0" ↕]   Special: [(none) ▼]   By: [↕]

Right: [0" ↕]

Spacing

Before: [0 pt ↕]   Line spacing: [Single ▼]   At: [↕]

After: [0 pt ↕]

☐ Don't add space between paragraphs of the same style

Preview

[preview text box]

[Tabs...]   [OK]   [Cancel]

[Context menu on left: Cut, Copy, Paste, Font..., Paragraph..., Bullets and Numbering..., Hyperlink..., Synonyms ▸, Select Text with Similar Formatting, Translate]

Selecting an alignment in the Alignment list and then OK aligns the text in the paragraph. Multiple paragraphs can be formatted by first selecting the paragraphs and then applying the alignment.

The Paragraph dialog box can also be displayed by right-clicking a paragraph and selecting Paragraph from the displayed menu.

The Align Left (▤), Center (▤), Align Right (▤), and Justify (▤) buttons on the toolbar can be used to format the alignment of a paragraph. Ctrl key shortcuts can also be used to format alignment:

SHORTCUT	ALIGNMENT
Ctrl+L	left align
Ctrl+E	center
Ctrl+R	right align
Ctrl+J	justify

5.10 Paragraph Formats - Line Spacing

Line Spacing Button

The Line Spacing button (▤▼) on the toolbar can be used to format line spacing for selected paragraphs. Clicking the arrow in the button displays a list from which the spacing can be selected:

The space between lines of text in a paragraph can be changed. *Single spacing* is the default. *Double spacing* adds more space between lines of text for notes or comments and makes a document more readable:

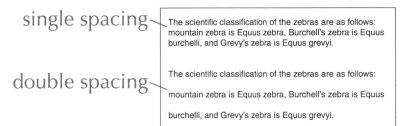

single spacing —⟨ The scientific classification of the zebras are as follows: mountain zebra is Equus zebra, Burchell's zebra is Equus burchelli, and Grevy's zebra is Equus grevyi.

double spacing —⟨ The scientific classification of the zebras are as follows: mountain zebra is Equus zebra, Burchell's zebra is Equus burchelli, and Grevy's zebra is Equus grevyi.

The Paragraph dialog box discussed in Section 5.9 can be used to format line spacing. Selecting Paragraph from the Format menu displays the dialog box. Selecting an option in the Line spacing list and then OK applies the formatting to the paragraph that contains the insertion point. Multiple paragraphs can be formatted by first selecting the paragraphs and then applying the line spacing.

Ctrl key shortcuts can also be used to format line spacing:

SHORTCUT	LINE SPACING
Ctrl+1	single spacing
Ctrl+2	double spacing

Practice 5 ♻

In this practice you will format paragraph alignment and spacing in WORKSHOP. Open WORKSHOP if it is not already displayed.

① *CENTER THE FIRST TWO LINES IN THE DOCUMENT*

    a. Scroll to the top of page 1 if it is not already displayed.

    b. Place the insertion point anywhere in the "Web Graphics Workshop" title at the top of page 1.

    c. Select Format → Paragraph. A dialog box is displayed.

        1. In the Alignment list, select Centered.

        2. Select OK. The dialog box is removed and the text is centered.

    d. Place the insertion point in the next line of the document "Malfas Web Design, Inc."

    e. On the toolbar, click the Center button (▤). The text is centered.

② *JUSTIFY THE PARAGRAPHS IN THE INTRODUCTION*

    a. Place the insertion point anywhere in the paragraph that begins "Welcome! All of us…."

    b. Hold down the Shift key and click in the last paragraph of the introduction, which begins "Now in our twentieth year…." Each paragraph in the Introduction now contains some selected text.

    c. On the toolbar, click the Justify button (▤). The selected paragraphs are justified.

    d. Click anywhere to remove the selection.

③ *DOUBLE SPACE THE SECOND PARAGRAPH OF THE INTRODUCTION*

    a. Right-click the second paragraph, which begins "All Malfas Web Design workshops…." A menu is displayed.

    b. Select Paragraph from the menu. A dialog box is displayed.

        1. In the Line spacing list, select Double.

        2. Select OK. The paragraph containing the insertion point is double spaced.

A Guide to Microsoft Office XP Professional

Check – Your document should look similar to:

Web·Graphics·Workshop¶
Malfas·Web·Design,·Inc.¶

¶
Introduction¶
¶
Welcome!·All· of· us· at· Malfas· Web· Design· are· pleased· that· you· chose· us· for· your· web· graphics· training· needs.· We· look· forward· to· helping· you· become· proficient· and· up· to· date· in· the· world· of· web· graphics.· Our· staff· is· highly· qualified,· with· advanced· degrees· from· accredited· universities· and· every· certification· imaginable.· The· instructor· and· assistants· for· your· workshop· have· extensive· experience· in· the· field· of· web· graphics· and· can·pass·their·knowledge·on·to·you.¶
¶
All·Malfas·Web·Design·workshops·are·organized·with·the·individual·in·mind.·In·addition·

to·the·instructor,·your·workshop·will·have·one·assistant·for·every·five·attendees·during·

the·hands-on·computer·sessions.·As·you·work·on·the·computers,·these·assistants·will·be·

right·there·with·you·to·help·you·and·answer·any·questions·you·may·have.¶

④ *DELETE THE DOUBLE-SPACED PARAGRAPH*

    a. Select the entire double-spaced paragraph.

    b. Press the Delete key. The paragraph is deleted.

    c. Press the Delete key again so that only one blank paragraph separates the two paragraphs in the Introduction.

⑤ *SAVE THE MODIFIED WORKSHOP*

5.11   Page Formats - Margins

Margins are shown in Print Layout view as the white region around the text on a page. The default margins in Word for an 8.5 inch by 11 inch page are 1.25 inches for the left and right and 1 inch for the top and bottom:

Paper Sizes

The size of paper used for a document can be changed using the Paper size list in the Paper tab options in the Page Setup dialog box:

Size	Measurements
Letter	8.5" x 11"
Tabloid	11" x 17"
Legal	8.5" x 14"
Executive	7.25" x 10.5"
A3	297mm x 420mm
A4	210mm x 297mm
A5	148mm x 210mm
B4 (JIS)	257mm x 364mm
B5 (JIS)	182mm x 257mm

1" top margin
1.25" left margin
1.25" right margin
11"
1" bottom margin
8.5"

Changes to the margins have an inverse affect on the amount of text that a page can contain. For example, widening the left and right margins decreases the number of characters that fit on a line. Narrowing the same margins increases the amount of text in a line. Similarly, larger top and bottom margins decrease the number of lines of text a page can contain and smaller top and bottom margins increase the amount of text on a page.

Selecting Page Setup from the File menu displays the Page Setup dialog box, and selecting the Margins tab displays those options:

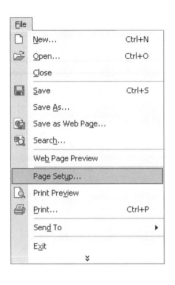

Margins are selected or typed in the Top, Bottom, Left, and Right boxes. Selecting OK applies the formatting. For example, the bottom margin is changed to 0.75 inches by selecting or typing the value 0.75 in the Bottom box and then selecting OK.

Changing the margins can affect the number of pages in a document. The Status bar at the bottom of the document window displays page information:

displayed page   total pages

Page 1   Sec 1   1/4

The status bar contains information about the currently displayed page and the total pages

---

Templates

Instead of creating similar documents over and over, a document can be created once and then saved as a template, which allows duplicates to be created as necessary. Templates are previously created documents that include only the basic elements.

A template is created by selecting Save As from the File menu and then selecting Template from the Save as type list. A template is opened by selecting the General tab in the New Office Document dialog box, selecting the template and OK.

Practice 6 ⟳

In this practice margins will be changed. Open WORKSHOP if it is not already displayed.

① CHANGE THE MARGINS

a. Select File → Page Setup. A dialog box is displayed.

 1. Click the Margins tab if the margin options are not already displayed.

 2. Change the Left margin to 2.5.

 3. Change the Right margin to 3.

 4. Select OK. The document now has a left margin of 2.5 inches and a right margin of 3 inches. Note that there is more white space on the left and right sides of the document, and the Status bar indicates that there are now 4 pages total in the document.

② PREVIEW THE DOCUMENT

a. Preview the document. Scroll to the first page in the document if it is not already displayed. Note that much more room appears on the left and right of the page because the margins have been increased:

b. Press Esc to return to the document window.

③ DECREASE THE MARGINS

a. Select File → Page Setup. A dialog box is displayed.

 1. Change the Left margin to 1.5.

 2. Change the Right margin to 1.5.

 3. Select OK. The document now has left and right margins of 1.5 inches.

④ SAVE THE MODIFIED WORKSHOP

Documents can be made more informative by including text at the top and bottom of each page in areas called the *header* and *footer*. Headers and footers are often used to include the current page number, the file name of the document, the author's name, or the date.

header

Selecting <u>H</u>eader and Footer from the <u>V</u>iew menu displays the Header and Footer toolbar, dims the text in the document, and places the insertion point in the header area at the top of the page:

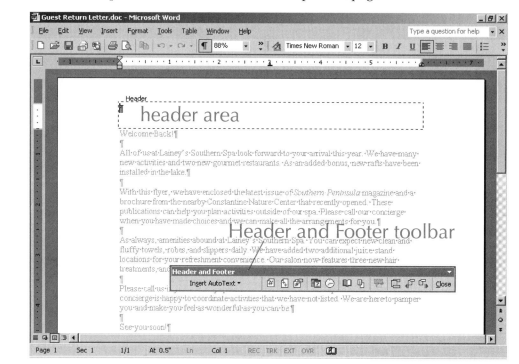

After typing text in the header area, the text can be selected and formatted.

footer

The insertion point is moved from the header to the footer by clicking the Switch Between Header and Footer button ( ) on the Header and Footer toolbar. Each time the button is clicked, Word scrolls the document until the header or footer is visible and places the insertion point. Text can then be typed and formatted. Headers or footers can be removed from a document by selecting the text and pressing the Delete key.

Note that the Header and Footer toolbar may need to be moved to view the document behind it. The toolbar can be moved by dragging its title bar.

Clicking the Close button (Close) in the Header and Footer toolbar removes the toolbar, dims the header and footer text, and displays the document.

editing a header or footer

An existing header or footer can be edited by double-clicking the header or footer area.

Displaying the Document

Another way to remove the Header and Footer toolbar and display the document is to double-click the dimmed text.

Text typed in the header or footer is printed on each page of the document. However, it is possible to have a different header and footer printed on the first page than on the rest of the pages. Selecting Page Setup from the File menu displays the Page Setup dialog box, and selecting the Layout tab displays those options:

Selecting the Different first page check box and then OK removes the contents from both the header and footer on the first page of the document. Text can then be added to the header and footer on the first page, or those areas can be left empty so that nothing prints in the header and footer on page 1.

5.13 Adding Page Numbers

Page numbers are often used in documents that have more than one page. Page numbers can be added by clicking the Insert Page Number button (⊞) on the Header and Footer toolbar:

Insert Page Number button

A page number is added at the insertion point, and can then be formatted. When the document is printed, the appropriate page number will appear at the top or bottom of every page in the document. A page number can be deleted from a header or footer by selecting it and pressing the Delete key.

Practice 7 ⟳

In this practice you will create a header and footer in WORKSHOP. Open WORKSHOP if it is not already displayed.

① *CREATE A HEADER*

    a. Scroll to the top of page 1 and place the insertion point anywhere on page 1.

    b. Select <u>V</u>iew → <u>H</u>eader and Footer. The text is dimmed and the insertion point is placed in the Header area. Note the Header and Footer toolbar.

    c. Type Web Graphics Workshop.

    d. Select all of the header text.

    e. On the toolbar, click the Italic button (*I*) and then the Center button (☰). The text in the header is italic and centered.

② *CREATE A FOOTER*

    a. On the Header and Footer toolbar, click the Switch Between Header and Footer button (🗐). The insertion point is placed in the Footer area.

    b. Type your name, followed by a space.

    c. On the Header and Footer toolbar, click the Insert Page Number button (⊞). The number 1 is inserted at the insertion point.

    d. Select all of the text in the footer, and then format it as 10 point bold Tahoma.

    e. On the Header and Footer toolbar, click the Close button (Close). The toolbar is removed and the header and footer are now dimmed.

③ *PREVIEW THE DOCUMENT*

    a. Preview the document. Page 1 of WORKSHOP is displayed. Note the text in the header and the text and page number in the footer.

    b. Scroll to view page 2. Note the page number is 2 in the footer.

    c. Preview the rest of the document and then close the Print Preview window.

④ *REMOVE THE HEADER AND FOOTER FROM THE FIRST PAGE*

    a. Select <u>F</u>ile → Page Set<u>u</u>p. A dialog box is displayed.

        1. Select the Layout tab.

        2. Select the **Different first page** check box.

        3. Select OK. The dialog box is removed and the header and footer are removed from page 1 of the document.

    b. Preview the document. Page 1 of WORKSHOP is displayed. Note that the header and footer are no longer visible on page 1.

    c. Scroll to view page 2. Note the header and footer.

    d. Preview the rest of the document and then close the Print Preview window.

⑤ *CREATE A DIFFERENT HEADER ON PAGE 1*

    a. Scroll to the top of page 1 and place the insertion point anywhere on page 1.

    b. Select <u>V</u>iew → <u>H</u>eader and Footer. The insertion point is placed in the Header area.

    c. Type your name.

    d. On the Header and Footer toolbar, click the Close button.

⑥ PREVIEW AND SAVE THE DOCUMENT

    a. Preview the document. Note the different headers on page 1 and the other pages.

    b. Close the Print Preview window.

    c. Save the modified WORKSHOP.

5.14 Page Formats - Pagination

Word automatically determines how much text will fit on a page based on the character, paragraph, and page formats. The process of determining where one page ends and the next begins is called *pagination*. As a document is edited, the pagination is automatically updated.

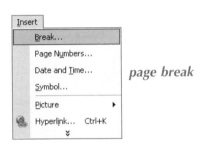

page break

A *page break* can be added to change pagination. Placing the insertion point where the new page should start and selecting <u>B</u>reak from the <u>I</u>nsert menu displays the Break dialog box:

Manual and Automatic Page Breaks

A page break that is added to a document using the Break dialog box is sometimes called a "manual" or "hard" page break. A place in a document where Word ends one page and begins another is sometimes called an "automatic" or "soft" page break.

Selecting OK accepts the default option of Page break and inserts a page break at the insertion point. If formatting marks are displayed in the document, a line is displayed with the words "Page Break":

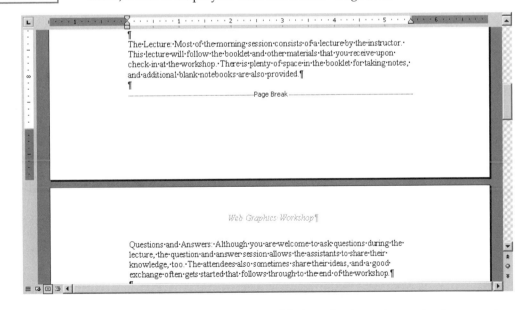

deleting a page break

A page break may also be added at the insertion point by pressing Ctrl+Enter. A page break is deleted by placing the insertion point to the left of the page break and pressing the Delete key. The document is then repaginated and text from the next page moves up to fill the current page.

In this practice you will add and remove page breaks. Open WORKSHOP if it is not already displayed.

① *INSERT A PAGE BREAK*

    a. Scroll to the beginning of the document and display formatting marks if they are not already displayed.

    b. Place the insertion point just before the "N" in the second paragraph that starts "Now in our twentieth year...."

    c. Select Insert → Break. A dialog box is displayed.

        1. Select OK. A Page break is added and text to the right of the insertion point is moved to the next page.

    d. Scroll up to view the top of page 1. A line is displayed with the words "Page Break."

② *PREVIEW WORKSHOP*

    a. Preview the document. Note the blank space at the bottom of page 1 as a result of the page break.

    b. Return to the document window.

③ *DELETE THE PAGE BREAK*

    a. Place the insertion point just to the left of the page break line.

    b. Press the Delete key. Text from page 2 is moved back up to page 1.

④ *INSERT TWO PAGE BREAKS*

    a. Scroll to the bottom of page 1.

    b. Place the insertion point just to the left of the words "Questions and Answers."

    c. Insert a page break. The text to the right of the insertion point is moved to the next page.

    d. Scroll to the bottom of page 2.

    e. Place the insertion point just to the left of the title "Our Computers."

    f. Insert a page break.

⑤ *SAVE AND CLOSE THE MODIFIED WORKSHOP*

5.15 Tabs and Tab Stops

Tab

Tabs are used to position text within a line. When the Tab key is pressed a tab is inserted and any text to the right of the insertion point is moved over to the position of the next tab stop. A *tab stop* specifies a location within the line of text. In Word, tab stops are displayed on the ruler above the document. A set of default tab stops are located at every half inch, but do not appear on the ruler.

A tab is deleted by placing the insertion point to the left of the tab and pressing the Delete key. Any text is automatically moved to the left to fill the space previously created by the tab.

In this practice you will format a new document and use tabs to indent text.

① CREATE A NEW DOCUMENT AND ENTER A TITLE

    a. Create a new document.

    b. Type City Diner Lunch Specials, and then press Enter.

    c. Type With guest chef and then type your name.

    d. Press Enter three times to add two blank paragraphs after the chef information.

② ENTER THE REST OF THE TEXT

    a. Type Choose Any Three Items for $6 and press Enter twice.

    b. Type the following text, pressing the Tab key as indicated (→) at the beginning of each line and pressing Enter (¶) at the end of each line:

          →   Chili¶
          →   Clam Chowder¶
          →   Garden Salad¶
          →   Turkey Sandwich (half)¶
          →   Tuna Sandwich (half)¶
          →   Hot Dog¶
          →   Brownie¶

③ FORMAT THE TEXT

    a. Select the title "City Diner Lunch Specials."

    b. Format the title as 26 point bold Tahoma, centered.

    c. Select the text "With guest chef *your name*."

    d. Format the text as 18 point bold Tahoma, centered.

    e. Select the text "Choose Any Three Items for $6."

    f. Format the text as 14 point bold and italic Tahoma.

    g. Select all the text below the titles you just formatted, starting with "Chili" and ending with "Brownie."

    h. Format the text as 14 point Tahoma.

    i. Click anywhere in the document. The text is no longer selected.

Check – Your document should look similar to:

a. Save the document naming it Lunch Specials.

b. Print a copy of Lunch Specials.

c. Close Lunch Specials.

5.16 Setting Individual Tab Stops

Tabs can be used to create a table of data. New tab stops are created at the appropriate intervals to arrange the data in columns:

Name	Age	Kennel	Feeding Time	Weight (kg)
Peach	12	29B	4 p.m	7.75
Jessie	3	6C	6 p.m	8.5
Duffy	10	20A	4:30 p.m.	9
Indy	7	5A	7 p.m	16

A tab stop can be set at any position on the ruler. When a tab stop is set, Word automatically removes the default tab stops to the left. For example, setting a tab stop at 1.4 inches automatically removes the default tab stops at 0.5 and 1.0 inches. The default stop at 1.5 inches is not affected.

When the Tab key is pressed, a tab is inserted and text to the right of the tab is aligned at the next tab stop according to the type of tab stop:

- **Left tab stop** (L) aligns the beginning of the text at the stop.

- **Right tab stop** (⌐) aligns the end of the text at the stop.

- **Center tab stop** (⊥) centers the text equidistant over the stop.

- **Decimal tab stop** (⊥) aligns the decimal point (a period) at the stop.

An example of each tab stop is shown below:

Name	→	Age	→	Kennel →	Feeding Time	→	Weight (kg)¶
Peach	→	12	→	29B	→	4·p.m	→	7.75¶
Jessie	→	3	→	6C	→	6·p.m	→	8.5¶
Duffy	→	10	→	20A	→	4:30·p.m.	→	9¶
Indy	→	7	→	5A	→	7·p.m	→	16¶

Tab stops are indicated by markers on the ruler

Tab stops are a paragraph format like alignment or line spacing. When tab stops are created, they are set for the paragraph that contains the insertion point, or for multiple paragraphs that are selected. As the insertion point is moved through the text, the ruler changes to show the tab stops set for the current paragraph.

Tab Leaders

A tab leader is a character that is repeated to fill the space spanned by a tab. Examples of tab leaders are ...., ----, and ___. The dotted pattern is often used in a table of contents or index. The solid line is used to represent a blank on a form or a test. Tab leaders are selected in the Tabs dialog box in the **Leader** section.

setting a tab stop

A tab stop is set by first clicking the Tab Selection button (L) on the ruler until the type of tab stop to be created is displayed:

A Guide to Microsoft Office XP Professional

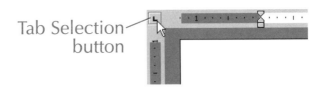

Tab Selection button

Clicking the white area of the ruler above the document places a tab stop that can then be dragged to any location. For example, clicking the Tab Selection button until the Right tab stop (⌐) is displayed and then clicking the ruler creates a right tab stop at that location.

removing a tab stop

A tab stop can be removed by dragging its marker downwards, off the ruler and into the document. Any text that was aligned at a deleted stop is then aligned to the next tab stop.

Tab stops can also be set by selecting Tabs from the Format menu, which displays the Tabs dialog box:

Tabs Dialog Box

The Tabs dialog box can be displayed by double-clicking a tab stop on the ruler or by clicking the Tabs button in the Paragraph dialog box.

Typing the Tab stop position that corresponds to the markings on the ruler, selecting the appropriate Alignment, and then selecting Set creates a tab stop at that position. This procedure can be repeated to create as many tab stops as needed. A tab stop can be removed by selecting it from the Tab stop position list in the Tabs dialog box and then selecting Clear. Selecting Clear All removes all the tab stops. Selecting OK removes the dialog box. Selecting OK removes the dialog box.

5.17 Selecting a Vertical Block of Text

Tables of data often have specific formatting applied to a column of data. A vertical block of text can be selected by holding down the Alt key and dragging:

Name		Age		Kennel	Feeding Time		Weight (kg)¶
Peach	→	12	→	29B	4·p.m.	→	7.75¶
Jessie	→	3	→	6C	6·p.m.	→	8.5¶
Duffy	→	10	→	20A	4:30·p.m.	→	9¶
Indy	→	7	→	5A	7·p.m.	→	16¶

Formatting can then be applied to the selected text. For example, clicking the Italic button when the data in the Feeding Time column is selected formats the data as italic:

Name		Age		Kennel	*Feeding Time*		Weight (kg)¶
Peach	→	12	→	29B	4 p.m.	→	7.75¶
Jessie	→	3	→	6C	6 p.m.	→	8.5¶
Duffy	→	10	→	20A	4:30 p.m.	→	9¶
Indy	→	7	→	5A	7 p.m.	→	16¶

Practice 10 ⟳

In this practice you will create a table by setting and deleting tab stops.

① OPEN WORKSHOP

Open WORKSHOP, which was last modified in Practice 8.

② LOCATE THE TABLE OF DATA IN THE WHAT TO EXPECT SECTION

Scroll to the "What to Expect" section, near the middle of page 1 in the document. In this table, there is a single tab between each column: one tab between "Event," "Time," and "Room." This table is difficult to read because tab stops have not been set.

③ SELECT THE TABLE

Select all of the paragraphs in the table, from the first "Event → Time → Room" to the last "Computer Instruction → 1:30 → C." Any tab stops set now will affect all of the selected paragraphs.

④ SET TAB STOPS FOR THE TABLE

    a. At the far left of the ruler, click the Tab Selection button until the right tab stop (⌐) is displayed in the button.

    b. Click the ruler near the 2" mark. A right tab stop is created and the "Time" column is aligned at the stop.

    c. Drag the tab stop to the 2.25" mark on the ruler, if it is not already there. The "Time" column is aligned at 2.25".

    d. Click the Tab Selection button until the left tab stop (L) is displayed in the button.

    e. Click the ruler near the 3" mark. A left tab stop is created and the "Room" column is aligned at the stop.

    f. Drag the tab stop to the 3" mark on the ruler, if it is not already there. The table is now formatted and is easier to read.

⑤ DELETE AN EXISTING TAB STOP AND CREATE A NEW TAB STOP

    a. Select the table if it is not still selected.

    b. Point to the left tab stop at the 3" mark on the ruler.

    c. Drag the tab stop downwards, off the ruler. The tab stop is removed. The "Room" column is now aligned at the next tab stop, which is the default tab stop at 2.5".

    d. Click the Tab Selection button until the center tab stop (⊥) is displayed in the button.

    e. Click the ruler near the 3" mark. A center tab stop is created and the "Room" column is aligned at the stop.

A Guide to Microsoft Office XP Professional

f. Drag the new tab stop to the 3" mark on the ruler, if it is not already there. The third column in the table is now centered.

g. Click anywhere to remove the selection.

⑥ *SELECT A VERTICAL BLOCK OF TEXT IN THE TABLE*

a. Hold down the Alt key and drag from the beginning of the "Event" title to the end of "Computer Instruction" in the last line of the table. Be sure that all of the events are entirely selected:

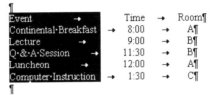

b. On the toolbar, click the Bold button. The first column in the table is formatted as bold text.

Check – Your document and ruler should look similar to:

Event	→	Time	→	Room¶
Continental Breakfast	→	8:00	→	A¶
Lecture	→	9:00	→	B¶
Q. & A. Session	→	11:30	→	B¶
Luncheon	→	12:00	→	A¶
Computer Instruction	→	1:30	→	C¶

¶
A·Networking·Breakfast:·Each·morning·begins·with·a·continental·breakfast·in·a·

⑦ *SAVE, PRINT, AND THEN CLOSE THE MODIFIED WORKSHOP*

a. Save the modified WORKSHOP.

b. Print the entire document. Note on the printed copy all of the formatting: headers, footers, paragraph formats, text formats, etc.

c. Close WORKSHOP.

⑧ *QUIT WORD*

Chapter Summary

This chapter introduced character, paragraph, and page formats that improve the appearance and readability of documents.

The effects of the last action are reversed by selecting the Undo command, or the action is performed a second time by selecting the Redo or Repeat command. The Undo button and the Redo button can also be used to reverse or repeat actions.

Text is selected by dragging the pointer over it. Pressing a key replaces selected text with the typed character. Pressing the Backspace key or Delete key removes selected text. Clicking anywhere in the document or pressing an arrow key removes the selection.

Selecting the Font command displays the Font dialog box, which is used to format the font, size, and style of selected text. A font refers to the shape of characters, and the size of text is measured in points. The Font box and the Font Size box can also be used to change the font and size of selected text. The way a character is emphasized is called its style. Common styles are bold, italic, and underline. In addition to options in the Font dialog box, the Bold, Italic, and Underline buttons can be used to apply character styles.

Superscript and subscript are formats that reduce the size of text and raise or lower it to the top or bottom of the current line. Check boxes in the Font dialog box are used to apply superscript and subscript formats.

A document can be previewed to see how it will appear when printed by selecting the Print Preview command or the Print Preview button. Clicking the magnifying glass pointer on the page zooms in, and clicking again displays the entire page. In Print Preview, selecting the Print button prints a copy of the document.

Selecting the Paragraph command displays the Paragraph dialog box, which is used to format the alignment and line spacing of selected text. The alignment of text in a paragraph refers to its position relative to the sides of the page. Buttons can also be used to format the alignment of a paragraph. The space between lines of text in a paragraph can be changed to double spacing or single spacing (the default).

Margins are the white region around text on a page. The default margins in Word for an 8.5" by 11" page are 1.25" for the left and right and 1" for the top and bottom. Margins can be changed for a document using the Page Setup command. Changing the margins can affect the number of pages in a document, which is displayed in the Status bar at the bottom of the document window.

The Header and Footer command is used to display the header and footer areas at the top and bottom of each page. The insertion point is moved between the header and footer by clicking the Switch Between Header and Footer button. Headers or footers can be removed from a document by selecting the text and pressing the Delete key. Clicking the Insert Page Number button adds a page number.

Word automatically determines where one page ends and the next begins in a process called pagination. A page break can be added at the insertion point using the Break command.

Tabs are used to position text within a line. A tab stop specifies a location within a line of text and is displayed on the ruler above a document. A tab stop is set by first clicking the Tab Selection button until the type of tab stop to be created is displayed, then clicking the white area of the ruler above the doucment. The tab stop can then be dragged to any location. A tab stop can be removed by dragging its marker off the ruler. A vertical block of text in a table can be selected by holding down the Alt key and dragging, and then formatting can be applied.

Alignment Position of text in a paragraph relative to the sides of the page. Left, right, centered, and justified are alignments.

Bold text Character format that prints text darker.

Center alignment Alignment format that positions text evenly between the left and right margins.

Character format A formatting level that affects the selected characters.

Dingbat A picture created by a special font such as Wingdings.

Double spacing Paragraph format that adds more space between each line of text.

Font Shape of a set of characters.

Footer Text that is printed at the bottom of each page.

Format The way text appears on a page.

Header Text that is printed at the top of each page.

Italic text Character format that makes text slanted.

Justified alignment Paragraph format where both sides of the paragraph are straight.

Left alignment Default paragraph format where the left edge of the paragraph is straight and the right edge is jagged.

Margin The white region around the text on a page.

Page break Changes the pagination in a document.

Page format A formatting level that affects the entire document.

Pagination The process of determining where one page ends and another begins.

Paragraph format A formatting level that affects the selected paragraph(s).

Point The unit used to measure character size. There are 72 points to an inch.

Right alignment Paragraph format where the right edge of the paragraph is straight and the left edge is jagged.

Selected text Text that is shown highlighted on the screen.

Single spacing The default paragraph format where there is no extra space between each line of text.

Smart menu A menu that changes to reflect the current situation.

Style The way in which a character is emphasized.

Subscript Text that is reduced in size and lowered to the bottom of the current line.

Superscript Text that is reduced in size and raised to the top of the current line.

Tabs Characters used to position text within a line.

Tab stop Specifies a location within a line of text.

Typeface Commonly referred to as font. See font.

Underlined text Character format that puts a line under text.

Word Commands and Buttons

Align Left button Left aligns the text in the selected paragraph. Found on the toolbar.

Align Right button Right aligns the text in the selected paragraph. Found on the toolbar.

Bold button Formats selected text as bold. Found on the toolbar.

Break **command** Displays a dialog box used to insert a page break at the insertion point. Found in the Insert menu.

Center button Centers the text in the selected paragraph. Found on the toolbar.

Close button Used to remove the Header and Footer toolbar, dim the header and footer text, and display the document. Found on the Header and Footer toolbar.

Close button Used to return to the document window. Found on the toolbar in the Print Preview window.

Font **command** Displays a dialog box used to apply character formats. Found in the Format menu.

Header and Footer **command** Displays the Header and Footer toolbar, dims the text in the document, and places the insertion point in the header area at the top of the page. Found in the View menu.

Insert Page Number button Adds a page number at the insertion point in a header or footer. Found in the Header and Footer toolbar.

Italic button Formats selected text as italic. Found on the toolbar.

Justify button Justifies the text in the selected paragraph. Found on the toolbar.

Page Setup **command** Displays a dialog box used to apply page formats. Found in the File menu.

Paragraph **command** Displays a dialog box used to apply paragraph formats. Found in the Format menu.

Print button Prints a copy of the document. Found on the toolbar in the Print Preview window.

Print Preview **command** Used to preview a document to see how it will appear when printed. Found in the File menu. The Print Preview button on the toolbar can be used instead of the command.

Redo **command** Performs the last action again. Found in the Edit menu. The Redo button on the toolbar can be used instead of the command.

Select All **command** Selects all the text in a document. Found in the Edit menu.

Switch Between Header and Footer button Moves the insertion point to either the header or footer area in a document. Found on the Header and Footer toolbar.

Tab Selection button Used to select the type of tab stop that will be created by clicking the ruler. Found on the ruler.

Tabs **command** Displays a dialog box used to set or clear individual tab stops. Found in the Format menu.

Underline button Formats selected text as underlined. Found on the toolbar.

Undo **command** Reverses the effects of the last action. Found in the Edit menu. The Undo button on the toolbar can be used instead of the command.

Review Questions

Sections 5.1 — 5.14

1. What are the three levels of formatting associated with a document?

2. List the steps required to remove the last sentence that was typed.

3. a) How is selected text shown on the screen?
   b) What happens if text is selected and then the Backspace key is pressed?

4. List two methods for selecting an entire paragraph of text.

5. a) What does font refer to?
   b) List five fonts available on your computer.

6. a) What is character size measured in?
   b) List the steps required to format a selected sentence as 24 point.

7. List the steps required to format a word as bold and italic.

8. List the steps required to remove bold formatting from a selected paragraph.

9. List the steps required to preview the open document, print a copy, and then return to the document window.

10. List the steps required to superscript the word up and subscript the word down in the sentence:

    Sea turtles come up for air and then swim down to the bottom.

11. a) List the four paragraph alignments and describe each one.
    b) List the steps required to right align the selected paragraph.

12. What is double spacing?

13. List the steps required to change the formatting of a paragraph from double spaced to single spaced.

14. a) What are margins?
    b) What are the default margins in Word?

15. a) List the steps required to change the margins of a document so that the left margin is 2" and the right margin 3".
    b) How long is a line of text after these margins have been set? (Assume an 8.5" x 11" sheet of paper.)

16. a) What is a header?
    b) What is a footer?
    c) What type of information is often included in a header or footer?

17. List the steps required to have Word print the text Proposal in the header and a page number in the footer on each page in a document.

18. What is pagination?

19. List the steps required to add a page break at the insertion point.

Sections 5.15 — 5.17

20. a) What are tabs used for?
    b) What does a tab stop do?
    c) Where are the default tab stops located?

21. List the four types of tab stops and describe each one.

22. a) List the steps required to set a center tab stop at 2.25".
    b) How can the tab stop described in part (a) be removed?
    c) How can you tell where tab stops have been set?

23. List the steps required to change a center tab stop at 2.5" to a left tab stop at 3".

Exercise 1 ⟲ ——————————————————— Ceramics Info Request

The request letter created in Chapter 4, Exercise 1 needs to be formatted. Open Ceramics Info Request and complete the following steps:

a) Format the alignment of the entire letter as justified.

b) Change the left and right margins to 1.5".

c) Create a left tab stop at 2" for the entire letter.

d) Insert a tab before the date at the top of the letter, at the bottom of the letter before the closing ("Sincerely"), and before your name.

e) Save the modified Ceramics Info Request and print a copy.

Exercise 2 ——————————————————————— OPENINGS

The OPENINGS document contains several introductions that can be used to start a short story. Open OPENINGS and complete the following steps:

a) Choose one of the introductions, delete the rest, then write a short paragraph using the remaining introduction as the beginning of the paragraph.

b) Format the paragraph as justified and double spaced.

c) Create a header with a title for the story centered. Format the title as 18 point and bold.

d) Create a footer with your name right aligned.

e) Check the document on screen for errors and misspellings and make any corrections.

f) Save the modified OPENINGS and print a copy.

Exercise 3 ⟲ ——————————————————— Entertainment Review

The review created in Chapter 4, Exercise 3 needs to be formatted. Open Entertainment Review and complete the following steps:

a) Create a bold, centered title that has the name of the event that was reviewed. Be sure there is a blank paragraph between the title and the first paragraph.

b) Format any titles in the review as italic, such as the title of a movie or a song title.

c) Format the alignment of the body of the review as justified.

d) Doubled space the body of the review.

e) Create a header with the text CRITIC'S CHOICE centered.

f) Create a footer with your name right aligned.

g) Save the modified Entertainment Review and print a copy.

1, 3, 5, 9
13, 16

Exercise 4 ——————————————— TELECOMMUTING

The TELECOMMUTING document contains information about the advantages of telecommuting. Open TELECOMMUTING and complete the following steps:

a) Format the following headings as 14 point, bold, Tahoma, and centered:

"Computers in the Home Office"
"The Process of Telecommuting"
"Advantages of Telecommuting"
"Telecommuting in Coral County"

b) Underline the first sentence of the second paragraph that begins "Telecommuting is possible because…."

c) Format the first paragraph that begins "Over the past ten years…" as justified.

d) Change the left and right margins to 0.75".

e) Insert a page break before the heading "Telecommuting in Coral County."

f) Create a header with the text TELECOMMUTING centered.

g) Create a footer with your name right aligned.

h) Format the entire table on page 2 with the following tab stops:

- at 2" create a right tab stop (for the number of people)
- at 3.5" create a right tab stop (for the percentage of population)

j) Format the column titles "Number of People" and "Percentage of Population" in the table to have only the following tab stops:

- at 1.75" create a center tab stop (for "Number of People")
- at 3.5" create a center tab stop (for "Percentage of Population")

k) Format the column titles in the table as bold.

l) Format the last line in the table that contains the totals as italic.

m) Save the modified TELECOMMUTING and print a copy.

Exercise 5 ——————————————— Geology Schedule

The memo created in Chapter 4, Exercise 5 needs to be formatted. Open Geology Schedule and complete the following steps:

a) Format the word "MEMORANDUM" as bold and italic.

b) Format the words "TO:," "FROM:," "DATE:," and "SUBJECT:" and the colons as bold.

c) Double space the paragraphs with "TO:," "FROM:," "DATE:," and "SUBJECT:."

d) Replace the spaces after the colons in the words "TO:," "FROM:," "DATE:," and "SUBJECT:" with a tab.

e) Format "TO:," "FROM:," "DATE:," and "SUBJECT:" with a left tab stop at 1".

f) Edit the data and column titles in the listing of research papers so that there is a single tab between each paper topic and due date. Delete any spaces that were previously used to separate the columns.

g) Create a header with the text Independent Study in Geology centered.

h) Create a footer with your name right aligned.

i) Format the entire table with a right tab stop at 1.5".

j) Modify the tab stop set in part (i) to a center tab stop at 1.5".

k) Format the column titles "Topic" and "Due Date" in the table as italic.

l) Save the modified Geology Schedule and print a copy.

Exercise 6 ———————————————————WELCOME

The WELCOME document contains a letter for new customers. Open WELCOME and complete the following steps:

a) Format the title "Marrelli's Gym" as 18 point, bold, in a different font, and centered.

b) Format all occurrences of "work" in the word "workout" as superscript and all occurrences of "out" in "workout" as subscript.

c) Change the top and left margins to 2".

d) Format all the paragraphs of the letter except for the "Marrelli's Gym" title as justified.

e) Create a footer with your name right aligned.

f) Format the entire table at the bottom of the letter with the following tab stops:

- at 1.25" create a left tab stop (for the hours on Monday – Friday)
- at 2.75" create a left tab stop (for the hours on Saturday)
- at 4.25" create a left tab stop (for the hours on Sunday)

g) Format the column titles in the table as bold and italic.

h) Save the modified WELCOME and print a copy.

Exercise 7 ———————————————————PROPOSAL

The Coral Research proposal modified in Chapter 4, Exercise 7 needs to be formatted. Open PROPOSAL and complete the following steps:

a) Bold and center align the headings "A PROPOSAL FOR CORAL RESEARCH" and "GROWTH STUDIES OF CORAL ON SOUTH FLORIDA REEFS."

b) Format the headings "Summary," "Purpose and Description," "Coral," and "Computerized Guide" as italic.

c) Change the top and bottom margins to 1.25" and the left and right margins to 1.5".

d) Create a footer with your name and the page number centered.

e) Insert a page break before the heading "Computerized Guide".

f) Format the "BUDGET" heading on page 2 as bold, in a larger size, and center aligned.

g) Format the table below the "BUDGET" heading with the following tab stops:

- at 0.75" create a left tab stop
- at 4.5" create a decimal tab stop

h) Insert a page break before the heading "Notes" at the bottom of page 2.

i) Save the modified PROPOSAL and print a copy.

Exercise 8 ⟳ ————————————————————— Journal

The journal created in Chapter 4, Exercise 8 needs to be formatted. Open Journal and complete the following steps:

a) Format all the text as italic.

b) Format all the text as justified.

c) Create a footer with your name right aligned.

d) Save the modified Journal and print a copy.

Exercise 9 ⟳ ————————————————————— Grand Opening

The store flyer created in Chapter 4, Exercise 9 needs to be formatted. Open Grand Opening and complete the following steps:

a) Bold all occurrences of the store's name.

b) Format the "20% OFF EVERYTHING!" title as 36 point. Since this is a flyer, increase the font size of the rest of the text so that the information fills the page.

c) Format appropriate paragraph alignments throughout the flyer.

d) Create a footer with your name right aligned.

e) Save the modified Grand Opening and print a copy.

Exercise 10 ————————————————————— PRESIDENTS

The PRESIDENTS document contains a list of all the presidents of the United States, which needs formatting with tab stops. Open PRESIDENTS and complete the following steps:

a) Format the entire document with left tab stops at 0.75" and 4" and a right tab stop at 3.5". The table should appear similar to the following:

Number	President	Years in Office	Party
1.	George Washington	1789-1797	(none)
2.	John Adams	1797-1801	Federalist
3.	Thomas Jefferson	1801-1809	Democratic-Republican
…	…	…	…

b) Save the modified PRESIDENTS.

c) Format the column titles in the table as bold.

d) Double space the entire table.

e) Create a header with your name centered.

f) Create a footer with the page number centered.

g) Save the modified PRESIDENTS and print a copy.

Exercise 11 — Water Conservation

The article created in Chapter 4, Exercise 11 needs to be formatted. Open Water Conservation and complete the following steps:

a) Create a byline by typing the text By *your name* under the title, using your full name. Insert a blank paragraph below the byline.

b) Format the document's title as 14 point and bold, and the byline as italic.

c) Format the text in the body of the article as justified.

d) Change the top and bottom margins to 3".

e) Create a header with the text Environmental Issue centered and bold.

f) Create a footer with your name right aligned and italic.

g) Save the modified Water Conservation and print a copy.

Exercise 12 — Ten Years

The local newspaper would like to print the essay created in Chapter 4, Exercise 12. Open Ten Years and complete the following steps:

a) Create a title at the top of the document that describes the essay, and insert two blank paragraphs between the title and the first paragraph.

b) Format the title as 20 point, bold, Tahoma, and centered.

c) Double space the text in the body of the essay.

d) Change the top and bottom margins to 1.5" and the left and right margins to 2".

e) Create a header with your name right aligned.

f) Save the modified Ten Years and print a copy.

Exercise 13 — Vitamins

In a new document create the following table, separating the columns with single tabs (do <u>not</u> precede the first column with a tab):

Vitamin	Usage in Body	Common Food Sources
A	skeletal growth, skin	green leafy or yellow vegetables
B1	metabolism of carbohydrates	whole grains, liver
B12	production of proteins	liver, kidney, lean meat
C	resistance to infection	citrus fruits, tomatoes
E	antioxidant	peanut, corn oils

Note: Your table will not look like the one above until tab stops have been set.

a) Save the document naming it Vitamins.

b) Format the entire table with the following tab stops:

- at 1.25" create a left tab stop (for the usage in body)
- at 3.5" create a left tab stop (for the common food sources)

c) Format the entire "Common Food Sources" column of data as italic.

d) At the top of the document, create a bold title with the text Vitamins and Their Usage. Insert a blank paragraph between the title and the table.

e) Format the column titles in the table as bold.

f) Subscript the "1" in "B1" and subscript the "12" in "B12."

g) Create a footer with your name right aligned.

h) Check the document on screen for errors and misspellings and make any corrections.

i) Save the modified Vitamins and print a copy.

Exercise 14 ———————————————————— Hawaiian Islands

In a new document create the following table, separating the columns with single tabs (do not precede the first column with a tab):

Island	Area (km2)	Tallest Peak	Peak Height (m)
Hawaii	6,501	Mauna Kea	4,139
Maui	1,174	Haleakala	3,007
Oahu	979	Kaala	1,208
Kauai	890	Kawaikini	1,573
Molokai	420	Kamakou	1,491
Lanai	225	Lanaihale	1,011
Niihau	118	Paniau	384
Kahoolawe	72	Lua Makika	443

Note: Your table will not look like the one above until tab stops have been set.

a) Save the document naming it Hawaiian Islands.

b) Format the entire table with the following tab stops:
- at 1" create a left tab stop (for the area)
- at 2.5" create a center tab stop (for the tallest peak)
- at 4" create a right tab stop (for the peak height)

c) In the paragraph with the column titles, change the right tab stop at 4" to a center tab stop at 3.75".

d) Format the column titles "Island," "Area (km2)," "Tallest Peak," and "Peak Height (m)" in the table as bold.

e) Format the entire "Area (km2)" column of data and the "Peak Height (m)" column of data as Tahoma.

f) At the top of the document, create a bold title with the text The Hawaiian Islands. Insert a blank paragraph between the title and the table.

g) Superscript the "2" in the column title "Area (km2)."

h) Format the entire document as 11 point Helvetica.

i) Create a footer with your name centered.

j) Check the document on screen for errors and misspellings and make any corrections.

k) Save the modified Hawaiian Islands and print a copy.

In a new document create the following table, separating the columns with single tabs (do <u>not</u> precede the first column with a tab):

Measurement	Units	Symbol	Formula
Area	square meter	m2	m2
Heat	joule	J	N x m
Power	watt	W	J/s
Force	newton	N	kg x m/s2
Pressure	pascal	Pa	N/m2
Velocity	meter per second	m/s	m/s

Note: Your table will not look like the one above until tab stops have been set.

a) Save the document naming it Science Review.

b) Format the entire table with the following tab stops:

- at 1.5" create a left tab stop (for the units)
- at 3.5" create a center tab stop (for the symbol)
- at 5" create a right tab stop (for the formula)

c) Format all occurrences of "2" in the table as superscript.

d) Insert three blank paragraphs after the first table, then create the following table, separating the columns with single tabs (do <u>not</u> precede the first column with a tab):

Formula	Name
C2H2	acetylene
H2O	water
K2SO4	potassium sulfate
NH3	ammonia
CH4	methane
C6H6	benzene

Note: Your table will not look like the one above until tab stops have been set.

e) Format the entire second table to have only one tab stop, a left tab stop at 1".

f) In the second table, format all occurrences of numbers as subscript.

g) At the top of the document, create a bold, centered title with the text Science Review Sheet. Insert a blank paragraph between the title and the first table.

h) Bold all of the column titles in both tables.

i) Create a header with your name left aligned.

j) Check the document on screen for errors and misspellings and make any corrections.

k) Save the modified Science Review and print a copy.

In a new document write a letter to a clothing company. Discuss your favorite garments, colors, and fabrics, and describe what you would like to wear next year. Include a table of at least five lines of text. Format the text as 10 point and a different font. Include a footer with the text From the desk of Name centered, using your name for Name. Save the letter naming it Garments and print a copy.

Chapter 6
Word Processor Features

Cut

Copy

Paste

Office Clipboard

Find

Replace

Thesaurus

Paragraph

Reveal Formatting

Footnote

Date and Time

Word Count

Clip art

Columns

Chapter 6 Expectations

After completing this chapter you will be able to:

1. Copy and move text.
2. Use the Office Clipboard.
3. Find text and special characters in a document.
4. Locate text and replace it.
5. Use the thesaurus to display a list of synonyms for words or phrases.
6. Indent paragraphs.
7. Copy and paste paragraph formats.
8. Display and use the Reveal Formatting task pane.
9. Format hanging indents and first line indents.
10. Format bulleted and numbered lists.
11. Create footnotes and endnotes.
12. Insert time stamps.
13. Display the number of words in a document.
14. Search for clipart.
15. Add a picture to a document and change the size of a picture.
16. Format a document with columns.

This chapter discusses several features including copying text and searching for text. Formatting such as hanging indents, bulleted lists, and columns are also covered. Adding clip art to a document is also discussed.

6.1 Copying and Moving Text

There are times when text needs to be repeated in a document. Rather than typing the text multiple times, it can be duplicated using the Copy button ( ) and the Paste button ( ) on the toolbar.

copying text

The steps for copying text in a document are:

1. Select the text to be copied.

2. Click the Copy button ( ) on the toolbar. A copy of the selected text is added to the Clipboard.

3. Place the insertion point in the document where the text is to be inserted.

4. Click the Paste button ( ) on the toolbar. The contents of the Clipboard are placed in the document at the insertion point, and the Paste Options button ( ) is displayed.

Clipboard

The *Clipboard* is a designated area in memory. Text in the Clipboard remains there until different text is copied or the computer is turned off.

moving text

Text may need to be moved from one place to another in a document. The Cut ( ) and Paste ( ) buttons on the toolbar can be used to move text. Clicking the Cut button ( ) on the toolbar moves the selected text from the document to the Clipboard. Placing the insertion point where the text is to be inserted and clicking the Paste button places a copy of the Clipboard contents in the document at the insertion point. Note that using the Cut button moves selected text, and using the Copy button creates a duplicate of selected text.

The Cut (Ctrl+X), Copy (Ctrl+C), and Paste (Ctrl+V) commands in the Edit menu can be used instead of the buttons. Alternatively, right-clicking selected text displays a menu with Cut, Copy, and Paste commands.

> **The Paste Options Button**
>
> Clicking the Paste Options button ( ) after pasting text into a document displays a list of options that can be used to change the default paste option of Keep Source Formatting.

6.2 The Office Clipboard

The *Office Clipboard* is a special clipboard available in Microsoft Office applications such as Word. Unlike the Clipboard, which only stores the last item cut or copied, the Office Clipboard stores up to 24 different items, including the last cut or copied item. Selecting Office Clipboard from the Edit menu displays the Office Clipboard task pane, with the last copied item in the top position:

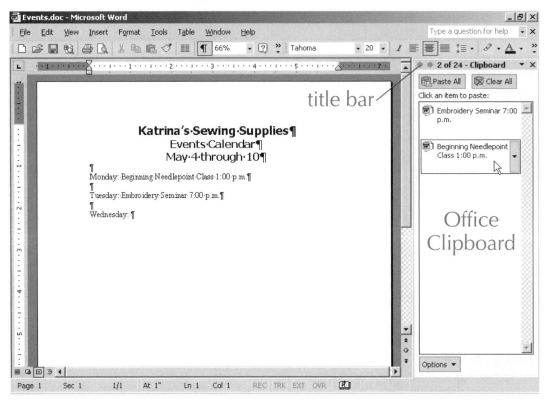

- The **title bar** indicates the number of items currently in the Office Clipboard. In the example shown above, 2 of 24 indicates there are two items in the Office Clipboard.

- **Paste All button** (![Paste All]) pastes copies of all the items in the Office Clipboard at the insertion point. Items are pasted in the order in which they were cut or copied.

- **Clear All button** (![Clear All]) removes all the items from the Office Clipboard.

pasting an item

In the Office Clipboard, pointing to an item changes it to a button, such as the second item in the Office Clipboard shown above. Clicking the button pastes a copy of that item in the document at the insertion point. Clicking ⋅ displays a menu from which Paste or Delete can be selected, to paste the item or remove it from the Office Clipboard. This menu is also displayed by right-clicking an item.

deleting an item

closing the task pane

The Office Clipboard can be removed from the document window by clicking the Close button (![X]) in the upper-right corner of the task pane.

Displaying the Office Clipboard

The Office Clipboard can also be displayed by clicking the Copy button twice in rapid succession.

In this practice you will cut, copy, and paste text and use the Office Clipboard.

① *OPEN MOCKINGBIRD MUSIC*

Open MOCKINGBIRD MUSIC, which is a data file for this text, and display formatting marks if they are not already displayed.

② *SELECT TEXT TO BE MOVED*

In the large paragraph near the top of page 1, select the last sentence, which begins "Our students have won…." Do not include the paragraph mark in the selection.

③ *MOVE SELECTED TEXT*

    a. On the toolbar, click the Cut button ( ). The selected text is removed from the document and placed on the Clipboard.

    b. Scroll down to the bottom of the page and place the insertion point in the last blank paragraph below the "Harps" paragraph.

    c. Press Enter to create a new paragraph.

    d. On the toolbar, click the Paste button ( ). The Clipboard contents are placed at the insertion point and the Paste Options button button ( ) is displayed. The Paste Options button will not be used and should be ignored.

④ *DISPLAY THE OFFICE CLIPBOARD*

Select Edit → Office Clipboard. The Office Clipboard task pane is displayed, and the text that was cut in step 3 is the first item in the Office Clipboard.

⑤ *COPY AND PASTE TEXT*

    a. In the large paragraph near the top of page 1, select the last sentence, which begins "We take pride…." Do not include the paragraph mark in the selection.

    b. On the toolbar, click the Copy button ( ). The copied text appears in the Office Clipboard as the top item.

    c. Scroll down to the bottom of the page and place the insertion point at the end of the last paragraph, after the exclamation point in "…make us proud!"

    d. Type a space.

    e. In the Office Clipboard, click the top item. The sentence is pasted at the insertion point as part of the last paragraph of the document. Ignore the Paste Options button.

    f. Scroll up in the document and note that the original sentence is still there.

⑥ *CLEAR AND CLOSE THE OFFICE CLIPBOARD*

    a. In the Office Clipboard task pane, select the Clear All button (Clear All). All of the items in the Office Clipboard are removed.

    b. In the upper-right corner of the Office Clipboard task pane, click the Close button (X). The Office Clipboard is removed from the document window.

⑦ *SAVE AND THEN CLOSE THE MODIFIED MOCKINGBIRD MUSIC*

6.3 Finding Text in a Document

search text

The text in a Word document can be scanned for *search text*, which is a specified single character, word, or phrase. Selecting Find (Ctrl+F) from the Edit menu displays the Find and Replace dialog box where search text is typed:

Selecting Less reduces the dialog box's size and hides the Search Options. Selecting More expands the dialog box again. Selecting Cancel ends the search and removes the dialog box.

In the example above, the word sailing has been entered as the search text. When Find Next is selected, Word starts searching from the position of the insertion point and continues through the document looking for the search text. If a match is found, Word stops searching and selects the text. Selecting Find Next continues the search. If the search text is not found, a message similar to the following is displayed:

Word could not find the search text

Match case

The Match case check box is used when occurrences of search text with the same capitalization are to be found. For example, with the Match case check box selected, a search for Cat will not find CAT or cat.

Find whole words only

The Find whole words only check box is used when occurrences of the search text that are not part of another word are to be found. For example, a search for fin will not only find fin but also finer, stuffing, and muffin unless the Find whole words only check box is selected. The Match case and Find whole words only check boxes can be used together to perform a precise search.

The Go To Tab

Selecting the Go To tab in the Find and Replace dialog box displays options used to display a specific page quickly.

A Guide to Microsoft Office XP Professional

6.4 Finding Special Characters

Special characters such as tab and paragraph characters can also be found using the Find and Replace dialog box. For example, it may be helpful to find all the occurrences of the word tip at the beginning of a paragraph. Since all (except the first) paragraphs in the document have a paragraph mark before them, a precise search would include a paragraph mark before the word tip. Selecting Special in the Find and Replace dialog box displays a list of special characters:

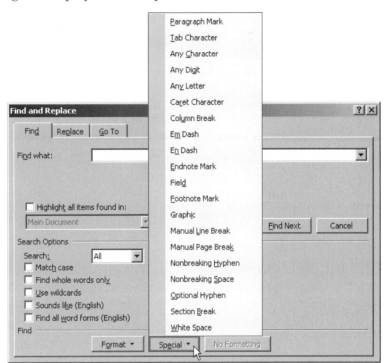

Special characters can be selected from this list

Finding Text in the Header and Footer

When searching for text using the Find and Replace dialog box, Word searches the entire document and then searches the header and footer. If the search text is found in the header or footer, the text is selected and displayed in a separate window at the bottom of the document.

finding a paragraph mark   Selecting Paragraph Mark from the list inserts ^p in the Find what box, and the rest of the search text can then be typed:

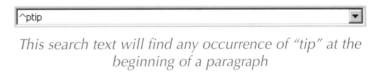

This search text will find any occurrence of "tip" at the beginning of a paragraph

finding a tab   Similarly, a tab can be found by selecting Tab Character from the list. The tab appears as ^t in the Find what box.

Practice 2

In this practice you will search for text and special characters.

① *OPEN WORKSHOP*

Open WORKSHOP, which was last modified in Chapter 5, Practice 10.

② *FIND SEARCH TEXT*

a. Make sure that the insertion point is at the top of page 1 in the document.

b. Select <u>E</u>dit → <u>F</u>ind. A dialog box is displayed.

    1. In the Find what box, type the word instruction.

    2. Select Find Next. The first occurrence of "instruction" is selected. Note that the selected word starts with a capital "I" even though the search text has a lowercase "i."

    3. Select Find Next to select the next occurrence of the search text.

    4. Continue to select Find Next until a message is displayed that Word has finished searching the document. Note that occurrences of both "instruction" and "Instruction" were found.

    5. Select OK. The message dialog box is removed.

    6. Select Cancel. The Find and Replace dialog box is removed. Note that the insertion point was returned to the top of page 1.

③ *MODIFY THE SEARCH TEXT*

Select <u>E</u>dit → <u>F</u>ind. A dialog box is displayed. The previously entered search text instruction is displayed and selected in the Find what box.

    1. Select More if the Search Options are not already displayed.

    2. Select the Match case check box so that only "instruction" with all lowercase letters will be found.

    3. Select Find Next. Note how the selected word has a lowercase "i."

    4. Select Find Next again. A message is displayed that Word has finished searching the document. This is because there are no more occurrences of "instruction" with a lowercase "i" in the document.

    5. Select OK. The message dialog box is removed.

    6. Select Cancel. The dialog box is removed.

④ *SEARCH FOR OCCURRENCES OF "LUNCHEON" AT THE BEGINNING OF A PARAGRAPH*

Select <u>E</u>dit → <u>F</u>ind. A dialog box is displayed. The previously entered text instruction is displayed and selected in the Find what box.

    1. Select More if the Search Options are not already displayed.

    2. Select Special. A list of special characters is displayed.

    3. Click Paragraph Mark at the top of the list to place ^p in the Find what box, replacing the selected text, then type luncheon. This will have Word locate all occurrences of "luncheon" that begin a paragraph. Your dialog box should look similar to:

4. Clear the Match case check box so that all occurrences of "luncheon" will be found.

5. Select Find Next to start the search. Note how the text and the paragraph mark in the line above it is selected.

6. Continue to select Find Next until a message is displayed that Word has finished searching the document.

7. Select OK and then Cancel. The dialog boxes are removed.

6.5 Replacing Text

replace text

In a Word document, search text can be found and then changed to other specified text called *replace text*. This makes it easy to create different versions of a document. For example, after creating and printing a letter to the Mount Pine Ski Resort, each occurrence of "Mount Pine" can be changed to "Livermore Peak" and a new letter printed. "Livermore Peak" can then be changed to another ski resort, and so on, creating several letters.

Selecting Replace (Ctrl+H) from the Edit menu displays the Find and Replace dialog box with the Replace tab selected:

Word will search for "Mount Pine" and replace it with "Livermore Peak"

Selecting Replace starts searching from the insertion point for the first occurrence of the search text, which is then selected in the document. Selecting Replace again changes the selected text to the replace text and then finds the next occurrence of the search text. Find Next can be selected to find the next occurrence of the search text without making changes to the selected text.

Replace All

All occurrences of the search text can be automatically replaced with the replace text by selecting Replace All. However, using Replace instead of Replace All is usually preferable because each replacement can be verified before it is made. For example, if the search text is "ease" and the replace text is "assist," selecting Replace All also changes "please" to "plassist," which is not a word.

Capitalization

If the Match case check box is not selected when replacing text, Word uses the capitalization of the located text. For example, using puppy as the search text and dog as the replace text, Word would replace Puppy with Dog.

Tabs and paragraph characters may be used in either the search or replace text. The Match case check box is used when only text that has the same capitalization as the search text is to be replaced. The Find whole words only check box is used when occurrences of the search text that are not part of another word are to be replaced.

6.6 Using the Thesaurus

synonym

A *thesaurus* is a collection of *synonyms*, which are words that have similar meanings. For example, "chilly" is a synonym for "cool." Word contains a thesaurus that can be used to display a list of synonyms for words or phrases. Selecting a word or phrase and then selecting Thesaurus (Shift+F7) from the Language submenu in the Tools menu displays the Thesaurus dialog box with a list of synonyms:

Because words can have several definitions, a list of Meanings is included with each meaning identified by its part of speech (adjective, noun, verb, and so on). The Replace with Synonym list contains words that correspond to the selected meaning. Clicking a meaning selects it and changes the list of synonyms. Clicking a synonym and selecting Replace replaces the word in the document with the selected synonym.

Synonyms can be displayed for any of the suggested meanings by first selecting the word in the list and then selecting Look Up. This procedure may be continued for as many words as desired. Selecting Cancel removes the dialog box, leaving the word in the document unchanged.

Word uses a file for the thesaurus which does not contain every possible word in the English language. If the selected word cannot be found, a dialog box is displayed with an alphabetical list of possible words:

Synonyms for Phrases

The Word thesaurus can list synonyms for some phrases. For example, Word displays anticipate, hope for, and expect as synonyms for the phrase "look forward to."

Note that the thesaurus will only replace the selected word or phrase. For example, the word "cool" might appear five times in a document, but only the selected "cool" will be replaced with the selected synonym.

Practice 3 ✑

In this practice you will replace text and use the thesaurus. Open WORKSHOP if it is not already displayed.

① *REPLACE ALL OCCURRENCES OF "INSTRUCTOR"*

    a. Select Edit → Replace. A dialog box is displayed. The previously entered search text ^pluncheon is displayed and selected in the Find what box.

        1. In the Find what box, type instructor, replacing the selected text.

        2. In the Replace with box, type trainer.

        3. Select Replace. The first occurrence of "instructor" is selected.

        4. Select Replace again. The selected text is replaced with "trainer" and the next occurrence of "instructor" is selected.

        5. Select Replace again. A message is displayed that Word has finished searching the document.

        6. Select OK. The message dialog box is removed.

        7. Select Close. The dialog box is removed.

② *LOCATE THE WORD TO BE CHANGED*

    At the top of page 1, in the sentence that begins "All of us...," select the word "pleased."

③ *SELECT THE DESIRED SYNONYM AND REPLACE THE WORD*

    a. Select Tools → Language → Thesaurus. A dialog box is displayed.

        1. In the Replace with Synonym list, select "delighted."

        2. Select Replace. The word "pleased" is replaced with "delighted" and the dialog box is removed.

④ *CHANGE THE WORD "FIELD"*

    a. In the last sentence of the same paragraph, which begins "The trainer and assistants...," select the word "field."

    b. Press Shift+F7. The Thesaurus dialog box is displayed with several meanings for "field."

        1. In the Meanings list, click "subject (n.)," because the definition of "field" that is being used in the sentence is most similar to "subject." Your dialog box should look similar to:

        2. Select "area" from the list of synonyms.

        3. Select Replace. The word "field" is replaced by "area" and the dialog box is removed.

⑤ *SAVE THE MODIFIED WORKSHOP*

6.7 Paragraph Formats - Indents

Margin settings apply to an entire document and cannot change from paragraph to paragraph. However, it is possible to decrease the width of lines of text in a specific paragraph by using *indents*. Indents are often used to set off paragraphs such as a quotation.

The default indents are 0 inches, meaning that lines of text extend from the left margin to the right margin. Specifying left and right indents causes a paragraph to have a shorter line length:

not indented — The scientific classification of the zebras are as follows: mountain zebra is Equus zebra, Burchell's zebra is Equus burchelli, and Grevy's zebra is Equus grevyi.

indented — The scientific classification of the zebras are as follows: mountain zebra is Equus zebra, Burchell's zebra is Equus burchelli, and Grevy's zebra is Equus grevyi.

The scientific classification of the zebras are as follows: mountain zebra is Equus zebra, Burchell's zebra is Equus burchelli, and Grevy's zebra is Equus grevyi.

Selecting Paragraph from the Format menu displays the Paragraph dialog box. Selecting the Indents and Spacing tab displays those options:

The indent amounts, in inches, are selected or typed in the Left and the Right boxes in the Indentation area. For example, a paragraph is indented by 1 inch on both the left and right by typing 1 in the Left box, 1 in the Right box, and then selecting OK.

Setting an indent affects only the paragraph that contains the insertion point. Multiple paragraphs can be formatted together by first selecting them and then applying the indents.

Units

The unit of measure used in dialog boxes and on the ruler may be one of the following units:

inches
centimeters
millimeters
points
picas

A Guide to Microsoft Office XP Professional

Indents can also be set by dragging markers on the ruler:

left indent marker   right indent marker

Dragging an indent marker changes the indent for the paragraph that contains the insertion point, or for all selected paragraphs. When an indent marker is dragged, a dotted line appears that helps line up text. This method of changing indents is usually less precise than using options in the Paragraph dialog box.

6.8 Copying and Pasting Paragraph Formats

Paragraph formats, such as indents, can be copied from one paragraph to another. Placing the insertion point in the paragraph that contains the formatting to be copied and clicking the Format Painter button () on the toolbar changes the pointer to 🖌. Clicking another paragraph applies the copied formatting.

6.9 The Reveal Formatting Task Pane

A listing of the character and paragraph formats that have been applied to text can be viewed in the Reveal Formatting task pane. Selecting Reveal Formatting from the Format menu displays the task pane:

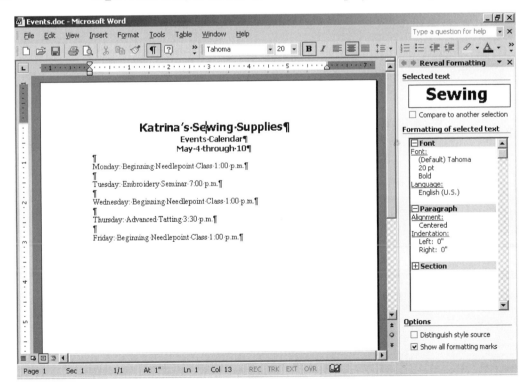

Selected text or, as in the example above, text around the insertion point is displayed in the Selected text box in the task pane. The character and paragraph formats of the text are listed in the Formatting of selected text list. In the example on the previous page, the insertion point is in the word "Sewing" in the first paragraph of the document, and formats that have been applied to the text (Tahoma font, 20 point size, bold style, centered alignment, and no indents) are listed in the pane. Note that the underlined headings Font, Language, Alignment, and Indentation in the pane are links that display the corresponding dialog box when clicked.

comparing formats   The Reveal Formatting task pane can be used to compare formats. Selecting the Compare to another selection check box in the task pane adds another Selected text box and changes the Formatting of selected text list to Formatting differences. Selecting text in the document displays it in the second Selected text box and the format differences of the two selections are displayed in the Formatting differences list:

<table>
<tr><td rowspan="8">

The What's This? Command

Selecting What's This? (Shift+F1) in the Help menu and then clicking text in a document displays the Reveal Formatting task pane with the formatting for the clicked text.

</td></tr>
</table>

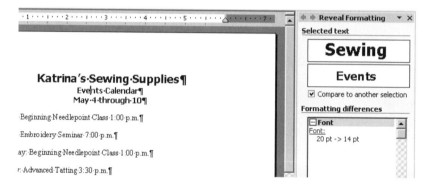

closing the task pane   The Reveal Formatting task pane can be removed from the document window by clicking the Close button ([X]) in the upper-right corner of the task pane.

Practice 4

In this practice you will indent paragraphs, compare formats, and copy formats. Open WORKSHOP if it is not already displayed.

① FORMAT A PARAGRAPH WITH INDENTS

   a. If the ruler is not displayed, select View → Ruler.

   b. Scroll to the bottom of page 1 and place the insertion point in the paragraph that begins "A Networking Breakfast...." Note the indent markers on the ruler.

   c. Select Format → Paragraph. A dialog box is displayed.

      1. Select the Indents and Spacing tab if those options are not already displayed.

      2. In the Indentation section, type 0.5 for the Left indent.

      3. In the Right box, type 0.75.

      4. Select OK. The dialog box is removed and the paragraph has left and right indents. Note the positions of the indent markers on the ruler.

② DISPLAY THE REVEAL FORMATTING TASK PANE

   a. Be sure the insertion point is still in the "A Networking Breakfast...." paragraph.

   b. Select Format → Reveal Formatting. The Reveal Formatting task pane is displayed. Note the left and right indents listed in the Formatting of selected text list.

③ *COMPARE FORMATS*

    a. Be sure the insertion point is still in the "A Networking Breakfast…." paragraph.

    b. In the Reveal Formatting task pane, select the Compare to another selection check box. Another Selected text box is added to the pane and the Formatting of selected text list is changed to Formatting differences.

    c. Place the insertion point in the next paragraph, which begins "The Lecture…." The Formatting differences list now indicates that the first paragraph has a left indent of 0.5" and a right indent of 0.75" and the second paragraph is different because it has 0" left and right indents.

④ *CHANGE THE RIGHT INDENT*

    a. Place the insertion point in the "A Networking Breakfast…." paragraph.

    b. On the ruler, drag the right indent marker (△) to the 5" mark. Note how the right indent of the paragraph changes, and the indents listed in the task pane are changed.

    c. In the upper-right corner of the Reveal Formatting task pane, click the Close button (❌). The task pane is removed from the document window.

⑤ *FORMAT SEVERAL PARAGRAPHS WITH INDENTS*

    a. Place the insertion point in the next paragraph, which begins "The Lecture…."

    b. Scroll down until the paragraph that begins "Computer Instruction…" is visible.

    c. Hold down the Shift key and click the "Computer Instruction…" paragraph. Several paragraphs are included in the selection.

    d. Select Format ➡ Paragraph. A dialog box is displayed.

       1. Select the Indents and Spacing tab if those options are not already displayed.

       2. In the Left box, type 0.5.

       3. In the Right box, type 0.5.

       4. Select OK. The dialog box is removed and the selected paragraphs now have left and right indents.

Check – Your document should look similar to:

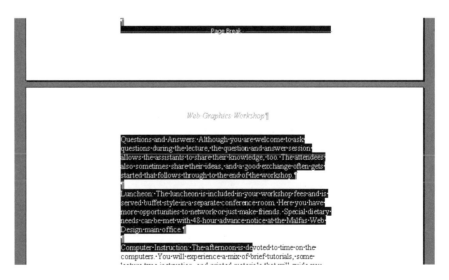

⑥ *COPY PARAGRAPH FORMATTING*

    a. Click the "Computer Instruction…" paragraph. The insertion point is placed in the paragraph.

    b. On the toolbar, click the Format Painter button (🖌). The pointer changes to 🖌 when moved over the text.

    c. Scroll to page 3 and click the paragraph under the "See You Soon" heading, the paragraph that begins "All of us at Malfas…." The indents that the Computer Instruction paragraph was formatted with are now also applied to the closing paragraph in the document.

⑦ *SAVE THE MODIFIED WORKSHOP*

6.10 Paragraph Formats - Hanging and First Line Indents

A paragraph can be formatted so that the first line is indented differently from the rest of the paragraph. When the first line of a paragraph is farther to the left than the rest of the paragraph, it is formatted with a *hanging indent*. A hanging indent is often used for lists, outlines, or for a bibliography entry:

hanging indent

> Riggi, Donna. *The Complete Guide to Stocking and Selling Mattresses.* Chicago: Winding Staircase Press, 1993.

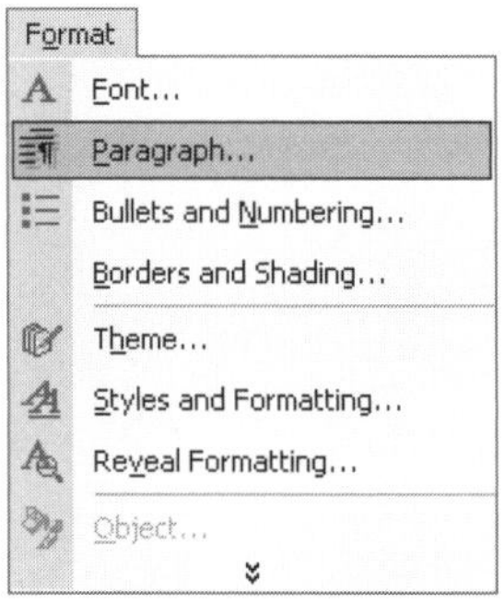

A hanging indent is created for the paragraph that contains the insertion point by first selecting Paragraph from the Format menu. Selecting the Indents and Spacing tab displays those options:

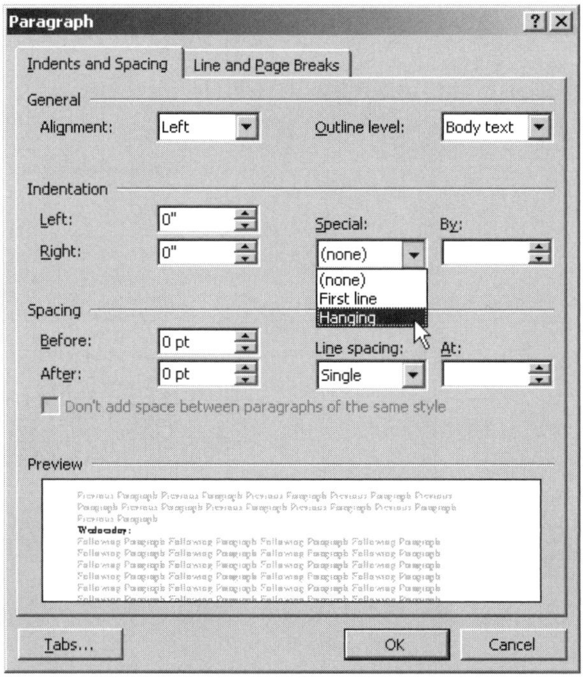

Selecting Hanging in the Special list and then OK formats the paragraph with a 0.5" hanging indent:

Contini, Constantine J. *Strawberries by the Quart: A Guide to New England Roadside Produce Stands*. Massachusetts: American Chowder Press, 1995.¶

Indent Markers

Each indent marker formats a different kind of indent:

first line indent
hanging indent
left indent

The default measurement for a hanging indent is 0.5" and appears in the By box. Changing this measurement changes the distance that the indent hangs beyond the rest of the paragraph.

A hanging indent can also be created for the paragraph containing the insertion point by dragging the hanging indent marker on the ruler:

hanging indent marker

first line indent

Another paragraph format is the *first line indent,* which indents the first line of the paragraph farther to the right than the rest of the paragraph. A first line indent is often used for text in a published book or paper. For example, this paragraph is formatted with a first line indent.

A first line indent is created for the paragraph that contains the insertion point by first selecting Paragraph from the Format menu and then the Indents and Spacing tab to display those options. Selecting First line in the Special list and then OK formats the paragraph with a 0.5" first line indent (the default). Changing this measurement in the By box changes the distance that the first line is indented. First line indents can also be created by dragging the first line indent marker (▽) on the ruler.

6.11   Creating Lists

bulleted list

One use for hanging indents is in the creation of *bulleted lists*. In a bulleted list, each item is a separate paragraph formatted with a hanging indent, a special character such as a bullet (•), and a tab. In Word, a bulleted list is created by first selecting the paragraphs in the list

There are many things to do at the Great Seas Resort:¶
Snorkel off the world famous Barracuda Beach in our high quality rental gear¶
Dine in one of five luxurious restaurants including the five-star Jacaranda Steak House¶
Lounge by one of luxury swimming pools¶
Shop in our promenade of 36 stores¶

and then clicking the Bullets button (▤) on the toolbar:

There are many things to do at the Great Seas Resort:¶
   • → Snorkel off the world famous Barracuda Beach in our high quality rental gear¶
   • → Dine in one of five luxurious restaurants including the five-star Jacaranda Steak House¶
   • → Lounge by one of luxury swimming pools¶
   • → Shop in our promenade of 36 stores¶

Note that Word automatically formats the paragraph with a hanging indent, and adds a bullet character and a tab to each paragraph. The bulleted items can be indented farther by clicking the Increase Indent button () on the toolbar.

numbered list

Bulleted lists are used when each item is equally important. *Numbered lists* show a priority of importance and are used, for example, for the steps in a recipe. Numbered lists are created by first selecting the paragraphs and then clicking the Numbering button (⧉) on the toolbar:

Chicken·Noodle·Soup:¶

1. → Pour·some·canned·chicken·broth·into·a·large·saucepan·with·a· small·amount·of·chopped·celery·and·bring·it·to·a·rolling·boil.¶
2. → Add·some·elbow·macaroni·and·cook·for·5-7·minutes,·stirring· occasionally.¶
3. → Reduce·the·heat,·add·some·small·chunks·of·chicken,·and·simmer· for·3-4·minutes.¶
4. → Serve·immediately·with·crackers·or·toast.¶

Automatic Formatting

The best way to create a bulleted or numbered list is to type all of the items first, each in a separate paragraph, and then click the Bullets or Numbering button. If Word continues to automatically format text in a list as it is typed, clicking the AutoCorrect Options button 🗲 that appears and selecting Undo Automatic Numbering will stop the list formatting.

Note that Word automatically formats the paragraph with a hanging indent, and adds a number followed by a period and a tab to each paragraph. The numbered items can be indented farther by clicking the Increase Indent button (⧉) on the toolbar.

The bullets or numbering formats can be removed from text by selecting the formatted paragraphs and then clicking the appropriate button on the toolbar.

Practice 5

In this practice you will create a bulleted list in WORKSHOP and then create a hanging indent in MOCKINGBIRD MUSIC. Open WORKSHOP and display formatting marks if they are not already displayed.

① *FORMAT A BULLETED LIST*

    a. Scroll to the middle of page 2 and locate the list of items in the "What to Bring" section.

    b. Select all four paragraphs in the list, from "Notepads and pens" to "Sweater or jacket."

    c. On the toolbar, click the Bullets button (⧉). The items in the list are formatted with bullets and a hanging indent.

② *SAVE AND CLOSE THE MODIFIED WORKSHOP*

③ *FORMAT A HANGING INDENT*

    a. Open MOCKINGBIRD MUSIC, which was last modified in Practice 1. Display formatting marks if they are not already displayed.

    b. Select all three paragraphs in the "Lessons Available" section, from "Mondays and..." to "...General Percussion."

    c. Select Format → Paragraph. A dialog box is displayed.

        1. Select the Indents and Spacing tab if those options are not already displayed.

        2. In the Special list, select Hanging.

        3. Select OK. The dialog box is removed and the selected paragraphs now have a 0.5" hanging indent.

④ *MODIFY THE HANGING INDENT*

On the ruler, drag the hanging indent marker (△) to the 2" mark. Click anywhere in the document to remove the selection. Your document and ruler should look similar to:

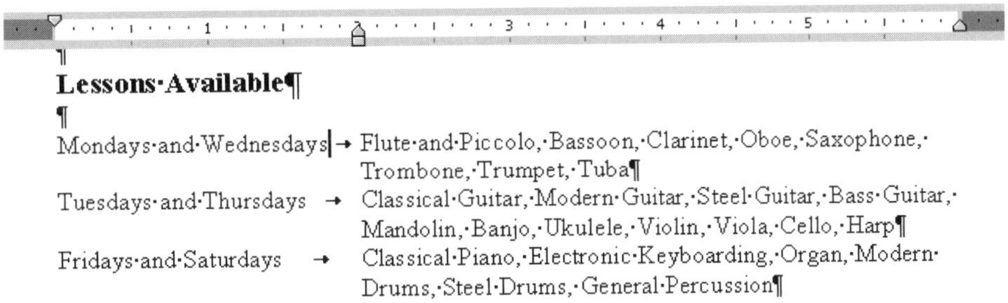

Lessons·Available¶
¶
Mondays·and·Wednesdays| → Flute·and·Piccolo,·Bassoon,·Clarinet,·Oboe,·Saxophone,·
Trombone,·Trumpet,·Tuba¶
Tuesdays·and·Thursdays → Classical·Guitar,·Modern·Guitar,·Steel·Guitar,·Bass·Guitar,·
Mandolin,·Banjo,·Ukulele,·Violin,·Viola,·Cello,·Harp¶
Fridays·and·Saturdays → Classical·Piano,·Electronic·Keyboarding,·Organ,·Modern·
Drums,·Steel·Drums,·General·Percussion¶

⑤ *FORMAT A NUMBERED LIST*

a. Locate the list in the "Tips on Learning to Play an Instrument" section.

b. Select all five paragraphs in the list, from "Purchase…" to the last "…Practice!"

c. On the toolbar, click the Numbering button (▤). The items in the list are formatted with numbers and a hanging indent.

⑥ *SAVE AND CLOSE THE MODIFIED MOCKINGBIRD MUSIC*

6.12 Creating Footnotes and Endnotes

Research papers and reports often include *footnotes* to document sources. Placing the insertion point in the text where the footnote number should appear and selecting Foot<u>n</u>ote from the Refere<u>n</u>ce submenu in the <u>I</u>nsert menu displays the Footnote and Endnote dialog box:

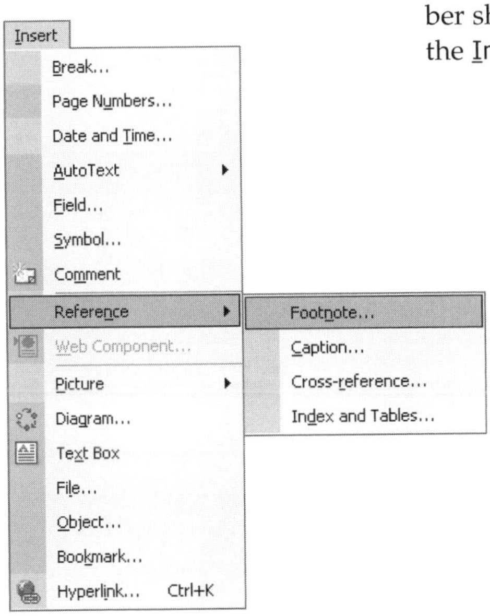

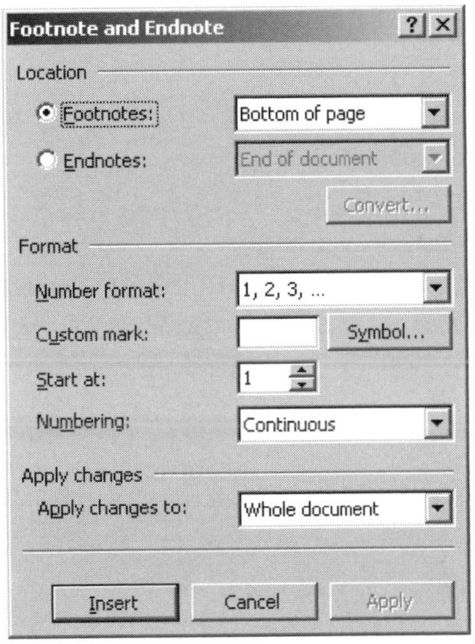

Footnotes and Bottom of page are the default options. Selecting Insert adds a superscripted number at the insertion point and also adds the same number at the bottom of the page. In Print Layout view, the footnote looks similar to:

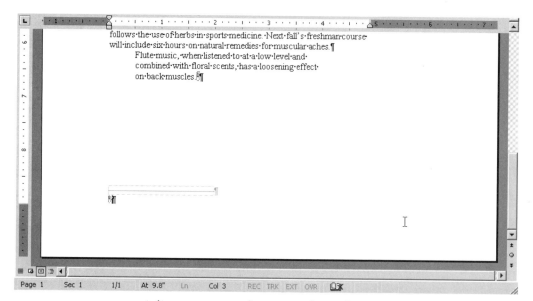

A line separates footnotes from the rest of the text in Print Layout view

In Normal view, an additional window appears at the bottom of the window with the footnote number:

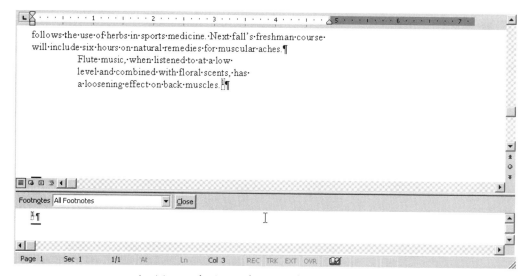

In Normal view, the window splits to show footnotes

In either view, the insertion point is automatically placed to the right of the footnote number so that the footnote can be typed. Footnote text can then be edited and formatted like any other text.

Word sequentially numbers footnotes, and automatically renumbers footnotes when one is moved, inserted, copied, or deleted. A footnote can be deleted by deleting the footnote number in the text, which automatically removes the reference from the bottom of the page.

endnotes

Endnotes appear separately on the last page of a document and are sometimes used instead of footnotes. Selecting the Endnotes option in the Footnote and Endnote dialog box creates endnotes instead of footnotes.

In this practice you will create a footnote.

① *OPEN WORKSHOP*

    Open WORKSHOP, which was last modified in Practice 5.

② *CREATE A FOOTNOTE*

    a. In the last paragraph of the document, place the insertion point at the end of the quote in italics, which ends "…since fire was discovered."

    b. Select Insert → Reference → Footnote. A dialog box is displayed.

        1. Select Insert. The dialog box is removed. Word inserts a 1 at the insertion point and the insertion point is moved to the bottom of the page where the footnote text can be typed. Note the horizontal line separating the reference from the rest of the text.

③ *ENTER THE FOOTNOTE TEXT*

    Type the following text, allowing Word to wrap the text:

        Grossman, Lucinda. From Cave Painting to Distance Learning: A Study of Global Education Systems (Atlanta: Brandenburg Press, 1988) 143.

④ *FORMAT THE FOOTNOTE TEXT*

    a. Select the book title, "From Cave Painting to Distance Learning: A Study of Global Education Systems."

    b. On the toolbar, click the Italic button. The book title is now italic.

    c. Click anywhere in the footnote text. The footnote is no longer selected and the insertion point is placed in the footnote.

    d. With the insertion point in the footnote text, drag the first line indent marker (▽) on the ruler to the 0.5" mark. The footnote now has a first line indent of 0.5 inches.

Check – The footnote should look similar to:

⑤ *SAVE, PRINT, AND THEN CLOSE THE MODIFIED WORKSHOP*

6.13   Inserting Time Stamps

It is easier to keep track of document revisions when printouts include the time they were printed. A *time stamp* is the current date and time and is created by selecting Date and Time from the Insert menu, which displays the Date and Time dialog box:

Selecting a format in the Available formats list and then OK places a time stamp at the insertion point:

```
  Header
Marketing·Report·for·1/22/2002·1:43·PM¶
```

Selecting the Update automatically check box will insert a time stamp composed of a code that is automatically updated when the file is later opened or printed.

The date and time can appear on each page in a document by placing a time stamp in a header or footer. Buttons on the Header and Footer toolbar can be used as well as the Date and Time command to place time stamps. Clicking the Insert Date button () or Insert Time button (⊘) inserts a time stamp at the insertion point:

Insert Date   Insert Time

Time stamps that are inserted using the Header and Footer toolbar buttons are updated automatically.

6.14 Displaying Document Information

write for space

It can be useful to know the number of pages, words, or characters contained in a document. For example, journalists often *write for space*, which means writing to fill a precise amount of newspaper or publication space. Some student assignments also require a certain number of words. Selecting Word Count from the Tools menu displays the Word Count dialog box:

A Guide to Microsoft Office XP Professional

```
Tools
ABC  Spelling and Grammar...   F7
     Language                     ▶
     Word Count...
     Letters and Mailings         ▶
     Tools on the Web...
     Customize...
     Options...
              ⌄
```

```
Word Count                    ? ✕
Statistics:
   Pages                        2
   Words                      672
   Characters (no spaces)   3,320
   Characters (with spaces) 3,992
   Paragraphs                   8
   Lines                       65

☐ Include footnotes and endnotes
      Show Toolbar          Close
```

Selecting the Include footnotes and endnotes check box adds the text in the footnotes and endnotes to the displayed information. Note that the page count and word count for the document is included in the statistics. The information for a portion of a document can be displayed by selecting the text before selecting Word Count.

Practice 7

In this practice you will add a time stamp to a header and footer and determine the number of words in a document.

① OPEN MOCKINGBIRD MUSIC

Open MOCKINGBIRD MUSIC, which was last modified in Practice 5.

② INSERT A TIME STAMP IN THE HEADER

a. Select View → Header and Footer. The insertion point is placed in the Header area and the Header and Footer toolbar is displayed.

b. Type Printed on and then type a space.

c. Select Insert → Date and Time. A dialog box is displayed.

1. Click the date and time format that appears similar to 3/22/2003 4:00 PM.

2. Select the Update automatically check box if it is not already selected.

3. Select OK. The current date and time is inserted at the insertion point.

③ INSERT A TIME STAMP IN THE FOOTER

a. On the Header and Footer toolbar, click the Switch Between Header and Footer button (⊞). The insertion point is placed in the Footer area.

b. Type your name, followed by a space.

c. On the Header and Footer toolbar, click the Insert Date button (▦). The date is inserted in the footer.

d. On the Header and Footer toolbar, click the Close button. The header and footer are now dimmed.

④ DETERMINE THE NUMBER OF WORDS IN THE DOCUMENT

a. Select Tools → Word Count. A dialog box is displayed. How many words are in the document?

b. Select Close. The dialog box is removed.

⑤ *DEMONSTRATE HOW THE TIME STAMP IS UPDATED*

    a. Save the modified MOCKINGBIRD MUSIC.

    b. The time stamp will be updated each time the document is opened or printed. Carefully note the current time, especially the minutes.

    c. Print a copy of MOCKINGBIRD MUSIC. The header printed at the top of the page reflects the time of printing, not the time the stamp was placed in the header. Also, the time stamp in the document has been updated on the screen.

    d. Close MOCKINGBIRD MUSIC.

6.15 Adding Clip Art to a Document

Microsoft Office includes pictures called *clip art* that can be used to make documents more interesting and informative. Selecting Clip Art from the Picture submenu in the Insert menu displays the Insert Clip Art task pane:

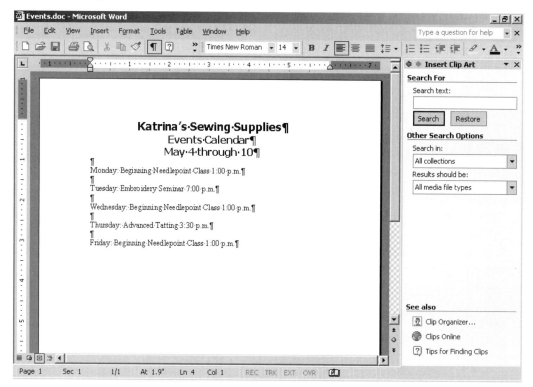

keyword

Options in the Search in list, which contains clip art collection names, and the Results should be list, which contains file formats, can be used to narrow a search. Typing a *keyword*, which is a descriptive word, in the Search text box and selecting Search finds all the clip art that have the keyword in their description. For example, typing homes in the Search text box and selecting Search displays three pictures:

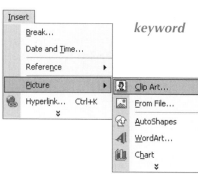

closing the task pane

Clicking a picture places it in the document at the insertion point. Selecting Modify displays the Search text box again, so that another search can be performed.

Clicking a picture in a document selects it and displays handles (■) for sizing:

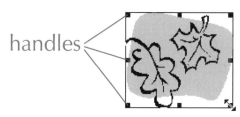

A picture can be sized by dragging a corner handle

Pointing to a corner handle changes the pointer to ↘, and then dragging sizes the picture. Dragging the center of the picture (not a handle) moves the picture. Wherever a picture is moved, text moves to make room. The Cut, Copy, and Paste buttons on the toolbar can be used to create copies or move a selected picture. Pressing the Delete key deletes the selected picture. Clicking anywhere in the document other than on the picture removes the handles.

In a document, a picture can have formats applied to the paragraph it is in. For example, a picture can be centered by placing the insertion point in the paragraph that contains the picture and clicking the Center button on the toolbar.

The Insert Clip Art task pane can be removed from the document window by clicking the Close button (☒) in the upper-right corner of the task pane.

6.16 Formatting a Document in Columns

Columns are commonly used in newspapers, newsletters, magazines, and other long publications to make lines of text easier to read. A document can be formatted in multiple columns by selecting Columns from the Format menu, which displays the Columns dialog box:

The number of columns per page can be selected using the Presets options or by selecting or typing a number in the Number of columns box. The Line between check box can be selected to include a line between the columns. Selecting OK applies the formatting to the document. Note that the column format is a page format, which means it applies to the entire document.

A document can also be formatted in multiple columns using the Columns button (▦) on the toolbar.

Practice 8

In this practice you will format a document with columns and insert clip art.

① OPEN WORKSHOP

Open WORKSHOP, which was last modified in Practice 6.

② FORMAT THE DOCUMENT IN TWO COLUMNS

a. At the top of page 1, place the insertion point just to the left of "Web Graphics" in the title of the document if it is not already there.

b. Select Format → Columns. A dialog box is displayed.

    1. In the Number of columns box, type 2.

    2. Select OK. The text in the entire document is formatted in two columns.

③ INSERT A PICTURE

a. Select Insert → Picture → Clip Art. The Insert Clip Art task pane is displayed. If the Add Clips to Organizer dialog box is displayed, select Later to remove the dialog box.

b. In the Insert Clip Art task pane, in the Search text box, type homes.

c. In the Insert Clip Art task pane, click the Search in list. Clip art collection names are displayed.

    1. Clear the My Collections check box. The Everywhere check box is automatically cleared.

    2. Clear the Web Collections check box.

    3. Click anywhere in the document. The list is removed.

d. In the Insert Clip Art task pane, click the Results should be list. File formats are displayed.

    1. Clear the Photographs, Movies, and Sounds check boxes. The All media types check box is automatically cleared.

    2. Click anywhere in the document. The list is removed.

e. In the Insert Clip Art task pane, select Search. Clip art is displayed in the task pane.

f. At the top of page 1, place the insertion point just to the left of "Web Graphics" in the title of the document.

g. Press Enter to create a new paragraph, then press the up arrow key to place the insertion point in the blank paragraph.

h. In the Insert Clip Art task pane, click the black and white clip art of a house. The clip art is placed in the document at the insertion point.

i. In the upper-right corner of the Insert Clip Art task pane, click the Close button (☒). The task pane is removed.

④ *SIZE THE PICTURE*

a. Click the picture. The picture is selected and handles are displayed.

b. Point to the handle in the bottom-right corner of the picture. The pointer changes to ↖.

c. With the double-headed arrow pointer on the handle, drag the handle upward and to the left a little. Note how the dotted lines move with the mouse to indicate the size of the picture. When the picture is a little smaller, release the mouse button.

d. Click anywhere in the document. The picture is no longer selected.

⑤ *PRINT PAGE ONE*

a. Save WORKSHOP.

b. Select File → Print. A dialog box is displayed.

    1. Select the Pages option and then type 1 in the Pages box.

    2. Select OK. The first page of the document is printed.

⑥ *DELETE THE PICTURE AND FORMAT THE DOCUMENT IN ONE COLUMN*

a. Click the picture to select it.

b. Press the Delete key. The picture is removed from the document.

c. Press the Delete key again. The empty paragraph is removed from the document.

d. Select Format → Columns. A dialog box is displayed.

    1. In the Presets area, click the One column option.

    2. Select OK. The text in the document is formatted in one column again.

⑦ *SAVE AND CLOSE THE MODIFIED WORKSHOP*

⑧ *QUIT WORD*

This chapter introduced several word processor features. Selected text can be moved or copied using the Copy, Cut, and Paste buttons on the toolbar or using commands in the Edit menu. When text is Cut or Copied it is placed on the Clipboard, which is a designated area in memory. The Office Clipboard is available in Microsoft Office applications. Clicking an item in the Office Clipboard pastes a copy of it at the insertion point.

A document can be scanned for search text using the Find command. The Match case check box and the Find whole words only check box are used to refine a search. Special characters can be included in search text. Search text can be changed to other text using the Replace command.

The Thesaurus command is used to display a list of synonyms for a selected word or phrase.

Indents are paragraph formats that decrease the width of lines of text. A hanging indent formats the first line of a paragraph farther to the left than the rest of the paragraph, and a first line indent formats the first line of a paragraph farther to the right. Indents are set using the Paragraph command or by dragging markers on the ruler.

Bulleted and numbered lists are paragraphs that are formatted with a hanging indent, a number or bullet, and a tab. Bulleted and numbered lists are created using the Bullets button or Numbering button on the toolbar. Items in bulleted or numbered lists can be indented farther by clicking on the Increase Indent button on the toolbar.

Paragraph formats can be copied from one paragraph to another using the Format Painter button. The Reveal Formatting task pane contains a list of the character and paragraph formats that have been applied to text, and can be used to compare the formats of two selections of text.

Footnotes and endnotes are created using the Footnote command. Word automatically places the appropriate number in the text and at the bottom of the page containing the footnote. A footnote is removed by deleting its number from the text.

A time stamp includes the current date and time in a document and is created using the Date and Time command or buttons on the Header and Footer toolbar.

The Word Count command displays a dialog box with information about the document, including the number of words in the document.

Pictures called clip art can be added to a document using the Clip Art task pane. In the task pane, clip art can be searched for using keywords. Clicking a picture in the task pane places it in the document and displays handles for sizing.

A document can be formatted in multiple columns using the Columns command or the Columns button on the toolbar.

Bulleted list List created with each item as a separate paragraph formatted with a hanging indent, a special character such as a bullet (•), and a tab.

Clip art Pictures used to make documents more informative.

Clipboard A designated area in memory that stores the last cut or copied text.

Endnote Used to document a source. Found on the last page of a document.

First line indent First line of a paragraph that is farther to the right than the rest of the paragraph.

Footnote Used to document a source. Usually located at the bottom of the page that contains the footnoted material.

Hanging indent First line of a paragraph that is farther to the left than the rest of the paragraph.

Indent Paragraph format that decreases the width of lines of text in a specific paragraph.

Keyword A descriptive word used to search for clip art.

Numbered list List created with each item as a separate paragraph formatted with a hanging indent, a number, and a tab character. Each number indicates an item's priority in the list.

Office Clipboard Special clipboard available in Microsoft Office applications that stores up to 24 different cut or copied items.

Replace text Text that search text is changed to in a document.

Search text A specified single character, word, or phrase that a document is scanned for.

Synonym A word that has a similar meaning to another word.

Thesaurus A collection of synonyms.

Time stamp The current date and/or time.

Write for space Writing to fill a precise amount of newspaper or publication space.

Word Commands and Buttons

Bullets button Formats a paragraph with a hanging indent and inserts a bullet and a tab to create a bulleted item in a list. Found on the toolbar.

Clear All button Removes all items from the Office Clipboard. Found in the Office Clipboard task pane.

Clip Art **command** Displays the Insert Clip Art task pane, which is used to insert clip art into a document at the insertion point. Found in the Picture submenu in the Insert menu.

Close button Removes the task pane from the document window.

Columns **command** Displays a dialog box used to format a document in multiple columns. Found in the Format menu. The Columns button on the toolbar can be used instead of the command.

Copy **command** Adds a copy of the selected text to the Clipboard, leaving the selected text at its location. Found in the Edit menu. The Copy button on the toolbar can be used instead of the command.

Cut **command** Moves the selected text to the Clipboard. Found in the Edit menu. The Cut button on the toolbar can be used instead of the command.

Date and Time **command** Displays a dialog box used to insert a time stamp at the insertion point. Found in the Insert menu.

Find **command** Displays a dialog box used to scan a document for search text. Found in the Edit menu.

Footnote **command** Displays a dialog box used to create footnotes or endnotes. Found in the Reference submenu in the Insert menu.

Format Painter button Used to copy paragraph formats from one paragraph to another. Found on the toolbar.

Increase Indent button Indents an item farther in a bulleted or numbered list. Found on the toolbar.

Insert Date button Inserts a time stamp in the form of a date at the insertion point. Found on the Header and Footer toolbar.

Insert Time button Inserts a time stamp at the insertion point. Found on the Header and Footer toolbar.

Numbering button Formats a paragraph with a hanging indent and inserts a number and a tab to create a numbered item in a list. Found on the toolbar.

Office Clipboard **command** Displays the Office Clipboard task pane. Found in the Edit menu.

Paragraph **command** Displays the Paragraph dialog box. Found in the Format menu.

Paste All button Pastes copies of all the items in the Office Clipboard at the insertion point. Found in the Office Clipboard task pane.

Paste **command** Places the contents of the Clipboard in the document at the insertion point. Found in the Edit menu. The Paste button on the toolbar can be used instead of the command.

Paste Options button Displayed when text is pasted into a document.

Replace **command** Displays a dialog box used to search a document for search text and change it to specified text. Found in the Edit menu.

Reveal Formatting **command** Displays the Reveal Formatting task pane. Found in the Format menu.

Thesaurus **command** Displays a dialog box that contains a list of synonyms. Found in the Language submenu in the Tools menu.

Word Count Displays a dialog box with information about the document. Found in the Tools menu.

Sections 6.1 — 6.11

1. List the steps required to copy the third paragraph in a document to a blank paragraph at the end of the document.

2. What is the difference between moving and copying text?

3. a) What happens when the Paste All button in the Office Clipboard is clicked?
   b) How is an item pasted from the Office Clipboard to the locations of the insertion point in a document?

4. List the steps required to remove all the items from the Office Clipboard.

5. List the steps required to find each occurrence of Jerome in a document.

6. In a search for the word hat, how can you avoid finding the word that?

7. List the steps required to find each occurrence of the word The at the beginning of a paragraph.

8. What is replace text?

9. List the steps required to find each occurrence of day and replace it with week in a document.

10. Why is it usually better to use the Replace button repeatedly instead of the Replace All button in the Find and Replace dialog box?

11. a) What is a thesaurus?
    b) What is a synonym?
    c) List the steps required to list the synonyms for the word house in a document.

12. a) What does a paragraph formatted with left and right indents of 2" look like compared to a paragraph with no indents?
    b) When are indents often used?

13. List the steps required to format a paragraph with 0.5" left and right indents.

14. List the steps required to use the Format Painter button to copy the formatting of the first paragraph to the last paragraph in a document.

15. What is listed in the Reveal Formatting task pane?

16. List the steps required to compare the formatting of the first paragraph to the last paragraph in a document.

17. List the steps required to format a paragraph with a hanging indent of 0.25".

18. List the steps required to format a paragraph with a first line indent of 0.5".

19. List the steps required to format six paragraphs as a bulleted list of six items.

20. When would a numbered list be used instead of a bulleted list?

21. List the steps required to format five paragraphs as a numbered list of five items.

Sections 6.12 — 6.16

22. a) What are footnotes used for?
    b) List the steps required to create a footnote for an indented paragraph in a document.

23. a) What happens to the numbers on the other footnotes when one is deleted?
    b) How can a footnote be deleted?

24. a) What is a time stamp?
    b) List two ways to insert a time stamp into the header in a document.

25. List the steps required to display the number of words in a document.

26. a) What is a keyword?
    b) List the steps required to add a picture at the insertion point in a document.

27. a) List the steps required to size a picture smaller.
    b) List the steps required to delete a picture.

28. a) List the steps required to format a document in three columns.
    b) How can a document formatted in three columns be changed to two columns?

Exercise 1 ——————————————— TAKING TESTS

The TAKING TESTS document gives directions on how to take a test, but the steps are listed out of order. Open TAKING TESTS and complete the following steps:

a) Use the Cut and Paste buttons on the toolbar to place the directions in proper order. Be sure there is a blank line between each step.

b) Create a header with your name right aligned.

c) Save the modified TAKING TESTS and print a copy.

Exercise 2 ——————————————— Favorite Quote

Create a new document that contains your favorite quote 40 times, each in a separate paragraph. Hint: consider duplicating a text block with more than 1 paragraph.

a) Format every other quote as bold with 1" left and right indents. Hint: consider using the Format Painter button.

b) In a new paragraph at the end of the document, insert a time stamp that includes the current time.

c) Create a header with your name right aligned.

d) Save the document naming it Favorite Quote and print a copy.

Exercise 3 ——————————————— Entertainment Review

The review modified in Chapter 5, Exercise 3 needs to be refined. Open Entertainment Review and complete the following steps:

a) Create 0.5" left and right indents for the first paragraph of your review.

b) In the footer, after your name, type a space and then insert a time stamp that includes the current date.

c) In a new paragraph at the end of the document, add a sentence that states the number of words in the document.

d) Format the document with two columns.

e) Save the modified Entertainment Review and print a copy.

Exercise 4 — TELECOMMUTING

The TELECOMMUTING document modified in Chapter 5, Exercise 4 needs to be refined. Open TELECOMMUTING and complete the following steps:

a) Create 0.5" left and right indents for the last paragraph on page 1, the one that begins "…if 10% to 20%…."

b) A footnote needs to be placed after the period ending the quote you just indented. Create the following footnote for the quote, formatting it with a 0.5" first line indent and formatting the title as italic:

    [1] Effy Oz, *Ethics for the Information Age* (Wm. C. Brown Communications, Inc., 1994).

c) Insert an appropriate clip art picture in a new paragraph at the top of the document above the heading "Computers in the Home Office." Center align the picture (Hint: format the paragraph containing the picture as center aligned). Resize the picture smaller so that the document prints on two pages.

d) Save the modified TELECOMMUTING and print a copy.

Exercise 5 — CAMPING TIPS

The CAMPING TIPS document contains a list of helpful information on camping. Open CAMPING TIPS and complete the following steps:

a) Find the word unwind in the document and then use the thesaurus to replace it with a synonym.

b) Format the entire document, except the title, as a numbered list.

c) Format the list of items after the first camping tip as a bulleted list. Use the Increase Indent button on the toolbar to indent the entire list farther so that it is a sub-list of the first camping tip.

d) Create a header with your name right aligned.

e) Save the modified CAMPING TIPS and print a copy.

Exercise 6 — Things To Do

The list created in Chapter 4, Exercise 6 needs to be refined. Open Things To Do and complete the following steps:

a) Format the list of eight things you want to do as a numbered list.

b) Create a right aligned header with your name followed by a space and a time stamp that includes the current date and time.

c) Save the modified Things To Do and print a copy.

Exercise 7 ✦ ——————————————————————— PROPOSAL

The research proposal modified in Chapter 5, Exercise 7 needs to be refined. Open PROPOSAL and complete the following steps:

a) Find the word greater in the proposal and then use the thesaurus to replace it with a synonym.

b) Replace all occurrences of aging with growth.

c) Format the three numbered paragraphs of stages on page 2 as a numbered list.

d) In a new paragraph at the end of the document, add a sentence to that states how many words are in the document.

e) Save the modified PROPOSAL and print a copy.

Exercise 8 ✦ ——————————————————————— Journal

The journal modified in Chapter 5, Exercise 8 needs to be refined. Open Journal and complete the following steps:

a) Format every paragraph with a 0.5" first line indent.

b) In the footer, after your name, type a space and then insert a time stamp that includes the current date and time.

c) Format the document with two columns.

d) Save the modified Journal and print a copy.

Exercise 9 ——————————————————————— SCIENCE MUSEUM

The SCIENCE MUSEUM document contains information on a museum. Open SCIENCE MUSEUM and complete the following steps:

a) Format the exhibits under each of the five departments in the museum as bulleted lists to make them more readable.

b) Create 0.5" left and right indents for the paragraph that begins "It is my dream that the Sunport Science Museum...."

c) A footnote needs to be placed after the period ending the quote you just indented. Create the following footnote for the quote, formatting it with a 0.5" first line indent:

    [1] Elaine Diver, Keynote address, Sunport Science Museum Dedication, Sunport, FL, 15 Feb. 1965.

d) Insert an appropriate clip art picture below the title and center align it (Hint: format the paragraph containing the picture as center aligned). Resize the picture if necessary so that all the information fits on one page.

e) Create a header with your name right aligned.

f) Save the modified SCIENCE MUSEUM and print a copy.

Exercise 10 ⚙ —————————————————————— Karate

The karate essay created in Chapter 4, Exercise 10 needs to be refined. Open Karate and complete the following steps:

a) Make a copy of the second sentence in the first paragraph and place it after the second paragraph. Leave a blank line between the second paragraph and the copied sentence.

b) Format the second paragraph with 0.5" left and right indents.

c) In a new paragraph at the end of the document, add a sentence that states the number of words in the document.

d) Create a header with your name right aligned.

e) Save the modified Karate and print a copy.

Exercise 11 ⚙ —————————————————————— Water Conservation

The environmental article modified in Chapter 5, Exercise 11 needs to be refined. Open Water Conservation and complete the following steps:

a) Insert two blank paragraphs after the second paragraph which ends "sprinklers are not," then add the text below, pressing Enter after each line:

> Here are three more easy things you can do to conserve water:
> Don't leave the water running when you are brushing your teeth or washing your hair.
> Only fill the bathtub up half way.
> When you are washing your car, do not leave the hose running while you are not using it.

b) Format the last three sentences you just typed as a bulleted list.

c) In a new paragraph at the end of the document, insert an appropriate clip art picture. Format the paragraph as center aligned.

d) Format the document as two columns and resize the picture, if necessary, so that it fits in the second column and the document prints on one page.

e) Save the modified Water Conservation and print a copy.

Exercise 12 —————————————————————— SUNPORT CAMPING

The SUNPORT CAMPING document contains a short article on the recent Sunport Camping Symposium. Open SUNPORT CAMPING and complete the following steps:

a) Find the word eat in the article and then use the thesaurus to replace it with a more descriptive word.

b) Format the symposium specials, starting with "Johnson Cooking" and ending with "The Camp Grounds Company," as a bulleted list.

c) Italicize the two book titles in the paragraph after the bulleted list.

d) Footnotes need to be placed after the punctuation marks at the end of each book title. Create the following footnotes, formatting each one with a 0.5" first line indent and formatting the titles as italic:

[1] Gordon Washington, *Mountain Streams are Nice but Ponds are Better* (New Haven: Persimmons Publishing, 1994) 133.

[2] Henrietta Lebon, *Good Dirt Bad Dirt* (Minneapolis: Baked Zucchini Press, 1995) 54.

e) Create a header with your name right aligned.

f) Save the modified SUNPORT CAMPING and print a copy.

Exercise 13 ☼ ——————————————————— Campsite Request

The letter created in Chapter 4, Exercise 13 needs to be refined. Open Campsite Request and complete the following steps:

a) Find the word arriving in the document and then use the thesaurus to replace it with a synonym.

b) Replace the date at the top of the letter with a time stamp that includes the current date.

c) Create a header with your name right aligned.

d) Save the modified Campsite Request and print a copy.

Exercise 14 (advanced) ——————————————— Web Service

The word processor can be used to make page-sized flyers.

a) In a new document create a flyer that announces your new business called "Indiana Internet Innovations." Include the following information:

- the phone number and fax number of your business (make them up).
- the Internet address of your Web page: http://www.inno.fake.
- a bulleted list of services such as web page design, web page maintenance, custom graphics, and custom forms.
- at least two of the following phrases: You can be on the WEB!, Special Service Packages Available, Now Available, Step Up to the Internet!
- one appropriate clip art picture

Also include any other text you need.

b) Format all of the text to be at least 18 point. You can use more than one font size, for example format the business name as larger.

c) Format the text with two different fonts and two different paragraph alignments.

d) Save the document naming it Web Service and print a copy.

In a new document create a newsletter on any topic. Save the document naming it Newsletter and print a copy when complete. Be sure to check the document on screen for errors and misspellings and make any corrections. Your newsletter should contain the following:

- At least two pages, formatted in two columns per page.
- At least four different stories.
- Two advertisements.
- Correct spelling.
- Justified paragraphs.
- Appropriate character formatting. The titles of each article should be bold and in a larger font size than the text of the article. Titles of books, magazines, songs, etc. should be italicized.
- At least one numbered or bulleted list.
- A header with the title of the newsletter.
- A footer with a centered page number.
- At least one table of information. Be sure that tabs and tab stops are used to align the information in the tables.
- At least one footnote.
- At least two clip art pictures.

Page one of an example newsletter could look similar to the following:

Exercise 16 (advanced) ———————————— Lunch Menu

In a new document create a lunch menu for a restaurant. Your menu should contain the following:

- The name of the restaurant.
- Two columns.
- At least one clip art picture.
- At least one bulleted or numbered list.
- A header with the name of the restaurant.
- A footer with a message, such as Personal Checks Not Accepted.

Be sure to use tabs and tab stops to align the prices. Format the menu appropriately, using emphasized text and different fonts and sizes. Check the document on screen for errors and misspellings and make any corrections. Save the document naming it Lunch Menu and print a copy.

Exercise 17 (advanced) ———————————— Basic Resume

In a new document create a résumé for yourself. Your résumé should contain the following:

- Four sections of information with the following titles: Education, Experience, Skills, and Accomplishments.
- At least one bulleted or numbered list.
- A header with your name, address, and phone number.
- A footer with the text References available upon request.

Format the résumé appropriately, using emphasized text, different fonts, different sizes, and tabs and tab stops. Check the document on screen for errors and misspellings and make any corrections. Save the document naming it Basic Resume and print a copy.

A Guide to Microsoft Office XP Professional

Advanced Word Processor Features

Table

Column

Row

Rows

Columns

Symbol

Hyphenation

Styles and Formatting

Outline

Index and Table

Break

Hyperlink

Envelopes and Labels

Record New Macro

Macros

Chapter 7 Expectations

After completing this chapter you will be able to:

1. Create a table structure and enter data.
2. Format the cell contents of a table.
3. Insert symbols into a document.
4. Hyphenate a document.
5. Apply styles to text and paragraphs.
6. Create a style.
7. View and modify a document in Outline view.
8. Create a table of contents.
9. Divide a document into sections.
10. Create different headers and footers in a document that is divided into sections.
11. Insert section page numbers.
12. Create hyperlinks to a web page and to a document heading.
13. Produce a newsletter using Word.
14. E-mail a document from Word.
15. Create labels.
16. Record and run macros.

This chapter introduces advanced features of Word that are used to organize and format long documents. Creating tables, labels, and macros are discussed.

7.1 Using Tables

Tables can be created by using tabs and tab stops similar to:

Element → Symbol → Atomic·Number → Atomic·Mass¶
Calcium → Ca → 20 → 40.1¶
Gold → Au → 79 → 197.0¶

However, Word includes a feature for creating tables that consist of rows and columns of cells. Cells have borders, which makes information easier to read:

Element	Symbol	Atomic·Number	Atomic·Mass
Calcium	Ca	20	40.1
Gold	Au	79	197.0

row
column
cell

The table above has three rows and four columns. *Rows* are horizontal and, in this example, the first row contains the titles. *Columns* are vertical. The intersection of a row and column is called a *cell*. Cells can contain text and clip art.

creating a table

A table is created by clicking the Insert Table button (▦) on the toolbar, which displays a grid of squares that represent cells. Moving the pointer over the grid selects the squares. For the three row, four column table shown above, the selected squares would appear similar to:

3 x 4 Table

Clicking creates a table at the insertion point. Text can then be typed into the individual cells.

Another way to create a table is by selecting <u>T</u>able from the <u>I</u>nsert submenu in the T<u>a</u>ble menu, which displays the Insert Table dialog box. Selecting or typing the number of rows and columns and then selecting OK creates a table.

entering text into cells

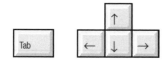

Clicking a cell places the insertion point so that text can be typed. Pressing the Tab key moves the insertion point to the next cell in the row. If the insertion point is in the last cell of a row, pressing the Tab key moves the insertion point to the first cell in the next row. The arrow keys can also be used to move the insertion point from cell to cell. Pressing the Enter key creates a new paragraph in the cell instead of moving the insertion point to another cell.

7.2 Formatting Cell Contents

selecting cells

Tables with cells are much easier to format than a table that uses tabs and tab stops. Cells can be selected individually, by row, by column, or by table, and then formatting applied. There are several methods for selecting cells:

- Pointing to the left edge of a cell changes the pointer to ➚, and then clicking selects the cell's contents.

- Pointing to the left of a row changes the pointer to ⇗, and then clicking selects the row. Dragging selects multiple rows.

- Pointing to the top of a column changes the pointer to ↓, and then clicking selects the column. Dragging selects multiple columns.

- Select A<u>ll</u> (Ctrl+A) from the <u>E</u>dit menu selects all the cells in the table that contains the insertion point.

- Commands from the Sele<u>c</u>t submenu in the T<u>a</u>ble menu can be used to select the <u>T</u>able, <u>C</u>olumn, <u>R</u>ow, or Ce<u>ll</u> that contains the insertion point.

formatting cells

Paragraph and character formats, such as alignment, indents, and fonts, can be applied to selected cells. Note that some formats affect the row height, for example formatting a row in a larger font size increases the row height.

boundary
changing width and height

When a table is created, Word automatically adjusts the column widths to be equal so that the table fills the space between the left and right margins. The lines separating the row and column are called *boundaries* and are used to change the width of a column or the height of a row:

- Pointing to the right boundary of a column changes the pointer to ◄‖►:

Symbol◻	◄‖►Atomic·Number◻
Ca◻	20◻
Au◻	79◻

Dragging the boundary to the left or right decreases or increases the column's width, respectively.

- Pointing to the bottom boundary of a row changes the pointer to ÷, and then dragging changes the row's height.

- Double-clicking a boundary changes the row or column so that it is just tall or wide enough to display the data entirely.

A Guide to Microsoft Office XP Professional

adding a row or column

After creating a table, a row or column may need to be added. Selecting a row and then clicking the Insert Rows button (⬛) on the toolbar adds a row above the selected row. A column is added to a table by clicking the Insert Columns button (⬛), which adds a column to the left of the selected column. Rows and columns can be added by using commands in the <u>I</u>nsert submenu in the T<u>a</u>ble menu.

deleting a row or column

deleting a table

A row or column can be deleted by placing the insertion point in a cell and then selecting <u>R</u>ows or <u>C</u>olumns from the <u>D</u>elete submenu in the T<u>a</u>ble menu. An entire table can be deleted by placing the insertion point in a cell and then selecting <u>T</u>able from the <u>D</u>elete submenu in the T<u>a</u>ble menu.

Practice 1

In this practice you will insert a table into a document and format it.

① *OPEN VOLCANOES*

Open VOLCANOES, which is a data file for this text, and display formatting marks if they are not already displayed.

② *INSERT A TABLE*

a. Near the bottom of page 2, place the insertion point in the blank paragraph after the sentence that ends "…the last eruption:"

b. On the toolbar, click the Insert Table button (⬛). Empty squares are displayed.

c. Move the pointer over the squares until four rows and three columns are selected (a 4 x 3 table) and then click. The table is inserted into the document.

③ *ENTER DATA INTO THE FIRST ROW*

a. Click the first cell of the first row to place the insertion point if it is not already there.

b. Type Name.

c. Press the Tab key. The insertion point is now in the second cell of the first row.

d. Type Country and then press the Tab key.

e. Type Last Erupted and then press the Tab key. The insertion point is now in the first cell of the second row.

④ *ENTER THE REMAINING DATA*

Follow the procedure in step 3 to enter the remaining rows of data:

Mt. Saint Helens	United States	1980
Mt. Etna	Italy	2001
Mt. Hekla	Iceland	2000

⑤ *FORMAT THE DATA*

a. Point to the top of the third column until the pointer changes to ↓ and then click. The last column is selected.

b. On the toolbar, click the Align Right button (⬛). The data is right aligned.

c. Point to the left of the first row until the pointer changes to ⤢ and then click. The first row is selected.

d. Format the data as 14 point and bold. The row height increases with the larger font size.

e. Click anywhere to remove the selection.

⑥ *FORMAT THE TABLE*

    a. Point to the boundary between the first and second column until the pointer changes to ◀▮▶.

    b. Drag the boundary to the left until the first column is just slightly wider than the data. Word automatically changes the column width of the second column so that the table still fills the space between the left and right margin.

    c. Repeat step 6, parts (a) and (b) for the second and third columns. The table no longer fills the space between the left and right margin.

⑦ *ADD A COLUMN AND FORMAT IT*

    a. Select the third column.

    b. On the toolbar, click the Insert Columns button (⌗). A new column is inserted.

    c. In the new column, type Height (m) as the column title.

    d. In the new column, type 2,549 in the second cell, 3,323 in the third cell, and 1,491 in the bottom cell.

    e. Double-click the boundary between the third and fourth columns. The column is widened just enough to display the data.

Check – The table should look similar to:

more·than·one·vent.·The·following·table·lists·three·volcanoes·and·the·date·of·the·last·eruption:¶

Name¤	Country¤	Height·(m)¤	Last·Erupted¤¤
Mt.·Saint·Helens¤	United·States¤	2,549¤	1980¤¤
Mt.·Etna¤	Italy¤	3,323¤	2001¤¤
Mt·Hekla¤	Iceland¤	1,491¤	2000¤¤

¶

⑧ *SAVE THE MODIFIED VOLCANOES*

7.3 Inserting Symbols

Symbols that do not appear on the keyboard, such as the copyright (©) and degree (°) symbols, can be inserted into a document by selecting Symbol from the Insert menu, which displays the Symbol dialog box:

A Guide to Microsoft Office XP Professional

Selecting a symbol and then Insert places the symbol at the insertion point. Selecting Close removes the dialog box. Other symbols can be displayed in the dialog box by selecting a font in the Font list.

7.4 Hyphenating a Document

Hyphenating a document is a process that divides words, if necessary, at the end of lines with a hyphen (-) so that part of a word wraps to the next line. Hyphenation can smooth out very ragged right edges in left-aligned text and can lessen the space between words in justified text.

Once a document is otherwise complete, hyphenation can be performed. Selecting Hyphenation from the Language submenu in the Tools menu displays the Hyphenation dialog box:

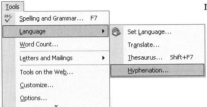

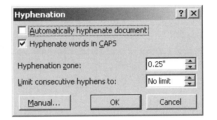

Manual Hyphenation

In the Hyphenation dialog box, selecting Manual displays each word selected for hyphenation in a dialog box. The hyphenation of the word can then be selected.

Selecting the Automatically hyphenate document check box and then OK hyphenates the entire document. Selecting the Hyphenate words in CAPS check box allows words that are all uppercase letters to be hyphenated. The Hyphenation zone box specifies the amount of space to leave between the last word in a line and the right margin. A smaller hyphenation zone results in a less ragged right edge. The Limit consecutive hyphens to box specifies how many consecutive lines of text can be hyphenated.

7.5 Styles

A *style* is a named set of formats. Styles make it easy to create documents that have consistent formatting. For example, long documents usually contain *headings*, which are titles that are often bold and in a larger and different font than the *body text*. A style can be used to apply all of these formats in one step.

headings
body text

Word has several styles, some used for formatting text, and others for formatting tables or lists such as bulleted lists. Style names and corresponding formats include:

Style	Formatting
Normal	Times New Roman 12 point left-aligned
Heading 1	**Arial 16 point bold left-aligned**
Heading 2	***Arial 14 point bold italic left-aligned***
Heading 3	**Arial 13 point bold left-aligned**

Normal style is automatically applied to paragraphs in a new document.

A style is applied using the Styles and Formatting task pane. Selecting Styles and Formatting from the Format menu displays the Styles and Formatting task pane:

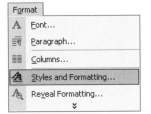

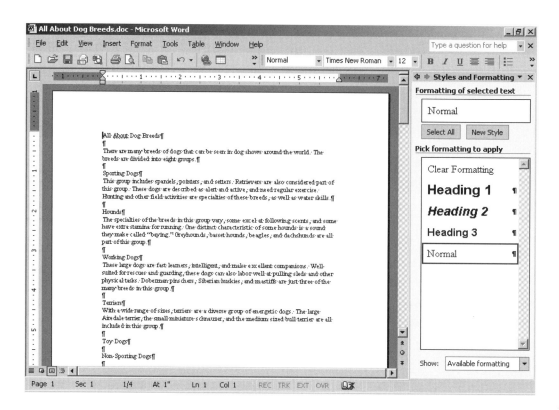

Styles are listed in the Pick formatting to apply list, and include Heading 1, Heading 2, Heading 3, and Normal. Clicking a style in the Pick formatting to apply list applies the style to the paragraph that contains the insertion point. Clicking Clear Formatting changes the formatting of the selected paragraph to Normal style. The Show list can be used to list the available styles or just the formatting in use.

closing the task pane

The Styles and Formatting task pane can be removed from the document window by clicking the Close button (☒) in the upper-right corner of the task pane.

A style can also be applied by selecting it from the Style list on the toolbar:

7.6 Creating a Style

A new style can be created when the built-in styles are not appropriate. A new style is created by selecting the New Style button (New Style) in the Styles and Formatting task pane, which displays the New Style dialog box:

A Guide to Microsoft Office XP Professional

Character Style Type

In the New Style dialog box, in the Style type list, selecting Character allows a style to be created that only affects selected text, and not an entire paragraph.

A name for the style is typed in the Name box. The type of style is selected in the Style type list. An existing style that this new style is based on is selected in the Style based on list. The style that is automtically applied to the next paragraph when the Enter key is pressed is selected in the Style for following paragraph list. All of the formats for the new style are selected in the Formatting area of the dialog box. Selecting OK creates the style and adds it to the Pick formatting to apply list in the Styles and Formatting task pane. The new style can then be applied to text by clicking the new style in the task pane.

Note that styles are saved with the document. If a new document is created, any styles created in other documents do not appear.

Practice 2 ♻

In this practice you will insert a symbol, apply styles, create a new style, and hyphenate a document. Open VOLCANOES and display formatting marks if they are not already displayed.

① INSERT A SYMBOL

   a. Scroll to the top of page 2 until the "Introduction" heading is displayed.

   b. In the second sentence of the next paragraph, place the insertion point between "2200" and "C."

   c. Select Insert → Symbol. A dialog box is displayed. If necessary, drag the title bar of the dialog box so that the insertion point is displayed.

      1. Select Times New Roman from the Font list if it is not already selected.

      2. Scroll the list of symbols until degree (°) is displayed. It will be near the ¼ symbol.

      3. Click the degree symbol (°).

      4. Select Insert. A degree symbol is placed into the document at the insertion point.

      5. In the same sentence, place the insertion point between "5000" and "C." Drag the title bar of the Symbol dialog box to move it out of the way if necessary. The degree symbol should still be selected.

      6. Select Insert. A degree symbol is inserted.

      7. Select Close. The dialog box is removed.

② APPLY A STYLE USING THE TOOLBAR

    a. At the top of page 2, place the insertion point in the "Introduction" heading.

    b. On the toolbar, from the Style list select the Heading 1 style. The Heading 1 style is now applied to the "Introduction" heading.

③ APPLY A STYLE USING THE STYLES AND FORMATTING TASK PANE

    a. Select Format → Styles and Formatting. The Styles and Formatting task pane is displayed.

    b. At the bottom of the Styles and Formatting task pane, in the Show list, select Available styles. Note the styles listed in the Pick formatting to apply list. Some styles were created just for this document, and have "Volcano" in the name of the style.

    c. Place the insertion point in the "Volcano Facts" heading, which is below the Introduction paragraph on page 1.

    d. In the Styles and Formatting task pane, click Heading 1.

    e. Scroll to the bottom of page 4 and apply the Heading 1 style to the "Conclusion" heading.

④ CREATE A NEW STYLE

    a. In the Styles and Formatting task pane, click New Style. A dialog box is displayed.

        1. In the Name box, type My Heading 2.

        2. In the Style type list, select Paragraph if it is not already selected.

        3. In the Style based on list, select Heading 2.

        4. In the Style for following paragraph list, select Normal.

        5. In the Font Size box, type 15.

        6. Select OK. The dialog box is removed and the new style is added to the Styles and Formatting task pane.

⑤ APPLY STYLES TO THE OTHER HEADINGS

    a. Scroll to the middle of page 2 and place the insertion point in the "Stages of Volcanic Activity" heading.

    b. In the Styles and Formatting task pane, click the My Heading 2 style.

    c. Scroll through the rest of the document and apply the My Heading 2 style to the "Types of Volcanoes" and "Types of Lava Rocks," headings.

    d. Scroll to the middle of page 2 and place the insertion point in the "Eruption Stage" heading.

    e. In the Styles and Formatting task pane, click the Heading 3 style.

    f. Scroll through the rest of the document and apply the Heading 3 style to the "Cooling and Inactive Stage," "Cinder Cones," "Shield Volcanoes," "Composite Volcanoes," "Basalt," "Obsidian," and "Andesite" headings.

    g. In the upper-right corner of the Styles and Formatting task pane, click the Close button (☒). The task pane is removed.

⑥ HYPHENATE THE DOCUMENT

Select Tools → Language → Hyphenation. A dialog box is displayed.

        1. Select the Automatically hyphenate document check box if it is not already selected.

        2. Select OK. The dialog box is removed and Word hyphenates the document. Scroll through the document and look for hyphenated words.

⑦ SAVE THE MODIFIED VOLCANOES

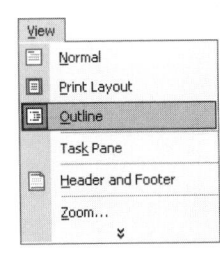

7.7 Using Outline View

Outline view displays the organization of a document. A document is displayed in Outline view by selecting <u>O</u>utline from the <u>V</u>iew menu. For example, the document on the left is displayed in Print Layout view, and the same document is displayed in Outline view on the right:

· Our·Solar·System¶

· Planets¶

· Mercury¶
Mercury·is·the·closest·planet·to·the·sun·at·57.9·million·km.·Unlike·Earth,·which·has·one·orbiting·satellite,·Mercury·does·not·have·any·known·satellites.·The·core·of·Mercury·is·a·large·dense·iron·core.·The·surface·is·lunar·like·and·contains·craters·from·earlier·collisions·of·asteroids.·Mercury·takes·approximately·58.7·days·to·rotate·about·its·axis.¶

· Venus¶
Venus·is·the·second·planet·from·the·sun·at·108.2·million·km.·It·also·has·no·known·satellites.·Its·atmosphere's·primary·gas·is·carbon·dioxide.·A·thick·cloud·layer·made·mostly·of·sulfuric·acid·covers·the·surface.·Venus·takes·approximately·243·days·to·rotate·about·its·axis.¶

· Earth¶
Earth·is·the·third·planet·from·the·sun·at·150·million·km·and·the·only·known·planet·that·contains·life.·It·has·one·orbiting·satellite·called·the·moon.·The·inner·core·is·believed·to·be·solid·with·a·liquid·outer·core.·The·surrounding·atmosphere·is·made·up·mostly·of·oxygen·and·nitrogen.·The·Earth·takes·24·hours·to·rotate·about·its·axis.¶

Print Layout view

⊕ **Our·Solar·System¶**
  ⊕ **Planets¶**
    ⊕ **Mercury¶**
      ▫ Mercury·is·the·closest·planet·to·the·sun·at·57.9·million·km.·Unlike·Earth,·which·has·one·orbiting·satellite,·Mercury·does·not·have·any·known·satellites.·The·core·of·Mercury·is·a·large·dense·iron·core.·The·surface·is·lunar·like·and·contains·craters·from·earlier·collisions·of·asteroids.·Mercury·takes·approximately·58.7·days·to·rotate·about·its·axis.¶
    ⊕ **Venus¶**
      ▫ Venus·is·the·second·planet·from·the·sun·at·108.2·million·km.·It·also·has·no·known·satellites.·Its·atmosphere's·primary·gas·is·carbon·dioxide.·A·thick·cloud·layer·made·mostly·of·sulfuric·acid·covers·the·surface.·Venus·takes·approximately·243·days·to·rotate·about·its·axis.¶
    ⊕ **Earth¶**
      ▫ Earth·is·the·third·planet·from·the·sun·at·150·million·km·and·the·only·known·planet·that·contains·life.·It·has·one·orbiting·satellite·called·the·moon.·The·inner·core·is·believed·to·be·solid·with·a·liquid·outer·core.·The·surrounding·atmosphere·is·made·up·mostly·of·oxygen·and·nitrogen.·The·Earth·takes·24·hours·to·rotate·about·its·axis.¶

Outline view

In Outline view, Word uses styles to determine heading levels and body text. Paragraphs are indented according to their levels, for example the Heading 1 style is at a higher level than Heading 2. In the example shown above, "Our Solar System" is formatted in the Heading 1 style. Paragraphs with the Normal style are body text and have the lowest level.

When a document is displayed in Outline view, the Outlining toolbar is also displayed:

⇐ ← Body text ▾ → ⇒ ↑ ↓ ✦ — Show All Levels ▾ ═ 🅰 Update TOC 🔁 ▢ ...

- **Promote button** (⇐) or **Demote button** (⇒) applies the next higher or lower level style, respectively, to the paragraph containing the insertion point.

- **Demote to Body Text button** (⇒) applies the Normal style to the paragraph containing the insertion point.

- **Move Up button** (↑) or **Move Down button** (↓) moves the paragraph containing the insertion point before or after the preceding paragraph, respectively.

- **Expand button** (✦) or **Collapse button** (—) displays or hides the body text under the heading containing the insertion point, respectively.

- **Show Level list** (Show All Levels ▾) is used to display different heading levels and the levels above. Body text is only displayed when Show All Levels is selected.

Icons in Outline view indicate levels:

▫ **Body text**

⊕ **Headings followed by a paragraph with a lower level**

▢ **Headings followed by a paragraph with the same level**

selecting and moving a topic   Entire topics can be selected by clicking a heading's plus sign, which selects that heading and the body text under it. Clicking the Move Up or Move Down button on the Outlining toolbar moves the selected topic. A topic can also be moved by dragging.

printing in Outline view   A document can be printed in Outline view by selecting <u>P</u>rint from the <u>F</u>ile menu or clicking the Print button on the toolbar. The printout will contain the same headings and body text as displayed on the screen. Selecting <u>P</u>rint Layout or <u>N</u>ormal from the <u>V</u>iew menu displays the document in a different view from Outline view.

Practice 3

In this practice you will display a document in Outline view, modify the document, and print the outline. Open VOLCANOES and display formatting marks if they are not already displayed.

① *DISPLAY VOLCANOES IN OUTLINE VIEW*

    a. Scroll to the top of page 2 and place the insertion point in the "Introduction" heading.

    b. Select <u>V</u>iew → <u>O</u>utline. The document is displayed in Outline view. Note the different levels in the document.

② *DISPLAY DIFFERENT LEVELS OF HEADINGS*

    a. On the Outlining toolbar, in the Show Level list select Show Level 1. Only the headings with the Heading 1 style are displayed.

    b. On the Outlining toolbar, in the Show Level list select Show Level 2. Heading levels 1 and 2 are displayed.

    c. On the Outlining toolbar, in the Show Level list select Show Level 3. All three heading levels are displayed.

③ *MOVE THE "TYPES OF LAVA ROCKS" TOPIC*

    a. Click the plus sign (✛) next to the "Types of Lava Rocks" heading. The entire topic, including lower level headings, is selected.

    b. On the Outlining toolbar, click the Move Up button (⬆). The selected headings are moved before the "Composite Volcanoes" heading.

    c. On the Outlining toolbar, click the Move Up button three more times. The selected topic is moved before the Types of Volcanoes topic and its headings.

    d. On the Outlining toolbar, in the Show Level list select Show All Levels. Note that the text under each heading also moved.

    e. On the Outlining toolbar, in the Show Level list select Show Level 3.

    f. Click anywhere to remove the selection.

④ *SAVE AND THEN PRINT THE DOCUMENT IN OUTLINE VIEW*

    a. Save the modified VOLCANOES.

    b. On the toolbar, click the Print button. An outline of the document is printed with only the headings displayed.

    c. Select <u>V</u>iew → <u>P</u>rint Layout. The document is again displayed in Print Layout view.

    d. Save the modified VOLCANOES.

7.8 Creating a Table of Contents

TOC

A *table of contents*, or *TOC*, is a list of headings and corresponding page numbers in a document. Word can automatically create a table of contents for a document based on the styles applied to its headings. A table of contents is created by first placing the insertion point where it should appear and then selecting Index and Tables from the Reference submenu in the Insert menu. Selecting the Table of Contents tab in the dialog box displays those options:

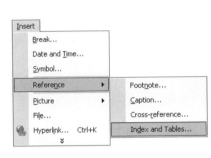

In the Formats list, the type of table of contents is selected. The Print Preview box displays a sample of what the selected format will look like. Selecting the Show page numbers check box includes the corresponding page numbers for headings and the Right align page numbers check box aligns the page numbers with the right margin. The Show levels box specifies the number of heading levels to include. Selecting OK creates a table of contents for the document and places it at the insertion point.

scrolling a document

Each entry in a table of contents created by Word is a hyperlink to the corresponding heading. Pointing to a table of contents entry displays a ScreenTip:

Our·Solar·System...→.................................2¶
  Pla Current Document ....→.................................2¶
      CTRL + click to follow link ....→.................................2¶
    Venus..→.................................3¶
    Earth ....→.................................3¶
    Mars ....→.................................3¶

Holding down the Ctrl key changes the pointer to a hand (🖑). Clicking scrolls the document and places the insertion point in the corresponding heading.

F9

Word does not automatically update a table of contents when changes are made to a document. A table of contents can be updated by clicking it and then pressing the F9 key, which displays the Update Table of Contents dialog box:

Selecting Update entire table and then OK updates any headings and the corresponding page numbers in the table of contents.

7.9 Creating Sections in a Document

Long documents often need to have different page formats applied to parts of the document. For example, page three of a five page report may need to be formatted with two columns, while the remaining pages need only one column. A document can be divided into different parts called *sections*, which allows different page formats to be applied to each section.

section break

A *section break* can be added to divide a document into sections. Placing the insertion point where the new section should start and selecting Break from the Insert menu displays the Break dialog box:

Next page inserts a section break and starts the next section on a new page. Continuous inserts a section break and starts the next section on the same page. Selecting OK inserts the section break.

The status bar at the bottom of the document window displays the section that contains the insertion point. When formatting marks are displayed, section breaks are identified by a double line and the type of break. For example, a continuous section break was added to the document:

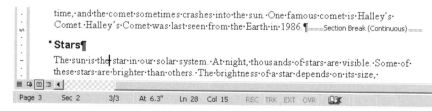

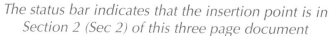

*The status bar indicates that the insertion point is in
Section 2 (Sec 2) of this three page document*

Text that was to the right of the insertion point is now in the next section of the document. Any page formats that are applied, such as margins and columns, affect only the section that contains the insertion point.

deleting a section break   A section break is deleted by placing the insertion point to the left of the section break and pressing the Delete key.

Practice 4

In this practice you will create a table of contents for VOLCANOES and divide the document into two sections. Open VOLCANOES and display formatting marks if they are not already displayed.

① INSERT A TABLE OF CONTENTS

   a. Scroll to the top of page 2.
   b. Place the insertion point in the blank paragraph above the "Introduction" heading.
   c. Type TABLE OF CONTENTS and then press Enter.
   d. Select Insert → Reference → Index and Tables. A dialog box is displayed.
      1. Select the Table of Contents tab to display those options.
      2. In the Formats list, select Formal.
      3. Select OK. A table of contents is inserted at the insertion point.
   e. Bold and center align the "TABLE OF CONTENTS" title.

② USE A HYPERLINK IN THE TABLE OF CONTENTS

   a. Point to "Obsidian" in the table of contents until a ScreenTip is displayed.
   b. Hold down the Ctrl key until the pointer changes to a hand (🖑) and then click the Obsidian entry. The document is scrolled to the Obsidian heading, and the insertion point is placed in the heading.

③ INSERT A SECTION BREAK

   a. Scroll to page 2 and place the insertion point to the left of the "I" at the beginning of the "Introduction" heading, below the table of contents.
   b. Select Insert → Break. A dialog box is displayed.
      1. Select Next page.
      2. Select OK. A section break is inserted between pages 2 and 3 and the main text of the report is moved to page 3. Note that the status bar displays Sec 2 because the insertion point is currently in Section 2 of the document.

④ UPDATE THE TABLE OF CONTENTS

   a. At the top of page 2, place the insertion point in the table of contents. The table of contents is selected and turns gray.
   b. Press the F9 key. A dialog box is displayed.
      1. Select OK. The table of contents now shows the correct page numbers.

Check – The table of contents should look similar to:

⑤ *SAVE THE MODIFIED VOLCANOES*

7.10   Using Section Headers and Footers

A document divided into sections can have different headers and footers in each section. For example, in a long report, the page numbers in the footer should start on the first page of the body of the report, not on the title page or on the table of contents page.

When a document is first divided into sections, each section header and footer contains the same text as the previous section. For example, if Solar System is entered as the header text in Section 1, the header in Section 2 automatically contains Solar System:

The header in Section 2 is based on the header in Section 1

A different header or footer can be created for a section by first placing the insertion point in the header or footer area then deselecting the Same as Previous button ( ) on the Header and Footer toolbar. The text can then be changed and will appear on all pages in that section.

7.11 Using Section Page Numbers

front matter

body

Different page numbering may be required for different parts of a document. For example, the front matter of a formal report usually uses separate page numbering from the body of the report. *Front matter* is information that comes before the body of a report, such as the title page, table of contents, and list of acknowledgments. The *body* of a report contains the information being presented. The front matter is usually numbered with small Roman numerals (i, ii, iii, and so on) and the body is numbered with Arabic numerals (1, 2, 3, and so on) starting at 1.

The steps for formatting different page numbering in a section are:

1. **Deselect the Same as Previous Button.** Place the insertion point in the header or footer area of the section and deselect the Same as Previous button on the Header and Footer toolbar.

2. **Add a page number.** Clicking the Insert Page Number button ([#]) on the Header and Footer toolbar inserts a page number.

3. **Format the page number.** Clicking the Format Page Number button ([#]) on the Header and Footer toolbar displays the Page Number Format dialog box:

Number Formats

Number formats available in the Page Number Format dialog box include:

Format	Type
1, 2, 3, …	Arabic
- 1 -, - 2 -, - 3 -,…	Arabic
a, b, c, …	letters
A, B, C, …	letters
i, ii, iii, …	Roman
I, II, III,…	Roman

changing the starting page number

The format of the page number is selected from the Number format list. Page numbering can be started at a number other than the actual page number by selecting Start at and then typing or selecting the beginning number. Selecting OK applies the formats.

Practice 5

In this practice you will insert and format different page numbers in the footers of Sections 1 and Section 2. Open VOLCANOES and display formatting marks if they are not already displayed.

① *INSERT A PAGE NUMBER IN THE FOOTER*

a. At the top of page 2, place the insertion point in the "TABLE OF CONTENTS" title. The insertion point in now in Section 1.

b. Select File → Page Setup. A dialog box is displayed.

1. Select the Layout tab to display those options.

2. Select the Different first page option.

3. Select OK.

c. Select <u>V</u>iew → <u>H</u>eader and Footer. The insertion point is placed in the header of Section 1.

d. On the Header and Footer toolbar, click the Switch Between Header and Footer button (⊞). The insertion point is placed in the footer of Section 1.

e. On the Header and Footer toolbar, click the Insert Page Number button (⊞). The page number is inserted in the footer.

f. On the toolbar, click the Center button. The page number is center aligned.

g. On the Header and Footer toolbar, click the Format Page Number button (⊞). A dialog box is displayed.

    1. In the **Number** format list, select i, ii, iii, ...

    2. Select **OK**. The dialog box is removed.

h. Close the Header and Footer toolbar.

② *FORMAT THE PAGE NUMBER IN THE FOOTER OF SECTION 2*

a. Scroll through the document to view the dimmed footer text. Note that the footer in Section 2 on page 3 contains page numbers that need to be formatted to start numbering at 1.

b. Place the insertion point anywhere in Section 2 if it is not already there. Note that the status bar indicates the section that currently contains the insertion point.

c. Select <u>V</u>iew → <u>H</u>eader and Footer. The insertion point is placed in the header of Section 2.

d. On the Header and Footer toolbar, click the Switch Between Header and Footer button (⊞). The insertion point is placed in the footer of Section 2.

e. On the Header and Footer toolbar, click the Same as Previous button (⊞) to deselect it. The footer in Section 2 will not be the same as the footer in Section 1.

f. On the Header and Footer toolbar, click the Format Page Number button (⊞). A dialog box is displayed.

    1. In the **Number** format list select 1, 2, 3, ... if it is not already selected.

    2. Select the **Start at** option. The insertion point is placed in the box.

    3. Type 1 if it is not already there. The page numbering in Section 2 will now start at 1 instead of 3.

    4. Select **OK**. The dialog box is removed.

g. Close the Header and Footer toolbar.

h. Preview the document. Zoom in and note the different page numbers, then close the print preview window.

③ *UPDATE THE TABLE OF CONTENTS*

a. Place the insertion point in any entry in the table of contents. The table of contents is selected and turns gray. Note the page numbers.

b. Press the F9 key. A dialog box is displayed.

    1. Select **OK**. The table of contents now shows the correct page numbers.

④ *SAVE, PRINT, AND THEN CLOSE THE MODIFIED VOLCANOES*

7.12   Creating a Hyperlink to a Web Page

In general, the purpose of a document is to communicate information. To help accomplish this, a document can include hyperlinks to web pages on the Internet:

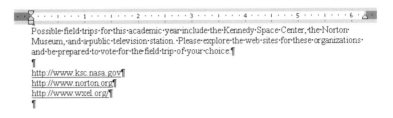

A hyperlink in a Word document is formatted as blue and underlined. Pointing to a hyperlink displays a ScreenTip:

Holding down the Ctrl key changes the pointer to a hand ($\sqrt[h]{}$). Clicking displays the web page in a browser window if the computer has Internet access.

A hyperlink is inserted into a document at the insertion point by clicking the Insert Hyperlink button (▓) on the toolbar, which displays the Insert Hyperlink dialog box. Selecting Existing File or Web Page displays those options:

Text typed in the Text to display box is displayed as the hyperlink. Entering a URL in the Address box and selecting OK places the text in the document and formats it as a hyperlink to the specified URL. The text http:// is automatically added to the beginning of the URL. Hyperlinks are automatically formatted as blue underlined text in a Word document. If no text is typed in the Text to display box, the URL is placed in the document as the text for the hyperlink.

The Insert Hyperlink dialog box can also be displayed by selecting Hyperlink (Ctrl+K) from the Insert menu.

removing a hyperlink   A hyperlink is removed by right-clicking the hyperlink and selecting Remove Hyperlink from the menu.

7.13 Creating a Hyperlink to a Heading

A hyperlink can be used to quickly scroll to a heading. For example, entries in a table of contents are hyperlinks to headings in the same document, but are not blue and underlined.

 A hyperlink to a heading in the open document is created at the insertion point by clicking the Insert Hyperlink button () on the toolbar, which displays the Insert Hyperlink dialog box. Selecting Place in This Document displays the current outline for the document:

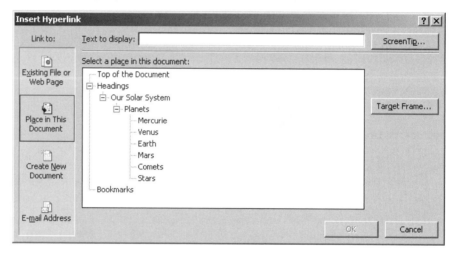

Clicking the plus or minus signs next to the headings displays other heading levels. Clicking a heading places it in the Text to display box, which can then be edited if needed. Selecting OK inserts a hyperlink to the selected heading.

7.14 Creating a Newsletter

Clubs and organizations often produce monthly newsletters to inform their members of upcoming events and issues.

title area   Newsletters have several common elements. Most newsletters have a title area, some text, and graphics. A *title area* is the section at the top of the first page that contains publication information such as the title and date. The pages in a newsletter are usually formatted in two or three columns with informative headers and footers. A table of contents is usually included on the first page.

Sections are used in a newsletter created in Word to allow for different page formats. The first page can be divided into sections with the title area in one section and the text in another section. The rest of the newsletter is in a third section. Additional sections can be added as needed for different page formats.

Practice 6

In this practice you will format the SPACE TRANSMISSIONS document as a newsletter with hyperlinks.

① *OPEN SPACE TRANSMISSIONS*

Open SPACE TRANSMISSIONS, which is a data file for this text. This document already contains text and a picture. Display formatting marks if they are not already displayed.

② *CREATE THE TITLE AREA*

a. Near the top of page 1, place the insertion point to the left of the "I" at the beginning of the "In This Issue" heading.

b. Select Insert → Break. A dialog box is displayed.

    1. Select Continuous.

    2. Select OK. Section 1 of the document is now the title area of the newsletter.

③ *FORMAT SECTION 2 IN TWO COLUMNS*

a. Place the insertion point in Section 2 of the document if it is not already there.

b. Select Format → Columns. A dialog box is displayed.

    1. In the Number of columns box, type 2.

    2. Select OK. The text in Section 2 is formatted in two columns.

④ *FORMAT THE REMAINING PAGES IN THREE COLUMNS*

a. Scroll to the top of page 2.

b. Insert a Continuous section break just before the heading "Space Exploration Facts."

c. Format Section 3 of the document in three columns.

⑤ *SAVE THE MODIFIED SPACE TRANSMISSIONS*

⑥ *INSERT A HYPERLINK*

a. In the second column of page 2, just above the "Mission to Mars" heading, place the insertion point to the right of the "t" at the end of "NASA's web site at" and type a space.

b. On the toolbar, click the Insert Hyperlink button (▨). A dialog box is displayed.

    1. Click Existing File or Web Page at the left side of the dialog box if it is not already selected.

    2. In the Address box type www.nasa.gov. Note that Word added http://.

    3. Select OK. A hyperlink is added to the document.

⑦ *SAVE THE MODIFIED SPACE TRANSMISSIONS*

⑧ *DISPLAY NASA'S WEB SITE*

a. Point to the http://www.nasa.gov hyperlink until a ScreenTip is displayed.

b. Hold down the Ctrl key until the pointer changes to a hand (🖑) and then click. If necessary, ask your instructor for help in connecting to the Internet. After connecting to the Internet, NASA's web page is displayed in a browser window.

c. Explore the web page. When finished, close the browser window.

⑨ *SAVE, PRINT, AND THEN CLOSE SPACE TRANSMISSIONS*

7.15 E-Mailing a Document

An existing document can be e-mailed from Word. For example, a business in Arizona could send a document to a printing company in Ohio.

 An open document can be sent as an e-mail message by first clicking the E-mail button (📧) on the toolbar, which displays the address information boxes:

The e-mail address of the recipient is typed in the To box, and the file name automatically appears in the Subject box, which can be edited. Text typed in the Introduction box appears above the document when the recipient opens the message. Clicking the Send a Copy button (📧 Send a Copy) sends a copy of the document as an e-mail message. Once the message is sent, the address information is removed and the document remains open and displayed.

Practice 7

In this practice you will send the WORKSHOP document as an e-mail message.

① *OPEN WORKSHOP*

Open WORKSHOP, which was last modified in Chapter 6, Practice 8.

② *SEND THE DOCUMENT AS AN E-MAIL MESSAGE*

a. On the toolbar, click the E-mail button (📧). The address information boxes are displayed at the top of the window.

b. In the To box, type office@lpdatafiles.com or an e-mail address specified by your instructor.

c. In the Subject box, replace the existing text with Workshop Information for You.

d. In the Introduction box, type Only four spaces left!

A Guide to Microsoft Office XP Professional

e. Click the Send a Copy button (☒ Send a Copy). If necessary, ask your instructor for help with connecting to the Internet. After connecting to the Internet, the message is sent and the address information boxes removed.

③ *SAVE AND CLOSE WORKSHOP*

7.16   Creating Labels

Multiple labels that contain the same text can easily be created in Word. For example, return address labels can be created to use on envelopes.

When printing labels, special adhesive paper with multiple labels on each page is used in the printer. The Avery® brand of adhesive labels is widely used, and the dimensions of many of its labels have been included in Word. Therefore only the Avery product number needs to be selected to create labels in the appropriate format.

Labels are created by selecting Envelopes and Labels from the Letters and Mailings submenu in the Tools menu, which displays the Envelopes and Labels dialog box. Selecting the Labels tab displays those options:

Clicking Options displays the Label Options dialog box. Selecting the appropriate Avery label in the Product number list and then OK displays the Envelopes and Labels dialog box again. The text for the labels is entered in the large Address box. The labels are now ready to be placed into a document by selecting New Document. The labels can then be saved, formatted, and printed.

Practice 8

In this practice you will print return address labels on plain paper.

① *CREATE A NEW DOCUMENT*

② CREATE THE RETURN ADDRESS LABELS

a. Select Tools → Letters and Mailings → Envelopes and Labels. A dialog box is displayed.

   1. Select the Labels tab if those options are not already displayed.
   2. Select Options. A dialog box is displayed.
      a. In the Product number list, scroll until 5267 - Return Address is displayed and then select it.
      b. Select OK. The Labels options are again displayed.
   3. Type your first and last name in the large Address box and then press Enter.
   4. Type your street address and then press Enter.
   5. Type your city, state, and zip (or province and postal code).
   6. Select New Document. The dialog box is removed and a new document is created with the labels displayed.

③ FORMAT THE LABELS

a. Select Edit → Select All. All of the text in the document is selected.

b. On the toolbar, in the Font Size box select 8. All of the text now fits on the labels.

④ SAVE, PRINT, AND CLOSE THE DOCUMENT

a. Save the document naming it My Return Labels.

b. Print a copy on plain paper.

c. Close My Return Labels.

7.17   Recording Macros

Macro Names

The name of a macro must begin with a letter and can have up to 255 letters and numbers. Spaces and other punctuation are not allowed.

▶	Macros...	Alt+F8
●	Record New Macro...	
	Security...	
📄	Visual Basic Editor	Alt+F11
🔗	Microsoft Script Editor	Alt+Shift+F11

When creating documents, a series of steps may need to be repeated. For example, every week a manager creates a table used as a sign-up sheet for employee work hours. Macros can be created in Word to help perform repetitive tasks. A *macro* is a named series of recorded commands and actions that perform a specific task.

A macro is recorded by selecting Record New Macro from the Macro submenu in the Tools menu, which displays the Record Macro dialog box:

A name for the macro is typed in the Macro name box. The name of the open document is selected in the Store macro in list so that the macro will be saved with the document. The description for the macro in the

Description box can be edited. Selecting OK begins the recording and the pointer changes to 🖐.

The sequence of steps are recorded by selecting the commands and options as usual. During recording, the mouse can be used to select commands from menus and options in dialog boxes but cannot be used in the document. For example, to format bold text as part of the macro, the text must be selected using the keyboard and not the mouse.

While a macro is being recorded, the Stop Recording toolbar (⬛) is displayed. Clicking the Stop Recording button (⬛) ends recording after all the macro's steps have been performed. Clicking the Pause Recording button (⬛) interrupts the recording.

A macro is run by selecting Macros (Alt+F8) from the Macro submenu in the Tools menu, which displays the Macros dialog box. Selecting the macro name and then Run runs the macro.

Practice 9

In this practice you will create a macro that inserts a formatted table into a document.

① *CREATE A NEW DOCUMENT*

② *CREATE A MACRO*

    a. Select Tools → Macro → Record New Macro. A dialog box is displayed.

        1. In the Macro name box, type TimeTable.

        2. In the Store macro in list, select Document1.

        3. In the Description box, replace the existing text with Inserts a formatted table.

        4. Select OK to begin recording the steps. The pointer changes to 🖐.

③ *RECORD STEPS TO CREATE AND FORMAT THE TABLE*

    a. Select Table → Insert → Table. A dialog box is displayed.

        1. In the Number of columns box, type 7 .

        2. In the Number of rows box, type 6.

        3. Select OK. The table is inserted and the insertion point is in the first cell.

    b. Type the following text in the first row of cells, using the Tab key or arrow keys to move the insertion point:

        Employee   Mon   Tue   Wed   Thu   Fri   Sat

    c. Type the following employee names in the first column, using the down arrow key to move the insertion point: Eklund, Lopez, Quinn, Rosen, Sladek.

    d. Using the arrow keys, move the insertion point to any cell in the first row (do not use the mouse).

    e. Select Table → Select → Row. The first row is selected.

    f. Format the selected row as bold and change the font size to 14 point.

    g. Using the arrow keys, place the insertion point in the second cell in the second row.

    h. On the Stop Recording Toolbar, click the Stop Recording button (⬛).

    i. Close the document without saving it.

④ *OPEN EMPLOYEE HOURS*

Open EMPLOYEE HOURS, which is a data file for this text.

⑤ *RUN THE MACRO*

    a. In the second blank paragraph below the sentence that reads "For week starting 3/3," place the insertion point.

    b. Select Tools → Macro → Macros. A dialog box is displayed.

        1. Select TimeTable in the Macro name list.

        2. Select Run. A formatted table is inserted into the document.

    c. Place the insertion point in the second blank paragraph below the sentence that reads "For week starting 3/10."

    d. Run the TimeTable macro again.

⑥ *SAVE, PRINT, AND THEN CLOSE THE MODIFIED EMPLOYEE HOURS*

⑦ *QUIT WORD*

7.18   Where can you go from here?

The last four chapters have introduced the concepts of using a word processor including how to create, edit, format, and print documents. Word has other features not discussed in this text which can be explored using the online help.

A powerful feature of Word is its ability to integrate information stored in a database with a Word document to produce personalized form letters. This process is called mail merge and is described in Chapter 16. In addition, Chapter 12 describes how to integrate spreadsheet data and charts into a document.

Chapter Summary

This chapter explained how to create tables and introduced features that help organize and format long documents. Creating labels and recording macros was also introduced.

A table consists of rows and columns of cells and is created using the Insert Table button or the Table command. Text is entered in a cell by clicking a cell and then typing. The Tab key and arrow keys are used to move the insertion point in a table. A row or column is selected by moving the pointer to the left of the row or top of the column and clicking. Selected cells can be formatted using character formats and some paragraph formats such as alignment.

The height of rows and width of columns can be changed by dragging a row's bottom boundary or a column's right boundary. Double-clicking a boundary changes a row or column to be just tall or wide enough to display the data entirely. A row or column can be added using the Insert Rows button or Insert Columns button. A row or column can be deleted using the Rows and Columns commands from the Delete submenu.

Documents can be refined by hyphenating and adding symbols. A document can be hyphenated using the Hyphenation command. Symbols such as copyright (©) and degrees (°) can be inserted in a document using the Symbol command.

A style is a named set of character and paragraph formats. Styles can also be applied using the Styles and Formatting task pane, which is displayed using the Styles and Formatting command. A style is applied by clicking a style in the Pick formatting to apply list. The Show list can be used to change what is displayed in the Pick formatting to apply list.

Outline view displays the organization of a document. A document is displayed in Outline view by selecting the Outline command. In Outline view, Word uses styles to determine heading levels and body text. When a document is displayed in Outline view, the Outlining toolbar is also displayed. Entire topics can be moved by clicking on a heading's plus sign and selecting the Move Up or Move Down button. A document can be printed in Outline view using the Print command or the Print button.

A table of contents, or TOC, is created by selecting the Index and Tables command. Each entry in a table of contents is a hyperlink to the corresponding heading. Pointing to a table of contents entry, holding down the Ctrl key, and clicking scrolls the document to the heading. A table of contents can be updated by selecting it and then pressing the F9 key.

A document can be divided into sections by inserting a section break using the Break command. Next page starts the next section on a new page, and Continuous starts the next section on the same page. The status bar displays the section of the document that contains the insertion point. Any page formats that are applied affect only the section that contains the insertion point. Sections can have different headers and footers by deselecting the Same as Previous button. Different page numbering can be applied to each section using the Format Page Number button.

A document can include a hyperlink to a web page on the Internet or to another part of the open document. A hyperlink in a Word document is formatted as blue and underlined. Pointing to a hyperlink, holding down the Ctrl key, and clicking displays the web page or other part of the document. A hyperlink is created using the Insert Hyperlink button.

Word processors are used for producing newsletters, which usually have a title area, some text, and graphics. The pages of a newsletter are usually formatted in two or three columns.

An open document can be e-mailed from Word by clicking the E-mail button, typing information in the address boxes, and then clicking the Send a Copy button.

Multiple labels that contain the same text can easily be printed in Word using the Envelopes and Labels command. The labels can be saved, formatted, and printed.

A macro is a named series of recorded commands and actions that perform a specific task and can be recorded by selecting the Record New Macro command. During recording, the mouse can only be used to select commands and options. The Stop Recording button is used to end recording. A macro can be run using the Macros command.

Vocabulary

Body   The information presented in a report.

Body text   The main paragraphs in a document.

Boundary   A line that separates cells in a table.

Cell   The intersection of a row and column in a table.

Column   Vertical cells in a table.

F9 key   Displays a dialog box used to update a table of contents.

Front matter   Information that comes before the body of a report.

Headings   Titles that are often bold and in a larger and different font than the body text.

Hyphenating   A process that divides a word, when necessary, at the end of a line with a hyphen (-) so part of the word wraps to the next line.

Macro   A named series of recorded commands and actions that perform a specific task.

Normal style   The 12 point, Times New Roman, left-aligned default style applied to text.

Outline view   Displays the organization of a document.

Row   Horizontal cells in a table.

Section break   Added to a document to divide it into sections.

Sections   Parts of a document that can have different page formatting.

Style   A named set of character and paragraph formats.

Table of contents   A list of the headings and the corresponding page numbers in a document.

Title area   A section at the top of a newsletter that contains information about the publication.

TOC   A table of contents.

Word Commands and Buttons

Break command   Displays a dialog box used to insert a section break at the insertion point. Found on the Insert menu.

Collapse button   Hides the body text under the heading containing the insertion point. Found on the Outlining toolbar.

Column command   Selects the column containing the insertion point in a table. Found in the Select submenu in the Table menu.

Columns command   Deletes a selected column or columns in a table. Found in the Delete submenu in the Table menu.

Demote button   Applies the next lower level style to the paragraph containing the insertion point. Found on the Outlining toolbar.

Demote to Body Text button   Applies the Normal style to the paragraph containing the insertion point. Found on the Outlining toolbar.

E-mail button   Used to send the currently open document as an e-mail message. Found on the toolbar.

Envelopes and Labels command   Displays a dialog box used to create labels. Found in the Letters and Mailings submenu in the Tools menu.

Expand button   Displays the body text under the heading containing the insertion point. Found on the Outlining toolbar.

Format Page Number button   Displays a dialog box used to format the numbering and change the starting number. Found on the Header and Footer toolbar.

Header and Footer command Dims the text in a document, places the insertion point in the header area, and displays the Header and Footer toolbar. Found in the View menu.

Hyperlink command Displays a dialog box used to insert a hyperlink at the insertion point. Found in the Insert menu. The Insert Hyperlink button on the toolbar can be used instead of the command.

Hyphenation command Displays a dialog box used to hyphenate a document. Found in the Language submenu in the Tools menu.

Index and Tables command Displays a dialog box used to insert a table of contents at the insertion point. Found in the Reference submenu in the Insert menu.

Insert Columns button Adds a column to the left of the selected column in a table. Found on the toolbar when a column is selected.

Insert Page Number button Inserts a page number at the insertion point. Found on the Header and Footer toolbar.

Insert Rows button Adds a row above the selected row in a table. Found on the toolbar when a row is selected.

Macros command Displays a dialog box used to select and run a macro. Found in the Macro submenu in the Tools menu.

Move Down button Moves the paragraph containing the insertion point to after the preceding paragraph. Found on the Outlining toolbar.

Move Up button Moves the paragraph containing the insertion point to before the preceding paragraph. Found on the Outlining toolbar.

New Style button Displays a dialog box used to create a new style. Found in the Styles and Formatting task pane.

Outline command Displays a document in Outline view. Found in the View menu.

Pause Recording button Interrupts the recording of a macro. Found on the Stop Recording toolbar.

Promote button Applies the next higher level style to the paragraph containing the insertion point. Found on the Outlining toolbar.

Record New Macro command Displays a dialog box used to name a macro and begin recording it. Found in the Macro submenu in the Tools menu.

Row command Selects the row containing the insertion point in a table. Found in the Select submenu in the Table menu.

Rows command Deletes a selected row or rows in a table. Found in the Delete submenu in the Table menu.

Same as Previous button Deselected to allow for different section headers or footers. Found on the Header and Footer toolbar.

Select All command Selects all the cells in the table that contains the insertion point. Found in the Edit menu.

Send a Copy button Connects the computer to the Internet and sends a copy of the currently open document as an e-mail message.

Stop Recording button Ends the recording of a macro. Found on the Stop Recording toolbar.

Styles and Formatting command Displays the Styles and Formatting task pane. Found in the Format menu.

Symbol command Displays a dialog box used to insert a symbol into a document. Found in the Insert menu.

Table command Displays a dialog box used to insert a table. Found in the Insert submenu in the Table menu. The Insert Table button on the toolbar can be used instead of the command.

Review Questions

Sections 7.1 — 7.7

1. What is a cell?

2. List the steps required to create a table with four columns and three rows.

3. List two ways to move the insertion point in a table.

4. List the steps required to right align the data in the first column of a table and then bold the data in the first row.

5. a) What is a boundary?
   b) What happens when the boundary of a column is double-clicked?

6. List the steps required to insert a row between rows three and four of a table.

7. a) List the steps required to delete a row in a table.
   b) List the steps required to delete an entire table.

8. List the steps required to insert the copyright (©) symbol at the beginning of a paragraph.

9. What does hyphenation do to justified text?

10. List the steps required to hyphenate the open document.

11. a) What is a style?
    b) What are headings?

12. What formatting does the Normal style apply to a paragraph?

13. a) List the steps required to view all the styles.
    b) List the steps required to apply the Heading 2 built-in style to a paragraph.

14. List the steps required to create a new style named Caption, based on the Normal style, that center aligns a paragraph.

15. a) What does Outline view display?
    b) List the steps required to display the open document in Outline view.

16. List the steps required to select a topic in Outline view and move it to after the topic below it.

17. List the steps required to only print the first two heading levels in a document.

Sections 7.8 — 7.17

18. a) What is a TOC?
    b) List the steps required to insert a table of contents at the insertion point.

19. List the steps required to use an entry in the table of contents display the corresponding heading in the document.

20. a) What is added to a document to divide it into sections?
    b) List the steps required to insert a Next page section break at the insertion point.
    c) What is the difference between Next page and Continuous section breaks?

21. List the steps required to have Gifts as a header on page 1 and Jewelry as a header on page 2.

22. a) List the steps required to have a footer with Roman numeral page numbers in Section 1 and Arabic page numbers in Section 2 in a document.
    b) List the steps required to start page numbering at 1 on the third page of a document.

23. List the steps required to insert a hyperlink to a web page at the insertion point.

24. List the steps required to insert a hyperlink at the insertion point to a heading in the document.

25. a) What is the title area of a newsletter?
    b) Why is a newsletter created in Word divided into sections?

26. List the steps required to send the open Word document as an e-mail message.

27. List the steps required to create return address labels.

28. a) What is a macro?
    b) During recording, how can text be selected?
    c) List the steps required to run a macro named Bold.

Exercise 1 ✥ ─────────────────── SCIENCE MUSEUM

The SCIENCE MUSEUM document last modified in Chapter 6, Exercise 9 needs a table that displays the hours of operations. Open SCIENCE MUSEUM and complete the following steps:

a) Insert a table with three rows and three columns (a 3 x 3 table) in the blank paragraph after the sentence that begins "The hours of operation…."

b) Enter the following data into the table starting in the first cell:

Day	Open	Close
Weekdays	9:00 a.m.	8:00 p.m.
Sunday	12:00 p.m.	5:00 p.m.

c) Bold the text in the first row.

d) Decrease the width of the columns appropriately.

e) Insert a row between the Weekdays and Sunday rows, and enter the following data into the new row:

| Saturday | 10:00 a.m. | 7:00 p.m. |

f) Resize the clip art at the top of the document as necessary so that all the information fits on one page.

g) Save the modified SCIENCE MUSEUM and print a copy.

Exercise 2 ─────────────────── ELEMENTS

The ELEMENTS document contains information on elements and chemical formulas. Open ELEMENTS and complete the following steps:

a) Insert a table with four rows and three columns (a 4 x 3 table) in the second blank paragraph after the "Alkali Metals" heading.

b) Enter the following data into the table starting in the first cell:

Element	Symbol	Atomic Number
Lithium	Li	3
Sodium	Na	11
Potassium	K	19

c) Insert a table with five rows and three columns (a 5 x 3 table) in the second blank paragraph after the "Nonmetals" heading.

d) Enter the following data into the table starting in the first cell:

Element	Symbol	Atomic Number
Carbon	C	6
Nitrogen	N	7
Oxygen	O	8
Fluorine	F	9

e) Insert a table with four rows and three columns (a 4 x 3 table) in the second blank paragraph after the "Noble Gases" heading.

f) Enter the following data into the table starting in the first cell:

Element	Symbol	Atomic Number
Helium	He	2
Neon	Ne	10
Argon	Ar	18

g) Bold and increase the size of the text in the first row of all the tables.

h) Decrease the width of the columns in each table appropriately.

i) Apply the Heading 1 style to the "Elements" heading and the Heading 2 style to the "Alkali Metals," "Nonmetals," and "Noble Gases" headings.

j) Create a header with your name right aligned.

k) Save the modified ELEMENTS and print a copy of the document in Outline view with the first and second level headings displayed.

l) Print a copy in Print Layout view.

Exercise 3 — SOLAR SYSTEM

The SOLAR SYSTEM document contains a report on our solar system. Open SOLAR SYSTEM and complete the following steps:

a) Have Word hyphenate the document.

b) Apply the Heading 1 style to the "Introduction," "Our Solar System," and "Conclusion" headings.

c) Apply the Heading 2 style to the "Planets," "Objects," and "Stars" headings.

d) Apply the Heading 3 style to each planet and the "Meteoroids" and "Comets" headings.

e) Use Outline view to move the topic "Objects" (including the headings and text underneath it) to after the "Stars" heading and text.

f) Save the modified SOLAR SYSTEM and print a copy of the document in Outline view with the first, second, and third level headings displayed.

g) Have Word insert a Formal format table of contents above the "Introduction" heading at the top of page 2. Include a title for the table of contents and format the title appropriately.

h) Insert a Next page section break after the table of contents you just inserted.

i) Create a Section 1 footer with your name followed by a space and a page number in the i, ii, iii, ... format. Center align the footer. No footer should appear on the first page in Section 1.

j) Create a Section 2 footer with your name followed by a space and a page number in the 1, 2, 3, ... format. The page numbers in the Section 2 footers should start at 1 and be center aligned.

k) Update the table of contents to reflect the new page numbering.

l) At the bottom of the first page of the document, change "Your Name" to your name.

m) Save the modified SOLAR SYSTEM and print a copy.

A Guide to Microsoft Office XP Professional

Exercise 4 ⚙ ——————————————————— WORKSHOP

The WORKSHOP document last modified in the Practice 7 needs formatting applied to different sections. Open WORKSHOP and complete the following steps:

a) Insert a Continuous section break before the heading "Our Computers."

b) Insert a Continuous section break in the blank paragraph before the quote that begins "To seek knowledge…" at the end of the document.

c) Format Section 2 as two columns.

d) Save the modified WORKSHOP and print a copy.

Exercise 5 ——————————————————— HONORS HANDOUT

The HONORS HANDOUT document contains information on different honors clubs at Ivy University. Open HONORS HANDOUT and complete the following steps:

a) Insert a table with four rows and four columns (a 4 x 4 table) in the blank paragraph after the last sentence under the "Fraternities" heading on page 3.

b) Enter the following data into the table starting in the first cell, using the Symbol command to insert the Greek letters into the table:

Name	Greek Letters	College	Members
Delta Epsilon Phi	ΔΕΦ	Business	45
Lambda Pi Sigma	ΛΠΣ	Liberal Arts	56
Xi Psi Zeta	ΞΨΖ	Engineering	34

c) Bold and increase the size of the text in the first row.

d) Decrease the width of the columns appropriately.

e) Apply the Heading 1 style to the "Honors Program," "Honors Societies," and "Honors Classes" headings.

f) Apply the Heading 2 style to the "Clubs" and "Fraternities" headings.

g) Apply the Heading 3 style to the following headings:

Business Honors Society	Delta Epsilon Phi
Honors Computer Club	Lambda Pi Sigma
Science Club of Honors	Xi Psi Zeta

h) Have Word insert a Formal format table of contents above the "Honors Program" heading at the top of page 2. Include a title for the table of contents and format the title appropriately.

i) Insert a Next page section break after the table of contents you just inserted.

j) Create a Section 1 footer with your name followed by a space and a page number in the i, ii, iii, … format. Center align the footer. No footer should appear on the first page in Section 1.

k) Create a Section 2 footer with your name followed by a space and a page number in the 1, 2, 3, … format. The page numbers in the Section 2 footers should start at 1 and be center aligned.

l) Update the table of contents to reflect the new page numbering.

m) Save the modified HONORS HANDOUT and print a copy.

Exercise 6

Documents often require page numbering in the footer. Create a macro that creates a footer similar to Page 1 center aligned. Name the macro PageNumberFooter.

Exercise 7 ⟳ ————————————————————————— PROPOSAL

E-mail the PROPOSAL document last modified in Chapter 6, Exercise 7 to office@lvp.com or to an address specified by your instructor. Type the text Proposal for Research as the Subject and type the text Donna, can you edit this for me? Thanks! as the Introduction.

Exercise 8 ————————————————————————————— My Labels

Create a sheet of labels with the appropriate information on each label depending on the type of label you create. Use regular paper to print the labels.

Exercise 9 (advanced) —————————————————— My Favorite Recipe

Recipes in a cookbook often appear with different page formats. In a new document enter your favorite recipe. Format the document into three continuous sections as follows:

Section 1: include the name of the recipe, your name, and a clip art graphic
Section 2: list the ingredients for the recipe and format the section in two columns
Section 3: a numbered list of the recipe steps

Save the document naming it My Favorite Recipe and print a copy.

Exercise 10 (advanced) —————————————————— Technology Research

Research a technology topic of your choice using the Internet. Write a report based on the information you found. The report should include a title page, a table of contents, the body of the report, and footnotes where appropriate. Include at least two hyperlinks, and create and use your own style using the Style dialog box. Save the report naming it Technology Research and print a copy.

Exercise 11 (advanced) —————————————————— Deluxe Newsletter

Create a four page newsletter using the information presented in Section 7.14. Format the newsletter with at least three different sections and at least two hyperlinks to web pages. Save the newsletter naming it Deluxe Newsletter and print a copy.

Exercise 12 (advanced) ——————————————————————————

Create a macro that saves the open document, prints a copy, and then closes the document. Save the macro with an appropriate name and description.

Chapter 8
Introducing the Spreadsheet

Print Preview

Page Setup

Cells

Ignore Error

Edit in Formula Bar

Down

Right

Chapter 8 Expectations

After completing this chapter you will be able to:

1. Define what a spreadsheet is.
2. Identify the different parts of the worksheet window.
3. Create a workbook and enter data into it.
4. Save, close, and print a workbook.
5. Create headers and footers in a worksheet.
6. Change the width of columns.
7. Demonstrate techniques for selecting cells.
8. Format a worksheet.
9. Use formulas to perform calculations.
10. Use cell references in formulas.
11. Use the SUM, AVERAGE, and ROUND functions.
12. Enter formulas by pointing.
13. Display formulas in cells.
14. Copy adjacent cells and formulas.
15. Understand relative cell references.

The History of the Spreadsheet

The earliest double-entry books, used to record business transactions, are from the 14th century. The transactions were recorded using a pencil and paper with the data in rows and columns. This method was essentially unchanged until the introduction of the PC in the 70s. In 1978 Dan Bricklin, a graduate student at the Harvard School of Business, and his friend Bob Frankston, developed the first spreadsheet application software called VisiCalc. VisiCalc, written for the Apple II, was one of the most widely used software products during the 80s and helped change how businesses did business. In 1983, Jonathan Sachs and Mitchell Kapor, founders of Lotus Development Corporation, introduced Lotus 1-2-3 for the IBM PC. Lotus 1-2-3 integrated operations of a spreadsheet with graphics to produce charts, and became one of the most successful application software products of all time. Today, spreadsheet applications are a standard business tool.

T his chapter introduces Microsoft Excel, a powerful spreadsheet application used to store numeric data and perform calculations.

8.1 What is a Spreadsheet?

Excel
workbook
worksheet

A *spreadsheet* is data displayed in rows and columns. The term comes from the field of accounting where business activities were tracked on large sheets of paper that spread out to form a "spreadsheet." The computerized spreadsheet application in Microsoft Office is *Excel*. In Excel, spreadsheet files are called *workbooks*, and each workbook contains three *worksheets*, also called sheets.

Worksheets are used to present data in an organized format:

	A	B	C	D	E	F
1	Name	Test 1	Test 2	Test 3	Test 4	Student Average
2		1/7/2003	2/9/2003	3/1/2003	4/1/2003	
3						
4	Jones, D.	85	73	88	95	85.3
5	Neave, C.	92	88	85	91	89.0
6	Garcia, E.	72	63	67	72	68.5
7	McCallister, T.	87	92	85	93	89.3
8	Smith, L.	94	91	93	84	90.5
9	Bell, M.	70	74	80	83	76.8

Spreadsheet Uses

Spreadsheets are widely used by businesses for payroll and inventory and by individuals for personal budgets and calculating education costs. They can also be used to perform calculations on data collected in a laboratory.

The name Jones, D., the test grades 85, 73, 88, 95, and the average 85.3 form a row. Rows 4 through 9 store the name, test grades, and average for six students. The title Test 1, date 1/7/2003, and test grades from 85 to 70 form a column. Columns B through E each store a title, date, and all of the grades for a single test.

Benefits of using a spreadsheet application include the ability to easily perform calculations on data and to automatically recalculate values when changes are made to the data. For example, the spreadsheet above is set up to calculate student averages. If a test grade is changed, the corresponding average will automatically recalculate.

8.2 Creating a New Excel Workbook

Blank Workbook

Selecting New Office Document from the Start menu on the Windows Taskbar displays the New Office Document dialog box. Clicking the Blank Workbook icon and then selecting OK starts Excel and creates a new, empty workbook. The first worksheet in the workbook is displayed:

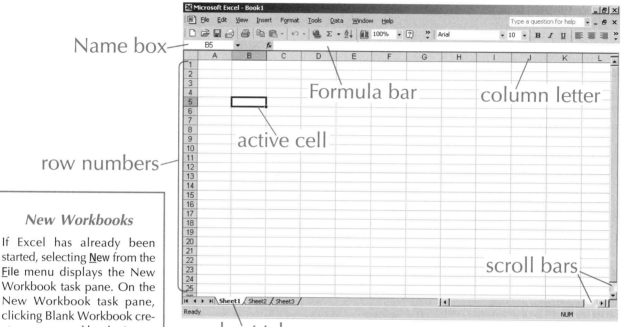

- **Letters** at the top of the worksheet identify individual **columns**. In Excel columns are lettered from A to Z and then AA to IV for a total of 256 columns. In the worksheet above, only columns A through L are displayed.

- **Numbers** down the left side of the worksheet identify individual **rows**. In Excel, rows are numbered from 1 to 65,536. In the worksheet above, only rows 1 through 25 are displayed.

- **Scroll bars** are used to display rows and columns that are not currently visible in the worksheet.

- A **cell** is the intersection of a row and column. Each cell can store a single item of data.

- A **cell reference** is the column letter and row number that identify a single cell. For example, B5 is the cell reference of the selected cell in the worksheet above.

- The selected cell is called the **active cell** and is displayed with a bold outline. In the worksheet above, cell B5 is the active cell. The column letter and row number corresponding to the active cell are blue. Data can only be entered into an active cell.

- The **Name box** displays the cell reference of the active cell, which is B5 in the worksheet above.

- The **Formula bar** displays the contents of the active cell.

- The **sheet tabs** are used to display the three worksheets in the workbook.

Scrolling

The active cell does not change when the scroll bars are used. If the active cell is not displayed after scrolling, pressing Ctrl+Backspace scrolls back to the active cell.

Date Interpretation

If a date is entered with a two-digit year, Excel interprets years 00 through 29 as the years 2000 through 2029 and interprets years 30 through 99 as the years 1930 through 1999.

8.3 The Active Cell

When the pointer is moved onto the worksheet, it changes to ⬦. Clicking a cell makes it the active cell.

The keyboard can also be used to change the active cell. Pressing an arrow key makes the next cell in that direction the active cell. Pressing the Home key changes the active cell to the first cell in the row. Pressing Ctrl+Home changes the active cell to cell A1. Pressing the Page Up or Page Down key changes the active cell to a cell one screen up or down, respectively.

8.4 Entering Data into a Worksheet

Worksheets can store three types of data: labels, values, and times/dates. *Labels* are text and cannot be used in calculations. *Values* are numeric and can be used in calculations. *Times/dates* are either a time, such as 12:10 PM, or a date, such as 6/4/2003. A time/date entry may be used in some calculations. In the worksheet in Section 8.1, student names and titles (such as Jones, D. and Test 1) are labels, test grades (such as 85) are values, and a date (such as 1/7/2003) is a time/date. Labels are left aligned and values and times/dates are right aligned in worksheet cells:

	A	B	C	D
1	Inventory	9/8/2003	1:30 PM	789
2				

Data is entered into a cell by selecting that cell and then typing the data. As data is typed, it appears in the cell and on the Formula bar, and the Cancel and Enter buttons are activated:

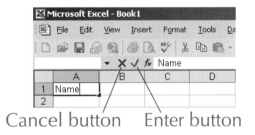

Cancel button   Enter button

Clicking the Enter button (☑) enters the data in the active cell. Clicking the Cancel button (☒) cancels data entry and restores the original contents of the cell. The keyboard can also be used to perform similar actions:

- Pressing the Enter key enters the data and then selects the next cell in the column.

- Pressing the Tab key enters the data and then selects the next cell in the row.

- Pressing an arrow key enters the data and then selects the next cell in the direction of the arrow key.

- Pressing the Esc key cancels data entry and restores the original contents of the cell.

AutoComplete

Excel uses a feature called AutoComplete to guess the current entry based on data in the cells above:

	A	B
1	Inventory	
2	Inventory	
3		

Pressing Enter accepts the entry, or continuing to type replaces the AutoComplete entry.

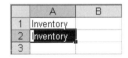

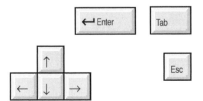

efficient data entry

An efficient method of entering data across a row is to use the Tab key, which enters the data and then selects the next cell in the row. Once the row is complete, Excel is able to recognize a pattern and pressing the Enter key selects the cell in the first column that contains data in the next row. For example, in the worksheet below cell A2 is selected when the Enter key is pressed:

	A	B	C	D	E
1	Item	Price	Quantity	Total	
2					

numeric keypad

The numeric keypad can make the entering of large amounts of numeric data more efficient. Most keyboards require pressing the Num Lock key on the numeric keypad before numbers can be entered.

replacing cell data

If a mistake is made when entering data, it can be corrected by selecting the cell and entering the correct data. The new data then replaces any previous data. If the mistake is noticed while typing the data, the Backspace key can be used to delete one character at a time.

8.5 Editing Cell Contents

> ### Editing in a Cell
>
> Cell contents can be edited by selecting a cell and then pressing the F2 key, which displays the insertion point in the cell.
>
> The insertion point is also displayed in the cell by double-clicking a cell.

Data in a cell is edited by first selecting the cell to display its contents on the Formula bar. Next, clicking the Formula bar creates an insertion point, which allows characters to be entered or deleted. The *insertion point* is a blinking vertical line that indicates where the next character typed will be placed. When the data has been corrected, the Enter button is clicked or the Enter key is pressed.

The contents of a selected cell are erased by pressing the Delete key. If a cell is cleared by mistake, immediately selecting Undo (Ctrl+Z) from the Edit menu or clicking the Undo button ( ) on the toolbar restores the contents of the cell. Clicking the Undo button arrow displays a list of the last 16 actions performed. Selecting an option from the list will undo that particular action. Note that saving a worksheet clears the list of any previous actions.

Practice 1

In this practice you will create a new workbook and enter data.

① *CREATE A NEW WORKBOOK*

   a. On the Taskbar, click Start → New Office Document. The New Office Document dialog box is displayed.

      1. Click the Blank Workbook icon to select it.
      2. Select OK. Excel starts and a new, empty workbook is created and the first worksheet in the workbook is displayed. Note the features of the Excel window.

② **ENTER COLUMN LABELS IN ROW 1**

    a. Note that A1 is the active cell. Type Name and then click the Enter button (☑). Cell A1 now contains the label Name. Note that the active cell's contents are displayed on the Formula bar.

    b. Press the right-arrow key to select cell B1, then type Test 1.

    c. Press the Tab key. The label is entered and the next cell in the row is active.

    d. Type Test 2.

    e. Press the Tab key. The label is entered and cell D1 is the active cell.

    f. Continue this procedure to place the labels Test 3 in cell D1 and Test 4 in cell E1.

③ **ENTER THE TEST DATES**

    a. Click cell B2 and type the date 1/7/2003. Click the Enter button. Note that Excel right aligns the date when it is entered into the cell.

    b. Select cell C2, type the date 2/9/2003 and then press the Tab key. The data is entered and D2 is now the active cell.

    c. Enter the date 3/1/2003 in cell D2 and the date 4/1/2003 in cell E2.

④ **ENTER THE STUDENT NAMES AND GRADES**

Enter the following labels and values starting in cell A4 by typing the label or value and pressing the Tab key to enter the data and move to the next cell in the row. Press Enter at the end of the row.

Jones, D.	85	73	88	95
Neave, C.	92	88	85	91
Garcia, E.	72	63	67	72
McCallister, T.	87	92	85	93
Smith, L.	94	91	93	84
Bell, M.	70	74	80	85

⑤ **EDIT A GRADE**

    a. Select cell E9.

    b. On the Formula bar, click to the right of the number 5. The insertion point appears.

    c. Press the Backspace key once to delete the number 5.

    d. Type a 3 and then press Enter. The grade is now an 83.

Check – Your worksheet should look similar to:

	A	B	C	D	E
1	Name	Test 1	Test 2	Test 3	Test 4
2		1/7/2003	2/9/2003	3/1/2003	4/1/2003
3					
4	Jones, D.	85	73	88	95
5	Neave, C.	92	88	85	91
6	Garcia, E.	72	63	67	72
7	McCalliste	87	92	85	93
8	Smith, L.	94	91	93	84
9	Bell, M.	70	74	80	83

Note that the appearance of the worksheet will be modified in Practice 2 and Practice 3.

8.6 Saving, Closing, and Opening a Workbook and Quitting Excel

Selecting <u>S</u>ave (Ctrl+S) from the <u>F</u>ile menu or clicking the Save button (🖫) on the toolbar saves the workbook. If the workbook is new and has not yet been named, the Save As dialog box is displayed. Excel uses the default name Book1 for a new workbook. This should be changed to a descriptive file name. Excel automatically adds the .xls extension to the file name. After saving a workbook, it should be closed if no longer needed by selecting <u>C</u>lose from the <u>F</u>ile menu or clicking the Close button (☒) in the upper-right corner of the workbook window.

If Excel is running, a workbook can be opened by selecting <u>O</u>pen (Ctrl+O) from the <u>F</u>ile menu or clicking the Open button (📂) on the toolbar, which displays the Open dialog box. A workbook can also be opened by selecting Open Office Document from the Start menu, which displays the Open Office Document dialog box.

When Excel is no longer needed, it should be quit properly so that any worksheets in memory are not damaged or lost. Quitting Excel means that the application window is closed and the program is no longer in the computer's memory. Excel is quit by selecting E<u>x</u>it from the <u>F</u>ile menu or clicking the Close button (☒) in the upper-right corner of the application window. Attempting to quit Excel with an open worksheet that has been edited but not saved displays a dialog box asking if you want to save the worksheet.

8.7 Previewing and Printing a Worksheet

Selecting Print Pre<u>v</u>iew from the <u>F</u>ile menu or clicking the Print Preview button (🔍) on the toolbar displays the worksheet as it will appear when printed. Features of Print Preview include:

    Zoom button   Enlarges the view so the data is easier to read.

    Close button   Returns to Normal view. Pressing the Esc key also returns to Normal view.

    Print button   Displays the Print dialog box.

The worksheet can be printed by clicking the Print button, which displays the Print dialog box. Selecting OK prints the portion of the worksheet that contains data. A worksheet should be saved before it is printed since a problem with the printer could cause the program to stop responding, resulting in the worksheet being lost.

A worksheet can also be printed by selecting <u>P</u>rint (Ctrl+P) from the <u>F</u>ile menu, which displays the Print dialog box. Selecting OK prints the portion of the worksheet that contains data. Clicking the Print button on the toolbar prints one copy of the worksheet using the default settings without displaying the Print dialog box.

gridlines
row and column headings

Gridlines and row and column headings can make a worksheet printout easier to read. *Gridlines* are solid lines that mark off the rows and columns, similar to what appears on the screen in Excel. *Row* and *column headings* are the row numbers and column letters. Selecting Page Setup from the File menu displays the Page Setup dialog box. Selecting the Sheet tab displays those options:

Selecting the Gridlines and Row and column headings check boxes and then selecting OK displays gridlines and row and column headings when the worksheet is previewed or printed.

8.8 Adding a Header and Footer

Information such as the date or the file name can be included in a header or footer to help identify printouts. Headers and footers are automatically printed at the top and bottom of each worksheet page, respectively. A header or footer is added to a worksheet by selecting Page Setup from the File menu, which displays the Page Setup dialog box. Selecting the Header/Footer tab displays those options:

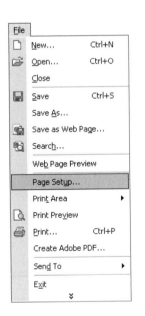

Headers and Footers

Headers and footers can also be added in Print Preview. In Print Preview, selecting the Setup button displays the Page Setup dialog box. Selecting the Header/Footer tab displays those options.

Selecting Custom Header or Custom Footer displays another dialog box where header or footer text is entered. For example, selecting Custom Header displays the Header dialog box:

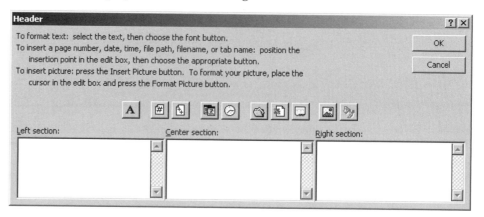

Text typed in the Left section, Center section, or Right section boxes is left, center, or right aligned in the header, respectively. Buttons in the dialog box are used to insert codes at the insertion point:

A Font button formats header and footer text.

Page Number button inserts the current page number.

Date button inserts the current date.

Time button inserts the current time.

When the worksheet is previewed or printed, the codes are replaced with the appropriate information.

Practice 2

In this practice you will add headers and footers to a worksheet and then save the worksheet. The worksheet created in Practice 1 should still be displayed.

① CREATE A HEADER AND A FOOTER

Select File → Page Setup. A dialog box is displayed.

1. Select the Header/Footer tab if those options are not already displayed.
2. Select Custom Header. The Header dialog box is displayed.
   a. Click in the Center section box. The insertion point appears.
   b. Click the Date button ( ). The code &[Date] is placed in the box.
   c. Select OK. The dialog box is removed.
3. Select Custom Footer. The Footer dialog box is displayed.
   a. Click in the Right section box and then type your name.
   b. Select OK. The dialog box is removed.
4. Select OK. The dialog box is removed.

② PREVIEW THE WORKSHEET

a. Select File → Print Preview. The worksheet is displayed in the Print Preview window. Note the header and footer. Also note how it is difficult to read the worksheet data because there are no gridlines or row and column headings.
b. Select Close to return to Normal view.

c. Select File → Page Setup. A dialog box is displayed.

  1. Select the Sheet tab to display those options.

  2. Select the Gridlines check box.

  3. Select the Row and column headings check box.

  4. Select OK. The dialog box is removed.

d. On the toolbar, click the Print Preview button (🔍). Note how much easier the worksheet is to read.

e. Select Close to return to Normal view.

③ *SAVE THE WORKBOOK AND THEN PRINT THE WORKSHEET*

a. Select File → Save. A dialog box is displayed.

  1. Use the Save in box and the contents box below it to select the appropriate location for the file to be saved.

  2. In the File name box, replace the existing text with Grades.

  3. Select Save. The workbook is saved and the dialog box removed.

b. Select File → Print. A dialog box is displayed.

  1. Select OK. The printout contains the worksheet with a header, footer, gridlines, and row and column headings.

④ *CLOSE GRADES*

  Select File → Close.

8.9 Changing the Width of a Column

The Width Command

The width of a column can be increased or decreased by selecting Width from the Column submenu in the Format menu, which displays the Column Width dialog box. Typing a number in the Column width box and then selecting OK changes the width of the column that contains the active cell.

The width of multiple columns can be changed to the same width by first selecting the columns and then dragging the right boundary of one of the columns or selecting the Width command.

The width of a column can affect the way Excel displays numeric data. If a cell is not wide enough to display its value, scientific notation is used. For example, the value 123456789012 is displayed as 1.23457E+11. Labels are displayed in their entirety until they encounter another cell that contains data. For example, typing This is a long label in cell A1 produces:

	A	B	C
1	This is a long label		
2			

Cell A1 stores This is a long label. Even though B1 appears to contain data, it is empty. Entering data in cell B1 produces:

	A	B	C
1	This is a lc	Label 2	
2			

Cell A1 still stores This is a long label, but only the characters that fit in the width of the cell are displayed. The full contents can be seen on the Formula bar when cell A1 is the active cell. The entire label in A1 can be displayed by changing the width of column A.

The width of a column is changed by dragging the right boundary of the column. Pointing to the *boundary*, the bar separating the column letters at the top of the worksheet, changes the pointer to ↔:

boundary

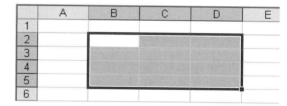

Dragging the boundary changes the width of column C

Dragging the boundary to the right increases the width of the column, and dragging to the left decreases the width. Note that the width of the entire column is changed. The width of a single cell cannot be changed.

Another technique for changing the width of a column is to double-click the right boundary of the column. This changes the column width so that it is just wide enough to display the data it contains.

8.10   Selecting Cells

Adjacent worksheet cells can be selected together to form a range. *Adjacent cells* are cells that are next to each other. A *range* is a selection of two or more cells. Dragging the pointer from one cell to another is one way to create a range:

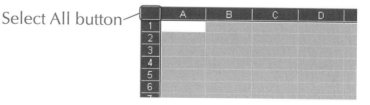

The pointer was placed on cell B2 and then dragged to cell D5 to create this range

Another way to create a range is to first select the starting cell, then hold down the Shift key and click the last cell in the range.

An entire row or column is selected by first pointing to a row number or column letter, which displays an arrow indicating what row or column is being selected, and then clicking the row number or column letter.

Clicking the Select All button selects the entire worksheet:

Select All button ―

The keyboard can also be used to select a range by first selecting the starting cell, then holding down the Shift key and using the arrow keys to define the range.

8.11   Alignments and Fonts

Formatting is applied to cells to make the data easier to understand. Formatting does not change the data stored in a cell, only the way it is displayed.

Changing Row Height

Row height can be increased or decreased by dragging the bottom boundary of the row number or by selecting H<u>e</u>ight from the <u>R</u>ow submenu in the F<u>o</u>rmat menu.

adjacent cells, range

Entering the Same Data

The same data can be entered into more than one cell by selecting a range of cells, typing the data, and then pressing Ctrl+Enter.

Shift

selecting rows and columns

select all

Selecting Non-adjacent Cells

A range can consist of non-adjacent cells. A range of non-adjacent cells is created by selecting the first cell or range of cells and then holding down the Ctrl key and selecting other cells or ranges.

A Guide to Microsoft Office XP Professional

Cell Alignment

The Orientation option in the Format Cells dialog box is used to rotate cell contents.

The Vertical list in the Format Cells dialog box is used to change the vertical alignment of data in a cell when the height of the cell is larger than the data in it.

Clearing Cell Formats

Selecting Formats from the Clear submenu in the Edit menu removes any formatting applied to the active cell and leaves the data unchanged.

Selecting All from the Clear submenu in the Edit menu removes the contents and formatting of the active cell.

Character Formatting

When the active cell is formatted, the entire contents of the cell are affected. To format only a few characters in an active cell, select the characters on the Formula bar and then apply the format.

Font Size

Changing the font size of worksheet labels can help distinguish between labels, such as titles and column headings, and the data. The row height adjusts automatically when the font size is changed.

Unless cells are formatted otherwise, labels are left aligned, and values and times/dates are right aligned. For this reason, labels and values displayed in the same column do not line up. For example, the test labels and dates in the Grades worksheet do not align in the column.

Selecting Cells from the Format menu displays the Format Cells dialog box. Selecting the Alignment tab displays those options:

Selecting Left (Indent), Center, or Right (Indent) from the Horizontal list and then selecting OK changes the alignment of the active cell accordingly. The Align Left (▤), Center (▤), and Align Right (▤) buttons on the toolbar can also be used to change the alignment of the active cell.

Selecting the Wrap text check box allows for more than one line of text within a cell. Excel automatically determines if the next word will fit or if it must go to the next line in the cell. This feature is useful for long column headings.

Selecting the Font tab in the Format Cells dialog box displays options for changing the font, font size, and style of the data in a selected cell:

8.12 Formatting Numeric Data

Cells storing numeric data should be properly formatted to reflect the type of value stored. For example, values representing money should display a $ sign and two decimal places. Selecting Cells (Ctrl+1) from the Format menu displays the Format Cells dialog box. Selecting the Number tab displays those options:

![Format Cells dialog box showing Number tab with Category list (General, Number highlighted, Currency, Accounting, Date, Time, Percentage, Fraction, Scientific, Text, Special, Custom), Sample area, Decimal places: 2, Use 1000 Separator (,) checkbox, and Negative numbers list (-1234.10 highlighted, 1234.10, (1234.10), (1234.10)). Text at bottom reads: "Number is used for general display of numbers. Currency and Accounting offer specialized formatting for monetary value." OK and Cancel buttons.]

- **Number** formats the active cell to display values with two decimal places.

- **Currency** formats the active cell to display values with a dollar sign and two decimal places.

- **Accounting** is similar to Currency except the dollar sign aligns itself at the left edge of the cell. Clicking the Currency Style button (**$**) on the toolbar is the same as applying the Accounting format.

- **Percentage** formats the active cell to display values as a percentage with two decimal places. For example, a cell storing the value 0.15 formatted as percentage displays 15.00%. Clicking the Percent Style button (**%**) on the toolbar formats the cell as percentage with no decimal places.

- **Scientific** formats the active cell to display values in scientific notation with two decimal places.

There are three options associated with numeric formats. The number of decimal places can be changed by selecting or typing a number in the Decimal places box. For large numbers, the Use 1000 Separator (,) check box displays values with separating commas, such as 1,000,000. The Negative numbers list displays different formats for negative numbers.

Merge and Center

Data entered into a single cell can be centered across several cells that are combined or merged together. Data is centered across several cells by first entering the data in the upper left-most cell, selecting the cells to merge, and then clicking the Merge and Center button (▦) on the toolbar.

Merged cells can be split by selecting the merged cells and then clicking the Merge and Center button.

Displaying the Format Cells Dialog Box

The Format Cells dialog box can also be displayed by right-clicking a cell or range of cells and then selecting Format Cells from the menu.

Getting Rid of

Formatting a value in a cell may add additional characters to the value. For example, selecting the Currency Style button adds a dollar sign, a decimal point, and two decimal places to the value.

If the column is not wide enough to display the additional characters, a series of number signs (###) is displayed in the cell. Increasing the width of the column removes the number signs and displays the value and its formatting.

> ### Decimal Places
>
> The number of decimal places in the format of the active cell can be changed by selecting the Increase Decimal button (⊞) or the Decrease Decimal button (⊞) on the toolbar.

A cell is automatically formatted if a $, %, or a decimal position is typed with the number. For example, entering $45.67 in a cell formats that cell to display any number with a dollar sign and two decimal places. If 34 is then entered in that cell, $34.00 is displayed. Entering 45% in a cell formats that cell to display any number with a percent sign and no decimal places. If 55.3 is then entered in that cell, 55% is displayed.

Formatting a cell does not change the value that is stored in the cell, only how that value is displayed. Number signs (####) are displayed if a cell is not wide enough to display the formatted number.

time/date   Time/date values can also be formatted by selecting one of the many Date or Time options in the Format Cells dialog box. Examples of date formats include 3-14-01 and March 14, 2001. Examples of time formats include 1:30:55 PM and 1:30 PM.

Format Painter button

Cell formatting can be copied to another cell or range of cells by first selecting the cell that contains the formatting to be copied and then selecting the Format Painter button (🖌) on the toolbar, which changes the pointer to ⊹🖌. Clicking a cell or range of cells copies the selected cell's formatting.

Practice 3 ↻

In this practice you will format the Grades workbook. Start Excel if it is not already running.

① *OPEN GRADES*

   a. Select File → Open. A dialog box is displayed.

   1. Use the Look in list and the contents box below it to display the file name Grades, which was last modified in Practice 2.

   2. In the contents box, click Grades.

   3. Select Open. The Grades workbook is displayed.

② *BOLD THE NAME LABEL*

   a. Select cell A1.

   b. On the toolbar, click the Bold button (**B**). The label is now bold.

③ *WIDEN COLUMN A BY DRAGGING*

   Note that the label in cell A7 is cut off because the column is too narrow to display it entirely.

   a. Point to the boundary between columns A and B. The pointer changes to ↔.

   b. Drag the boundary to the right approximately halfway across column B. Column A should be wide enough to display the entire label in cell A7. If not, drag the column boundary farther to the right.

④ *RIGHT ALIGN AND BOLD THE TEST LABELS*

   a. Drag the pointer from cell B1 to cell D1. Cells B1 through D1 are selected as a range.

   b. Select Format → Cells. A dialog box is displayed.

   1. Select the Alignment tab if those options are not already displayed.

   2. In the Horizontal list, select Right (Indent).

   3. In the Indent box, select or type 0 if it is not already displayed.

4. Select the Font tab. The font options are displayed.

5. In the Font style list, select Bold.

6. Select OK. The labels are right aligned and bold.

⑤ COPY CELL FORMAT

a. Select cell D1.

b. On the toolbar, click the Format Painter button (🖌). The pointer changes to ⬥🖌 when moved onto the worksheet.

c. Click cell E1. The format of cell D1 is copied to cell E1.

⑥ FORMAT THE DATES

a. Select cell B2.

b. Hold the Shift key down and then click cell E2. Cells B2 through E2 are selected as a range.

c. Select Format → Cells. A dialog box is displayed.

1. Select the Number tab. The number formatting options are displayed.

2. In the Category list, click Date if it is not already selected.

3. Scroll the Type list if necessary until a date similar to 3/14/01 is displayed.

4. Click the date to select it.

5. Select OK. The dates in row 2 now display the year with two digits.

⑦ SAVE AND CLOSE THE MODIFIED GRADES

a. Select File → Save. The workbook is saved.

b. Select File → Close. The workbook is removed from Excel.

⑧ QUIT EXCEL

Select File → Exit. Excel is removed from the screen.

8.13 Using Formulas to Perform Calculations

One benefit of using a worksheet is its ability to perform calculations using formulas. *Formulas* are mathematical statements used to calculate values. Every formula in Excel must begin with an equal sign (=). For example, entering the formula =25 * 3 in a cell displays the value 75.

The following mathematical operators can be used in a formula:

Exponentiation	^
Multiplication	*
Division	/
Addition	+
Subtraction	−

Exponentiation means to raise a value to a power and is represented by the caret (^) symbol. For example, $2^3 = 8$ is expressed as $2 \wedge 3 = 8$.

The Formula Bar

The Formula bar displays the contents of the active cell instead of the value displayed in the cell. For example, if the Formula bar shows =2+3, the cell displays 5. When looking for errors in a worksheet, the Formula bar is the first place to start.

Remembering the Order of Operations

To remember the order of operations, memorize this simple phrase:

Please
Excuse
My **D**ear
Aunt **S**ally

The initials correspond to the order in which a mathematical expression is evaluated:

Parenthesis
Exponents
Multiply **D**ivide
Add **S**ubtract

Excel evaluates a mathematical expression using a specific *order of operations*. Exponentiation is performed first, multiplication and division next, and then addition and subtraction. Two operators of the same precedence, for example + and –, are evaluated in order from left to right. For example, the expression 5 + 2 * 3 – 1 evaluates to 10 because multiplication is performed first and then the addition and subtraction. For example:

Formula	Resulting value
=2*2+3*2	10
=25*8/4	50
=35+12/3	39
=3+5*8+7	50

The order in which Excel evaluates a mathematical expression can be changed by including parentheses in the expression. Operations within parentheses are evaluated first. For example, the result of (5 + 2) * 3 – 1 is 20 because 5 and 2 were added before the multiplication and subtraction was performed. For example:

Formula	Resulting value
=(3+5)*(8+7)	120
=3^2*8-4	68
=6+2^2	10
=(6+2)^2	64

error checking

When a formula is entered in a cell, Excel automatically checks the formula for errors. Entering an invalid formula in a cell causes Excel to display an error value in the cell and a triangle in the upper-left corner of the cell. For example, a number cannot be divided by zero because the result is mathematically undefined. Therefore, entering =10/0 displays #DIV/0! in the cell.

Triangle Indicators

The triangle indicators that appear in cells have different meanings depending on the triangle's placement and color.

A green triangle in the upper-left corner of a cell indicates an error. A red triangle in the upper-right corner of a cell indicates a comment has been added to the cell. A comment is a note that explains the cell's contents. A purple triangle in the lower-right corner of a cell indicates a smart tag. Smart tags recognize certain types of data that are commonly used in other applications.

Selecting the cell with the error value displays the Trace Error button (◈) to the left of the cell. Clicking the Trace Error button displays a list of options:

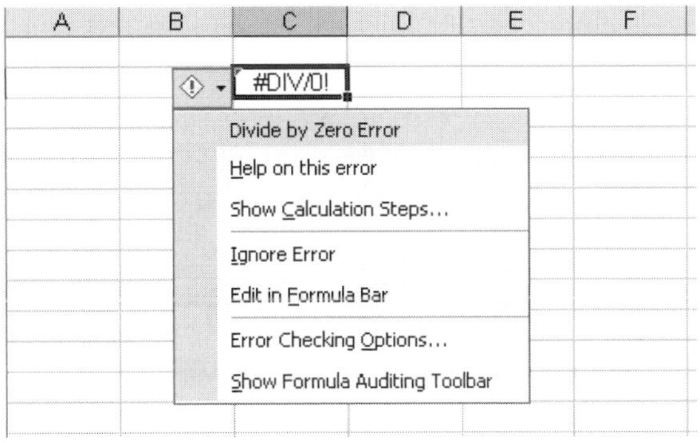

The error is described in the top gray line of the list. Selecting Ignore Error removes the Trace Error button and the triangle from the worksheet. Selecting Edit in Formula Bar places the formula on the Formula bar where it can be edited.

Practice 4

In this practice you will enter formulas into the cells of a new, empty workbook to perform calculations.

① **CREATE A NEW WORKBOOK**

② **ENTER LABELS**

    a. Enter the label Example Formulas in cell A1.

    b. Bold the label. Note that the text extends into the next cell.

    c. Double-click the boundary between columns A and B. Column A is widened just enough to display the label.

    d. Select cell A2 and enter the label Formula.

    e. Select cell B2 and enter the label Result.

    f. Italicize both labels and right align the label in cell B2.

③ **ENTER A LABEL AND A FORMULA**

    a. Select cell A3.

    b. Type 20/50 and then click the Enter button. The result is a label because it is not preceded by an equal sign.

    c. Select cell B3.

    d. Type =20/50 and then click the Enter button. The result 0.4 is displayed. Note that the formula is displayed on the Formula bar, and the result of the formula is shown in the cell:

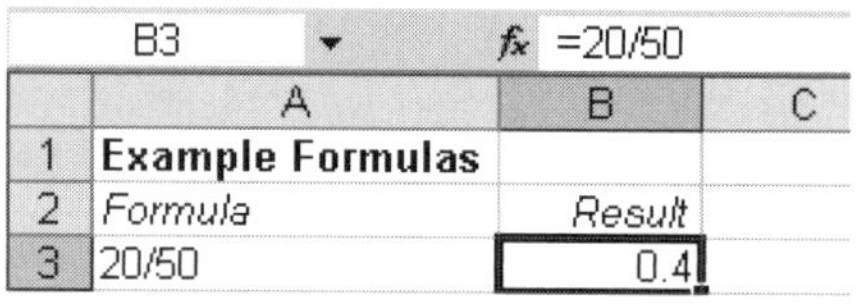

B3		▼	f_x =20/50	
	A		B	C
1	**Example Formulas**			
2	*Formula*		*Result*	
3	20/50		0.4	

④ **ENTER FORMULAS**

    a. Enter each of the labels and formulas shown below in the cells indicated. Note the resulting values of the formulas:

In cell **A4** enter	20*50	In cell **B4** enter	=20*50	to display	1000
A5	20–50	**B5**	=20–50		–30
A6	2+20*5+50	**B6**	=2+20*5+50		152
A7	(2+20)*(5+50)	**B7**	=(2+20)*(5+50)		1210
A8	20/0	**B8**	=20/0		#DIV/0!

    b. Select cell B8 if it is not already selected. Note the triangle in the top-left corner and the Trace Error button (⬦).

    c. Click the Trace Error button. A list of options is displayed. Note the first entry indicates the formula contains a "Divide by Zero Error".

        1. Select Ignore Error. The triangle and the Trace Error button are removed.

⑤ **SAVE THE WORKBOOK**

    Save the workbook in the appropriate folder naming it Formula Examples.

8.14 Using Cell References in Formulas

A cell reference may be used in a formula so that the value stored in the cell is used in the calculation of the formula. When Excel evaluates the formula, it uses the cell reference to locate the value needed in the calculation. For example, in the worksheet below cell C1 contains a formula that references values in cells A1 and B1:

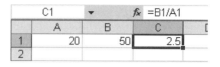

C1	▼	*fx* =B1/A1	
	A	B	C
1	20	50	2.5
2			

Circular References

A circular reference occurs when a cell's formula refers to itself. For example, placing the formula =B5–C1 in cell B5 creates a circular reference.

A circular reference also occurs when a cell's formula refers to another cell that contains a cell reference to the current cell. For example, placing the formula =B5–C1 in cell D10 creates a circular reference if either B5 or C1 contain a formula that references D10.

A dialog box is displayed if a circular reference occurs.

As a cell reference is typed, the border of the referenced cell is outlined in a colored border. Cell references can be typed in uppercase or lowercase letters. However, Excel automatically converts a cell reference to uppercase letters when entered.

Formulas that contain cell references are automatically recalculated when the value in a referenced cell changes. For example, in the worksheet below, cell D2 contains a formula that references cells B2 and C2. If the value in cell B2 or C2 changes, the formula will automatically recalculate:

D2	▼	*fx* =B2*C2		
	A	B	C	D
1	Item	Price	Quantity	Total
2	Pen	$1.00	100	$100.00
3				

A formula cannot reference the cell it is stored in. For example, the formulas above cannot be stored in cells B2 or C2 because this would cause an error called a *circular reference*.

Practice 5

In this practice you will enter formulas that contain cell references. Open Formula Examples if it is not already displayed.

① *ENTER A LABEL AND VALUES*

    a. Select cell A10 and enter the label Example Formulas with Cell References.

    b. Bold the label.

    c. Select cell A11 and enter the label Formula.

    d. Select cell B11 and enter the label Result.

    e. Italicize both labels and right align the label in cell B11.

    f. Select cell E10 and enter the value 20.

    g. Select cell F10 and enter the value 50.

② ENTER FORMULAS

    a. Select cell A12.

    b. Type E10/F10 and then click the Enter button. The result is a label because it is not preceded by an equal sign.

    c. Select cell B12.

    d. Enter the formula =E10/F10. Note that as a cell reference is typed, the border of the cell is outlined in a colored border. The result 0.4 is displayed.

    e. Enter each of the labels and formulas shown below in the cells indicated. Note the resulting values of the formulas:

In cell	enter		in cell	enter	to display
A13	E10*F10		**B13**	=E10*F10	1000
A14	E10-F10		**B14**	=E10–F10	–30
A15	2+E10*5+F10		**B15**	=2+E10*5+F10	152
A16	(2+E10)*(5+F10)		**B16**	=(2+E10)*(5+F10)	1210
A17	E10^2+F10^2		**B17**	=E10^2+F10^2	2900
A18	(E10+F10)^2		**B18**	=(E10+F10)^2	4900

③ CHANGE THE VALUE IN CELL E10

    a. Select cell E10.

    b. Enter 30 to replace the current value. Every formula in the worksheet referencing cell E10 is automatically recalculated. A key advantage of using formulas with cell references is that they automatically recalculate when values in the cells they reference change.

Check – Your worksheet should look similar to:

	A	B	C	D	E	F
1	**Example Formulas**					
2	*Formula*	*Result*				
3	20/50	0.4				
4	20*50	1000				
5	20-50	-30				
6	2+20*5+50	152				
7	(2+20)*(5+50)	1210				
8	20/0	#DIV/0!				
9						
10	**Example Formulas with Cell References**				30	50
11	*Formula*	*Result*				
12	E10/F10	0.6				
13	E10*F10	1500				
14	2+E10*5+F10	202				
15	(2+E10)*(5+F10)	1760				
16	E10^2+F10^2	3400				
17	(E10+F10)^2	6400				

④ SAVE, PRINT, AND THEN CLOSE THE MODIFIED FORMULA EXAMPLES

    a. Create a header with the date center aligned and a footer with your name right aligned.

    b. Save the modified Formula Examples.

    c. Print a copy of the worksheet.

    d. Close the workbook.

8.15 Using Functions to Perform Calculations

function
arguments

For performing common calculations, Excel contains built-in functions that can be included in a formula. A *function* performs a calculation that results in a single value. A function requires data, called *arguments*, to perform its calculation. The arguments of a function are enclosed in parentheses after the function name and are usually cell references.

SUM function

The *SUM function* adds the values of the cells in the range. For example, to add the values stored in cells A1, B5, and E7, a formula that contains the built-in SUM function can be used:

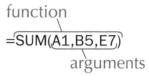

In the example above, the values to be summed are stored in nonadjacent cells. Therefore, the SUM arguments are separated by commas. When adjacent cells are the arguments of a function, a range of cells may be referenced by typing the first cell reference followed by a colon (:) and then the last cell reference. For example, to add the values in cells G1, G2, and G3, a range is used:

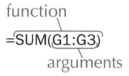

Typing Functions

Functions can be typed in uppercase or lowercase letters. However, Excel automatically converts a function to uppercase letters when entered.

As a range is typed, the border of the range is outlined with a colored border and the value produced from the calculation is formatted with the same format as the argument cells.

Functions are useful because they often make a formula shorter and less error-prone, especially when a large range of cells is involved. As a function is being typed, an argument tooltip is displayed illustrating the structure, or syntax, of the function:

```
=sum(
SUM(number1, [number2], ...)
```

AVERAGE function

Another function is AVERAGE, which adds the values of the cells in the range and then divides the result by the number of cells in the range. For example, the formula =AVERAGE(C12:C17) sums the values in cells C12, C13, C14, C15, C16, and C17 and then divides the total by 6.

The SUM and AVERAGE functions ignore cells that contain text or are empty when their cell references are included as arguments.

If a formula cannot produce a result, an error value is displayed in the cell. For example, the #DIV/0 error value indicates the formula is trying to divide by zero. Other common error values include:

#REF The formula contains a reference that is not valid.

#NUM A numeric value is invalid, such as a value that is too large or too small.

#VALUE The formula is using the wrong type of argument, such as a label instead of a value.

The result of the formula is too wide to fit in the column. If the result should fit in the column, check the formula for errors. This error value can also indicate that the result of the formula is a negative time or date value.

Selecting the cell with the error value displays the Trace Error button (⟐) to the left of the cell. Clicking the Trace Error button displays a list of options for correcting the error.

Practice 6

In this practice you will use functions to calculate the total and average sales for a candy store.

① *OPEN CANDY SALES*

Open CANDY SALES, which is a data file for this text.

② *FORMAT THE CELLS*

　a. Select cells B3 through B11. The sales amounts are selected as a range.

　b. Select Format → Cells. A dialog box is displayed.

　　　1. Select the Number tab if those options are not already displayed.

　　　2. In the Category list, select Currency.

　　　3. Select or type 2 in the Decimal places box if it is not already there.

　　　4. Select OK. The values are displayed as currency with 2 decimal places.

③ *USE A FUNCTION TO SUM THE VALUES*

Select cell B12 and enter the formula:

　　=SUM(B3:B11)

The sum $300,632.03 is displayed. Note how the total is also formatted as currency because it is summing values that have already been formatted as currency.

④ *USE A FUNCTION TO AVERAGE THE VALUES*

Select cell B13 and enter the formula:

　　=AVERAGE(B3:B11)

The average sales, $33,403.56, is displayed in cell B13.

⑤ *CREATE A HEADER AND FOOTER*

Create a header with the date center aligned and a footer with your name right aligned.

⑥ *SAVE, PRINT, AND THEN CLOSE THE MODIFIED CANDY SALES*

8.17   Entering Formulas - Pointing

When typing a formula, cell references can be entered by pointing. *Pointing* is a technique where a formula is typed up to where a cell reference should appear and then a cell is clicked, which places its reference in the formula. Selecting a range of cells places the cell range in the formula. Pointing is the best method for entering cell references into a formula because typing errors are avoided.

For example, in the worksheet below, =SUM(was typed into cell C5. The range was then entered into the formula by dragging the pointer from cell C2 to cell C4. The colon (:) is automatically inserted by Excel:

	A	B	C	D	E
SUM	▼ ✗ ✓ *ƒx* =sum(C2:C4				
1	Product Number	Product Name	Inventory		
2	001-787-0	Lawn Chair	529		
3	001-498-2	Umbrella	120		
4	006-211-8	Outdoor Table	70		
5		Inventory Total:	=sum(C2:C4		
6			SUM(**number1**, [number2], ...)		
7					

Selecting a block of cells enters its range into a formula

The formula is completed by clicking the Enter button or pressing the Enter key. Note that Excel automatically adds a right parenthesis.

8.18   Displaying Formulas

Worksheet formulas are displayed at their cell locations by pressing Ctrl+` (grave accent):

	A	B	C	D	E
1	Product Number	Product Name	Inventory	Unit Price	Total
2	001-787-0	Lawn Chair	529	$10.00	$5,290.00
3	001-498-2	Umbrella	120	$15.00	$1,800.00
4	006-211-8	Outdoor Table	70	$20.00	$1,400.00
5		Inventory Total:	719		$8,490.00

Before pressing Ctrl+`

	A	B	C	D	E
1	Product Number	Product Name	Inventory	Unit Price	Total
2	001-787-0	Lawn Chair	529	10	=C2*D2
3	001-498-2	Umbrella	120	15	=C3*D3
4	006-211-8	Outdoor Table	70	20	=C4*D4
5		Inventory Total:	=SUM(C2:C4)		=SUM(E2:E4)
6					
7		Formula Auditing ▼ ✗			
8					
9					

After pressing Ctrl+`

The grave accent key is located above the Tab key on the keyboard. When formulas are displayed, column widths may need adjusting. The Formula Auditing toolbar, which contains advanced formula editing features, is automatically displayed.

Displaying formulas does not change the worksheet, only the way it is displayed. Printing when formulas are displayed prints the formulas stored in the cells rather than the values. Pressing Ctrl+` again removes the Format Auditing toolbar and displays values in each cell, although any column widths that were increased remain wider and need to be reformatted.

Practice 7 ↻

In this practice you will enter formulas to calculate the average grade on a test and a student's average in the Grades worksheet.

① *OPEN GRADES*

Open Grades, which was last modified in Practice 3.

② *USE A FORMULA TO AVERAGE THE GRADES FOR TEST 1*

    a. Select cell B10.

    b. Type =AVERAGE(

    c. Select cells B4 to B9. Excel enters the cell references for the selected range into the formula.

    d. Press Enter. The average for Test 1, 83.33333, is displayed in cell B10.

③ *CALCULATE A STUDENT'S AVERAGE*

Select cell F4 and use pointing to enter the formula =AVERAGE(B4:E4). The average 85.25 is displayed.

④ *ADD TITLES FOR THE NEW INFORMATION*

    a. Select cell F1 and enter the label Student Average.

    b. Format the label as bold and right aligned if it is not already formatted.

    c. Change the column width so that the label is displayed entirely.

    d. Select cell A10 and enter the label Test Average.

    e. Format the label as italic and right aligned.

⑤ *VIEW AND PRINT THE FORMULAS*

    a. Save the modified Grades.

    b. Press Ctrl+` (located above the Tab key). Worksheet formulas are displayed at their cell locations and the Formula Auditing toolbar is displayed.

    c. Press Ctrl+` to again display only the values of each cell.

⑥ *SAVE THE MODIFIED GRADES*

8.19　Copying Adjacent Cells

Fill handle

Cell contents are copied to adjacent cells using the Fill handle. The *Fill handle* is the solid square in the lower-right corner of a selected cell or range:

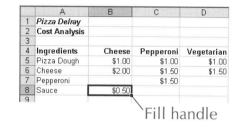

Fill handle

The pointer changes to **+** when placed on the Fill handle. Dragging the Fill handle copies the contents of the selected cell or range to the selected adjacent cells:

	A	B	C	D	E
1	*Pizza Delray*				
2	**Cost Analysis**				
3					
4	**Ingredients**	**Cheese**	**Pepperoni**	**Vegetarian**	
5	Pizza Dough	$1.00	$1.00	$1.00	
6	Cheese	$2.00	$1.50	$1.50	
7	Pepperoni		$1.50		
8	Sauce	$0.50	$0.50	$0.50	
9					

The contents of cell B8 is copied to adjacent cells by dragging the Fill handle

When the Fill handle is used to copy cell contents, the Auto Fill Options button (⊞) is displayed below and to the right of the last cell in the range. The Auto Fill Options button is removed when a key is pressed or a command is selected.

Commands from the Fill submenu in the Edit menu can also be used to copy the contents of a cell to adjacent selected cells. Down (Ctrl+D) is used if the selected cells are in a column, and Right (Ctrl+R) is used if the selected cells are in a row.

8.20　Copying Formulas

When a formula is copied, the cell references in the formula are automatically changed relative to the new row or column. For example, in the worksheet below, cell B10 contains the formula =SUM(B5:B9). Copying this cell to cells C10 and D10 creates the formula =SUM(C5:C9) in cell C10 and =SUM(D5:D9) in cell D10.

Series

If a cell contains a date, time, or a combination of text and a number, then a series is created when the Fill handle is dragged. For example, in the spreadsheet below, cells A1 through A3 were selected and then the Fill handle dragged to cell C3:

	A	B	C
1	Jan	Feb	Mar
2	2:00 PM	3:00 PM	4:00 PM
3	Test 1	Test 2	Test 3

A series of numbers is also created by selecting two cells and then dragging the Fill handle. For example, selecting a cell that contains 2 and an adjacent cell that contains 4 and then dragging the Fill handle produces a series of even numbers; 6, 8, 10, and so on.

The Auto Fill Options Button

Clicking the Auto Fill Options button displays a list of options including:

Copy Cells is the default setting that copies both the cell contents and formatting.

Fill Series creates a series out of the copied data.

Fill Formatting Only copies the format from the selected cell and not the content.

Fill Without Formatting copies the cell contents and not the formatting.

	A	B	C	D
1	*Pizza Delray*			
2	**Cost Analysis**			
3				
4	**Ingredients**	**Cheese**	**Pepperoni**	**Vegetarian**
5	Pizza Dough	$1.00	$1.00	$1.00
6	Cheese	$2.00	$1.50	$1.50
7	Pepperoni		$1.50	
8	Sauce	$0.50	$0.50	$0.50
9	Vegetables			$1.25
10	**Total Cost**	**$3.50**	**$4.50**	**$4.25**

relative cell references

Cell references that reflect the row or column they have been copied to are called *relative cell references*.

Rounding vs. Formatting

Formatting only affects the way information is displayed. Whereas, the ROUND function changes the value stored in a cell.

Excel follows certain rules when rounding numbers. A number with a decimal portion greater than or equal to 0.5 is rounded up and a number with a decimal portion less than 0.5 is rounded down.

A negative number as the second argument of the ROUND function rounds a value to the nearest 10s, 100s, etc. For example =ROUND(72.86,-1) displays 70. The formula =ROUND(72.866,-2) displays 100.

8.21   The ROUND Function

The ROUND function changes a value by rounding it to a specific number of decimal places. The first argument of the ROUND function is the value to be rounded, and the second argument is the number of decimal places to which the result is rounded. For example, to round the value stored in cell C16 to one decimal place, the formula =ROUND(C16,1) is used. If the value stored in C16 is 42.851, the rounded result is 42.9.

Often the result of a formula should be rounded. For example, the test averages should be rounded to 1 decimal places in the Grades worksheet. This means that the class average on Test 1 would be computed as 83.3, not 83.33333. To round the result of a formula, the formula is the first argument and the desired number of decimal places to round to is the second argument. For example, the average of all the Test 1 grades is rounded to 1 decimal place with the formula:

=ROUND(AVERAGE(B3:B8),1)

To round a value to the nearest whole number, a 0 can be used to indicate no decimal places: =ROUND(AVERAGE(B3:B8),0).

Practice 8

In this practice you will copy the formulas in the Grades worksheet and use the ROUND function. Open Grades if it is not already displayed.

① COPY A FORMULA USING THE FILL HANDLE

    a. Select cell B10. Note the Fill handle in the lower-right corner of the cell.

    b. Point to the Fill handle of the cell. The pointer changes to **+**.

    c. Drag the Fill handle from cell B10 to cell E10. The formula is copied to cells C10 through E10 and the Auto Fill Options button is displayed. The Auto Fill Options button will not be used and should be ignored.

    d. Select cell E10. Note that the formula displayed on the Formula bar shows how the cell references have been automatically changed.

② COPY ANOTHER FORMULA USING THE FILL HANDLE

    a. Select cell F4.

b. Drag the Fill handle from cell F4 to cell F9. The formula is copied. The first Auto Fill Options button is removed and another Auto Fill Options button appears below and to the right of cell F9. The Auto Fill Options button will not be used and should be ignored.

③ ROUND A TEST AVERAGE TO 1 DECIMAL PLACE
    a. Select cell B10.
    b. On the Formula bar, click between the equal sign and the word AVERAGE and type: ROUND(
    c. Click at the end of the formula and type ,1) so that the formula on the Formula bar is:

$$=ROUND(AVERAGE(B4:B9),1)$$

    Click the Enter button. The average is now rounded to 1 decimal place, 83.3.

④ ROUND ALL TEST AVERAGES TO 1 DECIMAL PLACE
    a. Select cell B10 if it is not already selected.
    b. Drag the Fill handle from cell B10 to cell E10. The formula is copied.

⑤ ROUND A STUDENT AVERAGE TO 1 DECIMAL PLACE
    a. Select cell F4.
    b. On the Formula bar, click between the equal sign and the word AVERAGE and type: ROUND(
    c. Move the cursor to the end of the formula and type ,1) so that the formula is:

$$=ROUND(AVERAGE(B4:E4),1)$$

    Click the Enter button. The average is now rounded to 1 decimal place, 85.3.

⑥ ROUND ALL STUDENT AVERAGES TO 1 DECIMAL PLACE
    a. Select cell F4 if it is not already selected.
    b. Use the Fill handle to copy the formula in cell F4 to cells F5 through F9.

⑦ FORMAT STUDENT AVERAGES TO DISPLAY 0 DECIMAL PLACES
    a. Select cells F4 through F9 if they are not already selected.
    b. Select Format ➡ Cells. A dialog box is displayed.
        1. Select the Number tab if those options are not already displayed.
        2. Select Number.
        3. Select or type 0 in the Decimal places box.
        4. Select OK. The averages are displayed with 0 decimal places.
        5. Click a blank cell to remove the selection. The selection is removed.

Check – Your worksheet should look similar to:

	A	B	C	D	E	F
1	Name	Test 1	Test 2	Test 3	Test 4	Student Average
2		1/7/03	2/9/03	3/1/03	4/1/03	
3						
4	Jones, D.	85	73	88	95	85
5	Neave, C.	92	88	85	91	89
6	Garcia, E.	72	63	67	72	69
7	McCallister, T.	87	92	85	93	89
8	Smith, L.	94	91	93	84	91
9	Bell, M.	70	74	80	83	77
10	Test Average	83.3	80.2	83	86.3	

⑧ *SAVE, PRINT, AND THEN CLOSE THE MODIFIED GRADES*

 a. Save the modified Grades.

 b. Display formulas. Change the column widths as necessary so all the formulas are displayed entirely.

 c. Print the worksheet.

 d. Close the workbook without saving changes. The only change that is not being saved is the displaying of the formulas.

⑨ *QUIT EXCEL*

Chapter Summary

A spreadsheet is data displayed in rows and columns. The computerized spreadsheet application in Microsoft Office is Excel. Benefits of using a spreadsheet application include the ability to easily perform calculations on data and to automatically recalculate values when changes are made to the data.

In Excel, spreadsheet files are called workbooks, and each workbook contains three worksheets, also called sheets. Worksheets are used to present data in an organized format.

Blank
Workbook

A new workbook is created by selecting the Blank Workbook icon. In the Excel window, rows are identified by numbers and columns by letters. A cell is the intersection of a row and column and is identified by its cell reference. For example, D4 is the cell reference of the cell located at the intersection of column D and row 4. The selected cell is called the active cell and is displayed with a bold outline. The Name box displays the cell reference of the active cell, and the Formula bar displays the contents of the active cell.

Worksheet cells can store three types of data: labels, values, and times/dates. Labels are text and cannot be used in calculations. Values are numeric and can be used in calculations. Times/dates are either times (10:30 AM) or calendar dates (9/21/2003), and both can be used in certain types of calculations.

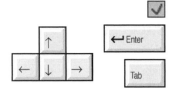

Data is entered into a cell by selecting that cell, typing the data and then pressing the Enter button. Pressing the Enter key, Tab key, or arrow key after typing data into a cell enters the data and then moves the active cell to an adjacent cell, in a direction depending on which key is pressed.

Data in a cell is edited by first selecting the cell to display its contents on the Formula bar. Next, clicking the Formula bar creates an insertion point, which allows characters to be entered or deleted. The contents of a selected cell are erased by pressing the Delete key. If a cell is cleared by mistake, immediately selecting the <u>U</u>ndo command or clicking the Undo button on the toolbar restores the contents of the cell.

Selecting the <u>S</u>ave command or clicking the Save button on the toolbar saves the workbook. A saved workbook that has been closed may be opened later by selecting the <u>O</u>pen command or selecting the Open button on the toolbar. Excel is quit by selecting the E<u>x</u>it command.

Selecting the Print Pre<u>v</u>iew command or clicking the Print Preview button on the toolbar displays the worksheet as it will appear when printed. In Print Preview, selecting the Print button displays the Print dialog box where selecting OK prints the portion of the worksheet that contains data. A worksheet can also be printed by selecting the <u>P</u>rint command. Gridlines and row and column headings can make a worksheet printout easier to read.

The width of a column is changed by dragging its right boundary or double-clicking the right boundary of the column.

Adjacent worksheet cells can be selected together to form a range. Adjacent cells are cells that are next to each other. A range is a selection of two or more cells.

Formatting is applied to cells to make the data easier to understand. Formatting does not change the data stored in a cell, only the way it is displayed. Selecting the C<u>e</u>lls command displays the Format Cells dialog box where formatting options can be selected. The toolbar can also be used to select formatting options.

Formulas are mathematical statements used to calculate values. All formulas must begin with an equal sign (=) and may contain cell references. Excel uses an order of operations when evaluating a formula. First it performs exponentiation, then multiplication and division, and finally addition and subtraction. Operations of the same priority are performed from left to right. The order of operations is changed by using parentheses.

When a formula is entered in a cell, Excel automatically checks the formula for errors. Entering an invalid formula in a cell causes Excel to display an error value in the cell and a triangle in the upper-left corner of the cell.

Excel contains built-in functions that are used to perform common calculations. The formula =SUM(B3:B8) includes the SUM function. The formula's argument, B3:B8, is called a range and defines the cells to be summed. The formula =AVERAGE(C3:C7) averages the values in the cells C3, C4, C5, C6, and C7. The formula =ROUND(C5,2) rounds the value stored in cell C5 to two decimal places. Similarly, the formula =ROUND(AVERAGE(B7:F7),1) rounds the average of the values in the range B7:F7 to one decimal place.

Cell references can be entered into a formula by clicking the cell. This technique is called pointing. The formulas in a worksheet are displayed by pressing Ctrl+`.

The contents of a selected cell or block of cells are copied to a row or column of adjacent cells by dragging the Fill handle or selecting the <u>D</u>own and <u>R</u>ight commands. When this is done, the cell references in the copied formulas automatically change to reflect the new row or column they are in. Cell references that reflect the row or column they have been copied to are called relative cell references.

Vocabulary

Active cell The selected cell displayed with a bold outline. Data can only be entered into an active cell.

Adjacent cells Cells that are next to each other.

Argument Data required by a function to perform calculations.

Arrow keys Enters data and then selects the next cell in the direction of the arrow key.

AVERAGE Function that adds the values of the cells in a range and divides the result by the number of cells in the range.

Boundary The bar separating the column letters at the top of the worksheet.

Cell The intersection of a row and column. Each cell can store a single item of data.

Cell reference The column letter and row number used to identify a cell, such as B3.

Circular reference An error that occurs when a formula references the cell it is stored in.

Column letter Letter at the top of the worksheet used to identify individual columns.

Date Data in the form of a calendar date.

Enter key Enters data and then selects the next cell in the column.

Esc key Cancels data entry and restores the original contents of the cell.

Excel The spreadsheet application in Microsoft Office.

Fill handle The solid square in the lower-right corner of a selected cell that is used to copy the contents of a cell to adjacent cells.

Formula Mathematical statement used to calculate a value. A formula must always begin with an equal sign. For example, =C5+D7+E8 is a formula.

Formula bar Area near the top of the worksheet window that displays the contents of the active cell.

Function Performs a calculation that results in a single value. The formula =SUM(B3:B8) contains the SUM function.

Gridlines Solid lines that mark off the rows and columns in a worksheet.

Insertion Point A blinking vertical line that indicates where the next character typed will be placed.

Label Text stored in a cell that cannot be used in calculations.

Name box Located near the top of the worksheet window. Displays the cell reference of the active cell.

Order of operations The rules Excel uses to evaluate a mathematical expression.

Pointing Clicking a cell to place its reference in a formula.

Range Selection of two or more cells.

Relative cell reference A cell reference that when copied reflects the row or column it has been copied to.

ROUND Function that changes a value by rounding it to a specific number of decimal places.

Row number The number down the left side of the worksheet used to identify individual rows.

Scroll bars Used to display rows and columns not currently visible in the worksheet.

Sheet tabs Used to display the three worksheets in the workbook.

Spreadsheet Data displayed in rows and columns.

SUM Function that adds the values in a range of cells.

Tab key Enters data and then selects the next cell in the row.

Time Data in the form of a time (i.e., 12:30 PM).

Value Numeric data that is stored in a cell that can be used in calculations.

Workbook An Excel spreadsheet file.

Worksheet Sheets in an Excel workbook used to present data in an organized format.

Excel Commands and Buttons

Align Left button Formats the active cell as left aligned. Found on the toolbar.

Align Right button Formats the active cell as right aligned. Found on the toolbar.

Auto Fill Options button Displayed when the Fill handle is used to copy cell contents.

Bold button Formats the active cell as bold. Found on the toolbar.

Cancel button Cancels data entry and restores the original contents of the cell. Found on the Formula bar.

C**e**lls **command** Displays a dialog box with alignment, font, and number formatting options. Found in the F**o**rmat menu.

Center button Formats the active cell as center aligned. Found on the toolbar.

Close **command** Closes a workbook. Found in the **F**ile menu. The Close button in the upper-right corner of the workbook can be used instead of the command.

Currency Style button Applies the Accounting format to the active cell. Found on the toolbar.

Down **command** Copies the cell contents into the selected cells of a column. Found in the F**i**ll submenu in the **E**dit menu.

Edit in Formula Bar **command** Places a formula on the Formula bar where it can be edited. Found in the list displayed by clicking the Trace Error button.

Enter button Enters data in the active cell. Found on the Formula bar.

E**x**it **command** Quits Excel. Found in the **F**ile menu. The Close button in the upper-right corner of the application window can be used instead of the command.

Font box Displays a list of fonts to choose from. Found on the toolbar.

Font Size box Displays a list of font sizes to choose from. Found on the toolbar.

Format Painter button Copies cell formatting. Found on the toolbar.

Ignore Error **command** Removes the Trace Error button and the triangle from the worksheet. Found in the list displayed by clicking the Trace Error button.

Italic button Formats the active cell as italic. Found on the toolbar.

New Office Document **command** Displays the New Office Document dialog box. Found in the **Start** menu.

Open Office Document **command** Displays the Open Office Document dialog box. Found in the **Start** menu.

Open **command** Displays a dialog box used to open an existing workbook. Found in the **F**ile menu. The Open button on the toolbar can be used instead of the command.

Page Set**u**p **command** Displays a dialog box with options for printing gridlines and row and column headings and creating a header or footer. Found in the **F**ile menu.

Percent Style button Formats the active cell as percentage with no decimal places. Found on the toolbar.

Print **command** Displays a dialog box used to print a worksheet. Found in the **F**ile menu. The Print button on the toolbar can be used instead of the command.

Print Pre**v**iew **command** Displays a worksheet as it will appear when printed. Found in the **F**ile menu. The Print Preview button on the toolbar can be used instead of the command.

Right **command** Copies the cell contents into the selected cells of a row. Found in the F**i**ll submenu in the **E**dit menu.

Save **command** Saves a workbook. Found in the **F**ile menu. The Save button on the toolbar can be used instead of the command.

Trace Error button Displays a list of options for correcting an error. Displayed when clicking a cell that contains an error.

Undo **command** Restores the previous action. Found in the **E**dit menu. The Undo button on the toolbar can be used instead of the command.

Underline button Formats the active cell as underlined. Found on the toolbar.

Review Questions

1. What is a spreadsheet?

2. a) What are spreadsheets called in Excel?
   b) How many worksheets does a new work-book contain?

3. List two benefits of using a spreadsheet application.

4. List the steps for creating a new Excel workbook.

5. a) How are individual columns identified on a worksheet?
   b) How are individual rows identified on a worksheet?
   c) What are scroll bars used for?

6. a) What is a cell?
   b) Give an example of a cell reference.
   c) Where can data be entered?
   d) What does the Name box display?
   e) What does the Formula bar display?
   f) What are the sheet tabs used to display?

7. List two ways to change the active cell.

8. How many of each of the following types of en-tries are stored in the Grades worksheet shown in Practice 1?
   a) labels
   b) values
   c) dates
   d) times

9. After selecting a cell and typing data, what hap-pens when you:
   a) click the Enter button?
   b) press the Enter key?
   c) press the Tab key?
   d) press the Esc key?

10. If a mistake has been made entering data into a cell, how can it be corrected?

11. List the steps required to edit data in a cell.

12. a) What is displayed when the Undo button arrow is clicked?
    b) What happens to the list of previous actions when a workbook is saved?

13. List two ways to save a worksheet.

14. a) List the steps required to view a worksheet as it will appear when printed.
    b) In Print Preview, what button can be selected to enlarge the view?

15. What options can be selected from the Page Setup dialog box to make a worksheet printout easier to read?

16. List the steps required to have your name left aligned and the current date right aligned in the header of a worksheet.

17. Is it possible to change the width of only a single cell?

18. List the steps required to increase the width of a column.

19. a) What is a range?
    b) List two ways to select the range B3 through C12.
    c) How is an entire column selected?
    d) What button selects the entire worksheet?

20. List the steps required to:
    a) format a cell to display a number with 3 deci-mal places.
    b) bold and right align the contents of a cell.
    c) format a cell to display a value in dollars to 2 decimal places.

21. What button can be used to copy a selected cell's format?

22. Briefly explain what a formula is and give two examples.

23. a) What is meant by order of operations?
    b) Which operation is performed first?
    c) Which operation is performed last?
    d) How can the order of operations be changed?

24. If 10/20 is entered into a cell, Excel considers it a label. How must the entry be changed so that 10 will be divided by 20?

25. What value would be calculated by Excel for each of the following formulas?
    a) =2+7*5+4
    b) =(2+7)*(5+4)
    c) =5+10/5
    d) =(5+10)/5
    e) =2^3+4

26. a) What is displayed in a cell if an invalid formula is entered?
    b) What button is displayed when a cell with an error value is selected?
    c) Where can a description of an invalid formula error be found?

27. In a formula, do cell references have to be typed in capital letters?

28. What value would be calculated by Excel for each of the following formulas if cell C15 stores a value of 16 and cell D8 a value of 4?
    a) =C15*D8
    b) =C15+5+D8
    c) =C15*5+D8
    d) =C15*(5+D8)
    e) =C15/D8

29. What is a circular reference?

30. a) What is a function?
    b) What does a function require to perform a calculation?

31. Write a formula that uses a function to calculate:
    a) the sum of the values stored in cells B4, B5, B6, and B7.
    b) the sum of the values stored in cells B4, C4, D4, and E4.
    c) the average of the values stored in the column of cells D7 to D35.
    d) the average of the values stored in the row of cells F3 to J3.

32. List and describe two common error values.

33. What is usually the best method for entering cell references in a formula?

34. How can the formulas stored in the cells of a worksheet be displayed instead of the values they calculate?

35. a) List the steps required to copy the contents of cell A1 into cells A2, A3, A4, and A5 using the Fill handle.
    b) List the steps required to copy the contents of cell C1 into cells D1, E1, and F1 using the Fill command.

36. a) What is a relative cell reference?
    b) List the steps required to copy the formula =AVERAGE(C5:C9) stored in cell C22 into the range of cells D22 to G22 so that the formula correctly calculates the average for each column.

37. What will be displayed in cell A2 if the value stored in cell C5 is 98.345 and the formula =ROUND(C5,2) is stored in cell A2?

38. Using functions, write a formula to calculate:
    a) the sum of the values in cells C5, C6, C7, C8, and C9 rounded to 2 decimal places.
    b) the sum of the values in cells B5, C5, D5, and E5 rounded to the nearest integer.
    c) the average of the values in cells A1, A2, A3, B1, B2, and B3 rounded to 1 decimal place.

Exercise 1 ————————————————————————Activity

A worksheet can be used to determine the time you spend on different activities during one week.

a) Create a new workbook.

b) Enter the following labels in row 1 starting in column A: Activity, Sun, Mon, Tue, Wed, Thu, Fri, Sat.

c) Bold all the labels in row 1. Right align all the days of the week labels.

d) Change the width of columns B through H so they are just wide enough to display the data entirely.

e) Starting in row 3, enter the appropriate label and number of hours you spend each day of the week on each of the following activities:

- school classes
- athletics
- extracurricular groups and clubs
- studying and doing homework
- eating
- sleeping
- watching television or listening to music
- talking on the phone
- doing housework
- working at a job

Change the width of column A to display all the labels entirely. Format all the hours to display 1 decimal place.

f) Save the workbook naming it Activity.

g) Most people's schedules do not account for all 24 hours in a day. Include a row, after the last activity, and enter formulas that use a function to calculate the amount of unaccounted time in your schedule for each day. Include an appropriate label for the unaccounted time.

h) In cell I1, enter the label Total Hours. Enter formulas that use a function to calculate the total hours spent for the week on each activity. Format the total hours as number with 1 decimal place if it is not already formatted.

i) In cell J1, enter the label Avg. Hours. Enter formulas that use a function to calculate the average number of hours spent per day on each activity for the week. Format the averages as number with to 1 decimal place.

j) Change the column widths as necessary so that all the data is displayed entirely.

k) Create a header with your name right aligned.

l) Save the modified Activity and print a copy with gridlines and row and column headings.

m) Display the formulas in the cells instead of values. Change the column widths as necessary so that the formulas are completely displayed. Print a copy with gridlines and row and column headings.

Exercise 2 ———————————————— Squeaky Clean Cars

The owner of Squeaky Clean Cars wants to use a worksheet to keep track of his budgeted and actual expenses.

a) Create a new workbook.

b) Enter the data as shown below. Change the column widths as necessary so that all the data is displayed entirely and format the numeric values as currency with 2 decimal places:

	A	B	C	D
1	Squeaky Clean Cars			
2				
3		June Expenses Budget		
4		Budgeted	Actual	
5				
6	Soap	$35.00	$28.65	
7	Wax	$50.00	$43.45	
8	Vinyl Cleaner	$25.00	$32.75	
9	Window Cleaner	$15.00	$20.50	
10	Sponges and Towels	$10.00	$12.56	
11				

c) Save the workbook naming it Squeaky Clean Cars.

d) The owner would like to know the difference between what was budgeted and what he actually spent. In cell D4, enter the label Difference. Enter formulas that use cell references to subtract the actual costs from the budgeted costs.

e) In cell A11, enter the label Total: and right align it. Enter formulas that use a function to total the Budgeted and Actual columns.

f) Bold the labels in column A and row 3. Italicize and right align the labels in row 4. Change the column widths as necessary so that all the data is displayed entirely.

g) Create a header with your name right aligned.

h) Save the modified Squeaky Clean Cars and print a copy with gridlines and row and column headings.

i) Display the formulas in the cells instead of values. Change the column widths as necessary so that the formulas are completely displayed. Print a copy with gridlines and row and column headings.

Exercise 3 ———————————————— Swim Meet

A swim team wants to use a worksheet to keep track of the last swim meet's results.

a) Create a new workbook.

b) Enter the data as shown on the next page. Change the column widths as necessary so that all the data is displayed entirely and format the average times with an appearance similar to 13:30:55:

	A	B	C	D	E
1	Swimming Event	Floyd	Abby	Eric	Katrina
2					
3	100 M Freestyle	2:54:00	2:45:40	2:55:06	2:23:36
4	100 M Breaststroke	3:07:17	3:12:40	2:56:27	3:28:16
5	100 M Butterfly	2:57:15	2:45:12	3:10:36	2:58:56
6	100 M Backstroke	3:00:30	2:45:18	2:55:09	3:12:16
7	200 M Individual Medley	3:56:50	5:25:25	4:34:07	4:24:36
8	400 M Medley Relay	5:34:08	5:45:02	5:46:25	5:51:32

c) Save the workbook naming it Swim Meet.

d) In cell F1, enter the label Avg. Time. Enter formulas that use a function to calculate the average time of each swimming event.

e) Italicize all the labels in row 1. Right align all the swimmers' names and the Avg. Time label in row 1. Change the column widths as necessary so that all the data is displayed entirely.

f) Create a header with your name right aligned.

g) Create a footer with the text September 10 Swim Meet Results center aligned.

h) Save the modified Swim Meet and print a copy with gridlines and row and column headings.

i) Display the formulas in the cells instead of values. Change the column widths as necessary so that the formulas are completely displayed. Print a copy with gridlines and row and column headings.

Exercise 4 ———————————————————— Student Stats

The Admissions department at a local university wants to use a worksheet to keep track of the statistics on the number of undergraduate and graduate students in each college.

a) Create a new workbook.

b) Enter the data as shown below. Change the column widths as necessary so that all the data is displayed entirely:

	A	B	C
1	College	Undergraduate	Graduate
2			
3	Business	3098	250
4	Education	1356	189
5	Liberal Arts	2589	180
6	Pharmacy	2398	212
7	Social Science	1586	98

c) Save the workbook naming it Student Stats.

d) In cell A8, enter the label Total: and then right align and italicize it. Enter formulas that use a function to calculate the total number of undergraduate students and the total number of graduate students at the university.

e) In cell A9, enter the label Average: and then right align and italicize it. Enter formulas that use a function to calculate the average number of undergraduate students and the average number of graduate students at the university.

f) Format the numeric values to display commas and 0 decimal places.

g) Bold all the labels in row 1. Right align the Undergraduate and Graduate labels. Change the column widths as necessary so that all the data is displayed entirely.

h) Create a header with your name right aligned.

i) Create a footer with the current date center aligned.

j) Save the modified Student Stats and print a copy with gridlines and row and column headings.

k) Display the formulas in the cells instead of values. Change the column widths as necessary so that the formulas are completely displayed. Print a copy with gridlines and row and column headings.

Exercise 5 ——————————————————— Coral Employees

The accountant for Coral county has decided to use a worksheet for the city hall payroll.

a) Create a new workbook.

b) Enter the data as shown below. Change the column widths as necessary so that all the data is displayed entirely and format the salaries as currency with 0 decimal places:

	A	B	C
1	First Name	Last Name	Salary
2			
3	Sang	Cho	$42,000
4	Jill	Grossman	$25,500
5	Jason	Jones	$26,000
6	Christa	Smith	$28,900
7	Tanya	White	$32,000

c) Save the workbook naming it Coral Employees.

d) Employees are paid weekly. In cell D1, enter the label Weekly Pay. Enter formulas that use cell references to calculate the weekly pay for each employee. Weekly pay is calculated by dividing the salary by 52 weeks in a year.

e) In cell B8, enter the label Average: and then right align and italicize it. Enter formulas that use a function to calculate the average salary and weekly pay for the employees. Format the average weekly pay as currency with 2 decimal places.

f) Bold all the labels in row 1. Right align the Salary and Weekly Pay labels. Change the column widths as necessary so that all the data is displayed entirely.

g) Modify the weekly pay formulas to use a function to round the weekly pay amounts in column D to 0 decimal places (do not round the average weekly pay formula). Note that the average weekly pay also changes because the numbers have been rounded.

h) Create a header with your name right aligned.

i) Save the modified Coral Employees and print a copy with gridlines and row and column headings.

j) Display the formulas in the cells instead of values. Change the column widths as necessary so that the formulas are completely displayed. Print a copy with gridlines and row and column headings.

Exercise 6 ———————————————————————— Dive Log

Researchers of a coral reef study want to use a worksheet to computerize their scuba diving log.

   a) Create a new workbook.

   b) Enter the following data starting in cell A1:

	A	B	C	D	E
1	Date	Depth (m)	Duration (min)	Water Temp (Celsius)	Visibility (m)
2					
3	5/8/2003	10	60	26	10
4	5/10/2003	18	45	25	12
5	5/11/2003	13	50	27	9
6	5/13/2003	27	15	23	10
7	5/14/2003	11	53	28	11

   c) Save the workbook naming it Dive Log.

   d) In cell A8, enter the label Average: and then right align and italicize it. Enter formulas that use a function to average the depth and duration of all five dives.

   e) Modify the average depth and duration formulas to use a function to round the results to 0 decimal places.

   f) Right align and italicize the labels in row 1. Change the column widths as necessary so that all data is displayed entirely.

   g) Create a header with your name right aligned.

   h) Save the modified Dive Log and print a copy with gridlines and row and column headings.

   i) Display the formulas in the cells instead of values. Change the column widths as necessary so that the formulas are completely displayed. Print a copy with gridlines and row and column headings.

Exercise 7 ———————————————————————— Pizza Palace

The owner of Pizza Palace wants to use a worksheet to keep track of expenses.

   a) Create a new workbook.

   b) Enter the data as shown below. Change the column widths as necessary so that all the data is displayed entirely and format the expenses as currency with 2 decimal places:

	A	B	C	D
1	Pizza Palace			
2	Expenses per Pizza			
3				
4	Ingredients	Everything	Vegetarian	Cheese
5				
6	Dough	$1.25	$1.25	$1.25
7	Cheese	$1.50	$1.50	$1.50
8	Sauce	$0.50	$0.50	$0.50
9	Pepperoni	$0.75	$0.00	$0.00
10	Sausage	$1.00	$0.00	$0.00
11	Onion	$0.15	$0.15	$0.00
12	Mushroom	$0.35	$0.35	$0.00
13	Green Pepper	$0.40	$0.40	$0.00

A Guide to Microsoft Office XP Professional

c) Save the workbook naming it Pizza Palace.

d) In cell A14, enter the label Cost of Pizza: and then right align and italicize it. Enter formulas that use a function to calculate the total cost of each pizza type.

e) Bold the labels in rows 1 and 2.

f) Bold the labels in row 4. Right align the pizza type labels. Change the column widths as necessary so that all the data is displayed entirely.

g) Create a header with your name right aligned.

h) Create a footer with the current date center aligned.

i) Save the modified Pizza Palace and print a copy with gridlines and row and column headings.

j) Display the formulas in the cells instead of values. Change the column widths as necessary so that the formulas are completely displayed. Print a copy with gridlines and row and column headings.

Exercise 8 — Balance Sheet

A company uses a balance sheet to list assets (what they own), liabilities (what they owe), and stockholder's equity (the owner's investments) as of a specific date. The owner of Northern Lights Gym wants use a worksheet to computerize the balance sheet.

a) Create a new workbook.

b) Enter the data and apply formatting as shown below:

	A	B	C	D	E	F
1			**Northern Lights Gym**			
2			**Balance Sheet**			
3			**Month Ended Jan 31, 2003**			
4						
5	*Assets:*			*Liabilities:*		
6		Cash	$12,000		Accounts Payable	$75,987
7		Accounts Receivable	$15,000	*Stockholder's Equity:*		
8		Gym Equipment	$45,000		Stockholder's Equity	$95,003
9		Office Computers	$98,990			
10						
11		**Total Assets:**		**Total Liabilities and Stockholder's Equity:**		

c) Save the workbook naming it Balance Sheet.

d) In cell C11, enter a formula that uses a function to calculates the total assets.

e) In cell F11, enter a formula that uses cell references to calculate the total liabilities and stockholder's equity.

f) Create a header with your name right aligned.

g) Create a footer with the current date center aligned.

h) Save the modified Balance Sheet and print a copy with gridlines and row and column headings.

i) Display the formulas in the cells instead of values. Change the column widths as necessary so that the formulas are completely displayed. Print a copy with gridlines and row and column headings.

Exercise 9 ———————————————————— Temp Conversion

The local university's Meteorology department wants to use a worksheet to convert Fahrenheit temperatures to the equivalent Celsius temperatures.

a) Create a new workbook.

b) Enter the data and apply formatting as shown below. In cell E3 enter the formula =5/9*(B3–32) to convert the Fahrenheit temperature stored in cell B3 to degrees Celsius:

	A	B	C	D	E
1	Temperature Conversion				
2					
3	Fahrenheit Temp:	20		Celsius Temp:	-6.66667

c) Save the workbook naming it Temp Conversion.

d) Modify the formula in cell E3 to use a function to round the result to 0 decimal places.

e) Enter the following Fahrenheit temperatures in cell B3, one at a time: 0, 32, and 80. What Celsius temperature does each of these convert to?

f) In row 5, have the worksheet convert temperatures from a Celsius temperature entered in cell B5 to a Fahrenheit temperature displayed in cell E5. Use 26 for the Celsius temperature. Include appropriate labels. The formula needed for converting from degrees Celsius to Fahrenheit is =9/5*B5+32. Use a function to round the result to 0 decimal places. Change the column widths as necessary so that all the data is displayed entirely.

g) Enter the following Celsius temperatures in cell B5, one at a time: 0, 12, and –21. What Fahrenheit temperature does each of these convert to?

h) Create a header with your name right aligned.

i) Create a footer with the current date center aligned.

j) Save the modified Temp Conversion and print a copy with gridlines and row and column headings.

k) Display the formulas in the cells instead of values. Change the column widths as necessary so that the formulas are completely displayed. Print a copy with gridlines and row and column headings.

Exercise 10 ———————————————————— Upgrade Costs

A technology coordinator wants to use a worksheet to project computer-related costs through the year 2007. Years 2002 and 2003 have already been established.

a) Create a new workbook.

b) Enter the following data starting in cell A1. Format the costs as currency with 0 decimal places:

	A	B	C	D
1	Year	Hardware	Software	Training
2				
3	2002	$15,750	$5,500	$2,500
4	2003	$0	$8,000	$2,500

c) Save the workbook naming it Upgrade Costs.

d) Hardware is upgraded every other year with an expected 15% increase over the last upgrade and software costs are expected to increase 7% each year starting in 2004. The training budget is $2,500 per year. Enter formulas that use cell references to calculate the costs for years 2004 through 2007.

e) Use a function to round the formulas for the hardware and software costs to 0 decimal places. Format all of the numeric values as currency with 0 decimal places.

f) Format the labels in row 1 as right aligned and bold. Change the column widths as necessary so that all the data is displayed entirely.

g) In cell E1, enter the label Total Expenses. Enter formulas that use a function to calculate the total expenses projected each year. Change the column width as necessary so that all the data is displayed entirely.

h) Note the triangle in the upper-left corner of cell E3 indicating an error. Select the cell and then click the Trace Error button. The error is described as Formula Omits Adjacent Cells and results from the dates in column A not being included in the formula that calculates the total expenses. Since the dates are not suppose to be included in the formula, select Ignore Error from the list of options.

i) Create a header with your name right aligned.

j) Create a footer with the current date center aligned.

k) Save the modified Upgrade Costs and print a copy with gridlines and row and column headings.

l) Display the formulas in the cells instead of values. Change the column widths as necessary so that the formulas are completely displayed. Print a copy with gridlines and row and column headings.

Exercise 11 ———————————————————— Class Scores

Worksheets can be used to keep track of your class grades. Create a worksheet of your grades in this class for the chapters you have covered so far. This exercise assumes assignments are graded using a point system. For example, review questions are worth 20 points and tests are worth 100 points.

a) Create a new workbook.

b) Enter your points for the practices, review questions, exercises, and tests. Also, enter the total points possible for each chapter. Include appropriate labels and proper formatting as shown below. Your worksheet will have different data but should look similar to:

	A	B	C	D	E	F	G
1		Ch 1	Ch 2	Ch 3	Ch 4	Ch 5	Ch 6
2							
3	Practices	None	25	25	30	27	25
4	Review Questions	20	15	20	20	18	20
5	Exercises	None	None	50	45	43	47
6	Test	91	89	85	94	85	90
7	Possible Points	120	150	200	200	200	200

c) Save the workbook naming it Class Scores.

d) In cell H1, enter the label Total Points. Enter formulas that use a function to calculate the total points you earned for the practices, review questions, exercises, and tests. Also calculate the total points possible and format the totals to display commas and 0 decimal places.

e) Change the column widths as necessary so that all the data is displayed entirely.

f) In cell A8, enter the label Current Grade and then right align, bold, and italicize it. In cells B8, enter a formula that uses cell references and a function to calculate your grade as a percentage. Your grade is calculated by dividing the total points you earned by the total points possible. Format your current grade as a percentage with 0 decimal places and bold.

g) Create a header with your name right aligned.

h) Create a footer with the text Computer Class Grades center aligned.

i) Save the modified Class Scores and print a copy with gridlines and row and column headings.

j) Display the formulas in the cells instead of values. Change the column widths as necessary so that the formulas are completely displayed. Print a copy with gridlines and row and column headings.

Exercise 12 ————————————————————————Checkbook

Worksheets can be helpful with personal financial management. Sally wants to organize her finances using a worksheet as a checkbook register.

a) Create a new workbook.

b) Enter the data and apply formatting as shown below:

	A	B	C	D	E
1	Date	Transaction	Description	Expenses	Income
2					
3	1-Feb-2003	Opening Deposit			$200.00
4	5-Feb-2003	Coral Gas	Gas for car	$20.00	
5	8-Feb-2003	Deposit	Paycheck		$100.00
6	10-Feb-2003	Sally's Diner	Dinner out	$15.35	
7	15-Feb-2003	Coral Square Cinema	Movie	$6.75	
8	17-Feb-2003	Deposit	Birthday check		$25.00
9	18-Feb-2003	Book Palace	Magazines	$15.98	
10	19-Feb-2003	Fully Belly	Dinner out	$10.50	
11	22-Feb-2003	Coral Square Mall	Lunch out	$5.75	
12	24-Feb-2003	Coral Gas	Gas for car	$15.00	
13	26-Feb-2003	Deposit	Paycheck		$100.00

c) Save the workbook naming it Checkbook.

d) In cell F1, enter the label Balance and right align and bold it if it is not already formatted.

e) In column F, enter formulas that use cell references to calculate the balance after each transaction. To calculate the balance, subtract the expense from the previous balance and add the income to the previous balance.

f) In cell C14, enter the label Total: and then right align and bold it. Enter formulas that use a function to calculate the total expenses and total income for the month.

g) Create a header with your name right aligned.

h) Create a footer with the text Personal Finances center aligned.

i) Save the modified Checkbook and print a copy with gridlines and row and column headings.

j) Display the formulas in the cells instead of values. Change the column widths as necessary so that the formulas are completely displayed. Print a copy with gridlines and row and column headings.

Exercise 13 ———————————————————Income Statement

An income statement lists a company's revenue (money they earn), expenses (money they pay out), and net income/loss (revenue minus expenses) for a specific time period. Fluffy Bakery is a small home business that wants to use a worksheet to produce an income statement.

a) Create a new workbook.

b) Enter the data and apply formatting as shown below:

	A	B	C	D	E
1			Fluffy Bakery		
2			Income Statement		
3			for the years 2002-2004		
4					
5		2002	2003	2004	
6	Revenue:				
7	Cookie Sales	$15,500	$16,896	$17,864	
8	Cake Sales	$27,589	$26,298	$25,982	
9	Bread Sales	$24,980	$25,298	$25,398	
10	Total Revenues:				
11	Expenses:				
12	Advertising	$5,000	$4,500	$4,500	
13	Baking Supplies	$2,000	$1,000	$2,750	
14	Ingredients	$13,275	$15,298	$16,490	
15	Salaries	$30,000	$30,000	$35,000	
16	Utilities	$6,570	$7,250	$8,090	
17	Total Expenses:				
18	Net Income/(Loss):				

c) Save the workbook naming it Income Statement.

d) In row 10, enter formulas that uses a function to calculate the total revenue for each year.

e) In row 17, enter formulas that use a function to calculate the total expenses for each year.

f) In row 18, enter formulas that use cell references to calculate the net income or loss for each year. The net income/loss is calculated by subtracting total expenses from total revenue. Format the values as currency with 0 decimal places, if necessary.

g) Create a header with your name right aligned.

h) Save the modified Income Statement and print a copy with gridlines and row and column headings.

i) Display the formulas in the cells instead of values. Change the column widths as necessary so that the formulas are completely displayed. Print a copy with gridlines and row and column headings.

Exercise 14 ——————————————————————Budget

A student wants to use a worksheet to create a personal budget for her fall semester in college.

a) Create a new workbook.

b) Enter the data and apply formatting as shown below:

	A	B	C	D	E	F	G	H	I
1	**Personal Budget**								
2									
3		Sep-03		Oct-03		Nov-03		Dec-03	
4		Budgeted	Actual	Budgeted	Actual	Budgeted	Actual	Budgeted	Actual
5	Income:								
6	Loan	$7,000	$7,000	$0	$0	$0	$0	$0	$0
7	Job	$1,000	$925	$500	$465	$500	$485	$600	$725
8	Parents	$5,500	$5,500	$0	$0	$0	$0	$0	$0
9	Total:								
10	Expenses:								
11	Tuition	$6,000	$5,943	$0	$0	$0	$0	$0	$0
12	Room/Board	$5,500	$5,575	$0	$0	$0	$0	$0	$0
13	Books	$700	$635	$0	$45	$0	$0	$0	$0
14	Food	$300	$315	$300	$325	$300	$320	$250	$375
15	Entertainment	$150	$0	$50	$80	$50	$0	$100	$100
16	Clothes	$50	$0	$50	$80	$50	$0	$100	$100
17	Total:								

c) Save the workbook naming it Budget.

d) In row 9, enter formulas that use a function to calculate the total budgeted and actual income for each month.

e) In row 17, enter formulas that use a function to calculate the total budgeted and actual expenses for each month.

f) In cell A18, enter the label Savings: and right align and italicize it. Enter formulas that use cell references to calculate the savings for each month. Savings are calculated by subtracting the total expenses from the total income.

g) Change the column widths as necessary so that all the data is displayed entirely.

h) Create a header with your name right aligned.

i) Save the modified Budget and print a copy with gridlines and row and column headings.

j) Display the formulas in the cells instead of values. Change the column widths as necessary so that the formulas are completely displayed. Print a copy with gridlines and row and column headings.

A Guide to Microsoft Office XP Professional

Exercise 15 ———————————————————— Brochure Costs

A worksheet can be used to calculate the costs of producing brochures in different quantities. The cost of the brochure is made up of fixed costs and variable costs. Fixed costs remain the same no matter how many brochures are produced. Variable costs change depending on the number of brochures produced.

a) Create a new workbook.

b) Enter the data and apply formatting as shown below:

	A	B	C	D	E	F
1	Brochure Costs					
2						
3	Number of Brochures:	100	250	500	750	1000
4						
5	Fixed Costs:					
6	Art work	$500.00	$500.00	$500.00	$500.00	$500.00
7	Salaries	$1,500.00	$1,500.00	$1,500.00	$1,500.00	$1,500.00
8	Initial setup fee	$1,000.00	$1,000.00	$1,000.00	$1,000.00	$1,000.00
9	Variable Costs:					
10	Paper					
11	Printing					
12	Labor					
13	Shipping					

c) Save the workbook naming it Brochure Costs.

d) The breakdown of variable costs per brochure are:

	100	250	500	750	1000
Paper	$0.20	$0.18	$0.15	$0.12	$0.10
Printing	$0.12	$0.11	$0.10	$0.09	$0.08
Labor	$0.07	$0.07	$0.06	$0.05	$0.04
Shipping	$0.10	$0.09	$0.08	$0.08	$0.07

Variable costs are calculated by multiplying the variable cost per brochure by the number of brochures produced. In cells B10 through F13, enter formulas that use cell references and the constant values listed above to calculate the variable costs. Format the cells as currency with 2 decimal places.

e) In cell A14, enter the label Total Costs: and right align and bold it. Enter formulas that use a function to calculate the total cost of producing the different quantity of brochures. Total cost is calculated by adding the fixed costs plus the variable costs.

f) In cell A15, enter the label Cost per Brochure: and right align and bold it. Enter formulas that use cell references to calculate the cost per brochure of producing the different quantities of brochures. Cost per brochure is calculated by dividing the total costs by the number of brochures produced.

g) Create a header with your name right aligned.

h) Save the modified Brochure Costs and print a copy with gridlines and row and column headings.

i) Display the formulas in the cells instead of values. Change the column widths as necessary so that the formulas are completely displayed. Print a copy with gridlines and row and column headings.

Exercise 16 (advanced) ——————————————— Club

Create a new workbook that stores relevant numbers about a club or organization that you belong to. The worksheet should contain at least five columns and five rows of data. Include at least two formulas in the worksheet. Format the worksheet appropriately and include informative headers or footers. Save the workbook naming it Club and print a copy with gridlines and row and column headings. Print a copy of the worksheet so that formulas are displayed in the cells instead of values.

Exercise 17 (advanced) ——————————— Vacation Costs

Create a new workbook that stores estimated costs for vacations to at least three different countries you would like to visit. The worksheet should contain at least four columns and four rows of data. Include at least two formulas and one function in the worksheet. Format the worksheet appropriately and include informative headers or footers. Save the workbook naming it Vacation Costs and print a copy with gridlines and row and column headings. Print a copy of the worksheet so that formulas are displayed in the cells instead of values.

Exercise 18 (advanced) ——————— Fund-raiser Finances

Create a new workbook that stores financial information about a fund-raiser you have participated in. The worksheet should contain at least six columns and six rows of data. Include at least three formulas and two functions in the worksheet. Format the worksheet appropriately and include informative headers or footers. Save the workbook naming it Fund-raiser Finances and print a copy with gridlines and row and column headings. Print a copy of the worksheet so that formulas are displayed in the cells instead of values.

Chapter 9
Spreadsheet Techniques

<u>F</u>ind

R<u>e</u>place

<u>F</u>unction

Insert

Delete

Page Set<u>u</u>p

Page <u>B</u>reak

Remove Page <u>B</u>reak

Chapter 9 Expectations

After completing this chapter you will be able to:
1. Determine how to present data in a logical and organized format.
2. Locate data and replace it.
3. Copy and move data.
4. Use the MAX and MIN functions.
5. Insert functions into a formula.
6. Understand absolute cell references.
7. Insert and delete rows and columns.
8. Change the print orientation and margins of worksheet.
9. Add and remove page breaks.
10. Use the IF function.

In this chapter, planning and modifying a worksheet are explained. Other functions are also introduced.

9.1 Planning a Worksheet

Planning a worksheet is the process of determining how to present data in a logical, organized, and easy-to-understand format. The planning process involves answering the following four questions:

1. What information will the worksheet produce?

2. What data will be required?

3. What formulas will be required?

4. How will the worksheet be organized?

For example, a company planning a worksheet for calculating their weekly payroll would answer the questions as follows:

1. The worksheet will produce each employee's gross and net pay for the week.

2. The worksheet requires the following data:

   - Employee number and name
   - Pay rate per hour and hours worked per week
   - Social security and tax rates

3. The worksheet requires the following formulas:

   - A formula to calculate gross pay. Gross pay is the amount earned before any deductions and is calculated by multiplying the hours worked by the employee's rate per hour.
   - A formula to calculate net pay. Net pay is the amount that the employee receives after deductions and is calculated by subtracting social security and taxes from the gross pay.
   - A formula to calculate social security. Social security is calculated by multiplying the gross pay by the social security rate.
   - A formula to calculate taxes. Taxes are calculated by multiplying the gross pay by the appropriate tax rate.

Expanding a Worksheet

Data can be added to a worksheet by simply making entries into empty columns and rows, but this should be done with care. If data is added without thought to the overall plan, the worksheet will quickly become unorganized. Expanding a worksheet requires the same careful planning as the initial worksheet.

4. Creating a sketch is the best way to illustrate how the data will be organized:

Net Provider Payroll												
Soc. Sec. Rate:	percent 2 decimals											
				Overtime Hours	Overtime Pay							
Last Name	First Initial	Rate/hr	Hours			Gross Pay	Soc. Sec.	Taxes	Net Pay			
text	text	currency 2 decimals	number 1decimal	number 1decimal	currency 2 decimals	currency 2 decimals	currency 2 decimals	currency 2 decimals	currency 2 decimals			

In the sketch above, note that descriptive column and row labels are used and the format of each column is specified.

Practice 1

In this practice you will plan a worksheet for Net Provider, a national Internet service provider that offers access to the Internet through dial-up and DSL service to the entire United States. A dial-up account is $17.95 per month and a DSL account is $45.95 per month. The owner of the company wants to know the monthly revenues from both dial-up and DSL accounts per state, as well as the total monthly revenue per state. Revenue is the money collected and is based on the monthly service price and the number of accounts using that service. Using paper and pencil, plan the worksheet by answering the four questions discussed in Section 9.1.

9.2 The Find and Replace Commands

A worksheet can be searched by selecting Find (Ctrl+F) from the Edit menu, which displays the Find and Replace dialog box where the data to be searched for is typed. Selecting Options expands the dialog box:

The data to be searched for, =SUM, has been entered in the Find what box. The Look in option is Formulas, which searches the worksheet by what is stored in the cell. The Look in list also contains the Values option, which searches the worksheet by what is displayed in the cell. Selecting Find Next starts the search from the active cell.

Selecting cell A1 before selecting the Find command starts the search at the beginning of the worksheet. A dialog box is displayed if the search data is not found.

Data can be searched for and replaced with other data by selecting Replace (Ctrl+H) from the Edit menu, which displays the Find and Replace dialog box with the Replace tab selected. The options include the Replace with box that is used to specify data to replace the data in the Find what box.

9.3 Copying and Moving Data

There are times when data needs to be repeated in a worksheet. Rather than entering the same data multiple times, it can be duplicated using the Copy button ( ) and Paste button( ) on the toolbar.

The steps for copying a range of cells are:

source

1. Select the *source*, which is the cell(s) to be copied.

2. Click the Copy button ( ) on the toolbar. A copy of the source is added to the Clipboard.

destination

3. Select the *destination*, which is the upper-left cell of the range where the data is to be pasted.

4. Click the Paste button ( ) on the toolbar. The contents of the Clipboard are placed in the cell(s) and the Paste Options button ( ) is displayed. Note that the source formatting is copied as well.

Clicking the Copy button ( ) on the toolbar outlines the source cells with a moving dashed line to show what will be copied. After pasting the cells, the Esc key is pressed to remove the dashed outline.

When pasting cell contents, only the upper-left cell of the destination range needs to be selected. Any existing cell contents at the new location are replaced by the Clipboard contents when the Paste button ( ) on the toolbar is clicked.

moving data

Data may need to be moved from one place to another on a worksheet. Clicking the Cut button ( ) on the toolbar places a copy of the source in the Clipboard and outlines the cells to be moved. Selecting the Paste button ( ) on the toolbar places the contents of the Clipboard in the new location and deletes the contents and formatting of the original, outlined cells.

The Cut (Ctrl+X), Copy (Ctrl+C), and Paste (Ctrl+V) commands in the Edit menu can be used instead of the buttons. Alternatively, right-clicking a cell displays a menu from which Cut, Copy, or Paste can be selected.

Using the Office Clipboard

Chapter 6 discussed how to use the Office Clipboard in Word to copy or cut up to 24 different items. The Office Clipboard works in the same manner in Excel.

The Paste Options Button

Clicking the Paste Options button ( ) displays a list of options that can be used to change the default paste option of Keep Source Formatting. Options include Formatting Only, which copies the formatting and not the cell contents.

Practice 2

In this practice you will search a worksheet and move labels and values.

① *OPEN NET PROVIDER*

Open NET PROVIDER, which is a data file for this text.

② *SEARCH FOR THE TEXT "Vermont"*

a. Select cell A1 if it is not already selected.

b. Select Edit → Find. A dialog box is displayed.

    1. In the Find what box, type Vermont.

    2. Select Find Next. The active cell changes to A51, which contains the label Vermont. To view cell A51, you may need to move the Find and Replace dialog box by dragging its title bar.

    3. Select Close. The dialog box is removed.

c. Select cell B51 and enter 101 as the new number of dial-up accounts.

③ REPLACE "N." WITH "North"

a. Select cell A1.

b. Select Edit → Replace. A dialog box is displayed.

    1. In the Find what box, type N. (be sure to type the period).

    2. In the Replace with box, type North (no period).

    3. Select Find Next. The active cell is the cell containing "N. Carolina."

    4. Select the Replace button. The current data in the cell is replaced and the active cell changes to the next cell containing the search data.

    5. Select Replace. The current data in the cell is replaced and the active cell remains on the cell indicating there are no more occurrences of the search data.

    6. Select Close. The dialog box is removed.

④ MOVE CELL CONTENTS

a. Select cells A57 through C57.

b. On the toolbar, click the Cut button (✂). A moving dashed line is placed around the cells.

c. Select cell A17.

d. On the toolbar, click the Paste button (📋▾). The label and values in cells A57 through C57 are moved to cells A17 through C17.

⑤ SAVE THE MODIFIED NET PROVIDER

9.4 The MAX and MIN Functions

Excel includes two functions that determine the maximum or the minimum value stored in a range of cells. The MAX function takes the form:

    =MAX(<range of cells>)

<range of cells> is the cell range to be checked to determine the maximum number. For example, =MAX(C2:C9) displays the maximum (largest) of all the values in the range C2 through C9.

The MIN function takes the form:

    =MIN(<range of cells>)

<range of cells> is the cell range to be checked to determine the minimum number. For example, =MIN(B2:F3) displays the minimum (smallest) of all the values in the range B2 through F3.

The COUNT and COUNTA Functions

The COUNT function determines the number of cells that contain values. For example, =COUNT(C1:C8) displays the number of cells in the range C1 through C8 that contain values.

The COUNTA function determines the number of cells that contain data regardless of the type. For example, =COUNTA(A1:A8) displays the number of cells in the range A1 through A8 that contain any type of data.

9.5 Inserting a Function into a Formula

Instead of typing the name of a function into a formula, selecting Function from the Insert menu displays the Insert Function dialog box, which lists available functions that can be inserted into a formula:

Selecting an option in the Or select a category list limits the functions that are displayed. Selecting a function in the Select a function list and then OK displays the Function Arguments dialog box for the selected function. For example, selecting AVERAGE and then OK displays the Function Arguments dialog box for the AVERAGE function:

A range of cells is automatically entered in the Number1 box based on the location of the active cell. Excel assumes the range of cells is to the right or above the active cell. For example, in the worksheet above, the active cell is A5 and there are a series of values above cell A5. Therefore, the range A1:A4 is entered in the Number1 box. The cell range can be changed, if necessary, by typing in the Number1 box or by pointing to cells on the worksheet. Selecting OK removes the Function Arguments dialog box and the function is entered into the formula. Excel automatically precedes the function with an equal sign if it is not already part of a formula.

Function Box

After typing an equal sign (=) in a cell, the Functions list appears on the Formula bar. The Functions list can be used as an alternative to typing a function name:

Selecting a function from the Functions list displays the Function Arguments dialog box. If the function is not listed, selecting **More Functions…** displays the Insert Function dialog box.

The AutoSum Button

Clicking the AutoSum button (Σ ▾) automatically creates a formula with the SUM function. The range placed in the SUM function is the series of cells to the right or above the active cell. Pressing the Enter key enters the formula.

Formulas created using the AutoSum button should always be double-checked for correctness since Excel guesses the range.

Clicking the AutoSum button arrow displays a list of other functions, such as AVERAGE and MAX, that can be selected.

The Function Arguments dialog box may need to be moved to view cells behind it. The dialog box can be moved by dragging its title bar.

 The Insert Function button (f_x) on the Formula bar can also be used to display the Insert Function dialog box.

Practice 3

In this practice you will compute the maximum and minimum number of dial-up and DSL accounts. Open NET PROVIDER if it is not already displayed.

① DETERMINE THE HIGHEST NUMBER OF DIAL-UP INTERNET ACCESS ACCOUNTS

  a. Select cell A57 and enter the label Max accounts: then right align and italicize the label.

  b. Select cell B57.

  c. Select Insert → Function. An equal sign is inserted into cell B57 and a dialog box is displayed.

     1. In the Or select a category list, select All.

     2. Scroll until MAX is visible in the Select a function list and then select it.

     3. Select OK. The Function Arguments dialog box is displayed and Excel automatically enters the range B7:B56 in the Number1 box.

       a. Select OK to accept the range entered by Excel. Oklahoma's dial-up accounts, 7,787, is displayed as the maximum value in the cell range specified in the function.

② DETERMINE THE LOWEST NUMBER OF DIAL-UP INTERNET ACCESS ACCOUNTS

  a. Select cell A58 and enter the label Min accounts: then right align and italicize the label.

  b. Select cell B58.

  c. Select Insert → Function. An equal sign is inserted into cell B58 and the Insert Function dialog box is displayed.

     1. Scroll until MIN is visible in the Select a function list and then select it.

     2. Select OK. The Functions Argument dialog box is displayed. Note the range B7:B57 in the Number1 box, which is not the correct range.

       a. In the Number1 box, change the range to B7:B56.

       b. Select OK. Georgia's dial-up accounts, 2, is displayed as the minimum value in the cell range specified in the function.

③ COPY THE MAX AND MIN FORMULAS

  a. Select cells B57 and B58.

  b. On the toolbar, click the Copy button ( ).

  c. Select cell C57.

  d. On the toolbar, click the Paste button ( ). The formulas are pasted into cells C57 and C58 and the cell references are automatically changed. The Paste Options button is displayed. The Paste Options button will not be used and should be ignored.

  e. Press the Esc key to remove the moving dashed outline.

④ SAVE THE MODIFIED NET PROVIDER

9.6 Absolute Cell References

As discussed in Chapter 8, relative cell references automatically change when copied. However, there may be times when a cell reference should remain the same. A cell reference that does not change when copied is called an *absolute cell reference*. An absolute cell reference contains dollar signs in front of both the column letter and row number. For example, $A$1.

In the worksheet below, shipping charges are calculated using a shipping rate stored in cell B4. In cell C7, the shipping for the first item is calculated using the formula =B7*B4. However, if this formula were copied to cells C8, C9, and C10, the cell reference B4 would become B5, B6, and B7 respectively, which is incorrect. To prevent this error, the formula in cell C7 was entered as =B7*$B$4 and then copied to cells C8 through C10:

	C10	▼	*fx*	=B10*$B$4	
	A			B	C
1	The Fresh Fruit Company				
2	Shipping Rates				
3					
4	Shipping per kg:			$1.75	
5					
6	Item			Weight (kg)	Shipping
7	Crate of Oranges			4	$7.00
8	Crate of Grapefruit			5	$8.75
9	Assorted Fruit Crate			8	$14.00
10	Seasonal Fruit Basket			7	$12.25

Note the formula in the Formula bar

F4

The F4 key can be used to place dollar signs in front of the column letter and row number in a cell reference. For example, the shipping formula in cell C7 was entered by first typing =B7*. Next, cell B4 was clicked and then the F4 key pressed to create the absolute cell reference, $B$4, in the formula.

Practice 4 ☼

In this practice you will use relative and absolute cell references to calculate revenue. Open NET PROVIDER if it is not already displayed.

① ENTER FORMULAS TO CALCULATE REVENUES

Revenue is calculated by multiplying the price per month by the number of accounts.

a. Select cell D7.

b. Type an equal sign (=).

c. Click cell B7. The cell reference is entered into the formula.

d. Type an asterisk (*).

e. Click cell B3 and then press the F4 key once. The absolute reference $B$3 appears in the formula.

f. Click the Enter button to enter the formula that calculates the revenue, $8,185.20.

g. In cell E7, enter the formula =C7*$C$3 to calculate the DSL revenue, $3,354.35.

h. In cell F7, enter the formula =D7+E7 to total the revenue for the state of Alabama.

② *COPY THE FORMULAS*

    a. Select cells D7 through F7.

    b. Drag the Fill handle in cell F7 down to cell F56. The formulas are copied for each state and the Auto Fill Options button is displayed. The Auto Fill Options button will not be used and should be ignored.

    c. Change the column widths as necessary so that all the data is displayed entirely.

③ *CREATE A HEADER AND FOOTER*

    Create a header with the date center aligned and a footer with your name right aligned.

④ *SAVE, PRINT, AND THEN CLOSE THE MODIFIED NET PROVIDER*

9.7 Inserting and Deleting Rows and Columns

The Insert Menu

A new row can be inserted by clicking the row number where the new row is to appear and then selecting Rows from the Insert menu. A new column can be inserted by clicking the column letter and then selecting Columns from the Insert menu.

The Insert Options Button

Clicking the Insert Options button (🖌) displays a list of options that can be used to change the default formatting of the new column or row to either Format Same As Right or Format Same As Below, respectively and an option to Clear Formatting.

Rows and columns can be inserted between data in a worksheet. A new row or column is inserted by right-clicking the row number or column letter where the new row or new column is to appear and then selecting Insert from the menu. If a new row is inserted, the selected row and all those below it move down to accommodate the newly inserted row. If a new column is inserted the selected column and all those after it are moved to the right. The Insert Options button (🖌) is displayed when a new row or column is inserted.

Newly inserted rows and columns are empty and contain no data or formulas. However, cells in the new row or column have the same formatting as the cells above or to the left of them respectively.

Rows and columns can also be deleted from a worksheet by right-clicking the row number or column letter and selecting Delete from the menu. If a row is deleted, all rows below the deleted row move up to fill its position. If a column is deleted, the columns to the right of the deleted column then move to the left.

Immediately selecting Undo from the Edit menu or clicking the Undo button (🔄▾) on the toolbar restores a deleted row or column.

When cells are inserted or deleted, Excel automatically changes the cell references in any affected formulas. For example, if row 3 is deleted, the formula =SUM(C1:C10) changes to =SUM(C1:C9). If a row is inserted between rows 1 and 10, the formula becomes =SUM(C1:C11).

Practice 5

In this practice you will add columns to a payroll worksheet to calculate social security, taxes, and net pay for each employee.

① *OPEN PAYROLL*

    Open PAYROLL, which is a data file for this text. The worksheet is based on the worksheet plan discussed in Section 9.1. Note that the worksheet already contains some formulas.

② ENTER A FORMULA TO CALCULATE SOCIAL SECURITY TAX

Social security tax is calculated by multiplying the gross pay by the social security rate, which is stored in cell B3.

    a. Select cell F7.

    b. Enter the formula =E7*$B$3. The social security deduction as 6.5% of the gross pay, $14.63 is displayed.

③ ENTER A FORMULA TO CALCULATE NET PAY

Net pay is calculated by subtracting the social security deduction, which is stored in cell G6, from the gross pay.

    a. Select cell G7.

    b. Enter the formula =E7–F7 to calculate the net pay, $210.38 is displayed.

④ COPY THE FORMULAS

Use the Fill handle to copy the formulas in cells F7 through G7 to cells F8 through G24. Ignore the Auto Fill Options button.

⑤ CHANGE THE SOCIAL SECURITY RATE

In cell B3, edit the value to display 6.0%. Note that Excel automatically recalculates all the values in columns F and G.

⑥ DELETE THE ROW CONTAINING DATA FOR EMPLOYEE OTIS, H.

    a. Select cell A1.

    b. Select Edit → Find. A dialog box is displayed.

        1. In the Find what box, type Otis and then select Find Next. The cell cursor is moved to the cell containing the search text "Otis."

        2. Select Close. The dialog box is removed.

    c. Right-click the row number of the row containing H. Otis' data. A menu is displayed.

    d. Select Delete. The row is deleted and all rows below it move up to fill the space. All the cell references in the formulas are automatically updated.

⑦ INSERT A COLUMN FOR THE TAXES

Taxes are calculated by multiplying the gross pay, which is stored in cell E7, by 15%.

    a. Right-click the column letter G. A menu is displayed.

    b. Select Insert. A new column is inserted. The Insert Options button is displayed. The Insert Options button will not be used and should be ignored.

    c. In cell G5, enter the label Taxes. Note that the label is automatically formatted.

    d. In cell G7, enter the formula =E7*15% to calculate 15% of the gross pay, $33.75 is displayed.

    e. Use the Fill handle to copy the new formula to cells G8 through G23. Ignore the Auto Fill Options button.

⑧ MODIFY THE NET PAY FORMULA

The Net Pay formula now needs to be edited. The social security deduction in cell F7, and the taxes deduction in cell G7, need to be subtracted from the Gross Pay.

    a. In cell H7, modify the formula to be: =E7–F7–G7. $177.75 is displayed.

    b. Use the Fill handle to copy the new formula to cells H8 through H23. Ignore the Auto Fill Options button.

9.8 Printing a Large Worksheet

A worksheet that has many columns of data is often too wide to print on a single sheet of paper. When this happens, Excel prints the worksheet on consecutive sheets starting from the leftmost column and proceeding to the right. However, changing the print orientation or the margins before printing can help fit the worksheet on a single page.

Selecting Page Setup from the File menu displays the Page Setup dialog box:

landscape orientation
portrait orientation

Selecting the Page tab and then clicking Landscape prints the worksheet across the widest part of the page in *landscape orientation.* This allows more columns and fewer rows to fit on a page. *Portrait orientation* is the default and allows more rows to be printed on a page.

One way to fit more rows and columns on a printout is to decrease the margins. Selecting the Margins tab in the Page Setup dialog box displays options that affect the margins. Decreasing the Top and Bottom margins may allow more rows to fit on a page, and decreasing the Left and Right margins may allow more columns to fit on a page.

page breaks

Page breaks are used to control how a worksheet is divided into pages. Page breaks are added by selecting Page Break from the Insert menu, which inserts a page break before the currently selected row or column. If a single cell is selected before selecting the command, the page break is created above and to the left of that cell.

A page break is indicated on the screen by a dashed line, and the effects of page breaks can be seen by previewing the worksheet. A page break is removed by selecting a cell in the row or column after the page break and then selecting Remove Page Break from the Insert menu.

Printing Labels

Specific rows and columns can be printed on every page by selecting the Sheet tab in the Page Setup dialog box and specifying the appropriate rows and columns in the Rows to repeat at top and Columns to repeat at left boxes.

9.9 The IF Function

Excel includes several built-in functions that make decisions based on the data stored in a worksheet. One of these functions is the IF function, which makes a decision based on a comparison. If the comparison is true, one value is displayed in the cell; if the comparison is false, a second value is displayed. The IF function has three arguments and takes the form:

=IF(<comparison>, <value if true>, <value if false>)

For example, the formula

=IF(C4<E7, 10, 20)

displays a 10 if the value in C4 is less than the value in E7. If the value in C4 is greater than or equal to the value in E7, 20 is displayed.

relational operators

The comparison argument of the IF function can contain one of the following *relational operators*, which are used to compare two values:

=	equal to
<	less than
>	greater than
<=	less than or equal to
>=	greater than or equal to
<>	not equal to

Nested Functions

A nested function is created when a function is used as one of the arguments of another function. For example, =IF(SUM(A1:A10) > 100, 100, 0) uses a nested SUM function.

The arguments of an IF function can contain values, cell references, or calculations as shown in the following formulas:

=IF(N1<=25, 50, 100)

=IF(B2<K25, 0, B2*15%)

=IF(C9>MIN(C2:C7), C11, C14)

=IF(D22<>F25, 0, SUM(E1:E10))

an IF example

The IF function can be used in a worksheet when a comparison is needed to make a calculation. For example, a business needs to determine if the weight of an item is over 7 kg. If it is, $5.00 is added to the charge.

Using Large Numbers with the IF Function

When entering a large number in the comparison argument of the IF function, do not include commas as thousands separators. This causes an error because Excel expects commas to separate each argument.

D7	▼	*fx*	=IF(B7>$D$3, (C7+$D$4), C7)	
	A	B	C	D	E
1	Shipping Department				
2					
3			Products Weighing Over:	7	kg
4			Additional Charge:	$5.00	
5					
6	Product	Weight (kg)	Shipping	Total	
7	garden hose	11	$14.00	$19.00	
8	lawn chair	8	$9.99	$14.99	
9	outdoor table	12	$24.99	$29.99	
10	chair cushion	3	$18.00	$18.00	

The formula in cell D7 checks if the weight value stored in cell B7 is greater than the value in cell E3, 7. If this is true, the total is calculated by adding the value stored in cell E4, $5.00, to the cost in cell C7. If the weight is less than or equal to the value in cell E3, 7, then the current cost in cell

C7 is displayed as the total. Absolute cell references are used for cells E3 and E4 so they do not change when copied.

using cell references   Note that by using cell references in the example formulas on the previous page, if the weight stored in cell E3 or shipping cost stored in cell E4 changes, formulas in cells D7 through D10 automatically recalculate.

Practice 6 ☯

In this practice you will modify the PAYROLL worksheet to calculate gross pay that includes overtime pay. Open PAYROLL if it is not already displayed.

① INSERT A COLUMN FOR THE OVERTIME HOURS

    a. Right-click the column letter E. A menu is displayed.

    b. Select Insert. A new column is inserted. Ignore the Insert Options button.

    c. In cell E5, enter the label Overtime Hours. Note that the label is automatically formatted.

    d. In cell E5, select Format → Cells. A dialog box is displayed.

        1. Select the Alignment tab if the those options are not already displayed.

        2. Select the Wrap text check box.

        3. Select OK. The label Overtime Hours is displayed on two lines in the cell. The dialog box is removed.

    e. Widen column E just enough to fit the entire word Overtime on one line and Hours below it.

② ENTER A FORMULA TO CALCULATE OVERTIME HOURS

The worksheet requires a formula that checks to see if the Hours value stored in cell D7 is greater than 40. If the value is greater than 40, overtime hours should be calculated and displayed in the cell. If not, zero should be displayed. Overtime hours are calculated by subtracting the Hours, which is stored in cell D7, from 40.

    a. In cell E7, enter the formula =IF(D7>40, D7–40, 0) to calculate any hours over 40. Note that an argument tooltip is displayed as the formula is being typed. Since the Hours value is less than 40, 0.0 is displayed.

    b. Use the Fill handle to copy the formula in cell E7 to cells E8 through E23. Ignore the Auto Fill Options button.

③ INSERT A COLUMN FOR THE OVERTIME PAY

    a. Right-click the column letter F. A menu is displayed.

    b. Select Insert. A new column is inserted. Ignore the Insert Options button.

    c. In cell F5, enter the label Overtime Pay. Note that the label is automatically formatted.

④ ENTER A FORMULA TO CALCULATE OVERTIME PAY

The worksheet requires a formula that calculates the overtime pay. Overtime pay is calculated by multiplying the overtime hours by the overtime rate, which is $15.00 per hour.

    a. In cell F7, enter the formula =E7*15 to calculate the overtime pay, 0.0 is displayed.

    b. Use the Fill handle to copy the formula in cell F7 to cells F8 through F23. Ignore the Auto Fill Options button.

    c. Format cells F7 through F23 as Currency, 2 decimals.

⑤ *ENTER A NEW GROSS PAY FORMULA*

    a. The Gross Pay formula needs to be modified to add the Overtime Pay. Modify the formula in cell G7 to be =(D7*C7)+F7. Because the value in cell F7 is 0, the gross pay does not change.

    b. Use the Fill handle to copy the formula in cell G7 to cells G8 through G23. Note the Gross Pay changes for employees who worked more than 40 hours. Ignore the Auto Fill Options button.

Check – Your worksheet should look similar to:

	A	B	C	D	E	F	G
1	Net Provider Payroll						
2							
3	Soc. Sec. Rate:	6.0%					
4							
5	Last Name	First Initial	Rate/Hr	Hours	Overtime Hours	Overtime Pay	Gross Pay
6							
7	Alban	B.	$7.50	30.0	0.0	$0.00	$225.00
8	Angulo	M.	$8.00	29.5	0.0	$0.00	$236.00
9	Balto	Y.	$8.00	29.0	0.0	$0.00	$232.00
10	Cruz	S.	$7.75	13.0	0.0	$0.00	$100.75
11	Del Vecchio	E.	$9.00	43.5	3.5	$52.50	$444.00

⑥ *VIEW THE WORKSHEET AS IT WILL APPEAR WHEN PRINTED*

    a. Select File ➞ Print Preview. The Print Preview window is displayed. Note that in portrait orientation the worksheet is displayed on two pages. Use the scroll bar to preview page 2.

    b. Select Close. The worksheet window is again displayed.

    c. Select File ➞ Page Setup. A dialog box is displayed.

        1. Select the Page tab to display those options if they are not already displayed.

        2. Select the Landscape option.

        3. Select OK. The dialog box is removed.

    d. Preview the worksheet. Note that in landscape orientation the worksheet is displayed on one page.

    e. Select Close. The worksheet window is again displayed.

⑦ *CREATE A HEADER AND FOOTER*

    Create a header with the date center aligned and a footer with your name right aligned.

⑧ *SAVE, PRINT, AND THEN CLOSE THE MODIFIED PAYROLL*

9.10 Using Text in the IF Function

Text can also be used in the IF function:

C3	▼	*fx* =IF(B3>=70, "Plenty", "Reorder")		
	A	B	C	D	E
1	Tool Inventory				
2	Item	In Stock	Status		
3	Drill	78	Plenty		

Cell C3 contains the formula

=IF(B3>=70, "Plenty", "Reorder")

which displays Plenty if the value in cell B3 is greater than or equal to 70. Otherwise, Reorder is displayed. Notice that quotation marks must surround text in a function.

Cell references of a cell storing a label can also be used in the IF function. For example, if Plenty is stored in cell E1 and Reorder in cell E2, then the formula =IF(B3>=70, E1, E2) produces the same result as the formula above.

To check to see if a cell's contents are empty, two adjacent quotation marks can be used. For example, =IF(B20="", "Yes", "No") displays Yes if the cell contents are empty and No if there is data in the cell. Two adjacent quotation marks can also be used to display nothing in a cell. For example, =IF(B3>=70, "", "Reorder") displays a blank cell if the value in cell B3 is greater than or equal to 70. Otherwise, Reorder is displayed.

Text can also be used in the comparison part of the IF function. When compared, the alphabetical order of the text is determined. For example, the following formula displays True because apple comes before orange alphabetically:

=IF("apple"<"orange", "True", "False")

Cells that store labels can also be compared. If apple is stored in cell B3 and orange is stored in cell B5, the formula =IF(B3<B5, B3, B5) displays apple.

The COUNTIF Function

The COUNTIF function is used to determine how many cells meet a certain condition. For example, the formula =COUNTIF(D1:D50, "Reorder") determines how many cells in the range D1 through D50 contain the label Reorder. The COUNTIF function can include relational operators. For example, the formula =COUNTIF (D1:D15, ">80") determines how many cells in the range D1 through D15 contain a value greater than 80.

Practice 7 ⟳

In this practice the Grades workbook will be modified to display each student's status.

① *OPEN GRADES*

Open Grades, which was last modified in Chapter 8, Practice 8.

② *ENTER A LABEL AND FORMAT IT*

In cell G1, enter the label Status and then center align it. The label is automatically formatted in bold.

③ **ENTER FORMULAS TO DETERMINE THE STUDENTS' STATUS**

    a. In cell G4, enter the formula:

        =IF(F4>=70, "Passing", "Below Average")

    Note that an argument tooltip is displayed as the formula is being typed. Since the value in cell F4 is greater than or equal to 70, Passing is displayed in cell G4.

    b. Center align the label in cell G4.

    c. Copy the formula in cell G4 to cells G5 through G9. Note that since the value in cell F6 is less than 70, Below Average is displayed in cell G6.

    d. Widen column G to display all the labels entirely.

    e. Click on a blank cell to remove the selection.

Check – Your worksheet should look similar to:

	A	B	C	D	E	F	G
1	**Name**	**Test 1**	**Test 2**	**Test 3**	**Test 4**	**Student Average**	**Status**
2		1/7/03	2/9/03	3/1/03	4/1/03		
3							
4	Jones, D.	85	73	88	95	85	Passing
5	Neave, C.	92	88	85	91	89	Passing
6	Garcia, E.	72	63	67	72	69	Below Average
7	McCallister, T.	87	92	85	93	89	Passing
8	Smith, L.	94	91	93	84	91	Passing
9	Bell, M.	70	74	80	83	77	Passing
10	*Test Average*	83.3	80.2	83	86.3		

④ **SAVE, PRINT, AND THEN CLOSE THE MODIFIED GRADES**

⑤ **QUIT EXCEL**

Chapter Summary

This chapter covered planning and modifying large worksheets. Worksheets should be carefully planned before creating them in Excel by first deciding what information the worksheet will produce, what data is required, what formulas are required, and how the worksheet will be organized. A sketch of the worksheet is the best way to illustrate how the data will be organized.

A worksheet can be searched by selecting the Find command. Selecting the Replace command locates data and then replaces it with other data supplied by the user.

Data can be duplicated using the Copy button (⧉) and Paste button(⧉▾) on the toolbar. Data can be moved to a different location in the worksheet using the Cut button (✂)and Paste button(⧉▾) on the toolbar.

The MAX and MIN functions display the maximum and minimum values stored in a specified range of cells, respectively.

An alternative to typing a function name into a formula is to select the Function command or click the Insert Function button on the Formula bar, which displays a dialog box where a function can be selected.

A cell reference that does not change when copied is called an absolute cell reference. An absolute cell reference contains a dollar sign in front of both the column letter and row number. For example, $A$1. The F4 key can be used to place dollar signs in a cell reference.

Rows and columns can be inserted between data in a worksheet by right-clicking the row number or column letter and selecting Insert from the menu. Rows and columns are deleted from a worksheet by right-clicking the row number or column letter and selecting Delete from the menu. When cells are inserted or deleted, Excel automatically changes the cell references in any affected formulas.

Modifying the margins or print orientation by selecting the Page Setup command changes the way a worksheet is printed. Printing a worksheet in landscape orientation prints more columns and fewer rows on a page. A page break can be used to control how a worksheet is divided into pages. A page break is added by selecting the Page Break command. A page break is removed by selecting the Remove Page Break command.

A decision can be made based on the data in a worksheet by using the IF function. When a comparison is true, the second argument in the function is displayed in the current cell. When a comparison is false, the third argument is shown. For example, evaluating the formula =IF(A5>B4, 30, 15) displays 30 when the value in A5 is greater than the value in B4, and 15 when the value in A5 is less than or equal to the value in B4. The comparison argument of the IF function uses relational operators (=, <, <=, >, >=, <>).

Relational operators can also be used to compare text in the comparison part of the IF function. For example, if cell A5 contains George and B12 contains Andrews, then the formula =IF(A5<B12, "Yes", "No") displays No since George comes before Andrews alphabetically.

Text can be used in the IF function. For example, the formula =IF(A5<30, "Cheap", "Expensive") displays Cheap if A5 is less than 30 and Expensive if A5 is greater than or equal to 30. The cell reference of a cell storing a label can also be used in the IF function. To check to see if a cell's contents are empty, two adjacent quotation marks can be used. Two adjacent quotation marks can also be used to display nothing in a cell.

Vocabulary

Absolute cell reference A cell references that does not change when copied because a dollar sign has been placed in front of both the column letter and row number, such as $A$5.

Destination The upper-left cell of the range where data is to be pasted.

F4 key Places dollar signs in front of the column letter and row number in a cell reference.

IF Function that makes a decision based on a comparison.

Landscape orientation A print orientation that prints a worksheet across the widest part of the page.

MAX Function that displays the largest value in a range of cells.

MIN Function that displays the smallest value in a range of cells.

Portrait orientation The default print orientation that allows more rows to be printed on a page.

Relational operators Used to compare two values. Operators include =, <, >, <=, >=, <>.

Source Selected cells that are to be copied.

Excel Commands and Buttons

Copy button Places the selected cell(s) on the Clipboard. Found on the toolbar. Copy in the Edit menu can be used instead of the button.

Cut button Removes the selected cell(s) and places them on the Clipboard. Found on the toolbar. Cut in the Edit menu can be used instead of the button.

Delete command Deletes a selected column or row from a worksheet. Found in the menu displayed by right-clicking a row or column.

Find command Displays a dialog box that allows the user to search a worksheet for data. Found in the Edit menu.

Function command Displays a dialog box that can be used to insert a function into a formula. Found in the Insert menu. The Insert Function button on the Formula bar can be used instead of the command.

Insert command Inserts a row or column. Found in the menu displayed by right-clicking a row number or column letter.

Insert Options button Displayed when a new row or column is inserted.

Page Break command Inserts a page break before the currently selected row or column. Found in the Insert menu.

Page Setup command Displays a dialog box with margin and the print orientation options. Found in the File menu.

Paste Options button Displayed when contents of the Clipboard are placed in cells.

Paste button Places the Clipboard contents in a worksheet starting at the selected cell. Found on the toolbar. Paste in the Edit menu can be used instead of the button.

Remove Page Break command Removes a page break. Found in the Insert menu.

Replace command Displays a dialog box that allows the user to search a worksheet for data and replace it with other data. Found in the Edit menu.

Undo command Restores the previous action. Found in the Edit menu. The Undo button on the toolbar can be used instead of the command.

Review Questions

Sections 9.1 — 9.6

1. What four questions should be answered when planning a large worksheet?

2. Sketch the layout for a worksheet that will contain an automobile dealership's inventory. The worksheet should include model names, quantity in stock, and asking prices.

3. a) List the steps required to find each cell in a worksheet that contains the SUM function.
   b) List the steps required to find each cell in a worksheet that contains the label Jamie and replace it with the label Pat.

4. List the steps required to copy the contents of cell B4 into cell A9.

5. List the steps required to move the values stored in cells A1, A2, and A3 to cells T1, T2, and T3.

6. What key is pressed to remove the dashed outline from the source cells once the cells have been pasted?

7. When pasting cell contents in the range G1 through H10, what cell needs to be selected before selecting the Paste command?

8. Write a formula that calculates:
   a) the maximum value stored in the range of cells D4 to Y5.
   b) the minimum value stored in the range of cells C1 to C9.

9. List the steps required to enter a function into a formula without typing the function.

10. What is the difference between a relative cell reference and an absolute cell reference?

11. List the steps required to create a formula in cell G5 that multiplies the value in cell F5 with the value in cell B1 so that when the formula is copied, the cell reference to B1 remains constant.

Sections 9.7 — 9.10

12. List the steps required to insert a column between column A and column B.

13. List the steps required to delete row 8.

14. a) What formatting is in a newly inserted row?
    b) What formatting is in a newly inserted column?

15. a) The formula =SUM(C3:C22) is used to sum the values in cells C3 to C22. If a row is inserted directly above row 20, what must be done to include the new cell in the sum?
    b) If a row is inserted directly above row 24, what must be done to include the new cell in the sum?
    c) If row 20 is deleted, what must be done to the formula so that the deleted cell is no longer in the range?

16. a) List the steps required to print a worksheet across the widest part of the paper.
    b) What can be decreased in order to fit more rows and columns on a printout?

17. What can be used to control how a worksheet is divided into pages?

18. What will be displayed by the following formulas if cell D4 stores a value of 30 and cell E7 stores a value of –12?
    a) =IF(D4<=E7, 10, 20)
    b) =IF(E7*D4<-5, E7, D4)
    c) =IF(D4–42=E7, D4*2, E7*3)

19. Write a formula that:
    a) displays 50 if the value stored in D20 equals the value in C70, or 25 if they are not equal.
    b) displays the value in B40 if the sum of the range of cells C20 to C30 exceeds 1000, otherwise displays a 0.
    c) displays the value of R20*10 if R20 is less than 30, otherwise displays the value in R20.

20. Write formulas using the IF function for each of the following:
    a) If B3 is less than or equal to C12 display Low, if greater than display High.
    b) If A5 is equal to Z47 display Jonathan, if not equal to display Judith.
    c) If cell C6 is empty, display the contents of cell D3, otherwise display New Student.

Exercises

Exercise 1 ———————————————MULTIPLICATION

An elementary school teacher wants to use a worksheet to create multiplication tables for her students. Open MULTIPLICATION and complete the following steps:

a) Copy the contents of cells A3 through E13 to cells A15 through E25.

b) In cell A15, type 1 to replace the 0. Note that the table now contains a multiplication table for 1.

c) In columns A through E, create multiplication tables for numbers 2 through 5 by copying and pasting the values and formulas in cell A3 through E13, replacing the bold number appropriately. Leave a blank row between each table.

d) In columns G through K, create multiplication tables for numbers 6 through 11 by copying and pasting the values and formulas in cell A3 through E13, replacing the bold number appropriately. Leave a blank row between each table.

e) Change the print orientation to landscape and adjust the margins appropriately so that none of the multiplication tables are split on separate pages when the worksheet is printed.

f) Create a header with your name right aligned.

g) Save the modified MULTIPLICATION and print a copy with gridlines and row and column headings.

Exercise 2 ⟳ ———————————— Squeaky Clean Cars

The budget created in Chapter 8, Exercise 2 needs to be modified to include July's budgeted expenses. Open Squeaky Clean Cars and complete the following steps:

a) Copy the contents of cells B3 and B4 to cells F3 and F4. In cell F3, change June to July.

b) July's budgeted expenses are based on the differences between the budgeted and actual expenses for June stored in column D. July's budgeted expenses will be the same as those for June when the difference is greater than or equal to 0, otherwise they will be 30% more. In column F, enter formulas that use a function to calculate the budgeted expenses for July. Include proper formatting.

c) Copy the formula in cell B11 to cell F11.

d) Save the modified Squeaky Clean Cars and print a copy with gridlines and row and column headings.

e) Display the formulas in the cells instead of values. Change the column widths as necessary so that the formulas are completely displayed. Print a copy.

Exercise 3 ✍ ————————————————————— Swim Meet

The swim meet workbook created in Chapter 8, Exercise 3 needs to be modified. Open Swim Meet and complete the following steps:

a) Pats's scores need to be added to the worksheet. The following are the times for Pat: 2:45:55, 3:12:07, 2:45:19, 3:02:00, 4:45:57, and 5:45:10. Insert a column between columns E and F, and then enter the values and an appropriate column heading.

b) In the next available columns, enter formulas that use functions to calculate the fastest time and slowest time for each event (remember the fastest time in swimming is the lowest time). Include appropriate column headings and right align the labels. Change the column widths so that all the data is displayed entirely, if necessary.

c) Save the modified Swim Meet and print a copy in landscape orientation with gridlines and row and column headings.

d) Display the formulas in the cells instead of values. Change the column widths as necessary so that the formulas are completely displayed. Print a copy.

Exercise 4 ✍ ————————————————————— Student Stats

The student statistics workbook created in Chapter 8, Exercise 4 needs to be modified. Open Student Stats and complete the following steps:

a) The Engineering and Nursing colleges need to be added to the worksheet. Insert the new data shown below into the worksheet so the colleges remain in alphabetical order:

College	Undergraduate	Graduate
Engineering	1,645	179
Nursing	876	45

b) In rows 12 and 13, enter formulas that use functions to calculate:

- the maximum number of undergraduate students and the maximum number of graduate students in college
- the minimum number of undergraduate students and the minimum number of graduate students in college

Include appropriate labels and proper formatting. Change the column widths so that all the data is displayed entirely, if necessary.

c) Save the modified Student Stats and print a copy with gridlines and row and column headings.

d) Display the formulas in the cells instead of values. Change the column widths as necessary so that the formulas are completely displayed. Print a copy.

Exercise 5 ⚙ ——————————————— Coral Employees

The payroll workbook created in Chapter 8, Exercise 5 needs to be modified. Open Coral Employees and complete the following steps:

a) The comptroller has hired two more employees. Insert the new data shown below into the worksheet so that the employee names remain in alphabetical order by last name:

First Name	Last Name	Salary
Dedra	Roberts	$42,000
Philip	Jorge	$28,000

Copy the weekly pay formula for the new employees into cells D6 and D7.

b) Tax deductions are calculated by multiplying 15% by the weekly pay when the salary is less than $30,000, and 28% by the weekly pay when the salary is equal to or higher than $30,000. In column E, enter the label Taxes and then enter formulas that use a function and cell references to calculate the taxes. Right align the label and format the values as currency with 2 decimals.

c) Social security deductions also need to be calculated. Insert two blank rows at the top of the worksheet. In cell A1, enter the label Soc. Sec. Rate:. In cell C1, enter the value 6%. In column F, enter the label Soc. Sec., right align it, and then enter formulas that use absolute and relative cell references to calculate social security of each employee by multiplying the rate by the weekly pay.

d) Net pay is computed by making the necessary deductions from the weekly pay. In column G, enter the label Net Pay, right align it, and then enter formulas that use cell references to deduct the taxes and social security from the weekly pay of each employee to get the net pay.

e) The employees of Coral County receive yearly bonuses based on the position they hold. Cho, Roberts, and White are managers. The rest of the employees are assistants. Insert a column after the salary column, and enter the label Position. Enter the appropriate position for each person, either Manager or Assistant and center align the entire column.

f) Every year, managers receive a bonus of 20% of their weekly pay and assistants receive a bonus of 10% of their weekly pay. In column I, enter the label Bonus, right align it, and enter formulas that use a function and cell references to calculate the bonus amounts for each employee.

g) Format all the data appropriately. Change the column widths so that all the data is displayed entirely and fits on one page.

h) Save the modified Coral Employees and print a copy with gridlines and row and column headings.

i) Display the formulas in the cells instead of values. Change the column widths as necessary so that the formulas are completely displayed. Print a copy.

Exercise 6 ☼ —————————————————————————— Dive Log

The dive log workbook created in Chapter 8, Exercise 6 needs to be modified. Open Dive Log and complete the following steps:

a) Two dives were not recorded. Insert the new data shown below into the worksheet so that the dates remain in chronological order:

Date	Depth (m)	Duration (min)	Water Temp (Celsius)	Visibility (m)
5/9/2003	15	45	28	11
5/12/2003	20	40	24	9

b) In rows 11 and 12, enter formulas that use functions to calculate:

- the maximum depth of the dives and the maximum duration of the dives
- the minimum depth of the dives and the minimum duration of the dives

Include appropriate labels and proper formatting. Change the column widths as necessary so that all the data is displayed entirely.

c) Save the modified Dive Log and print a copy with gridlines and row and column headings.

d) Display the formulas in the cells instead of values. Change the column widths as necessary so that the formulas are completely displayed. Print a copy.

Exercise 7 ☼ —————————————————————————— Pizza Palace

The expense workbook created in Chapter 8, Exercise 7 needs to be modified. Open Pizza Palace and complete the following steps:

a) Pepperoni pizza needs to be added to the worksheet between the Vegetarian and Cheese pizza columns. Enter an appropriate column heading and values for the pepperoni pizza. Copy the cost of pizza formula for the pepperoni pizza into cell D14.

b) Change the column widths so that all the data is displayed entirely, if necessary.

c) The menu price for each pizza needs to be added to the worksheet in row 15. When the cost of pizza is less than or equal to $4.00 the price is one and a half (1.5) times the cost, and it is two (2) times the cost when it is greater than $4.00. Enter formulas that use a function and cell references to calculate the menu price of the pizzas. Include an appropriate label and proper formatting.

d) Save the modified Pizza Palace and print a copy with gridlines and row and column headings.

e) Display the formulas in the cells instead of values. Change the column widths as necessary so that the formulas are completely displayed. Print a copy.

Exercise 8 ─────────────────────────────PROFIT

The PROFIT workbook contains income and expenses for a company. Open PROFIT and complete the following steps:

   a) In row 6, enter formulas that use a function to calculate the total income for each year. Total income is calculated by summing the three type of sales.

   b) Change the column widths as necessary so that all the data is displayed entirely.

   c) In row 14, enter formulas that use a function to calculate the total expenses for each year. Total expenses are calculated by summing all the expense categories.

   d) In row 15, enter formulas that use cell references to calculate the profit for each year. Profit is calculated by subtracting total expenses from the total income.

   e) In rows 18 and 19, enter formulas that use functions to calculate the highest and lowest sales amounts of the three types of sales for each year.

   f) Row 15 stores the profit and row 16 stores the profit that the company wanted to obtain. In row 20, enter formulas that use a function to display Yes if the profit goal was reached or No if the actual profit was less than the profit goal.

   g) Center align the labels in cells B20 through E20.

   h) Create a header with your name right aligned.

   i) Save the modified PROFIT and print a copy with gridlines and row and column headings.

   j) Display the formulas in the cells instead of values. Change the column widths as necessary so that the formulas are completely displayed. Print a copy.

Exercise 9 ───────────────────────────── DANCE

The DANCE workbook contains income and expenses information for a dance. The dance coordinator wants to know how much profit the dance will make depending on the number of people attending. Open DANCE and complete the following steps:

   a) In row 4, enter formulas that use absolute and relative cell references to calculate expected income from tickets when 50, 100, 200, or 300 people attend the dance.

   b) In row 5, enter formulas that use absolute and relative cell references to calculate expected income from food when 50, 100, 200, or 300 people attend the dance.

   c) In row 6, enter formulas that use absolute and relative cell references to calculate expected income from beverages when 50, 100, 200, or 300 people attend the dance.

   d) In row 8, enter formulas that use absolute and relative cell references to calculate the ticket printing expense when 50, 100, 200, or 300 people attend the dance.

   e) In row 9, enter formulas that use absolute and relative cell references to calculate the food expense when 50, 100, 200, or 300 people attend the dance.

   f) In row 10, enter formulas that use absolute and relative cell references to calculate the beverages expense when 50, 100, 200, or 300 people attend the dance.

   g) In row 11, enter formulas that use functions to calculate the profit (total income less total expenses) for the different number of people attending the dance.

   h) Change the column widths as necessary so that all the data is displayed entirely.

i) Create a header with your name right aligned.

j) Save the modified DANCE and print a copy with gridlines and row and column headings.

k) Display the formulas in the cells instead of values. Change the column widths as necessary so that the formulas are completely displayed. Print a copy.

Exercise 10 ———————————————————————————— STOCKS

The STOCKS workbook contains stock information. Open STOCKS and complete the following steps:

a) Determine how much was originally paid for each stock. Insert a column between the Purchase Price and Jan columns. Enter the label Original Value and then enter formulas that use cell references to calculate the original value of each stock. The original value of each stock is calculated by multiplying the shares purchased by the purchase price.

b) Determine how much each stock is worth in March. In column H, enter the label March Value and then enter formulas that calculate the value of each stock in March. The value is calculated by multiplying the shares purchased by the price they are selling for in March.

c) Change column widths as necessary so that all the data is displayed entirely.

d) In rows 17 and 18, enter formulas that use functions to calculate:

- the maximum original value and the maximum March value
- the minimum original value and the minimum March value

Include appropriate labels in columns C and G and proper formatting. Change column widths as necessary so that all the data is displayed entirely.

e) It would be best to sell those stocks in March which have a value at least 25% higher than their original value. In column I, enter formulas that use a function to display Sell for stocks that should be sold or Retain for stocks that should be held. Include an appropriate column heading and proper formatting. Size the column as necessary so that all the data is displayed entirely.

f) Center align the data in Column I.

g) Create a header with your name right aligned.

h) Save the modified STOCKS and print a copy in landscape orientation with gridlines and row and column headings.

i) Display the formulas in the cells instead of values. Change the column widths as necessary so that the formulas are completely displayed. Print a copy.

A Guide to Microsoft Office XP Professional

The manager of an amphitheater wants to use a worksheet to calculate ticket prices. There are three types of tickets: Floor, Balcony, and General Admission. The price of the tickets are different for each act and the amphitheater charges a handling fee for all tickets.

a) Create a new workbook.

b) Enter the following data starting in cell A1:

	A	B	C
1	Act	Seats	Price
2			
3	The Motherboards	Floor	$55
4		Balcony	$40
5		General Adm.	$28
6	Blue Knights	Floor	$65
7		Balcony	$40
8		General Adm.	$28
9	The Altairs	Floor	$85
10		Balcony	$65
11		General Adm.	$28

c) Bold the labels in row 1, italic the act titles, and right align the Price label. Change column widths as necessary so that all the data is displayed entirely. Save the worksheet naming it Tickets.

d) Replace all occurrences of "General Adm." with General Admission.

e) In the next available column, enter formulas that use a function to calculate the handling fee. The handling fee is $5 when the price of the ticket is less than or equal to $50, and $10 when the ticket price is greater than $50. Include an appropriate label and proper formatting.

f) In the next available column, enter formulas that use cell references to calculate the total price. The total price of the ticket is the price of the ticket plus the handling fee. Include an appropriate label and proper formatting.

g) Change column widths as necessary so that all the data is displayed entirely.

h) Create a header with your name right aligned.

i) Save the modified Tickets and print a copy with gridlines and row and column headings.

j) Display the formulas in the cells instead of values. Change the column widths as necessary so that the formulas are completely displayed. Print a copy.

Exercise 12 ———————————————— Track Progress

A track team coach wants to use a worksheet to keep track of the team's progress of the 100 meter and 200 meter runs. The worksheet should record the names of the members, the time in seconds, and the distance in meters for each month January through April.

a) Create a new workbook.

b) At the top of a new worksheet in separate cells, include labels and values for the state record of 13.5 seconds for the 100 meter and 26.7 seconds for the 200 meter. Bold the labels.

c) Enter the following data into the worksheet starting in cell A4:

	A	B	C	D	E	F
1	**100 meter**	13.5				
2	**200 meter**	26.7				
3						
4	Meters	Student	January	February	March	April
5						
6	100	Hannah Otis	16.5	16.3	16	15.8
7	100	Russel Rosen	16.8	16.9	16.5	16.2
8	100	Rolanda Lopez	15.5	14.4	14	14.4
9	100	Paul Quinn	18.5	18.3	18	17.8
10	200	Hannah Otis	34.9	34.8	34.8	34.7
11	200	Emma Del Vecchio	32.5	32.4	32	31.8
12	200	Paul Quinn	35.5	35.3	35	34.8
13	200	Callie Ramis	30.7	30.3	30.3	30.2

d) In row 4, bold the labels and right align the labels in columns C through F. Left align the data in column A. Format all the times as number with 1 decimal place. Change column widths as necessary so that all the data is displayed entirely. Save the worksheet naming it Track Progress.

e) In column G, enter formulas that use a function to calculate the fastest time during the four months for each student (remember the fastest time in running is the lowest time).

f) In column H, enter formulas that use a function to calculate the slowest time during the four months for each student.

g) In column I, enter formulas that use a function to calculate the difference between the fastest time and the state record depending on the type of race. (Hint: You should do a comparison using the IF function with absolute and relative cell references to determine the type of race.)

h) In columns G through I, include appropriate labels and proper formatting. Format all the times as number with 1 decimal place. Change column widths as necessary so that all the data is displayed entirely.

i) Paul Quinn's February time for the 200 meter should be 35.8. Update the worksheet.

j) Create a header with your name right aligned.

k) Save the modified Track Progress and print a copy in landscape orientation with gridlines and row and column headings.

l) Display the formulas in the cells instead of values. Change the column widths as necessary so that the formulas are completely displayed. Print a copy.

A Guide to Microsoft Office XP Professional

Exercise 13 —————————————————————— Coins

A coin collector wants to use a worksheet to keep track of the value of each coin in the collection. The worksheet should record the coin name, year of coin, condition, and estimated value.

a) Create a new workbook.

b) The condition of a coin is called its grade, and it is a major factor in determining a coin's worth. Coins are rated using the Mint State (MS) grade scale, which ranges from 60 (low) to 70 (high). Enter the following coin data starting in cell A1:

	A	B	C	D
1	Coin	Year	Grade	Value
2				
3	Half Dollar	1860	Mint State-63	$679
4	Half Dollar	1917	Mint State-63	$125
5	Half Dollar	1937	Mint State-63	$39
6	Half Dollar	1942	Mint State-64	$34
7	Half Dollar	1946	Mint State-65	$109
8	Quarter Eagle	1913	Mint State-62	$449
9	Eagle	1901	Mint State-62	$495

Bold the labels in row 1 and right align the Year and Value labels. Center align column C. Format the coin values as currency with 0 decimal places. Change column widths as necessary so that all the data is displayed entirely. Save the worksheet naming it Coins.

c) Replace all occurrences of "Mint State" with MS.

d) In rows 10, 11, and 12, enter formulas that use a function to calculate:

- the maximum value of a single coin in the collection
- the minimum value of a single coin in the collection
- the total value of the collection

Include appropriate right aligned and bold labels in column C. Change column widths as necessary so that all the data is displayed entirely.

e) The collector has decided that it would be best to trade those coins which have a value less than or equal to $150. In the next available column, enter the label Status and bold it. Enter formulas that use a function to display Trade for the coins that should be traded or Keep for coins that should not be traded.

f) Center align the data in column E.

g) Create a header with your name right aligned.

h) Save the modified Coins and print a copy with gridlines and row and column headings.

i) Display the formulas in the cells instead of values. Change the column widths as necessary so that the formulas are completely displayed. Print a copy.

The Meteorology department at the local university wants to use a worksheet to record the average yearly temperatures for a city.

a) Create a new workbook.

b) Enter the data below starting in cell A1. To save typing, use a formula to calculate and display the years:

	A	B
1	Year	Temp (Celsius)
2		
3	1984	18
4	1985	14
5	1986	19
6	1987	20
7	1988	22
8	1989	23
9	1990	19
10	1991	22
11	1992	23
12	1993	19
13	1994	22
14	1995	18
15	1996	18
16	1997	22
17	1998	21
18	1999	22
19	2000	19
20	2001	22
21	2002	19
22	2003	22

c) Bold and right align the labels in row 1. Change column widths as necessary so that all the data is displayed entirely. Save the worksheet naming it City Temp.

d) In rows 23 and 24, enter formulas that use a function to calculate:

- the highest temperature within the 20 years
- the lowest temperature within the 20 years

Include appropriate labels and proper formatting. Change column widths as necessary so that all the data is displayed entirely.

e) Create a header with your name right aligned.

f) Save the modified City Temp and print a copy with gridlines and row and column headings.

g) Display the formulas in the cells instead of values. Change the column widths as necessary so that the formulas are completely displayed. Print a copy.

Exercise 15 ——————————————— Retirement Contributions

The owner of a small appliance company wants to keep track of employee retirement contributions.

  a) Create a new workbook.

  b) Enter the data below starting in cell A1:

	A	B	C
1	Alberto's Appliances		
2			
3	Employee	Full-time Salary	Part-time Hourly
4			
5	Anderson	$50,000	
6	Boyd		$18.00
7	Carlson	$35,000	
8	Dugan	$28,500	
9	Evans		$13.50
10	Niemiec	$44,000	
11	Rodriguez		$10.00

  c) Bold the labels in rows 1 and 3. Right align the labels in columns B and C. Format the values in column B as currency with 0 decimal places and format the values in column C as currency with 2 decimal places. Change column widths as necessary so that all the data is displayed entirely. Save the worksheet naming it Retirement Contributions.

  d) In cell D3, enter the label Retirement Contribution. Bold and right-align the label. Change column width as necessary so that all the data is displayed entirely.

  e) In column D, enter formulas that use a function to calculate the retirement contributions. Only Full-time Salary employees make retirement contributions and they contribute 4% of their salary. Include proper formatting.

  f) Create a header with your name right aligned.

  g) Save the modified Retirement Contributions and print a copy with gridlines and row and column headings.

  h) Display the formulas in the cells instead of values. Change the column widths as necessary so that the formulas are completely displayed. Print a copy.

Exercise 16 (advanced) ——————————————— My Finances

A worksheet is a good way to manage your personal finances. Plan a worksheet to record your income and expenses each month for a year. A number of categories such as food, movies, and clothing should be selected so that few of your expenses fall into a miscellaneous category. Include a savings category that uses an IF function to either display a zero if you spent more money than you had or display the percent of income you saved based on the amount of income and expenses for that month. The worksheet should also include formulas that use functions to total the income and expenses for each month and for each category for the year. Format all the data appropriately. Save the workbook naming it My Finances and print a copy.

Exercise 17 (advanced) —————————— My Checking Account

Plan a worksheet to keep track of your checking account. The worksheet should include a starting balance, transaction dates, check numbers, transaction amounts, and descriptions. It should also be able to handle deposits. The worksheet should use formulas that contain cell references to determine the new balance after each transaction. Format all the data appropriately. Save the workbook naming it My Checking Account and print a copy.

Exercise 18 (advanced) ———————————————————————

Modify one of the worksheets created in Exercises 16, 17, or 18 in Chapter 8 to include four additional rows and one additional column of data. Also include at least one formula containing the IF function. Format the worksheet appropriately. Save the modified workbook and print a copy.

A Guide to Microsoft Office XP Professional

Chapter 10
Worksheets and Charts

Chapter 10 Expectations

After completing this chapter you will be able to:
1. Organize data using multiple sheets in a workbook.
2. Copy and move data between sheets.
3. Refer to data in different sheets.
4. Link cells.
5. Print an entire workbook.
6. Create pie, bar, and line charts.
7. Modify, format, and print charts.

This chapter discusses how to use multiple worksheets in a workbook. Creating charts using the data stored in a worksheet is also explained.

10.1 Using Multiple Sheets

Multiple sheets within a workbook can be used to organize, store, and link related information. For example, a workbook named Clothing Sales could contain a sheet for the 2002 Sales data, a sheet for the 2003 Sales, and a sheet for the 2004 Forecast:

	A	B	C	D	E
1	Clothing Sales				
2	2002 Sales Summary				
3					
4	Store	First Quarter	Second Quarter	Third Quarter	Fourth Quarter
5					
6	Seattle West	$87,989.00	$105,586.80	$52,793.40	$81,829.77
7	Seattle East	$123,898.00	$148,677.60	$74,338.80	$115,225.14
8	Los Angeles	$767,898.00	$921,477.60	$460,738.80	$714,145.14
9	Toronto	$898,999.00	$1,078,798.80	$539,399.40	$836,069.07
10	Oakville	$345,982.00	$415,178.40	$207,589.20	$321,763.26
11	Mississauga	$123,897.00	$148,676.40	$74,338.20	$115,224.21
12	Miami	$987,222.00	$1,184,666.40	$592,333.20	$918,116.46
13	Tampa	$123,897.00	$148,676.40	$74,338.20	$115,224.21
14	New York	$457,230.00	$548,676.00	$274,338.00	$425,223.90
15	Denver	$500,034.00	$600,040.80	$300,020.40	$465,031.62
16					

I◄ ◄ ► ►I \ **2002 Sales** ╱ 2003 Sales ╱ 2004 Forecast ╱   I◄

Ready   NUM

displaying a sheet   The sheets that make up a workbook are displayed, or made *active*, by clicking the appropriate tab at the bottom of the Excel window:

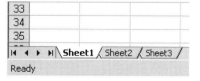

Sheet1 is the active sheet

renaming a sheet   Sheets are given the default names of Sheet1, Sheet2, and Sheet3. A sheet can be renamed by double-clicking its tab to select it, typing a new name, and then pressing Enter. Changing the default name to a name that is descriptive of the worksheet contents makes working with multiple sheets easier.

adding and deleting sheets

The number of worksheets in a workbook can be changed. A new sheet is inserted in front of the active sheet by selecting <u>W</u>orksheet from the <u>I</u>nsert menu. A sheet is deleted by right-clicking its tab and selecting Delete from the menu.

moving and copying sheets

Sheet order can be changed by dragging a sheet tab to a new location within the sheet tabs. When a sheet tab is dragged, a solid triangle is displayed indicating where the sheet is being moved to and the pointer changes to ◻:

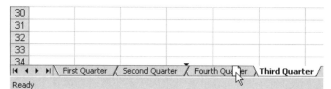

The Third Quarter sheet is being moved in front of the Fourth Quarter sheet

The sheet is moved when the mouse button is released. Similarly, a sheet can be copied by dragging its tab to the desired location while holding down the Ctrl key.

Scrolling Sheets

Renaming sheets and adding sheets to a workbook may result in some of the sheet tabs not being displayed. Tab scrolling buttons are displayed to the left of the sheet tabs, and are used to scroll the sheet tabs:

From left to right, the buttons scroll to the first sheet tab, previous sheet tab, next sheet tab, and last sheet tab.

10.2 Copying and Moving Data Between Sheets

Data can copied and moved between sheets. The steps for copying or moving a range of cells between sheets are:

1. Select the source, which is the cell(s) to be copied.

2. Click the Copy button (▤) on the toolbar to copy data or the Cut button (✂) on the toolbar to move data. A copy of the source is added to the Clipboard.

3. Click the sheet tab of the worksheet that is to receive the copied data.

4. Select the destination, which is the upper-left cell of the range where the data is to be pasted.

5. Click the Paste button (▤▾) on the toolbar. The contents of the Clipboard are placed in the cell(s) and the Paste Options button (▤) is displayed. Note that the source formatting is copied as well.

The Cu<u>t</u> (Ctrl+X), <u>C</u>opy (Ctrl+C), and <u>P</u>aste (Ctrl+V) commands in the <u>E</u>dit menu can be used instead of the buttons.

Edit

↶	Can't <u>U</u>ndo	Ctrl+Z
✂	Cu<u>t</u>	Ctrl+X
▤	<u>C</u>opy	Ctrl+C
▤	<u>P</u>aste	Ctrl+V
🔍	<u>F</u>ind...	Ctrl+F
	⌄	

Practice 1

In this practice you will modify a workbook that contains three different sheets.

① *OPEN CAR SALES*

Open CAR SALES, which is a data file for this text. This workbook contains data in three different sheets: New Car Sales, Sheet2, and Used Car Sales. The Total Sales column in the New Car Sales sheet contains formulas.

> a. Click the Sheet2 tab at the bottom of the workbook. The second sheet in the workbook is displayed.
>
> b. Click the Used Car Sales tab. The third sheet in the workbook is displayed.

③ *CHANGE THE ORDER OF THE SHEETS*

> a. Drag the Used Car Sales tab to the Sheet2 tab. Note that the pointer changes to 📄 and a solid triangle appears between the New Car Sales and Sheet2 tabs.
>
> b. Release the mouse button. The Used Car Sales tab now appears between the two tabs.

④ *RENAME SHEET2*

> a. Double-click the Sheet2 tab. The sheet name is selected.
>
> b. Type Total Sales and then press Enter. The default name is replaced.

⑤ *SAVE THE MODIFIED CAR SALES*

10.3 Using Cell References from Different Sheets

When using multiple sheets, it is possible for a formula to contain a cell reference to a cell on another sheet. Referring to a cell on a different sheet takes the form:

<sheet name>!<cell reference>

For example, in the 2004 Forecast sheet, the Seattle West store is expected to have First Quarter sales that are 20% higher than its 2003 First Quarter sales:

B6		f_x 87989	
	A	**B**	**C**
1	Clothing Sales		
2	2003 Sales Summary		
3			
4	Store	First Quarter	Second Quarter
5			
6	Seattle West	$87,989.00	$105,586.80
7	Seattle East	$123,898.00	$148,677.60
8	Los Angeles	$767,898.00	$921,477.60
9	Toronto	$898,999.00	$1,078,798.80
10	Oakville	$345,982.00	$415,178.40

◄ ◄ ► ►► \ 2002 Sales \ **2003 Sales** / 2004 Forecast /

B6		f_x ='2003 Sales'!B6*1.2	
	A	**B**	**C**
1	Clothing Sales		
2	2004 Forecast		
3			
4	Store	First Quarter	Second Quarter
5			
6	Seattle West	$105,586.80	$126,704.16
7	Seattle East	$148,677.60	$178,413.12
8	Los Angeles	$921,477.60	$1,105,773.12
9	Toronto	$1,078,798.80	$1,294,558.56
10	Oakville	$415,178.40	$498,214.08

◄ ◄ ► ►► \ 2002 Sales / 2003 Sales \ **2004 Forecast** /

Cell B6 in the 2004 Forecast sheet displays $105,586.80 because it contains a formula that references cell B6 in the 2003 Sales sheet and then multiplies its value by 1.2, ='2003 Sales'!B6*1.2. If the data in cell B6 in the 2003 Sales sheet changes, then the formula in cell B6 in the 2004 Forecast sheet will automatically recalculate.

The formula in cell B6 in the 2004 Forecast sheet can be created by making cell B6 the active cell, typing =, and then clicking the 2003 Sales tab, which displays the 2003 Sales sheet. In that sheet, clicking cell B6, typing *1.2, and then pressing Enter displays the 2004 Forecast sheet and adds the formula ='2003 Sales'!B6*1.2 in cell B6 of that sheet.

10.4   Linking Cells

Data stored in cells can be linked to cells on a different worksheet. When the data is modified, the linked cells automatically update. For example, the store locations in column A of the 2003 Sales sheet are linked to the 2002 Sales sheet:

	A	B	C	D	E
	A6		='2002 Sales'!A6		
2	2003 Sales Summary				
3					
4	Store	First Quarter	Second Quarter	Third Quarter	Fourth Quarter
5					
6	Seattle West	$87,989.00	$105,586.80	$52,793.40	$81,829.77
7	Seattle East	$123,898.00	$148,677.60	$74,338.80	$115,225.14
8	Los Angeles	$767,898.00	$921,477.60	$460,738.80	$714,145.14

Note that cell A6 displays Seattle West, but contains the formula ='2002 Sales'!A6. If a mistake was made entering the contents of cell A6 and it had to be changed to Seattle North West, changing the contents in the 2002 Sales sheet automatically updates the linked cell in the 2003 Sales sheet.

The steps for linking cells are:

1.   Select the source, which is the cell(s) to link to.

2.   Click the Copy button (🖺) on the toolbar. A copy of the source is added to the Clipboard.

3.   Click the sheet tab of the worksheet that is to receive the linked data.

4.   Select the destination, which is the upper-left cell of the range where the linked data is to be pasted.

5.   Click the Paste button (🖺▾) on the toolbar. The contents of the Clipboard are placed in the cell(s) and the Paste Options button (🖺) is displayed. Note that the source formatting is copied as well.

6.   Click the Paste Options button (🖺). A list of options is displayed:

Miami	$1,184,666.40	$1,421,599.68	$710,799.84
Tampa	$148,676.40	$178,411.68	$89,205.84
New York	$548,676.00	$658,411.20	$329,205.60
Denver	$600,040.80	$720,048.96	$360,024.48

🖺 ▾
- ⦿ Keep Source Formatting
- ○ Match Destination Formatting
- ○ Values and Number Formatting
- ○ Keep Source Column Widths
- ○ Formatting Only
- ○ Link Cells

7.   In the Paste Options list, select Link Cells.

A Guide to Microsoft Office XP Professional

10.5   Printing Sheets

The Print dialog box is used to specify which sheets are printed:

Selecting Active sheet(s) and then OK prints only the active sheet. Selecting Entire workbook prints all the sheets in the workbook. The active sheet can also be printed by clicking the Print button on the toolbar.

Headers, footers, and orientation are saved with the active sheet. This makes it possible for sheets to be printed differently. For example, Sheet1 can be printed in portrait orientation and Sheet2 in landscape orientation. Selecting Page Setup from the File menu displays the Page Setup dialog box where these options are selected.

Practice 2

In this practice you will reference data between three sheets in CAR SALES. Open CAR SALES if it is not already displayed.

① *LINK LABELS TO THE TOTAL SALES SHEET*

    a. Display the New Car Sales sheet.

    b. Select cells A4 through A23.

    c. Click the Copy button (📋).

    d. Display the Total Sales sheet.

    e. Select cell A4.

    f. Click the Paste button (📋▾). The Paste Options button is displayed.

    g. Click the Paste Options button. A list of options is displayed.

        1. Select Link Cells.

    h. Click cell A4. Note that ='New Car Sales'!A4 is displayed on the Formula bar.

    i. Display the New Car Sales sheet and then press Esc. The moving dashed line is removed.

    j. In the New Car Sales sheet, follow steps a) through g) above to link the labels in cells B3 through E3 to cells B3 through E3 in the Total Sales sheet.

② MODIFY LABELS

    a. Display the New Car Sales sheet and press the Esc key. The moving dashed line is removed.

    b. Select cell A6.

    c. Edit the cell contents so that the name is Base.

    d. Display the Total Sales sheet. Note that in cell A6 the cell contents have been automatically updated because the cell was linked to cell A6 in the New Car Sales sheet.

    e. Display the Used Car Sales sheet. Note that in cell A6 the cell contents have not been updated because the cell is not linked.

    f. In the Used Car Sales sheet, modify the contents of cell A6 to read Base.

③ TOTAL NEW AND USED CAR SALES

    a. Display the Total Sales sheet.

    b. Select cell B4 and type an equal sign (=).

    c. Display the New Car Sales sheet. Note that ='New Car Sales'! is displayed in the Formula bar.

    d. Click cell B4. The Formula bar now displays ='New Car Sales'!B4.

    e. Type a plus sign (+).

    f. In the Used Car Sales sheet, click cell B4. The Formula bar should now display ='New Car Sales'!B4+'Used Car Sales'!B4.

    g. Click the Enter button. The Total Sales sheet is displayed and cell B4 displays $156,217.

    h. Use the Fill handle to copy the formula in cell B4 to cells C4 and D4. Employee Alfred's total new and used car sales for January, February, and March are displayed. Ignore the Auto Fill Options button.

    i. Use the Fill handle to copy the formulas in cells B4 through D4 to cells B5 through D23. Ignore the Auto Fill Options button.

④ TOTAL THE SALES FOR ALL THREE MONTHS

    a. In the Total Sales sheet, select cell E4.

    b. Enter the formula =SUM(B4:D4) to total the sales for the three months, $479,861 is displayed.

    c. Use the Fill handle to copy the formula in cell E4 to cells E5 through E23. Ignore the Auto Fill Options button.

⑤ SET PRINT OPTIONS FOR A SHEET

    a. In the Total Sales sheet, select File → Page Setup. A dialog box is displayed.

        1. Select the Sheet tab if those options are not already displayed.

        2. Select the Gridlines check box.

        3. Select the Row and column headings check box.

        4. Select OK. The dialog box is removed.

a. Display the New Car Sales sheet.

b. In the New Car Sales, Used Car Sales, and Total Sales sheets, create a header with the date center aligned and a footer with your name right aligned.

c. Save the modified CAR SALES.

d. Select File ➜ Print. A dialog box is displayed.

1. In the Print what section of the dialog box, select Entire workbook.

2. Select OK. All three sheets in the workbook are printed. Note that only the Total Sales sheet contains gridlines and row and column headings.

e. Close CAR SALES.

10.6 Charts

Worksheet data can be used to create a chart. A *chart* is a visual representation of worksheet data. A chart can enhance and simplify the understanding of numerical data in a worksheet by illustrating a relationship between the data.

titles, labels, legend   A chart usually contains titles, data labels, a legend, and at least one
data series   data series. *Titles* and *labels* are used to describe what is charted. A *legend* contains labels that identify the data series. A *data series*, or series, is a set of related data to be plotted on the chart. The data to be charted dictates what type of chart to use. The three most commonly used chart types are pie, bar, and line.

pie chart, slice   A *pie chart* can include only one series of data, with each *slice* representing a value from the series. The size of a slice varies with its percentage of the total. Pie charts are best for charting data that is a percentage of a whole:

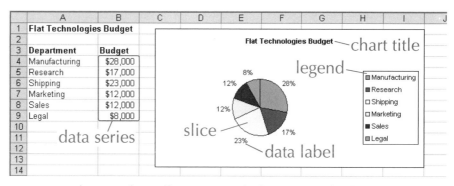

The pie chart illustrates each department budget as a percentage of the entire budget

bar chart   A *bar chart* can include several series of data, with each bar representing a value. The height of the bar is proportional to the value it represents. Bar charts are therefore useful for comparing the differences between values. Excel can create bar charts with either vertical bars or horizontal bars. In Excel, a horizontal bar chart is called a bar chart and a vertical
column chart   bar chart is called a *column chart*. In the column chart on the following page, only one series is charted:

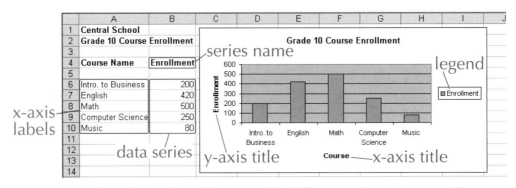

The column chart illustrates the differences in course enrollment

line chart   A *line chart* can include several series of data with each line representing a series. The values in a series are represented by a point on the line. Line charts are therefore useful for displaying the differences of data over time:

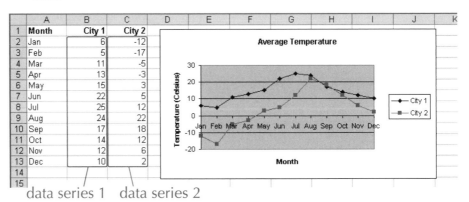

The line chart illustrates temperature changes over a year

10.7   Creating a Pie Chart

planning a chart   Before creating any chart, it should be planned by answering the following questions:

1. What series will the chart contain?

2. What type of chart should be used?

3. What titles, labels, and legends will make the chart easier to read and understand?

Chart Wizard   In Excel, a chart can be created using the *Chart Wizard*, which provides dialog boxes for specifying how the data will be charted. The steps for using the Chart Wizard to create a pie chart are:

data range

1. **Select the data to be charted.** The portion of the worksheet to be charted is called the *data range*. The data range should include the data series and corresponding labels:

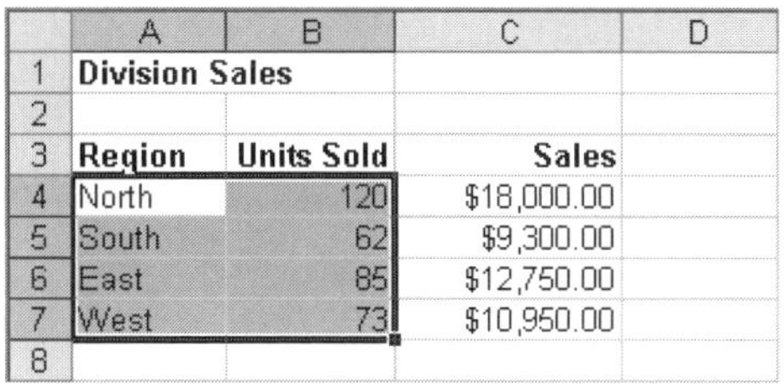

	A	B	C	D
1	Division Sales			
2				
3	Region	Units Sold	Sales	
4	North	120	$18,000.00	
5	South	62	$9,300.00	
6	East	85	$12,750.00	
7	West	73	$10,950.00	
8				

The labels will be used in the legend to explain the data.

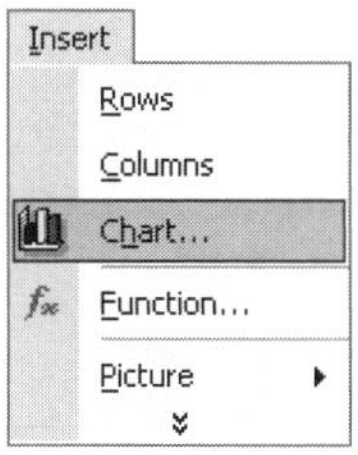

2. **Start the Chart Wizard.** Selecting Chart from the Insert menu or clicking the Chart Wizard button ( ) on the toolbar displays the first Chart Wizard dialog box.

3. **Select the Pie chart type.** Clicking Pie in the Chart type list creates a Pie chart:

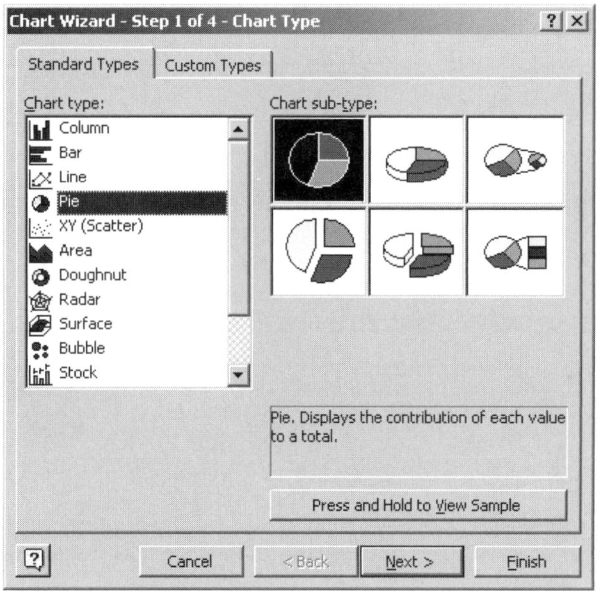

Selecting Next displays the second Chart Wizard dialog box.

4. **Verify the source data and chart appearance.** The Series in options are used to indicate whether the series of data is in Rows or Columns. Note that the Data range box includes the name of the sheet in addition to the range of cells selected:

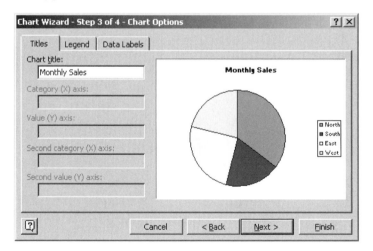

If the Chart appearance is not correct, clicking the Collapse Dialog button (▥) minimizes the Chart Wizard dialog box and returns to the worksheet so that a new data range can be selected. Selecting a new data range and pressing the Enter key returns to the Source Data dialog box. Selecting Next displays the third Chart Wizard dialog box.

5. **Enter the chart title and select data labels.** A descriptive title can be typed in the Chart title box, such as Monthly Sales:

Since pie charts are useful for showing parts of a whole, data labels for the percentage each slice represents should be added to make the chart more descriptive. Selecting the Data Labels tab displays options, such as Percentage and Category name. Selecting an option displays the data labels on the chart. In the example below, the Percentage check box was selected to show the percentage of sales for each division:

The Finish Button

Selecting Finish in any Chart Wizard dialog box displays a chart on the active sheet. The chart will contain the information provided before Finish was selected. The chart can then be deleted (discussed in Section 10.8) or modified (discussed in Section 10.11).

Chart Wizard - Step 3 of 4 - Chart Options

Selecting Next displays the last Chart Wizard dialog box.

6. **Select the placement of the chart.** The As new sheet option creates a new sheet named Chart1 in the workbook, which contains only the chart. The As object in option places the chart in a specified sheet in the workbook:

Chart Placement

A chart that is large and complex should be placed as a new sheet. To view the data in the spreadsheet and its associated chart at the same time, the chart should be placed as an object in the active sheet.

Chart Wizard - Step 4 of 4 - Chart Location

Selecting Finish creates the pie chart and displays it. The Chart toolbar, which is used to edit charts, is automatically displayed. Note that the Chart toolbar may need to be moved to view the chart behind it. The Chart toolbar can be moved by dragging its title bar.

Once created, a chart is linked to the worksheet data. Therefore, if a number that is part of a chart data series is changed in the worksheet, the chart automatically changes to reflect the new data. When a workbook is saved, any charts that were created are saved with it. Therefore, it is important to save a workbook each time a chart is created or modified.

Practice 3

In this practice you will create a pie chart using the data stored in the CONTINENTS workbook.

① OPEN CONTINENTS

Open CONTINENTS, which is a data file for this text. The CONTINENTS workbook contains the area in square kilometers of the seven continents.

② CREATE A PIE CHART

a. Select cells A2 through B8. The data range is selected.

b. Select Insert → Chart. The first Chart Wizard dialog box is displayed.

    1. In the Chart type list, click Pie.

    2. Select Next. The second Chart Wizard dialog box is displayed.

    3. Verify that the correct range =Sheet1!$A$2:$B$8 is displayed in the Data range box. An example of the pie chart is displayed in the dialog box.

    4. Select Next. The third Chart Wizard dialog box is displayed.

    5. In the Chart title box, type Area of Continents (sq km).

    6. Select the Data Labels tab to display those options.

    7. Select the Percentage check box. Note that the pie chart example now displays percentages next to each slice.

    8. Select Next. The fourth Chart Wizard dialog box is displayed.

    9. Select the As object in option if it is not already selected.

    10. Select Finish to display the pie chart as an object in the worksheet. The Chart toolbar is also displayed.

③ CHANGE A VALUE IN THE WORKSHEET

a. Note that the size of the Africa slice in the pie chart is 11% of the pie.

b. Select cell B2.

c. A mistake was made when recording the area of Africa. Type the correct value of 30,330,000 and then press the Enter key. Note how the slices of the pie chart have adjusted. The Africa slice is now 20% of the pie.

Check – Your chart should look similar to:

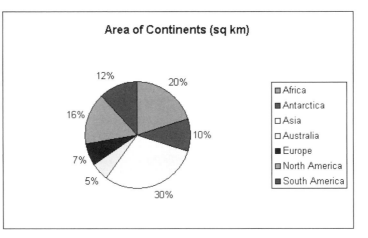

④ SAVE THE MODIFIED CONTINENTS

The chart is saved with the workbook.

10.8 Moving, Sizing, and Deleting Charts

selecting a chart, Chart area, handles

A chart is *selected* by clicking the Chart area. The *Chart area* is the blank portion of the chart. When a chart is selected, it is displayed with *handles*, and the corresponding data series and labels are outlined in color on the worksheet:

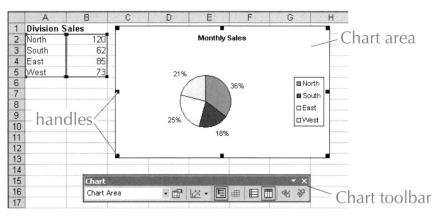

Selected charts are displayed with handles

moving a chart

A chart is moved by positioning the pointer in the Chart area and dragging the chart. This is often necessary to display data stored in cells behind the chart.

sizing a chart

A chart is sized proportionately by dragging one of the corner handles. Pointing to a corner handle changes the pointer to ↖. Dragging a corner handle changes the pointer to +:

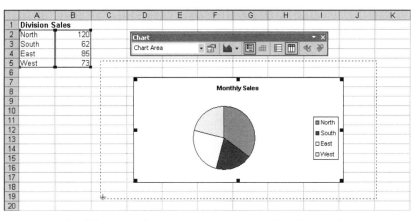

Dashed lines indicate the new size of a chart when dragging a corner handle

deleting a chart

A selected chart can be deleted by pressing the Delete key or by selecting All from the Clear submenu in the Edit menu. If a chart is deleted by mistake, selecting Undo from the Edit menu or clicking the Undo button on the toolbar restores the chart.

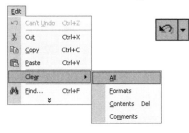

10.9 Printing a Chart

A chart that appears as an object in a worksheet is printed when the worksheet is printed. Selecting Print from the File menu or clicking the Print button on the toolbar prints the active worksheet.

Selecting a chart that appears as an object in a worksheet before selecting the Print command prints only the chart on a single sheet of paper in landscape orientation. Note that a chart printed in this manner will not contain the worksheet header or footer. A header or footer can be added to a chart by first selecting the chart and then selecting Page Setup from the File menu, which displays the Page Setup dialog box. Selecting the Header/Footer tab displays options to add a header or footer.

Before printing a chart, Print Preview from the File menu should be selected to determine if the chart will fit completely on a page. The Print Preview button on the toolbar can also be used to preview the chart. Sizing or moving a chart may be necessary to fit it on a single sheet of paper. Changing the orientation to landscape or changing the margins may also help fit a worksheet with a chart onto a single sheet of paper.

If a chart is in its own sheet, it is printed by making the chart sheet active and then selecting Print from the File menu or clicking the Print button on the toolbar. A header and footer can be added to a chart sheet the same way it is added to a worksheet.

Practice 4

In this practice you will size, move, and print the pie chart and data stored in the CONTINENTS workbook. Open CONTINENTS if it is not already displayed.

① SIZE AND MOVE THE CHART

a. If the chart handles are not displayed, move the pointer into an empty portion of the chart until a ScreenTip with the words Chart Area ( ) is displayed. Click to display handles.

b. Move the pointer over the handle in the bottom-right corner of the chart. The pointer changes to ↖ .

c. Drag the handle down and to the right a little. The chart is larger.

d. Move the pointer into the Chart area so the Chart Area ScreenTip is displayed.

e. Drag the chart so that it is below the worksheet data.

② SAVE, PRINT, AND THEN CLOSE THE MODIFIED CONTINENTS

a. Click a cell in the worksheet to remove the chart handles.

b. Create a header with the date center aligned and a footer with your name right aligned.

c. Make sure the chart is not selected and then print preview the worksheet. If necessary, size and move the chart on the sheet so that all the data and chart fit on one page.

d. Close the Print Preview window and save the modified CONTINENTS.

e. Make sure the chart is not selected and then click the Print button on the toolbar. The worksheet is printed with the chart.

f. Close CONTINENTS.

File

📂	Open...	Ctrl+O
	Close	
	Save As...	
📓	Save as Web Page...	
	Page Setup...	
📄	Print Preview	
📇	Print...	Ctrl+P
	⌄	

10.10 Creating Bar and Line Charts

The steps for creating a bar or line chart are:

1. **Select the data to be charted.** The data range should include the data series and corresponding labels:

	A	B	C	D	E	F
1	Central School Sports Fundraiser					
2	T-Shirt Sales					
3						
4		T-Shirt Colors				
5	Team	Red	Blue	Yellow	Black	Team Total
6						
7	Basketball	25	42	22	27	116
8	Hockey	32	28	23	32	115
9	Soccer	24	32	30	38	124
10	Volleyball	22	24	36	38	120
11	Color Total:	103	126	111	135	

Note that the column labels in row 5 are not selected as part of the data range since a blank line separates the column labels and chart data.

> ### Blank Cells
>
> When selecting the data to be charted, avoid selecting blank cells. If blank cells are selected as part of the chart data, they will represent either the value 0 in a data series or a blank label on the chart, making the chart incorrect.

2. **Start the Chart Wizard.** Selecting Chart from the Insert menu or clicking the Chart Wizard button (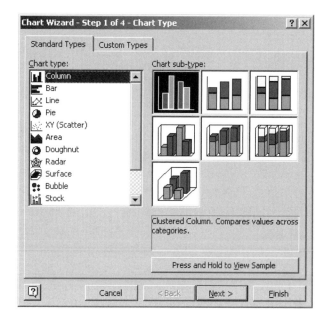) on the toolbar displays the first Chart Wizard dialog box.

3. **Select the desired chart type.** The chart type is selected by clicking a chart type in the Chart type list. In this example, Column is selected:

Selecting Next displays the second Chart Wizard dialog box.

4. **Verify the source data and chart appearance.** The Series in options are used to indicate whether the series of data are in Rows or Columns. In this example, the series to be charted are in rows so the Rows option must be selected:

> ### Presentation of Bar and Column Charts
>
> The data series of a bar or column charts can be presented differently by selecting the Chart type Cylinder, Cone, or Pyramid. These three types of charts use their named shape to represent the data series. For example, a Pyramid chart:

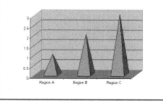

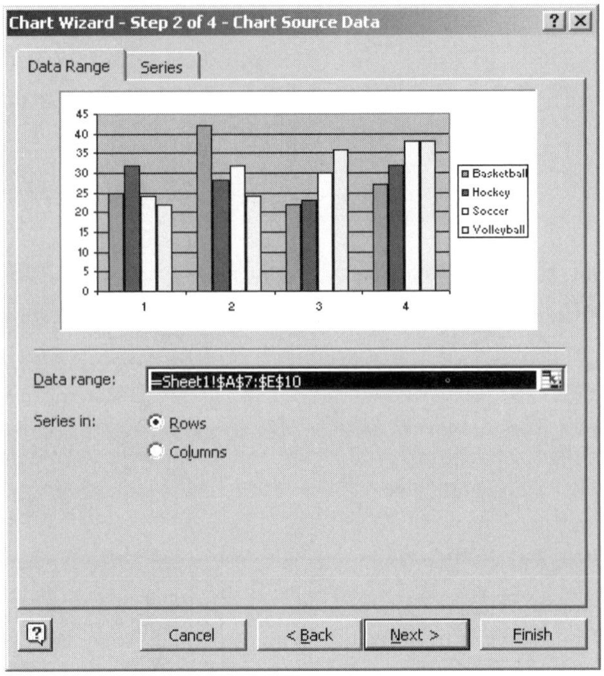

5. **Display options for adding the x-axis labels**. Selecting the Series tab displays those options:

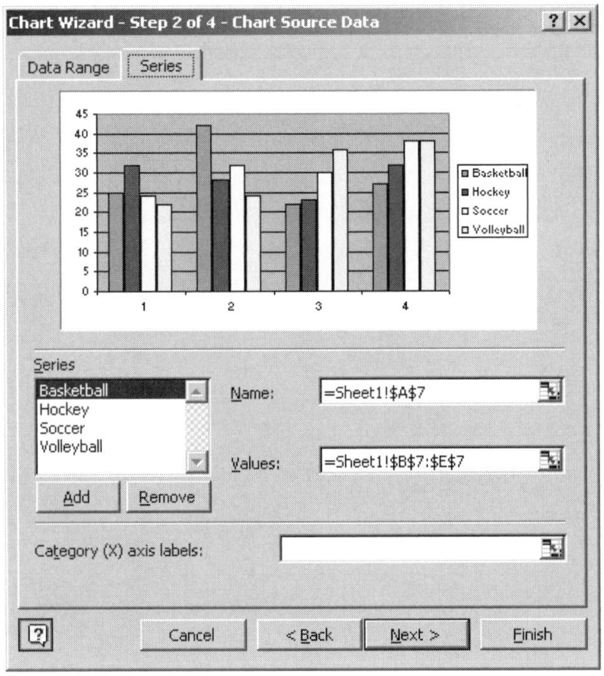

The Legend

The **Series** box contains a list of the data series labels that are displayed in the legend. Selecting a label in the **Series** box displays the cell reference for the label in the **Name** box.

If the Chart Wizard is unsure of the labels, it displays Series 1, Series 2, and so on as the labels. This can be modified by selecting a label, such as Series 1, in the **Series** box and then selecting the **Name** box and selecting or typing the correct label.

6. **Add the x-axis labels.** Clicking the Category (X) axis labels box places the insertion point and then selecting the x-axis labels on the worksheet outlines the selected labels with a moving dashed line:

	A	B	C	D	E	F
2	T-Shirt Sales					
3						
4		T-Shirt Colors				
5	Team	Red	Blue	Yellow	Black	Team Total
6						
7	Basketball	25	42	22	27	116
8	Hockey	32	28	23	32	115
9	Soccer	24	32	30	38	124
10	Volleyball	22	24	36	38	120

Chart Wizard - Step 2 of 4 - Chart Source Data - Category (X) ax... ? ✕

=Sheet1!$B$5:$E$5

Selecting Next displays the third Chart Wizard dialog box.

7. **Enter chart and axes titles.** Descriptive titles for the chart and each axis can be typed:

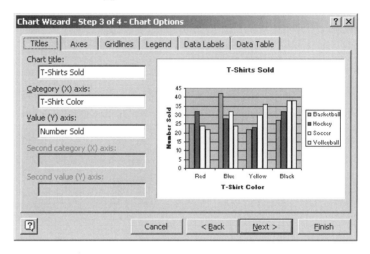

Selecting Next displays the last Chart Wizard dialog box.

8. **Select the placement of the chart.** Selecting the location of the chart determines how it will be displayed in the workbook.

9. **Display the chart.** Selecting Finish creates the chart and displays it.

Practice 5

In this practice you will create a line chart that displays the results of a plant growth experiment.

① *OPEN PLANT GROWTH*

Open PLANT GROWTH, which is a data file for this text.

② CREATE A LINE CHART

a. Select cells A5 through E5. The label and results for the first four weeks of control group A are selected.

b. On the toolbar, click the Chart Wizard button (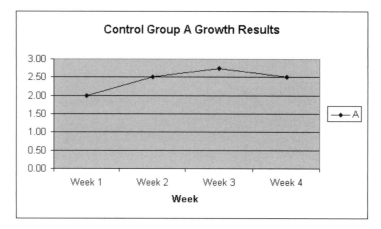). The first Chart Wizard dialog box is displayed.

    1. In the Chart type list, click Line.

    2. Select Next. The second Chart Wizard dialog box is displayed.

    3. Verify that the correct range =Sheet1!$A$5:$E$5 is displayed in the Data range box. An example of the line chart is displayed in the dialog box.

    4. Select the Series tab to display those options.

    5. Click the Category (X) axis labels box to place the insertion point.

    6. On the worksheet, select cells B3 through E3. The range =Sheet1!$B$3:$E$3 is displayed in the Category (X) axis labels box.

    7. Select Next. The third Chart Wizard dialog box is displayed. Select the Titles tab if those options are not already displayed.

    8. In the Chart title box, modify the title to read Control Group A Growth Results.

    9. In the Category (X) axis box, type Week.

    10. Select Finish to skip the last dialog box and have the chart appear as an object in the active sheet.

Check – Your chart should look similar to:

Control Group A Growth Results

③ MOVE THE CHART

Move the chart so that it is below the worksheet data.

④ SAVE THE MODIFIED PLANT GROWTH

Chart
Chart Type...
Source Data...
Chart Options...
Add Data...
3-D View...
⌄

10.11 Modifying a Chart

The contents of a selected chart can be modified by selecting Chart Options from the Chart menu, which displays the Chart Options dialog box:

This dialog box is similar to the third Chart Wizard dialog box. Changes can be made to the chart using the options in the dialog box:

- The Titles tab contains options for editing the chart title, x-axis title, and y-axis title.

- The Axes tab contains options for hiding or displaying each axes.

- The Gridlines tab contains options that affect the gridlines behind the chart. A chart may be easier to read if gridlines are displayed. Vertical and horizontal gridlines are displayed by selecting the Major gridlines check boxes in the Category (X) axis and Value (Y) axis sections, respectively. When these options are selected, gridlines are displayed both on the screen and when printed.

- The Legend tab contains a check box that can be used to turn off the display of the legend as well as options for specifying the placement of the legend (bottom, corner, top, right, and left).

- The Data Labels tab contains options for displaying data labels on a chart.

Selecting OK applies the changes to the chart.

Titles and axis labels can also be modified by clicking the chart title or axis label to select it, then clicking again to place the insertion point, typing new text, and pressing the Enter key.

10.12 Adding Adjacent Series and Labels

An adjacent data series can be added to a selected chart by dragging one of the handles of the outlined original data to include the new series. This method can only be used if the new series is adjacent to the data already charted. For example, in the worksheet on the next page, the range A2:B6 has already been charted:

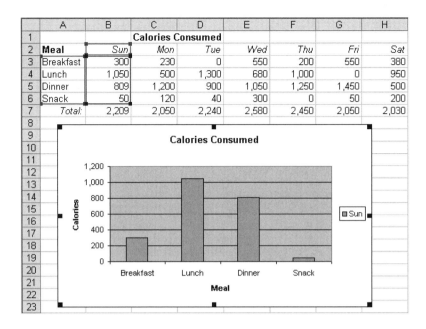

	A	B	C	D	E	F	G	H
1		Calories Consumed						
2	**Meal**	*Sun*	*Mon*	*Tue*	*Wed*	*Thu*	*Fri*	*Sat*
3	Breakfast	300	230	0	550	200	550	380
4	Lunch	1,050	500	1,300	680	1,000	0	950
5	Dinner	809	1,200	900	1,050	1,250	1,450	500
6	Snack	50	120	40	300	0	50	200
7	*Total:*	2,209	2,050	2,240	2,580	2,450	2,050	2,030

Cell B2 is outlined because it is in the legend as a label for the data series. Cells A3 through A6 are outlined because they are the x-axis labels. Cells B3 through B6 are the data series. The data series and label in column C can be added to the chart by dragging the handle in the lower-right corner of cell B6 to include column C.

An adjacent data series and label can also be added to an existing chart by selecting Source Data from the Chart menu, which displays a dialog box similar to the second Chart Wizard dialog box.

Practice 6

In this practice you will modify the chart stored in PLANT GROWTH. Open PLANT GROWTH if it is not already displayed.

① *MODIFY THE LINE CHART*

    a. Note that there is no title for the y-axis values along the left side of the chart.

    b. Click the Chart Area to select the chart if it is not already selected.

    c. Select Chart → Chart Options. A dialog box is displayed.

        1. Select the Titles tab if those options are not already displayed.

        2. In the Value (Y) axis box, type Centimeters.

        3. Select the Axes tab to display those options.

        4. Click the Value (Y) axis check box to clear it.

        5. Select the Gridlines tab. The gridlines options are displayed.

        6. In the Category (X) axis options, select the Major gridlines check box.

        7. Select the Data Labels tab to display those options.

        8. Select the Value check box.

        9. Select OK to remove the dialog box. The chart is modified.

②ADD DATA TO THE CHART

    a. Click the line chart if it is not already selected. The corresponding data in the worksheet displays colored outlines. Note that the last week of data for control group A is in cell F5 and its corresponding label is in cell F3 and it is not charted.

    b. Drag the handle in the lower-right corner of cell E3 to the right until cells F3 and F5 are included in the colored outlines. The new data is added to the chart.

③ADD A NEW SERIES TO THE CHART AND MODIFY THE CHART TITLE

    a. Click the line chart if it is not already selected. Note that only control group A is charted.

    b. Drag the handle in the lower-right corner of cell F5 down until cells A6 through F6 are included in the colored outlines. The data for control group B is added as new series to the chart.

    c. Click the chart title to select it and then click the chart title again to place the insertion point.

    d. Modify the chart title to read "Control Group A and B Growth Results."

④SAVE THE MODIFIED PLANT GROWTH AND PRINT THE LINE CHART

    a. Select the line chart if it is not already selected.

    b. Create a header with the date center aligned and a footer with your name right aligned. A header and footer is added only to the chart.

    c. Print preview the chart. Note the header and footer.

    d. Select **Close**. The worksheet window is again displayed.

    e. Save the modified PLANT GROWTH.

    f. On the toolbar, click the Print button. Only the chart is printed.

    g. Click a blank cell. The chart is no longer selected.

10.13 Adding Nonadjacent Series and Labels

It is possible to add a data series to an existing chart even if the data series is not stored in cells adjacent to those already specified for the chart.

nonadjacent series   A nonadjacent data series is added to a chart by selecting Add Data from the Chart menu, which displays the Add Data dialog box. Selecting the range of cells that contain the new data series places the range in the Range box. For example, the Calories Consumed chart currently has the Sunday data series charted. The Friday and Saturday data series can be added to the chart by selecting the range of cells containing the new data series and labels (G2:H6):

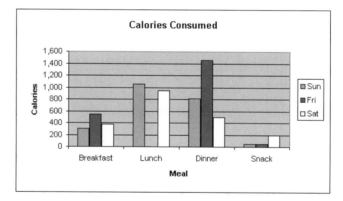

	A	B	C	D	E	F	G	H
1			Calories Consumed					
2	Meal	Sun	Mon	Tue	Wed	Thu	Fri	Sat
3	Breakfast	300	230	0	550	200	550	380
4	Lunch	1,050	500	1,300	680	1,000	0	950
5	Dinner	809	1,200	900	1,050	1,250	1,450	500
6	Snack	50	120	40	300	0	50	200
7	Total:	2,209	2,050	2,240	2,580	2,450	2,050	2,030

The range of cells containing the new data series can also be typed in the Range box. Note that any cells containing labels for the chart legend should also be included in the range. Selecting OK displays the modified chart:

Calories Consumed chart

nonadjacent labels   When labels are not adjacent to the series of data they are describing, they can be added to a chart by selecting Source Data from the Chart menu and then selecting the Series tab in the displayed dialog box. For example, in the chart on the page, the cells containing the days of the week need to be added as the x-axis labels to replace the default labels:

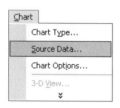

Nonadjacent series and their corresponding labels can be included when initially creating a chart by separating the cell ranges of the nonadjacent series by commas in the **Data range** box in the second Chart Wizard dialog box.

Nonadjacent x-axis labels and pie slice labels can be included when initially creating a chart by selecting the **Series** tab in the second Chart Wizard dialog box and selecting or typing the cell range in the **Category (x) axis labels** box or the **Category Labels** box.

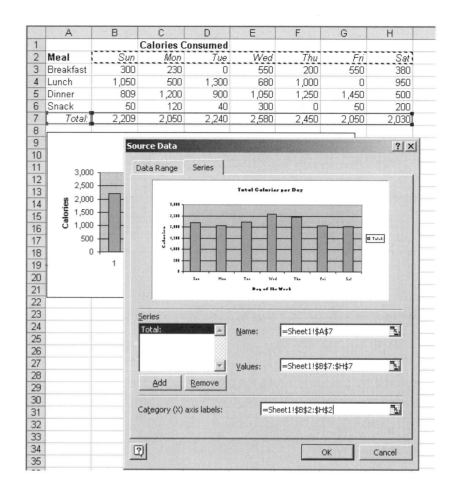

The labels are added by clicking the Category (X) axis labels box and then selecting the appropriate cells in the worksheet. Selecting OK removes the dialog box.

Nonadjacent labels for pie chart slices can be added to an existing pie chart using the Series tab similar to the method stated above, except the cell range is entered in the Category Labels box.

10.14 Formatting a Chart

There are many ways to modify the appearance of a chart. For example, the chart on the next page has been formatted so that the chart title is in a different font, the y-axis title is vertical, and the data series are in a different order (Yellow now comes before Blue):

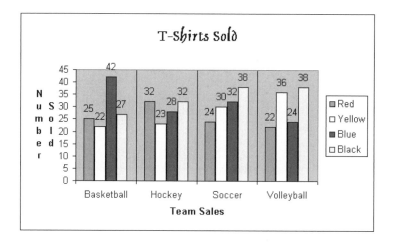

Double-clicking any object in a chart displays a Format dialog box. For example, double-clicking the legend of a chart displays the Format Legend dialog box:

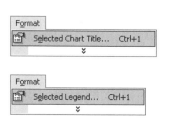

In this dialog box, options for the pattern, font, and placement of the legend can be changed.

Commands in the Format menu can also be used to display a Format dialog box. The Format menu changes depending on the chart object that is selected. For example, if the chart title is selected, then the Format menu displays Selected Chart Title. If the legend is selected, the Format menu displays Selected Legend. This method of formatting can be used to format the y-axis, x-axis, titles, data series, gridlines, and Chart Area.

A chart can also be formatted using the Chart toolbar, which is automatically displayed when a chart is selected:

Chart Objects list   Angle Counterclockwise
Format   Angle Clockwise

 Selecting an option from the Chart Objects list and then selecting the Format button () displays the appropriate format dialog box. For example, on the Chart toolbar, selecting Chart Title and then clicking the Format button displays the Format Chart Title dialog box:

The Format Chart Title dialog box provides options such as font, alignment, and color for changing the format of the Chart Title.

Other options on the Chart toolbar include the Angle Clockwise button (🖉) and the Angle Counterclockwise button (🖉) which allow titles and axes labels to be displayed on an angle. For example, selecting Category Axis in the Chart Objects list and then clicking the Angle Counterclockwise button (🖉) angles the x-axis labels counterclockwise in the chart.

Practice 7

In this practice you will create a column chart and format it. Open PLANT GROWTH if it is not already displayed.

① *RENAME SHEET1*

     a. Double-click the Sheet1 tab. The sheet name is selected.

     b. Type Results and then press Enter. The default name is replaced.

② CREATE A COLUMN CHART

a. Select cells G5 through G11. The data for the total plant growth is selected.

b. On the toolbar, click the Chart Wizard button (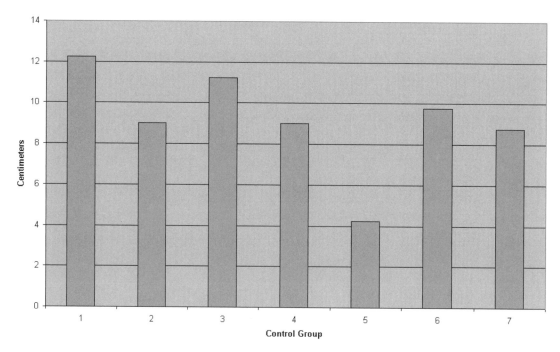). A dialog box is displayed.

1. In the Chart type list, click Column if it is not already selected.

2. Select Next. The second Chart Wizard dialog box is displayed.

3. Verify that the correct range =Results!$G$5:$G$11 is displayed in the Data range box and that the Columns option is selected.

4. Select Next. The third Chart Wizard dialog box is displayed.

5. Select the Titles tab to display those options if those options are not already displayed.

6. In the Chart title box, type Experiment Results.

7. In the Category (X) axis box, type Control Group.

8. In the Value (Y) axis box, type Centimeters.

9. Select the Legend tab to display those options.

10. Click the Show legend check box to clear it. The legend is removed from the chart.

11. Select Next. The fourth Chart Wizard dialog box is displayed.

12. Select the As new sheet option and enter Total Growth Chart in the box. A new sheet will be added to the workbook to display the chart in.

13. Select Finish. The chart is displayed in its own sheet. Note that a tab labeled Total Growth Chart has been created to display the chart sheet.

Check – Your chart should look similar to:

Experiment Results

A Guide to Microsoft Office XP Professional

③ ADD LABELS TO THE CHART

Note that the control group letters are not displayed on the x-axis. The letters in cells A5 through A11 in the Results sheet need to be added to the chart.

a. Select the Total Growth Chart tab if it is not already selected. The chart sheet is displayed.

b. Select Chart → Source Data. A dialog box is displayed.

    1. Select the Series tab if those options are not already displayed.

    2. Click the Category (X) axis labels box.

    3. Display the Results sheet and then select cells A5 through A11 on the worksheet. Verify that the correct range =Results!$A$5:$A$11 is displayed in the dialog box.

    4. Select OK. The dialog box is removed and the chart sheet is displayed with the control group letters added as x-axis labels.

④ FORMAT THE COLUMN CHART

a. Double-click the chart title (Experiment Results). A dialog box is displayed.

    1. Select the Font tab to display those options.

    2. Change the Font, Font style, and Size to options of your choice.

    3. Select OK. The dialog box is removed and the chart title has been formatted.

b. Double-click the y-axis title (Centimeters). A dialog box is displayed.

    1. Select the Alignment tab to display those options.

    2. In the Degrees box, change the existing number to 0.

    3. Select OK. The dialog box is removed and the y-axis title is displayed horizontally.

c. Click one of the bars to select the data series.

d. Select Format → Selected Data Series. A dialog box is displayed.

    1. Select the Patterns tab if those options are not already displayed.

    2. In the Area section, select a color of your choice.

    3. Select OK. The dialog box is removed. The color of the data series has changed.

⑤ SAVE, PRINT, AND THEN CLOSE THE MODIFIED PLANT GROWTH

a. Display the Total Growth Chart sheet if it is not already displayed.

b. Create a header with the date center aligned and a footer with your name right aligned. A header and footer is added only to the chart sheet.

c. Save the modified PLANT GROWTH.

d. On the toolbar, click the Print button. The chart sheet is printed.

e. Close PLANT GROWTH.

⑥ QUIT EXCEL

This chapter explained how to use multiple worksheets in a workbook and how to create charts using data stored in a worksheet.

A sheet is displayed by clicking its tab at the bottom of the Excel window. A sheet can be renamed by double-clicking its name. A new sheet is inserted in front of the active sheet by selecting the Worksheet command. A sheet is deleted by right-clicking its tab and selecting the Delete command. Sheet order can be changed by dragging a sheet tab to a new location within the sheet tabs.

Data can copied and moved between the sheets in a workbook. Formulas can contain a cell reference to a cell on another sheet. For example, Sheet1!A4 refers to cell A4 on Sheet1. Data stored in a cell can also be linked to a cell on a different worksheet.

Options in the Print dialog box are used to specify whether the entire workbook or the active sheet should be printed. Print Preview should be used to determine if the chart will fit completely on a page before it is printed.

A chart is a visual representation of worksheet data. A pie chart shows the percentage relationship between different parts of a whole quantity, a bar chart compares different values, and a line chart tracks data over time. In Excel, a vertical bar chart is called a column chart. A new chart is created by selecting the Chart command or clicking the Chart Wizard button on the toolbar. The Chart Wizard displays a series of dialog boxes for specifying how the data should be charted.

Before it can be moved, sized, or deleted, an existing chart must first be selected by clicking in the Chart area. The entire worksheet and any charts it contains can be printed by selecting the Print command or clicking the Print button on the toolbar. A selected chart can be printed by itself on a single sheet of paper by selecting the Print command.

A chart can be modified by first selecting it and then selecting the Chart Options command. Double-clicking a chart also displays the Chart Options dialog box.

An adjacent data series can be added to a selected chart by dragging one of the handles of the original data to include the new series. An adjacent data series and label can also be added to an existing chart by selecting the Source Data command. A nonadjacent data series is added to a chart by selecting the Add Data command.

Double-clicking any object in a chart displays a Format dialog box where options can be selected to change the appearance of the chart.

Active sheet The currently displayed sheet.

Bar chart Data graphed as a series of bars.

Chart A visual representation of data stored in a worksheet.

Chart area The blank portion of a chart.

Chart Wizard Displays dialog boxes where the user can select options to create a chart.

Column chart Data graphed as a series of vertical bars.

Data range The data to be charted.

Data series A set of related data to be plotted on a chart.

Destination The upper-left cell of the range where data is to be pasted.

Handles Used to size a selected chart or data series.

Label Describes what is charted.

Legend Labels that identify the different data series in a chart.

Line chart Data graphed using a continuous line.

Pie chart Data graphed as segments of a circular pie.

Selected chart A chart that displays handles.

Slice Part of a pie chart that represents one fractional part of a whole.

Source The cells to be copied, moved, or linked.

Title Describes what is charted.

Add Data **command**   Displays a dialog box where a nonadjacent data series can be added to an existing chart. Found in the Chart menu.

All **command**   Deletes the active chart. Found in the Clear submenu in the Edit menu.

Chart **command**   Displays the Chart Wizard dialog box used to create a chart. Found in the Insert menu. The Chart Wizard button on the toolbar can be used instead of the command.

Chart Options **command**   Displays a dialog box with options for changing the titles, axes, gridlines, legend, and data labels. Found in the Chart menu.

Collapse Dialog button   Minimizes the Chart Wizard dialog box in the worksheet so that a new data range can be selected. Found in the second Chart Wizard dialog box.

Copy button   Places the selected cell(s) on the Clipboard. Found on the toolbar. The Copy command in the Edit menu can be used instead of the command.

Cut button   Removes the selected cell(s) and places them on the Clipboard. Found on the toolbar. The Cut command in the Edit menu can be used instead of the command.

Delete **command**   Removes a sheet from the workbook. Found in the menu displayed by right-clicking a sheet tab.

Link Cells **command**   Links cell contents to a cell on a different worksheet.

Page Setup **command**   Displays a dialog box with page options for the active sheet. Found in the File menu.

Paste button   Places the Clipboard contents in a worksheet starting at the selected cell. Found on the toolbar. The Paste command in the Edit menu can be used instead of the command.

Print **command**   Displays a dialog box used to print the entire workbook or the active sheet. Also used to print charts in a workbook. Found in the File menu.

Print Preview **command**   Displays the worksheet as it will appear when printed. Found in the File menu. The Print Preview button on the toolbar can be used instead of the command.

Selected Chart Title **command**   Displays a dialog box used to format a chart title. Found in the Format menu when a chart title is selected.

Selected Legend **command**   Displays a dialog box used to format a legend. Found in the Format menu when a legend is selected.

Source Data **command**   Displays a dialog box used to add an adjacent data series and label to an existing chart. Nonadjacent labels can also be added to an existing chart using this command. Found in the Chart menu.

Undo **command**   Restores the previous action. Found in the Edit menu. The Undo button on the toolbar can be used instead of the command.

Worksheet **command**   Inserts a new sheet in front of the active sheet. Found in the Insert menu.

Review Questions

Sections 10.1 — 10.5

1. How is a sheet made active?

2. a) What are the default names given to sheets in a workbook?
   b) List the steps required to rename Sheet1 to Jan Sales.

3. a) Can a workbook contain more than 3 sheets?
   b) List the steps required to insert a new worksheet.
   c) List the steps required to change the sheet order.

4. List the steps required to copy or move data between sheets in a workbook?

5. List the steps required to reference cell B5 on Sheet1 and multiply its value by 3.6 in a formula stored in cell C4 on Sheet2?

6. List the steps required to link cells.

7. a) List the steps required to print all the sheets in a workbook at one time.
   b) List the steps required to print only the second sheet in a workbook.

8. List the steps required to print Sheet1 in landscape orientation and Sheet2 in portrait orientation.

9. In a workbook, is it possible for Sheet1 to contain a header and Sheet2 not to contain a header?

Sections 10.6 — 10.14

10. What is a chart?

11. a) What does a legend contain?
    b) What is a data series?

12. What are the three most commonly used chart types? *S*

13. What type of chart (bar, line, or pie) is best suited to display:
    a) a student's GPA over four years. *line*
    b) the percentage each department spent of a company's total budget. *pie chart*
    c) the number of full-time, part-time, and temporary employees in a company. *bar*
    d) the number of books sold each day for a month at the college bookstore. *bar*

14. In Excel, what is a vertical bar chart called? *column chart*

15. What three questions should be answered when planning a chart? *1. what series will the chart contain? 2. what type of chart should be used? 3. what titles, labels, and legends will make the chart easier to read & understand*

16. What is a data range? *The portion of w.s. to be charted.*

17. What happens to a chart when the data in the spreadsheet is changed? *The chart automatically changes to reflect the new data.*

18. a) List the steps required to move a chart.
    b) List the steps required to size a chart.

19. a) List the steps required to print a chart that is stored on the same sheet as the charted data so that the chart and data are both printed.
    b) List the steps required to print a chart that is stored on the same sheet as the charted data so that only the chart is printed.

20. List the steps required to create a bar or line chart.

21. List the steps required to modify a chart's title without selecting a command.

22. List the steps required to modify a chart to include an additional adjacent series of data.

23. List the steps required to modify a chart to include an additional nonadjacent series of data.

24. List two ways to format a legend in a chart. *C*

*18 a) Position pointer in chart area and drag chart.
b) drag on corner handles*

*Select print in File menu
b) 1st select the chart & then press print in File menu*

20.

Exercises

When creating the charts in the exercises of this chapter, your charts may look different than those shown. It is the content of the chart (height and number of bars, labels, legend, title, etc.) that is important, not that its appearance exactly match that shown in the text. The font size of the labels in the chart may need to be changed or the chart may need to be sized in order to display all the labels clearly.

Exercise 1 ——————————————————— Theater Attendance

A local theater wants to use a worksheet to keep track of the attendance for their performances for the last two years.

a) In a new workbook enter the following data:

	A	B	C	D
1		Students	Adults	Senior Citizens
2				
3	Romeo and Juliet	356	125	89
4	Othello	259	98	175
5	Bus Stop	289	125	112

Bold and right align the labels in row 1 and italicize the labels in column A. Change the column widths as necessary so that all the data is displayed entirely.

b) Save the workbook naming it Theater Attendance.

c) Rename **Sheet1** to 2002 Attendance and rename **Sheet2** to 2003 Attendance.

d) Copy all the labels from the **2002 Attendance** sheet into the **2003 Attendance** sheet, pasting them into the same cell locations. Change the column widths as necessary so that all the data is displayed entirely.

e) Enter the attendance for 2003 into the second sheet:

	A	B	C	D
1		Students	Adults	Senior Citizens
2				
3	Romeo and Juliet	389	255	110
4	Othello	188	145	175
5	Bus Stop	97	112	99

f) Rename **Sheet3** to Total Attendance and copy all the labels from the **2003 Attendance** sheet into the **Total Attendance** sheet, pasting them into the same cell locations. Change the column widths as necessary so that all the data is displayed entirely.

g) In the **Total Attendance** sheet, enter formulas that use cell references to the first two sheets to calculate:

- the total number of students, adults, and senior citizens attending Romeo and Juliet
- the total number of students, adults, and senior citizens attending Othello
- the total number of students, adults, and senior citizens attending Bus Stop

h) Create a header on each sheet with your name right aligned.

i) Create a footer on each sheet with the name of the sheet center aligned.

1,5, 8, 11, 13

j) Save the modified Theater Attendance and print a copy of all the sheets with grid-lines and row and column headings.

k) In the Total Attendance sheet, display the formulas in the cells instead of values. Change the column widths as necessary so that the formulas are completely displayed. Print a copy.

Exercise 2   ♻ ———————————————————— Squeaky Clean Cars

The owner of Squeaky Clean Cars wants the data reorganized and charted for the budget worksheet modified in Chapter 9, Exercise 2. Open Squeaky Clean Cars and complete the following steps:

a) Rename Sheet1 to June's Budget and rename Sheet2 to July's Budget.

b) Copy all the labels in column A from the June's Budget sheet into the July's Budget sheet, pasting them into the same cell locations. Change the column width as necessary so that all the data is displayed entirely.

c) Move the labels and formulas in column F from the June's Budget sheet into the July's Budget sheet, pasting them into the same row locations in column B. Note that the formulas automatically update to refer to the cells on the first sheet.

d) Produce a pie chart on a new sheet named July's Expense Chart that displays the percentage of the budgeted expenses for July. Include the title, legend, and data labels as shown below:

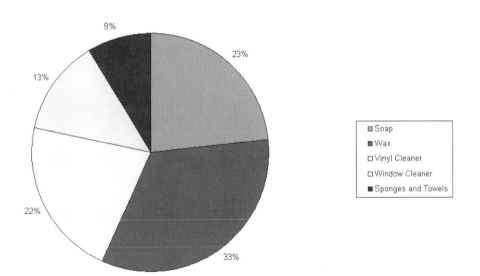

July's Budgeted Expenses

- Soap
- Wax
- Vinyl Cleaner
- Window Cleaner
- Sponges and Towels

e) Change the sheet order so that the July's Expense Chart sheet is behind the July's Budget sheet.

f) Create a header with your name right aligned in the July's Budget sheet and the July's Expense Chart sheet.

g) Save the modified Squeaky Clean Cars and print a copy of the July's Budget sheet with gridlines and row and column headings and a copy of the July's Expense Chart sheet.

Exercise 3

The swim coach wants the data charted for the swim meet worksheet modified in Chapter 9, Exercise 3. Open Swim Meet and complete the following steps:

a) Produce a column chart on the active sheet that displays the times for the first event. Include the title, legend, and axes labels as shown below:

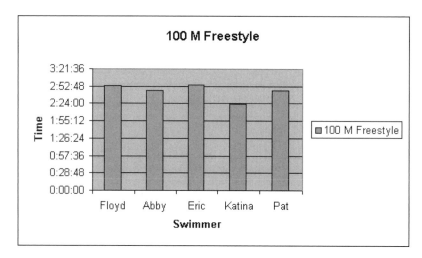

b) Modify the chart to include all six events. Edit the chart title appropriately.

c) Angle the x-axis labels counterclockwise.

d) Print preview the worksheet, then size and move the chart so it and the data fit on one page in landscape orientation. Save the modified Swim Meet and print a copy of the worksheet in landscape orientation with gridlines and row and column headings.

The university wants the data charted for the student statistics worksheet modified in Chapter 9, Exercise 4. Open Student Stats and complete the following steps:

a) Produce a pie chart on the active sheet that displays the percentage of undergraduate students in each college. Remove the legend and include the title and data labels as shown below:

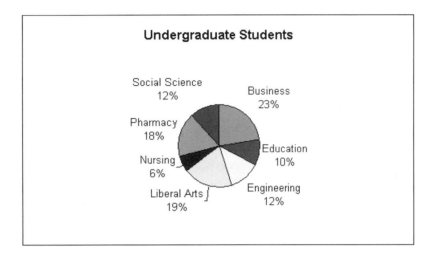

b) Produce a pie chart on the active sheet that displays the percentage of graduate students in each college. Remove the legend and include the title and data labels as shown below:

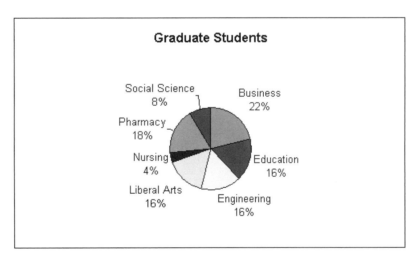

c) Print preview the worksheet, then size and move the charts so that the charts and data fit on one page. Make sure the labels in the chart are displayed clearly. Save the modified Student Stats and print a copy with gridlines and row and column headings.

The AQUARIUM worksheet contains the ammonia, nitrite, and nitrate levels for a new salt water aquarium. Open AQUARIUM and complete the following steps:

a) Rename Sheet1 to Aquarium.

b) Produce a line chart on a new sheet named Water Cycle Chart that displays the ammonia, nitrite, and nitrate levels for each day since set-up. Include the title, legend, and axes labels as shown below:

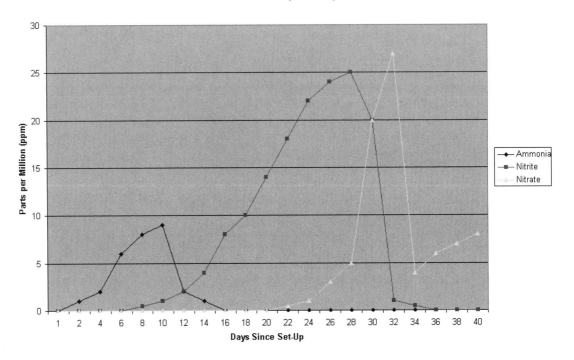

c) Create a header with your name right aligned in the Water Cycle Chart sheet.

d) Save the modified AQUARIUM and print the chart sheet.

Exercise 6 ———————————————— BREAK EVEN

In business, the break even point is when the sales revenue (money earned) equals the expenses (money paid out). A line chart can be used to determine the break even point. Open BREAK EVEN and complete the following steps:

a) Produce a line chart on the active sheet that displays the revenues and expenses per units sold. Include the title, legend, and axes labels as shown below:

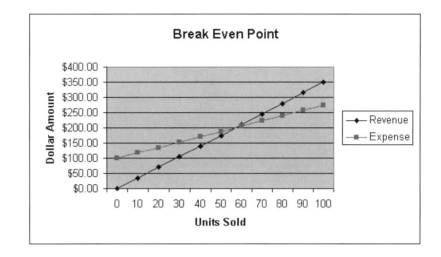

The chart shows that approximately 60 units must be sold for the company to break even.

b) Create a header with your name right aligned in the worksheet.

c) Print preview the worksheet, then size and move the chart so that it and the data fit on one page in landscape orientation. Make sure the labels in the chart are displayed clearly. Save the modified BREAK EVEN and print a copy with gridlines and row and column headings.

Exercise 7 ✧ ─────────────────────────── Pizza Palace

The owner of Pizza Palace wants the data charted for the expense worksheet modified in Chapter 9, Exercise 7. Open Pizza Palace and complete the following steps:

a) Produce a pie chart on the active sheet that displays the ingredients and the percentage of their costs for the Everything pizza. Include and format the title, legend, and data labels as shown below:

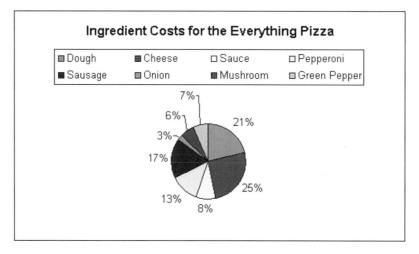

b) Print preview the worksheet, then size and move the chart so that it and the data fit on one page. Make sure the labels in the chart are displayed clearly. Save the modified Pizza Palace and print a copy with gridlines and row and column headings.

Exercise 8 ✧ ─────────────────────────── Balance Sheet

The accountant wants data added to the balance sheet created in Chapter 8, Exercise 8. Open Balance Sheet and complete the following steps:

a) Rename Sheet1 to Jan 2003, rename Sheet2 to Feb 2003 and rename Sheet3 to March 2003.

b) Copy all the data from the Jan 2003 sheet into the Feb 2003 and March 2003 sheets, pasting them into the same cell locations. Change the column widths as necessary so that all the data is displayed entirely.

c) Clear all the assets, liabilities, and stockholder's equity values in the Feb 2003 and March 2003 sheets (do not delete the formulas).

d) Edit the date in cell C3 in the Feb 2003 and March 2003 sheets appropriately. Note that there are 28 days in February 2003 and 31 days in March 2003.

e) Using the data below, enter the appropriate values into the Feb 2003 and March 2003 sheets:

	Feb	March
Cash	$12,250	$17,500
Accounts Receivable	$14,750	$8,500
Gym Equipment	$40,000	$38,900
Office Computers	$43,500	$42,750
Accounts Payable	$80,525	$79,525
Stockholder's Equity	$29,975	$28,125

f) Create a header with your name right aligned on the Feb 2003 and March 2003 sheets.

g) Create a footer with the current date center aligned on the Feb 2003 and March 2003 sheets.

h) Save the modified Balance Sheet and print a copy of the Feb 2003 and March 2003 sheets with gridlines and row and column headings.

Exercise 9 ☼ ——————————————————— DANCE

The dance coordinator wants the data charted for the profit worksheet modified in Chapter 9, Exercise 9. Open DANCE and complete the following steps:

a) Produce a column chart on the active sheet that displays the profit when 50, 100, 200, and 300 people attend the dance. Include and format the title and axes labels as shown below:

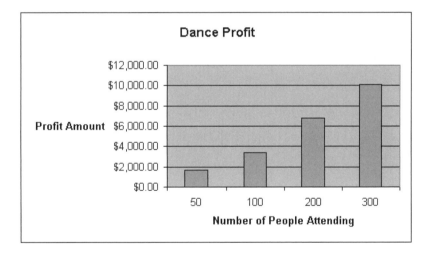

b) Print preview the worksheet, then size and move the chart so that it and the data fit on one page. Make sure the labels in the chart are displayed clearly. Save the modified DANCE and print a copy with gridlines and row and column headings.

The stockbroker wants the data charted for the worksheet modified in Chapter 9, Exercise 10. Open STOCKS and complete the following steps:

a) Rename Sheet1 to Investments.

b) Produce a column chart on a new sheet named Stock Value Chart that displays the original values of the stocks. Remove the legend and include the title and axes labels as shown below:

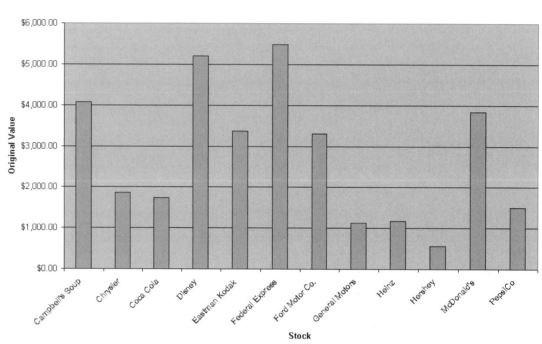

c) Create a header with your name right aligned in the Stock Value Chart sheet.

d) Modify the chart to include the March values of the stocks as a new data series.

e) Modify the title and Y axis label appropriately.

f) Save the modified STOCKS and print the chart sheet.

Exercise 11 ⟳ ——————————————————— Tickets

The amphitheater manager wants the data reorganized for the worksheet created in Chapter 9, Exercise 11. Open Tickets and complete the following steps:

a) Rename Sheet1 to The Motherboards, rename Sheet2 to Blue Knights and rename Sheet3 to The Altairs.

b) Copy the labels in row 1 to the new sheets, pasting them into the same cell locations.

c) Move the appropriate data so that each act's data is in the appropriate sheet starting in row 3. Change the column widths as necessary so that all the data is displayed entirely.

d) Create a header with your name right aligned on the second and third sheets.

e) Create a footer on each sheet with the name of the sheet center aligned.

f) Save the modified Tickets and print a copy of all the sheets with gridlines and row and column headings.

Exercise 12 ⟳ ——————————————————— Track Progress

The track coach wants the data charted for the progress worksheet created in Chapter 9, Exercise 12. Open Track Progress and complete the following steps:

a) Produce a line chart on the active sheet that displays the progress of the track team in the 100 meter run over the four months. Include the title, legend, and axes labels as shown below:

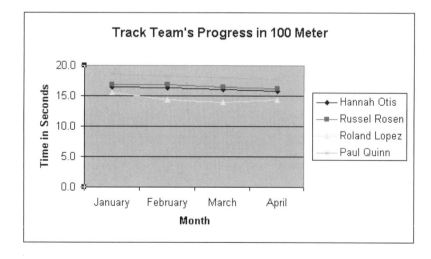

b) Produce a line chart on the active sheet that displays the students' progress in the 200 meter run over the four months. Include the title, legend, and axes labels as shown below:

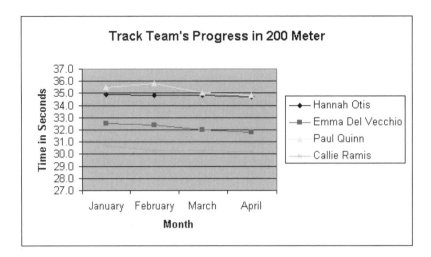

c) Print preview the worksheet, then size and move the charts so that the charts and data fit on one page in landscape orientation. Make sure that all the chart labels are displayed. Save the modified Track Progress and print a copy in landscape orientation with gridlines and row and column headings.

Exercise 13 ⟳ ──────────────────────── Income Statement

The accountant want the data charted for the income statement created in Chapter 8, Exercise 13. Open Income Statement and complete the following steps:

a) Rename Sheet1 to Fluffy Bakery.

b) Produce a line chart on a new sheet named Income Chart that displays the net income/loss for 2002–2004. Include and format the title and axes labels as shown below:

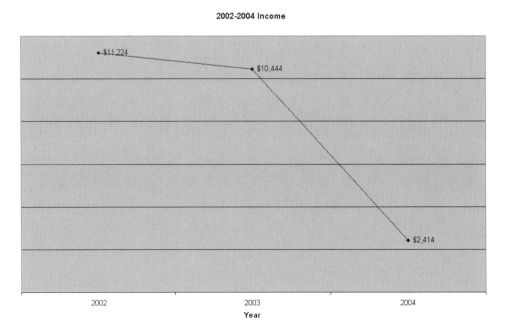

c) Create a header with your name right aligned on the Income Chart sheet.

d) Produce a line chart on the Fluffy Bakery sheet that charts the total revenues for 2002 and 2003. Remove the legend and include the title and axes labels as shown below:

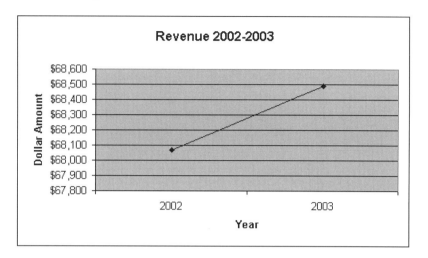

e) Modify the revenue chart to include all three years 2002–2004. Edit the title appropriately.

f) Move the chart so that it is below the worksheet data.

g) Select the chart and then create a header with your name right aligned.

h) Save the modified Income Statement and print each chart separately.

Exercise 14 ⟳ ——————————————————————— City Temp

The Meteorology department wants the data modified to include Fahrenheit temperatures and charted for the worksheet modified in Chapter 9, Exercise 14. Open City Temp and complete the following steps:

a) Rename Sheet1 to Celsius and Rename Sheet2 to Fahrenheit.

b) Copy all the data in column A from the Celsius sheet to the Fahrenheit sheet, pasting them into the same cell locations.

c) In the Fahrenheit sheet, enter formulas that use cell references to the Celsius sheet to convert the Celsius temperatures to Fahrenheit. The formula needed to convert from degrees Celsius to Fahrenheit is 9/5*(Celsius Temp)+32.

d) Title the column heading appropriately and include proper formatting. Change the column widths as necessary so that all the data is displayed entirely.

e) Copy the formulas in cells B23 and B24 from the Celsius sheet to the Fahrenheit sheet, pasting them into the same cell locations.

f) Create a line chart on the Celsius sheet that displays the temperature for the years 1984 to 1994. Include the title and axes labels as shown on the next page:

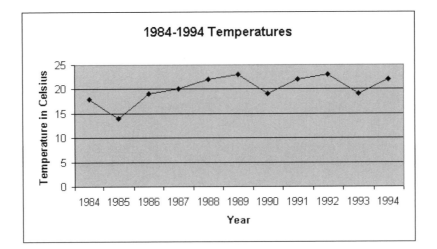

g) Create the same line chart for the Fahrenheit temperatures in the Fahrenheit sheet, changing the y-axis label appropriately.

h) Modify both charts to include the data for all 20 years and edit the titles appropriately.

i) Create a header with your name right aligned in the Fahrenheit sheet.

j) Create a footer with the sheet name centered.

k) Print preview both sheets, then size and move the charts so that the charts and data fit on each sheet in landscape orientation. Make sure all of the labels in the charts are displayed clearly. Save the modified City Temp and print a copy of both sheets in landscape orientation with gridlines and row and column headings.

Exercise 15 (advanced) ♻ ———————————— My Finances

Modify the My Finances worksheet created in Chapter 9, Exercise 16 so that it contains a line chart of your savings. Save the modified workbook and then print a copy of only the chart.

Exercise 16 (advanced) ———————————— New Charts

This chapter only discussed pie, line, and bar charts. Excel allows many different types of charts to be created. Enter data into a new workbook so that it can be charted. Create three charts besides pie, line, or bar from the data. Save the workbook naming it New Charts and then print a copy.

Exercise 17 (advanced) ♻ ————————————

Modify one of the workbooks created in Exercise 17 or 18 in Chapter 8 to include a chart on its own sheet. Save the modified workbook and then print the chart sheet.

Sort

From File

Freeze Panes

Unfreeze Panes

Set Print Area

Clear Print Area

Hyperlink

Save as Web Page

Chapter 11 Expectations

After completing this chapter you will be able to:

1. Determine how changing data impacts results by asking "What If" questions.
2. Sort the data in a spreadsheet.
3. Add a picture to a worksheet.
4. Use the CHOOSE and VLOOKUP functions.
5. Name a cell or range.
6. Freeze selected rows and columns.
7. Use text in CHOOSE and VLOOKUP functions.
8. Create an amortization table using the PMT function.
9. Print a selected worksheet area.
10. Create hyperlinks to a worksheet location.
11. E-mail a worksheet from Excel.
12. Save Excel data in HTML format.

$\mathbf{T}$his chapter discusses how to use a worksheet to answer "What If?" questions. The CHOOSE and VLOOKUP functions are introduced. Creating hyperlinks within a workbook and e-mailing worksheets are also discussed.

11.1   Asking "What If ?"

A worksheet is often used to answer "What If?" questions. A *What If* question asks how changing data will impact results. For example, a cookie manufacturer determines the selling price of a cookie by calculating the production cost per cookie and then adding a markup of 50%. The worksheet on the left uses the current price of sugar. On the right, the same worksheet has been modified to answer, "What if the price of sugar increased from $1.75 to $2.75?":

	A	B
1	**Cost of Production per Batch (100 cookies)**	
2		
3		**Production Costs**
4	Sugar	$1.75
5	Dairy Products	$1.80
6	Spices and Flavorings	$0.80
7	Flour	$0.90
8	Packaging	$2.75
9	Labor	$12.00
10	*Total Cost per Batch:*	$20.00
11		
12	*Production Cost (per cookie)*	$0.20
13	*Selling Price (per cookie)*	$0.30

Original sugar cost of $1.75

	A	B
1	**Cost of Production per Batch (100 cookies)**	
2		
3		**Production Costs**
4	Sugar	$2.75
5	Dairy Products	$1.80
6	Spices and Flavorings	$0.80
7	Flour	$0.90
8	Packaging	$2.75
9	Labor	$12.00
10	*Total Cost per Batch:*	$21.00
11		
12	*Production Cost (per cookie)*	$0.21
13	*Selling Price (per cookie)*	$0.32

What if sugar costs $2.75?

model

Note that the increased price of sugar results in the selling price increasing from $0.30 to $0.32 per cookie. A worksheet modified to answer What If? questions is called a *model*. Many businesses use models to help make decisions.

In this practice you will answer some "What If?" questions for a cookie manufacturer.

① OPEN COOKIE COSTS

Open COOKIE COSTS, which is a data file for this text. The COOKIE COSTS workbook contains the production costs per batch of cookies.

② ANSWER WHAT IF QUESTIONS

a. In cell B9, increase the Labor cost from $12.00 to $15.00. Note how the Production Cost (per cookie) and Selling Price (per cookie) are affected.

b. In cell B8, increase the Packaging cost from $2.75 to $3.75. Note how the Production Cost (per cookie) and Selling Price (per cookie) are affected.

③ ADD A HEADER AND FOOTER

Create a header with the text Increased Labor and Packaging Costs Model center aligned and a footer with your name right aligned.

④ SAVE, PRINT, AND THEN CLOSE THE MODIFIED COOKIE COSTS

11.2 Sorting Data

Placing data in a specified order is called *sorting*. In Excel, rows can be sorted in either *ascending* (low to high) or *descending* (high to low) order based on the data in a specified column. Ascending order is also called *alphabetical* order when the data is text, and *chronological* order when the data is times or dates.

ascending, descending

alphabetical, chronological

Data is sorted by first selecting the range to sort:

	A	B	C
1	Vacation Expenses		
2			
3	Item	Price	
4	Food	$429.00	
5	Hotel	$650.00	
6	Airfare	$1,025.00	
7	Rental Car	$198.00	
8	Total:	$2,302.00	

Note that only the expenses and their corresponding prices are selected. Clicking the Sort Ascending button () places the selected data in alphabetical order based on the values displayed in the first column of selected data, which is column A in the example:

	A	B	C
1	Vacation Expenses		
2			
3	Item	Price	
4	Airfare	$1,025.00	
5	Food	$429.00	
6	Hotel	$650.00	
7	Rental Car	$198.00	
8	Total:	$2,302.00	

The selected block has been sorted by column A

Clicking the Sort Descending button () sorts selected data in descending order.

key sort column

The Sort Ascending and Sort Descending buttons use the first selected column as the key sort column. The *key sort column* is the column that contains the values that a sort is based on. In the example above, column A is the key sort column. A different column can be designated as the key sort column by selecting Sort from the Data menu, which displays the Sort dialog box:

Selecting a column label from the Sort by list and selecting the method of sort, such as Descending, and then OK sorts the selected rows.

When a column and order are specified in the Then by area, rows that have the same data in the key sort column are sorted based on the data in the Then By area. For example, in the dialog box above, selecting Price in the first Then by list and Ascending sorts rows by Price when the Item data is the same.

Practice 2

In this practice the Grades worksheet will be sorted.

① OPEN GRADES

Open Grades, which was last modified in Chapter 9, Practice 7.

② SORT ALL THE STUDENT DATA

a. Point to the row number for row 4 and drag down to the row number for row 9 to select all the rows containing student data.

b. On the toolbar, click the Sort Ascending (⟨≜↓⟩) button. The selected rows are sorted in alphabetical order based on the data in column A.

c. Click anywhere in the worksheet to remove the selection.

③ SAVE AND THEN CLOSE THE MODIFIED GRADES

11.3   Adding a Picture

A picture, such as a business logo, can be added to a worksheet to give it a professional appearance:

	A	B
1		
2	**Contini's**	
3	**Cookie Company**	
4		
5		
6	**Cost of Production per Batch (100 cookies)**	
7		
8		**Production Costs**
9	Sugar	$2.75
10	Dairy Products	$1.80
11	Spices and Flavorings	$0.80
12	Flour	$0.90
13	Packaging	$2.75
14	Labor	$12.00
15	*Total Cost per Batch:*	$21.00
16		
17	*Production Cost (per cookie):*	$0.21
18	*Selling Price (per cookie)*	$0.32

A picture should be placed on an area of the worksheet where there are enough blank cells to display the picture without covering any data.

A picture is added by selecting <u>F</u>rom File from the <u>P</u>icture submenu in the <u>I</u>nsert menu, which displays the Insert Picture dialog box:

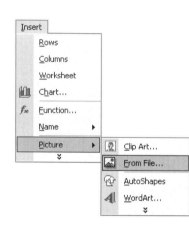

The Look in list and contents box below it are used to display the picture file name. When the contents box displays the appropriate file name, clicking that file name and then selecting Insert adds the picture.

Templates

Rather than recreating a workbook over and over again, it can be created once and then saved as a template. Templates are previously created files that include basic elements such as formatting, labels, and pictures.

Selecting Save <u>A</u>s from the <u>F</u>ile menu and then selecting Templates from the **Save as type** list saves the current workbook as a template. A template is used by selecting it from the **General** tab in the New Office Document dialog box.

Clicking a picture selects it and displays handles:

sizing a picture

Pointing to a handle changes the pointer to ↖, and then dragging sizes the picture. Dragging on a corner handle sizes the picture proportionately, which means that the width and height remain in the same ratio as the original to prevent the picture from looking distorted. Dragging a handle in the middle of a side, top, or bottom stretches and distorts the picture.

A picture is moved by positioning the pointer on the picture and then dragging the picture to a new location. The rotate handle is used to rotate the picture. The Pictures toolbar, which contains options for modifying pictures, is automatically displayed when a picture is selected.

The Cut, Copy, and Paste commands in the Edit menu can be used to move a selected graphic or create a copy. Pressing the Delete key deletes the selected picture. Gridlines should be turned off when printing a worksheet that contains a picture.

Practice 3

In this practice you will modify the PAYROLL worksheet by adding a picture.

① *OPEN PAYROLL*

Open PAYROLL, which was last modified in Chapter 9, Practice 6.

② *INSERT ROWS*

   a. Select rows 1 through 5 by selecting the row numbers.
   b. Right-click a row number in the selected area. A menu is displayed.
   c. Select Insert. Five new rows are inserted and the existing data moves down.

③ *ADD A PICTURE*

   a. Select cell A1.
   b. Select Insert → Picture → From File. A dialog box is displayed.
      1. Use the Look in list and the contents box below it to display the data files for this text.
      2. Click the Net Provider.gif file name.
      3. Select Insert. The dialog box is removed and the picture is inserted.
   c. Click the picture to select it if it is not already selected. Handles and the Picture toolbar are displayed.
   d. Drag the picture so the bottom of the picture is aligned with row 4. The left edge of the picture should be in column A.

④ *SAVE AND PRINT THE MODIFIED PAYROLL*

11.4 The CHOOSE Function

The CHOOSE function is used to return a value from a list of many values. The CHOOSE function takes the form:

$$=CHOOSE(<choice>, <option_1>, <option_2>, ..., <option_N>)$$

<choice> is a number between 1 and 29 or a formula or reference to a cell containing a number between 1 and 29. <option1>, <option2>, ... store the possible values to return. CHOOSE returns the value in the list of arguments that corresponds to <choice>. If <choice> is 1, CHOOSE returns <option_1>; if <choice> is 2, then <option_2> is returned, and so on.

For example, with the formula =CHOOSE(A1, 500, 400, 250, 100) in cell C2:

C2	▼	f_x =CHOOSE(B2, 500, 400, 250, 100)		
	A	B	C	D	E
1	Employee	Department	Bonus		
2	Buckley, S.	2	$400		
3	George, B.	3	$250		
4	McCabe, M.	1	$500		
5	Wilson, J.	4	$100		

Excel displays 500 if the value stored in cell A1 is 1, 400 if the value is 2, 250 if the value is 3, and 100 if it is 4. If <choice> is less than 1 or greater than N, which is 4 in this example, #VALUE! is displayed, meaning that a corresponding value is not available.

Only the integer portion of <choice> is used to determine which value to return. For example, if A1 stores 1.6, 500 is displayed because only the integer portion of the value, 1, is used. The options (<option_1>, <option_2>, ...) in the CHOOSE function can include values, formulas, cell references, and labels.

Practice 4 ❄

In this practice you will modify the PAYROLL worksheet to calculate a contribution amount using the CHOOSE function. Open PAYROLL if it is not already displayed.

① INSERT COLUMNS

    a. Right-click the column letter H. A menu is displayed.

    b. Select Insert. A new column is inserted with the same formatting as the column to the left and the Insert Options button is displayed.

    c. Click the Insert Options button. A list of options is displayed.

        1. Select Clear Formatting. The formatting of the new column is removed.

    d. Right-click the column letter I. A menu is displayed.

    e. Select Insert. A new column is inserted with the same formatting as the column to the left and the Insert Options button is displayed.

    f. Click the Insert Options button. A list of options is displayed.

        1. Select Format Same As Right. The formatting of the new column is changed to be the same as column J, which is Currency with 2 decimals.

A Guide to Microsoft Office XP Professional

② ENTER LABELS

    a. In cell H10, enter the label Code. Note that the label is formatted the same as the other labels in the row even though the column formatting was removed.

    b. In cell I10, enter the label Contribution. Note that the label is formatted the same as the other labels in the row.

    c. Adjust the column widths to display the labels entirely.

③ ENTER THE CONTRIBUTION CODES

    a. There are four codes numbered 1 through 4 that determine the percentage of the employee's gross pay deducted for a contribution. Enter the code numbers below into the indicated cells in column H:

In cell	H12	enter	2		In cell	H21	enter	4
	H13		2			H22		1
	H14		1			H23		1
	H15		3			H24		2
	H16		1			H25		3
	H17		1			H26		3
	H18		1			H27		4
	H19		2			H28		1
	H20		2					

④ ENTER FORMULAS TO CALCULATE CONTRIBUTIONS

Each of the codes above corresponds to the following percentages which are used to calculate the contribution deduction:

Code	Percentage
1	0%
2	1%
3	2%
4	5%

    a. In cell I12, enter the formula:

        =CHOOSE(H12, 0, G12*1%, G12*2%, G12*5%)

The CHOOSE function first looks in cell H12 to determine the value of <choice>. Because the value in cell H12 is 2, this corresponds to <option$_2$> and Excel calculates G12*1% to compute the contribution. Cell I12 displays $2.25, the result of $225.00*1%.

    b. Use the Fill handle to copy the formula in cell I12 to cells I13 through I28. Ignore the Auto Fill Options button.

⑤ *RECALCULATE THE NET PAY*

    a. In cell L12, modify the existing formula to be:

        =G12–I12–J12–K12

    Net pay is now computed by subtracting social security, taxes, and contribution from the gross pay, and $175.50 is displayed in cell L12.

    b. Use the Fill handle to copy the formula in cell L12 to cells L13 through L28. Ignore the Auto Fill Options button.

⑥ *SAVE THE MODIFIED PAYROLL*

11.5   Naming a Cell or Range

The Name box can be used to name a cell or range of cells. A cell or range of cells is named by selecting the cell(s) and then typing a descriptive name in the Name box. For example, in the worksheet below, the selected range is named Test1:

Name box —

	A	B	C	D	E
1	Name	Test 1	Test 2	Test 3	Test 4
2		1/7/03	2/9/03	3/1/03	4/1/03
3					
4	Bell, M.	70	74	80	83
5	Garcia, E.	72	63	67	72
6	Jones, D.	85	73	88	95
7	McCallister, T.	87	92	85	93
8	Neave, C.	92	88	85	91
9	Smith, L.	94	91	93	84

(Name box: Test1 ▾   *fx* 70)

The named range can then be used in formulas. For example, the formula =AVERAGE(Test1) would calculate the average of the test scores in cells B4 through B9. A named range is an absolute reference.

11.6   The VLOOKUP Function

The VLOOKUP function is used to return a value from a table of values stored in the worksheet. The VLOOKUP function takes the form:

    =VLOOKUP(<value>, <range>, <column>)

<value> is a number to be looked up in a table of values and <range> is the cell range where the VLOOKUP table is stored. VLOOKUP finds the largest number in the first column of <range> which is less than or equal to <value>, and then returns the value stored in the same row in column <column> of the VLOOKUP table. The value of <column> is usually 2 to indicate that the second column in the VLOOKUP table stores the value to be returned.

A Guide to Microsoft Office XP Professional

For example, with the formula =VLOOKUP(B5,$D$10:$E$14,2) in cell C5:

	C5	▼		f_x =VLOOKUP(B5, $D$10:$E$14, 2)	
	A	B	C	D	E
1	Boca Distributing				
2					
3	Customer	Amount	Shipping Cost		
4					
5	Garcia	$39.75	$7.49		
6	Keating	$100.00	$12.49		
7	Marotta	$52.50	$7.49		
8	Postma	$176.75	$14.99		
9				Shipping Cost	
10				$0.00	$4.99
11				$30.00	$7.49
12				$60.00	$10.49
13				$100.00	$12.49
14				$150.00	$14.99

1. Excel looks in cell B5 for its value, which is $39.75.

2. Excel then looks in the first column of the VLOOKUP table for the largest value which is less than or equal to $39.75, in this case $30 (stored in D11).

3. The corresponding value in the second column of the table, in this case $7.49, is then displayed in cell C5.

   In a similar manner, the function displays $12.49 in cell C6 because cell D13 stores the largest value in the VLOOKUP table which is less than or equal to $100.00 (the value stored in cell B6).

The values in the first column of a VLOOKUP table must be in ascending order for VLOOKUP to work correctly. If <value> is less than the first value stored in the VLOOKUP table, #N/A! is displayed. For this reason, the first value stored in the VLOOKUP table must be less than or equal to any value that will be looked up.

In the VLOOKUP function, absolute references should be used for the VLOOKUP table range so that the range does not change when the formula containing the VLOOKUP function is copied.

named range   The range that defines the VLOOKUP table can also be specified as a named range. For example, in the worksheet below, the table range D10 through E14 has been named Shipping and the VLOOKUP function modified accordingly:

	C5	▼		f_x =VLOOKUP(B5, Shipping, 2)	
	A	B	C	D	E
1	Boca Distributing				
2					
3	Customer	Amount	Shipping Cost		
4					
5	Garcia	$39.75	$7.49		
6	Keating	$100.00	$12.49		
7	Marotta	$52.50	$7.49		
8	Postma	$176.75	$14.99		
9				Shipping Cost	
10				$0.00	$4.99
11				$30.00	$7.49
12				$60.00	$10.49
13				$100.00	$12.49
14				$150.00	$14.99

11.7   Freezing Cells

One difficulty encountered when working with a large worksheet is that rows and columns that contain descriptive labels may scroll off the screen. This makes it difficult to determine which columns or rows the displayed cells are in. One way to solve this problem is to *freeze* selected rows and columns in place so they will not scroll when the rest of the worksheet is scrolled.

Selecting Freeze Panes from the Window menu designates every row above the active cell and every column to the left of the active cell as frozen. For example, selecting cell C11 and then selecting Freeze Panes freezes the cells in columns A and B and rows 1 through 10 from scrolling:

Frozen cells are displayed with solid borders

When scrolling vertically, frozen rows remain on the screen. Frozen columns remain on the screen when scrolling horizontally. Selecting Unfreeze Panes from the Windows menu unfreezes all the frozen cells.

Freezing cells does not affect how the worksheet is printed, only how the data is viewed on the screen.

Practice 5

In this practice PAYROLL will be modified to allow for four tax rates. Cells will be frozen to keep the employee names and column titles on the screen. Open PAYROLL if it is not already displayed.

① ADD A VLOOKUP TABLE TO THE WORKSHEET

The following tax rates will be used in calculating taxes:

Salary	Tax Rate
under $51	0%
$51 – $524	15%
$525 – $1,124	28%
$1,125 and above	31%

a. In cell J30, enter the label Tax Rate Table and then bold it.

b. Enter the following values into the indicated cells to create the VLOOKUP tax table:

In cell		enter		In cell		enter	
J31	enter	$0		**K31**	enter	0%	
J32		$51		**K32**		15%	
J33		$525		**K33**		28%	
J34		$1,125		**K34**		31%	

② *FREEZE TITLES*

    a. Select cell C11. Be sure that cell A1 is displayed on the screen as well.

    b. Select Window → Freeze Panes. The frozen cells are indicated by solid borders.

    c. Click the right scroll arrow several times to scroll horizontally until column L is displayed beside column B. Note that columns A and B remain displayed while other columns are scrolled off the screen.

    d. Click the down scroll arrow until row 45 is displayed in the window. Note that rows 1 through 10 remain on the screen.

    e. Press Ctrl+Home to return to cell C11.

③ *NAME THE TABLE RANGE*

    a. Select cell J31 through K34.

    b. Click in the Name box.

    c. Type Rate and press the Enter key. Rate is now displayed in the Name box.

④ *CALCULATE TAXES USING THE VLOOKUP FUNCTION*

    a. In cell K12, replace the existing formula with

        =G12*VLOOKUP(G12, Rate, 2)

    The gross pay stored in cell G12 is $225.00, which is multiplied by 15% to compute the tax deduction of $33.75.

    b. Use the Fill handle to copy the formula in cell K12 to cells K13 through K28. Ignore the Auto Fill Options button.

    c. Click any cell to remove the selection.

Check – Your worksheet should look similar to:

	A	B	C	D	E	F	G	H	I	J	K	L
1												
2												
3	**Net Provider** ▲											
4												
5												
6	Net Provider Payroll											
7												
8	Soc. Sec. Rate:	6.0%										
9												
10	Last Name	First Initial	Rate/Hr	Hours	Overtime Hours	Overtime Pay	Gross Pay	Code	Contribution	Soc. Sec.	Taxes	Net Pay
11												
12	Alban	B.	$7.50	30.0	0.0	$0.00	$225.00	2	$2.25	$13.50	$33.75	$175.50
13	Angulo	M.	$8.00	29.5	0.0	$0.00	$236.00	2	$2.36	$14.16	$35.40	$186.44
14	Balto	Y.	$8.00	29.0	0.0	$0.00	$232.00	1	$0.00	$13.92	$34.80	$183.28
15	Cruz	S.	$7.75	13.0	0.0	$0.00	$100.75	3	$2.02	$6.05	$15.11	$79.59
16	Del Vecchio	E.	$9.00	43.5	3.5	$52.50	$444.00	1	$0.00	$26.64	$66.60	$350.76

⑤ *SAVE, PRINT, AND THEN CLOSE THE MODIFIED PAYROLL*

    a. Select Window → Unfreeze Panes. Cells are no longer frozen.

    b. Save the modified PAYROLL and print a copy.

    c. Close PAYROLL.

11.8 Using Text in the CHOOSE and VLOOKUP Functions

As with the IF function, text can be used in both the CHOOSE and VLOOKUP functions. For example, the formula

=CHOOSE(C3, "Beginner", "Intermediate", "Advanced", "Expert")

displays the word Beginner if the value stored in cell C3 is 1, Intermediate if C3 stores the value 2, Advanced if C3 stores the value 3, and Expert if C3 stores the value 4. Cell references of cells that store labels can be used as well.

The VLOOKUP function can also be used to display text by storing labels in the VLOOKUP table. For example, the formula =VLOOKUP(B2, $B$10:$C$12, 2) in cell C3 below displays High Normal because cell B11 stores the largest value in the VLOOKUP table less than or equal to the value in cell B3:

	C3	▼	f_x =VLOOKUP(B3,$B$10:$C$12,2)	
	A	B	C	D
1	Patient	Blood Pressure	Diagnosis	
2				
3	Hajdu, B.	130	High Normal	
4	Palombi, R.	128	Normal	
5	Thomas, M.	150	High	
6	Wells, J.	129	Normal	
7				
8				
9		**Systollic Blood Pressure Table**		
10		0	Normal	
11		130	High Normal	
12		140	High	

Practice 6 ✎

In this practice the Grades worksheet will be modified to display each student's letter grade.

① *OPEN GRADES*

Open Grades, which was last modified in Practice 2.

② *ENTER AND FORMAT A LABEL*

In cell H1, enter the label Grade and then center align the label.

③ *ADD A VLOOKUP TABLE*

a. In cell B12, enter the label Letter Grade Table and then bold it.

b. Enter the following data into the indicated cells to create the VLOOKUP table:

In cell	**B13**	enter	0		In cell	**C13**	enter	F
	B14		60			**C14**		D
	B15		70			**C15**		C
	B16		80			**C16**		B
	B17		90			**C17**		A

④ *NAME THE TABLE RANGE*

    a. Select cell B13 through C17.

    b. In the Name box, type Grade and press the Enter key. Grade is now displayed in the Name box.

⑤ *ENTER FORMULAS TO DETERMINE THE STUDENTS' GRADES*

    a. In cell H4, enter the formula:

        =VLOOKUP(F4, Grade, 2)

    Since 70 is the largest number less than or equal to the value in cell F4, C is displayed.

    b. Center align the letter grade in cell H4.

    c. Copy the formula in cell H4 to cells H5 through H9. Ignore the Auto Fill Options button.

    d. Click any cell to remove the selection.

Check - Your worksheet should look similar to:

	A	B	C	D	E	F	G	H
1	Name	Test 1	Test 2	Test 3	Test 4	Student Average	Status	Grade
2		1/7/03	2/9/03	3/1/03	4/1/03			
3								
4	Bell, M.	70	74	80	83	77	Passing	C
5	Garcia, E.	72	63	67	72	69	Below Average	D
6	Jones, D.	85	73	88	95	85	Passing	B
7	McCallister, T.	87	92	85	93	89	Passing	B
8	Neave, C.	92	88	85	91	89	Passing	B
9	Smith, L.	94	91	93	84	91	Passing	A
10	Test Average	83.3	80.2	83	86.3			
11								
12		Letter Grade Table						
13		0	F					
14		60	D					
15		70	C					
16		80	B					
17		90	A					

⑥ *CHANGE NEAVE'S SCORE ON TEST 3*

    A mistake was made when Neave's Test 3 score was entered. Select cell D8 and enter 95, the correct score. Note how Excel automatically recalculated all formulas that refer to the cell containing the test score.

⑦ *SAVE, PRINT, AND THEN CLOSE THE MODIFIED GRADES*

    a. Save the modified Grades.

    b. Print a copy of the worksheet in landscape orientation.

    c. Save the modified Grades and then close the worksheet.

11.9 Amortization Tables and the PMT Function

installment loan

A useful application of a worksheet is an amortization table. *Amortization* is a method for computing equal periodic payments for an *installment loan*. Car loans and mortgages are often installment loans. Each installment, or payment, is the same and consists of two parts: a portion to pay interest due on the principal for that period and the remainder which reduces the principal. The *principal* is the amount of money owed, and decreases with each payment made.

principal

An *amortization table* displays the interest and principal amounts for each payment of an installment loan. For example, the monthly payment on a 30 year loan of $100,000 borrowed at 12% interest (1% per month) is $1,028.61. In the first payment, $1,000.00 pays the interest due (1% × $100,000) and $28.61 goes to reduce principal ($1,028.61 – $1,000.00). In the next payment, $999.71 pays the interest due and $28.90 goes to reduce principal. As payments are made, the interest due decreases because there is less principal to charge interest on. In the final payment, $10.18 pays the interest due and $1,018.43 pays off the principal.

The PMT function is used to calculate the equal periodic payment for an installment loan. Three arguments are needed by the PMT function. The PMT function takes the form:

=PMT(<rate>, <term>, <principal>)

<rate> is the interest rate per period, <term> is the total number of payments to be made, and <principal> is the amount borrowed. For example, the PMT function would be used to determine the monthly payment on a mortgage. The formula below calculates the monthly payments on a 30-year, $100,000 loan with an annual interest rate of 12%:

=PMT(12%/12, 360, –100000)

Since the payments are made monthly, the interest rate must also be computed monthly by dividing the annual interest rate of 12% by 12. The number of payments is 360, 30 years × 12 months. The principal is negative because it is the amount borrowed and it does not include a dollar sign or commas. This formula computes the monthly payment as $1,028.61.

11.10 Printing a Selected Worksheet Area

Instead of printing an entire worksheet, it is possible to print part of a worksheet. The printable worksheet area is set by selecting the range to be printed and then selecting Set Print Area from the Print Area submenu in the File menu. Selecting Print from the File menu then prints only the specified print area. Once the print area is set, only those cells will be displayed in print preview and included in a printout.

The entire worksheet can be set as the print range by selecting Clear Print Area from the Print Area submenu in the File menu.

In this practice you will complete an amortization table.

① *OPEN LOAN*

Open LOAN, which is a data file for this text. The displayed worksheet is a partially completed amortization table.

② *ENTER THE LOAN'S INFORMATION*

    a. In cell B3, enter the yearly interest rate 12%.

    b. In cell B4, enter the number of payments 360 (30 years × 12 monthly payments).

    c. In cell B5, enter the principal $100,000.

③ *CALCULATE THE MONTHLY PAYMENT*

In cell B7, enter the formula:

    =PMT(B3/12, B4, –B5)

The division by 12 is needed to convert the yearly interest rate in cell B3 to a monthly value. $1,028.61 is displayed.

④ *CALCULATE TOTAL PAID AND TOTAL INTEREST*

    a. In cell B9, enter the formula:

        =ROUND(B4*B7, 2)

    This formula computes the total paid for the loan, $370,300.53, including principal and interest.

    b. In cell B10, enter the formula =B9–B5 to display the total interest paid over the 30 years, $270,300.53.

⑤ *ENTER THE FIRST PAYMENT DATA*

    a. In cell A13, enter 1.

    b. In cell B13, enter =B5.

    c. In cell C13, enter the formula

        =B13*($B$3/12)

    to calculate one month's interest on the loan. $1,000.00, which is 1% (12%/12) of the principal, is displayed. The cell reference B3 contains dollar signs because the interest rate will be the same for each payment.

    d. In cell D13, enter the formula

        =IF(C13<0.01, 0, $B$7–C13)

    to calculate the amount of the payment which is applied to the principal, $28.61. If the value in cell C13 is less than 0.01 (less than a penny), then 0 is displayed.

    e. In cell E13, enter the formula =B13–D13 to calculate the new principal owed.

⑥ **ENTER FORMULAS FOR THE SECOND PAYMENT**

    a. In cell A14, enter the formula: =A13+1.

    b. In cell B14, enter =E13 to display the new principal.

    c. Copy the formulas in cells C13 through E13 into cells C14 through E14. Ignore the Auto Fill Options button. This completes the data for the second payment and the principal owed, $99,942.49 is displayed in cell E14.

⑦ **COMPLETE THE TABLE**

    a. Copy the formulas in cells A14 through E14 into cells A15 through E372. Ignore the Auto Fill Options button. The principal owed is $0.00 in cell E372, which indicates the loan has been paid in full.

    b. Click any cell to remove the selection.

Check – Your worksheet should look similar to:

	A	B	C	D	E
1	**Loan Amortization Table**				
2					
3	Interest rate =	12%			
4	Number of payments =	360			
5	Principal =	$100,000.00			
6					
7	Monthly payment =	$1,028.61			
8					
9	Total paid =	$370,300.53			
10	Total interest =	$270,300.53			
11					
12	**Payment**	**Principal**	**Pay to Interest**	**Pay to Principal**	**Principal Owed**
13	1	$100,000.00	$1,000.00	$28.61	$99,971.39
14	2	$99,971.39	$999.71	$28.90	$99,942.49
15	3	$99,942.49	$999.42	$29.19	$99,913.30
16	4	$99,913.30	$999.13	$29.48	$99,883.82
17	5	$99,883.82	$998.84	$29.77	$99,854.05

⑧ **ADD A HEADER AND FOOTER AND PRINT A PORTION OF THE WORKSHEET**

    a. Create a header with the date center aligned and a footer with your name right aligned.

    b. Select cells A1 through E15.

    c. Select File → Print Area → Set Print Area. Note the dashed lines around the cells indicating the print area.

    d. Click a blank cell to remove the selection.

    e. Print preview the worksheet. Note that only the cells designated as the print area are displayed.

    f. Save the modified LOAN and then print the worksheet.

    g. Select File → Print Area → Clear Print Area. The print area is now set to the entire worksheet.

⑨ **CREATE AN AUTO LOAN MODEL**

The LOAN worksheet currently represents a house loan. Because the data is stored in cells, it is easy to answer What If? questions. Therefore, the worksheet can be used to calculate the payments for a car loan.

    a. In cell B3, enter the new yearly interest rate 10%.

    b. The car loan is a 5 year loan; therefore, the number of monthly payments will be 5 × 12. In cell B4, enter the new number of payments 60.

    c. In cell B5, enter the new principal $12,000.

d. Note how the worksheet has been recalculated. Scroll down to row 72 which contains the last payment. The worksheet can easily model loans with less than 360 payments.

e. Save the modified LOAN.

⑩ ENTER YOUR OWN VALUES INTO THE LOAN WORKSHEET

a. Experiment by changing the rate, term, and principal of the LOAN worksheet to any values you like. Change the number of payments to see how that affects the interest paid.

b. Select File → Close. Click No in the dialog box when prompted to save the file. The only change that is not saved is the experimenting with values in step 10 (a).

11.11 Creating a Hyperlink to a Worksheet Location

In addition to numeric data and text, a worksheet can include hyperlinks to a worksheet location.

A hyperlink to a specific worksheet location is inserted into the active cell by clicking the Insert Hyperlink button (⬚) on the toolbar, which displays the Insert Hyperlink dialog box. Selecting Place in This Document displays those options:

Insert Hyperlink	? X
Link to:	**Text to display:** Tax Rate Table ScreenTip...
Existing File or Web Page	Type the cell reference: J30
Place in This Document	Or select a place in this document: Cell Reference — Sheet1 — Sheet2 — Sheet3 — Defined Names
Create New Document	
E-mail Address	OK Cancel

Text typed in the Text to display box is displayed as the hyperlink. The cell reference typed in the Type the cell reference box is the location selected when the hyperlink is clicked. Selecting OK creates the hyperlink that is formatted in blue underlined text.

Clicking a hyperlink moves the active cell to the specified worksheet location. For example, in the worksheet on the next page, cell G8 contains a hyperlink:

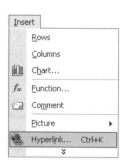

	A	B	C	D	E	F	G	H
1								
2								
3	**Net Provider** ▲							
4								
5								
6	Net Provider Payroll							
7								
8	Soc. Sec. Rate:	6.0%				Tax Rate:	Tax Rate Table	
9								
10	Last Name	First Initial	Rate/Hr	Hours	Overtime Hours	Overtime Pay	Gross Pay	Code
11								
12	Alban	B.	$7.50	30.0	0.0	$0.00	$225.00	2

Clicking <u>Tax Rate Table</u> moves the active cell to J30.

The Insert Hyperlink dialog box can also be displayed by selecting Hyperlink (Ctrl+K) from the <u>I</u>nsert menu.

editing a hyperlink
removing a hyperlink

A hyperlink is edited by right-clicking the hyperlink and selecting Edit Hyperlink. A hyperlink is removed by right-clicking the hyperlink and selecting Remove Hyperlink.

Practice 8 ↻

In this practice you will insert a hyperlink to a worksheet location in the PAYROLL workbook.

① *OPEN PAYROLL*

Open PAYROLL, which was last modified in Practice 5.

② *ADD A HYPERLINK TO A WORKSHEET LOCATION*

a. Select cell F8.

b. Type the label Tax Rates: and then right align and bold the label.

c. Select cell G8.

d. On the toolbar, click the Insert Hyperlink button (📋). A dialog box is displayed.

1. Select Place in This Document if it is not already selected.

2. In the Text to display box, replace the existing text with Tax Rate Table.

3. In the Type the cell reference box, replace the existing cell reference with J30.

4. Select OK. A hyperlink is displayed in cell G8.

③ *DISPLAY THE TAX RATE TABLE*

a. Select cell A1 to make it the active cell.

b. Move the pointer over the hyperlink you just entered in cell G8 until the hand (🖑) is displayed and click. The active cell is moved to the hyperlink destination, cell J30.

④ *SAVE THE MODIFIED PAYROLL*

11.12 E-mailing a Worksheet

A worksheet can be sent as the body of an e-mail message from Excel. For example, an accountant could send a payroll worksheet to the clerk who prepares the checks.

An open worksheet is sent as the body of an e-mail message by first clicking the E-mail button ( ) on the toolbar, which displays the address information boxes above the worksheet:

E-mailing a Workbook as an Attachment

A workbook can be sent as an e-mail attachment. Selecting Mail Recipient (as Attachment) from the Send To submenu in the File menu displays the New Message dialog box with the workbook file name displayed in the Attach box.

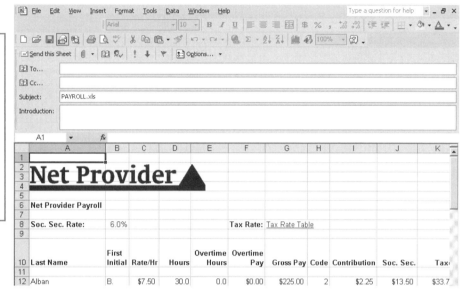

The e-mail address of the recipient is typed in the To box. The Subject box automatically contains the workbook file name. Clicking the Send this Sheet button (Send this Sheet) sends the worksheet as an e-mail message. Once the message is sent, the address information is removed and the worksheet remains open and displayed.

receiving the e-mail message

When the e-mail message is viewed by the recipient, the worksheet is in the message area:

From: Jan
Subject: PAYROLL.xls

To:
Cc:

Net Provider ▲

Net Provider Payroll

Soc. Sec. Rate: 6.0%   Tax Rate: Tax Rate Table

Last Name	First Initial	Rate/Hr	Hours	Overtime Hours	Overtime Pay	Gross Pay	Code	Contribution	Soc. Sec.	Taxes	Net Pay
Alban	B.	$7.50	30.0	0.0	$0.00	$225.00	2	$2.25	$13.50	$33.75	$175.50
Angulo	M.	$8.00	29.5	0.0	$0.00	$236.00	2	$2.36	$14.16	$35.40	$186.44
Balto	Y.	$8.00	29.0	0.0	$0.00	$232.00	1	$0.00	$13.92	$34.80	$183.28
Cruz	S.	$7.75	13.0	0.0	$0.00	$100.75	3	$2.02	$6.05	$15.11	$79.59

In Outlook, right-clicking the message area of the e-mail and selecting Open in Microsoft Excel 10 starts Excel and opens the worksheet.

e-mailing a range

A range of cells can also be sent in the body of an e-mail message by first selecting the range on the worksheet and then clicking the E-mail button.

In this practice you will e-mail a worksheet. This practice assumes you have access to the Internet and an e-mail account. Open PAYROLL if it is not already displayed.

① E-MAIL A WORKSHEET

a. On the toolbar, click the E-mail button (📇). The address information boxes are displayed above the worksheet.

b. In the To box, type office@lpdatafiles.com or an address specified by your instructor. Note that the Subject box already contains the name of the file.

c. Click the Send this Sheet button (⊟ Send this Sheet). If necessary, ask your instructor for help with connecting to the Internet. After connecting to the Internet, the message is sent and then the address information boxes are removed.

② SAVE AND THEN CLOSE THE MODIFIED PAYROLL

③ QUIT EXCEL

11.13 Saving Excel Data in HTML Format

An Excel worksheet can be saved in HTML format, which allows the data to be viewed in a web browser. This feature allows anyone with a web browser to view a worksheet on their computer, even if they do not have Excel. Selecting Save as Web Page from the File menu displays the Save As dialog box:

The Save in list displays a location name, with the location contents displayed in the box below. When the Save in list displays the appropriate location for the file to be saved, a descriptive file name should be typed in the File name box. Selecting Save copies the workbook data to a file with the extension .htm. The file can now be viewed in a web browser by opening a web browser, such as Internet Explorer, and selecting Open from the File menu.

Chapter Summary

This chapter explained how worksheets can be used to answer "What If?" questions. A What If question asks how changing data will impact results. A worksheet modified to answer What If? questions contains data relating to a particular situation and is called a model.

 The Sort Ascending and Sort Descending buttons on the toolbar are used to sort data in a worksheet in alphabetical or numerical order.

A picture, such as a business logo, can be added to a worksheet to give it a professional appearance. A picture is added by selecting the From File command from the Picture submenu.

The CHOOSE function can select one value from a list of many. When given a choice, 1 to 29, the CHOOSE function returns the value in the position corresponding to choice. For example, if cell C3 stores the value 2, then the formula =CHOOSE(C3, "Red", "Blue", "Green") displays Blue.

The Name box can be used to name a cell or range of cells. The named range can then be used in formulas.

The VLOOKUP function selects values from a table that is stored in a range of cells. When given a numeric expression and the cell range where values are stored, VLOOKUP finds the largest number in the VLOOKUP table which is less than or equal to the numeric expression. It then returns the value stored in the specified column of the table. The range that defines the VLOOKUP table can also be specified as a named range. Both the CHOOSE and VLOOKUP functions can be used to display text.

Excel allows rows and columns to remain on the screen by selecting the Freeze Panes command. This feature is especially useful for keeping rows and columns containing labels from scrolling off the screen.

An amortization table displays how much interest and principal make up each payment of an installment loan. The PMT function is used to calculate the periodic payments of an installment loan.

Only part of a worksheet can be printed by selecting the range to be printed and then selecting the Set Print Area command from the Print Area submenu.

 A hyperlink to a specific worksheet location is created in the active cell by clicking the Hyperlink button on the toolbar or selecting the Hyperlink command.

 A worksheet can be sent as the body of an e-mail message from Excel by clicking the E-mail button on the toolbar. A worksheet can also be saved in HTML format, which allows the data to be viewed in a web browser.

Vocabulary

Alphabetical Sorting text in ascending order form A to Z.

Amortization A method for computing equal periodic payments for an installment loan.

Amortization table Displays the interest and principal amounts for each payment of an installment loan.

Ascending Increasing in value from low to high, such as alphabetical order.

CHOOSE Function that returns a value from a list of many values.

Chronological Sorting times or dates in ascending order.

Descending Decreasing in value from high to low.

Installment loan Loan that is repaid in a series of periodic payments.

Key sort column The column that contains the values that a sort is based on.

Model A worksheet containing data relating to a particular situation.

PMT Function that calculates the periodic payment for an installment loan.

Principal The amount of money owed on a loan.

Sorting Placing rows of data in a specified order.

VLOOKUP Function that returns a value from a table of values stored in the worksheet.

What If? question A question that is answered using a worksheet model.

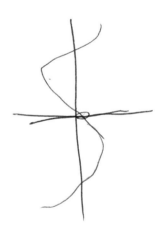

Clear Print Area **command**   Restores the print area to the entire worksheet. Found in the Print Area submenu in the File menu.

Copy button   Places the selected cell(s) on the Clipboard. Found on the toolbar. Copy in the Edit menu can be used instead of the button.

Cut button   Removes the selected cell(s) and places them on the Clipboard. Found on the toolbar. Cut in the Edit menu can be used instead of the button.

E-mail button   Displays options for e-mailing the current worksheet. Found on the toolbar.

From File **command**   Displays a dialog box used to place a picture on the worksheet. Found in the Picture submenu in the Insert menu.

Freeze Panes **command**   Keeps rows and columns from scrolling off the screen. Found in the Window menu.

Hyperlink button   Displays a dialog box used to insert a hyperlink into the active cell. Found on the toolbar. Hyperlink in the Insert menu can be used instead of the command.

Paste button   Places the Clipboard contents in a worksheet starting at the selected cell. Found on the toolbar. Paste in the Edit menu can be used instead of the button.

Print **command**   Displays a dialog box used to print a worksheet. Found in the File menu.

Save as Web Page **command**   Displays a dialog box used to save a worksheet in HTML format. Found in the File menu.

Send this Sheet button   Sends the open worksheet as an e-mail message. Displayed after selecting the E-mail button.

Set Print Area **command**   Designates a specific range of cells to be printed. Found in the Print Area submenu in the File menu.

Sort Ascending button   Places selected rows of data in order from low to high based on the column that was selected first. Found on the toolbar.

Sort **command**   Displays a dialog box where options to select the key sort column and sort order can be selected. Found in the Data menu.

Sort Descending button   Places selected rows of data in order from high to low based on the column that was selected first. Found on the toolbar.

Unfreeze Panes **command**   Unfreezes all the cells on a worksheet. Found in the Window menu.

$$-\pi \quad -\frac{5\pi}{6} \quad -\frac{3\pi}{4} \quad -\frac{2\pi}{3} \quad -\frac{\pi}{2} \quad -\frac{\pi}{3} \quad -\frac{\pi}{4} \quad -\frac{\pi}{6} \quad 0$$

$$0 \quad -\frac{1}{2} \quad -\frac{\sqrt{2}}{\sqrt{2}} \quad -\frac{\sqrt{3}}{2} \quad -1 \quad -\frac{\sqrt{3}}{2} \quad -\frac{\sqrt{2}}{2} \quad -\frac{1}{2} \quad 0 \quad \frac{1}{2}$$

$$-1 \quad -\frac{\sqrt{3}}{2} \quad \frac{\sqrt{3}}{2} \quad -\frac{1}{2} \quad 0 \quad \frac{1}{2} \quad \frac{\sqrt{3}}{2} \quad \frac{\sqrt{3}}{2} \quad 1 \quad \frac{\sqrt{3}}{2} \quad \frac{\sqrt{2}}{2} \quad \frac{1}{2} 0$$

$$-\frac{1}{2}$$

$$0 \qquad \frac{1}{2} \quad \frac{2}{\sqrt{3}}$$

under

$$\frac{2\sqrt{3}}{2\sqrt{3}} \qquad \frac{2\sqrt{3}}{6}$$

$$6 \qquad \frac{\sqrt{3}}{3}$$

$$\sqrt{3}$$

Review Questions

Sections 11.1 — 11.8

1. a) Give an example of how a worksheet be used to answer "What If?" questions?
   b) What is a model?

2. Make a list of five "What If?" questions that can be answered using the PAYROLL workbook.

3. a) List the steps required to sort the data in the PAYROLL workbook in descending order based on the employee's last name.
   b) What is the key sort column?

4. a) List the steps required to add a picture to a worksheet.
   b) List the steps required to size a picture.
   c) List the steps required to move a picture.

5. List three situations in which the CHOOSE function could be used.

6. Write a CHOOSE function that displays 100 if cell B20 contains a value of 1, 500 if a 2, 900 if a 3, and 1200 if a 4.

7. a) List the steps required to name a range.
   b) Does a named range change when copied?

8. List three situations in which a VLOOKUP table could be used.

9. The Lawrenceville Widget Company uses the following discount rates when large numbers of widgets are ordered:

Number of Widgets	Discount
100 - 149	10%
150 - 999	20%
1000 - 1999	30%
2000 and above	70%

   a) Convert this into a VLOOKUP table and make a sketch of the table.
   b) Write a formula that uses the VLOOKUP function to display the proper discount percent if cell C12 stores the number of widgets and cells A1 through B5 store the VLOOKUP table created in part (a).

10. List the steps required to keep the row containing the labels that identify the columns in PAYROLL from scrolling off the screen.

11. Does freezing cells affect the way a worksheet is printed?

12. Write a CHOOSE function that displays the word Excellent if cell B20 contains a value of 1, Good if a 2, Fair if a 3, and Poor if a 4.

Section 11.9 — 11.13

13. Briefly explain what an amortization table is.

14. a) How much interest is paid in the first month of a loan of $5,000 borrowed for 5 years at 12% per year interest?
    b) Show what PMT function is used to calculate the monthly payments on the above loan.

15. a) List the steps required to print only the values displayed in the cell range A3:D17.
    b) List the steps required to print the entire worksheet after a print area was previously set.

16. List the steps required to insert a hyperlink in cell B7 that links to cell K38.

17. List the steps required to e-mail an open worksheet from Excel.

18. Where can the data be viewed if an Excel worksheet is saved in HTML format?

19. What file extension is added to a worksheet saved in HTML format?

 A Guide to Microsoft Office XP Professional

2,5,8,12,14

Exercise 1 ———————————————————— FLORIDA FLIGHTS

A small commuter airline wants to use a worksheet to calculate revenue (money they collect). Open FLORIDA FLIGHTS and complete the following steps:

a) Revenue is based on the number of tickets purchased and the type of ticket. Column B contains the type of ticket, 1 for coach and 2 for first class. The price for tickets will be determined by the following scale:

Ticket Type	Ticket Price
1	$99
2	$150

b) Revenue is calculated by multiplying the ticket price by the number of tickets purchased. In column D, enter the label Revenue and right align it. Enter formulas that use the CHOOSE function to calculate and display the revenue earned for each route.

c) Format the revenue as currency with 0 decimal places. Change the column width as necessary so that all the data is displayed entirely.

d) Create a header with your name right aligned.

e) Save the modified FLORIDA FLIGHTS and print a copy with gridlines and row and column headings.

f) Display the formulas in the cells instead of values. Change the column widths as necessary so that the formulas are completely displayed. Print a copy.

Exercise 2 ———————————————————— Used Books

A university bookstore buys used textbooks based on their condition. A student wants to use a worksheet to determine how much the bookstore will pay for last semester's books.

a) In a new workbook enter the following data starting in cell A1:

	A	B	C
1	Book Title	Original Price	Condition
2			
3	Introduction to Digital Logic Design	$75.80	1
4	A Guide to Computing Fundamentals	$125.25	1
5	Introduction to Arthurian Legend	$32.50	3
6	Fiction Writing Basics	$15.45	2

b) Bold the labels in row 1 and right align the Original Price and Condition labels. Change the column widths as necessary so that all the data is displayed entirely.

c) Save the workbook naming it Used Books.

d) The bookstore buys used textbooks at a percentage of the original price based on the condition of the book:

Condition	Percentage
1	40%
2	20%
3	10%

The used price is calculated by multiplying the original price by the appropriate percentage. In column D, enter the label Used Price. Enter formulas that use the CHOOSE function to calculate and display the used price for each book.

e) Bold and right align the label in cell D1. Format the values in column D as currency with 2 decimal places.

f) The student has decided that if the used price is over $20, it would be best to sell the book, otherwise it is best to donate the book to the library. In column E, enter the label What To Do. Enter formulas that use a function to display Sell for the books that will be sold or Donate for books that will be donated to the library.

g) Center align all the data in column E. Change the column widths as necessary so that all the data is displayed entirely.

h) Create a header with your name right aligned.

i) Save the modified Used Books and print a copy with gridlines and row and column headings.

j) Display the formulas in the cells instead of values. Change the column widths as necessary so that the formulas are completely displayed. Print a copy.

Exercise 3 ——————————————————— Target Zone

A gym wants to use a worksheet to determine the target heart rate zone for its members.

a) In a new workbook enter the following data starting in cell A1:

	A	B
1	Gym Member	Age
2		
3	Brian	25
4	Christine	20
5	Stephanie	32
6	Marchello	44

b) Bold the labels in row 1 and right align the Age label. Change the column widths as necessary so that all the data is displayed entirely.

c) Save the workbook naming it Target Zone.

A Guide to Microsoft Office XP Professional

d) The target heart rate is based on a person's age. In cell A8, enter the label Target Heart Rate Table and bold it. Starting in cell A9, create a VLOOKUP table based on the following criteria:

Age	Target Zone
20 – 24	100 to 150
25 – 29	98 to 146
30 – 34	95 to 142
35 – 39	93 to 138
40 – 44	90 to 135
45 – 49	88 to 131
50 – 54	85 to 127
55 – 59	83 to 123
60 – 64	80 to 120
65 – 69	78 to 116
70 and older	75 to 113

e) Name the table range Zone.

f) In column C, enter the label Target Zone and bold it. Enter formulas that use the VLOOKUP function to display the target zone for each gym member.

g) Center align all the data in column C. Change the column width as necessary so that all the data is displayed entirely.

h) Insert 5 blank rows starting in row 1.

i) In cell A1, insert the picture BARBELL.gif.

j) Create a header with your name right aligned.

k) Save the modified Target Zone and print a copy with gridlines and row and column headings.

l) Display the formulas in the cells instead of values. Change the column widths as necessary so that the formulas are completely displayed. Print a copy.

Exercise 4 ———————————————————— MUSIC SALE

The MUSIC SALE workbook contains an inventory of used musical instruments. Open MUSIC SALE and complete the following steps:

a) The worksheet would be better organized if the instruments in column A were in alphabetical order. Sort the worksheet so that the instruments and their corresponding information are in alphabetical order.

b) The selling price is a percentage of the original price based on the condition of the instrument:

Condition	Percentage
1	60%
2	50%
3	40%
4	30%
5	20%

The selling price is calculated by multiplying the original price by the appropriate percentage. In column D, enter the label Selling Price and bold and right align it. Enter formulas that use the CHOOSE function to calculate and display the selling price for each instrument. Format the values as currency with 2 decimal places.

c) Each instrument will either be sold, donated, or thrown away based on the selling price. In cell A12, enter the label What To Do Table. Starting in cell A13, create a VLOOKUP table based on the following criteria:

Sale Price	What to Do?
under $100	Throw Away
$100 – $499	Donate
$500 and above	Sell

d) Name the table range Action.

e) In column E, enter the label What To Do and bold it. Enter formulas that use the VLOOKUP function to display what to do with each instrument.

f) Center align all the data in column E. Change the column widths as necessary so that all the data is displayed entirely.

g) Create a header with your name right aligned.

h) Save the modified MUSIC SALE and print a copy with gridlines and row and column headings.

i) Display the formulas in the cells instead of values. Change the column widths as necessary so that the formulas are completely displayed. Print a copy.

Exercise 5 ❄ ———————————————————————— AQUARIUM

The AQUARIUM workbook modified in Chapter 10, Exercise 5 can be modified to evaluate the toxicity of the water to marine animals. Open AQUARIUM and complete the following steps.

a) The toxicity of water in a marine aquarium is based on the nitrite levels. In cell B27, enter the label Nitrite Table and bold it. Starting in cell B28, create a VLOOKUP table based on the following criteria:

ppm	Result
under 0.25	safe
0.25 – 0.49	OK
0.5 – 0.99	unsafe
1 – 1.99	very unsafe
2 – 3.99	toxic
4 and above	very toxic

b) Name the table range Result.

c) In column E, enter the label Water is:. Enter formulas that use the VLOOKUP function to display the toxicity of the water. Center align all the data in column E.

d) Format all the data appropriately. Change the column widths as necessary so that all the data is displayed entirely.

e) Create a header with your name right aligned.

f) Save the modified AQUARIUM and print a copy of the worksheet with gridlines and row and column headings.

g) Display the formulas in the cells instead of values. Change the column widths as necessary so that the formulas are completely displayed. Print a copy.

Exercise 6 ———————————————— BOOKSTORE PAYROLL

The BOOKSTORE PAYROLL workbook contains the monthly payroll information for a bookstore's employees. Open BOOKSTORE PAYROLL and complete the following steps:

a) The worksheet would be better organized if the employees were listed in alphabetical order. Sort the worksheet so that the employees and their corresponding information are in alphabetical order.

b) The taxes for each employee need to be calculated. Tax deductions are based on the number of dependents each employee has:

Dependents	Percentage
1	8%
2	7%
3	6%

Taxes are calculated by multiplying the monthly gross pay by the appropriate percentage. In column D, enter the label Taxes and right align and bold it. Enter formulas that use the CHOOSE function to calculate and display the tax for each employee.

c) Social security is calculated by multiplying the social security rate in cell B3 by the monthly gross pay. In column E, enter the label Soc. Sec.. Enter formulas that use absolute and relative cell references to calculate the social security deductions.

d) The net pay for each employee is calculated by making the necessary deductions from the monthly gross pay. In column F, enter the label Net Pay. Enter formulas that use cell references to deduct the taxes and social security from the gross pay of each employee to get the net pay.

e) Format all data appropriately. Change the column widths as necessary so the data is displayed entirely.

f) Create a header with your name right aligned.

g) Save the modified BOOKSTORE PAYROLL and print a copy with gridlines and row and column headings.

h) Display the formulas in the cells instead of values. Change the column widths as necessary so that the formulas are completely displayed. Print a copy.

Exercise 7 ⟳ ———————————————————— Pizza Palace

Pizza Palace wants to use the expense workbook modified in Chapter 10, Exercise 7 to ask What If? questions. Open Pizza Palace and answer the following questions:

a) The owner of pizza palace wants to determine what affect switching suppliers would have on the cost of the pizzas. The new supplier has better quality items but the cost of dough would increase from $1.25 to $1.40, and the cost of cheese would increase for each pizza to $1.75. Update the worksheet to calculate the new cost of the pizzas.

b) The owner has decided to change the way the menu prices are calculated because of the higher costs. The menu price will now be calculated by multiplying the cost of pizza by 225%. Update the worksheet to calculate the new pizza prices.

c) Save the modified Pizza Palace. Print a copy of only the cells containing data (not the chart) with gridlines and row and column headings.

d) Display the formulas in the cells instead of values. Change the column widths as necessary so that the formulas are completely displayed. Print a copy.

Exercise 8 ———————————————————— FLOWER STORE

The FLOWER STORE workbook contains the items sold at a discount flower retailer. Open FLOWER STORE and complete the following steps:

a) The worksheet would be better organized if all the flowers in column A were in alphabetical order. Sort the worksheet so the flowers and their corresponding information are in alphabetical order.

b) The selling price of the flower arrangements are based on a percentage markup. In cell B14, enter the label Markup Table and bold it. Starting in cell A15, create a VLOOKUP table based on the following criteria:

Cost	Markup
$25 and under	35%
from $26 to $45	45%
$46 and above	35%

c) Name the table range Markup.

d) Insert a column between columns B and C, and enter the label Selling Price. The selling price is calculated by multiplying the cost by the markup percentage and then adding that total to the cost. Enter formulas in the new column that use the VLOOKUP function to display the selling price.

e) Frequent buyers receive discounts that vary depending on the flower. Column D contains the discount codes 1 through 4. The discount on the selling price is determined by the following percentages:

Discount Code	Percentage
1	20%
2	15%
3	10%
4	5%

The discount price is calculated by multiplying the selling price by the appropriate percentage and then subtracting all of that from the selling price. In column E, enter the label Discount Price. Enter formulas that use the CHOOSE function and cell references to calculate and display the discounted selling price for each item.

f) Format all the data appropriately. Change the column widths as necessary so that all the data is displayed entirely.

g) Create a header with your name right aligned.

h) Save the modified FLOWER STORE and print a copy with gridlines and row and column headings.

i) Display the formulas in the cells instead of values. Change the column widths as necessary so that the formulas are completely displayed. Print a copy.

Exercise 9 ———————————————————— SCHOOL LOAN

The SCHOOL LOAN workbook contains a loan amortization table. Open SCHOOL LOAN and answer the following What If? questions about different school loans:

a) The tuition and room/board fees for one year at the state university are $8,250. The loan options are:

- 7% interest for a five year loan
- 8% interest for a three year loan
- 6% interest for a ten year loan

In cells B3, B4, and B5, enter the appropriate data for the first loan (7% for five years).

b) In cell B7, enter a formula that uses the PMT function with cell references to calculate the periodic payment for the five year loan option.

c) In cells C3, C4, and C5, enter the appropriate data for the three year loan option and calculate the monthly payment, total amount paid, and total interest paid.

d) In cells D3, D4, and D5, enter the appropriate data for the ten year loan option and calculate the monthly payment, total amount paid, and total interest paid.

e) Create a header with your name right aligned.

f) Save the modified SCHOOL LOAN and print a copy of cells A1 through E17 with gridlines and row and column headings.

g) Display the formulas in the cells instead of values. Change the column widths as necessary so that the formulas are completely displayed. Print a copy.

Exercise 10

The stock workbook modified in Chapter 10, Exercise 10 can be modified to evaluate the stock portfolio. Open STOCKS and complete the following steps:

a) A commission must be paid to a stockbroker when a stock is sold. The commission rate is based on the number of shares purchased. In cell G20, enter the label Commission Table and bold it. Starting in cell G21, create a VLOOKUP table based on the following criteria:

Number of Shares	Commission
0 – 29	5%
30 – 69	4%
70 – 99	2%
100 – 149	1%
150 and above	0.5%

b) Name the table range Commission.

c) The dollar amount of the commission is calculated by multiplying the March value of the stock by the appropriate commission percent. In column J, enter the label Commission. Enter formulas that use the VLOOKUP function to calculate and display the sales commission on each of the stocks.

d) Modify the formulas in column J to display N/A for stocks that are retained, and display the dollar amount of the commission otherwise.

e) Format all the data appropriately. Change the column widths as necessary so that all the data is displayed entirely and fits on one page.

f) In cell D1, type the label Commission and then make the label a hyperlink to cell G20.

g) Save the modified STOCKS. Print a copy with gridlines and row and column headings.

h) Display the formulas in the cells instead of values. Change the column widths as necessary so that the formulas are completely displayed. Print a copy.

Exercise 11

The class scores workbook created in Chapter 8, Exercise 11 can be modified to display letter grades. Open Class Scores and complete the following steps:

a) Create a VLOOKUP table starting in cell A11 of percentages and their corresponding letter grade in the worksheet based on the grading scale at your school.

b) Name the table range Grade.

c) In cell C8, enter a formula that use the VLOOKUP function with the named table range to calculate and display your letter grade. Bold and italicize the letter grade.

d) Save the modified Class Scores and print a copy with gridlines and row and column headings.

e) Display the formulas in the cells instead of values. Change the column widths as necessary so that the formulas are completely displayed. Print a copy.

Exercise 12 ———————————————————————— Car Loan

A loan amortization table can be used for any kind of loan, including car loans. Amortization tables can also be combined with What If? questions to help make decisions when purchasing a new car.

a) In a new workbook enter the data and apply formatting as shown below:

	A	B	C	D	E
1	New Car Loan Amortization Table				
2					
3		3 Year Loan	3 Year Loan	5 Year Loan	5 Year Loan
4					
5	Interest rate =	7%	10%	7%	10%
6	Number of payments =	36	36	60	60
7	Principal =				
8					
9	Monthly payment =				
10					
11	Total paid =				
12	Total interest =				

b) Save the workbook naming it Car Loan.

c) Using the Internet or a newspaper, find an ad for a new car.

d) Enter the price of the car in the ad as the principal of the car loan in row 7 of the worksheet.

e) In row 9, enter formulas that use the PMT function with cell references to calculate the periodic payment for the different loan interest rates and payment periods.

f) In row 11, enter formulas that use cell references to calculate the total amount paid (number of payments multiplied by the monthly payment).

g) In row 12, enter formulas that use cell references to calculate the total interest paid (total amount paid minus the principal).

h) Create a header with your name right aligned.

i) Save the modified Car Loan and print a copy with gridlines and row and column headings.

j) Display the formulas in the cells instead of values. Change the column widths as necessary so that the formulas are completely displayed. Print a copy.

Exercise 13 (advanced) ———————————————————————————

Modify one of the advanced exercises created in Chapter 8, 9, or 10 to include either the VLOOKUP or CHOOSE function. Format the worksheet appropriately. Save the modified workbook and print a copy with gridlines and row and column headings.

Exercise 14 (advanced) ———————————————————— Credit

Credit cards can be used to borrow money. This is usually an expensive method of borrowing and best used for only short periods of time or not at all. Create a new workbook that stores the amount of money to borrow, the number of months to pay back the borrowed money, and the annual interest rate. Include columns for annual interest rates ranging from 5% to 25% in increments of 5%. The worksheet should calculate the monthly payment, total amount paid, and total interest paid for each of the different interest rates. Experiment by changing the amount borrowed and the length of time. Save the workbook naming it Credit and print a copy with gridlines and row and column headings. The worksheet model shows that borrowing at a low interest rate for a short period of time saves substantial amounts of money. Often credit card companies charge 20% or more to borrow money while banks usually charge considerably less.

Exercise 15 (advanced) ———————————————————— My Loan

Create an amortization table in a new workbook to display the interest and principal amounts for an installment loan. Use Practice 6 from this chapter as a guide. Format the worksheet appropriately. Save the workbook naming it My Loan and print a copy with gridlines and row and column headings.

Chapter 12
Integrating Data Between Word and Excel

Open

Close

Copy

Paste

Hyperlink

Edit Hyperlink

Remove Hyperlink

Paste Special

Chapter 12 Expectations

After completing this chapter you will be able to:

1. Work with multiple files in an application.
2. Copy text between Word documents.
3. Copy data between Excel workbooks.
4. Work with files from multiple applications.
5. Copy data between applications.
6. Use the Office Clipboard to paste information from several files.
7. Copy a chart object into a Word document.
8. Create hyperlinks to files.
9. Create embedded and linked objects in Excel worksheets and Word documents.

This chapter explains how to copy data between files. Creating hyperlinks to files and embedding and linking data are also discussed.

12.1 Working with Multiple Files in an Application

opening files

In Office, more than one file can be open at the same time. After opening a Word or an Excel file, additional files in the same application are opened by selecting Open (Ctrl+O) from the File menu or clicking the Open button ( ) on the toolbar.

displaying an open file

The Taskbar at the bottom of the screen displays a button for each open file. For example, if two Word documents are open, the Taskbar looks similar to:

Start
GRETA LEE.doc - Micro...
ON STAGE.doc - Microsof...

The displayed file's button appears pushed in

A file is displayed by clicking its button on the Taskbar.

The Window menu in Word and Excel can also be used to switch between open files. Selecting Window in the menu bar displays a list of open files in that application:

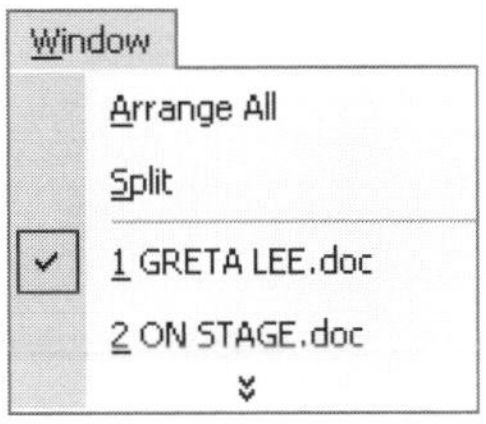
Window
Arrange All
Split
1 GRETA LEE.doc
2 ON STAGE.doc

File Status

Each open file is maintained independently in its own window, including any changes to the file's window size or the location of the insertion point. Therefore, when switching from file to file, each document is displayed exactly as it was left. Also note that an option set in one window has no effect on any other window.

active file

The *active file* is designated by a check mark and is the file currently displayed. The active file is changed by selecting a different file name in the Window menu.

12.2 Saving and Closing Multiple Files

When multiple files are open, selecting Save from the File menu or clicking the Save button (🖫) on the toolbar saves only the active file. It is a good practice to save any open files as edits are made.

When work on an open file is complete, the file should be closed by selecting Close from the File menu or clicking the Close button (☒) in the upper-right corner of the document window. Closing a file frees some of the computer's memory and avoids accidental changes to the file. When a file is closed, its window is removed from the screen, and the next open file is displayed and made active.

12.3 Copying Text Between Word Documents

In previous chapters, data was copied using the Copy and Paste buttons. This method can also be used to copy text from one Word document to another because the contents of the Clipboard remain the same regardless of which file is displayed.

Copying text from one Word document to another can save time typing and help to maintain consistency between documents. The steps for copying text between open Word documents are:

1. Select the text to be copied.

2. Click the Copy button (📋) on the toolbar. A copy of the selected text is added to the Clipboard.

3. Display the document that is to receive the copied text.

4. Place the insertion point in the document where the text is to be inserted.

5. Click the Paste button (📋) on the toolbar. The contents of the Clipboard are placed in the document at the insertion point, and the Paste Options button (📋) is displayed.

Paragraph formatting is retained when text is copied if the corresponding paragraph mark (¶) is included in the selection. If the paragraph mark is not copied, pasted text is given the format of the paragraph in the receiving document. Character formats are always retained when text is copied.

The Cut (Ctrl+X), Copy (Ctrl+C), and Paste (Ctrl+V) commands in the Edit menu can be used instead of the buttons. Alternatively, right-clicking a cell displays a menu from which Cut, Copy, or Paste can be selected.

Practice 1

In this practice you will copy text from multiple Word documents to another Word document.

① *OPEN THE GRETA LEE DOCUMENT*

Open GRETA LEE, which is a Word data file for this text.

② *OPEN ANOTHER WORD DOCUMENT*

    a. Select <u>F</u>ile ➜ <u>O</u>pen. A dialog box is displayed.

        1. Use the Look in list and the contents box below it to display the file name ON STAGE, which is a data file for this text.

        2. In the contents box, click ON STAGE.

        3. Select Open. ON STAGE, an empty newsletter, is displayed in its own window as the active document. Note the two Word document buttons on the Taskbar.

③ *DISPLAY GRETA LEE*

    a. Display the <u>W</u>indow menu. Note that there are two Word documents open.

    b. From the <u>W</u>indow menu, select GRETA LEE. The GRETA LEE document is now the active document.

④ *COPY TEXT TO THE CLIPBOARD*

    a. Select <u>E</u>dit ➜ Select A<u>l</u>l. All of the text in the GRETA LEE document is selected.

    b. On the toolbar, click the Copy button (⧉). A copy of the selected text is added to the Clipboard.

    c. Select <u>F</u>ile ➜ <u>C</u>lose. The GRETA LEE document is removed and ON STAGE is displayed. Note on the ruler that the newsletter is already formatted with two columns.

⑤ *PASTE THE CLIPBOARD CONTENTS INTO THE ON STAGE NEWSLETTER*

    a. Place the insertion point in the last blank paragraph of the document if it is not already there.

    b. On the toolbar, click the Paste button (📋). The Clipboard contents are placed at the insertion point and the Paste Options button is displayed. The Paste Options button will not be used and should be ignored.

Check – Your document should look similar to:

⑥ **COPY ANOTHER STORY TO THE NEWSLETTER**

    a. Open ARTS COUNCIL MEMBERS, which is a Word data file for this text.

    b. Select Edit → Select All. All of the text in the ARTS COUNCIL MEMBERS document is selected.

    c. On the toolbar, click the Copy button (⧉).

    d. Close ARTS COUNCIL MEMBERS. The ON STAGE document is again displayed.

    e. In the blank paragraph at the end of the document below the "The Coral Playhouse to Host Greta Lee…" story, place the insertion point if it is not already there and press Enter. A blank paragraph is created.

    f. On the toolbar, click the Paste button (⧉). The Clipboard contents are placed at the insertion point. Ignore the Paste Options button.

⑦ **COPY MORE TEXT TO THE NEWSLETTER**

    a. Open ART EXHIBITS, which is a Word data file for this text.

    b. Select Edit → Select All. All of the text in the ART EXHIBITS document is selected.

    c. On the toolbar, click the Copy button (⧉).

    d. Close ART EXHIBITS. The ON STAGE newsletter is again displayed.

    e. In the blank paragraph at the end of the document below the "Coral Arts Council Membership Growing" story, place the insertion point if it is not already there and press Enter. A blank paragraph is created.

    f. On the toolbar, click the Paste button (⧉). The Clipboard contents are placed at the insertion point. Ignore the Paste Options button.

⑧ **SAVE AND THEN CLOSE THE MODIFIED ON STAGE**

⑨ **QUIT WORD**

12.4 Copying Data Between Excel Workbooks

The Paste Options Button

Clicking the Paste Options button (⧉) after pasting data into an Excel document displays a list of options that can be used to change the default paste option of Keep Source Formatting. Options include Match Destination Formatting, which will keep the formatting of the destination cell.

Data can be copied from one Excel workbook to another in the same way text is copied between Word documents. The steps for copying data between open Excel workbooks are:

1. Select the source, which is the cell(s) to be copied.

2. Click the Copy button (⧉) on the toolbar. A copy of the source is added to the Clipboard.

3. Display the workbook that is to receive the copied data.

4. Select the destination, which is the upper-left cell of the range where the data is to be pasted.

5. Click the Paste button (⧉ ▾) on the toolbar. The contents of the Clipboard are placed in the cell(s) and the Paste Options button (⧉) is displayed.

Keep Source Formatting

Match Destination Formatting

Values and Number Formatting

Keep Source Column Widths

Formatting Only

Link Cells

Column widths do not copy, but can be retained by clicking the Paste Options button (⬛) and selecting Keep Source Column Widths.

When pasting data within existing data, room must be made in the receiving workbook. For example, to copy a row from one workbook into the center of another, a blank row must be inserted in the receiving workbook. If blank space is not created in the receiving workbook, the pasted data will overwrite existing data.

Practice 2

In this practice you will copy a range of cells from one Excel workbook to another Excel workbook.

① *OPEN TWO EXCEL WORKBOOKS*

    a. Open GRODER, which is an Excel data file for this text.

    b. Open EXHIBITS, which is an Excel data file for this text.

② *INSERT AN EMPTY ROW IN THE EXHIBITS WORKBOOK*

    a. Right-click row number 6. A menu is displayed.

    b. Select Insert. A new row is inserted.

③ *COPY DATA TO THE CLIPBOARD*

    a. On the Taskbar, click **GRODER**. The GRODER workbook is displayed.

    b. Select cells A1 through D1, the four cells containing data.

    c. On the toolbar, click the Copy button (⬛).

    d. Close GRODER. The EXHIBITS workbook is displayed.

④ *PASTE THE CLIPBOARD CONTENTS INTO THE EXHIBITS WORKBOOK*

    a. Select cell A6.

    b. On the toolbar, click the Paste button (⬛▾). The Clipboard contents are placed in the empty cells. Ignore the Paste Options button.

    c. Click a blank cell to remove the selection.

Check – Your workbook should look similar to:

	A	B	C	D
1		Douglas Powers Center for the Arts		
2				
3	Exhibit	Attendance	Cost of Exhibit	Donations
4	Local Sculptors	510	$380	$790
5	Jo Marten: Watercolors	200	$575	$438
6	The Groder Collection	450	$610	$532
7	Winter Photography	560	$420	$816

⑤ *SAVE THE MODIFIED EXHIBITS*

12.5 Working with Multiple Applications

More than one Office application can be running at the same time. The **Open Office Document** command from the **Start** menu on the Taskbar can be used to open files in different applications.

The Taskbar is used to switch between open files, regardless of the application. For example, if two Word documents and two Excel workbooks are both open, the Taskbar looks similar to:

| Start | | EXHIBITS.xls | GRODER.xls | GRETA LEE.doc (R... | ON STAGE.doc (R... |

The active file's button appears pushed in

On the Taskbar, the ⊞ symbol on a button indicates a Word document and the ⊞ symbol indicates an Excel workbook.

12.6 Copying Data Between Applications

integrated package

Office is an *integrated package*, which means that data from a file created in one application can be easily copied into a file created in a different application. For example, data from an Excel workbook can be integrated into a Word document.

from Excel to Word

The steps for copying data from an open Excel workbook to an open Word document are:

1. Select the source, which is the cell(s) to be copied.

2. Click the Copy button (⊞) on the toolbar. A copy of the source is added to the Clipboard.

3. On the Taskbar, select the Word document that is to receive the copied data.

4. Place the insertion point in the document where the data is to be inserted.

5. Click the Paste button (⊞) on the toolbar. The contents of the Clipboard are placed in the document at the insertion point, and the Paste Options button (⊞) is displayed.

When data is copied from an Excel workbook to a Word document the data is automatically placed in a table.

from Word to Excel

Data from a Word document can be copied into an Excel workbook. This allows calculations to be performed on the data. Before the data is copied, it needs to be either separated by tabs or stored in a table.

The Paste Options Button

Clicking the Paste Options button (⊞) after pasting Excel data into a Word document displays a list of options that can be used to change the default paste option of **Keep Source Formatting**. One option, **Match Destination Table Style**, formats the copied data the same as the destination text.

The steps for copying data separated by tabs or in a table from an open Word document to an open Excel workbook are:

1. Select the source, which is the data separated by tabs or in a table to be copied.

2. Click the Copy button (⊞) on the toolbar. A copy of the selected data is added to the Clipboard.

3. On the Taskbar, select the Excel workbook that is to receive the copied data.

4. Select the destination, which is the upper-left cell of the range where the data is to be pasted.

5. Click the Paste button (⊞▾) on the toolbar. The contents of the Clipboard are placed in the cell(s) and the Paste Options button (⊞) is displayed.

When data separated by tabs is copied into an Excel workbook, each line in the table is placed in a row and each tab identifies a new column. When data in a table is copied into an Excel workbook, each row of the table is placed in a row of the workbook with each column corresponding to a column in the workbook.

> ### Removing Borders
>
> When data is copied from a Word table to an Excel worksheet, the cells storing the copied data are formatted with borders. The borders can be removed from the selected cells by selecting the **Border** tab in the Format Cells dialog box.

Practice 3 ♻

In this practice you will copy data from an Excel workbook to a Word document. Open EXHIBITS if it is not already displayed.

① COPY DATA TO THE CLIPBOARD

a. In the EXHIBITS workbook, select cells A3 through B7.

b. On the toolbar, click the Copy button (⊞).

② OPEN A WORD DOCUMENT

a. On the Taskbar, click Start ➛ Open Office Document. The Open Office Document dialog box is displayed.

   1. Use the Look in list and the contents box below it to display the file name ON STAGE, which was last modified in Practice 1.

   2. In the contents box, click ON STAGE.

   3. Select Open. The ON STAGE document is displayed. Note there are two buttons on the Taskbar. One button is for the Word document and the other is for the Excel workbook.

③ PASTE THE CLIPBOARD CONTENTS INTO THE ON STAGE DOCUMENT

a. In the "Art Exhibits Draw Crowds and Donations" story in the middle of the second column, place the insertion point in the blank paragraph after the paragraph that ends "…have drawn large crowds and donations:."

b. Press Enter. A blank paragraph is created.

c. On the toolbar, click the Paste button (⊞). The Clipboard contents are placed at the insertion point. Ignore the Paste Options button.

Check – Your document should look similar to:

Ms. Lee is considered to be the world genius on pan flutes, partially due to her travels and collection, but also due to her skills. Not only is she a natural musician, but she also studied under the pan flute master Jean Claude Moll for several years.¶

¶

The concerts will be held January 13, 14, and 15 in the auditorium. Tickets are available at the box office and prices are as follows: $6.50 for students and educators, and $13.00 for the general public.¶

Donations¶
¶
The last four exhibits at the Douglas Powers Center for the Arts have drawn large crowds and donations:¶

¶

Exhibit	Attendance
Local Sculptors	510
Jo Marten Watercolors	200
The Groder Collection	450
Winter Photography	560

¶

④ *SAVE AND CLOSE THE MODIFIED ON STAGE*

⑤ *QUIT WORD*

Quit Word. The EXHIBITS workbook is again displayed.

12.7 Using the Office Clipboard to Copy Data

A document may need information from several files. In this case, the Office Clipboard is convenient to use because it stores up to 24 cut and copied items from any number of Office files:

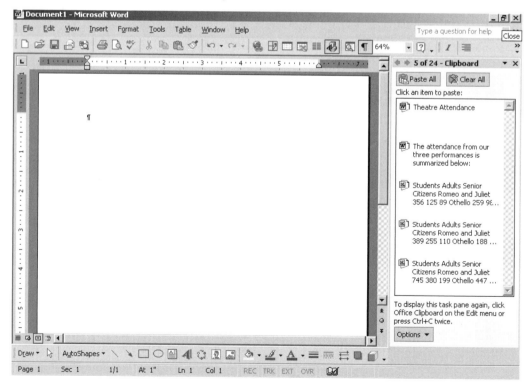

The Office Clipboard currently stores two Word items and three Excel items

In the Office Clipboard task pane, the ⊞ symbol indicates the item was copied from a Word document and the ⊞ symbol indicates the item was copied from an Excel workbook. Items in the Office Clipboard task pane can be pasted into any Office document. For example, in the window on the previous page, any of the stored items could be pasted into the displayed Word document by placing the insertion point and then clicking an item in the Office Clipboard task pane.

Practice 4 ⟳

In this practice you will create a new Excel workbook named Donations using information from several files in different applications. Open EXHIBITS if it is not already displayed.

① COPY DATA TO THE OFFICE CLIPBOARD

    a. Display the Office Clipboard task pane if it is not already displayed.

    b. If there are items in the Office Clipboard, click the Clear All button (🗙 Clear All) in the task pane. The Office Clipboard is empty.

    c. Select cell B1.

    d. On the toolbar, click the Copy button (🗈). The Office Clipboard contains one Excel item.

    e. Close EXHIBITS.

② OPEN DONATION POLICY AND COPY TEXT

    a. Open DONATION POLICY, which is a Word data file for this text.

    b. Display the Office Clipboard if it is not already displayed. Note the Excel item stored on the Office Clipboard.

    c. In the last paragraph in the document, select the last sentence, which begins "All donations are…."

    d. On the toolbar, click the Copy button (🗈). The Office Clipboard contains two items.

    e. Close DONATION POLICY and exit Word. Excel is displayed.

③ PASTE ITEMS FROM THE OFFICE CLIPBOARD INTO A NEW EXCEL WORKBOOK

    a. Create new Excel workbook.

    b. Display the Office Clipboard task pane if it is not already displayed.

    c. Select cell A3.

    d. Click the second item in the Clipboard, which begins "Douglas Powers…." The item is placed in the cell. Ignore the Paste Options button.

    e. Select cell A1.

    f. Click the first item in the Clipboard, which begins "All donations…." The item is placed in the cell. Ignore the Paste Options button.

    g. Close the Office Clipboard task pane.

    h. Save the workbook naming it Donations.

④ OPEN SUMMARY AND COPY DATA TO THE OFFICE CLIPBOARD

    a. Open SUMMARY, which is an Excel data file for this text.

    b. Select cells A1 through B5.

    c. On the toolbar, click the Copy button (🗈).

    d. From the Window menu, select Donations. The Donations workbook is displayed.

    e. Select cell A5.

f. On the toolbar, click the Paste button (). The Clipboard contents are placed in the active cell. The Paste Options button is displayed.

g. Click the Paste Options button. A menu is displayed.

 1. Select Keep Source Column Widths. The original column widths are applied.

⑤ *SAVE THE MODIFIED DONATIONS WORKBOOK*

⑥ *CLOSE SUMMARY*

 a. On the Taskbar, click SUMMARY. The SUMMARY workbook is displayed.

 b. Close SUMMARY. Donations is again displayed.

12.8 Copying a Chart Object into a Word Document

Businesses often include charts in documents to enhance and simplify the understanding of the text. Office allows an Excel workbook chart to be copied to a Word document as an object.

The steps for copying a chart object from an open Excel workbook to an open Word document are:

1. Select the chart to be copied by clicking its Chart Area.

2. Click the Copy button () on the toolbar. A copy of the chart is added to the Clipboard.

3. From the Taskbar, select the Word document that is to receive the copied chart.

4. Select the destination by placing the insertion point where the chart is to appear.

5. Click the Paste button () on the toolbar. The chart is placed in the document and the Paste Options button () is displayed.

sizing a chart

inline object

floating object

A pasted chart can be sized by clicking the chart to select it and then dragging a handle. A chart is pasted as an inline object as long as the original workbook remains open. An *inline object* is placed in the text at the insertion point. The inline object can then be positioned by using paragraph alignments, indents, and tabs. If the workbook containing the copied chart is closed before pasting, the chart object is pasted as a floating object. A *floating object* is positioned in a document by dragging the object.

Object Formatting

A chart that is pasted as a floating object can change its Wrapping style to options such as Behind text or Square by right-clicking the floating object and selecting Format Object from the menu, which displays the Format Object dialog box. Selecting the Layout tab displays those options.

Practice 5

In this practice you will create and copy an Excel chart to a Word document. Open Donations if it is not already displayed.

① *CREATE A PIE CHART*

 a. Select cells A6 through B9.

b. Select <u>I</u>nsert → C<u>h</u>art. The first Chart Wizard dialog box is displayed.

    1. In the **Chart type** list, click Pie.

    2. Select Next. The second Chart Wizard dialog box is displayed.

    3. Verify that the correct range =Sheet1!$A$6:$B$9 is displayed in the **Data range** box.

    4. Select Next. The third Chart Wizard dialog box is displayed.

    5. Select the **Titles** tab if it is not already selected.

    6. In the **Chart title** box, type Exhibit Donations.

    7. Select the **Data Labels** tab to display those options.

    8. Select the **Percentage** check box.

    9. Select Finish. The pie chart is displayed.

c. Size the chart to about half its original size.

d. Save the modified Donations.

Check – Your chart should look similar to:

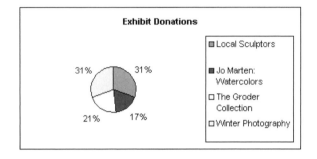

② COPY THE CHART TO THE CLIPBOARD

a. Select the pie chart if it is not already selected.

b. On the toolbar, click the Copy button (⧉).

③ PASTE THE CLIPBOARD CONTENTS INTO THE NEWSLETTER

a. Open the ON STAGE Word document, which was last modified in Practice 3.

b. At the bottom of the second column, place the insertion point in the blank paragraph below the workbook data you previously pasted.

c. Press Enter. A blank paragraph is created.

d. On the toolbar, click the Paste button (⧉). The chart is placed at the insertion point. Ignore the Paste Options button.

e. If necessary, size the chart smaller so that it appears at the bottom of the second column on the first page of the newsletter.

④ SAVE THE MODIFIED ON STAGE

⑤ CLOSE DONATIONS AND QUIT EXCEL

a. Display Donations and then close it.

b. Quit Excel. ON STAGE is again displayed.

12.9   Creating a Hyperlink to a File

A hyperlink can be used in a Word document or an Excel workbook to display another Office file.

A hyperlink to a file is inserted by clicking the Insert Hyperlink button (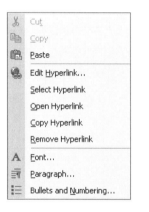) on the toolbar, which displays the Insert Hyperlink dialog box. Selecting Existing File or Web Page displays those options:

Text typed in the Text to display box is displayed as the hyperlink. The Look in list is used to display the appropriate file name in the contents box. Selecting the file name and OK inserts the hyperlink at the insertion point or in the active cell.

In Excel, pointing to a hyperlink changes the pointer to a hand (🖑). In Word, the Ctrl key must be held down while pointing to the hyperlink. Clicking starts the appropriate application and opens the file.

The Insert Hyperlink dialog box can also be displayed by selecting Hyperlink (Ctrl+K) from the Insert menu.

editing a hyperlink
removing a hyperlink

A hyperlink is edited by right-clicking the hyperlink and selecting Edit Hyperlink. A hyperlink is removed by right-clicking the hyperlink and selecting Remove Hyperlink.

Practice 6 ⟳

In this practice you will create a hyperlink to an Excel workbook. Open ON STAGE if it is not already displayed.

① *CREATE A HYPERLINK TO THE EXHIBITS WORKBOOK FILE*

a. At the bottom of the second column, place the insertion point after the pie chart and then press Enter twice.

b. Type the following sentence:

Refer to for more information on the exhibits.

c. If necessary, size the chart smaller so the document fits on one page.

d. Save the modified ON STAGE.

e. Place the insertion point after "to" in the "Refer to for ..." sentence and type a space.

f. On the toolbar, click the Insert Hyperlink button (⬛). A dialog box is displayed.

    1. Select **Existing File or Web Page** if it is not already selected.

    2. In the **Text to display** box, type Exhibits.

    3. Use the **Look in** list to display EXHIBITS, which was last modified in Practice 4, in the contents box.

    4. Click EXHIBITS.

    5. Select **OK**. The hyperlink is inserted in the document.

② *SAVE THE MODIFIED ON STAGE*

③ *USE THE HYPERLINK TO DISPLAY THE WORKBOOK*

a. Point to the hyperlink until a ScreenTip is displayed.

b. Hold down the Ctrl key until the pointer changes to a hand (🖑) and then click. The EXHIBITS workbook is displayed.

④ *QUIT EXCEL*

Quit Excel. EXHIBITS is closed and ON STAGE is again displayed.

⑤ *PRINT AND THEN CLOSE THE MODIFIED ON STAGE*

a. Add a footer with your name right aligned.

b. Save and then print ON STAGE.

c. Quit Word. ON STAGE is closed.

12.10 Embedding and Linking a Word Document Object

static

When the Copy and Paste buttons are used to integrate data, the pasted data is *static*, which means it is not connected to the source file or to the source application. Selecting **Paste Special** from the **Edit** menu displays a dialog box with options for pasting data as an embedded or linked object.

embedded object

An *embedded object* keeps the features of the application it was created in. For example, Word data can be placed in an Excel worksheet as an embedded object:

	A	B	C	D	E	F	G	H	I
1	Name	Test 1	Test 2	Test 3	Test 4	Student Average	Status	Grade	
2		1/7/03	2/9/03	3/1/03	4/1/03				
3									
4	Bell, M.	70	74	80	83	77	Passing	C	
5	Garcia, E.	72	63	67	72	69	Below Average	D	
6	Jones, D.	85	73	88	95	85	Passing	B	
7	McCallister, T.	87	92	85	93	89	Passing	B	
8	Neave, C.	92	88	95	91	92	Passing	A	
9	Smith, L.	94	91	93	84	91	Passing	A	
10	Test Average	83.3	80.2	84.7	86.3				
11									
12		Letter Grade Table							
13		0	F			• Final grades must be turned in by January 6th			
14		60	D			• Students eligible for honors are to be notified by			
15		70	C			January 4th			
16		80	B						
17		90	A						
18									

The bulleted list is an embedded object

OLE

OLE is a technology that allows an application to contain an object created by another Windows application.

activating a Word object

Double-clicking the embedded object activates it and displays Word's ruler, menus and toolbars in the Excel window:

Word menu bar ─

Word toolbar ─

Word ruler

active object

Activating the object allows it to be edited and updated in Excel. An embedded object should be used if the pasted data will need to be modified using features unique to the source application without modifying the source file.

linked object

Word data can also be integrated into an Excel worksheet as a linked object. A *linked object* is similar to an embedded object. However, the data in a linked object can only be modified by editing the source file. The source file is edited by double-clicking the linked object, which starts Word and opens the source file. Modifying the source file automatically updates the linked object. A linked object should be used if an up-to-date display of data is needed. For example, a Word document that is handed out at a weekly sales meeting could contain a table of current inventory. Instead of recreating the Word document every week, the inventory table could be placed as a linked object which is automatically updated when the source file is updated.

The steps for embedding or linking an object from an open Word document into an open Excel workbook are:

1. Select the source, which is the data to be embedded or linked as an object.

2. Click the Copy button (⬚) on the toolbar. A copy of the selected text is added to the Clipboard.

3. Display the Excel workbook that is to receive the embedded or linked object.

4. Select the destination, which is the upper-left cell where the object is to be placed.

5. Select Paste Special from the Edit menu, which displays the Paste Special dialog box:

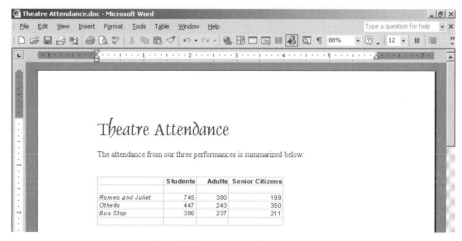

Note that the Word source file must remain open until after the Paste <u>S</u>pecial command is selected.

6. Select Paste to create an embedded object or select Paste link to create a linked object.

7. Select Microsoft Word Document Object from the As list and then select OK.

When an object from a Word document is embedded in or linked to an Excel worksheet, the object is placed as a floating object and can be positioned by dragging it.

12.11 Embedding and Linking an Excel Worksheet Object

Excel data can be an embedded or linked object in a Word document. For example, the Word document below contains an embedded Excel worksheet object:

The table is an embedded object

activating an Excel object   Double-clicking the embedded object activates it and displays Excel's menus and toolbars:

Excel menu bar ⟶
Excel toolbars ⟵
Excel Formula bar ⟶

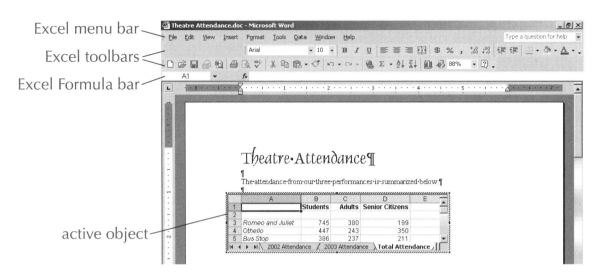

active object ⟶

Note that when the object is active, the entire workbook is accessible and the object can be edited and updated in Word.

The steps for embedding or linking an object from an open Excel workbook into an open Word document are:

1. Select the source, which is the Excel data to be embedded or linked as an object.

2. Click the Copy button ( ) on the toolbar. A copy of the source is added to the Clipboard.

3. Display the Word document that is to receive the embedded or linked object.

4. Place the insertion point where the object is to appear.

5. Select Paste Special from the Edit menu, which displays the Paste Special dialog box:

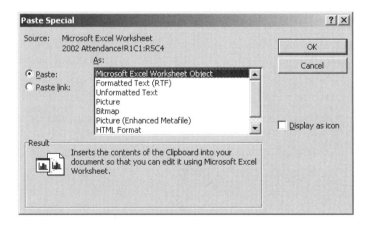

Note that the source file must remain open until after the Paste Special command is selected.

6. Select Paste to create an embedded object or select Paste link to create a linked object.

7. Select Microsoft Excel Worksheet Object from the As list and then select OK.

Embedding a New Excel Worksheet Object

A new Excel worksheet object can be embedded into a Word document by placing the insertion point where the embedded object is to appear and then selecting Object from the Insert menu, which displays the Object dialog box. Selecting the Create New tab and then selecting Microsoft Excel Worksheet from the Object type list and OK creates a new active Excel worksheet object.

When an Excel worksheet object is embedded or linked in a Word document, the object is placed as an inline object and can be positioned by using paragraph alignments, indents, and tabs.

Practice 7

In this practice you will use data in the 2002 SALES workbook to create an embedded object in the PAST SALES MEMO document.

① *OPEN THE PAST SALES MEMO DOCUMENT*

Open PAST SALES MEMO, which is a Word data file for this text.

② *OPEN THE 2002 SALES WORKBOOK AND COPY DATA*

a. Open 2002 SALES, which is an Excel data file for this text.

b. Select cells A1 through E5.

c. On the toolbar, click the Copy button (⬚).

③ *EMBED THE OBJECT*

a. Display the PAST SALES MEMO document.

b. Place the insertion point in the last blank paragraph of the document.

c. Select Edit → Paste Special. A dialog box is displayed.

    1. Select the Paste option if it is not already selected.

    2. In the As list, select Microsoft Excel Worksheet Object.

    3. Select OK. The data is embedded as an object in the Word document.

④ *MODIFY THE EMBEDDED OBJECT*

a. Double-click the embedded object to activate it. Note how Excel's menus, toolbars, and Formula bar are displayed even though a Word document is displayed.

b. Drag the middle-right handle of the object so that column F is displayed.

c. In cell F1, enter the label Total.

d. In cell F2, enter the formula: =SUM(B2:E2)

e. Use the Fill handle to copy the formula in cell F2 to cells F3 through F5. Ignore the Auto Fill Options button.

f. Click any place outside the embedded object. Word's menus and toolbars are again displayed.

⑤ *PRINT AND THEN CLOSE THE MODIFIED PAST SALES MEMO*

a. Create a footer with your name right aligned.

b. Save and then print the document.

c. Close PAST SALES MEMO.

d. Quit Word. The 2002 SALES workbook is displayed.

⑥ *CLOSE THE 2002 SALES WORKBOOK AND QUIT EXCEL*

a. Note that column F contains no data even though data was added to the embedded object in the Word document.

b. Close 2002 SALES.

c. Quit Excel

12.12 Embedding and Linking an Excel Chart Object

Charts created in Excel can be an embedded or linked object in a Word document.

The steps for embedding or linking a chart object from an open Excel workbook into an open Word document are:

1. Select the source, which is the chart to be embedded or linked.

2. Click the Copy button ( ) on the toolbar. A copy of the chart is added to the Clipboard.

3. Display the Word document that is to receive the embedded or linked object.

4. Place the insertion point near where the chart is to appear.

5. Select Paste Special from the Edit menu, which displays the Paste Special dialog box:

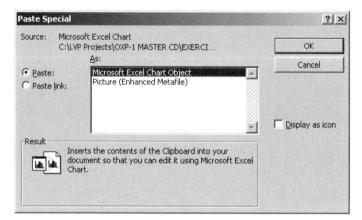

Note that the source file containing the chart must remain open until after the Paste Special command is selected.

6. Select Paste to create an embedded object or select Paste link to create a linked object.

7. Select Microsoft Excel Chart Object in the As list and then select OK.

When an Excel chart is embedded in or linked to a Word document, the chart object is placed as an inline object and can be positioned by using paragraph alignments, indents, and tabs.

activating a chart object   Double-clicking an embedded or linked Excel chart object has similar effects as double-clicking an Excel worksheet object as discussed in Section 12.11.

In this practice you will use data in the 2003 SALES Excel workbook to create a linked object in the CURRENT SALES MEMO Word document.

① *OPEN THE CURRENT SALES MEMO DOCUMENT*

Open CURRENT SALES MEMO, which is a Word data file for this text.

② *OPEN THE 2003 SALES WORKBOOK AND COPY DATA*

a. Open 2003 SALES, which is an Excel data file for this text.

b. Select cells A1 through C11.

c. On the toolbar, click the Copy button ().

③ *LINK THE OBJECT*

a. Display the CURRENT SALES MEMO document.

b. Place the insertion point in the last blank paragraph of the document.

c. Select Edit → Paste Special. A dialog box is displayed.

1. Select the Paste link option.

2. In the As list, select Microsoft Excel Worksheet Object.

3. Select OK. A linked object is inserted into the Word document.

④ *CLOSE THE 2003 SALES WORKBOOK AND QUIT EXCEL*

⑤ *MODIFY THE WORKBOOK DATA*

a. Display the CURRENT SALES MEMO document if it is not already displayed.

b. Double-click the worksheet object. Excel is started and the linked file, 2003 SALES, is displayed. Note how it is displayed in an Excel window, unlike an embedded workbook object.

c. In cell C2, enter the value $25,000.

d. Save the modified 2003 SALES workbook.

e. Quit Excel. The 2003 SALES workbook is also closed. The CURRENT SALES MEMO document is displayed. Note that the workbook object displays the new value because it is linked to the 2003 SALES workbook file.

f. Create a footer with your name right aligned.

⑥ *SAVE, PRINT, AND THEN CLOSE THE MODIFIED CURRENT SALES MEMO*

⑦ *QUIT WORD*

This chapter presented the steps necessary to copy data between files and between applications.

In an application, more than one file in the same application can be open at the same time, each in its own window. The Window menu displays the names of open files with the active file designated by a check mark. When work has been completed on a file, it should be saved and then closed.

More than one Office application can be running at one time and have files open. The Taskbar is used to switch between open files, regardless of the application.

This chapter explained how data can be copied between:

- Word documents (Section 12.3)

- Excel workbooks (Section 12.4)

- an Excel workbook and a Word document (Section 12.6 and Section 12.8)

Information from a number of different files can be pasted into any Office document using the Office Clipboard. The Office Clipboard stores up to 24 cut and copied items.

Office is an integrated package, which means that data from a file created in one application can be easily copied into a file created in a different application. The steps for coping data between two open files are:

1. Select the source, which is the data to be copied.

2. Click the Copy button. A copy of the selected data is added to the Clipboard.

3. Make the file receiving the data active.

4. Select the destination by placing the insertion point or selecting the upper-left cell of the range where the data is to be pasted.

5. Click the Paste button.

A hyperlink can be used in a Word document or an Excel workbook to display another Office file. Clicking the hyperlink displays the file, opening it if necessary. A hyperlink is added by selecting the Hyperlink command or clicking the Insert Hyperlink button.

When the Copy and Paste buttons are used to copy data, the pasted data is static, which means it is not connected to the source file or to the source application. The Paste Special command displays a dialog box with options for pasting data as an embedded or linked object. An embedded object keeps the features of the source application. Double-clicking an embedded object activates it so that it can be edited and updated. A linked object can only be modified by editing the source file.

Vocabulary

Active file   The file currently displayed.

Embedded object   An object that keeps the features of the source application.

Floating object   An object that can be positioned by dragging the object.

Inline object   An object that is placed in the text at the insertion point. It can then be positioned by using paragraph alignment, indents, and tabs.

Linked object   An object that can only be modified by editing the source file.

Static   Pasted data that is not connected to the source file or to the source application.

Word and Excel Commands and Buttons

☒ **Close command**   Closes an open file. Found in the File menu. The Close button in the upper-right corner of the document window can be used instead of the command.

▣ **Copy button**   Places a copy of the selected data on the Clipboard. Found on the toolbar. Copy in the Edit menu can be used instead of the button.

Edit Hyperlink command   Used to edit a hyperlink. Found in the menu displayed by right-clicking a hyperlink.

▣ **Hyperlink button**   Displays a dialog box used to insert a hyperlink to a different file. Found on the toolbar. Hyperlink in the Insert menu can be used instead of the command.

▣ **Open command**   Displays a dialog box used to open an existing file. Found in the File menu. The Open button on the toolbar can be used instead of the command.

Open Office Document command   Displays the Open Office Document dialog box. Found in the Start menu.

▣ ▣▾ **Paste button**   Places the Clipboard contents in a worksheet starting at the selected cell. Found on the toolbar. Paste in the Edit menu can be used instead of the button.

▣ **Paste Options button**   Displayed when Clipboard contents are placed in cells.

Paste Special command   Displays a dialog box that can be used to paste the Clipboard contents as an embedded or linked object. Found in the Edit menu.

Remove Hyperlink command   Used to remove a hyperlink. Found in the menu displayed by right-clicking a hyperlink.

▣ **Save command**   Saves the active file. Found in the File menu. The Save button on the toolbar can be used instead of the command.

Sections 12.1 — 12.9

1. List the steps required to open two Word documents.

2. a) What is an "active" file?
   b) Explain how an active file is designated in the Windows menu.

3. List two ways to switch from one open file to another open file in the same application.

4. Why should you close an open file after work on the file is complete?

5. The Word document NEWS contains a paragraph that describes the inauguration of a new president. List the steps required to copy this paragraph into a Word document named PRESIDENT.

6. List the steps required to copy two columns of data from an Excel workbook named OWED and insert them between two existing columns in a workbook named ASSETS.

7. List the steps required to open a Word document and then an Excel workbook.

8. List the steps required to switch from an open Word document to an open Excel workbook.

9. What does "integrated packaged" mean?

10. List the steps required to copy cells A1, A2, B1, and B2 from an Excel workbook into an open Word document.

11. How must the data being copied from a Word document to an Excel workbook be organized?

12. a) How many cut and copied items can the Office Clipboard store?
    b) In the Office Clipboard, what does the 🖼 symbol indicate?

13. a) List one reason why businesses might include a chart in a document.
    b) List the steps required to copy a chart object from an open Excel workbook into an open Word document.

14. What is the difference between an inline object and a floating object?

15. List the steps required to create a hyperlink in a Word document to a file named Budget.

Sections 12.10 — 12.12

16. What is static data?

17. What is an embedded object?

18. What happens when an embedded workbook object in a Word document is activated?

19. List the steps required for embedding an object from an open Word document into a new Excel workbook.

20. What is the difference between an embedded object and a linked object?

21. A Word document that contains a linked workbook object is opened. Then, Excel is started and the workbook file that the linked object was created from is opened. Next, the workbook is modified, and then saved. If the Word document is displayed, is the linked workbook object updated?

22. How is an embedded or linked Excel chart object positioned in a Word document?

Exercises

Exercise 1 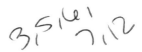 ———————————————— SUNPORT CAMPING

The CAMPING TIPS document last modified in Chapter 6, Exercise 5 contains a list of helpful camping tips. The SUNPORT CAMPING document modified in Chapter 6, Exercise 12 contains a short article on the Sunport Camping Symposium. The SUNPORT CAMPING article would be more informative if the CAMPING TIPS list was added to it. Open CAMPING TIPS and SUNPORT CAMPING and complete the following steps:

a) Insert two blank lines after the last paragraph in SUNPORT CAMPING and then enter the following sentence:

To make your next camping trip easier, here are a few helpful tips:

b) Place a copy of the numbered list in the CAMPING TIPS document after the line you just entered. Do not copy the "Camping Tips" title. Include a blank line between the new sentence and the numbered list.

c) Delete the entire bulleted list from the first numbered camping tip.

d) Delete the sentence that begins "The following list…" at the end of the first numbered camping tip.

e) Save the modified SUNPORT CAMPING and print a copy.

Exercise 2 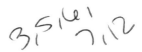 ———————————————— Student Stats

The Student Stats workbook last modified in Chapter 10, Exercise 4 contains statistics on the number of undergraduate and graduate students in each college at a university. The DOCTORATE STATS workbook contains statistics on the number of doctoral students in each college at the university. The doctoral information needs to be added to the Student Stats workbook. Open Student Stats and DOCTORATE STATS and complete the following steps:

a) The data stored in DOCTORATE STATS needs to be copied to Student Stats starting in cell D1. In Student Stats, move and size the charts as necessary so that column D is completely visible.

b) Place a copy of all the data in the DOCTORATE STATS workbook into the Student Stats workbook starting in cell D1. Size the column as necessary so that all the data is displayed entirely.

c) Copy the total, average, maximum, and minimum formulas in column C to the new doctoral information in column D.

d) Save the modified Student Stats and print a copy.

Exercise 3 ———————————————— Estimated Candle Sales

The CANDLE MEMO document contains sales figures which can be copied into a new workbook to ask What If? questions. Open the CANDLE MEMO document and complete the following steps:

a) Create a new Excel workbook.

b) Place a copy of the entire table containing the sales figures from the CANDLE MEMO document in the new workbook starting in cell A1.

c) Change the font of the copied data to Arial 10 point, bold the labels in row 1, and right align the October, November, and December labels. Size columns as necessary so that all the data is displayed entirely.

d) Save the workbook naming it Estimated Candle Sales.

e) In cell A8, enter the label Total: and bold and right align it. In row 8, enter formulas that use a function to total the sales for each month.

f) In cell E1, enter the label Q4 Total. In column E, enter formulas that use a function to total the fourth quarter sales for each item. Fourth quarter sales are calculated by summing the October, November, and December sales.

g) Insert a row at the top of the workbook. In cell F1, enter the label Expected Quarter 1 Sales and bold it.

h) In cell F2, enter the label 3% Increase and in cell G2 enter the label 8% Increase.

i) The sales manager wants to know the expected sales for the first quarter of next year if the first quarter sales increase 3% from the fourth quarter totals. In column F, enter formulas that use cell references to calculate the expected first quarter sales for each item if there is a 3% sales increase.

j) The sales manager wants to know the expected sales for the first quarter of next year if the first quarter sales increase 8% from the fourth quarter totals. In column G, enter formulas that use cell references to calculate the expected first quarter sales for each item if there is an 8% sales increase.

k) Format the values in columns F and G as currency with 0 decimal places. Size the columns as necessary so that all the data is displayed entirely.

l) In cell A11, insert a hyperlink to the CANDLE MEMO document.

m) Create a header with your name right aligned.

n) Save the modified Estimated Candle Sales and print a copy in landscape orientation with gridlines and row and column headings.

Exercise 4 ☼ ———————————————————— Upgrade Memo

The data in the Upgrade Costs workbook created in Chapter 8, Exercise 10 needs to be added to a memo. Open Upgrade Costs and complete the following steps:

a) Create a pie chart that displays the hardware, software, and training costs for the year 2004. Title the chart 2004 Upgrade Costs and display percentage data labels.

b) In a new Word document create the following memo, substituting your name for Your Name and inserting tabs and setting a 1" tab stop:

MEMORANDUM

TO: Duncan MacKenzie, Controller

FROM: Your Name, Technology Coordinator

DATE: January 3, 2004

SUBJECT: Upgrade Costs

The technology department has finished its upgrade cost estimates. The chart below shows the expected hardware, software, and training upgrade cost percentages for this year:

The table below shows the expected hardware, software, and training upgrade costs for years 2002 through 2007:

   c) Save the document naming it Upgrade Memo.

   d) Place a copy of the chart in the Upgrade Costs workbook after the second sentence in the memo. There should be a single blank line before and after the pasted chart.

   e) Place a copy of the data in cells A1 through E8 in the Upgrade Costs workbook at the end of the memo. There should be a blank line between the pasted workbook data and the last sentence in the memo.

   f) Save both files and print a copy of the Upgrade Memo document.

Exercise 5 ———————————————————— BREAKFAST

The BREAKFAST document contains a letter introducing a bakery's products to nearby stores. The GOODIE workbook contains price information on the products. Open BREAKFAST and GOODIE and complete the following steps:

   a) Place a copy of the data in cells A3 through B8 in the GOODIE workbook into the letter after the paragraph that ends "...quite a variety:." There should be a single blank line before and after the pasted workbook data.

   b) The chart in the GOODIE workbook also needs to be added to the BREAKFAST letter. Place a copy of the chart into the letter after the paragraph that ends "...you a tidy profit:." There should be a single blank line before and after the pasted chart.

   c) In the BREAKFAST letter, replace the text "To Whom It May Concern" with your name.

   d) Size and move the chart so that the letter fits on one page. Make sure the labels in the chart are displayed clearly. Save the modified BREAKFAST and print a copy.

Exercise 6 —————————————————————FRANKLIN TOURS

The FRANKLIN TOURS document contains a partial newsletter. The TOURS document and the TOUR PRICES workbook contain information for the newsletter. Open FRANKLIN TOURS, TOURS, and TOUR PRICES and complete the following steps:

a) Place a copy of all the text in the TOURS document into the FRANKLIN TOURS document in the blank paragraph at the end of the newsletter.

b) The data in cells A1 through B5 in the TOUR PRICES workbook needs to be added to the FRANKLIN TOURS newsletter. Place a copy of the data into the newsletter in the blank paragraph at the end of the newsletter.

c) The chart in the TOUR PRICES workbook also needs to be added to the FRANKLIN TOURS newsletter. Place a copy of the chart into the letter below the workbook data. There should be a blank line between the pasted chart and the pasted workbook data.

d) In the FRANKLIN TOURS document, create a footer with your name right aligned.

e) Save the modified FRANKLIN TOURS and print a copy.

Exercise 7 —————————————————————— Contest

A university is holding a community service contest. The college (College of Business, College of Nursing, and so on) whose students perform the most community service hours receives ten new computers. The SERVICE HOURS workbook contains the number of community service hours completed so far. Open SERVICE HOURS and complete the following steps:

a) In a new Word document create a one page document that promotes the contest. The document should include a short description of the contest and a paragraph about why community service is important. It should also include the deadline, which is the end of the semester. The document will be e-mailed to each college.

b) Save the document naming it Contest.

c) Insert two blank lines after the last line of text in the document and enter the following sentence:

> To date, students have performed the following community service hours:

d) The document needs to display the number of community service hours completed for each college. Using all the data in the SERVICE HOURS workbook, insert a linked object into the Contest document after the sentence you just entered. There should be a single blank line between the linked object and the last paragraph.

e) In the Contest document, create a header with your name right aligned.

f) The undergraduate students in the College of Business have just completed a total of 650 hours of community service. Edit the workbook appropriately.

g) Save the modified Contest and print a copy.

Exercise 8 ✍ ——————————————————————————— Pizza Palace

The owner of Pizza Palace wants to add some information to the expense workbook last modified in Chapter 11, Exercise 7. Open Pizza Palace and complete the following steps:

a) Change the page orientation to landscape.

b) Delete the chart.

c) In a new Word document, enter a sentence explaining how the menu prices were calculated. In a second sentence, give an example. Format both sentences as a bulleted list.

d) Using all the data in the Word document, place an embedded Word document object in the Pizza Palace workbook.

e) Move and size the Word document object so it starts in column F near the Menu Price row and the entire workbook fits on one page in landscape orientation.

f) Save the modified Pizza Palace and print a copy.

Exercise 9 ✍ ——————————————————————————— Grand Opening

The Grand Opening document last modified in Chapter 5, Exercise 9 needs to include the sale prices of some of the special items sold at the store. Open Grand Opening and complete the following steps:

a) The list of special items is going to be replaced with an embedded object. Cut the list of special items from the document.

b) Create a new Excel workbook.

c) Paste the cut list of special items starting in cell A2.

d) In cell A1 in the workbook, enter the label Item. In cell B1, enter the label Original Price. In cell C1, enter the label Sale Price. Bold all of the labels.

e) In column B, enter original prices for the items.

f) In column C, enter formulas that use cell references to display the item's sale price. The sale price is 20% off of the original price.

g) Using all of the data in the Excel workbook, place an embedded Worksheet object in the Grand Opening document in the blank paragraph under "Special Items Available:."

h) Activate the embedded object and center align all of the data. Increase the size of the font in the entire workbook object to match the rest of the flyer. Format the numeric data as currency with 2 decimal places. Size the workbook columns as necessary so that all the data is displayed entirely. Size the embedded object if necessary so that only the three columns of data are displayed.

i) Adjust margins if necessary so that the flyer prints on one page.

j) Save the modified Grand Opening and print a copy.

Exercise 10 ✿ ───────────────────────────── Track Memo

The Track Progress workbook last modified in Chapter 10, Exercise 12 contains information on the track team's progress for the season. The coach wants to include some of this information in a memo to the head of the athletics department. Open Track Progress and complete the following steps:

a) In a new Word document create a memo to the head of the athletics department summarizing how the track season went. The document should contain a separate paragraph about the progress of the students running the 100 Meter and a paragraph about the progress of the students running the 200 Meter. Format the memo appropriately and include your name in the **FROM:** line.

b) Save the document naming it Track Memo.

c) Insert two blank lines after the paragraph about the 100 Meter progress. Using the Track Team's Progress in 100 Meter chart in the Track Progress workbook, insert a linked chart object into the memo after the paragraph. There should be a single blank line before and after the chart object.

d) Insert two blank lines after the paragraph about the 200 Meter progress. Using the Track Team's Progress in 200 Meter chart in the Track Progress workbook, insert a linked chart object into the memo after the paragraph. There should be a single blank line before the chart object.

e) The coach realized that the Track Team's Progress in 200 Meter chart had a mistake. Callie Ramis' January time in the 200 Meter should be 32.0. Edit the workbook appropriately.

f) Size the charts appropriately so that the memo fits on one page.

g) Save the modified Track Memo and print a copy.

Exercise 11 (advanced) ✿ ───────────────────── Newsletter

The Newsletter document created in Chapter 6, Exercise 15 needs to be modified. Open Newsletter and complete the following steps:

a) In a new Excel workbook, enter data that is relevant to the newsletter.

b) Using all of the data in the Excel workbook, create an embedded Worksheet object in the Newsletter document.

c) Size the object appropriately.

d) In Word, format the data in the embedded object appropriately.

e) Save the modified Newsletter and print a copy.

Exercise 12 (advanced) ✿ ──────────────────────────────

Use the My Finances workbook last modified in Chapter 10, Exercise 15 as a basis for a letter to a financial planner requesting his or her advice. You would like to invest the money you will be saving. Copy the chart of your savings information from the workbook into the letter. Also include a hyperlink to the workbook file.

Introducing the Relational Database

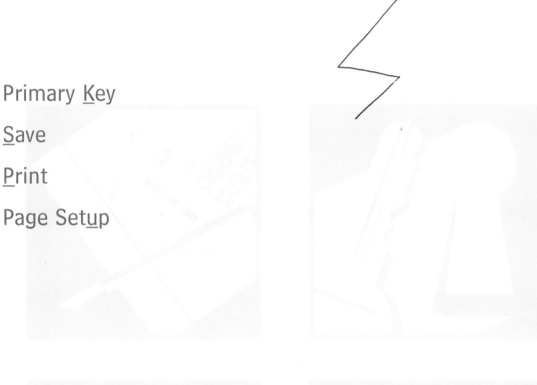

Primary <u>K</u>ey

<u>S</u>ave

<u>P</u>rint

Page Set<u>u</u>p

Chapter 13 Expectations

After completing this chapter you will be able to:

1. Describe a relational database and its structure.
2. Define fields.
3. Design a relational database.
4. Create a relational database.
5. View tables in Design view and Datasheet view.
6. Create a form for a table.
7. Enter records using forms.
8. Format Datasheet view.
9. Print records.
10. Create and use filters to query a database table.
11. Save a filter.
12. Create and use complex queries.

The History of the Database

The broad category of data handling refers to the tools and techniques used to manipulate large amounts of data. One of the earliest significant achievements in data handling was the 1951-1952 Sort-Merge Generator developed by Betty Holberton for the UNIVAC 1, which initiated the development and widespread use of data processing tools. Early data processing environments used a flat-file system to maintain separate files of data for each application. For example, a company would maintain an employee file for payroll purposes and another employee file for job classification. However, maintaining duplicate data in separate files proved time-consuming and error-prone. The DBMS (Database Management System) model maintained data by combining files into a common framework. In 1971, CODASYL (Conference on Data Systems Language) set standards for the DBMS model. Oracle was among the first DBMS applications to implement this model which is still used today.

$\mathbf{T}$his chapter introduces database terminology and discusses using Microsoft Access for creating a relational database. An Access database will be created, records will be added, and queries will be performed to limit the records displayed.

13.1   What is a Database?

Our present time is referred to as the "Information Age" because the computer's fast retrieval and large storage capabilities enable us to store and manipulate vast amounts of information. Related information is often stored in a *computerized database.* A piece of information in a database, called *data*, must be in digital format but can include text, numerical data, photos and graphics, sound files, e-mail addresses, and hyperlinks.

data

Microsoft Access is the database application in Microsoft Office. An Access database can be used to generate forms, queries, and reports from the data it stores. A form is used for entering and viewing data, a query is used for displaying specific data, and a report is used for formatting and organizing data for printing:

Access

A Microsoft Access database displaying a query (top left), a form (top right), and a report (bottom)

13.2 Defining Fields

field

A database is organized into *fields* that store data. A field is defined by its name, type, size, and format. A well designed database has fields that store one piece of data only. For example, a field named FullName that stores both a first and last name is considered poor design because it limits the sorting and searching capabilities of the database. A better design would include FirstName and LastName fields to separate name data.

field name

A field has a name that should be descriptive of its contents. The following guidelines should be used when choosing field names:

- **Make field names unique.** Duplicate field names cannot be used to represent similar data. For example, a sales ID and a customer ID cannot be represented by two fields that are both named ID. Instead, SalesID and CustomerID could be used as field names.

- **Choose the shortest possible name that accurately describes the contents of the field.** In Access, field names may be up to 64 characters. When multiple words are used for a field name, each word should begin with an uppercase letter. As a matter of good design, the field name should not contain spaces. For example, ItemName is a field name that contains multiple words but no spaces.

- **Use complete words instead of numbers or abbreviations.** For example, FirstName is better than 1stName, or FName. Some users may not understand abbreviations.

- **Avoid special characters.** For example, #1Name, ?Name, and *Name, are poor choices for field names. Some special characters are not permitted.

field type

Fields are classified by the type of data they store:

- *text fields* store characters (letters, symbols, words, a combination of letters and numbers, etc.).
- *number fields* store only numeric values.
- *date/time fields* store a date or time.
- *currency fields* store dollar amounts.
- *memo fields* store several lines of text.
- *AutoNumber fields* automatically store a numeric value that is one greater than that in the last record added. An AutoNumber field is often used as the primary key for a table since each value is automatically unique.

Fields Containing Numbers

A field should be of type text if its entries are numbers that would not be used in a numeric calculation. For example, a Zip field should be a text field because the numbers are not used as numeric values.

---

field size

The *size* of a field is the number of characters or the type of number it can store. Text fields can store up to 255 characters. The size of a number field is defined by the type of value it stores. For fields that store a number with a decimal portion, the field size *single* is used. Fields that store only whole numbers use the *long integer* field size. A size cannot be defined for date/time and currency fields.

single
long integer

field format   The *format* of a field determines how its data is displayed. Numeric field formats include:

- *general number*, which is the default and displays the number exactly as entered.

- *fixed*, which displays a field value to a specified number of decimal places.

- *percent*, which multiplies the value entered by 100 and displays it with a % sign.

- *standard*, which displays a field value with the thousands separator, usually a comma.

Date/time field formats include:

- *long* (e.g., Saturday, June 24, 2003 or 10:12:30 AM)

- *medium* (e.g., 24-June-03 or 10:12 AM)

- *short* (e.g., 6/24/03 or 10:12)

Text and memo fields usually have no format.

decimal places   Decimal places can be set as appropriate for numeric field types. A number field with the long integer field size should have the number of decimal places set to 0. A number greater than 0 results in the long integer data value being rounded.

13.3   Tables and Records

table   Access is a relational database, which uses *tables* to group related fields. For example, The Kite Company uses a relational database that contains a table for inventory, another for customer information, and a third for sales transactions:

> ### RDBMS
>
> A <u>d</u>ata<u>b</u>ase <u>m</u>anagement <u>sys</u>tem (*DBMS*) is a set of programs that together are used to create a database and then access the data. One type of DBMS is the *relational database*, which uses tables for organizing data. Access is a relational <u>d</u>atabase <u>m</u>anagement <u>s</u>ystem (*RDBMS*).

The Kite Company relational database has three tables

record   A table contains rows of records and columns of fields. A *record* is the data for a set of fields. The Kites table contains six inventory records:

a record ← | ItemID | ItemName |
▶ BOX | Box
DRA | Dragon
DRF | Dragonfly
LAD | Ladybug ← a field
SEA | Seagull
SPA | Space Shuttle
✳

primary key

Field names are shown at the top of a table and data in the columns below. Each table must have a *primary key*, which is a field designated to contain unique data, which means that no two values are the same. A primary key ensures that each record in a table is unique. If a duplicate value is entered in the primary key field, Access displays a warning dialog box. In the Kites table shown above, the ItemID is the primary key. Note that each record is unique. The primary key may also be a combination of fields designated to have a unique combination of entries.

13.4 Designing a Relational Database

A database should be created based on a design. Designing a database is a three-step process:

1. **Determine what information should be stored.** This decision requires considering the purpose of the database.

   For example, The Kite Company is a wholesaler of kites and needs a database to keep track of inventory, customers, and sales transactions. Therefore, information such as item names, customer names, and so on should be stored.

2. **Divide information into named tables.** This should be done by grouping related information and then choosing a short descriptive name for each group. These named groups will be made into tables when the database is created.

   For example, The Kite Company database should contain inventory information (item ID, item name), customer information (company ID, company name), and sales information (sales ID, date, company ID, item ID, and quantity). Appropriate names for each group are Kites, Customers, and Sales, respectively.

3. **Define the fields and determine the primary key for each table.** The guidelines in Section 13.2 should be used to define fields with appropriate field names, types, sizes, and formats, if any. A primary key for each table must also be designated.

   For example, the fields and primary key for the Kites table are:

   ItemID   text field, 3 characters (primary key)
   ItemName   text field, 20 characters

Table Relationships

A relational database designer will also be sure that a table is related to at least one other table in the database. When two tables contain the same field, they are said to be "related" by this field. A table with no relationship to another table may not belong in the database. Relationships are discussed in Chapter 14.

Practice 1

In this practice you will use pencil and paper to design two tables for The Kite Company database.

① *DEFINE FIELDS FOR THE SALES TABLE*

The Sales table should contain a sales ID (a unique number automatically generated), date of sale (similar to 6/24/03), customer ID (a maximum three-letter abbreviation), item ID (a three-letter abbreviation), and quantity sold.

a. Write appropriate field names for the Sales table information and next to each field name write down its type, size (keep in mind that date/time fields do not have a size), and field format, if any (keep in mind that text fields do not have a format).

b. Determine the primary key for the Sales table, which is the field that will have a unique value for each record. Write primary key next to this field.

Check – Your field definitions should look similar to:

SalesID	AutoNumber field (primary key)
Date	date field, short form
CustomerID	text field, maximum 3 characters
ItemID	text field, 3 characters
Quantity	number, long integer

② *DEFINE FIELDS FOR THE CUSTOMERS TABLE*

The Customers table should contain a customer ID (a maximum three-letter abbreviation) and company name. Define the fields, including the primary key, for the Customers table.

13.5 Creating a New Relational Database

Blank Database

Selecting New Office Document from the Start menu on the Taskbar displays the New Office Document dialog box. Clicking the Blank Database icon and then selecting OK starts Access and displays the File New Database dialog box:

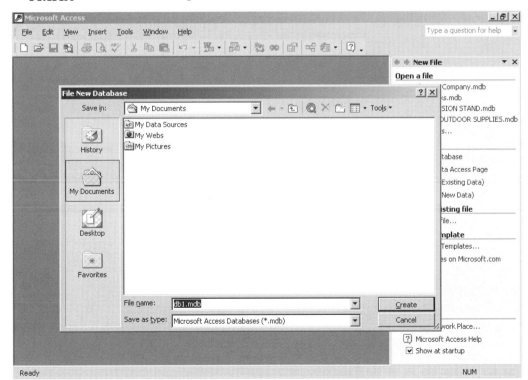

The name of the new database must be typed in the File name box. The Save in box and the contents box below it are used to select the folder where the new database is to be stored. Access automatically periodically saves the database to the file and folder specified when the database is created. Selecting Create creates the new database and opens the Database window in Access. The Kite Company database is displayed below:

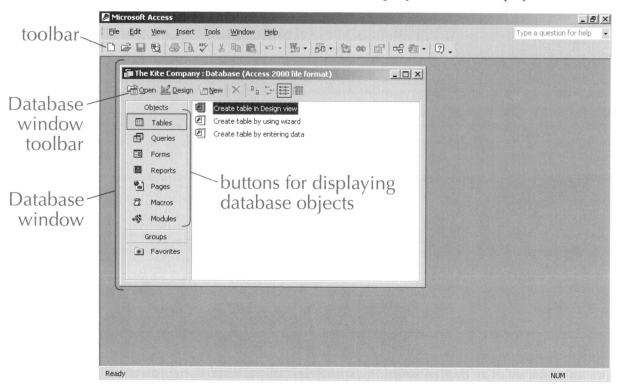

- The **toolbar** contains buttons that represent different actions.

- The **Database window** is used to display and create objects for the open database.

- **Buttons** in the Database window are used to display database objects and icons that can be clicked to create new objects.

- The **Database window toolbar** contains buttons that represent different actions.

13.6 Creating Tables and Fields

Design view

[Tables]

[Create table in Design view]

creating fields

A table is created by clicking Tables in the Database window and then double-clicking the Create table in Design view icon, which displays a new table in Design view. *Design view* shows the field definitions for a table. Fields are added by using the following steps:

1. **Type the field name.** The name of the field should be typed in the first empty Field Name box.

2. **Select the field type.** The field type should be selected from the Data Type box next to the corresponding field name.

3. **Type a description.** A description of the data expected in the field should be typed in the corresponding Description box. A field's description is displayed in the status bar of Access.

4. **Type the field size**. A field size should be typed in the Field Size box of the General options found in the Field Properties part of the window. For a text field, the size is the greatest number of characters allowed. For a number field, either Long Integer or Single should be selected. Date/time and currency fields do not have a field size.

5. **Select a field format**. A field format should be selected in the Format box of the General options found in the Field Properties part of the window. Text and memo fields do not have a format.

6. **Designate the number of decimal places**. For Single and Currency fields, the number of decimal places should be typed in the Decimal Places box of the General options found in the Field Properties part of the window.

primary key

active field

To complete a table, a primary key must be designated. Clicking the Primary Key button () on the toolbar or selecting Primary Key from the Edit menu selects the active field as the primary key. The *active field* contains the insertion point and has the ▶ symbol to the left of its row. Clicking a field makes it active. For the Kites table on the previous page, ItemID is the primary key, as indicated by the ▼ marker.

Required option

The primary key field should also have the Required option in the Field Properties part of the table Design view window set to Yes. This ensures that each record has data in the primary key field.

In the table below, fields for the Kites table have been created. Note the primary key field and its Required option in the Field Properties:

| ⚷▶ | ItemID | Text | Three character item ID |
| | ItemName | Text | Item name |

field properties

General	Lookup
Field Size	3
Format	
Input Mask	
Caption	
Default Value	
Validation Rule	
Validation Text	
Required	No
Allow Zero Length	Yes
Indexed	Yes (No Duplicates)
Unicode Compression	Yes
IME Mode	No Control
IME Sentence Mode	None

A field name can be up to 64 characters long, including spaces. Press F1 for help on field names.

A table with two fields in Design view

multiple-field primary key

Sometimes it is necessary to designate two fields as the primary key. Multiple fields can be selected by clicking the gray box to the left of the first field, holding down the Ctrl key, and then clicking the gray box to the left of the second field. Next, clicking the Primary Key button on the toolbar selects both fields as the primary key.

13.7　Saving and Closing a Table

A new table is saved by selecting <u>S</u>ave (Ctrl+S) from the <u>F</u>ile menu or clicking the Save button (🖫) on the toolbar. The first time a table is saved, the Save As dialog box is displayed so that a descriptive table name can be entered. After a table has been saved, its name appears as a table object in the Database window.

A table is closed by clicking the Close button (✖) in the upper-right corner of table window.

13.8　Closing and Opening a Database and Quitting Access

When finished working on a database, it should be closed properly. A database is closed by selecting <u>C</u>lose from the <u>F</u>ile menu or clicking the Close button (✖) in the upper-right corner of the Database window. When a database is closed, Access automatically saves any changes.

If Access is running, a database can be opened by selecting <u>O</u>pen (Ctrl+O) from the <u>F</u>ile menu or clicking the Open button (📂) on the toolbar, which displays the Open dialog box. A database can also be opened by selecting Open Office Document from the Start menu, which displays the Open Office Document dialog box.

When Access is no longer needed, it should be quit properly. Quitting Access means that the application window is closed and the program is no longer in the computer's memory. Access is quit by selecting E<u>x</u>it from the <u>F</u>ile menu or clicking the Close button (✖) in the upper-right corner of the application window.

Practice 2

In this practice you will create The Kite Company relational database and its tables.

① *CREATE A NEW DATABASE*

    a. On the Taskbar, select Start → New Office Document. A dialog box is displayed.

        1. Click the Blank Database icon to select it.

        2. Select OK. Access is started and the File New Database dialog box is displayed.

            a. In the File name box, type The Kite Company.

            b. Use the Save in box and the contents box below it to select the appropriate folder for storing the database.

            c. Select Create. The Kite Company : Database window is displayed.

② *CREATE A NEW TABLE*

    a. In The Kite Company : Database window, click Tables if it is not already selected.

    b. Double-click the Create table in Design view icon. A new table is displayed in Design view.

③ CREATE THE FIELDS FOR THE KITES TABLE

a. In the first Field Name box, type ItemID.

b. Press the Tab key to select the Data Type box. Text is the default type, which is appropriate for this field.

c. Press Tab to move the insertion point to the Description box. Type Three character item ID.

d. In the Field Properties part of the window, click the Field Size box.

e. Delete the current field size number and type 3, which is the maximum number of characters allowed for an entry in this field.

f. In the next Field Name box, create a field named ItemName, of type Text, with the description Item name, and a field size of 20.

Check – Your table should look similar to:

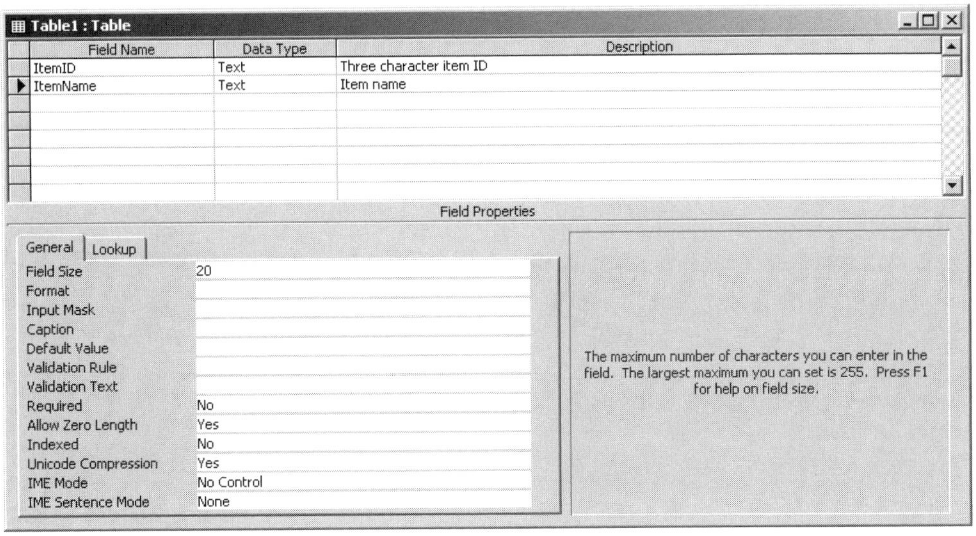

④ SELECT THE PRIMARY KEY FOR THE TABLE

The ItemID field is the primary key for this table because each item ID is unique.

a. Click the ItemID Field Name box to make it active.

b. On the toolbar, click the Primary Key button (🔑). A 🔑 symbol is displayed next to the ItemID field indicating that it is now the primary key for the table.

c. In the Field Properties part of the window, click the Required box and then select Yes from the list.

⑤ SAVE THE TABLE

a. Select File → Save. A dialog box is displayed.

    1. In the Table Name box, type Kites.

    2. Select OK. The Kites table is saved with the database.

b. In the upper-right corner of the table, click the Close button. The table is closed. Note how Kites appears as a table name in the Database window.

⑥ CREATE THE CUSTOMERS TABLE

    a. Double-click the Create table in Design view icon. A new table is displayed in Design view.

    b. Create the CustomerID and CompanyName fields using the design below. Enter appropriate descriptions for each of the fields.

CustomerID	Text field, maximum 3 characters
CompanyName	Text field, 50 characters

    c. Make CustomerID the primary key.

    d. In the Field Properties part of the window, select Yes in the Required box for the CustomerID field.

Check – Your table should look similar to:

    e. Save the table naming it Customers.

    f. Close the Customers table.

⑦ CREATE THE SALES TABLE

    a. Create a new table in Design view.

    b. In the first Field Name box, type SalesID.

    c. In the SalesID Data Type list, select AutoNumber.

    d. In the SalesID Description, type Sales ID.

    e. In the Field Properties part of the window, select Long Integer for the Field Size if it is not already displayed.

    f. Make SalesID the primary key.

    g. In the next Field Name box, type Date.

    h. In the Date Data Type box, select Date/Time.

    i. In the Date Description box, type Date of transaction.

    j. In the Field Properties part of the window, click the Format box and then select Short Date from the list.

    k. In the next Field Name box, create a field named CustomerID, of type Text, with description Customer ID, and a field size of 3.

    l. In the next Field Name box, create a field named ItemID, of type Text, with description Item ID, and a field size of 3.

m. In the next Field Name box, create a field named Quantity, of type Number, with description Number of items purchased, and a field size of Long Integer. In the Field Properties part of the window, set the number of decimal places to 0.

Check – Your table should look similar to:

n. Save the table naming it Sales.

o. Close the Sales table.

⑧ *CLOSE THE KITE COMPANY AND QUIT ACCESS*

a. Select File → Close. The Kite Company Database window is removed from Access.

b. Quit Access.

13.9   Creating a Form

A *form* is a window that contains the fields of a table and is used for entering data and viewing records. A form displays only one record at a time, making data entry less error-prone. It is similar to a paper form, such as an order form or employment application. For example, a form for the Kites table in The Kite Company database looks similar to:

columnar form   The Kites form is a *columnar form*, which displays a record with one field below the other in a column. Note that only blank field boxes are displayed since there are no records in the table.

Forms

In Access, a form is created by first clicking Forms in the Database window, which displays the form objects:

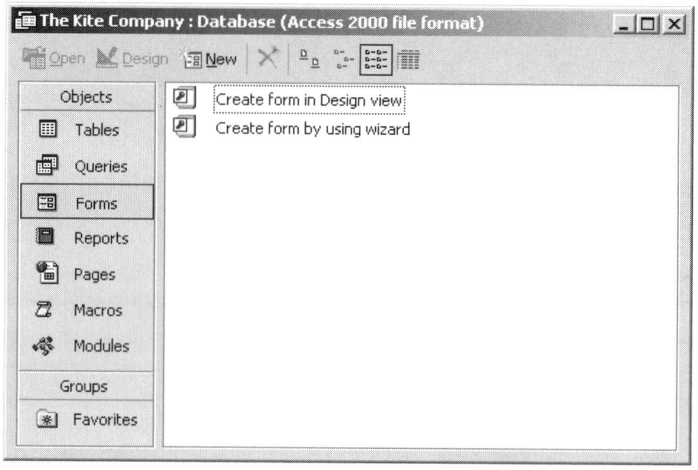

Create form by using wizard

Double-clicking the Create form by using wizard icon starts the Form Wizard, which provides dialog boxes for selecting fields to be included in the form and for selecting form layout options:

1. **Select the appropriate table and fields.** The table for the form is selected from the Tables/Queries list. The fields from that table are displayed in the Available Fields list. Since a form for a table usually includes all the fields of that table, clicking >> moves all the fields of the selected table to the Selected Fields list:

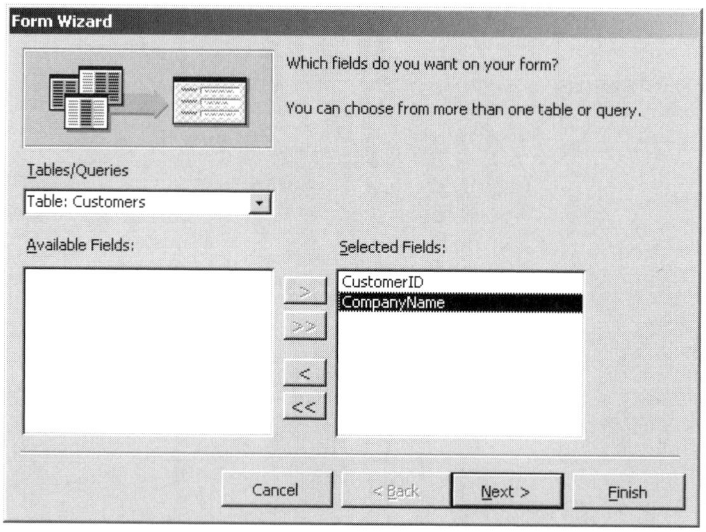

Selecting Next displays the next Form Wizard dialog box.

2. **Select the form layout.** Clicking Columnar creates a columnar form:

Selecting Next displays the next Form Wizard dialog box.

3. **Select the form style.** Clicking Standard gives the form a plain gray background:

Selecting Next displays the next Form Wizard dialog box.

4. **Type the form title.** A form title can be typed and the option to open the form for data entry can be selected:

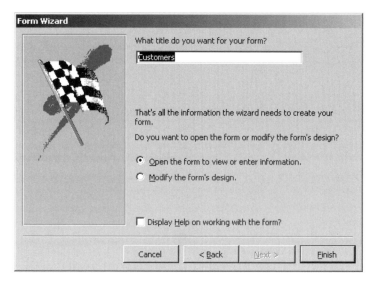

Selecting Finish displays the new form.

13.10 Using Forms and Entering Records

opening a form

record controls

After a form is created, its title is displayed as a form object in the Database window. Double-clicking a form name or selecting a form name and then the Open button () on the Database window toolbar opens the form. *Record controls* are displayed at the bottom of a form and are used for displaying a specific record in a table. The number of the active record and the total number of records in the table are displayed next to controls that scroll records:

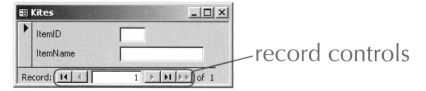

record controls

Sizing a Form

A form may not be large enough to completely display its record controls. A form is sized by dragging its lower-right corner.

⏮ displays the first record.

⏭ displays the last record.

▶ displays the next record.

◀ displays the previous record.

▶* displays a new record.

Record controls are dimmed if they cannot be used at the current time. For example, the ▶* control is dimmed when a new record is displayed.

If a table contains no data, then its corresponding form will display a record with empty boxes for all fields but number fields. A number field box automatically displays a 0 until it is replaced by another value. AutoNumber field data are not displayed until another field of the record is entered.

adding a record

A record is added by typing data into a blank record. If records already exist, then the control is clicked to display a new blank record. Clicking a field box places the insertion point in that box. However, data entry is usually faster when hands remain on the keyboard. In this case, the Enter key or the Tab key can be pressed to move the insertion point from field box to field box. Pressing Shift+Tab moves the insertion point to the previous field box in the record. When the insertion point is in the last field box of a record, pressing Enter or Tab displays the next record in the table, if there is one, or a blank record otherwise.

editing existing data

An existing value can be changed by moving the insertion point to that field box and then editing the data.

When a form is active, the Status bar at the bottom of the Access window displays the description of the active field. A field description is the text that was entered in the Description box in table Design view.

closing a form

A form is closed by clicking the Close button (**X**) in the upper-right corner of the form window.

13.11 Viewing Records in Datasheet View

opening a table

A table displayed in *Datasheet view* shows existing records in rows one after the other. A table is opened in Datasheet view by first clicking Tables in the Database window to display table objects. Next, double-clicking a table name or selecting a table name and then clicking the Open button (Open) on the Database window toolbar opens the table. For example, the Customers table with three records opened in Datasheet view looks similar to:

Customers : Table	
CustomerID	CompanyName
CK	Cool Kites
GFK	Go Fly a Kite
SKC	Southern Kite Company
*	

datasheet

A table in Datasheet view is also called a *datasheet*.

record selector
active record

The asterisk (*) that appears to the left of the row below the last record indicates where the next record entered will appear. It is not a blank record and it cannot be deleted or removed. The gray box to the left of each record is a *record selector*. Clicking a record selector makes that record the *active record* and displays the ▶ symbol. Note that the first record in the datasheet above is the active record.

The View button ( ) on the toolbar can be used to switch a table between Design view and Datasheet view.

In this practice you will use forms to add records to The Kite Company relational database and then view records in Datasheet view.

① *OPEN THE KITE COMPANY DATABASE*

   a. Select Start → Open Office Document. A dialog box is displayed.

      1. Use the Look in list and the contents box below it to display the file name The Kite Company, which was last modified in Practice 2.

      2. In the contents box, click The Kite Company.

      3. Select Open. The Kite Company Database window is displayed.

② *CREATE A NEW FORM*

   a. In The Kite Company : Database window, click Forms.

   b. Double-click the Create form by using wizard icon. A dialog box is displayed.

      1. In the Tables/Queries list, select Table: Kites. The fields of the Kites table are displayed in the Available Fields list.

      2. Click >> . All the fields from the Available Fields list are moved to the Selected Fields list.

      3. Select Next. The form layout options are displayed.

      4. Select Columnar if it is not already selected.

      5. Select Next. The form style options are displayed.

      6. Select Standard if it is not already selected.

      7. Select Next. More options are displayed.

      8. In the What title do you want for your form? box, type Kites if it not already displayed.

      9. Select Open the form to view or enter information if it is not already selected.

      10. Select Finish. The Kites form is displayed with the first record's data. Since there are no records in the Kites table, the field boxes are blank.

③ *ADD A RECORD USING A FORM*

   a. Move the insertion point to the ItemID box if it is not already there. The Status bar at the bottom of the Access window displays Three character item ID, the description of the field.

   b. Type SEA and then press Enter. The cursor is moved to the next field.

   c. In the ItemName field, type Seagull.

   d. Press Enter. A new blank record is displayed. Note the record controls indicate that record 2 is displayed.

④ *ADD FIVE MORE RECORDS TO THE DATABASE*

   Follow step 2 above to enter the next five records:

      BOX; Box

      DRA; Dragon

      DRF; Dragonfly

      LAD; Ladybug

      SPA; Space Shuttle

⑤ *VIEW THE RECORDS OF THE KITES TABLE*

    a. In the record controls, click ▮◂ to view the first record in the table.

    b. Click ▸▮ to view the next record in the table.

    c. Click ▸▮ to view the last record in the table.

    d. Click the form's Close button to remove it. The Kites Company : Database window should still be displayed. Note how Kites now appears as a form name in the window.

    e. In The Kite Company : Database window, click Tables. Table names are displayed.

    f. Double-click Kites. The Kites table is displayed in Datasheet view. Note the Kites records.

    g. Click the Close button (☒) in the Kites: Table window to remove it. The Kite Company : Database window should again be displayed.

⑥ *CREATE A FORM FOR THE CUSTOMERS TABLE*

    a. In The Kite Company : Database window, click Forms.

    b. Double-click the Create form by using wizard icon. A dialog box is displayed.

    c. Continue with the Form Wizard to create a form for the Customers table using all the fields from the Customers table. Refer to step 2 for form options and name the form Customers.

⑦ *ADD CUSTOMER RECORDS*

    a. Add the following records using the Customers form:

        SKC; Southern Kite Company

        GFK; Go Fly a Kite

        CK; Cool Kites

    b. Close the Customers form.

⑧ *CREATE A FORM FOR THE SALES TABLE AND ADD SALES RECORDS*

    a. Use the Form Wizard to create a form for the Sales table using all the fields from the Sales table. Refer to step 2 for the form options and name the form Sales.

    b. Note the new form is displayed with (AutoNumber) highlighted in the SalesID field. Press the Enter key. The cursor is moved to the Date field.

    c. Type 9/22/03. The SalesID value changes to a 1 since this is the first record entered.

    d. Type CK in the CustomerID field, SPA in the ItemID field, and 6 in the Quantity field.

    e. Add the remaining six order records:

        9/22/03; SKC; SEA; 32

        9/30/03; GFK; DRF; 12

        9/30/03; GFK; SEA; 24

        10/17/03; CK; LAD; 18

        10/17/03; SKC; DRF; 10

        10/21/03; GFK; DRF; 8

    f. Close the Sales form. Note that The Kite Company : Database window displays the names of three forms.

13.12 Formatting Datasheet View

When a table is created, the columns in Datasheet view have a default width that may or may not entirely display a field's name and data. For example, after three customer records have been entered, the Customers table in Datasheet view looks similar to:

	CustomerID	CompanyName
▶	CK	Cool Kites
	GFK	Go Fly a Kite
	SKC	Southern Kite C
✳		

A column may not be wide enough to entirely display its field name and data

changing column width boundary

The width of a column is changed by dragging the right boundary of the column. Pointing to the *boundary*, the bar separating the field names at the top of a table, changes the pointer to ↔:

	CustomerID ↔	CompanyName
▶	CK	Cool Kites
	GFK	Go Fly a Kite
	SKC	Southern Kite C
✳		

Dragging the boundary to the right increases the width of the column. Columns that are unnecessarily wide should be narrowed by dragging the boundary to the left.

Another technique for changing column width is to double-click the right boundary of the column. This method will size a column so that it is just wide enough to display its field name and data entirely.

changing field order

The order in which the fields appear in a table can be changed by dragging a selected field to a new location. A field is selected by pointing to its field name until the pointer changes to ⬇:

	CustomerID	CompanyName
▶	CK	Cool Kites
	GFK	Go Fly a Kite
	SKC	Southern Kite Company
✳		

Clicking ⬇ selects the field. The selected field can then be dragged to the new position. Note the heavy dark line indicating the field will be moved after the CompanyName field:

	CustomerID	CompanyName	
▶	CK	Cool Kites	
	GFK	Go Fly a Kite	▸
	SKC	Southern Kite Company	
✳			

When the mouse button is released, the column is moved:

	CompanyName	CustomerID
	Cool Kites	CK
	Go Fly a Kite	GFK
▶	Southern Kite Company	SKC
＊		

 After formatting Datasheet view, the table must be saved to retain the new layout.

13.13 Printing Records

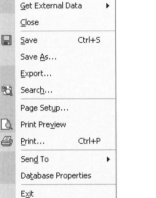

A table displayed in Datasheet view can be printed by selecting Print (Ctrl+P) from the File menu. If the table is too wide to fit on a single sheet of paper, columns are printed on consecutive sheets starting from the leftmost field and proceeding to the right. If the table is too long to fit on a single sheet, rows are printed on consecutive sheets starting from the first record and proceeding to the last.

More columns can be printed on a sheet of paper by printing the table in landscape orientation. This can be useful for tables with many columns or very wide columns. The print orientation of a table is changed by selecting Page Setup from the File menu, which displays the Page Setup dialog box. Selecting the Page tab and then selecting Landscape and OK changes the print orientation. When Print is selected, the table is printed across the widest part of the paper allowing more columns, but fewer rows.

printing selected records

The Selected Record(s) option in the Print dialog box is used to indicate that only the active record should be printed. Multiple records can be selected for printing by holding down the Ctrl key and clicking in the record selector boxes to the left of the records.

printing forms

Selecting the Print command when a form is displayed prints all the records of the form, one right after the other, in a column. The Selected Record(s) option in the Print dialog box is selected to print the displayed record only.

 The Print button () on the toolbar can be used to print one copy of a datasheet or a set of records in forms one after the other.

Practice 4

In this practice you will format and print the tables in The Kite Company database. The Sales form will also be printed. Open The Kite Company if it is not already displayed.

① *DISPLAY THE CUSTOMERS TABLE IN DATASHEET VIEW*

   a. In The Kite Company : Database window, click Tables. The Customers, Kites, and Sales table names are listed.

   b. Double-click the Customers table name. The Customers table is displayed in Datasheet view.

② CHANGE THE WIDTH OF COLUMNS

    a. Point to the boundary between the CustomerID and CompanyName fields. The pointer changes to ↔.

    b. Double-click the ↔ pointer. The column narrows so that it is just wide enough to display the field name and field data.

    c. Double-click the boundary to the right of the CompanyName field. The CompanyName field column expands so that it is just wide enough to display the field name and field data entirely.

Check – Your Customers table should look similar to:

CustomerID	CompanyName
CK	Cool Kites
GFK	Go Fly a Kite
SKC	Southern Kite Company

Customers : Table

③ PRINT THE CUSTOMERS TABLE

    a. Select File → Save. The modified table is saved.

    b. Select File → Print. A dialog box is displayed.

        1. Select OK. The table is printed.

    c. Close the Customers table.

④ FORMAT AND PRINT THE KITES TABLE

    a. Open the Kites table in Datasheet view.

    b. Double-click each field's right boundary. The columns are sized appropriately.

    c. Save the modified Kites table.

    d. Print and then close the Kites table.

⑤ FORMAT THE SALES TABLE

    a. Open the Sales table in Datasheet view.

    b. Double-click each field's right boundary. The columns are sized appropriately.

    c. Save, print, and then close the modified Sales table.

⑥ PRINT THE SALES RECORDS

    a. In the Kites Company : Database window, click Forms. The Customers, Kites, and Sales form names are listed.

    b. Double-click the Sales form name. The Sales form is displayed.

    c. Select File → Print. A dialog box is displayed.

        1. Select OK. The records are printed one after the other in a column.

    d. Close the Sales form.

13.14 Filtering

query

filter

A powerful feature of a relational database is its ability to perform queries. A *query* limits the records displayed to those that meet certain criteria. For example, The Kites Company database could be queried to display the records of Seagull kite sales. In Access, a *filter* can be used to to query a database.

criteria

The first step in filtering is to determine the criteria. The filter *criteria* specifies the data that a record must contain in order to be displayed. For example, the criteria when filtering for Seagull kite records is "SEA" in the ItemID field.

Filter by Form view

A filter can be applied to a displayed datasheet or form by clicking the Filter By Form button () on the toolbar, which displays a datasheet or form in *Filter by Form view*. For example, the Sales table in Filter by Form view looks similar to:

The Filter by Form view displays blank fields

Query criteria is specified by clicking a field box and selecting from the field list or typing a value. For example, clicking the ItemID field and then clicking the arrow displays a list of data in that field:

Clicking SEA enters it as the criteria.

After specifying the criteria, a filter is applied by clicking the Apply Filter button (⧩) on the toolbar. When the Sales filter is applied, there are 2 records that contain "SEA" in the ItemID field. The records that do not meet filter criteria are filtered from view, and are said to be hidden. *Hidden records* have not been deleted, they are just not currently displayed. The record controls at the bottom of the table or form indicate how many records meet the query criteria:

hidden records

Filtering Commands

Selecting <u>F</u>ilter by Form from the <u>F</u>ilter submenu in the <u>R</u>ecords menu displays a form or table in Filter by Form view. After entering the query criteria, a filter can be applied by selecting App<u>l</u>y Filter/Sort from the Filte<u>r</u> menu. Selecting <u>R</u>emove Filter/Sort from the <u>R</u>ecords menu will again display all the records in the table.

	SalesID	Date	CustomerID	ItemID	Quantity
▶	2	9/22/2003	SKC	SEA	32
	4	9/30/2003	GFK	SEA	24
✱	)Number)				0

Record: I◄ ◄ 1 ► ►I ►✱ of 2 (Filtered)

Two records meet the criteria

 All the records in a table or form are again displayed by clicking the Remove Filter button (🔽) on the toolbar.

13.15 Using Saved Filters

saving a filter

 Filters can be named and saved so that they can be applied again and again without having to repeatedly select criteria. A filter is saved by clicking the Save As Query button (💾) on the toolbar, which displays the Save As Query dialog box:

Save As Query ? ✕

Query Name:

Query1

OK

Cancel

The Save As Query Command

The Save As Query from the File menu can be used instead of the Save As Query button.

Typing a descriptive name for the filter and selecting OK adds a named query to the database. The Save As Query button is available in Filter by Form view before a filter is applied.

applying a saved filter

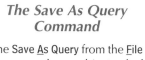

A saved filter is applied by first clicking Queries in the Database window to display the Query objects. Next, double-clicking a filter name or selecting a filter name and then clicking the Open button () on the Database window toolbar applies the filter and displays the results in Datasheet view.

deleting a saved filter

A saved filter is deleted by selecting its name in the Database window and then pressing the Delete key.

Practice 5 ⟳

In this practice you will apply and save filters. Open The Kite Company if it is not already displayed.

① DISPLAY THE SALES FORM

    a. In The Kite Company : Database window, click Tables if table names are not already displayed.

    b. Double-click the Sales table name. The Sales table is displayed.

② FILTER THE SALES RECORDS

    a. On the toolbar, click the Filter By Form button (🔳). The Sales table is displayed in Filter by Form view, which displays fields where criteria can be entered.

        1. Click the ItemID field and then click the arrow. A list is displayed that contains all the data in the ItemID field.

2. In the list, click SEA. The ItemID field displays "SEA".

3. On the toolbar, click the Apply Filter button (▽). Two records meet the criteria.

b. On the toolbar, click the Remove Filter button (▽). All the Sales records are again available.

③ *SAVE A FILTER*

a. On the toolbar, click the Filter By Form button (▦). The Sales table is displayed in Filter by Form view.

    1. In the ItemID field, select DRF.

    2. On the toolbar, select the Save As Query button (▥). A dialog box is displayed.

        a. Type Dragonfly Kite Sales.

        b. Select OK. The query is saved.

    3. On the toolbar, click the Apply Filter button (▽). Three records meet the criteria.

b. On the toolbar, click the Remove Filter button (▽). All the Sales records are again available.

c. Close the Sales table without saving changes.

④ *APPLY AND PRINT A SAVED FILTER*

a. In The Kite Company : Database window, click Queries. The Dragonfly Kite Sales query name is displayed.

b. Double-click the Dragonfly Kite Sales query to run it. The filter results are displayed.

c. Select File → Print. A dialog box is displayed.

    1. Select OK. The filter results are printed in a datasheet.

d. Close the datasheet.

13.16 Advanced Filtering

complex query

and

Criteria can be entered for more than one field in Filter by Form view. This type of query is called a *complex query* because the records are checked for more than one value. For example, The Kite Company Sales records could be filtered to display only the records of Dragonfly kites sold to the Go Fly a Kite company. The criteria for this filter is "DRF in the ItemID field *and* GFK in the CustomerID field"

or

Another type of complex query checks records for one value or another. For example, the Sales records could be filtered to display the records of Seagull and Ladybug kites sold. The criteria for this filter is "SEA in the ItemID field *or* LAD in the ItemID field". This kind of criteria is entered by using the Or tab at the bottom of the Filter by Form view window:

The Or tab allows multiple filter criteria to be used

Clicking the Or tab displays a blank Filter by Form view where additional criteria can be entered. Also, when the Or tab is clicked, a second Or tab appears making another Filter by Form view available, and so on. After the criteria is selected or typed, the filter is applied or saved as usual. For the Seagull and Ladybug Sales query, selecting SEA in the ItemID field of the first Filter by Form view, clicking the Or tab, selecting LAD in the ItemID field of the next Filter by Form view, and then applying the filter displays three records.

Practice 6

In this practice you will filter The Kite Company database. Open The Kite Company if it is not already displayed.

① *DISPLAY THE SALES TABLE*

② *APPLY A FILTER*

    a. On the toolbar, click the Filter By Form button (▦). The Sales table is displayed in Filter by Form view.

        1. In the ItemID field, select DRF.

        2. In the CustomerID field, select GFK.

        3. On the toolbar, click the Apply Filter button (▼). Two records meet the criteria.

    b. Print the filter results.

③ *FILTER THE SALES TABLE USING THE OR TAB*

    a. On the toolbar, click the Filter By Form button. The Sales table is displayed in Filter by Form view.

        1. In the ItemID field, select SEA.

        2. Delete any other criteria on the table.

        3. At the bottom of the Filter by Form view window, click the Or tab. A new, empty Filter by Form view is displayed.

        4. In the ItemID field, select LAD.

        5. On the toolbar, click the Apply Filter button. Three records meet the criteria.

    b. Print the filter results.

    c. On the toolbar, click the Remove Filter button. All the Sales records are again available.

④ *QUIT ACCESS*

Close the Sales table without saving it and then quit Access.

Chapter Summary

A computerized database is used to store related information. The Microsoft Access relational database can be used to store data and generate forms, queries, and reports from the stored data.

A database is organized into fields that store data. A field is defined by its name, type, size, and format. A field name should describe its contents and be unique. Field types include text, number, date/time, currency, memo, and AutoNumber. The size of a field is the number of characters or type of number it can store. Field format refers to how a field's data is displayed.

In a relational database, related fields are separated into tables that a rows of records and columns of fields. A record is data for a set of fields. A table must have a primary key, which is a field designated to contain unique data. The primary key of a table may also be a combination of fields designated to have a unique combination of entries.

A database should have a design, which is based on the three-step process of determining what information should be stored, dividing information into named tables, and defining the fields and determining the primary key for each table.

A relational database is created by selecting New Office Document from the Start menu. Access automatically periodically saves a database to the file and folder specified when the database was created.

Fields for a table are created when a new table is displayed in Design view. A field's name, type, size, and if necessary, the field's format including number of decimal places are entered in Design view. After the fields are created, the primary key is selected and then the table saved using a descriptive name. The Save command or the Save button on the toolbar is used to save the table.

A database should be closed when finished working on it by selecting the Close command or clicking the Close button in the Database window. A database can be opened by selecting the Open command or clicking the Open button on the toolbar. A database can also be opened by selecting Open Office Document from the Start menu. Access should be quit when no longer needed by selecting the Exit command.

A form is based on the fields of a table, and is used for entering and viewing records. A columnar form displays a record as one field below the other in a column. A form can be easily created using the Form Wizard.

The record controls at the bottom of a form are used for displaying a specific record in a table. A record is added to a database by typing data into a blank form. A blank form is displayed by clicking the (▶✱) control. The insertion point is moved from field to field by clicking a field box or by pressing the Tab or Enter keys. Existing entries can be changed by moving the insertion point to the field box and editing the data.

The View button on the toolbar is used to switch between Design view and Datasheet view. In Datasheet view, each row corresponds to a record and each column corresponds to a field. The record selector is the gray box to the left of each record and is used to make a record active.

In Datasheet view, column width is changed by dragging the right boundary of a column. Double-clicking on the right boundary of a column sizes the column so that it is just wide enough to display its field name and data entirely. A selected column is moved by dragging it to a new position.

A table displayed in Datasheet view can be printed by selecting the Print command or clicking the Print button. Printing a table in landscape orientation allows more columns on a sheet of paper. Selecting Print when a form is displayed prints the records one right after the other in a column. Only the active record is printed when the Select Record(s) option in the Print dialog box is selected.

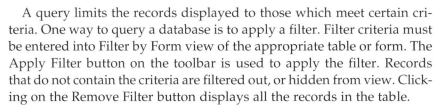

A query limits the records displayed to those which meet certain criteria. One way to query a database is to apply a filter. Filter criteria must be entered into Filter by Form view of the appropriate table or form. The Apply Filter button on the toolbar is used to apply the filter. Records that do not contain the criteria are filtered out, or hidden from view. Clicking on the Remove Filter button displays all the records in the table.

A filter is named and saved by clicking the Save As Query button on the toolbar. A saved filter can be applied again and again without having to repeatedly select criteria.

An "And" complex query is used to display records with data spcified for two or more fields. An "Or" complex query displays records with data that matches one of the specified entries for a particular field. This type of complex query uses the Or tab at the bottom of a Filter by Form view window.

Active field The field in Design view that contains the insertion point and displays ▶ to the left of its row.

Active record The record in a datasheet that displays ▶ to the left of its row.

And Used to describe criteria that requires a record to contain more than one value.

AutoNumber field A field that automatically stores a numeric value that is one greater than that in the last record added.

Boundary The bar separating the field names at the top of a table.

Columnar form A form that displays a record with one field below the other in a column.

Complex query A query that checks records for more than one value.

Computerized database Used to store related information.

Criteria The data a record must contain in order to be displayed by a filter.

Currency field A field that stores dollar amounts.

Data A piece of information in a database.

Datasheet A table in datasheet view.

Datasheet view The view used for displaying records in rows one after the other.

Date/Time field A field that stores a date or time.

Design view The table view that shows the field definitions for a table.

Field Used to store data in a database.

Filter Used to query an Access database.

Filter by Form view The view used for creating a filter.

Fixed A field format that displays a value to a specified number of decimal places.

Form A window that contains the fields of a table. Used for entering and viewing records.

Format The way in which data in a field is displayed.

General number A field format that displays a number exactly as entered.

Hidden records Records that have not been deleted, but are no longer displayed.

Long form A date/time format that displays data in a form similar to Friday, May 9, 2003 or 10:12:30 AM.

Long integer A field size that indicates a whole number.

Medium form A date/time format that displays data in a form similar to 24-June-03 or 10:12 AM.

Memo field A field that stores several lines of text.

Microsoft Access The database application in Microsoft Office.

Number field A field that stores only numeric values.

Or Used to describe criteria that requires a record to contain one value or another.

Percent A field format that multiplies the value entered by 100 and displays it with a % sign.

Primary key A field designated to contain unique data.

Query Used to limit the records displayed to those that meet certain criteria.

Record Data for a set of fields.

Record controls Used for displaying a specific record in a table. Located at the bottom of a form.

Record selector A gray box clicked to select a record in a datasheet. Located to the left of each record.

Required option Used to require data in the primary key field of a table. Located in the Field Properties part of a table in Design view.

Short form A date/time format that displays data in a form similar to 6/24/03 or 10:12.

Single A field size that indicates a number with a decimal portion.

Size The number of characters or the type of number a field can store.

Standard A field format that displays a value with the thousands separator, usually a comma.

Table A group of related fields.

Text field A field that stores characters (letters, symbols, words, a combination of letters and numbers).

Access Commands and Buttons

Apply Filter button   Applies a filter. Also used to remove a filter. Found on the toolbar.

Close button   Closes a table. Found in the upper-right corner of a table.

Close command   Closes a database. Found in the File menu. The Close button in the Database window can be used instead of the command.

Exit command   Quits Access. Found in the File menu. The Close button in the upper-right corner of the application window can be used instead of the command.

Filter By Form button   Displays a form or table in Filter by Form view. Found on the toolbar.

Forms   Displays the form objects. Found in the Database window.

New Office Document command   Displays the New Office Document dialog box. Found in the Start menu.

Open button   Opens a selected form, table, or query. Found on the Database window toolbar.

Open command   Displays a dialog box used to select a database to open. Found in the File menu. The Open button on the toolbar can be used instead of the command.

Open Office Document command   Displays the Open Office Document dialog box. Found in the Start menu.

Page Setup command   Displays a dialog box with print orientation options.

Primary Key command   Makes the active field the primary key. Found in the Edit menu. The Primary Key button on the toolbar can be used instead of the command.

Print command   Displays a dialog box used for printing a datasheet or form. Found in the File menu. The Print button on the toolbar can be used instead of the command.

Queries   Displays the query objects. Found in the Database window.

Save As Query button   Displays a dialog box for saving a filter. Found on the toolbar.

Save command   Saves a table. Found in the File menu. The Save button on the toolbar can be used instead of the command.

Tables   Displays the table objects. Found in the Database window.

View button   Switches a table between Design view and Datasheet view. Found on the toolbar.

Review Questions

Sections 13.1 — 13.13

1. a) Why is the present time called the Information Age?
    b) What is used to store related information?
    c) What is data?
    d) List two examples of digital information.

2. a) What is Microsoft Access?
    b) List three things an Access database can generate.

3. a) What is a field?
    b) What are four considerations when defining a field?
    c) Explain why a field that stores more than one piece of data is considered poor design.

4. List four guidelines that should be followed when choosing field names.

5. List six types of data that can be stored in a field.

6. a) What does the size of a field indicate?
   b) What field size should be used when a field will store numbers with a decimal portion?
   c) What field size should be used when a field will store whole numbers?

7. a) What does the format of a field determine?
   b) List four numeric field formats.
   c) List three data/time field formats.
   d) Do text fields have a field format?

8. a) What is used to group related fields?
   b) What is contained in a row in a table?
   c) What is a table?
   d) What is contained in a column in a table?

9. a) What is a primary key?
   b) Why is a primary key used?

10. List the three steps for designing a relational database.

11. a) Where is the name of a new database typed?
    b) How is a database saved?
    c) Why is it important to select the proper folder for a database when the database is created?
    d) Is it possible to save the database to a different folder after it is created?

12. Where is the Database window toolbar located?

13. a) What view is a new table created in?
    b) List the steps for creating a field in Design view.

14. a) What must be done to designate a primary key?
    b) What indicates a field is active?
    c) How can a different field be made active?
    d) What is the Required option in the Design view window used for?
    e) List the steps required to make two fields the primary key of a table.

15. a) What command or button is used to save a new table?
    b) List the steps required to close a table.

16. a) List the steps required to close a database.
    b) List the steps required to open an existing database.
    c) List the steps for quitting Access.

17. a) What is a form?
    b) How does a form make entering records less error-prone?
    c) What is a columnar form?

18. List the steps required to create a form.

19. List the steps required to open an existing form.

20. a) Where are the record controls located?
    b) What are they used for?

21. List the steps required to use a form to add a new record to a table that already contains records.

22. a) What is Datasheet view?
    b) List the steps required to make a record in a datasheet active.
    c) List the steps required to switch a table between Design view and Datasheet view.

23. a) What is the boundary in a datasheet?
    b) List two ways to change a column's width.
    c) List the steps required to change the order of fields.

24. a) How can more columns be printed on a sheet of paper?
    b) What option is used to print only the selected records?

Sections 13.14 — 13.16

25. a) What is a query?
    b) What is a filter?

26. What is criteria?

27. List the steps required to filter a database for records that have LAD in the ItemID field.

28. a) What are hidden records?
    b) How can hidden records be displayed?

29. List the steps required to save a filter.

30. List the steps required to apply a saved filter.

31. a) What is a complex query?
    b) What is the difference between an "or" query and an "and" query?

Exercise 1 ———————————————————————— FL COLLEGES

The FL COLLEGES database file contains one table with data about some of Florida's cities. An additional table is needed to complete the relational database. Open FL COLLEGES and complete the following steps:

a) Create a table that will store information on Florida colleges. After creating the fields below, save the table naming it Colleges:

Field Name	Data Type	Description	Size	Format	Decimals
Name 🔑	Text	Name of college	50		
City	Text	City location of college	25		
Enrollment	Number	Students attending	Long Integer	Standard	0

b) Create a form named Colleges for the Colleges table and enter the following seven records:

University of Central Florida; Orlando; 29,821
University of Florida; Gainesville; 42,000
Florida Atlantic University; Boca Raton; 19,562
Florida International University; Miami; 30,092
Florida State University; Tallahassee; 31,193
University of South Florida; Tampa; 23,502
University of West Florida; Pensacola; 8,081

c) Format the Colleges table in Datasheet view appropriately.

d) Print the Colleges table.

e) Create and save a filter named Dade County that displays the records of cities in Dade county. Display the Query objects and then apply Dade County. Print the query datasheet.

f) Create and save a filter named South Florida Colleges that displays the records of colleges in Boca Raton and Miami. Display the Query objects and then apply South Florida Colleges. Print the query datasheet.

Exercise 2 ———————————————————————— Museum Exhibits

Sunport Science Museum wants to use a relational database to store exhibit information.

a) Using Access, create a relational database naming it Museum Exhibits.

b) Create a table that contains the fields for the exhibits data. After creating the fields below, save the table naming it Exhibits:

Field Name	Data Type	Description	Size	Format
ExhibitID 🔑	Text	ID of permanent exhibit	4	
Name	Text	Name of exhibit	30	
Department	Text	Department exhibit is in	30	
Updated	Date/Time	Date exhibit was last updated		Short Date

c) Create a table that contains the fields for the attendance data for years 2002 through 2004. After creating the fields below, save the table naming it Attendance:

Field Name	Data Type	Description	Size	Format	Decimals
ExhibitID ⚷	Text	ID of permanent exhibit	4		
Year ⚷	Text	Year of attendance	4		
Attendance	Number	Number of people	Long Integer	Standard	0

Refer to page 13-7 for creating a multiple-field primary key. The ExhibitID and Year fields are the primary key because there can be only one record for a specific exhibit in a specific year.

d) Create a form named Exhibits for the Exhibits table and enter the following eight records:

LWL1; Minerals and Rocks; Land We Live On; 1/5/03
LWL2; Earth's Interior; Land We Live On; 3/6/02
LWL3; Atmosphere and Weather; Land We Live On; 5/3/01
SWD1; Oceans; Secrets of Water Depths; 5/3/02
SWD2; Fresh Water; Secrets of Water Depths; 7/12/03
SWD3; Lakes, Rivers & Streams; Secrets of Water Depths; 1/1/00
WDH2; Earthquakes & Hurricanes; Why Does That Happen; 2/7/02
WDH3; Volcanoes; Why Does That Happen; 11/23/01

e) Create a form named Attendance for the Attendance table and enter the following 27 records:

LWL1; 2002; 1,560   LWL1; 2003; 1,540   LWL1; 2004; 1,494
LWL2; 2002; 1,298   LWL2; 2003; 1,600   LWL2; 2004; 1,678
LWL3; 2002; 1,364   LWL3; 2003; 1,467   LWL3; 2004; 1,645
SWD1; 2002; 1,254   SWD1; 2003; 1,374   SWD1; 2004; 1,575
SWD2; 2002; 1,156   SWD2; 2003; 1,245   SWD2; 2004; 1,312
SWD3; 2002; 1,324   SWD3; 2003; 1,437   SWD3; 2004; 1,545
WDH1; 2002; 1,256   WDH1; 2003; 1,345   WDH1; 2004; 1,512
WDH2; 2002; 1,224   WDH2; 2003; 1,435   WDH2; 2004; 1,442
WDH3; 2002; 1,381   WDH3; 2003; 1,483   WDH3; 2004; 1,547

f) Format the Exhibits and Attendance tables in Datasheet view appropriately.

g) Print both tables.

h) Create and save a filter named Attendance for 2002 that displays the attendance records for the year 2002. Display the Query objects and then apply Attendance for 2002. Print the query datasheet.

Exercise 3 ——————————————————————— Library

The local library wants to use a relational database to store information on its books.

a) Using Access, create a relational database naming it Library.

b) Create a table that contains the fields for the books data. After creating the fields below, save the table naming it Books:

Field Name	DataType	Description	Size
ISBN ⚷	Text	International Standard Book Number	13
Title	Text	Title of book	50
Type	Text	Type of book	10
AuthorID	Text	ID of author	4

c) Create a table that contains the fields for the authors data. After creating the fields below, save the table naming it Authors:

Field Name	Data Type	Description	Size	Format
AuthorID 🔑	Text	ID of author	4	
FirstName	Text	First name of author	15	
LastName	Text	Last name of author	30	
Birth	Date/Time	Birth date		Short Date
Death	Date/Time	Death date		Short Date

d) Create a form named Books for the Books table and enter the following 12 records:

1-879233-01-0; My Wedding - Your Wedding; Family; KW23
1-879233-39-8; All The Presidents' Wives; History; CB12
1-879233-42-8; The Complete College Guide; Reference; TB22
1-879233-44-4; Appeasement In The Republic; History; CB12
1-879233-51-7; Build Your Muscles; Health; SZ04
1-879233-56-8; The Orange Tide; Drama; KW23
1-879233-57-6; Effective Management Skills; Business; MS12
1-879233-59-0; The Dog Wore a Red Coat; Mystery; ZT19
1-879233-62-2; Asian Alliances; History; CB12
1-879233-82-7; Healthy Eating; Health; SZ04
1-879233-84-3; Reading the Butler's Writing; Mystery; ZT19
1-879233-92-4; The Gold Necklace; Mystery; ZT19

e) Create a form named Authors for the Authors table and enter the following six records:

CB12; Carrie; Brennan; 6/12/1909; 12/3/1996
KW23; Karen; Willamson; 10/23/1974
MS12; Monica; Saliguero; 10/12/1912; 3/16/1990
SZ04; Slim; Zhorbyzki; 2/4/1959; 11/11/1993
TB22; Tomica; Broswell; 7/22/1921; 9/6/1992
ZT19; Zachery; Toening; 3/19/1923; 6/20/1989

f) Format the Books and Authors tables in Datasheet view appropriately.

g) Print both tables.

h) Create and save a filter named Mystery Novels that displays the records of books that are mystery novels. Display the Query objects and then apply Mystery Novels. Print the query datasheet.

Exercise 4 — Space Shuttle Missions

Orbiter vehicles, astronauts, and mission data can be maintained in a relational database.

a) Using Access, create a relational database naming it Space Shuttle Missions.

b) Create a table that contains the fields for the orbiter vehicle data. After creating the fields below, save the table naming it Orbiter Vehicles:

Field Name	Data Type	Description	Size	Format
OrbiterID 🔑	Text	ID of vehicle	6	
Name	Text	Name of vehicle	15	
RolloutDate	Date/Time	Date vehicle completed		Short Date

c) Create a table that contains the fields for the astronaut data. After creating the fields below, save the table naming it Astronauts:

Field Name	Data Type	Description	Size	Format	Decimals
AstronautID ⚷	Text	ID of astronaut	4		
FirstName	Text	First name of astronaut	15		
LastName	Text	Last name of astronaut	30		
BirthYear	Number	Year born	Long Integer	Fixed	0
TotalMissions	Number	Completed missions	Long Integer	Standard	0

d) Create a table that contains the fields for the mission data. After creating the fields below, save the table naming it Missions:

Field Name	Data Type	Description	Size
MissionID ⚷	Text	ID of mission	6
CommanderID	Text	ID of commander	4
OrbiterID	Text	ID of vehicle	6
LaunchDate	Date/Time	Date of launch	Short Date

e) Create a form named Orbiter Vehicles for the Orbiter Vehicles table and enter the following four records:

OV-102; Columbia; 3/8/79
OV-103; Discovery; 10/16/83
OV-104; Atlantis; 3/6/85
OV-105; Endeavour; 4/25/91

f) Create a form named Astronauts for the Astronauts table and enter the following four records:

EC-1; Eileen; Collins; 1956; 3
JC-1; John; Casper; 1943; 4
LS-1; Loren; Shriver; 1944; 3
RC-1; Robert; Cabana; 1949; 4

g) Create a form named Missions for the Missions table and enter the following eight records:

STS-31; JC-1; OV-103; 4/24/90   STS-65; RC-1; OV-102; 7/8/94
STS-46; LS-1; OV-104; 7/31/92   STS-77; JC-1; OV-105; 5/19/96
STS-54; JC-1; OV-105; 1/13/93   STS-88; RC-1; OV-105; 12/4/98
STS-62; JC-1; OV-102; 3/4/94   STS-93; EC-1; OV-102; 7/23/99

h) Format the tables in Datasheet view appropriately.

i) Print the tables.

j) Create and save a filter named OV-102 Missions that displays the missions of the orbiter vehicle with ID OV-102. Display the Query objects and then apply OV-102 Missions. Print the query datasheet.

Exercise 5 ———————————————————————— Boat Storage

Sunport Boat Storage wants to use a relational database to store information on its business.

a) Using Access, create a relational database naming it Boat Storage.

b) Create a table that contains the fields for the employee data. After creating the fields below, save the table naming it Employees:

Field Name	Data Type	Description	Size
EmployeeID 🔑	Text	ID of employee	4
FirstName	Text	First name of employee	15
LastName	Text	Last name of employee	30
Address	Text	Street address of employee	50
City	Text	City employee lives in	15
State	Text	State employee lives in	2
Zip	Text	Zip code of employee	10
Phone	Text	Phone number of employee	14

c) Create a table that contains the fields for the boat data. After creating the fields below, save the table naming it Boats:

Field Name	Data Type	Description	Size	Decimals
Boat 🔑	Text	Name of boat	30	
SlotNumber	Number	Slot boat is stored	Long Integer	
EmployeeID	Text	Employee in charge of boat	4	
Fee	Currency	Monthly maintenance fee		0
OwnerID	Number	ID of boat's owner	Long Integer	

d) Create a table that contains the fields for the boat owners data. After creating the fields below, save the table naming it Boat Owners:

Field Name	Data Type	Description	Size
OwnerID 🔑	AutoNumber	ID of owner of a boat	Long Integer
FirstName	Text	First name of owner	15
LastName	Text	Last name of owner	30
Address	Text	Street address of owner	50
City	Text	City owner lives in	15
State	Text	State owner lives in	2
Zip	Text	Zip code of owner	10
Phone	Text	Phone number of owner	14

e) Create a form named Employees for the Employees table and enter the following five records:

DK86; Denita; Kilcullen; 86 Hampshire Road; Cody; WA; 12232-1207; (617) 555-1229
HW28; Hillary; Walker; 1221 Rockledge Ave.; Cody; WA; 12232-1209; (617) 555-9800
NG12; Nate; Gervin; NE 66th Plaza; Rostock; WA; 12241; (617) 555-9462
SM23; Sherman; MacGragor; 2334 12th Ave.; Cody; WA; 12232-1207; (617) 555-0993
YA12; Yvette; Archibald; 13 Cypress Creed Rd.; Rostock; WA; 12241; (617) 555-7822

f) Create a form named Boats for the Boats table and enter the following 10 records:

Donned Upon You; 10; NG12; 70; 6
Jenny; 5; YA12; 62; 4
Just Desserts; 4; SM23; 50; 3
Monkey Business; 3; HW28; 86; 2
Shooting Star; 16; HW28; 77; 1

SteadyAsSheGoes; 13; DK86; 60; 5
The Sugar Queen; 12; NG12; 45; 4
Tidal Wave; 17; SM23; 55; 2
UR Behind Me; 9; DK86; 65; 5
Viking 5; 2; SM23; 55; 1

g) Create a form named Boat Owners for the Boat Owners table and enter the following six records:

Rachell; Gundarssohn; 1671 Westchester Ave.; Poliney; WA; 12245; (232) 555-0912
Pamela; Hogart; 12 Street; Monterey; WA; 12259-4761; (232) 555-7021
Dermont; Voss; 1087 67th Terrace; Monterey; WA; 12259-4761; (232) 555-9000
Zane; McCaffrey; 689 King Blvd.; Poliney; WA; 12245-3309; (232) 555-7492
Bethany; Mulberry; 8625 West View Drive Apt. 9; Rostock; WA; 12241; (617) 555-6524
Damon; Deitrich; 4567 Sandalwood Ave.; Poliney; WA; 12245; (232) 555-2651

h) Format the Employees, Boats, and Boat Owners tables in Datasheet view appropriately.

i) Print all the tables in landscape orientation.

j) Create and save a filter named OwnerID 5 Boats that displays the boat records with OwnerID 5. Display the Query objects and then apply OwnerID 5 Boats. Print the query datasheet.

Exercise 6 ———————————————— Ivy U Athletics

Ivy University's Athletic department wants to use a relational database to store information on Ivy University's sports teams.

a) Using Access, create a relational database naming it Ivy U Athletics.

b) Create a table that contains the fields for the players data. After creating the fields below, save the table naming it Players:

Field Name	Data Type	Description	Size
StudentID 🔑	Text	ID of student	5
FirstName	Text	First name of student	15
LastName	Text	Last name of student	30
Sport	Text	Sport the student plays	20
Position	Text	Position the student plays	20

c) Create a table that contains the fields for the sports data. After creating the fields below, save the table naming it Sports:

Field Name	Data Type	Description	Size	Decimals
Sport 🔑	Text	Name of sport	20	
Semester	Text	Semester sport is played	10	
Budget	Currency	Budget for sport		0

d) Create a table that contains the fields for the coaches data. After creating the fields below, save the table naming it Coaches:

Field Name	Data Type	Description	Size	Decimals
CoachID 🔑	Text	ID of coach	5	
FirstName	Text	First name of coach	15	
LastName	Text	Last name of coach	30	
Sport	Text	Sport coached	20	
CoachTitle	Text	Title of coach	20	
Salary	Currency	Yearly salary for coach		0

e) Create a form named Players for the Players table and enter the following eight records:

AS918; Adam; Schneider; Basketball; Shooting Guard
AY245; Alyssa; Yaniv; Basketball; Center
DM887; Derek; Mohatheny; Football; Linebacker
EW265; Emilia; Watson; Softball; Pitcher
JW387; Jody; Wainwright; Softball; First Base
LP338; Lorenzo; Pearson; Football; Tailback
MD286; Myrna; Dixon; Softball; Centerfield
MS416; Matt; Silverstein; Basketball; Power Forward

f) Create a form named Sports for the Sports table and enter the following three records:

Basketball; Spring; 451,000
Football; Fall; 891,000
Softball; Spring; 256,000

g) Create a form named Coaches for the Coaches table and enter the following six records:

AR729; Alex; Rodriguez; Football; Head Coach; 102,000
BK122; Brian; Klitch; Basketball; Assistant Coach; 23,000
DW655; Diane; Whitman; Football; Defensive Coach; 41,000
JD113; Jeffrey; Dytko; Basketball; Head Coach; 86,000
MK541; Mary; Klinghoffer; Softball; Manager; 56,000
RB918; Regina; Baker; Softball; First Base Coach; 31,000

h) Format the Players, Sports, and Coaches tables in Datasheet view appropriately.

i) Print all the tables.

j) Create and save a filter named Softball Pitchers that displays the players records where softball is the sport and pitcher is the position. Display the Query objects and then apply Softball Pitchers. Print the query datasheet.

Exercise 7 —————————————————————— Second Ocean

Second Ocean specializes in relocating injured sea animals to facilities that can care for them.

a) Using Access, create a relational database naming it Second Ocean.

b) Create a table that contains the fields for the animals data. After creating the fields below, save the table naming it Animals:

Field Name	Data Type	Description	Size	Format
AnimalID 🔑	AutoNumber	ID number of animal		
DateOfRescue	Date/Time	Date animal was rescued		Short Date
Type	Text	Type of animal		
ApproxAge	Number	Approximate age of animal	Long Integer	
Gender	Text	Gender of animal - M/F	1	
Facility	Text	Facility animal relocated to	20	

c) Create a table that contains the fields for the facilities data. After creating the fields below, save the table naming it Facilities:

Field Name	Data Type	Description	Size
Facility 🔑	Text	Name of facility	20
State	Text	State facility is located	2
FirstName	Text	First name of contact person	15
LastName	Text	Last name of contact person	30

d) Second Ocean checks on the progress of the animals they have relocated. Create a table that contains the fields for the facilities checks data. After creating the fields below, save the table naming it Facility Checks:

Field Name	Data Type	Description	Size	Format
CheckID 🔑	AutoNumber	ID of facility check		
Date	Date/Time	Date of check		Short Date
Facility	Text	Name of facility	20	
AnimalID	Number	ID number of animal checked	Long Integer	

e) Create a form named Animals for the Animals table and enter the following five records:

8/11/03; Dolphin; 2; F; Ocean World   2/1/03; Whale; 20; F; Ocean Care
6/5/03; Manatee; 3; M; Animal Help   4/20/03; Dolphin; 10; M; Ocean World
7/15/03; Manatee; 6; F; Animal Help

f) Create a form named Facilities for the Facilities table and enter the following three records:

Animal Help; FL; Mike; Gershberg
Ocean Care; FL; Caitlin; Porter
Ocean World; CA; Paula; Angelocci

g) Create a form named Facility Checks for the Facility Checks table and enter the following eight records:

3/25/03; Ocean World; 1   10/14/03; Ocean World; 5
6/19/03; Animal Help; 2   10/14/03; Ocean World; 1
6/19/03; Animal Help; 3   11/12/03; Animal Help; 3
8/15/03; Ocean Care; 4   12/22/03; Ocean Care; 4

h) Format the Animals, Facilities, and Facility Checks tables in Datasheet view appropriately.

i) Print all the tables.

j) Create and save a filter named Rescued Dolphins that displays the dolphin records. Display the Query objects and then apply Dolphins. Print the query datasheet.

Exercise 8 ——————————————————————— Green Thumb

Green Thumb is a plant nursery that wants to use a relational database to store information on its plants and sales.

a) Using Access, create a relational database naming it Green Thumb.

b) Create a table that contains the fields for the plants data. After creating the fields below, save the table naming it Plants:

Field Name	Data Type	Description	Size	Decimals
PlantID 🔑	Text	ID of plant	3	
Plant	Text	Name of plant	15	
InStock	Number	Number of plants in stock	Long Integer	
Reorder	Number	When to reorder plants	Long Integer	
Cost	Currency	Price paid for plant		2
Retail	Currency	Selling price of plant		2
VendorID	Text	ID of vendor	2	

c) Create a table that contains the fields for the plant sales data. After creating the fields below, save the table naming it Transactions:

Field Name	Data Type	Description	Size	Format
TransID 🔑	AutoNumber	ID of transaction		
Date	Date/Time	Date of transaction		Short Date
PlantID	Text	ID of plant purchased	3	
Quantity	Number	Number of plants purchased	Long Integer	

d) Create a table that contains the fields for the vendors data. After creating the fields below, save the table naming it Vendors:

Field Name	Data Type	Description	Size
VendorID 🔑	Text	ID of vendor	2
Name	Text	Name of vendor	30
Address	Text	Street address of vendor	50
City	Text	City where vendor is	15
State	Text	State where vendor is	2
Zip	Text	Zip code where vendor is	10
Phone	Text	Phone number of vendor	14
ContactFirstName	Text	First name of contact	15
ContactLastName	Text	Last name of contact	30

e) Create a form named Plants for the Plants table and enter the following five records:

Cac; Cactus; 60; 35; 4.99; 8.25; V2   Tul; Tulip; 15; 25; 7.99; 10.50; V3
Frn; Fern; 60; 50; 3.50; 5.75; V1   VF; Venus Flytrap; 45; 25; 7.99; 13.50; V2
Hib; Hibiscus; 10; 40; 10.99; 25.00; V1

f) Create a form named Transactions for the Transactions table and enter the following 11 records:

10/23/03; Frn; 10   11/10/03; VF; 10
10/25/03; Tul; 3   11/15/03; Cac; 2
10/25/03; Cac; 12   11/17/03; Hib; 3
11/3/03; Frn; 3   11/24/03; Tul; 5
11/6/03; Hib; 2   11/29/03; VF; 6
11/7/03; Tul; 2

g) Create a form named Vendors for the Vendors table and enter the following three records:

V1; Plantsalot; 1661 S. Yancy Ct.; Norman; OK; 44541; (617) 555-6122; Herbert; Mancini

V2; All Things Green; 30 Benton Dr.; Durango; CO; 89904-0768; (912) 555-0265; Zeke; Mowatt

V3; Green Machines; 8429 W. 45th Ave.; Peducha; KY; 54426; (662) 555-2815; Abigail; Vanover

h) Format the Plants, Transactions, and Vendors tables in Datasheet view appropriately.

i) Print all the tables in landscape orientation.

j) Create and save a filter named Frn Transactions that displays the transactions records for PlantID Frn. Display the Query objects and then apply Frn Transactions. Print the query datasheet.

Exercise 9 — Pizza Payroll

The owner of Pizza Palace wants to use a relational database to store information on the company's employees and payroll.

a) Using Access, create a relational database naming it Pizza Payroll.

b) Create a table that contains the fields for the employees data. After creating the fields below, save the table naming it Employees:

Field Name	Data Type	Description	Size
EmployeeID 🔑	Text	ID of employee	2
FirstName	Text	First name of employee	15
LastName	Text	Last name of employee	30
Address	Text	Street address of employee	50
City	Text	City employee lives in	15
State	Text	State employee lives in	2
Zip	Text	Zip code of employee	10
Phone	Text	Phone number of employee	14

c) Create a table that contains the fields for the payroll data. After creating the fields below, save the table naming it Payroll:

Field Name	Data Type	Description	Size	Format	Decimals
EmployeeID 🔑	Text	ID of employee	2		
Date 🔑	Date/Time	Date of paycheck		Short Date	
GrossPay	Currency	Employee's gross pay			2
Taxes	Currency	Tax deductions			2

Refer to page 13-7 for creating a multiple-field primary key. The EmployeeID and Date fields are the primary key because there can be only one record for a specific employee on a specific date.

d) Create a form named Employees for the Employees table and enter the following five records:

EI; Edna; Incahatoe; 254 20th St.; Armine; CT; 19154-7901; (332) 555-1765
JF; Jess; Frank; 101 Red Villa Circle; Armine; CT; 19154-7901; (332) 555-2792
RD; Rita; DiPasquale; 5672 56th Ct.; Weidner; CT; 77165-3342; (332) 555-0276
TW; Thomas; Warner; 11 Roni Dr.; Weidner; CT; 77165-3342; (332) 555-2665
WF; Wimberly; Franco; 86 Luther Ct.; Weidner; CT; 77165-9088; (332) 555-1711

e) Create a form named Payroll for the Payroll table and enter the following 10 records:

EI; 3/13/03; 244; 36.60
EI; 3/20/03; 254; 38.10
JF; 3/20/03; 191.67; 28.75
JF; 3/27/03; 210.75; 31.50
RD; 3/6/03; 175; 26.25

RD; 3/13/03; 180; 27
TW; 3/6/03; 210.24; 31.53
TW; 3/13/03; 225.64; 33.84
WF; 3/13/03; 187.82; 28.17
WF; 3/20/03; 195.25; 29.28

f) Format the Employees and Payroll tables in Datasheet view appropriately and then print all the tables in landscape orientation.

g) Create and save a filter named WF 3/13/03 Payroll that displays the payroll for the employee with ID WF for the pay date 3/13/03. Display the Query objects and then apply WF 3/13/03 Payroll. Print the query datasheet.

The researchers who created the coral reef study proposal you edited in previous chapters want to create a relational database to store their research findings.

a) Using Access, create a relational database naming it Coral Research.

b) Create a table that contains the fields for the coral data. After creating the fields below, save the table naming it Coral Sites:

Field Name	Data Type	Description	Size
SiteID 🔑	AutoNumber	ID of site location	Long Integer
CoralName	Text	Name of coral	20
Color	Text	Main color of coral	15
Description	Text	Identifying features	30

c) Create a table that contains the fields for the growth data. After creating the fields below, save the table naming it Growth Research:

Field Name	Data Type	Description	Size	Format	Decimals
Date 🔑	Date/Time	Date of observation		Short Date	
SiteID 🔑	Number	Location of the coral	Long Integer		
Time	Date/Time	Time of observation		Medium Time	
Size	Number	Coral size in meters	Single		3

Refer to page 13-7 for creating a multiple-field primary key. The Date and SiteID fields are the primary key because there can only be one record for a specific site on a specific date.

d) Create a form named Coral Sites for the Coral Sites table and enter the following five records:

Slimy Sea Plume; violet; feather-like
Yellow Sea Whip; bright yellow; branched colonies
Knobby Brain Coral; tan; hemispherical heads
Scroll Coral; light gray; rounded, thin blades
Venus Sea Fan; lavender; network of branches

e) Create a form named Growth Research for the Growth Research table and enter the following six records:

5/8/03; 1; 6:10 AM; 0.8378
5/12/03; 2; 8:15 AM; 0.2045
5/25/03; 3; 7:25 AM; 0.144

6/2/03; 4; 6:35 AM; 1.387
5/11/04; 2; 8:15 AM; 0.205
6/4/04; 4; 6:35 AM; 1.389

f) Format the Coral Sites and Growth Research tables in Datasheet view appropriately.

g) Print both tables.

h) Create and save a filter named Growth Data for Site 2 that displays the growth research records for the site with ID 2. Display the Query objects and then apply Growth Data for Site 2. Print the query datasheet.

Exercise 11 ————————————————————————

The Hot Spot travel agency wants to use a relational database to store travel bookings.

a) Using Access, create a relational database naming it Travel Agency.

b) Create a table that contains the fields for the clients data. After creating the fields below, save the table naming it Clients:

Field Name	Data Type	Description	Size
ClientID 🔑	Text	ID of client	2
FirstName	Text	First name of client	15
LastName	Text	Last name of client	30
Address	Text	Street address of client	50
City	Text	City client lives in	15
State	Text	State client lives in	2
Zip	Text	Zip code of client	10
Phone	Text	Phone number of client	14

c) Create a table that contains the fields for the vacation packages data. After creating the fields below, save the table naming it Vacations:

Field Name	Data Type	Description	Size	Decimals
Package 🔑	Text	Name of vacation package	20	
Cost	Currency	Cost of vacation		0
Nights	Number	Number of nights	Long Integer	
Location	Text	State/Country of vacation	30	
Type	Text	Type of vacation	15	

d) Create a table that contains the fields for the purchased packages data. After creating the fields below, save the table naming it Booked Vacations:

Field Name	Data Type	Description	Size	Format
ClientID 🔑	Text	ID of client	2	
Date 🔑	Date/Time	Date vacation started		Short Date
Package	Text	Name of vacation package	20	

The primary key for the Booked Vacations table is the ClientID and Date fields together because there can be only one record for a specific client on a specific date.

e) Create a form named Clients for the Clients table and enter the following six records:

DM; Diane; Mason; 8 Westchester Place; Bedrock; IL; 56224-9987; (445) 555-1552
GM; Gail; Mintzer; 8891 SW 63rd Circle; Wilbraham; IL 76209-0324; (298) 555-7392
HQ; Harvey; Quay; 33 Buren Blvd. Apt. 452; Wilbraham; IL 76209-0324; (298) 555-7782
JU; Juan; Ulloa; 352 Eagle Trace Blvd.; Bedrock; IL; 56224-9987; (445) 555-0287
RP; Richard; Pompeneur; 240 Keisha St.; Bedrock; IL; 56224-9988; (445) 555-0208
SV; Sandy; Vanderhorn; 12 343rd Terrace; Wilbraham; IL; 56624-9988; (445) 555-8927

f) Create a form named Vacations for the Vacations table and enter the following seven records:

Beach Fun; 475; 7; Bahamas; Relaxing
City Dude; 725; 5; Texas; Adventure
French Getaway; 1,525; 7; France; Sightseeing
HighRiser Crusade; 823; 8; New York; Sightseeing
Honolulu Hideaway; 950; 3; Hawaii; Relaxing
Mountain Explorer; 420; 3; Vermont; Ski
Summit Skiing; 1,250; 5; Switzerland; Ski

g) Create a form named Booked Vacations for the Booked Vacations table and enter the following nine records:

DM; 4/21/03; HighRiser Crusade   JU; 5/20/03; Beach Fun
GM; 1/5/03; Honolulu Hideaway   JU; 12/13/03; Summit Skiing
GM; 11/4/03; HighRiser Crusade   RP; 11/23/03; Mountain Explorer
HQ; 2/16/03; Mountain Explorer   SV; 10/18/03; City Dude
JU; 12/8/02; French Getaway

h) Format the Clients, Vacations, and Booked Vacations tables in Datasheet view appropriately.

i) Print all the tables in landscape orientation.

j) Create and save a filter named Adventure or Relaxing Vacations that displays the vacation records that are adventure or relaxing types. Display the Query objects and then apply Adventure or Relaxing Vacations. Print the query datasheet.

Exercise 12 (advanced) ———————————————— Club

Design a relational database that organizes and stores information on a club or organization you belong to. Follow the four guidelines in Section 13.4 to design the database. Use Access to create the relational database naming it Club. Create a form for each table and enter at least five records in each table. Format the tables in Datasheet view appropriately. Print all the tables in your relational database in the appropriate orientation. Create and save a filter that queries one of the tables and print the results.

Exercise 13 (advanced) ———————————————— Music

Design a relational database that organizes and stores information on past or upcoming music events and performers. Follow the four guidelines in Section 13.4 to design the database. Use Access to create the relational database naming it Music. Create a form for each table and enter at least five records in each table. Format the tables in Datasheet view appropriately. Print all the tables in your relational database in the appropriate orientation. Create and save a filter that queries one of the tables and print the results.

Exercise 14 (advanced) ———————————————— Sports

Design a relational database that organizes and stores information on your favorite sports teams or sports event. Follow the four guidelines in Section 13.4 to design the database. Use Access to create the relational database naming it Sports. Create a form for each table and enter at least five records in each table. Format the tables in Datasheet view appropriately. Print all the tables in your relational database in the appropriate orientation. Create and save a filter that queries one of the tables and print the results.

Relational Database Techniques

Delete Rows

Sort Ascending

Sort Descending

Delete Record

Relationships

Save

Expand All

Collapse All

Run

Show Table

Save As

Chapter 14 Expectations

After completing this chapter you will be able to:
1. Add, rename, and delete a field.
2. Sort records.
3. Add, update, and delete a record.
4. Define relationships.
5. View a table's subdatasheets.
6. Create and use select queries.
7. Modify a select query.
8. Sort select query results.
9. Create range queries.
10. Create and use complex select queries.
11. Create queries using wildcards.

This chapter explains how to modify a table and the records in a table. Changing the order that records are displayed in a datasheet is introduced, and querying with select queries is explained.

14.1 Modifying a Table and Updating a Form

A table can be modified by adding a new field, changing a field name, or deleting a field. Modifications should be done only after carefully considering and reviewing the original database design.

A table should be modified in Design view, which is displayed by clicking **Tables** in the Database window, selecting a table name, and then selecting the Design button ( ) on the Database window toolbar. A table displayed in Datasheet view can be switched to Design view by clicking the View button ( ) on the toolbar.

adding a field

A field is added by typing a name, selecting a type, and typing a description in the blank row after the last existing field in table Design view. Next, the field size, format, and decimal places, if necessary, are selected in the **Field Properties** part of the window.

renaming a field

A field is renamed by placing the insertion point in a **Field Name** box in table Design view, editing the existing text, and then pressing Enter.

deleting a field

A field is deleted by right-clicking a field name in table Design view and then selecting **Delete Rows** from the menu, which displays a warning dialog box:

| Primary Key |
| Cut |
| Copy |
| Paste |
| Insert Rows |
| **Delete Rows** |
| Build... |
| Properties |

Microsoft Access   ☒

⚠ **Do you want to permanently delete the selected field(s) and all the data in the field(s)?**
To permanently delete the field(s), click Yes.

[Yes]   [No]

Selecting **Yes** removes the field and any data in that field from every record in the table. Selecting **No** retains the field.

updating a form

A form is not automatically updated when a table is modified. The best way to update a form is by creating a new one as explained in Chapter 13. The new form should be given the same name as the original, which displays a warning dialog box. Selecting **Yes** replaces the existing form with the new, updated form.

14.2 Sonting Records

alphabetical
chronological

Placing records in a specified order is called *sorting*. In Access, records can be sorted in either ascending or descending order based on the data in a specified field. Ascending order is also called *alphabetical order* when a sort is based on a text field, and *chronological order* when a sort is based on a date/time field.

The Sort Ascending (⬆) and Sort Descending (⬇) buttons on the toolbar are used to sort records. Clicking a sort button orders records in a table based on the data in the field that contains the insertion point. For example, to place the records in The Kite Company Sales table in alphabetical order by customer ID, the CustomerID field is clicked to place the insertion point in that field. Next, clicking the Sort Ascending button orders the records based on customer ID.

Sorting the records of a table does not affect the order of the records in a form. The records in a form are ordered by clicking a field box and then clicking the appropriate sort button.

⬆ Sort Ascending
⬇ Sort Descending

The Sort Ascending and Sort Descending commands in the Sort submenu in the Records menu can also be used to sort records.

Practice 1 ↻

In this practice you will modify the Sales table of The Kite Company database, update the Sales form, and sort the Sales table and form.

① *OPEN THE KITE COMPANY*

Open The Kite Company database, which was last modified in Chapter 13, Practice 6.

② *DISPLAY THE SALES TABLE IN DESIGN VIEW*

a. In The Kite Company : Database window, click Tables if table names are not already displayed.

b. Click Sales to select it.

c. On The Kite Company : Database window toolbar, click the Design button (🔨 Design). The Sales table is displayed in Design view.

③ *EDIT THE DATE FIELD*

a. Edit the Date field name so that it now reads SalesDate.

b. Select File → Save. The modified Sales table is saved.

c. On the toolbar, click the View button (▦ ▾). The Sales table is displayed in Datasheet view. Note the SalesDate field in place of the Date field.

d. Close the Sales table.

④ *UPDATE THE SALES FORM*

a. In The Kite Company : Database window, click Forms.

b. Double-click the Create form by using wizard icon. A dialog box is displayed.

1. In the Tables/Queries list, select Table: Sales. The fields of the Sales table are displayed in the Available Fields list.

2. Click >> . All the fields from the Available Fields list are moved to the Selected Fields list.

A Guide to Microsoft Office XP Professional

3. Select Next. The form layout options are displayed.

4. Select Columnar if it is not already selected.

5. Select Next. The form style options are displayed.

6. Select Standard if it is not already selected.

7. Select Next. The dialog box displays a box for the form title and an option for viewing the form.

8. In the What title do you want for your form? box, replace the current name with Sales.

9. Select Open the form to view or enter information if it is not already selected.

10. Select Finish. A dialog box is displayed.

    a. Select Yes. The new form replaced the existing form. Note the SalesDate field name.

⑤ *SORT THE SALES FORM*

  a. Click in the CustomerID field box. The insertion point is in the CustomerID field.

  b. On the toolbar, click the Sort Descending button (Z↓).

  c. Use the record controls at the bottom of the form to scroll through the records. Note that the records are now in reverse alphabetical order by customer ID.

  d. Save and then close the form.

⑥ *SORT THE SALES TABLE*

  a. Display the Sales table. Note the table is not sorted based on customer ID.

  b. Click a data entry in the CustomerID field. The insertion point is in the CustomerID field.

  c. On the toolbar, click the Sort Ascending button (A↓). Note that the records are now in alphabetical order by customer ID.

  d. Save and then close the table.

14.3 Modifying Records

Records can be modified by adding new records, changing the data in existing records, and deleting records. Records should be modified using the appropriate form because a form displays only one record at a time, which reduces the possibility of errors.

adding a record

A new record is added by clicking the ▶∗ record control at the bottom of a form to display a blank record and then typing the data for the new record.

updating

Changing the data in an existing record is called *updating*. The record controls at the bottom of a form can be used to scroll until the record for updating is displayed. Alternatively, a filter may be applied to quickly find a record. Double-clicking a data entry and then typing replaces the existing data. Clicking a data entry places the insertion point so that the data can be edited.

The Delete Record button (⊠) on the toolbar is used to delete the current record displayed in a form. Delete Record from the Edit menu may also be used. The record controls at the bottom of a form can be used to display the record for deleting. Access displays a warning dialog box before a record is deleted:

```
Microsoft Access                                    [X]

    ⚠    You are about to delete 1 record(s).

         If you click Yes, you won't be able to undo this Delete operation.
         Are you sure you want to delete these records?

              [   Yes   ]        [   No   ]
```

Selecting Yes removes the active record. Selecting No retains the record.

Practice 2 ⟳

In this practice you will modify records in The Kite Company database. Open The Kite Company if it is not already displayed.

① ADD A NEW SALES RECORD

    a. Display the Sales form.

    b. At the bottom of the form, click ▶✳ to display an empty record.

    c. Since the SalesID field is type AutoNumber, there is no need to type data in that field. Starting with the SalesDate field, type the remaining data for the new transaction record:

       10/24/03; SKC; LAD; 15

    d. Close the form.

    e. Display the Sales table. Note the new record.

    f. Close the Sales table.

② UPDATE A KITES RECORD

    a. Display the Kites form.

    b. On the toolbar, click the Filter By Form button. The Kites form is displayed in Filter by Form view.

       1. In the ItemName field, select the Box entry.

       2. Delete any other criteria, if any appears.

       3. On the toolbar, click the Apply Filter button. The Box kite record is displayed.

    c. Click the ItemName box to place the insertion point.

    d. Change the data to Winged Box.

    e. On the toolbar, click the Remove Filter button.

    f. Close the Kites form.

    g. Display the Kites table. Note the updated record.

    h. Save and then close the Kites table.

14.4 Defining Relationships

related   Two tables are *related* when a field in one table corresponds to a field in another table. Every table in a relational database must be related to at least one other table in the database. For example, in The Kite Company database, the Sales and Kites tables are related by the ItemID field and the Customers table is related to the Sales table by the CustomerID field.

Access needs to know the relationships between tables so that data can be joined appropriately. For two fields to define a relationship, the type of data they store must be the same, such as two text fields or two numeric fields. The field names are also typically the same, but this is not required.

Relationships are defined by clicking the Relationships button () on the toolbar or selecting Relationships from the Tools menu, which displays the Relationships window. If relationships have not yet been defined for a database, the Show Table dialog box is automatically displayed:

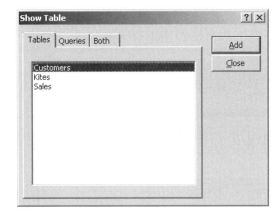

Clicking a table name and then selecting Add adds that table to the Relationships window. Clicking Close removes the Show Table dialog box. All of the tables in a database must be added to the Relationships window if relationships have not been defined. For The Kite Company database, the Relationships window with all the tables added looks similar to:

A relationship is created by dragging a field from one table to a related field in another table. When a field is dragged into another table, it appears as a small box. For The Kite Company database, the relationship between the Customers and Sales tables is defined by dragging the CustomerID field of the Customers table to the CustomerID field of the Sales table:

Displaying the Show Table Dialog Box

The Show Table dialog box may not be displayed automatically in the Relationships window. The Show Table dialog box can be displayed by clicking the Show Table button ( ) on the toolbar or selecting Show Table from the Relationships menu.

Releasing the mouse button displays the Edit Relationships dialog box:

Deleting a Relationship

If a relationship was created by mistake, it can be deleted by selecting the line that indicates the relationship and then pressing the Delete key. A relationship line is selected by clicking it, which makes it appear thicker.

After verifying the related fields, **Create** is selected to define the relationship. **Cancel** can be selected if the listed fields do not correspond. A line is displayed between the related fields in the tables to indicate a relationship. When all the relationships in The Kite Company database are defined, the Relationships window looks similar to:

Relationships are saved by selecting <u>S</u>ave (Ctrl+S) from the <u>F</u>ile menu or clicking the Save button (🖫) on the toolbar. The Relationships window is closed by selecting <u>C</u>lose from the <u>F</u>ile menu or clicking the Close button (✖) in the upper-right corner of the window.

14.5 Using Subdatasheets

Subdatasheets are available in Datasheet view when relationships have been defined for a database. A *subdatasheet* shows records from another table that are related to a particular record. A ➕ is displayed next to each record of a table when subdatasheets are available. Clicking ➕ displays the subdatasheet for that record. For example, in The Kite Company database, the Kites table is related to the Sales table by the ItemID field. Therefore, a subdatasheet in the Kites table shows a record's relation to Sales records:

Kites : Table

	ItemID	ItemName				
➕	BOX	Winged Box				
➕	DRA	Dragon				
➖	DRF	Dragonfly				
			SalesID	**SalesDate**	**CustomerID**	**Quantity**
			7	10/21/2003	GFK	8
			3	9/30/2003	GFK	12
			6	10/17/2003	SKC	10
			＊ (Number)			0
➕	LAD	Ladybug				
➕	SEA	Seagull				
➕	SPA	Space Shuttle				

Record: ◀◀ ◀ [1] ▶ ▶▶ ▶＊ of 6

Format menu:
- A Font...
- Datasheet...
- Row Height...
- Column Width...
- Rename Column
- Hide Columns
- Unhide Columns...
- Subdatasheet ▶
  - ⊕≣ Expand All
  - ⊟≣ Collapse All
  - Remove

A subdatasheet is displayed by clicking ➕

In this case, the subdatasheet shows that the Dragonfly kite was ordered by customers GFK and SKC. A ➕ changes to ➖ when a subdatasheet is displayed. Clicking ➖ removes the subdatasheet.

Commands from the Subdatasheet menu in the Format menu can be used to Expand All datasheets or Collapse All datasheets.

Practice 3

In this practice you will define the relationships of The Kite Company database and then view subdatasheets. Open The Kite Company if it is not already displayed.

① DEFINE RELATIONSHIPS

a. On the toolbar, click the Relationships button ([⬚]). The Relationships window is displayed with the Show Table dialog box on top.

  1. Click Customers and then select Add. The Customers table is added to the window.
  2. Click Kites and then select Add. The Kites table is added to the window.
  3. Click Sales and then select Add. The Sales table is added to the window.
  4. Select Close to remove the Show Table dialog box.

b. In the Customers table, drag the CustomerID field to the CustomerID field in the Sales table. A dialog box is displayed:

1. Verify that the CustomerID field of the Customers table and the CustomerID field of the Sales table appear in the dialog box. If not, select Cancel and then drag the field again. If correct, select Create. A line is shown between the two fields indicating their relationship. Note that the Kites table may be on top of the line.

c. In the Kites table, drag the ItemID field to the ItemID field in the Sales table. A dialog box is displayed:

1. Verify that the ItemID field of the Kites table and the ItemID field of the Sales table appear in the dialog box. If not, select Cancel and then drag the field again. If correct, select Create. A line is shown between the two fields indicating their relationship.

② CLOSE THE RELATIONSHIPS WINDOW

Note that all the tables of the database are related. This is an important aspect of a relational database.

a. Select File → Save. The database relationships are saved.

b. In the upper-right corner of the Relationships window, click the Close button. The Relationships window is closed.

③ VIEW A SUBDATASHEET

a. Display the Kites table. Note that each record displays a +.

b. Next to ItemID DRF, click +. A subdatasheet is displayed. Note the sales for this item.

c. Next to ItemID BOX, click +. A subdatasheet is displayed. Note there are no sales for this item.

d. Next to each subdatasheet, click – to close the subdatasheets.

e. Close the Kites table. If a dialog box is displayed, select Yes to save changes.

14.6 Using Select Queries

In Chapter 13, filtering was used to limit the records displayed in a table. Another way to view specific data in a relational database is by applying a select query. A *select query* can include fields from any table and uses the relationships between tables to determine which data to display. The results of a select query are displayed in a datasheet.

The steps for creating a select query in Design view are:

Create query in Design view

1. **Display a new select query in Design view.** Clicking Queries in the Database window displays the query objects. Next, double-clicking the Create query in Design view icon displays the Select Query window and the Show Table dialog box:

2. **Add the required tables to the select query.** The Show Table dialog box is used to add tables. The Select Query Design view window with two tables added looks similar to:

Add Only Required Tables

Only tables required for the query criteria should be added to the Select Query Design view window. Adding tables that will not be used could result in duplicate records being displayed in the query datasheet.

Note the line indicating that the tables are related. The tables in a select query must be related for the query to work properly.

design grid 3. **Add fields to the design grid.** The *design grid* is where fields to be displayed by the select query must appear. A field is added to the design grid by dragging it from the table in the top of the Select Query Design view window to a Field box in the design grid, or clicking a Field box in the design grid and selecting the field from the list. A field is also added by double-clicking it, which adds it to the next empty column. The design grid with fields added looks similar to:

4. **Add criteria to the design grid.** The Criteria row is where criteria is typed. Special characters such as $ and commas should not be used in numeric criteria. A query for companies purchasing dragonfly kites would have criteria similar to:

5. **Display the query results.** Clicking the Run button (▮) on the toolbar or selecting Run from the Query menu applies the query. The select query results are shown in Datasheet view:

6. **Save the select query.** A select query is saved by clicking the Save button () on the toolbar or selecting <u>S</u>ave from the <u>F</u>ile menu, which displays the Save As dialog box where a descriptive name can be typed.

applying a saved select query

A saved select query is applied by first clicking Queries in the Database window to display the query objects. Next, double-clicking a query name applies the query and displays the results in Datasheet view.

Practice 4 ↻

In this practice you will create a select query. Open The Kite Company if it is not already displayed.

① *ADD TABLES TO THE SELECT QUERY WINDOW*

a. In The Kite Company : Database window, click Queries. The query objects are displayed.

b. Double-click the Create query in Design view icon. The Select Query window is displayed with the Show Table dialog box on top.

  1. Click Customers if it is not already selected and then select Add. The Customers table is added to the Select Query.

  2. Add the Sales table to the Select Query.

  3. Select Close. The Show Table dialog box is removed.

② *ADD FIELDS TO THE DESIGN GRID*

a. Drag the CompanyName field from the Customers table to the first Field box in the design grid.

b. Double-click the ItemID field in the Sales table. The ItemID field is added to the second Field box.

c. Add the Quantity field in the Sales table to the third Field box. The design grid should look similar to:

Field:	CompanyName	ItemID	Quantity		
Table:	Customers	Sales	Sales		
Sort:					
Show:	☑	☑	☑	☐	
Criteria:					
or:					

③ ADD CRITERIA TO THE DESIGN GRID

In the Criteria box of the ItemID Field, type DRF. The design grid should look similar to:

④ APPLY THE SELECT QUERY

a. On the toolbar, click the Run button (![]). The database is queried and the results shown in a datasheet. Note that three records are displayed:

b. Select File → Save. A dialog box is displayed.
  1. In the Query Name box, type DRF Sales.
  2. Select OK. The query is saved.
c. Select File → Print. A dialog box is displayed.
  1. Select OK. The datasheet is printed.
d. Close the select query datasheet.

14.7 Modifying and Deleting a Select Query

A select query can be modified in Design view. If the select query datasheet is displayed, clicking the View button ( ) on the toolbar switches to Design view. A query can also be displayed in Design view by clicking Queries in the Database window, clicking the query name, and then clicking the Design button on the Database window toolbar.

removing and adding tables to the design grid

A table is removed from Select Query Design view by clicking the table and then pressing the Delete key. When a table is removed, any of its fields and corresponding criteria are removed from the design grid. A table is added to Select Query Design view using the Show Table dialog box, which is displayed by selecting Show Table from the Query menu or clicking the Show Table button ( ) on the toolbar.

adding a field between existing fields

Dragging a field to the design grid adds the field and moves existing fields to the right. For example, to place a LastName field between FirstName and CustomerID fields already in the design grid, the LastName field is dragged to the CustomerID field, which is then automatically moved to the right to make room for the new field.

deleting a column

A column is deleted from the design grid by selecting it and then pressing the Delete key. The gray box at the top of a field in the design grid is called the *column selector*. Clicking the column selector selects the field. A field can also be deleted by selecting Delete Columns from the Edit menu, which removes the column containing the insertion point.

column selector

changing field order

The order in which fields appear in a select query datasheet is changed by reordering the fields in the design grid. A field is moved by clicking its column selector and then dragging the field by its column selector to a new location.

creating similar queries

Queries with similar criteria can be created by modifying one query and saving it with a new name. For example, a query named DRF Sales could be modified to query for SEA sales and then named SEA Sales. Selecting Save As from the File menu displays a dialog box where a new query name is typed:

A modified query can be saved under a different name

The DRF Sales query remains in the database and the SEA Sales query is added to the Queries.

deleting a select query

A query is deleted by selecting its name in the Database window and then pressing the Delete key. Access displays a warning dialog box, where selecting Yes permanently removes the query.

14.8   Sorting Select Query Results

The results of a select query can be ordered based on the entries of a particular field. A sort order is specified by selecting an order from the Sort list of a field in the Select Query design grid. For example, Select Query Design view for the DRF Sales query looks similar to the following after modifying it to display records in order by quantity:

A Sort box contains a list for specifying a sort order

When the query is run, records in the select query datasheet are sorted:

Practice 5

In this practice you will modify the DRF Sales query and create a SEA Sales query. Open The Kite Company if it is not already displayed.

① MODIFY THE DRF SALES SELECT QUERY

  a. In The Kite Company : Database window, click Queries if query objects are not already displayed.

  b. Click DRF Sales and then select the Design button on the Database window toolbar. The DRF Sales select query is displayed in Design view.

  c. In the Quantity column of the design grid, click the Sort box. A Sort arrow is displayed.

d. From the Sort list, select Ascending. The design grid should look similar to:

e. Run the query. The DRF Sales query results are displayed in order by quantity sold.

f. Save the DRF Sales select query.

g. Print and then close the datasheet.

② *CREATE A SEA SALES SELECT QUERY*

a. Open the DRF Sales query in Design view.

b. Change the criteria of the ItemID field to SEA. The design grid should look similar to:

c. Run the query. The records of SEA sales are displayed.

d. Select File → Save As. A dialog box is displayed.

   1. Type SEA Sales as the new query name.

   2. Select OK. The new query is saved and DRF Sales remains in the database.

e. Print and then close the datasheet.

③ *CLOSE THE KITE COMPANY DATABASE*

14.9 Range Queries

A *range query* has criteria that include different values. For example, a query that displays sales after 9/30/03 requires checking the Date field for every date later than 9/30/03. This kind of criteria is specified using *relational operators*, which are used to compare values:

relational operators

=	equal to
<	less than
>	greater than
<=	less than or equal to
>=	greater than or equal to
<>	is not equal to

For the sales after 9/30/03, the criteria is >9/30/03.

Similarly, relational operators can be used to query for a range of numbers. For example, to display the records of sales in which 15 or more items were purchased, the criteria ">=15 in the Quantity field" is used.

Relational operators can also be used to compare text. For example, the criteria for querying for customers with names that come before the letter M alphabetically is "<M in the Name field."

Practice 6

In this practice you will query the BEACH RENTALS relational database, which contains Rentals, Renters, and Conditions tables.

① *OPEN BEACH RENTALS*

Select File → Open. A dialog box is displayed.

1. Use the Look in list and the contents box below it to display the data files for this text.
2. In the contents box, click BEACH RENTALS.
3. Select Open. The BEACH RENTALS : Database window is displayed.

② *DETERMINE RENTALS AT OR AFTER 3:00 PM*

a. In the BEACH RENTALS : Database window, click Queries.

b. Double-click the Create query in Design view icon. The Select Query window is displayed with the Show Table dialog box on top.

1. Click Rentals and then select Add. The Rentals table is added to the select query.
2. Add the Renters table to the select query.
3. Select Close. The Show Table dialog box is removed.

c. Add the ItemName field in the Rentals table to the first Field box in the design grid.

d. Add the TimeOut field in the Renters table to the second Field box.

e. Add the Date field in the Renters table to the third Field box.

f. In the Criteria box of TimeOut type >=3:00 PM. The design grid should look similar to:

g. Run the query. The select query datasheet displays two rentals.

h. Save the query naming it Rentals At or After 3:00 PM.

i. Print and then close the datasheet.

③ CREATE AND APPLY A TEXT RANGE QUERY

a. In the BEACH RENTALS : Database window, double-click the Create query in Design view icon. The Select Query window is displayed with the Show Table dialog box on top.

1. Add the Renters table to the select query and then close the Show Table dialog box.

b. Add the FirstName field in the Renters table to the first Field box in the design grid.

c. Add the LastName field in the Renters table to the second Field box.

d. In the Criteria box of LastName type <=M.

e. Click the LastName Sort box and then select Ascending from the list. The design grid should look similar to:

f. Run the query. The select query datasheet displays customers with names that start with a letter in the first half of the alphabet.

g. Save the query naming it A - M Renters.

h. Print and then close the datasheet.

14.10 Select Queries Involving "And"

Complex queries with "and" in the criteria can require multiple entries in the Criteria row of a select query design grid. For example, the BEACH RENTALS database could be queried to determine the June 8, 2003 half day rentals. The criteria for this query is June 8, 2003 in the Date field *and* Half Day in the ReservedTime field:

Boolean expression
And Boolean operator

Some complex queries with "and" in the criteria require a Boolean expression. A *Boolean expression* is formed with a logical operator, such as And. This type of criteria is required when checking for a range of values in the same field. For example, a query with criteria "rentals between June 8, 2003 and June 14, 2003" requires >6/8/2003 And <6/14/2003 to be typed in the Criteria box of the Date field. Only records with dates greater than 6/8/2003 *and* less than 6/14/2003 meet the criteria.

Practice 7

In this practice you will create queries involving "and" for the BEACH RENTALS database. Open BEACH RENTALS if it is not already displayed.

① *DETERMINE THE JUNE 8, 2003 HALF DAY RENTALS*

    a. In the BEACH RENTALS : Database window, click Queries if query names are not already displayed.

    b. Double-click the Create query in Design view icon. The Select Query window is displayed with the Show Table dialog box on top.

        1. Add the Renters and Rentals tables to the select query and then close the Show Table dialog box.

    c. Add the Date field in the Renters table to the first Field box in the design grid.

    d. Add the ItemName field in the Rentals table to the second Field box.

    e. Add the ReservedTime field in the Renters table to the third Field box.

    f. In the Criteria box of Date, type =6/8/03.

    g. In the Criteria box of ReservedTime, type =Half Day. The design grid should look similar to:

h. Run the query. The select query datasheet displays three rentals. Note that each record displayed has a date of June 8, 2003 and a reserved time of Half Day.

i. Save the query naming it 6/8/03 Half Day Rentals.

j. Print and then close the datasheet.

② *DETERMINE THE RENTALS BETWEEN JUNE 8, 2003 AND JUNE 14, 2003*

a. Double-click the Create query in Design view icon. The Select Query window is displayed with the Show Table dialog box on top.

    1. Add the Renters and Rentals tables to the select query and then close the Show Table dialog box.

b. Add the Date field in the Renters table to the first Field box in the design grid.

c. Add the ItemName field in the Rentals table to the second Field box.

d. In the Criteria box of Date, type >6/8/2003 And <6/14/2003.

e. In the Date column of the design grid, select Ascending in the Sort list. The design grid should look similar to:

f. Run the query. The select query datasheet displays six rentals. Note that each record displayed has a date between June 8, 2003 and June 14, 2003.

g. Save the query naming it Rentals Between 6/8/03 and 6/14/03.

h. Print and then close the datasheet.

14.11 Select Queries Involving "Or"

Complex queries with "or" in the criteria require the or row of a select query design grid. For example, the BEACH RENTALS database could be queried to determine half day and full day rentals on June 8, 2003. The criteria for this select query is "6/8/03" in the Date field and "Half Day" in the ReservedTime field *or* "Full Day" in the ReservedTime field:

Note that the date criteria is required in both rows. If the date criteria is in the first row only, the query displays half day rentals on 6/8/03 and full day rentals on any date.

expanding the design grid   The design grid of a select query may need to be expanded to accommodate multiple "or" criteria. Dragging the bottom of the select query window expands the window to display more rows for or criteria.

As another example, the BEACH RENTALS database could be queried to determine rentals of the cooler and the metal detector:

Practice 8 ⟳

In this practice you will create queries involving "or" for the BEACH RENTALS database. Open BEACH RENTALS if it is not already displayed.

① DETERMINE THE EARLY MORNING AND LATE AFTERNOON RENTALS

a. In the BEACH RENTALS : Database window, click Queries if query names are not already displayed.

b. Double-click the Create query in Design view icon. The Select Query window is displayed with the Show Table dialog box on top.

    1. Add the Rentals and Renters tables to the select query and then close the Show Table dialog box.

c. Add the ItemName from the Rentals table to the first Field box in the design grid.

d. Add the Date and TimeOut fields from the Renters table to the second and third Field boxes, respectively.

e. In the Criteria box of TimeOut, type <9 AM.

f. In the or box of TimeOut, type >3 PM. The design grid should look similar to:

g. Run the query. The select query datasheet displays 10 records. Note that each record displayed has a time less than 9 AM or greater than 3 PM.

h. Save the query naming it Early Morning and Late Afternoon Rentals.

i. Print and then close the datasheet.

② DETERMINE THE 6/8/03 HALF DAY AND FULL DAY RENTALS

a. In the BEACH RENTALS : Database window, click Queries if query names are not already displayed.

b. Double-click the Create query in Design view icon. The Select Query window is displayed with the Show Table dialog box on top.

    1. Add the Rentals and Renters tables to the select query and then close the Show Table dialog box.

c. Add fields and criteria to the design grid as shown below:

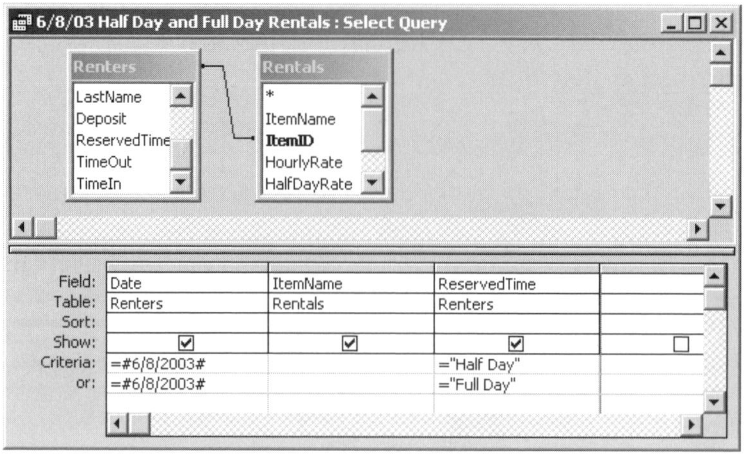

d. Run the query. The select query datasheet displays four records.

e. Save the query naming it 6/8/03 Half Day and Full Day Rentals.

f. Print and then close the datasheet.

14.12 Query Criteria Wildcards

Query criteria can include wildcards. A *wildcard* is a character that matches any one or more characters. The asterisk (*) and question mark (?) are two wildcards. The * wildcard matches any number of characters or no characters at all. For example, a BEACH RENTALS query with the criteria C* in the ItemID field would display all beach and lounge chair records because their ItemIDs begin with C. As another example, the criteria S* in the FirstName field displays the records for Sy, Sarah, and Sue because they all begin with the letter S.

asterisk (*)

question mark (?)

The ? wildcard matches any one character or no character at all. For example, a query with criteria Ann? displays the records for Ann and Anne, but not Annette.

Like operator

When wildcards are used in criteria, Access uses the Like operator to determine a match. The *Like operator* is displayed in criteria after the query is run, as in the criteria below:

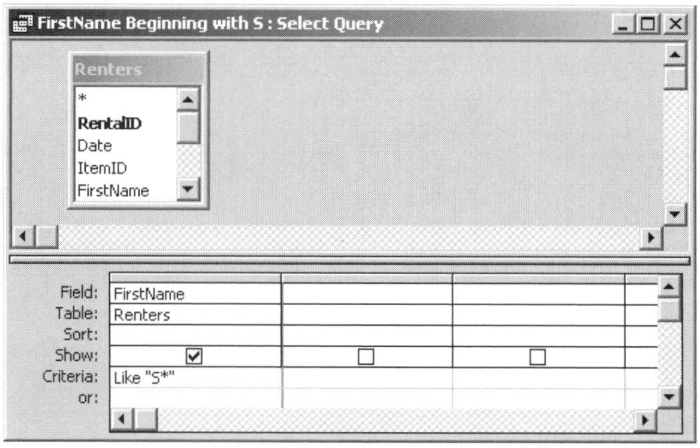

A Guide to Microsoft Office XP Professional

In this practice you will query the BEACH RENTALS database using criteria with wildcards. Open BEACH RENTALS if it is not already displayed.

① *DETERMINE THE BICYCLE RENTALS*

    a. In the BEACH RENTALS : Database window, click Queries if query names are not already displayed.

    b. Double-click the Create query in Design view icon. The Select Query window is displayed with the Show Table dialog box on top.

        1. Add the Rentals and Renters tables to the select query and then close the Show Table dialog box.

    c. Add fields and criteria to the design grid as shown below:

Field:	ItemID	ItemName	Date	ReservedTime	
Table:	Rentals	Rentals	Renters	Renters	
Sort:					
Show:	☑	☑	☑	☑	
Criteria:	K*				
or:					

    d. Run the query. The select query datasheet displays six records.

    e. Save the query naming it Bicycle Rentals.

    f. Print and then close the datasheet.

② *CLOSE BEACH RENTALS*

③ *QUIT ACCESS*

Chapter Summary

In this chapter, tables and records were modified and select queries were used to display specific records. A table can be modified to include a new field and an existing field can be renamed or deleted. Modifications to a table should be done from Design view. After modifying a table, its corresponding form is updated by creating a new form and saving it with the same name as the original.

Records can be sorted in ascending or descending order using the Sort buttons on the toolbar or the Sort command.

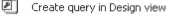

Records can be added, changed, and deleted. Records are added using the record control. Changing the entries in an existing record is called updating. Records are deleted using the Delete Record button on the toolbar or the Delete <u>R</u>ecord command.

In a relational database, each table must be related to another table by a field. Relationships between tables are defined using the Relationships button on the toolbar or the <u>R</u>elationships command. After relationships have been defined, subdatasheets are available in a table. A subdatasheet shows records from another table that are related to a particular record.

A select query can include fields from any table and uses the relationships between table to determine which data to include. Select query results are displayed in a datasheet. There are six steps for creating a select query:

1. Display a new select query in Design view.

2. Add the required tables to the select query.

3. Add fields to the design grid.

4. Add criteria to the design grid.

5. Display the query results by clicking the Run button on the toolbar.

6. Save the select query.

An existing select query is run by clicking Queries in the Database window and then double-clicking a select query name.

Select query results can be sorted. The order of a select query's records is designated by selecting an order from the Sort list in the design grid.

A range query has criteria that includes many different entries. The criteria for this type of query is defined using relational operators (>, >=, <, <=, <>). Complex queries may require multiple entries in the Criteria row of the design grid for queries involving and. Some complex queries require the logical operator And. The or row in the select query design grid is also used for specifying complex query.

Wildcards include the * and ? characters, and can be used in criteria to match any one or more characters. The * matches any number of characters or no characters at all. The ? matches any one character or no characters at all.

A select query can be modified by first displaying the query in Design view. A table is removed by clicking it and then pressing the Delete key. A table is added to Select Query Design view by using the Show Table dialog box. A field is added between existing fields in the design grid by dragging it to a column, which automatically moves existing fields to the right to make room for the new field. A column is deleted from the design grid by selecting it and then pressing the Delete key, which removes the column and any field and criteria it contained.

A select query can also be created by modifying an existing query and then saving it with a different name by selecting the Save <u>A</u>s command. A select query is deleted by clicking its name in the Database window and then pressing the Delete key.

Alphabetical order   Records sorted in ascending order based on the data in a text field.

And   A logical operator in a Boolean expression.

Asterisk (*)   A wildcard character that matches any number of characters or no character at all.

Boolean expression   Criteria formed with a logical operator, such as And.

Chronological order   Records sorted in ascending order based on the data in a date/time field.

Column selector   The gray box at the top of a field in the design grid of a select query.

Design grid   The part of Select Query Design view that contains fields and criteria.

Like   Operator displayed in criteria that uses wildcards.

Question mark (?)   A wildcard character matches any one character or no character at all.

Range query   A query with criteria that includes many different values.

Related   Two tables with corresponding fields.

Relational operators   Used in criteria to compare values. Operators include =, <, >, <=, >=, and <>.

Select query   A query that uses the relationships between tables to determine the data to display.

Sorting   Placing records in a specified order.

Subdatasheet   Shows records from another table that are related to a particular record.

Updating   Changing the data in an existing record.

Wildcard   A character used in criteria that matches any one or more characters.

Access Commands and Buttons

⊟ Collapse All command Closes all subdatasheets. Found in the Format menu. **⊟** can be clicked instead to remove a single subdatasheet.

⊠ Delete Record command Used to delete the record currently displayed in a form. Found in the Edit menu. The Delete Record button on the toolbar can be used instead of the command.

Delete Rows command Deletes a field in table Design view. Found in the menu displayed by right-clicking a field name in table Design view.

⊞ Design Design button Displays a selected table in Design view. Also displays a select query in Design view. Found on the Database window toolbar.

⊞ Expand All command Opens all subdatasheets. Found in the Format menu. **⊞** can be clicked instead to open a single subdatasheet.

⊞ Queries Displays the query objects. Found in the Database window.

⊞ Relationships command Used to define a relationship between two tables. Found in the Tools menu. The Relationships button on the toolbar can be used instead of the command.

⚡ Run command Applies a select query. Found in the Query menu. The Run button on the toolbar can be used instead of the command.

Save As command Displays a dialog box used for duplicating a query. Found in the File menu.

⊟ Save command Used to save defined relationships. Also used to save a select query. Found in the File menu. The Save button on the toolbar can be used instead of the command.

⊞ Show Table command Used to add a table to Select Query Design view. Found in the Query menu. The Show Table button on the toolbar can be used instead of the command.

⊞ Sort Ascending command Sorts a table in order from lowest to highest based on the data in a specified field. Found in the Sort submenu in the Records menu. The Sort Ascending button on the toolbar can be used instead of the command.

⊞ Sort Descending command Sorts a table in order from highest to lowest based on the data in a specified field. Found in the Sort submenu in the Records menu. The Sort Descending button on the toolbar can be used instead of the command.

⊞ ▾ View button Used to switch a table between Datasheet view and Design view. Also used to switch a select query from a datasheet to Design view. Found on the toolbar.

Sections 14.1 — 14.5

1. What view should a table be displayed in to modify its fields?

2. List the steps required to:
   a) add a field.
   b) rename a field.
   c) delete a field.

3. What must be updated after a field is added to an existing table?

4. What is sorting?

5. List the steps required to sort a table by the FirstName field in descending order.

6. Why should a table's form be used to modify a record?

7. How is a new, blank record displayed in a form?

8. a) What is updating?
   b) What can be used to quickly find a record for updating?

9. List the steps required to delete a record.

10. Explain the basis of a relationship between two tables.

11. List the steps required to define a relationship between the two tables with the fields shown below:

    CDs Table   **Songs Table**
    CDNumber   SongNumber
    Title   Title
    Type   CDNumber
                     SongLength

12. If a table is added to a database whose relationships have already been defined, how is the table added to the Relationships window?

13. a) What is a subdatasheet?
    b) When is a subdatasheet available?
    c) How is a subdatasheet viewed?
    d) How is a displayed subdatasheet removed from view?

Sections 14.6 — 14.12

14. a) What is a select query?
    b) What is a design grid?

15. a) List the steps required to create and run a select query.
    b) List the steps required to run a previously created select query.

16. List the steps required to add a field between existing fields in the design grid of a select query.

17. List the steps required to delete a field from the design grid of a select query.

18. List the steps required to create a query named Bicycle Rentals that is based on an exiting query named Beach Chair Rentals.

19. List the steps required to sort select query results based on the data in the ItemID field.

20. a) What is a range query?
    b) What are the relational operators that can be used in a range query?

21. List two ways to specify the criteria for a complex query using "and." Explain the circumstances required for each method.

22. What is the or row of a select query design grid used for?

23. List two criteria wildcards that can be used in a select query and explain when each would be used.

24. What does the Like operator in the design grid of a select query indicate?

Exercise 1 ♻ ──────────────────────────── FL COLLEGES

The FL COLLEGES relational database modified in Chapter 13, Exercise 1 needs to be updated and select queries applied to it. Open FL COLLEGES and complete the following steps:

a) In the Colleges table, change the Name field to CollegeName.

b) Update the Colleges form appropriately.

c) Add the following record to the Colleges table:

Florida A&M University; Tallahassee; 10,702

d) Sort the Cities table by Population in descending order. Save and print the table.

e) The Cities and Colleges tables are related by the City field. Create the appropriate relationship between the Cities and Colleges tables.

f) Create a select query that displays the CollegeName, County, and Enrollment fields for those colleges located in Leon county. Save the select query naming it Leon County Colleges. Print the select query datasheet.

g) Create a select query that displays the CollegeName, City, Population, and Enrollment fields for those colleges that are in cities with a population greater than 300,000 and have an enrollment less than 30,000. Save the select query naming it Population > 300,000 and Enrollment < 30,000. Print the select query datasheet.

Exercise 2 ♻ ──────────────────────────── Museum Exhibits

The Museum Exhibits relational database created in Chapter 13, Exercise 2 needs to be updated and queries applied. Open Museum Exhibits and complete the following steps:

a) In the Exhibits table, change the Name field to ExhibitName. Update the Exhibits form appropriately.

b) Add the following record to the Exhibits table:

WDH1; Physics; Why Does That Happen; 5/28/04

c) The attendance at the Earth's Interior exhibit (LWL2) in 2003 was recorded incorrectly. The correct attendance was 1,815. Update the appropriate Attendance record.

d) Sort the Exhibits table by ExhibitName in ascending order. Save and print the table.

e) The Exhibits and Attendance tables are related by the ExhibitID field. Create the appropriate relationship between the Exhibits and Attendance tables.

f) Create a select query that displays the ExhibitID, ExhibitName, Attendance, and Year fields of exhibits with an attendance over 1,500 in 2003. The query results should be sorted in descending order by attendance. Save the select query naming it 2003 Attendance over 1,500. Print the select query datasheet.

g) Create a select query that displays the ExhibitName, Updated, Attendance, and Year fields of exhibits with an attendance less than 1,500 in 2003 and last updated before 1/1/02. Save the select query naming it 2003 Attendance < 1,500 & Updated before 02. Print the select query datasheet.

h) Create a select query that displays the ExhibitID, ExhibitName, Year, and Attendance fields. Use the appropriate wildcard in the criteria to display all the Exhibits with ExhibitIDs that begin WDH. Save the select query naming it Why Does That Happen Exhibits. Print the select query datasheet.

Exercise 3 — Library

The Library relational database created in Chapter 13, Exercise 3 needs to be updated and queries applied. Open Library and complete the following steps:

a) The ISBN for The Complete College Guide was recorded incorrectly. The correct ISBN is 1-879233-03-7. Update the appropriate record in the Books form.

b) Add the following records to the Books table:

   1-879233-94-0; The Graduate College Guide; Reference; TB22
   1-879233-88-6; The Green Door; Drama; ZT19

c) Sort the Books table by Title in ascending order. Save and print the table.

d) The Books and Authors tables are related by the AuthorID field. Create the appropriate relationship between the Books and Authors tables.

e) Create a select query that displays the AuthorID, FirstName, LastName, and Title fields of books authored by AuthorID TB22. Save the select query naming it Books by TB22. Print the select query datasheet.

f) Create a select query that displays the FirstName, LastName, Title, and Type fields of books that are of drama or mystery type. The query results should be sorted in ascending order by the author's last name. Save the select query naming it Drama or Mystery. Print the select query datasheet.

g) Create a select query that displays the FirstName, LastName, Title, and ISBN fields. Use the appropriate wildcard in the criteria to display all the authors with last names that begin with B. Save the select query naming it Authors beginning with B. Print the select query datasheet.

Exercise 4 — Space Shuttle Missions

The Space Shuttle Missions relational database created in Chapter 13, Exercise 4 needs to be updated and queries applied. Open Space Shuttle Missions and complete the following steps:

a) The Orbiter Vehicles and Missions tables are related by the OrbiterID fields. The Astronauts and Missions tables are related by the AstronautID and CommanderID fields. Create the appropriate relationships between the tables.

b) Create a select query that displays the FirstName, LastName, Name, and LaunchDate fields of all John Casper's missions. Save the select query naming it Casper Missions. Print the select query datasheet.

c) Create a select query that displays the FirstName, LastName, and LaunchDate of all missions after 1995. Save the select query naming it Missions after 1995. Print the select query datasheet.

d) Create a select query that displays the Name, FirstName, LastName, and LaunchDate fields of all missions in which the orbiter vehicle Columbia was used. Save the select query naming it Columbia Shuttle Missions. Print the select query datasheet.

Exercise 5 ⟳ ──────────────────── Boat Storage

The Boat Storage relational database was created in Chapter 13, Exercise 5. Open Boat Storage and complete the following steps:

a) Add the following record to the Boats table:

   Sunshine; 1; NG12; 70; 4

b) The Employees and Boats tables are related by the EmployeeID field. The Boats table and Boat Owners table are related by the OwnerID field. Create the appropriate relationships between the Employees, Boats, and Boat Owners tables.

c) Create a select query that displays the Boat, OwnerID, FirstName of owner, LastName of owner, and Fee fields for those boats owned by OwnerID 2. Save the select query naming it OwnerID 2 Boats. Print the select query datasheet.

d) Create a select query that displays the Boat, Fee, FirstName of owner, and LastName of owner fields of those boats with a monthly fee greater than or equal to $70. The query should be sorted in ascending order by the owner's last name. Save the select query naming it Fees >= $70. Print the select query datasheet.

e) Create a select query that displays in ascending order by SlotNumber the FirstName of employee, LastName of employee, Boat, and SlotNumber fields of those boats stored in the first five slots. Save the select query naming Slots 1 through 5. Print the select query datasheet.

Exercise 6 ⟳ ──────────────────── Ivy U Athletics

The Ivy U Athletics relational database created in Chapter 13, Exercise 6 needs to be updated and queries applied. Open Ivy U Athletics and complete the following steps:

a) Add the following record to the Sports table:

   Women's Basketball; Spring; 451,000

b) Add the following records to the Players table:

   CS341; Clarissa; Sladek; Women's Basketball; Shooting Guard
   MA276; Marie; Angulo; Women's Basketball; Power Forward

c) Add the following record to the Coaches table:

   BS912; Barbara; Suppa; Women's Basketball; Head Coach; 86,000

d) Format all of the tables in Datasheet view appropriately.

e) Sort the Players table by LastName in ascending order. Save and print the table.

f) The Players and Sports tables are related by the Sport field. The Sports table and Coaches table are also related by the Sport field. Create the appropriate relationships between the Players, Sports, and Coaches tables.

g) Create a select query that displays the FirstName of player, LastName of player, Sport, and Semester fields of all those players who play sports in the Spring semester. The query results should be sorted in ascending order by the player's last name. Save the select query naming it Spring Sports. Print the select query datasheet.

h) Create a select query that displays the FirstName of coach, LastName of coach, Salary, Sport, and Budget fields of all those coaches with a salary less than $50,000 who have a sport's budget over $500,000. Save the select query naming it Salary < $50,000 & Budget > $500,000. Print the select query datasheet.

Exercise 7 ✿ ———————————————————— Second Ocean

The Second Ocean relational database created in Chapter 13, Exercise 7 needs to be updated and queries applied. Open Second Ocean and complete the following steps:

a) In the Facility Checks table, change the Date field to DateOfCheck. Update the Facility Checks form appropriately.

b) Format the Facility Checks table in Datasheet view appropriately.

c) Add the following records to the Animals table:

    8/13/03; Manatee; 5; F; Ocean Care
    9/4/03; Manatee; 7; F; Ocean Care

d) The whale has recovered and been released back into the ocean. Delete her record from the Animals table.

e) The Animals and Facility Checks tables are related by the AnimalID field. The Facility Checks and Facilities tables are related by the Facility field. Create the appropriate relationships between the Animals, Facility Checks, and Facilities tables.

f) Create a select query that displays the AnimalID, Type, Gender, DateOfRescue, Facility, and DateOfCheck fields for all the animals. Save the select query naming it Statistics on Animals. Print the select query datasheet.

g) Create a select query that displays the Facility, DateOfCheck, AnimalID, and Type fields for facility Ocean World. Save the select query naming it Ocean World Facility Checks. Print the select query datasheet.

h) Create a select query that displays the Facility, State, AnimalID, DateofRescue, Type, and Gender fields. Use the appropriate wildcard in the criteria to display all the records of facilities starting with O. The query results should be sorted in descending order by the DateofRescue. Save the select query naming it Facilities Starting with O. Print the select query datasheet.

Exercise 8 ⟳ ——————————————————————— Green Thumb

The Green Thumb relational database was created in Chapter 13, Exercise 8. Open Green Thumb and complete the following steps:

a) The Transactions and Plants tables are related by the PlantID field. The Plants and Vendors table are related by the VendorID field. Create the appropriate relationships between the Transactions, Plants, and Vendors tables.

b) Create a select query that displays the Plant, Retail, Date, and Quantity fields of all ferns sold. Save the select query naming it Ferns Sold. Print the select query datasheet.

c) Create a select query that displays the Name, Plant, and Cost fields for all the plants. Save the select query naming it Cost of Plants. Print the select query datasheet.

d) Create a select query that displays the Plant, InStock, Cost, and Name fields of those plants costing less than $10.00 and with less than 50 in stock. Save the select query naming it Plants < $10 and < 50 InStock. Print the select query datasheet.

e) Create a select query that displays the Plant, Retail, Cost, Date, and Quantity fields of all plants sold in a quantity greater than or equal to 10. Save the select query naming it Plants Sold >= 10. Print the select query datasheet.

Exercise 9 ⟳ ——————————————————————— Pizza Payroll

The Pizza Payroll relational database was created in Chapter 13, Exercise 9. Open Pizza Payroll and complete the following steps:

a) The Employees and Payroll tables are related by the EmployeeID field. Create the appropriate relationship between the Employees and Payroll tables.

b) Create a select query that displays the FirstName, LastName, Date, GrossPay, and Taxes fields of all payroll checks where gross pay is less than $250 and taxes are less than $30. Save the select query naming it Gross Pay < $250 & Tax < $30. Print the select query datasheet.

c) Create a select query that displays the EmployeeID, FirstName, LastName, Date, GrossPay, and Taxes fields for employeeID EI. Save the select query naming it Employee EI Payroll. Print the select query datasheet.

Exercise 10 ⟳ ——————————————————————— Coral Research

The Coral Research relational database was created in Chapter 13, Exercise 10. Open Coral Research and complete the following steps:

a) The Coral Sites and Growth Research tables are related by the SiteID field. Create the appropriate relationship between the Coral Sites and Growth Research tables.

b) Create a select query that displays the CoralName, Color, Description, Date, and Size fields for the coral named Knobby Brain Coral. Save the select query naming it Knobby Brain Coral. Print the select query datasheet.

c) Create a select query that displays the SiteID, CoralName, Date, and Size fields for all those corals larger than 1 meter in size. Save the select query naming it Size > 1. Print the select query datasheet.

d) Create a select query to display the SiteID, CoralName, and Date fields for all those corals in sites with SiteID 1 or 2. Save the select query naming it Sites 1 or 2. Print the select query datasheet.

Exercise 11 ✑ ———————————————————————— Travel Agency

The Travel Agency relational database was created in Chapter 13, Exercise 11. Open Travel Agency and complete the following steps:

a) The Clients and Booked Vacations tables are related by the ClientID field. The Booked Vacations and Vacations tables are related by the Package field. Create the appropriate relationships between the Clients, Booked Vacations, and Vacations tables.

b) Create a select query that displays the FirstName, LastName, and Package fields for those clients who have booked a Mountain Explorer or Summit Skiing vacation package. Save the select query naming it Mountain Explorer/Summit Skiing. Print the select query datasheet.

c) Create a select query that displays the ClientID, Date, Package, and Cost fields of those vacations booked by client with ClientID JU. Save the select query naming it Vacations Booked by JU. Print the select query datasheet.

d) Create a select query that displays the Package, Cost, and Date fields for all those vacations booked that are costing more than $500. Save the select query naming it Booked > $500. Print the select query datasheet.

e) Create a select query that displays the FirstName, LastName, Package, Cost, Location, Date, and Type fields for all those vacations booked which cost less than $1,000 and that are a relaxing Type. Save the select query naming it Booked Relaxing < $1,000. Print the select query datasheet.

Exercise 12 ———————————————————————— VIDEO STORE

The VIDEO STORE relational database contains information on a video store's members, videos, and rentals. Open VIDEO STORE and complete the following steps:

a) The Members table should also include the Address, City, State, and Zip fields for each member. Add the appropriate text fields to the Members table.

b) Update the Members form appropriately and enter the following ten records:

CS; 654 First St.; Sunport; FL; 33654-7786   JS-2; 285 Boca Lane; Medusa; FL; 33656
JF; 274 Boca Lane; Medusa; FL; 33656   LP; 655 First St.; Sunport; FL; 33654-7786
JH; 9876 Dolphin St.; Medusa; FL; 33656   NL; 983 Jefferson Ave.; Medusa; FL; 33656
JM; 985 Jefferson Ave.; Medusa; FL; 33656   RG; 9821 Dolphin St.; Medusa; FL; 33656
JS; 9898 Dolphin St.; Medusa; FL; 33656   RG-2; 987 First St.; Sunport; FL; 33654-7786

c) Add a record for yourself to the Members table.

d) Format the Members table in Datasheet view appropriately.

e) Sort the Members table by LastName in ascending order. Save and print the table in landscape orientation.

f) Create a select query that displays the FirstName, LastName, and InDate fields of those members who have not returned a video. If a video has not been returned, the InDate field is blank. To display fields that are blank, Is Null is entered as the criteria. Save the select query naming it Not Returned. Print the select query datasheet.

g) Create a select query that displays the Name, Type, and OutDate fields for all those movies checked out before 2/7/03 that are Sci-Fi movies. Save the select query naming it Sci-Fi < 2/7/03. Print the select query datasheet.

Exercise 13 ——————————————————————— INVENTIONS

The INVENTIONS relational database contains information on inventions and inventors. Open INVENTIONS and complete the following steps:

a) In the Inventors table, rename the Country field BirthCountry. Update the Inventors form appropriately.

b) Delete the Cash Register record from the Inventions table.

c) Sort the Inventions table in ascending order by Inventor. Save and print the table.

d) Sort the Inventors table in ascending order by the year born. Save and print the table.

e) Create a select query that displays the FirstName, LastName, BirthCountry, Invention, and Year fields of those inventions created after 1799 by inventors born in the United States. Save the select query naming it US > 1799. Print the select query datasheet.

f) Save the US > 1799 query as England > 1799 and modify the criteria to display the those inventions created after 1799 by inventors born in England. Print the select query datasheet.

Exercise 14 (advanced) ☼ ——————————————————————— Club

Modify the Club relational database created in Chapter 13, Exercise 12 to include at least two select queries. Be sure that at least one of the queries is a range criteria. Another query should involve criteria with an "and" or an "or" or a wildcard.

Exercise 15 (advanced) ☼ ——————————————————————— Music

Modify the Music relational database created in Chapter 13, Exercise 13 to include at least two select queries. Be sure that at least one of the queries is a range criteria. Another query should involve criteria with an "and" or an "or" or a wildcard.

Exercise 16 (advanced) ☼ ——————————————————————— Sports

Modify the Sports relational database created in Chapter 13, Exercise 14 to include at least two select queries. Be sure that at least one of the queries is a range criteria. Another query should involve criteria with an "and" or an "or" or a wildcard.

Relational Database Reports and Advanced Database Techniques

Chapter 15 Expectations

After completing this chapter you will be able to:

1. Create a report.
2. Add summary values to a report.
3. Use fields in select query criteria.
4. Create a calculated field.

In this chapter database reports are introduced. Report summaries for making a report more informative are also explained. Creating calculated fields in a select query is discussed.

15.1   Reports

Reports are a powerful database feature that present data for printing in an organized manner with a descriptive title and headings. The simplest report uses a single table or select query datasheet. However, a report can include any combination of fields from multiple tables. For example, an informative report from the Beach Rentals database looks similar to:

Rentals Report

ItemName	ItemID	Date	ReservedTime
Beach Chair			
	C001		
		Saturday, June 07, 2003	Full Day
		Tuesday, June 10, 2003	Half Day
		Sunday, June 15, 2003	Half Day
	C002		
		Saturday, June 07, 2003	Half Day
Bicycle			
	K001		
		Sunday, June 01, 2003	Half Day
		Sunday, June 08, 2003	Half Day
		Sunday, June 15, 2003	Full Day
	K002		
		Tuesday, June 03, 2003	Full Day
	K003		
		Sunday, June 15, 2003	Full Day
Boogie Board			
	B001		
		Saturday, June 14, 2003	Hourly
	B002		
		Saturday, June 14, 2003	Hourly
		Sunday, June 15, 2003	Half Day
Cooler			
	L001		
		Tuesday, June 10, 2003	Half Day
Inline Skates			
	N001		
		Sunday, June 01, 2003	Hourly
		Wednesday, June 04, 2003	Half Day
		Thursday, June 12, 2003	Half Day

Monday, June 16, 2003   *Page 1 of 3*

Page 1 of a Beach Rentals report

15.2 Creating a Report

Create report by using wizard

A report is created by clicking Reports in the Database window, which displays the report objects. Double-clicking the Create report by using wizard icon starts the Report Wizard, which provides dialog boxes for selecting fields for the report and report formatting options:

1. **Add fields to the report.** The Tables/Queries list is used to select a table or query. The fields from the selected table/query are displayed in the Available Fields list. Selecting a field and then clicking ⟩ moves the field to the Selected Fields list. The process of selecting a table or query and then moving fields to the Selected Fields list can be repeated to add fields from different tables or queries to a report. For example, the Selected Fields list below contains fields from multiple tables:

Report Wizard

Which fields do you want on your report?

You can choose from more than one table or query.

Tables/Queries

Table: Renters

Available Fields:

RentalID
ItemID
FirstName
LastName
Deposit
TimeOut
TimeIn

Selected Fields:

ItemID
ItemName
Date
ReservedTime

Cancel   < Back   Next >   Finish

Selecting Next displays the next Report Wizard dialog box.

2. **Select a view.** Clicking a view determines how the report data is organized. If only one table is used in the report, then there is only one possible way to organize the data and the dialog box is not displayed. When multiple tables are used in a report, the views correlate to the fields shown in each table's subdatasheet. In the following dialog box, the data is organized by Rentals:

Report Wizard

How do you want to view your data?

by Rentals
by Renters

ItemID, ItemName

Date, ReservedTime

» Show me more information

Cancel   < Back   Next >   Finish

Selecting Next displays the next Report Wizard dialog box.

3. **Select the data grouping.** Selecting a field and then clicking ⊡ groups the data in the report by this field's data. For example, the report can be grouped on ItemName:

Report Wizard

Do you want to add any grouping levels?

Date
ReservedTime

> <

Priority

ItemName

ItemID

Date, ReservedTime

| Grouping Options ... | Cancel | < Back | Next > | Finish |

Selecting Next displays the next Report Wizard dialog box.

grouping data

Grouping data can make a report easier to comprehend. For example, the two reports on the next page contain exactly the same data. However, the one on the left has been grouped on the ItemName field and the one on the right has no grouping:

Rentals Report

ItemName	ItemID	Date	ReservedTime
Beach Chair			
	C001		
		Saturday, June 07, 2003	Full Day
		Tuesday, June 10, 2003	Half Day
		Sunday, June 15, 2003	Half Day
	C002		
		Saturday, June 07, 2003	Half Day
Bicycle			
	K001		
		Sunday, June 01, 2003	Half Day
		Sunday, June 08, 2003	Half Day
		Sunday, June 15, 2003	Full Day
	K002		
		Tuesday, June 03, 2003	Full Day
	K003		
		Sunday, June 15, 2003	Full Day
Boogie Board			
	B001		
		Saturday, June 14, 2003	Hourly
	B002		
		Saturday, June 14, 2003	Hourly
		Sunday, June 15, 2003	Half Day
Cooler			
	L001		
		Tuesday, June 10, 2003	Half Day
Inline Skates			
	N001		
		Sunday, June 01, 2003	Hourly
		Wednesday, June 04, 2003	Half Day
		Thursday, June 12, 2003	Half Day

Monday, June 16, 2003   *Page 1 of 3*

Rentals Report (no grouping)

Date	ItemID	ItemName	ReservedTime
Sunday, June 01, 2003	N001	Inline Skates	Hourly
Sunday, June 01, 2003	S001	Surf Board	Half Day
Sunday, June 01, 2003	K001	Bicycle	Half Day
Monday, June 02, 2003	K005	Tandem Bicycle	Hourly
Tuesday, June 03, 2003	C005	Lounge Chair	Half Day
Tuesday, June 03, 2003	K002	Bicycle	Full Day
Wednesday, June 04, 2003	F004	Mask/Fins/Snorkel	Half Day
Wednesday, June 04, 2003	M001	Metal Detector	Hourly
Wednesday, June 04, 2003	F001	Mask/Fins/Snorkel	Half Day
Wednesday, June 04, 2003	N001	Inline Skates	Half Day
Wednesday, June 04, 2003	F005	Mask/Fins/Snorkel	Half Day
Saturday, June 07, 2003	F002	Mask/Fins/Snorkel	Half Day
Saturday, June 07, 2003	C002	Beach Chair	Half Day
Saturday, June 07, 2003	C001	Beach Chair	Full Day
Saturday, June 07, 2003	U001	Umbrella	Full Day
Saturday, June 07, 2003	F004	Mask/Fins/Snorkel	Half Day
Sunday, June 08, 2003	K001	Bicycle	Half Day
Sunday, June 08, 2003	S001	Surf Board	Half Day
Sunday, June 08, 2003	N004	Inline Skates	Half Day
Sunday, June 08, 2003	S002	Surf Board	Full Day
Tuesday, June 10, 2003	L001	Cooler	Half Day
Tuesday, June 10, 2003	C001	Beach Chair	Half Day
Thursday, June 12, 2003	U001	Umbrella	Half Day
Thursday, June 12, 2003	N001	Inline Skates	Half Day
Thursday, June 12, 2003	C004	Lounge Chair	Half Day
Friday, June 13, 2003	N001	Inline Skates	Hourly
Saturday, June 14, 2003	B002	Boogie Board	Hourly
Saturday, June 14, 2003	N007	Inline Skates	Half Day

Monday, June 16, 2003   *Page 1 of 2*

4. **Select the sort order.** A report can be sorted based on the data in a field. For example, the Date field has been selected below:

The button to the right of the sort field indicates the sort order. In this case, ascending. Clicking Ascending reverses the sort order and displays Descending . Selecting Next displays the next Report Wizard dialog box.

5. **Select the layout.** Clicking a Layout option shows a portion of the layout style in the left side of the dialog box:

Landscape orientation allows more fields to fit across the paper. Selecting Next displays the next Report Wizard dialog box.

6. **Select the report style.** Clicking Corporate will give the report a professional appearance:

Selecting Next displays the next Report Wizard dialog box.

7. **Enter the report title.** A report title can be typed and the option to preview the report can be selected:

closing a report

Selecting Finish displays the new report. Clicking the displayed report alternates between magnified and full-page views. A report is closed by clicking the Close button (✕) in the upper-right corner of the report window.

The Report Wizard makes creating a report simple and fast so that many reports with different grouping, sorting, layouts, and styles can be created. Reports cannot be edited from the report shown after the Report Wizard is finished. Therefore, it may be necessary to generate several reports until the best presentation for the data is achieved.

opening a report

A report is opened by first clicking Reports in the Database window to display report objects. Next, double-clicking a report name or selecting a report name and then clicking the Open button () on the Database window toolbar opens the report. Any changes made to the tables or queries used in a report are automatically reflected each time a report is displayed.

In this practice you will create two reports for the BEACH RENTALS database.

① *OPEN BEACH RENTALS*

Open BEACH RENTALS, which was last modified in Chapter 14, Practice 9.

② *CREATE A RENTALS REPORT*

a. In the BEACH RENTALS : Database window, click Reports.

b. Double-click the Create report by using wizard icon. A dialog box is displayed.

  1. In the Tables/Queries list, select Table: Rentals. The fields of the Rentals table are displayed in the Available Fields list.

  2. Click ItemName and then click ⟩. The ItemName field is moved to the Selected Fields list.

  3. Move the ItemID field to the Selected Fields list.

  4. In the Tables/Queries list, select Table: Renters. The fields of the Renters table are displayed in the Available Fields list.

  5. Move the Date and ReservedTime fields to the Selected Fields list.

  6. Select Next. Viewing options are displayed. Click by Rentals if it is not already selected.

  7. Select Next. The grouping levels are displayed.

  8. Click ItemName if it is not already selected and then click ⟩. The report data will be grouped at three levels.

  9. Select Next. Sorting options are displayed.

  10. In the first sort list, select Date. Ascending should be displayed.

  11. Select Next. Layout options are displayed.

  12. Select Stepped if it is not already selected.

  13. Select Next. Style options are displayed.

  14. Select Corporate if it is not already selected.

  15. Select Next. The last dialog box is displayed.

  16. In the What title do you want for your report? box, type Rentals Report to replace the existing title.

  17. Select Preview the report if it is not already selected.

  18. Select Finish. The Rentals Report is displayed.

c. At the bottom of the report window, use the scroll buttons to view the pages of the report.

d. Select File → Print. A dialog box is displayed.

  1. Select Pages. In the From box, type 1 and in the To box, type 1.

  2. Select OK. The first page of the report is printed and looks similar to that shown on page 15-1.

③ *CLOSE THE REPORT*

In the upper-right corner of the Rentals Report window, click the Close button (✕). The report is closed and the report name is displayed in the BEACH RENTALS : Database window.

④ *CREATE A BICYCLE RENTALS REPORT*

    a. In the BEACH RENTALS : Database window, double-click the Create report by using wizard icon. A dialog box is displayed.

        1. In the Tables/Queries list, select Query: Bicycle Rentals. The Available Fields list displays the fields used in the Bicycle Rentals query.

        2. Move the ItemName, Date, and ReservedTime fields to the Selected Fields list.

        3. Select Next. Viewing options are displayed.

        4. Click by Renters. The report is organized by the Renters records.

        5. Select Next. The grouping level is displayed.

        6. No further grouping will be used. Therefore, select Next. Sorting options are displayed.

        7. In the first sort list, select Date. Ascending should be displayed.

        8. Select Next. Layout options are displayed.

        9. Select Tabular if it is not already selected.

        10. Select Next. Style options are displayed.

        11. Select Corporate if it is not already selected.

        12. Select Next. The last dialog box is displayed.

        13. In the What title do you want for your report? box, type Bicycle Rentals to replace the existing title.

        14. Select Preview the report if it is not already selected.

        15. Select Finish. The Bicycle Rentals report is displayed as shown on the next page:

Bicycle Rentals

Date	ItemName	ReservedTime
Sunday, June 01, 2003	Bicycle	Half Day
Monday, June 02, 2003	Tandem Bicycle	Hourly
Tuesday, June 03, 2003	Bicycle	Full Day
Sunday, June 08, 2003	Bicycle	Half Day
Sunday, June 15, 2003	Bicycle	Full Day
Sunday, June 15, 2003	Bicycle	Full Day

    b. Select File → Print. A dialog box is displayed.

        1. Select OK. The report is printed.

⑤ *CLOSE THE REPORT*

    Close the report. The report name is displayed in the Database window.

15.3 Report Summaries

Statistics on a number field, such as an average or minimum value, can be displayed as a *summary* in a report. For example, the following Beach Rentals report displays a summary of the average temperature:

June Temperatures

Date by Month	Date	AirTemp
June 2003		
	Sunday, June 01, 2003	32
	Monday, June 02, 2003	30
	Tuesday, June 03, 2003	31
	Wednesday, June 04, 2003	31
	Thursday, June 05, 2003	32
	Friday, June 06, 2003	32
	Saturday, June 07, 2003	31
	Sunday, June 08, 2003	32
	Monday, June 09, 2003	32
	Tuesday, June 10, 2003	34
	Wednesday, June 11, 2003	32
	Thursday, June 12, 2003	34
	Friday, June 13, 2003	34
	Saturday, June 14, 2003	33
	Sunday, June 15, 2003	33
Summary for 'Date' = 6/15/2003 (15 detail records)		
Avg		32.2

A summary can be added to a report that has at least one grouping level and at least one numeric field. A summary is added by selecting Summary Options in the sorting options Report Wizard dialog box, which displays the Summary Options dialog box with a list of the numeric fields included in the report. For the June Temperatures report, the dialog box lists the AirTemp field, which is the only numeric field included in the report. The Avg check box can be selected to display the average of the temperatures in the report:

A Guide to Microsoft Office XP Professional

Other summary values can be added using the check boxes:

- the Sum check box adds the data
- the Min check box determines the smallest value in the data
- the Max check box determines the largest value in the data.

After selecting a summary check box, OK is selected to remove the dialog box and continue with the other Report Wizard dialog boxes.

Practice 2 ♺

In this practice you will create a report with a summary. Open BEACH RENTALS if it is not already displayed.

① *CREATE A JUNE TEMPERATURES REPORT WITH A SUMMARY*

a. In the BEACH RENTALS : Database window, click Reports if report names are not already displayed.

b. Double-click the Create report by using wizard icon. A dialog box is displayed.

1. In the Tables/Queries list, select Table: Conditions. The fields of the Conditions table are displayed in the Available Fields list.

2. Move the Date and AirTemp fields to the Selected Fields list.

3. Select Next. The grouping level is displayed.

4. Click Date and then click ⊒. A grouping level is added to the report.

5. Select Next. Sort order and summary options are displayed.

6. In the first sort list, select Date. Ascending should be displayed.

7. Select Summary Options. A dialog box is displayed.

   a. Select the Avg check box.

   b. Select OK. The sort order and summary options dialog box is again displayed.

8. Select Next. Layout options are displayed.

9. Select Stepped if it is not already selected.

10. Select Next. Style options are displayed.

11. Select Corporate if it is not already selected.

12. Select Next. The last dialog box is displayed.

13. In the What title do you want for your report? box, type June Temperatures to replace the existing title.

14. Select Preview the report if it is not already selected.

15. Select Finish. The June Temperatures report is displayed. Note the average summary at the bottom of the report.

② *PRINT AND THEN CLOSE THE REPORT*

③ *CLOSE BEACH RENTALS*

15.4 Using Fields in Query Criteria

The criteria of a select query can refer to a field in the database. For example, a candy store uses a database to maintain sales information. A select query could be used to determine which products have a retail price that is more than a 200% markup (a 200% markup equals three times the cost). This query criteria is "greater than 3×Cost" in the Retail field:

In the **Criteria**, the format [Table Name]![Field Name] is used to refer to a field. Field references are not case sensitive. For example, [Products]![Cost] is the same as [products]![cost]. However, spaces in a field reference generate an error. For example, [Products] ! [Cost] is invalid. In the criteria above, an asterisk (*) is used to indicate multiplication. When run, the select query displays the following datasheet:

Field Reference Considerations

A table name or field name that has been typed incorrectly produces an unexpected dialog box when the query is run:

Selecting **Cancel** removes the dialog box so that the query criteria can be checked.

Practice 3

In this practice you will create a select query that uses a field in the criteria.

① *OPEN CANDY*

Open the CANDY database, which is a data file for this text.

② *QUERY FOR PRODUCTS WITH A MARKUP OVER 200%*

a. In the CANDY : Database window, click Queries.

b. Double-click the Create query in Design view icon. The Select Query window is displayed with the Show Table dialog box on top.

   1. Add the Products table to the select query and then close the Show Table dialog box.

c. Drag the ProductName, Cost, and Retail fields from the Products table to the first, second, and third Field boxes in the design grid, respectively.

d. In the Criteria box of Retail type >3*[Products]![Cost]

e. Run the query. The select query datasheet looks similar to that shown in Section 15.4. Note how each of the records have a retail price more than three times that of the cost.

f. Save the query naming it Over 200% Markup.

g. Print and then close the datasheet.

15.5 Calculated Fields

A *calculated field* displays the result of a mathematical expression that is defined in a select query. For example, a Profit field can be added to a select query in the CANDY database. A calculated field is created in a Field box of the select query design grid by typing a new field name followed by a colon and then an expression to calculate the values to be displayed in that field:

A field reference is in an expression should be in the format [Table Name]![Field Name]. In the Profit field above, the expression subtracts the Cost field value from the Retail field value to determine the value displayed in the new Profit field. The calculated field and its expression in the design grid shown on the previous page are completely displayed because the column was widened by dragging its right boundary. Running the select query displays the following datasheet:

ProductName	Cost	Retail	Profit
Boston Baked Beans	$0.25	$0.75	$0.50
Candy Necklace	$0.40	$1.00	$0.60
Cinnamon Hearts	$0.20	$0.75	$0.55
Gold Mine Bubble Gum	$0.40	$1.00	$0.60
Licorice Laces	$0.01	$0.05	$0.04
Ring Pop	$0.20	$0.50	$0.30
Rootbeer Barrels	$0.02	$0.05	$0.03
Swedish Fish	$0.01	$0.05	$0.04
Wax Bottles (6 pack)	$0.30	$0.50	$0.20
Wax Lips	$0.20	$0.50	$0.30
*	$0.00	$0.00	

Record: 1 of 10

Note that the Profit field is based on an expression entered in the select query, and is not a field in one of the tables. Calculation fields are not stored in a table and data cannot be directly entered into the field.

Practice 4

In this practice you will create a select query that includes a calculated field. Open CANDY if it is not already displayed.

① CREATE A PROFIT CALCULATION FIELD

a. In the CANDY : Database window, click Queries if query names are not already displayed.

b. Double-click the Create query in Design view icon. The Select Query window is displayed with the Show Table dialog box on top.

 1. Add the Products table to the select query and close the Show Table dialog box.

c. Add the ProductName, Cost, and Retail fields to the first, second, and third Field boxes in the design grid, respectively.

d. In the fourth Field box, type the calculated field Profit:[Products]![Retail]-[Products]![Cost] and then press Enter.

e. Size the calculated field column so that the formula is displayed entirely:

Field:	ProductName	Cost	Retail	Profit: [Products]![Retail]-[Products]![Cost]
Table:	Products	Products	Products	
Sort:				
Show:	☑	☑	☑	☑
Criteria:				
or:				

f. Run the query. Format the select query datasheet appropriately. The select query datasheet looks similar to that shown in section 15.5.

g. Save the query naming it Profit.

h. Print and then close the datasheet.

② *CLOSE THE CANDY DATABASE*

③ *QUIT ACCESS*

15.6 Where can you go from here?

The last three chapters have introduced the concepts of relational databases. You can now create tables, forms, select queries, and reports in a relational database. The relational database has other options and applications not discussed in this text which you may want to explore using the Access online help.

Microsoft Office includes a powerful integration feature called mail merge. Mail merge combines data in an Access database with a Word document to produce personalized form letters. Mail merge is discussed in Chapter 16.

Reports and forms can be customized in Design view. Appendix C introduces creating and editing forms and reports in Design view.

Chapter Summary

Create report by using wizard

This chapter explained how to produce reports, which present data for printing in an organized manner with a descriptive title and headings. A report is easily created using the Report Wizard, which provides dialog boxes for selecting fields to be included in the report as well as report formatting options.

Statistics about a number field in a report can be displayed as a summary. Summary options are available when a report has at least one grouping level and at least one numeric field. Summary Options displays a dialog box where Sum, Avg, Min, and/or Max check boxes can be selected for displaying statistics.

Select queries can include fields in their criteria by using the format [Table Name]![Field Name] to refer to a field. This format is also used when creating a calculated field, which displays the result of an expression. Calculated fields are created in a select query and are not stored in a table. Data cannot be directly entered into a calculated field.

Vocabulary

Calculation field   Displays the result of a mathematical expression that is defined in a select query.

Grouping data   Organizing data in a report by a field's data to eliminate displaying duplicate entries and increase readability.

Report   A powerful database feature that is used to present data for printing in an organized manner with a descriptive title and headings.

Report Wizard   Provides dialog boxes for selecting fields for the report and report formatting options.

Sort order   The order in which records are listed in a report.

Summary   Displays statistics for a number field.

Access Commands and Buttons

Open button   Opens a selected report. Found on the Database window toolbar.

Displays the report objects. Found in the Database window.

Review Questions

Section 15.1 — 15.3

1. What is a database report?

2. If a change is made to a table used in a report, is the change displayed the next time the report is viewed?

3. If a database contains five tables, fields from how many of the tables may be included in a report?

4. What does the view in a report determine?

5. Explain how grouping data in a report can make the report easier to understand.

6. a) Explain what sort order is in a report.
   b) How can the sort order be changed from ascending to descending?

7. List a report style and explain how it affects the appearance of a report.

8. a) What is a report summary?
   b) List the steps required to add a report summary that sums the values in a number field.

Section 15.4 — 15.6

9. What is the format used to refer to a field name in the Criteria row of a design grid?

10. a) What is a calculated field?
    b) Can a calculated field be a field in a table?

Exercise 1 ✺ ─────────────────────────── VIDEO STORE

The VIDEO STORE database last modified in Chapter 14, Exercise 12 contains information on a video store's members, videos, and rentals. Open VIDEO STORE and create the following reports and query:

a) Create a report that displays the FirstName, LastName, Phone, and Credit fields from the Members table. Group the report by the Credit field, and sort the report on the LastName field in ascending order. Select appropriate layout and style options. Title the report Members Report. Print the report.

b) Create a select query that displays the TapeID, Name, Year, and Type fields of movies that are of drama type. Save the select query naming it Drama Movies.

c) Create a report that displays the Name and Year fields from the Drama Movies query. Sort the report on the Name field in ascending order. Select appropriate layout and style options. Title the report Drama Movies Report. Print the report.

Exercise 2 ✺ ─────────────────────────── Museum Exhibits

The Museum Exhibits database last modified in Chapter 14, Exercise 2 contains information on exhibits and attendance. Open Museum Exhibits and create the following reports and query:

a) Create a report that displays the ExhibitID, ExhibitName, and Department fields from the Exhibits table and the Year and Attendance fields from the Attendance table. View the report by Exhibits, and group the report by the Department field. Sort the report on the Attendance field in descending order, and include a summary that averages the Attendance field. Select appropriate layout and style options. Title the report Exhibits Attendance Report. Print the report.

b) Create a report that displays all the fields from the Why Does That Happen Exhibits query. View the report by Exhibits and group the report by the ExhibitID field. Include a summary that totals the Attendance field. Select appropriate layout and style options. Title the report Why Does That Happen Exhibits Report. Print the report.

c) Create a select query that displays the ExhibitID, ExhibitName, Department, Year, and Attendance fields for all exhibits in the year 2004 and includes a calculated field named Predicted2004Attendance. Sunport Science Museum predicts that the attendance in 2004 will be 10% higher than the attendance in 2003. Therefore, the predicted 2004 attendance is calculated by multiplying the Attendance field by 1.1. Format the calculated field by right-clicking the formula in the design grid, selecting Properties, and then selecting Standard from the Format list and 0 from the Decimal Places list. Format the select query datasheet appropriately. Save the select query naming it Predicted 2004 Attendance. Print a copy in landscape orientation.

Exercise 3 ⟳ ———————————————————————————Library

The Library database last modified in Chapter 14, Exercise 3 contains information on books and authors. Open Library and create the following reports:

a) Create a report that displays all the fields from the Books table. Group the report by the Type field. Select appropriate layout and style options. Title the report Books Report. Print the report.

b) Create a report that displays the FirstName and LastName fields from the Authors table and the Title and Type fields from the Books table. View the report by Authors, and sort the report on the Title field in ascending order. Select appropriate layout and style options. Title the report Authors and Their Books. Print the report.

Exercise 4 ⟳ ——————————————————————— INVENTIONS

The INVENTIONS database last modified in Chapter 14, Exercise 13 contains information on inventions and inventors. Open INVENTIONS and create the following queries and reports:

a) Create a select query that displays the Invention, Country, Year, FirstName, and LastName fields of all inventions created in the United States. Save the select query naming it United States Inventions.

b) Create a report that displays the Invention, Year, FirstName, and LastName fields from the United States Inventions query. Sort the report on the Year field in ascending order. Select appropriate layout and style options. Title the report United States Inventions Report. Print the report.

c) Create a select query that displays the FirstName, LastName, Country, and Born fields for all the inventors born in the 1800s. You will need to enter >=1800 And <=1899 as the criteria for the Born field. Save the select query naming it Inventors Born in the 1800s.

d) Create a report that displays all of the fields from the Inventors Born in the 1800s query. Group the report by the Country field, and sort the report on the LastName field in ascending order. Select appropriate layout and style options. Title the report Inventors Born in the 1800s Report. Print the report.

Exercise 5 ⟳ ——————————————————————— Boat Storage

The Boat Storage database last modified in Chapter 14, Exercise 5 contains information on employees, boats, and boat owners. Open Boat Storage and create the following reports and query:

a) Create a report that displays the FirstName, LastName and Phone fields from the Employees table. Sort the report on the LastName field in ascending order. Select appropriate layout and style options. Title the report Employee Phone List. Print the report.

b) Create a report that displays the FirstName and LastName fields from the Boat Owners table and the Boat, SlotNumber, and Fee fields from the Boats table. View the report by Boat Owners. Include a summary that totals the Fee field. Select appropriate layout and style options. Title the report Boat Fees Report. Print the report.

c) Create a select query that displays the Boat, Fee, FirstName of boat owner, and LastName of boat owner fields for all boat owners and includes a calculated field named AnnualRenewal. The annual renewal charge is calculated by multiplying the Fee field by 30% (0.30). Format the calculated field by right-clicking the formula in the design grid, selecting Properties, and then selecting Currency from the Format list. Format the datasheet appropriately. Save the select query naming it Annual Renewal Charges. Print a copy.

Exercise 6 ☼ ———————————————————————— Ivy U Athletics

The Ivy U Athletics database last modified in Chapter 14, Exercise 6 contains information on players, sports, and coaches. Open Ivy U Athletics and create the following reports and queries:

a) Create a report that displays the FirstName, LastName, Sport, and Salary fields from the Coaches table. Group the report on the Sport field, and sort the report on the LastName field in ascending order. Include a summary that totals the Salary field. Select appropriate layout and style options. Title the report Coaches Salary Report. Print the report.

b) Create a report that displays the FirstName, LastName, and Sport fields from the Players table and the Semester field from the Sports table. View the report by Sports, and group the report by the Sport field. Sort the report on the LastName field in ascending order. Select appropriate layout and style options. Title the report Players Report. Print the report.

c) Create a select query that displays the FirstName of the coach, LastName of the coach, Sport, and Salary fields for all the coaches and includes a calculated field named Bonus. The bonus is calculated by multiplying the Salary field by 0.15. Format the calculated field by right-clicking the formula in the design grid, selecting Properties, and then selecting Currency from the Format list. Format the select query datasheet appropriately. Save the select query naming it Coach Bonuses and print a copy.

d) Create a select query that displays the Sport, Semester, and Budget fields for all sports and includes a calculated field named BudgetProposal. The budget proposal is calculated by multiplying the Budget field by 1.15. Format the calculated field by right-clicking the formula in the design grid, selecting Properties, and then selecting Currency from the Format list. Format the select query datasheet appropriately. Save the query naming it Budget Proposal and print a copy.

Exercise 7 ☼ ———————————————————————— Second Ocean

The Second Ocean database last modified in Chapter 14, Exercise 7 contains information on animals, facilities, and facility checks. Open Second Ocean and create a report that displays all the fields from the Statistics on Animals query. View the report by Facility Checks, and group the report by the Facility field. Sort the report on the DateOfCheck field in descending order. Select appropriate layout and style options. Title the report Animal Statistics Report. Print the report.

Exercise 8 ✸ ————————————————————— Green Thumb

The Green Thumb database last modified in Chapter 14, Exercise 8 contains information on plants, transactions, and vendors. Open Green Thumb and create the following reports and queries:

a) Create a report that displays the Plant, InStock, Cost, and Retail fields from the Plants table. Sort the report on the Plant field in ascending order. Select appropriate layout and style options. Title the report Plants Report. Print the report.

b) Create a report that displays the Name, Address, City, State, and Zip fields from the Vendors table. Sort the report on the Name field in ascending order. Select appropriate layout and style options. Title the report Current Vendors. Print the report.

c) Create a report that displays all the fields from the Cost of Plants query. View the report by Vendors and sort the report on the Plant field in ascending order. Select appropriate layout and style options. Title the report Cost of Plants. Print the report.

d) Create a report that displays the Plant field from the Plants table and the Date and Quantity fields from the Transactions table. View the report by Plants, and sort the report on the Date field in descending order. Include a summary that totals the Quantity field. Select appropriate layout and style options. Title the report Transactions Report. Print the report.

e) Create a select query that displays the Name, Phone, Plant, InStock, and Reorder fields for all plants that have less stock than their reorder number. Save the select query naming it Plants to Reorder. Print the select query datasheet.

f) Create a select query that displays the Plant, Cost, and Retail fields for all plants and includes a calculated field named Profit. The profit of a plant is calculated by subtracting the Cost field from the Retail field. Format the select query datasheet appropriately. Save the query naming it Plant Profit. Print the select query datasheet.

g) Create a select query that displays the TransID, Date, PlantID, Quantity, and Retail fields for all transactions and includes a calculated field named Revenue. The revenue of a transaction is calculated by multiplying the Retail field by the Quantity field. Format the select query datasheet appropriately. Save the query naming it Transaction Revenues. Print the select query datasheet.

h) Create a report that displays all the fields from the Transaction Revenues select query. Group the report on the PlantID field, and sort the report on the TransID field in ascending order. Include a summary that totals the Quantity, Retail, and Revenue fields. Select appropriate layout and style options. Title the report Transaction Revenues Report. Print the report.

Exercise 9 ✸ ————————————————————— Pizza Payroll

The Pizza Payroll database last modified in Chapter 14, Exercise 9 contains information on employees and payroll. Open Pizza Payroll and create the following reports and queries:

a) Create a report that displays the LastName, FirstName, Address, City, State, and Zip fields from the Employees table. Sort the report on the LastName field in ascending order. Select appropriate layout and style options. Title the report Current Employees. Print the report.

b) Create a report that displays the EmployeeID, Date, GrossPay, and Taxes fields from the Employee EI Payroll query. View the report by Employees, and sort the report on the Date field in descending order. Include a summary that averages the GrossPay and Taxes fields. Select appropriate layout and style options. Title the report Employee EI Report. Print the report.

c) Create a report that displays the FirstName and LastName fields from the Employees table and the Date, GrossPay, and Taxes fields from the Payroll table. View the report by Employees, and sort the report on the Date field in descending order. Include a summary that totals the GrossPay and Taxes fields. Select appropriate layout and style options. Title the report Payroll Report. Print the report.

d) Create a select query that displays the EmployeeID, Date, GrossPay, and Taxes fields for all employees and includes a calculated field named NetPay. Net pay is calculated by subtracting the Taxes field from the GrossPay field. Format the query datasheet appropriately. Save the query naming it Net Pay. Print the select query datasheet.

Exercise 10 ✇ ———————————————————————— Coral Research

The Coral Research database last modified in Chapter 14, Exercise 10 contains information on coral sites and growth research. Open Coral Research and create a report that displays the CoralName field from the Coral Sites table and the Date and Size fields from the Growth Research table. View the report by Coral Sites, and sort the report on the Date field in ascending order. Select appropriate layout and style options. Title the report Coral Growth Report. Print the report.

Exercise 11 ✇ ———————————————————————— Travel Agency

The Travel Agency database last modified in Chapter 14, Exercise 11 contains information on clients, vacations, and booked vacations. Open Travel Agency and create the following report and query:

a) Create a report that displays the FirstName and LastName fields from the Clients table, the Package and Cost fields from the Vacations table, and the Date field from the Booked Vacations table. View the report by Clients, and sort the report on the Date field in ascending order. Include a summary that totals the Cost field. Select appropriate layout and style options. Title the report Booked Vacations Report. Print the report.

b) Create a select query that displays the Package and Cost fields for all vacations and includes a calculated field named Discount. The discount is calculated by multiplying the Cost field by 0.20 and then subtracting that amount from the Cost field. Format the calculated field by right-clicking on the formula in the design grid, selecting Properties, and then selecting Currency from the Format collapsible list. Format the select query datasheet appropriately. Save the query naming it Early Booking Discounts. Print the select query datasheet.

Exercise 12 (advanced) ⟳ ───────────────────────── Club

Modify the Club database created in Chapter 13, Exercise 12 to include at least one report. Include a summary in one of the reports, if possible. Create a select query that uses either a field in the criteria or includes a calculated field.

Exercise 13 (advanced) ⟳ ───────────────────────── Music

Modify the Music database created in Chapter 13, Exercise 13 to include at least one report. Include a summary in one of the reports, if possible. Create a select query that uses either a field in the criteria or includes a calculated field.

Exercise 14 (advanced) ⟳ ───────────────────────── Sports

Modify the Sports database created in Chapter 13, Exercise 14 to include at least one report. Include a summary in one of the reports, if possible. Create a select query that uses either a field in the criteria or includes a calculated field.

Chapter 16
Integrating Data Between Access, Word, and Excel

Select **A**ll Records

Database

Analyze It with Microsoft Excel

Rename

Mail Merge Wizard

Chapter 16 Expectations

After completing this chapter you will be able to:

1. Copy data from Access to Word.

2. Insert and link Access data into a Word document.

3. Create an Excel workbook from Access data.

4. Use Excel data to create an Access table.

5. Use the Mail Merge Wizard to create form letters and mailing labels from Access data.

This chapter discusses integrating data between Access, Word, and Excel. Mail merge is also introduced.

16.1 Copying Data From Access to Word

The data in an Access datasheet can be copied to a Word document. Businesses sometimes use this feature to include data from tables or queries in letters or annual reports.

The steps for copying data from an Access table or query displayed in Datasheet view to an open Word document are:

1. Select the data to be copied. All of the records can be selected by selecting Select All Records from the Edit menu.

2. Click the Copy button (📋) on the toolbar. A copy of the data is added to the Clipboard.

3. Display the Word document that is to receive the copied data.

4. Place the insertion point in the document where the data is to be inserted.

5. Click the Paste button (📋) on the toolbar. The contents of the Clipboard are placed in the document at the insertion point, and the Paste Options button (📋) is displayed.

The pasted data is placed in a Word table as an inline object:

October·14,·2003¶
¶
Dear·Frank:¶
¶
The·current·inventory·is·summarized·below:¶
¶

Inventory·Table¤		
Item·Number	Item·Name¤	Quantity¤
200303¤	Outdoor·Table¤	21¤
301902¤	Garden·Hose¤	450¤
409081¤	Lawn·Chair¤	329¤
559920¤	Lawn·Sprinkler¤	88¤
876532¤	Umbrella¤	345¤
895822¤	Barbecue¤	299¤

static The pasted data is *static*, which means it will not change if data in the source file changes.

Techniques for Selecting Records

In Datasheet view, an entire record is selected by clicking its record selector. Multiple records are selected by dragging a record selector.

Selecting Data

Data in a field box can be selected by placing the pointer just to the left of the data until the pointer changes to ⊕ and clicking. Adjacent data can then be selected by dragging.

In this practice you will copy Access data to a Word document. A select query will be used to display only the desired data.

① *OPEN THE CONCESSION STAND MEMO DOCUMENT*

Open CONCESSION STAND MEMO, which is a Word data file for this text.

② *OPEN THE CONCESSION STAND DATABASE*

Open CONCESSION STAND, which is an Access data file for this text.

③ *APPLY A SELECT QUERY*

Run the Reorder query. The ProductName and InStock fields for the products that have less than 100 in stock are displayed in a datasheet.

④ *COPY DATA TO THE CLIPBOARD*

a. Select Edit → Select All Records. All of the records in the query are selected.

b. On the toolbar, click the Copy button (🔳). A copy of the selected data is added to the Clipboard.

c. Close the select query datasheet. The CONCESSION STAND : Database window is displayed.

⑤ *PASTE THE CLIPBOARD CONTENTS INTO THE CONCESSION STAND MEMO*

a. Display the CONCESSION STAND MEMO document.

b. In the blank paragraph below the sentence that begins "The following…", place the insertion point.

c. Press Enter. A blank paragraph is created.

d. On the toolbar, click the Paste button (🔳). The Clipboard contents are placed at the insertion point in a Word table. Ignore the Paste Options button.

Check - Your memo should look similar to:

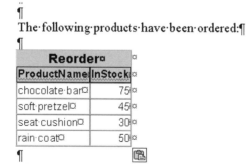

⑥ *PRINT AND THEN CLOSE THE MODIFIED CONCESSION STAND MEMO*

a. Create a footer with your name right aligned.

b. Save and then print the document.

c. Close CONCESSION STAND MEMO and Quit Word.

⑦ *CLOSE THE CONCESSION STAND DATABASE AND QUIT ACCESS*

16.2 Inserting and Linking Access Data into a Word Document

Data from a saved Access table or query can be inserted into a Word document and linked, which allows the data to be updated in Word if there are changes to the Access table or query.

displaying the Database toolbar

Data from a saved Access table or query is inserted by placing the insertion point in the Word document where the table or query is to appear and then selecting Database from the Toolbars submenu in the View menu, which displays the Database toolbar:

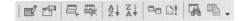

inserting data

Clicking the Insert Database button ( ) on the Database toolbar displays the Database dialog box:

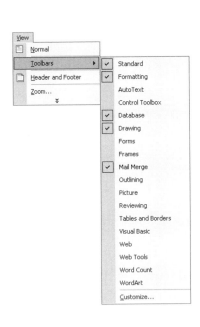

Selecting Get Data displays the Select Data Source dialog box:

The Look in list and contents box below it are used to display the Access database file name that contains the table or query to be inserted. When the contents box displays the appropriate file name, clicking that file name and then selecting Open displays the Select Table dialog box:

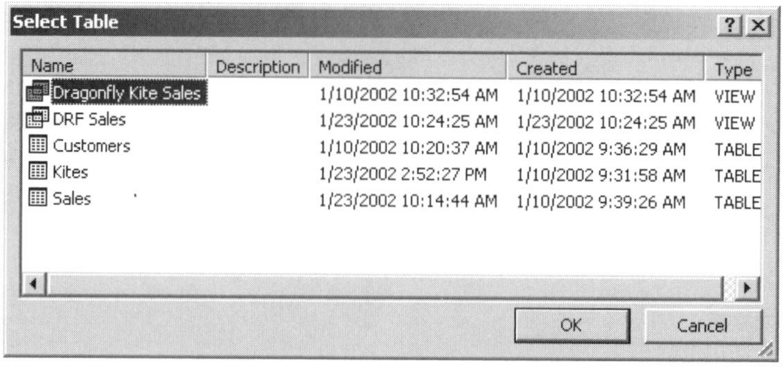

Clicking the name of a table or query and then selecting OK displays the Database dialog box:

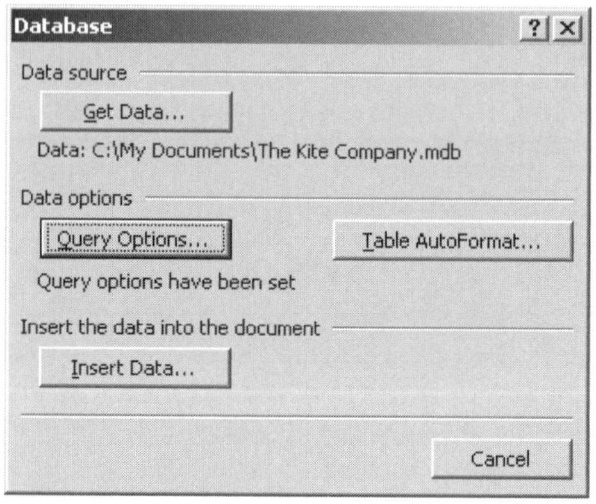

Table AutoFormat

Selecting Table AutoFormat in the Database dialog box displays another dialog box used to select a style for the table, such as Classic or Elegant.

Note the database file name in the Data source area. Selecting Insert Data displays the Insert Data dialog box:

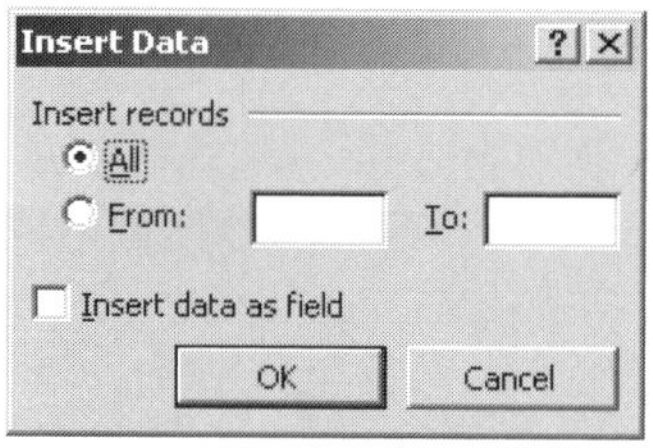

linking data

Selecting All inserts all of the records from the data source or specific records can be specified in the From and To boxes. Selecting the Insert data as field check box inserts the records as database fields and creates a link to the source file, which allows the fields to be updated if the Access table or query changes. Selecting OK displays the records in a Word table:

SalesID¤	SalesDate¤	CustomerID¤	ItemID¤	Quantity¤	¤
3¤	9/30/2003¤	GFK¤	DRF¤	12¤	¤
6¤	10/17/2003¤	SKC¤	DRF¤	10¤	¤
7¤	10/21/2003¤	GFK¤	DRF¤	8¤	¤

updating the Word table

If the Access source table or query is updated, clicking the Word table and then clicking the Update Field button () on the Database toolbar or pressing the F9 key updates the data in the Word table. Note that the modified Access table or query must be saved and closed and the source database window left open in order for the Word table to be updated.

A Guide to Microsoft Office XP Professional

modifying the Word table

In Word, buttons on the Database toolbar can be used to modify the inserted table. Clicking the Add New Record button () adds a new record to the Word table and clicking the Delete Record button () removes the record in the row that the insertion point is placed. Data can be sorted by placing the insertion point in the column to base the sort on and clicking the Sort Ascending button () or the Sort Descending button ().

Practice 2

In this practice you will insert and link data from an Access table into a Word document.

① *OPEN THE GARDEN DEPARTMENT DOCUMENT*

    a. Open GARDEN DEPARTMENT, which is a Word data file for this text.

    b. Place the insertion point in the last blank paragraph in the document.

    c. Select View ➜ Toolbars ➜ Database to display the Database toolbar if it is not already displayed.

② *INSERT DATA*

    a. On the Database toolbar, click the Insert Database button (◰). A dialog box is displayed.

        1. Select Get Data. A dialog box is displayed.

            a. Use the Look in list and the contents box below it to display the file name GARDEN INVENTORY, which is an Access data file for this text.

            b. In the contents box, click GARDEN INVENTORY.

            c. Select Open. The dialog box is removed and another dialog box is displayed.

        2. Select the Inventory table name and then OK. The dialog box is removed and another dialog box is displayed. Note that the selected data source is displayed in the dialog box.

        3. Select Insert Data. A dialog box is displayed.

            a. Select All if it is not already selected.

            b. Select the Insert data as field check box.

            c. Select OK. The dialog box is removed and the data is displayed in a Word table. Note that all the data in the table is selected.

③ *OPEN THE GARDEN INVENTORY DATABASE*

    a. Open GARDEN INVENTORY, which is an Access data file for this text.

    b. Display the Inventory table in Datasheet view.

④ *UPDATE INVENTORY RECORDS*

    a. Change the Outdoor Table quantity from 21 to 100.

    b. Change the Umbrella item name to Sun Umbrella.

    c. Save the modified Inventory Table.

    d. Close the Inventory table. The GARDEN INVENTORY : Database window is again displayed.

⑤ *UPDATE THE WORD TABLE*

    a. Display the GARDEN DEPARTMENT document.

    b. Click the Word table. The insertion point appears in the table.

    c. On the Database toolbar, click the Update Field button (◰). The table is updated to match the Access table.

⑥ *SORT THE DATA*

a. Place the insertion point in the Quantity column. All the data in the table is selected.

b. On the Database toolbar, click the Sort Ascending button (![A-Z down arrow]). The table is sorted in ascending order based on the Quantity data.

⑦ *DELETE A RECORD*

a. Place the insertion point in the Outdoor Table row.

b. On the Database toolbar, click the Delete Record button (![icon]). The record is deleted from the Word table.

⑧ *SAVE, PRINT, AND THEN CLOSE THE MODIFIED GARDEN DEPARTMENT*

a. Create a footer with your name right aligned.

b. Save and then print the document.

c. Close GARDEN DEPARTMENT.

⑨ *QUIT WORD*

Quit Word. The GARDEN INVENTORY : Database window is again displayed.

16.3   Creating a Workbook from Access Data

Access data that is in a table can be displayed and saved as an Excel workbook. Displaying Access data in Excel allows calculations to be performed on the data, What If? questions to be asked, and charts created. Opening a database file and clicking Tables in the Database window displays the table objects:

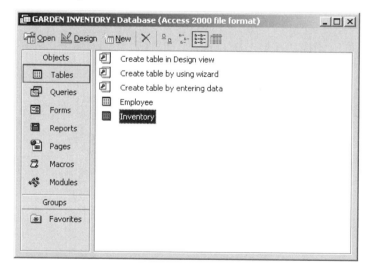

Selecting a table object and then selecting Analyze It with Microsoft Excel from the Office Links submenu in the Tools menu displays the selected Access table as an Excel workbook in a new window:

	A	B	C	D	E
1	Item Number	Item Name	Quantity		
2	200303	Outdoor Table	100		
3	301902	Garden Hose	450		
4	409081	Lawn Chair	329		
5	559920	Lawn Sprinkler	88		
6	876532	Sun Umbrella	345		
7	895822	Barbecue	299		
8					

The displayed data is automatically saved as an Excel workbook with the same name as the Access table name it was created from. Note the title bar above.

The Analyze It with Microsoft Excel command can also be applied to queries, forms, and reports. The OfficeLinks button ( ) on the toolbar can be used instead of the command.

Practice 3

In this practice you will display an Access table as an Excel workbook. Open the GARDEN INVENTORY database if it is not already displayed.

① SELECT THE INVENTORY TABLE

Display the Inventory table in Datasheet view.

② DISPLAY THE TABLE AS AN EXCEL WORKBOOK

Select Tools → Office Links → Analyze It with Microsoft Excel. The table is displayed in a new Excel window. Note the Inventory file name in the title bar, which indicates the table has been automatically saved as an Excel workbook.

③ CREATE A CHART

a. Select cells B2 through C7. The item name and quantity for each of the inventory items are selected.

b. On the toolbar, click the Chart Wizard button ( ). The first Chart Wizard dialog box is displayed.

    1. In the Chart type list, click Column if it is not already selected.

    2. Select Next. The second Chart Wizard dialog box is displayed.

    3. Verify that the correct range =Inventory!$B$2:$C$7 is displayed in the Data range box. An example of the column chart is displayed in the dialog box.

    4. Select Next. The third Chart Wizard dialog box is displayed. Select the Titles tab if those options are not already displayed.

    5. In the Chart title box, type Garden Inventory.

    6. In the Category (X) axis box, type Item.

    7. In the Value (Y) axis box, type Inventory.

    8. Select Finish to skip the last dialog box and have the chart appear as an object in the active sheet.

9. Delete the legend from the chart.

10. Click a blank cell. The chart is no longer selected.

④ *SAVE THE MODIFIED INVENTORY WORKBOOK*

    a. Create a header with the date center aligned and a footer with your name right aligned.

    b. Size and move the chart so that the worksheet fits on one page.

    c. Save the modified Inventory workbook.

    d. Print a copy of the worksheet with gridlines and row and column headings.

⑤ *QUIT EXCEL*

Quit Excel. The Inventory workbook is closed. The GARDEN INVENTORY: Database window is again displayed.

⑥ *QUIT ACCESS*

Quit Access. The GARDEN INVENTORY: Database window is closed.

16.4 Using Excel Data to Create an Access Table

Excel worksheet data can be used to create a table in an existing Access database so that queries and reports can be performed on the data.

The steps for using Excel data to create a table in an open Access database are:

1. Select the source, which is the range of cells to be used to create the table.

2. Click the Copy button (📋) on the toolbar. A copy of the source is added to the Clipboard.

3. Display the Database window that is to receive the table and select Tables. Note that the workbook must remain open until the copied data is pasted into a new table.

4. Click the Paste button (📋) on the toolbar. Access displays a dialog box asking if the first row of the copied data contains column headings:

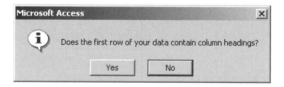

Selecting Yes uses the first row of data as field names. Selecting No uses the first row of data as a record. If No is selected, the table will need to be displayed in Design view so that appropriate field names can be defined.

renaming a table   When data from an Excel worksheet is pasted into an Access database, Access creates a table naming it the same as as the sheet it was copied from. For example, Sheet1. A table name is changed by right-clicking it in the Database window and then selecting Rename from the menu, which selects that table name and displays the insertion point. The new name can then be typed and Enter pressed to rename the table.

completing the table   After the table is renamed, it should be displayed in Design view to select the primary key and check the field types and formats. Descriptions should also be added for each of the fields. The new table's relationship to the other tables in the database must be defined before the new table can be used in a select query or report.

Practice 4

In this practice you will create a new Access database table from Excel worksheet data.

① *OPEN THE CONCESSION STAND EMPLOYEES WORKBOOK*

Open CONCESSION STAND EMPLOYEES, which is an Excel data file for this text.

② *COPY THE SPREADSHEET DATA*

a. Select cells A3 through C7.

b. On the toolbar, click the Copy button (🖹). A copy of the selected data is added to the Clipboard.

③ *CREATE A NEW TABLE*

a. Open the CONCESSION STAND database, which is an Access data file for this text.

b. In the CONCESSION STAND : Database window, click **Tables**.

c. On the toolbar, click the Paste button (🖺). A dialog box is displayed.

    1. Select **Yes**. A new table is created and another dialog box is displayed.

    2. Select **OK**. The dialog box is removed.

d. Right-click the name of the new table, Sheet1. A menu is displayed.

e. Select **Rename**. The menu is removed and the table name is selected.

f. Type Employees and then press Enter to replace the existing table name.

④ *QUIT EXCEL*

Quit Excel. The CONCESSION STAND EMPLOYEES workbook is closed.

⑤ *MODIFY THE NEW TABLE*

a. Display the Employees table in Design view.

b. Enter appropriate descriptions for each field.

c. Click the EmployeeID **Field Name** box.

d. On the toolbar, click the Primary Key button.

e. In the **Required** list in the **Field Properties** part of the window, select Yes.

f. Change the **Field Size** to 4 for the EmployeeID field, 20 for the FirstName field, and 30 for the LastName field.

g. Save and close the modified table. If warning dialog boxes are displayed, select **Yes** in each one.

⑥ *DEFINE THE RELATIONSHIP BETWEEN THE EMPLOYEES AND SALES TABLES*

    a. Select <u>T</u>ools → <u>R</u>elationships. The Relationships window is displayed.

    b. On the toolbar, click the Show Table button ( ). A dialog box is displayed.

        1. Add the Employees table.

        2. Select **Close**. The dialog box is removed.

    c. In the Employees table, drag the EmployeeID field to the EmployeeID field in the Sales table. A dialog box is displayed.

        1. Verify that the EmployeeID field of the Employees and Sales table appear in the dialog box.

        2. Select **Create**. The dialog box is removed.

    d. Save the modified relationships.

    e. Close the Relationships window.

⑦ *QUERY THE DATABASE*

    a. Create a select query that includes the LastName field from the Employees table, the ProductName field from the Products table, and the EventID and Quantity fields from the Sales table. The criteria for the query is bottled water in the ProductName field.

    b. Run the query. Four records are displayed.

    c. Save the query naming it Bottled Water Sales and then print the query datasheet.

⑧ *QUIT ACCESS*

    Quit Access. The CONCESSION STAND : Database window is closed.

16.5   Mail Merge - Form Letters

form letter
merge fields

In Word, the Mail Merge Wizard can be used to integrate data stored in an Access database with a Word document. Mail merge is commonly used to create personalized form letters. A *form letter* is a Word document that includes *merge fields*, which are placeholders that indicate where data from an Access table or query should be inserted. For example, a business may create a letter to mail to thousands of recipients that is personalized by merging name and address data from an Access table.

A mail merge form letter is created by first creating a new Word document and then selecting <u>M</u>ail Merge Wizard from the <u>L</u>etters and Mailings submenu in the <u>T</u>ools menu, which displays the Mail Merge task pane:

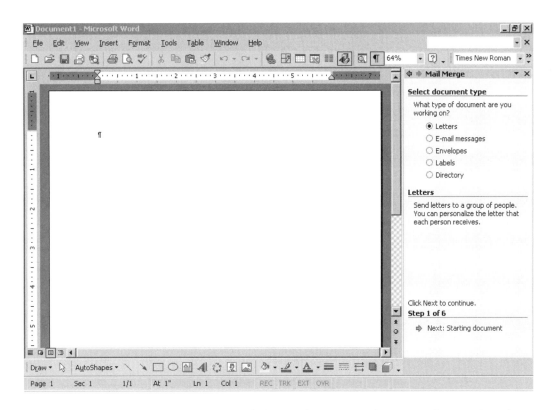

Note that the bottom of the Mail Merge task pane indicates that there are six mail merge steps that need to be completed. The six steps are:

1. **Select the document type.** In the Mail Merge task pane shown above, selecting Letters indicates form letters are to be created. Clicking <u>Next: Starting document</u> displays the next set of options.

2. **Select the starting document.** Selecting Use the current document starts the form letter in the displayed new Word document:

Clicking <u>Next: Select recipients</u> displays the next set of options.

3. **Select the recipients.** Selecting Use an existing list indicates the merge fields for the letter will come from an Access database:

Clicking <u>Browse</u> displays the Select Data Source dialog box:

The Look in list and the contents box below it are used to display the appropriate Access database file. When the contents box displays the correct file name, clicking that file name and then selecting Open displays the Select Table dialog box, which lists all of the tables and queries in the database:

Selecting the table or query name that contains the merge field data and then OK displays the Mail Merge Recipients dialog box:

A Guide to Microsoft Office XP Professional

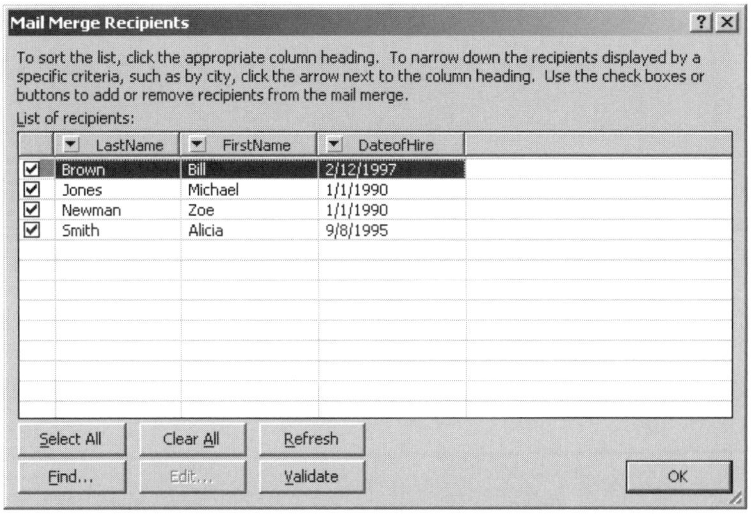

The Mail Merge Recipients dialog box displays a list of the data stored in the selected Access database table or query. Selecting OK accepts the list of recipients to be included in the mail merge.

Clicking Next: Write your letter displays the next set of options.

4. **Write the letter.** Type the text that will appear in every letter and insert merge fields where appropriate. For example, the letter below has three merge fields:

November·3,·2003¶
¶
¶
¶
Dear·«FirstName»·«LastName»:¶
¶
The·Human·Resources·department·is·currently·creating·a·company·seniority·list.·Please·verify·that·your·date·of·hire·is·accurate.·According·to·our·records,·your·date·of·hire·is·«DateofHire».·¶
¶
If·the·information·is·incorrect,·please·notify·the·Human·Resources·department·immediately.¶
¶
Sincerely,¶
¶
¶
Monica·Keating¶
Human·Resources·Manager¶

A merged field is inserted by placing the insertion point where the merged text is to appear and then clicking More Items in the Mail Merge task pane:

The Insert Merge Field dialog box is then displayed with a list of the fields from the source Access table or query:

Clicking a field name in the Field list and then selecting Insert displays the merge field in the Word document. Selecting Close removes the dialog box. The merge field can then be formatted just like any other text.

Clicking <u>Next: Preview your letters</u> displays the next set of options.

5. **Preview the merged letter.** The letter for the first recipient is displayed in the Word window:

November·3,·2003¶
¶
¶
¶
Dear·Bill·Brown:¶
¶
The·Human·Resources·department·is·currently·creating·a·company·seniority·list.·Please·
verify·that·your·date·of·hire·is·accurate.··According·to·our·records,·your·date·of·hire·is·
2/12/1997.·¶
¶
If·the·information·is·incorrect,·please·notify·the·Human·Resources·department·
immediately.¶
¶
Sincerely,¶
¶
¶
Monica·Keating¶
Human·Resources·Manager¶

The Mail Merge task pane contains options for previewing other letters and editing the recipient list:

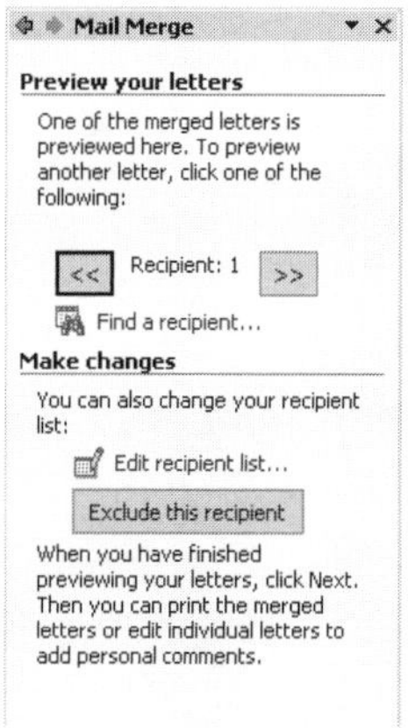

Clicking >> displays the next form letter and clicking << displays the previous form letter. The list of recipients can be edited by clicking Edit recipient list.

Clicking Next: Complete the merge displays the next set of options.

6. **Print the form letters.** The Mail Merge task pane contains options to print and edit the form letters:

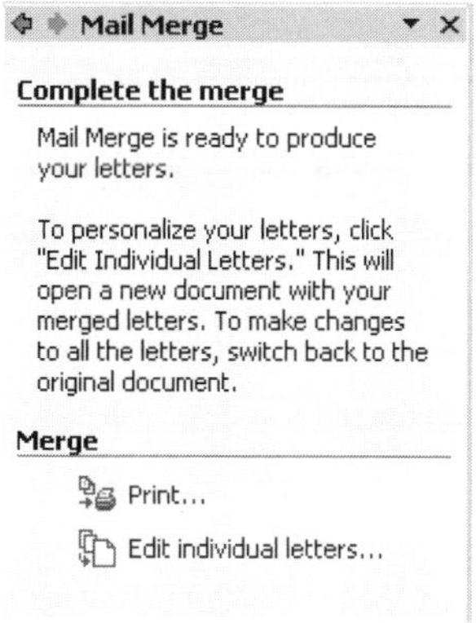

Clicking Print displays the Merge to Printer dialog box:

Selecting All prints all of the merged letters. Selecting Current record prints the displayed letter and specific letters can be printed by typing a number in the From and To boxes. Selecting OK displays the Print dialog box. In the Print dialog box, selecting OK prints the merged letter(s).

Practice 5 ♻

In this practice you will create and print mail merged letters.

① CREATE A NEW WORD DOCUMENT

② CREATE A FORM LETTER

    a. Select Tools → Letters and Mailings → Mail Merge Wizard. The Mail Merge task pane is displayed.

        1. In the Mail Merge task pane, select Letters if it is not already selected.

        2. Click Next: Starting document. The next set of options is displayed.

        3. In the Mail Merge task pane, select Use the current document if it is not already selected.

        4. Click Next: Select recipients. The next set of options is displayed.

        5. In the Mail Merge task pane, select Use an existing list if it is not already selected.

        6. Click Browse. A dialog box is displayed.

            a. Use the Look in list and the contents box below it to display the file name CONCESSION STAND, which was last modified in Practice 4.

            b. In the contents box, click CONCESSION STAND.

            c. Select Open. Another dialog box is displayed.

            d. Select the Employees table and then OK. Another dialog box is displayed.

            e. Select OK. The dialog box is removed and the Word document is displayed.

        7. In the Mail Merge task pane, click Next: Write your letter. The next set of options is displayed.

    b. In the Word document, type today's date and then press Enter five times.

    c. Type Dear and a space.

    d. In the Mail Merge task pane, click More Items. A dialog box is displayed.

        1. Click the FirstName field and then select Insert. A merge field is inserted in the document.

        2. Select Close. The dialog box is removed.

    e. Type a space and then insert the LastName merge field.

    f. Type a colon (:) and then press Enter twice.

g. Type the rest of the letter and insert the FirstName merge field as shown below, substituting your name for Your Name and allowing Word to wrap the text:

```
August·2,·2003¶
¶
¶
¶
¶
Dear·«First_Name»·«Last_Name»·:¶
¶
Thank·you·«First_Name»·for·your·excellent·work·this·past·year.·Due·to·record·sales,·I·
have·decided·to·award·you·a·bonus·in·your·next·paycheck.·Keep·up·the·good·work!·¶
¶
Sincerely,¶
¶
¶
¶
Your·Name¶
Manager¶
```

h. Save the form letter naming it Concession Stand Bonus.

③ PREVIEW A MERGED COPY OF THE FORM LETTER

In the Mail Merge task pane, click <u>Next: Preview your letters</u>. The next set of options is displayed and the letter for the first recipient is displayed in the Word window. Note that the merge fields are replaced by data from the Employees table.

④ VIEW THE MERGED DATA

a. In the Mail Merge task pane, click <u>>></u>. The letter for the next recipient is displayed.

b. Continue to click <u>>></u> to view the rest of the merged letters.

⑤ PRINT THE MAIL MERGED LETTERS AND THEN CLOSE THE DOCUMENT

a. Click <u>Next: Complete the merge</u>. The next set of options is displayed.

b. In the Mail Merge task pane, click <u>Print</u>. A dialog box is displayed.

    1. Select All if it is not already selected.

    2. Select OK. The dialog box is removed and another dialog box is displayed.

    3. Select OK. Four letters are printed, with each personalized for the employees in the database.

c. Save and close Concession Stand Bonus.

16.6   Mail Merge - Mailing Labels

The Mail Merge Wizard can also be used to create mailing labels. Like a mail merge form letter, mailing labels are created in a document that includes merge fields.

When printing mailing labels, adhesive paper with multiple labels to a page is used in the printer. The Avery® brand of adhesive labels is widely used, and the dimensions of many of its labels have been included in Word. Therefore only the Avery product number needs to be selected for Word to automatically print labels in the appropriate format.

Mailing labels are created by first creating a new Word document and then selecting <u>M</u>ail Merge Wizard from the <u>L</u>etters and Mailings submenu in the <u>T</u>ools menu, which displays the Mail Merge task pane. Note that just like creating a form letter, there are six steps to complete in the Mail Merge task pane. The six steps are:

1. **Select the document type.** In the Mail Merge task pane, selecting Labels indicates mailing labels are to be created:

Clicking <u>Next: Starting document</u> displays the next set of options.

2. **Select the starting document.** Selecting Change document layout allows a label size to be selected:

Clicking <u>Label options</u> displays the Label Options dialog box:

Selecting the appropriate Product number and any other necessary options and then selecting OK displays outlined mailing labels in the document.

Clicking <u>Next: select recipients</u> displays the next set of options.

3. **Select the recipients.** Selecting Use an existing list indicates the names and addresses for the labels will come from an Access database:

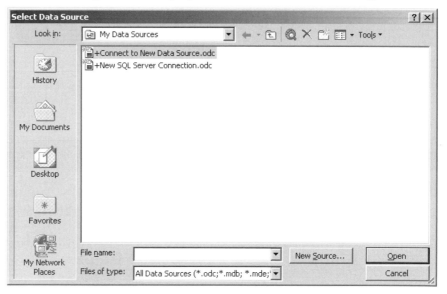

Clicking <u>Browse</u> displays the Select Data Source dialog box:

The Look in list and the contents box below it are used to display the appropriate Access database file. When the contents box displays the correct file name, clicking that file name and then selecting Open displays the Select Table dialog box, which lists all of the tables and queries in the database:

Selecting the table or query name that contains the names and addresses for the mailing labels and then selecting OK displays the Mail Merge Recipients dialog box:

Mail Merge Recipients

To sort the list, click the appropriate column heading. To narrow down the recipients displayed by a specific criteria, such as by city, click the arrow next to the column heading. Use the check boxes or buttons to add or remove recipients from the mail merge.

List of recipients:

	N...	Address	City	State	Z...	Ph...	VendorID	
☑	Sports...	98 1st Street	Sunport	FL	33568	(407)55...	V101	Ju
☑	The S...	8766 Wire ...	Ann A...	MI	48107	(303)55...	V102	Ge
☑	Glend...	5463 N.W. ...	Cairo	GA	31768	(912)55...	V103	Vir

Select All   Clear All   Refresh

Find...   Edit...   Validate   OK

The Mail Merge Recipients dialog box displays a list of the data stored in the selected Access database table or query. Selecting OK accepts the list of recipients to be included in the mail labels and displays «Next·Record» on each mailing label in the Word document.

Clicking Next: Arrange your labels displays the next set of options.

4. **Insert merge fields.** Using the first outlined label in the Word document, layout the label by placing merged fields. A proper address format can be selected by clicking Address block in the Mail Merge task pane

Mail Merge

Arrange your labels

If you have not already done so, lay out your label using the first label on the sheet.

To add recipient information to your label, click a location in the first label, and then click one of the items below.

⊞ Address block...

⊡ Greeting line...

⊡ Electronic postage...

‖‖ Postal bar code...

▤ More items...

When you have finished arranging your label, click Next. Then you can preview each recipient's label and make any individual changes.

Replicate labels

You can copy the layout of the first label to the other labels on the page by clicking the button below.

Update all labels

which displays the Insert Address Block dialog box:

Insert Address Block

Specify address elements

☑ Insert recipient's name in this format:

Joshua
Joshua Randall Jr.
Joshua Q. Randall Jr.
Mr. Josh Randall Jr.
Mr. Josh Q. Randall Jr.
Mr. Joshua Randall Jr.

☑ Insert company name

☑ Insert postal address:

◉ Never include the country/region in the address
○ Always include the country/region in the address
○ Only include the country/region if different than:

Preview

Mr. Joshua Randall Jr.
Blue Sky Airlines
1 Airport Way
Kitty Hawk, NC 27700

Match Fields...   OK   Cancel

Selecting the appropriate options and OK displays «‹AddressBlock›» in the first label. In the Mail Merge task pane, clicking **Update all labels** copies the layout of the first label to the other labels on the page.

Clicking <u>Next: Preview your labels</u> displays the next set of options.

5. **Preview the labels.** The merged fields are replaced by merged data in the Word document:

Sports Stuff 98 1st Street Sunport, FL 33568	The Soda Fountain 8766 Wire Lane Ann Arbor, MI 48107	Glendor Incorporated 5463 N.W. 21st Lane Cairo, GA 31768

Note that the label text can be formatted just like any other text and may need to be sized to fit in the outlined label.

Clicking <u>Next: Complete the merge</u> displays the next set of options.

6. **Print the labels.** The Mail Merge task pane contains options to print and edit the mailing labels:

Clicking <u>Print</u> displays the Merge to Printer dialog box:

Selecting All prints the merged labels. Selecting Current record prints the displayed label and specific labels can be printed by typing a number in the From and To boxes. Selecting OK displays the Print dialog box. In the Print dialog box, selecting OK prints the labels(s).

Practice 6 ♻

In this practice you will create mailing labels and print the labels on plain paper.

① *CREATE A NEW WORD DOCUMENT*

② *CREATE MAILING LABELS*

    a. Select <u>T</u>ools → <u>L</u>etters and Mailings → <u>M</u>ail Merge Wizard. The Mail Merge task pane is displayed.

       1. In the Mail Merge task pane, select Labels.

       2. Click <u>Next: Starting document</u>. The next set of options is displayed.

       3. In the Mail Merge task pane, select Change document layout if it is not already selected.

       4. Click <u>Label options</u>. A dialog box is displayed.

          a. In the Product number list, select 5260 – Address.

          b. Select OK. The dialog box is removed.

       5. Click <u>Next: Select recipients</u>. The next set of options is displayed.

       6. In the Mail Merge task pane, select Use an existing list if it is not already selected.

7. Click <u>Browse</u>. A dialog box is displayed.

    a. Use the Look in list and the contents box below it to display the file name CONCESSION STAND, which was last modified in Practice 5.

    b. In the contents box, click CONCESSION STAND.

    c. Select Open. Another dialog box is displayed.

    d. Select the Vendors table and then OK. Another dialog box is displayed.

    e. Select OK. The dialog box is removed and the Word document displays outlined mailing labels.

8. In the Mail Merge task pane, click <u>Next: Arrange your labels</u>. The next set of options is displayed.

9. In the Mail Merge task pane, click <u>Address Block</u>. A dialog box is displayed.

    a. Select OK. The dialog box is removed and the «AddressBlock» merge field is displayed in the first label.

10. In the Mail Merge task pane, click Update all labels. The layout of the first label is copied to the other labels on the page. Note that the other labels also display the Next Record merge field which indicates the data is to come from the next record in the Vendors table.

③ VIEW THE MERGED DATA

In the Mail Merge task pane, click <u>Next: Preview your labels</u>. The next set of options is displayed and the merged fields are replaced by data from the Vendors table.

④ SAVE, PRINT THE MERGED LABELS, AND THEN CLOSE THE DOCUMENT

a. Save the document naming it Vendor Labels.

b. Click <u>Next: Complete the merge</u>. The next set of options is displayed.

c. In the Mail Merge task pane, click <u>Print</u>. A dialog box is displayed.

    1. Select All if it is not already selected.

    2. Select OK. The dialog box is removed and another dialog box is displayed.

    3. Select OK. The labels are printed.

d. Save and close Vendors Labels.

⑤ QUIT WORD

Chapter Summary

This chapter presented the steps necessary to integrate an Access database with a Word document or Excel workbook. Mail Merge was also covered.

The steps for copying the data in an Access table or query displayed in Datasheet view to an open Word document are:

1.   Select the data to be copied.

2.   Click the Copy button on the toolbar. A copy of the data is added to the Clipboard.

3.   Display the Word document that is to receive the copied data.

4. Place the insertion point in the document where the data is to be inserted.

5. Click the Paste button on the toolbar. The contents of the Clipboard are placed in the document at the insertion point, and the Paste Options button is displayed.

Data from a saved Access table or query can be inserted into a Word document and linked using buttons on the Database toolbar. This allows the data to be updated in Word if there are changes to the Access table or query.

Access data that is in a table can be displayed and saved as an Excel workbook by using the Analyze It with Microsoft Excel command or clicking the OfficeLinks button. Displaying Access data in Excel allows calculations to be performed, What If? questions to be asked, and charts created.

Excel worksheet data can be used to create a new table in an existing Access database so that queries and reports can be performed on the data.

In Word, the Mail Merge Wizard can be used to integrate data stored in an Access database with a Word document. Mail merge is commonly used to create personalized form letters. A form letter is a Word document that includes merge fields, which are placeholders that indicate where data from an Access table or query should be inserted. Mail merge is also used to create mailing labels. Mail merge form letters or mailing labels are created using the Mail Merge Wizard command. Before printing mailing labels, special adhesive paper needs to be inserted into the printer.

Vocabulary

F9 key Updates the data in a Word table that is linked to an Access table or query.

Form letter A Word document that includes merge fields.

Mailing labels A type of mail merge document used to print addresses on special adhesive paper.

Merge fields Placeholders that indicate where data from an Access table or query should be inserted.

Static Pasted data that does not change if the data in the source file changes.

Access and Word Commands and Buttons

Analyze It with Microsoft Excel command Displays Access data in an Excel workbook. Found in the Office Links submenu in the Tools menu. The OfficeLinks button on the toolbar can be used instead of the command.

Copy button Places a copy of the selected data on the Clipboard. Found on the toolbar.

Database command Displays the Database toolbar in Word. Found in the Toolbars submenu in the View menu.

Mail Merge Wizard command Displays the Mail Merge task pane that is used to select options for creating form letters or mailing labels. Found in the Letters and Mailings submenu in the Tools menu.

Paste button Places the Clipboard contents in a worksheet starting at the selected cell. Found on the toolbar.

Paste Options button Displayed when Clipboard contents are placed in cells.

Rename command Used to rename an Access table. Found in the menu displayed by right-clicking a table name.

Select All Records command Selects all the records in a datasheet. Found in the Edit menu.

Review Questions

Sections 16.1 — 16.4

1. List the steps required to copy all the records in an Access database table to an open Word document.

2. What happens to Access data when it is pasted into a Word document?

3. What is static data?

4. What is the advantage of inserting and linking data from an Access table into a Word document instead of just copying and pasting the data?

5. List the steps required to update linked Access data in a Word table.

6. List the steps required to display and save the data in an Access table as an Excel workbook.

7. List three reasons why you would display and save Access data in an Excel workbook.

8. List the steps required to create an Access table named Customers from data in an Excel worksheet.

Sections 16.5 — 16.6

9. What can the Mail Merge Wizard be used to do?

10. What is a form letter?

11. What are merge fields?

12. Give an example of when you would use the Mail Merge Wizard.

13. What are mailing labels?

Exercise 1   ⟳ ————————————————————————————Vacations

The owner of Hot Spot travel agency wants to ask What If? questions about the data stored in the Travel Agency database last modified in Chapter 15, Exercise 11. Open Travel Agency and complete the following steps:

   a) Display the Vacations table as a new Excel workbook.

   b) Insert two columns between columns C and D (Nights and Location).

   c) In cell D1, enter the label Cost per Night. In column D, enter formulas that use cell references to calculate the cost per night of the vacation packages. Cost per night is calculated by dividing the cost by the number of nights. Include appropriate formatting. Change the column width as necessary.

   d) In cell E1, enter the label Price. The owner has decided that if the cost per night is less than $200, then the price of the vacation package is 20% more than the cost, otherwise the price of the vacation package is 50% more than the cost. In column E, enter formulas that use the IF function to calculate and display the price. Change the column width as necessary.

   e) Format the worksheet appropriately.

   f) Create a header with your name right aligned.

   g) Save the modified Vacations and print a copy with gridlines and row and column headings.

Exercise 2   ⟳ ————————————————————————— Exhibits Memo

The board members of Sunport Science Museum want a list of the exhibits and the last time they were updated. The information is stored in the Museum Exhibits database last modified in Chapter 15, Exercise 2. Open Museum Exhibits and complete the following steps:

   a) In a new Word document create the following memo, substituting your name with Your Name, allowing Word to wrap the text, and formatting as shown:

> **Memorandum**¶
> ¶
> **TO:** → Board·Member¶
> ¶
> **FROM:**→Your·Name¶
> ¶
> **DATE:**→February·1,·2003¶
> ¶
> **RE:** → Exhibit·List¶
> ¶
> The·following·list·shows·the·exhibits·currently·showing·at·Sunport·Science·Museum,·the·
> department·they·are·in,·and·the·last·time·the·exhibits·have·been·updated:¶

   b) Copy the ExhibitName, Department, and Updated data in the Exhibits table to the memo after the last paragraph. Make sure there is a blank line between the paragraph and the copied data.

c) Save the memorandum naming it Exhibits Memo.

d) Open the BOARD MEMBERS workbook that contains information on all the board members of Sunport Science Museum.

e) Create a new table in the Museum Exhibits database from the data stored in the BOARD MEMBERS workbook.

f) Rename the new table Board Members.

g) Define the FirstName and LastName fields as the primary key. Add descriptions and modify the Field Properties for each field appropriately.

h) The Exhibits and Board Members tables are related by the Department and DepartmentHead fields. Create the appropriate relationship between the Exhibits and Board Members tables.

i) Using the Museum Exhibits database, modify the memorandum to mail merge the board members' first and last names in place of the words "Board Member."

j) Save the modified Exhibits Memo.

k) Print a non-mail merged copy of Exhibits Memo and then print the mail merged memos.

Exercise 3 ✪ ──────────── Plants, Green Thumb Vendor Labels

The owner of a plant nursery wants to ask What If? questions about the data stored in the Green Thumb database last modified in Chapter 15, Exercise 8. Open Green Thumb and complete the following steps:

a) Display the Plants table as a new Excel workbook.

b) Delete the PlantID column.

c) Insert a column between columns C and D (Reorder and Cost).

d) In cell D1, enter the label Reorder Now. Change the column width as necessary. Plants need to be reordered when the amount in stock is less than the reorder number. In column D, enter formulas that use the IF function to display Reorder when more plants need to be reordered, or No Reorder if not. Include appropriate formatting.

e) Insert two columns between columns F and G (Retail and VendorID).

f) In cell G1, enter the label Profit. In column G, enter formulas that use cell references to calculate the profit made on each plant. The profit is calculated by subtracting the cost of the plant from the retail price of the plant. Change the column width as necessary.

g) In cell H1, enter the label Total Profit. In column H, enter formulas that use cell references to calculate the total profit made when all the plants are sold. The total profit is calculated by multiplying the profit per plant by the number of plants in stock. Change the column width as necessary.

h) Format the worksheet appropriately.

i) Create a footer with your name right aligned.

j) Save the modified Plants workbook and print a copy in landscape orientation with gridlines and row and column headings.

k) In a new Word document create mailing labels (5260 - Address) using the Vendors table in the Green Thumb database.

l) Save the document naming it Green Thumb Vendor Labels and then print the merged labels on plain paper.

Exercise 4 ———————————————————— Activity Letter

The ROBOTICS CLUB relational database contains information on the history and activities of the robotics club. The president of the club wants to send a letter to all the members informing them of the upcoming meeting. Open ROBOTICS CLUB and complete the following steps:

a) In a new Word document create the following letter, substituting your name with Your Name and allowing Word to wrap the text:

> January·1,·2003¶
> ¶
> ¶
> ¶
> ¶
> Dear·Member:¶
> ¶
> This·semester·is·going·to·be·a·great·semester·for·the·Robotics·Club.·With·your·help·and·
> dedication,·I·hope·to·increase·our·membership·to·15·people.·For·the·meeting·on·January·
> 15,·please·look·over·the·following·activities·we·have·done·in·the·past·and·bring·
> suggestions·and·ideas·for·new·activities:¶
> ¶
> Sincerely,¶
> ¶
> ¶
> ¶
> Your·Name¶
> President¶

b) In the ROBOTICS CLUB database, create a select query that displays the Date, Activity, and Attendance fields from the Activities table. Save the query naming it List of Activities.

c) Copy all the records in the List of Activities select query to the letter after the last sentence in the body of the letter, which ends "…for new activities:." Be sure there is a single blank line before and after the copied data.

d) Save the letter naming it Activity Letter.

e) Open the ROBOTICS CLUB MEMBERS workbook that contains information on the members of the robotics club.

f) Create a new table in the ROBOTICS CLUB database from the data stored in cells A3 through E11 in the ROBOTICS CLUB MEMBERS workbook.

g) Rename the new table Members.

h) Define the StudentID field in the Members table as the primary key. Add descriptions and modify the Field Properties for each field appropriately.

i) The Activities and Members tables are related by the InCharge and StudentID fields. The Members and Club History tables are related by the StudentID field. Create the appropriate relationships between the Activities, Members, and Club History tables.

j) Create a select query that displays the FirstName, LastName, and Status fields of the Members table of those members who still have an active status. Save the query naming it Active Members.

k) Using the Active Members query in the ROBOTICS CLUB database, modify the letter to mail merge the active members' first and last names in place of the word "Member."

l) Scroll through the merged letters to make sure only active members will receive the letter. Make any necessary corrections.

m) Save the modified Activity Letter.

n) Print a non-mail merged copy of the letter and then print the mail merged letters.

Exercise 5 ———————————————— Repair Request Letter

The ARCADE relational database contains information on the games owned by a local arcade. The owner of the arcade needs to send letters to all the manufacturers regarding broken games. Open ARCADE and complete the following steps:

a) Open the ARCADE MAINTENANCE RECORD workbook that contains all the maintenance information on the games at the arcade.

b) Create a new table in the ARCADE database from the data stored in cells A3 through H13 of the ARCADE MAINTENANCE RECORD workbook.

c) Rename the new table Maintenance.

d) Define the JobNumber field in the Maintenance table as the primary key. Add descriptions and modify the Field Properties for each field appropriately.

e) The Games and Maintenance tables are related by the Game field. Create the appropriate relationship between the Games and Maintenance tables.

f) Create a select query that displays the Name, ContactFirstName, ContactLastName, Game, Problem, Date, and Fixed fields of those games that have not been fixed. Save the select query naming it Broken Games.

g) In a new Word document create the following letter, substituting your name with Your Name, entering the merge fields as shown (using the Broken Games query in the ARCADE database), and allowing Word to wrap the text:

> July·15,·2003¶
> ¶
> ¶
> ¶
> ¶
> Dear·<<ContactFirstName>>·<<ContactLastName>>:¶
> ¶
> I·own·the·<<Game>>·game.·However,·the·game·is·not·working·properly·because·of·the· following·reason:·<<Problem>>.·It·has·been·out·of·service·since·<<Date>>.·Please·send·a· maintenance·representative·from·your·company·as·soon·as·possible.¶
> ¶
> Thank·you,¶
> ¶
> ¶
> ¶
> Your·Name¶
> Owner·of·Nickel·and·Dime·Arcade¶

h) Scroll through the merged letter to make sure only the manufactures of the broken game will receive the letter. Make any necessary corrections.

i) Save the letter naming it Repair Request Letter.

j) Print a non-mail merged copy of the letter and then print the mail merged letters.

Exercise 6 (advanced)

Create an informative form letter based on Exercise 12, 13, or 14 in Chapter 13. The form letter should be merged based on a query resulting in less than five letters being printed. Also the form letter should contain information from the database that will be printed on every page. Save the form letter with an appropriate name. Print a non-mail merged copy of the letter and then print the mail merged letters.

Exercise 7 (advanced)

Create a database that contains a table that can be used as an address book. The table should contain at least 20 records of friends or family members. Create mailing labels that could be used to send on envelopes for holiday cards. Save the mailing labels with an appropriate name. Print the mail merged labels.

Chapter 17
PowerPoint Presentations

<u>V</u>iew Show

End Show

Slide Navigator

<u>N</u>ew Slide

<u>D</u>elete Slide

<u>C</u>lip Art

Print Pre<u>v</u>iew

<u>H</u>eader and Footer

Slide <u>T</u>ransition

Animation S<u>c</u>hemes

<u>S</u>lide Master

Notes <u>P</u>age

Chapter 17 Expectations

After completing this chapter you will be able to:

1. Explain what a presentation is.
2. Create a new presentation based on a template.
3. Display a presentation in different views.
4. Display different slides.
5. View a presentation.
6. Edit text on a slide.
7. Add and delete slides, and change the order of slides.
8. Add a picture to a slide.
9. Print a presentation.
10. Add footers to slides.
11. Add slide transitions and animation to slides.
12. Add a chart from an Excel workbook to a slide.
13. Plan and design a presentation.
14. Use the Slide Master.
15. Create and print speaker notes.

The History of Presentations

In the past, visuals included slides, handwritten or typed overheads, chalkboards, and poster boards. Some slide presentations required teams of artists to spend days or weeks laying out the slides using special expensive equipment. Today, presentations are easily created electronically, which simplifies the preparation time and allows more time for refinement.

With advances in technology, it is becoming easier to use a computer to play the presentation, whether it is displayed on a large screen in an auditorium or on a monitor at eye level. One of the bestselling presentation software applications is Microsoft PowerPoint.

$\mathbf{T}$his chapter describes how to create presentations that include text, charts, spreadsheet data, and clip art using Microsoft PowerPoint.

17.1   What is a Presentation?

visuals

Professionals and students all give presentations at one time or another. A *presentation* is an informative talk, such as a lecture or speech, that usually includes visuals. These *visuals* are often slides that are projected onto a large screen while the speaker talks. For example, a sales representative for a paper bag company visits a grocer and gives a presentation on why the grocer should buy paper bags. The sales representative uses slides to outline and emphasize the most important points of the presentation. Some slides contain pictures and charts which convey information that would otherwise be difficult to describe in words.

PowerPoint presentation
slide

Professional-looking visuals can be produced quickly on a computer using a presentation application such as *Microsoft PowerPoint*, the presentation application in Microsoft Office. A *PowerPoint presentation* is a collection of slides stored in a file, where each *slide* is an individual screen of the presentation. The presentation can be viewed on a screen by connecting the computer to a projector or a large monitor.

17.2   Creating a New PowerPoint Presentation

PowerPoint template

PowerPoint contains files called templates that are used to create a presentation. A *PowerPoint template* is an already formatted presentation that can be modified to fit specific needs. A new presentation based on a template is created by first selecting New Office Document from the Start menu, which displays the New Office Document dialog box. Selecting the Presentations tab displays the templates:

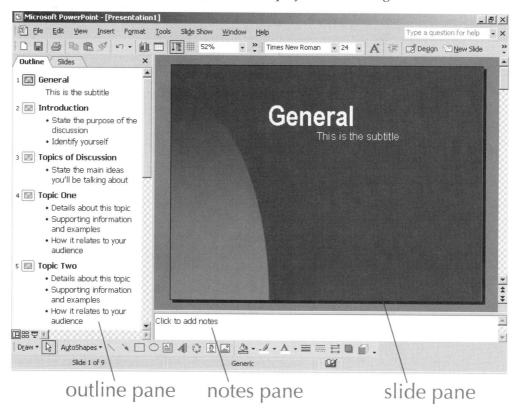

Starting PowerPoint and Creating a New Presentation

PowerPoint can be started by selecting **Microsoft PowerPoint** from the **Programs** submenu in the **Start** menu. A new presentation can be created by selecting <u>General Templates</u> in the New Presentation task pane, which displays a dialog box similar to the New Office Document dialog box.

Selecting one of the templates and then OK starts PowerPoint and creates an untitled presentation that contains several slides. The presentation is displayed in Normal view, which has three panes. For example, clicking the Generic icon and then OK displays the following:

outline pane   notes pane   slide pane

- **Outline pane** contains the text of all the slides in a format similar to Outline view in Word.

- **Notes pane** contains notes for the speaker that correspond to the displayed slide.

- **Slide pane** displays one slide at a time as it will appear in the presentation.

saving a presentation

A new presentation should be saved with a descriptive file name by selecting <u>S</u>ave from the <u>F</u>ile menu.

17.3   PowerPoint Views

PowerPoint has three views that can be used to display slides. Each view is selected by clicking one of the buttons in the lower-left corner of the PowerPoint window:

Normal view — Slide Show view
Slide Sorter view

- **Normal view** divides the window into three panes, which allows a slide, the outline, and speaker notes to be edited without changing views. Each pane can be sized by dragging on its top or right border.
- **Slide Sorter view** displays miniature slides that allow the order of slides in a presentation to be modified. Slide transitions and animations, discussed later, can be added in this view.
- **Slide Show view** displays the current slide in full-screen size as it appears during a presentation.

Commands in the <u>V</u>iew menu can also be used to change the view.

17.4   Displaying Slides

In Normal view, one slide is displayed at a time in the slide pane. The next or previous slide in the presentation can be displayed by:

- clicking the vertical scroll bars, box, or arrows
- pressing the Page Up or Page Down key

The outline pane can be used to display a specific slide. Clicking a slide icon () in the outline pane displays that slide in the slide pane. Clicking the Slides tab in the outline pane displays a picture of each slide in miniature:

Clicking a slide in the outline pane displays it in the slide pane.

display the next/previous slide

Page Up   Page Down

display a specific slide

Restoring the Panes

In Normal view, if the outline pane has been closed, selecting <u>N</u>ormal (Restore Panes) from the <u>V</u>iew menu restores the outline pane.

View

- Normal
- Sli<u>d</u>e Sorter
- Slide Sho<u>w</u>   F5
- <u>M</u>aster   ▶
- <u>C</u>olor/Grayscale   ▶
- <u>T</u>oolbars   ▶
- <u>H</u>eader and Footer...
- <u>Z</u>oom...
- ⌄⌄

Slide Buttons

The Previous Slide (⬆) and Next Slide (⬇) buttons are located below the vertical scroll bar. These buttons can be clicked to display the previous or next slide, respectively.

---

slide indicator   The *slide indicator* at the bottom of the window indicates the current slide and the total number of slides in the presentation:

slide indicator

The slide indicator is displayed in Normal view.

17.5   Viewing a Presentation

Slide Show view is used to play a completed presentation. The presentation can be started at the currently displayed slide by selecting the Slide Show button (⬛) in the lower-left corner of the window. Selecting View Show from the Slide Show menu or pressing the F5 key starts the presentation from Slide 1, regardless of which slide is currently displayed.

Once the presentation is started, the slides are displayed in full-screen size and the PowerPoint window is no longer visible. The keyboard and mouse are used during the presentation to control the slides:

- The next slide is displayed by either clicking, or pressing the N key, the Page Down key, or the spacebar.

- The previous slide is displayed by either pressing the P key or the Page Up key.

- The slide show is ended by pressing the Esc key, or by clicking the right mouse button and then selecting End Show from the menu.

In Slide Show view, a specific slide can be displayed by right-clicking anywhere on the screen and then selecting Slide Navigator from the Go submenu, which displays a dialog box. Selecting a slide and then Go To displays that slide.

Practice 1

In this practice you will create a new PowerPoint presentation using a template.

① **CREATE A NEW PRESENTATION**

    a. On the Taskbar, click Start. A menu is displayed.

    b. Select New Office Document. A dialog box is displayed.

        1. Click the Presentations tab to display the template icons.

        2. Click the Generic icon and then select OK. PowerPoint is started and the first slide of a generic presentation is displayed in Normal view. Note the three panes.

② **VIEW THE SLIDE SHOW**

    a. At the bottom of the PowerPoint window, click the Slide Show button (⬛). PowerPoint starts the presentation by filling the screen with the first slide:

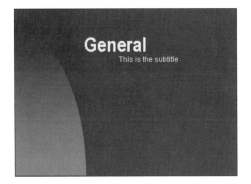

b. Click the mouse button. The show is advanced to the next slide, titled "Introduction."

c. Press the N key. The next slide is displayed.

d. Press the P key. The previous slide is displayed.

e. Press the Esc key. The presentation is again displayed in Normal view.

③ CHANGE VIEWS

a. In the lower-left corner of PowerPoint window, click the Slide Sorter view button (⊞). The entire presentation is displayed in miniature slides.

b. In the lower-left corner of PowerPoint window, click the Normal view button (⊡). The presentation is again displayed in Normal view.

④ DISPLAY DIFFERENT SLIDES AND VIEW THE SLIDE INDICATOR

a. In the slide pane, click the down scroll arrow. The slide indicator displays "Slide 3 of 9" and the "Topics of Discussion" slide is displayed.

b. In the outline pane, click the slide icon (▦) next to the "Topic One" text. The slide indicator now displays "Slide 4 of 9" and the slide is displayed in the slide pane.

c. Press the Page Down key. Slide 5 of 9 is displayed.

d. Press the Page Up key. Slide 4 of 9 is displayed again.

⑤ SAVE THE FILE NAMING IT GEMSTONE

Save the file naming it Gemstone.

17.6   Editing Text

The text in a slide can be edited in the slide pane or in the outline pane.
placeholder   Clicking the text in the slide pane displays the outline of a *placeholder* and places the insertion point in the box:

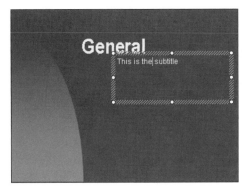

The text in the placeholder can then be edited. For example, the subtitle was clicked in the slide shown on the previous page to place the insertion point in the placeholder. Note that the word "General" is in a separate placeholder. The word "General" can be edited, but it must first be clicked to place the insertion point in its placeholder.

Text can be edited in the outline pane by selecting the Outline tab and then clicking text, which places the insertion point. Editing text in the outline pane is convenient because the slide that corresponds to the location of the insertion point is automatically displayed in the slide pane.

The text in the outline pane can be collapsed or expanded by clicking the Expand All button (⬇⬛) on the toolbar. Collapsing the text displays only the title for each slide, which can help give an overview of the slides.

17.7 Adding and Deleting Slides

When using a template, slides usually need to be deleted or added to the presentation.

adding a slide

A new slide can be added after the current slide by clicking the New Slide button (⬛ New Slide) on the toolbar, which adds a slide and displays the Slide Layout task pane:

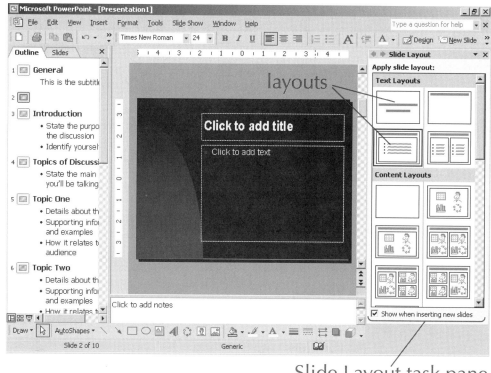

Slide Layout task pane

Clicking a layout in the task pane changes the appearance of the new slide. The new slide can then be edited. The task pane can be removed from the window by clicking the Close button (☒) in the upper-right corner of the task pane.

Another way of adding a slide is by selecting New Slide (Ctrl+M) from the Insert menu, which adds a slide and displays the task pane.

deleting a slide

The slide displayed in the slide pane in Normal view is deleted by selecting Delete Slide from the Edit menu. Another way to delete a slide is by selecting it in the outline pane, with either the Outline tab or the Slides tab selected, and then pressing the Delete key.

Practice 2 ⟳

In this practice you will add a slide, delete slides, and edit text in a presentation. Open Gemstone and display the presentation in Normal view if it is not already displayed.

① ADD A NEW SLIDE

a. Display slide 6.

b. On the toolbar, click the New Slide button (New Slide). A slide is added after slide 6 and the Slide Layout task pane is displayed.

c. In the task pane, click the layout that looks similar to:

Check - The new slide in the slide pane should now look similar to:

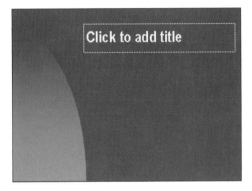

② ENTER THE TITLE

a. In the slide pane, click the text "Click to add title." The outline of the placeholder is displayed, the text disappears, and the insertion point is placed.

b. Type Mohs Hardness Scale, then click anywhere on the slide outside of the placeholder. The placeholder is no longer selected. This slide will have contents added to it in a later practice.

③ DELETE SLIDES

a. Display slide 3.

b. Select Edit ➞ Delete Slide. The slide is deleted and slide 3 of 9 is now displayed.

c. Display slide 7.

d. Select Edit ➞ Delete Slide. Slide 7 of 8 is now displayed.

④ DELETE A SLIDE USING THE OUTLINE PANE

a. In the outline pane, click the slide icon (▦) next to the "What This Means" text. The entire slide's text is highlighted.

b. Press the Delete key. The slide is deleted.

⑤ ENTER TEXT FOR THE FIRST SLIDE

   a. Display slide 1, then double-click the word "General" in the slide pane. The placeholder is made active and the word is selected.

   b. Type Gemstone Lecture.

   c. Click the text "This is the subtitle." The insertion point is placed.

   d. Select the text "This is the subtitle."

   e. Type By and then type a space and your name.

⑥ ENTER THE REST OF THE TEXT

   a. In the outline pane, in the text for slide 2, edit the two bulleted items under the title "Introduction" to:

> Gemstones are made of minerals
> One type of mineral can form several types of gemstones

   b. Change the "Topic One," "Topic Two," and "Topic Three" slides (slides 3, 4, and 5) to the following titles and bulleted items:

> Quartz
> • Occurs in crystals
> • Very common mineral
> • Examples: amethyst, citrine
>
> Corundum
> • Aluminum oxide material
> • Found in USA, India, South Africa
> • Examples: ruby, sapphire
>
> Beryl
> • Very large crystals
> • Found in Colombia, Australia, Russia
> • Examples: emerald, aquamarine

   c. Change the "Next Steps" slide (slide 7) to the following:

> Summary
> • Quartz: amethyst, citrine
> • Corundum: ruby, sapphire

   d. With the insertion point at the end of the word sapphire, press Enter. A new bulleted item is added.

   e. Type Beryl: emerald, aquamarine.

⑦ SAVE THE MODIFIED GEMSTONE

17.8   Adding a Picture to a Slide

Clip art can be placed on a slide and then moved and sized as needed. Selecting Clip Art from the Picture submenu in the Insert menu displays the Insert Clip Art task pane. Typing a keyword in the Search text box and selecting Search finds all the clip art that have the keyword in their description. Options in the Search in list and Results should be list can be used to narrow a search. Clicking a picture in the task pane places it in the slide in the slide pane.

Clicking a picture in a slide selects it and displays handles (○) for sizing. Dragging a corner handle sizes the picture. Dragging the center of the picture (not a handle) moves it. The Cut, Copy, and Paste buttons on the toolbar can be used to move or copy a selected picture. Pressing the Delete key deletes a selected picture. Clicking outside the selected picture removes the handles.

17.9   Changing the Order of Slides

Clicking the Slide Sorter View button (⊞) in the lower-left corner of the window displays all of the slides in a presentation:

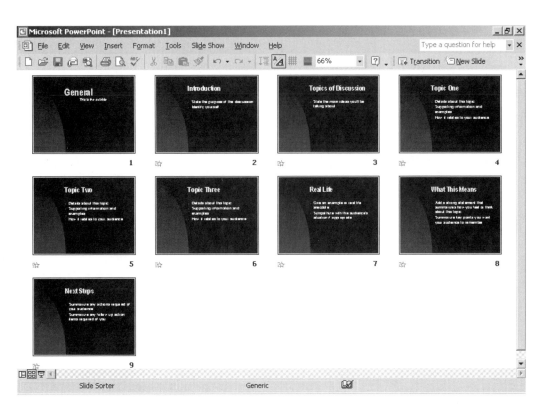

The order of slides in a presentation can be changed in Slide Sorter view by dragging a slide to another position.

The order of slides can also be changed in Normal view in the outline pane by dragging a slide's icon (▦) in the Outline tab or a slide in the Slides tab to another position.

17.10 Printing a Presentation

The Print Preview window is used to view the different ways a presentation can be printed. Selecting Print Preview from the File menu or clicking the Print Preview button (🔍) on the toolbar displays the Print Preview window:

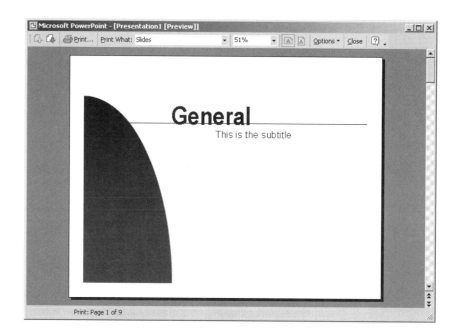

Options in the Print What list and Options list on the toolbar can be selected to change how the presentation appears on paper. The Print What list contains the following options:

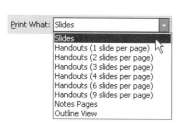

- Slides prints one slide per page.

- Handouts prints the indicated number of miniature slides on each page.

- Notes Pages prints one slide in the top half of each page and any text that was in typed in the notes pane in the bottom half of the page. Notes are discussed later in this chapter.

- Outline View prints the outline of the presentation as it appears in the outline pane.

headers and footers on a printout

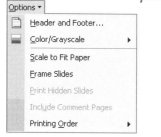

Headers and footers can be added to the printout of a presentation by selecting Header and Footer in the Options list, which displays a dialog box, and selecting the Notes and Handouts tab displays those options:

- A date can be typed in the Fixed box, or Update automatically can be selected to insert a time stamp. The location of the inserted date varies depending on the Print What option selected.

- Text for the top of the printouts is typed in the Header box.

- The Page number check box is selected to include a page number in the printouts. Page numbers will not print if the Print What option is Slides.

- Text for the bottom of the printouts is typed in the Footer box.

Selecting Apply to All applies the selected options, which can then be viewed in the Preview window.

In print preview, the pages that will print can be viewed by pressing the Page Up key or Page Down key or by clicking the Previous Page (⬆) or Next Page (⬇) buttons. The previous or next page can also be displayed using the vertical scroll bar. Selecting the Close button (Close) on the toolbar or pressing the Esc key returns to the presentation window without printing the presentation. Selecting the Print button (Print...) on the toolbar displays a dialog box similar to:

The Print dialog box varies depending on the printer

Options in the Print range section of the dialog box affect how much of the presentation is printed:

- The All option prints the entire presentation.
- The Current slide option prints only the displayed slide.

Selecting OK prints the presentation.

In this practice you will add a picture to the presentation, change the order of slides, add a footer, and then print a copy. Open Gemstone if it is not already displayed.

① *ADD A PICTURE*

    a. Display slide 1 in Normal view.

    b. Select Insert → Picture → Clip Art. The Insert Clip Art task pane is displayed. If the Add Clips to Organizer dialog box is displayed, select Later to remove the dialog box.

    c. In the Insert Clip Art task pane, in the Search text box, type instructors.

    d. In the Insert Clip Art task pane, click the Search in list. Clip art collection names are displayed.

        1. Clear the My Collections check box, the Everywhere check box, and the Web Collections check box if they are not already cleared.

        2. Click anywhere in the task pane. The list is removed.

    e. In the Insert Clip Art task pane, click the Results should be list. File formats are displayed.

        1. Clear the Photographs, Movies, Sounds, and All media types check boxes if they are not already cleared.

        2. Click anywhere in the task pane. The list is removed.

    f. In the Insert Clip Art task pane, select Search. Clip art is displayed in the task pane.

    g. In the Insert Clip Art task pane, click the picture of a teacher. The picture is placed in slide 1.

    h. In the upper-right corner of the Insert Clip Art task pane, click the Close button (☒). The task pane is removed.

② *SIZE AND MOVE THE PICTURE*

    a. Drag the lower-right handle of the picture downwards and to the right. When the outline is approximately twice the size, release the mouse button.

    b. Drag the center of the picture so that it is centered below the subtitle "By *your name*."

③ *CHANGE THE ORDER OF SLIDES*

    a. In the lower-left corner of the PowerPoint window, click the Slide Sorter view button (▦). The presentation is displayed in Slide Sorter view.

    b. Drag slide 6 to between slides 2 and 3. The "Mohs Hardness Scale" slide is now slide 3.

    c. In the lower-left corner of PowerPoint window, click the Normal view button (▣). The presentation is again displayed in Normal view.

④ *PREVIEW THE PRESENTATION*

    a. Save the modified Gemstone.

    b. On the toolbar, click the Print Preview button (▣). The first page is displayed in the print preview window.

    c. On the toolbar, click the Next Page button (▣). The next page is displayed.

    d. On the toolbar, click the Previous Page button (▣). The previous page is displayed.

    e. On the toolbar, in the Print What list select Outline View. The preview changes to display the outline of the presentation.

    f. On the toolbar, in the Print What list select Handouts (9 slides per page). The preview changes to show up to nine miniature slides (this presentation has seven slides) on a piece of paper.

⑤ *ADD A FOOTER*

    a. On the toolbar, in the Options list select Header and Footer. A dialog box is displayed.

        1. Select the Notes and Handouts tab if those options are not already displayed.

        2. In the Footer box, type your name.

        3. Select Apply to All. The dialog box is removed and the footer is added to the preview.

⑥ *PRINT THE PRESENTATION*

    a. On the toolbar, click the Print button (🖨 Print...). A dialog box is displayed.

        1. Select OK. The Gemstone presentation is printed.

    b. On the toolbar, click the Close button (Close). The Print Preview window is closed and the presentation is displayed in Normal view.

⑦ *SAVE THE MODIFIED GEMSTONE*

17.11 Adding Footers to Slides

Information about a presentation can be included at the bottom of each slide. Selecting Header and Footer from the View menu displays a dialog box, and selecting the Slide tab displays options for the footer:

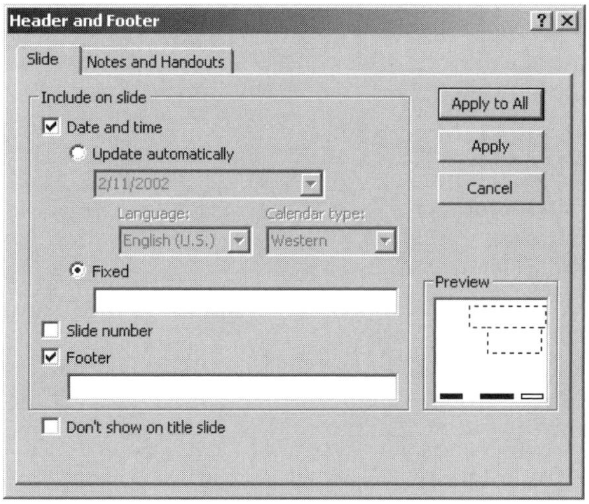

* Update automatically inserts a time stamp.

* The Slide number check box adds the slide number to the footer.

* Text for the footer can be typed in the Footer box.

Selecting Apply applies the selected options to the currently displayed slide. Selecting Apply to All applies the selected options to all the slides in the presentation.

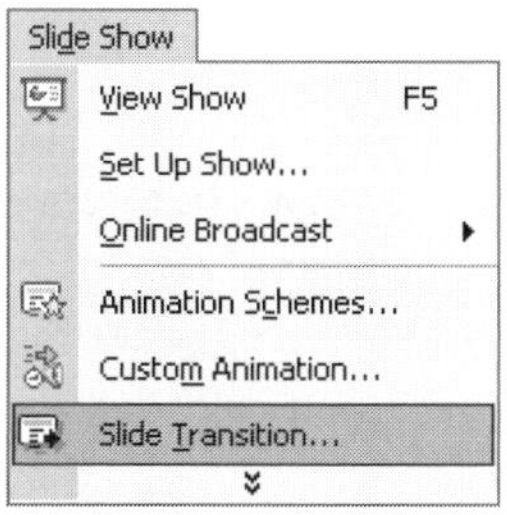

17.12 Slide Transitions

A *slide transition* is the way one slide changes to the next in Slide Show view. For example, the current slide can appear to fall off the screen to reveal the next slide, or it can dissolve into the next slide.

A slide transition is added in Normal view by selecting Slide Transition from the Slide Show menu, which displays the Slide Transition task pane:

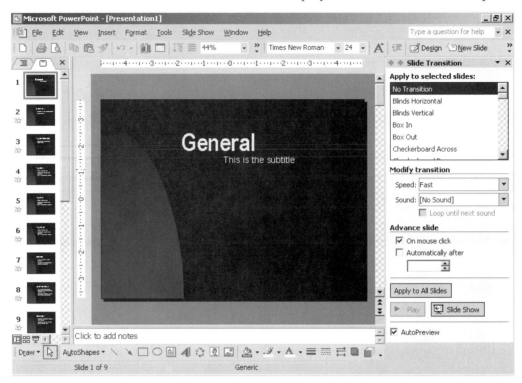

In the task pane, clicking a transition in the Apply to selected slides list applies the transition to the displayed slide. Clicking Apply to All Slides applies the transition to the entire presentation. Except for special circumstances, all the slides in a presentation usually have the same transition. Varied transitions are confusing when viewing a presentation.

A transition can be removed from the displayed slide by clicking No Transition in the Apply to selected slides list. Clicking Apply to All Slides removes transitions from the entire presentation.

A transition icon (🌠) is displayed next to each slide in the Slides tab of the outline pane and in Slide Sorter view. The transition can be previewed by clicking the icon.

Selecting Multiple Slides

In the Slides tab in the outline pane, multiple slides can be selected by holding down the Ctrl key and clicking slides.

17.13 Animation

A slide can have animation added to it so that the separate items in the slide appear one by one in Slide Show view. *Animation* refers to the way items move onto a slide. For example, each item on a slide can appear by sliding in from the left side, or it can dissolve into place.

Animation is added in Normal view by selecting Animation Schemes from the Slide Show menu, which displays the Slide Design task pane with Animation Schemes selected:

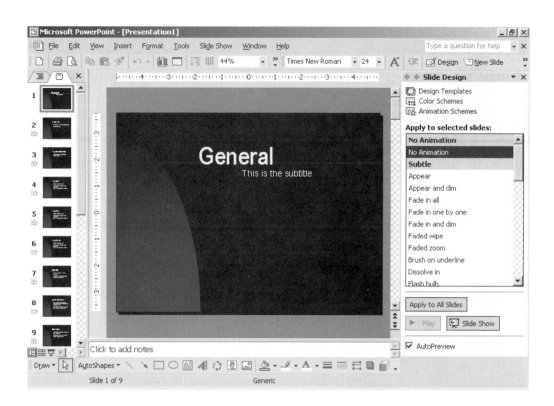

In the task pane, clicking an animation in the Apply to selected slides list applies the animation to the displayed slide. Clicking Apply to All Slides applies the animation to the entire presentation. Like transitions, all the slides in a presentation usually have the same animation to avoid confusion when viewing the presentation.

An animation can be removed from the displayed slide by clicking No Animation in the Apply to selected slides list. Clicking Apply to All Slides removes animations from the entire presentation.

The transition icon (⚡) next to each slide in the Slides tab of the outline pane and in Slide Sorter view can be used to preview animations.

Once the Slide Design task pane is displayed, selecting <u>Animation Schemes</u>, <u>Color Schemes</u>, or <u>Design Schemes</u> at the top of the pane displays those options. Design Schemes are covered later in this chapter.

Transitions and Animations in Slide Sorter View

Slide transitions and animations can also be added to selected slides in Slide Sorter view by first selecting the slide or slides and then selecting the transition in the task pane.

Practice 4 ⟳

In this practice you will add information to the bottom of each slide and then add slide transitions and animation. Open Gemstone if it is not already displayed.

① *ADD A FOOTER WITH THE SLIDE NUMBER AND TEXT*

   a. Display slide 1 in Normal view.

   b. Select <u>V</u>iew → <u>H</u>eader and Footer. A dialog box is displayed.

       1. Select the Slide tab if those options are not already displayed.

       2. Clear the Date and time check box.

       3. Select the Slide number check box.

       4. In the Footer box, type Science Lecture Series.

       5. Select Apply to All. The footer text and slide number appear at the bottom of slide 1.

   c. Display slide 2. Note the footer information.

② *ADD TRANSITIONS TO THE ENTIRE PRESENTATION*

    a. Select Slide Show → Slide Transition. The Slide Transition task pane is displayed.

    b. In the Slide Transition task pane, in the Apply to selected slides list, click Cover Down. The transition is applied to the displayed slide.

    c. In the Slide Transition task pane, click Apply to All Slides. The transition is applied to all the slides in the presentation.

    d. In the outline pane, click the transition icon (🖾) next to any slide. The slide is displayed and the transition is previewed.

③ *ADD ANIMATION TO THE ENTIRE PRESENTATION*

    a. Select Slide Show → Animation Schemes. The Slide Design task pane is displayed.

    b. In the Slide Design task pane, in the Apply to selected slides list, click Fade in one by one. The animation is applied to the displayed slide.

    c. In the Slide Design task pane, click Apply to All Slides. The animation is applied to all the slides in the presentation.

    d. In the outline pane, click the transition icon (🖾) next to any slide. The slide is displayed and the transition and animation are previewed.

    e. In the upper-right corner of the task pane, click the Close button (🗙). The task pane is removed.

④ *VIEW THE SLIDE SHOW*

    a. Press the F5 key. The presentation starts with slide 1. Notice the subtitle is not yet displayed.

    b. Click once. The subtitle fades in.

    c. Click again. Slide 2 drops down. Only the title of slide 2, "Introduction," fades in.

    d. Click once. The first bulleted item fades in.

    e. Click again. The second bulleted item fades in.

    f. Click again. Slide 3 drops down and covers slide 2.

    g. Press Esc. The presentation is displayed in Normal view.

⑤ *SAVE THE MODIFIED GEMSTONE*

17.14 Adding a Chart to a Slide

Slides can include charts of data from an Excel workbook. Charts can be added to any slide using the Copy and Paste buttons on the toolbar. The steps for copying a chart from an open Excel workbook onto a slide in an open PowerPoint presentation are:

1. Select the chart to be copied.

2. Click the Copy button (📋) on the toolbar. A copy of the chart is added to the Clipboard.

3. Display the PowerPoint window, and display the slide in the slide pane in Normal view.

4. Click the Paste button (📋) on the toolbar. The chart is placed in the slide, and the Paste Options button (📋) is displayed.

The Paste Options Button

Clicking the Paste Options button (📋) after pasting a chart into a slide displays a list of options that can be used to change the default paste option of Excel Chart (entire workbook) to Picture of Chart (smaller file size).

On a slide, a chart can be moved and sized like a picture. Clicking a chart selects it and displays handles for sizing. Pressing the Delete key removes the selected chart from the slide.

Practice 5 ⟳

In this practice you will add a chart to a slide. Open Gemstone if it is not already displayed.

① OPEN A WORKBOOK AND ADD A CHART

a. Open MOHS SCALE, which is an Excel data file for this text. This workbook contains data on the Mohs hardness scale, which is used to determine the strength of gemstones.

b. Click the chart to select it if it is not already selected.

c. On the toolbar, click the Copy button (⧉). The chart is copied to the Clipboard.

d. Display the PowerPoint window. The Gemstone presentation is displayed.

e. Display slide 3 in Normal view.

f. On the toolbar, click the Paste button (⧉). The chart is pasted onto the slide. Ignore the Paste Options button.

g. Drag the chart until it is centered under the slide's title.

h. Display the workbook.

i. Close MOHS SCALE and quit Excel without saving changes.

② SAVE, PRINT, AND THEN CLOSE THE MODIFIED GEMSTONE

a. Save the modified Gemstone.

b. Print the presentation as Handouts with 9 slides per page.

c. Close Gemstone.

17.15 Planning a Presentation

A successful presentation is carefully planned before it is created. Even the most experienced lecturers spend time planning each detail of their presentation. Planning a presentation is a three step process:

1. **Carefully plan the lecture or speech** that will accompany the presentation, including what to say and how to say it:

   • Identify the purpose of the presentation. For example, will it be used to persuade opinions or present ideas?

   • Identify the audience so that appropriate language and speech styles can be determined. For example, young children require a different vocabulary than adult lawyers.

   • Keep remarks short and to the point. At the end of the presentation, the audience should want to hear more, not be relieved it is over.

2. **Sketch the slides** using pencil and paper.

   • Make sure that the slides emphasize the key points to be made in the lecture.

- Separate information over several slides to avoid putting too many concepts and ideas on one slide.

3. **Create the presentation using PowerPoint.**

- Limit your design to two or three fonts. Also, avoid text that is all uppercase letters because it is more difficult to read.

- Keep the text short and in a color different from the background color, preferably a light color on a dark background or vice versa.

17.16 Presentation Design

elements
layout

Any presentation can be made more effective if the elements on each slide reflect the presentation's purpose or subject matter. *Elements* are the text, pictures, colors, and fonts on a slide. The *layout* of a slide refers to the placement and choice of the elements. For example, a presentation on financial information could have a blue background and a plain font, which are more appropriate than a pink background and a script font.

The background and fonts of an entire presentation can be changed by selecting the Design button (Design) on the toolbar, which displays the Slide Design task pane with <u>Design Templates</u> selected:

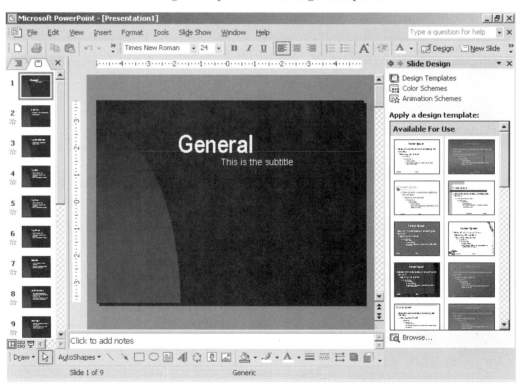

In the task pane, clicking a design in the Apply a design template list applies the design to the entire presentation.

Slide Master

The font can be changed on all the slides at once using the *Slide Master*. Displaying any slide except slide 1 in Normal view and then selecting <u>S</u>lide Master from the <u>M</u>aster submenu in the <u>V</u>iew menu displays the Slide Master:

Any formatting applied to text in the Slide Master is applied to all the slides in the presentation. Note that the Slide Master View toolbar is automatically displayed, and can be moved by dragging its title bar.

Clicking a view button in the lower-left corner of the PowerPoint window closes the Slide Master and displays the presentation another view.

Practice 6

In this practice you will format a presentation.

① *OPEN WINTER TRIP*

Open WINTER TRIP, which is a data file for this text. This presentation contains three slides.

② *VIEW THE SLIDE SHOW*

a. Press the F5 key. The presentation starts with slide 1.

b. Click once. Slide 2 is displayed.

c. Continue clicking until the slide show has been viewed and is displayed in Normal view.

③ *CHANGE THE DESIGN TEMPLATE*

a. On the toolbar, click the Design button (Design). The Slide Design task pane is displayed.

b. In the Slide Design task pane, in the Apply a design template list, click any design. The design is applied to the entire presentation.

c. In the Slide Design task pane, in the Apply a design template list, scroll until a design that looks like the ocean is displayed:

d. Click the Ocean design. The design is applied to the entire presentation.

④ *CHANGE THE TEXT FORMATTING*

a. Display slide 2 in Normal view.

b. Select <u>V</u>iew → <u>M</u>aster → <u>S</u>lide Master. The Slide Master slide is displayed.

c. At the top of the slide, click the text "Click to edit Master title style."

d. On the toolbar, in the Font list select Times New Roman.

e. On the toolbar, click the Bold button. The text is now bold.

f. In the lower-left corner of PowerPoint window, click the Normal view button (▣). The presentation is again displayed in Normal view. Note the title is in a different font.

⑤ *VIEW THE SLIDE SHOW*

    a. Press the F5 key. The presentation starts with slide 1.

    b. Click once. Slide 2 is displayed.

    c. Continue clicking until the slide show has been viewed and is displayed in Normal view.

⑥ *SAVE AND THEN PRINT THE MODIFIED WINTER TRIP*

    a. Save the modified WINTER TRIP.

    b. Print the presentation as Handouts with 3 slides per page and your name in the footer or the printout. The three slides print on one page.

17.17 Creating and Printing Speaker Notes

Notes for the speaker can be entered into the notes pane for each slide. Clicking the notes pane places the insertion point, and text can then be typed. Dragging the top boundary of the pane expands it. Selecting Notes Page from the View menu displays one slide and the corresponding notes as they will appear when printed, and also allows the notes to be edited.

The notes can be printed by selecting Notes Pages in the Print What list in the Print Preview window, which prints one slide and the corresponding notes on each page.

Practice 7

In this practice you will create and print notes. Open WINTER TRIP if it is not already displayed.

① *EXPAND THE NOTES PANE*

    a. Display slide 1 in Normal view if it is not already displayed. The notes pane is displayed below the slide pane.

    b. Drag upwards on the top boundary of the notes pane until the notes pane is taller.

② *TYPE NOTES FOR EACH SLIDE*

    a. In the notes pane, click the text "Click to add notes." The text is removed and the insertion point is placed.

    b. Type the following text, pressing Enter at the end of the first line:

        At Ryder Resort in Islamorada.
        Goal: to observe marine life in a natural environment.

    c. Click the slide pane, then press the Page Down key to display slide 2.

    d. In the notes pane, type the following text, pressing Enter at the end of each line:

        Temperatures of 70 to 90 degrees F.
        Prepare for rain, sun, and mosquitoes.

    e. Click the slide pane, then press the Page Down key to display slide 3.

    f. Select View → Notes Page. The slide is displayed in Notes Page view.

g. In the notes area, type the following text, pressing Enter at the end of each line:

No radios or electronics that cannot fit into your bag.
Divers need to bring a full set of scuba gear.
All meals are paid for.

③ *SAVE, PRINT, AND THEN CLOSE THE MODIFIED WINTER TRIP*

a. Save the modified WINTER TRIP.

b. Print the presentation as Notes Pages. Three pages print with the notes below each slide.

c. Close WINTER TRIP.

④ *QUIT POWERPOINT*

17.18 Where can you go from here?

This chapter introduced the concepts of creating a presentation, formatting slides, and adding transitions and animations to produce a professional-looking presentation. PowerPoint has other options not discussed in this text which can be explored using the online help.

Presentation applications are commonly used in academic and business environments. Because you have learned how to use PowerPoint, you will easily be able to learn and use other presentation applications.

Chapter Summary

This chapter discussed how to make presentations using Microsoft PowerPoint. A new presentation is created by selecting New Office Document from the Start menu and selecting a template in the Presentations tab. Slides are displayed in three views. Normal view divides the window into three panes, Slide Sorter view displays miniature slides, and Slide Show view displays the current slide in full-screen size.

In Normal view, the slide indicator indicates the current slide and total number of slides. The order of slides can be changed in Slide Sorter view.

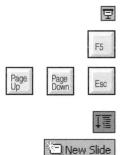

Slide Show view is used to play a presentation, which is started by selecting the Slide Show button, the <u>V</u>iew Show command, or the F5 key. The next slide is displayed by clicking once, pressing the N key, the Page Down key, or the spacebar. The previous slide is displayed by pressing the P key or the Page Up key. Pressing the Esc key ends the slide show.

Text is edited in the slide pane by clicking the outline of a placeholder. The text in the outline pane can be collapsed or expanded by clicking the Expand All button. A slide is added by clicking the New Slide button and deleted by selecting the <u>D</u>elete Slide command.

Clip art can be placed on a slide by selecting the <u>C</u>lip Art command. The Cut, Copy, and Paste buttons can be used to add a chart from an open Excel workbook. Clicking a picture or chart selects it and displays handles for sizing. Dragging the center moves the picture or chart, and pressing the Delete key removes it.

A presentation can be printed in different ways, which can be viewed and changed by selecting the Print Preview command. Headers and footers are added to a printout in the Print Preview window. Footers can be added to slides by selecting the Header and Footer command.

A slide transition is added by selecting the Slide Transition command. Animation is added by selecting the Animation Schemes command. Transitions and animations are previewed by clicking the transition icon. The background and fonts are changed by selecting the Design button.

A successful presentation is carefully planned before it is created using a three step process: carefully plan the lecture or speech, sketch the slides, and then create the presentation in PowerPoint.

Formatting applied to text in the Slide Master is applied to all the slides. The Slide Master is displayed by selecting the Slide Master command.

Notes for the speaker can be entered into the Notes pane for each slide. Selecting the Notes Page command displays one slide and the corresponding notes as they will appear when printed as Notes Pages.

Vocabulary

Animation The way items move onto a slide.

Elements The text, pictures, colors, and fonts on a slide.

F5 key Pressing the F5 key starts the slide show.

Layout The placement and choice of the elements on a slide.

Microsoft PowerPoint The presentation application in Microsoft Office.

Normal view Displays a presentation in a window divided into three panes, which allows a slide, the outline, and speaker notes to be edited.

Notes pane Contains notes for the speaker that correspond to the displayed slide.

Outline pane Contains the text of all the slides in a format similar to Outline view in Word.

Placeholder An object on a slide that contains text.

PowerPoint presentation A collection of slides stored in a file.

PowerPoint template An already formatted presentation which can be modified to fit specific needs.

Presentation An informative talk, such as a lecture or speech, that usually includes visuals.

Slide An individual screen of a presentation.

Slide indicator Indicates the current slide and the total number of slides in a presentation.

Slide Master A slide that is used to change the font on all the slides in a presentation.

Slide pane Displays one slide at a time as it will appear in the presentation.

Slide Show view Displays the current slide in full-screen size as it appears during a presentation.

Slide Sorter view Displays miniature slides that allow the order of slides to be modified.

Slide transition The way one slide changes to the next in Slide Show view.

Visuals Slides projected onto a large screen while a speaker talks.

Exercise 1 ———————————————————————— Catsharks

Create a new presentation based on the Generic template. Save the presentation naming it Catsharks and complete the following steps:

a) Modify the presentation so that it contains five slides with the following text:

Catsharks
  A Brief Introduction

Characteristics
  • Bottom-dwellers
  • Small, up to 1 meter long

Coral Catshark
  • Found in the Pacific Ocean
  • White spots on dark body

Swellshark
  • Found in the Pacific Ocean
  • Dark brown mottled color

Striped Catshark
  • Found in the Atlantic Ocean
  • Dark horizontal stripes

b) Apply an appropriate design template to the presentation.

c) Add the slide number and your name in the footer of each slide.

d) Add the Dissolve transition and Highlights animation to each slide.

e) Save the modified Catsharks.

f) Print the presentation, with a footer that includes your name, so that all the slides are printed on one page.

Exercise 2 ⚙ ——————————————————————— Volcano Presentation

The VOLCANOES document, last modified in the practices of Chapter 7, can be used as the basis for a presentation. Print a copy of the VOLCANOES document and complete the following steps:

a) Using paper and pencil, sketch five slides for the presentation.

b) Using PowerPoint, create a new presentation based on the Generic template. Save the presentation naming it Volcano Presentation.

c) Modify the existing slides so that the presentation contains the following:

  • five slides containing the appropriate text
  • an appropriate design template applied to the presentation
  • the slide number and your name in the footer of each slide
  • the Box In transition and Zoom animation added to each slide

- Arial font formatting for the title of each slide
- at least one clip art picture
- an increased font size on slide 1

d) Save the modified Volcano Presentation.

e) Print the presentation, with a footer that includes your name, so that all the slides are printed on one page.

Exercise 3 ——————————————————— Maple Trees

Create a new presentation based on the Generic template. Save the presentation naming it Maple Trees and complete the following steps:

a) Modify the presentation so that it contains five slides with the following text:

Maple Trees
    Broad-leafed Tree Series

Sugar Maple
    • Sap is used for maple syrup
    • Height - 24 meters

Silver Maple
    • Leaves have large teeth
    • Height - 15 meters

Red Maple
    • Bright red flowers and buds
    • Height - 30 meters

Tree Heights

b) In a new Excel workbook, enter the tree names and their height data, and create a column chart titled Maple Trees. Save the workbook naming it Maples.

c) Place a copy of the chart on slide 5, the slide with the title "Tree Heights." Size and move the chart appropriately.

d) Apply an appropriate design template to the presentation.

e) Add the slide number and your name in the footer of each slide.

f) Add the Cover Left transition and Float animation to each slide.

g) Save the modified Maple Trees.

h) Print the presentation, with a footer that includes your name, so that all the slides are printed on one page.

Exercise 4 ✿ ———————————— Track Team Performance

Create a new presentation based on the Generic template. Save the presentation naming it Track Team Performance and complete the following steps:

a) Modify the presentation so that it contains four slides with the following text:

Track Team 2003
  Performance Plan

Team Progress - 100 Meter

Team Progress - 200 Meter

Improving our Performance
  • Nutrition
  • Cross training
  • Attitude seminar

b) On slide 1, add a clip art picture. Size and move the picture appropriately.

c) Open the Track Progress workbook last modified in Chapter 12, Exercise 10. Place a copy of the "Track Team's Progress in 100 Meter" chart on slide 2. Size and move the chart appropriately.

d) Place a copy of the "Track Team's Progress in 200 Meter" chart on slide 3. Size and move the chart appropriately.

e) Apply an appropriate design template to the presentation.

f) Add the slide number and your name in the footer of each slide.

g) Add the Comb Horizontal transition and Wipe animation to each slide.

h) Save the modified Track Team Performance.

i) Print the presentation, with a footer that includes your name, so that all the slides are printed on one page.

Exercise 5 (advanced) ——————— Computer History Presentation

Plan a presentation on the history of computers using the information in Chapter 1, Sections 1.1 through 1.9. Using paper and pencil, sketch the slides of the presentation. Using PowerPoint, create a new presentation based on the Generic template. Save the new presentation naming it Computer History Presentation. Include appropriate clip art, footer text, slide transitions, and animation. Create speaker notes for each slide. Print the presentation so that all the slides are printed six slides to a page and then print all the slide notes.

Exercise 6 (advanced) ——————— Environmental Presentation

Plan a presentation on an environmental issue of your choice. Using paper and pencil, sketch the slides of the presentation. Using PowerPoint, create a new presentation based on the Generic template. Save the new presentation naming it Environmental Presentation. Include appropriate clip art, footer text, slide transitions, animation, and a chart. Create speaker notes for each slide. Print the presentation so that all the slides are printed six slides to a page and then print all the slide notes.

Exercise 7 (advanced) ——————— Persuade Investors

Plan a presentation in which you propose a business plan for a company you wish to start. Using PowerPoint, create a new presentation based on the Generic template. Save the presentation naming it Persuade Investors. Include appropriate clip art, footer text, slide transitions, animation, and a chart. Create speaker notes for each slide. Print the presentation so that all the slides are printed six slides to a page and then print all the slide notes.

Appendix A
Using Microsoft Office Help

A.1 The Assistant

When working in a Microsoft Office application, a small animated character called the *Assistant* may appear. The default Assistant is named Clippit and resembles a paper clip. The Assistant provides help and suggestions in response to actions performed, such as typing text or clicking a button. For example, as text is typed into a Word document, a light bulb may appear indicating that the Assistant has a helpful tip. Clicking the light bulb displays the helpful tip in a balloon:

The balloon is removed by clicking OK.

moving the Assistant

The Assistant can be moved by dragging. The location of the balloon may change depending on where the Assistant is on the screen.

removing the Assistant
displaying the Assistant

The Assistant can be removed by selecting Hide the Office Assistant from the Help menu. The Assistant can be displayed again by selecting Show the Office Assistant from the Help menu or clicking the Microsoft Help button (⊞) on the toolbar.

A.2 Finding a Help Topic

The Assistant can be used to find helpful information. Clicking the Assistant displays a balloon with a What would you like to do box:

Help on the Web

Selecting the "None of the above, look for more help on the Web" topic in the Assistant's balloon of suggestions displays options for searching the Microsoft Office Web site for help.

Typing a question and then selecting Search displays a balloon with a list of topics. Selecting a topic displays the Microsoft Word Help window next to the application window:

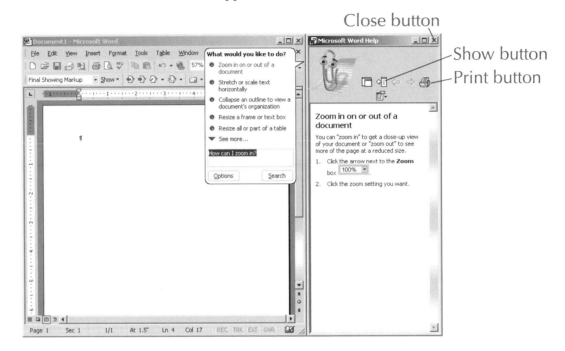

Close button
Show button
Print button

navigation pane

Clicking the Show button (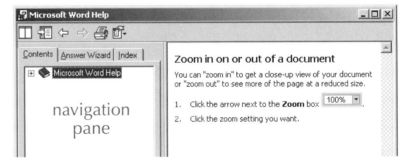) expands the Help window and displays the navigation pane:

Displaying Help

The Help window can be displayed by selecting Microsoft *Program Name* Help from the Help menu in a Microsoft application. For example, in PowerPoint the command is Microsoft PowerPoint Help and in Outlook the command is Microsoft Outlook Help.

---

browse help topics

Tabs in the navigation pane can be used to search for help in different ways. The list in the Contents tab is used to browse help topics. Clicking the plus sign next to Microsoft Word Help in the Contents tab expands a list of help topics:

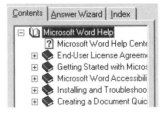

The plus signs next to each topic can be clicked to display more topics, and clicking a topic displays it in the right side of the window.

ask a question

Options in the Answer Wizard tab are used to ask a question. Clicking the Answer Wizard tab displays a What would you like to do box. Typing a question and selecting Search displays a list of topics:

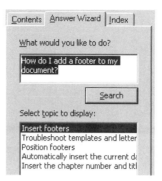

Help Content

Each Office application includes help topics specific to that application.

Clicking a topic displays it in the right side of the window.

search the index

Options in the Index tab are used to search help topics for keywords. Clicking the Index tab displays a Type keywords box and an Or choose keywords list. Typing a keyword and selecting Search or clicking a keyword displays a list of topics:

Clicking a topic displays it in the right side of the window.

Ask a Question box

Help topics can be found quickly using the Ask a Question box in the upper-right corner of an application's window:

Typing a question in the Ask a Question box and then pressing Enter displays a list of topics below the box. Clicking a topic displays it in the Microsoft Help window.

closing the Help window

When finished using Help, the window can be removed by clicking the Close button (☒) in the upper-right corner of the task pane.

A.3 Displaying the Contents of a Topic

Show All may be displayed in the upper-right corner of a topic. Clicking Show All displays the definitions of keywords in the topic, which are designated by a different color. Selecting Hide All hides the definitions again:

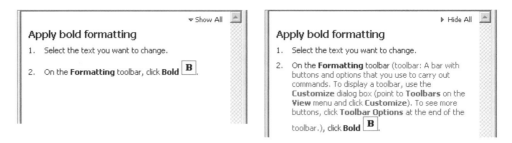

Apply bold formatting

1. Select the text you want to change.

2. On the **Formatting** toolbar, click **Bold** [B].

Apply bold formatting

1. Select the text you want to change.

2. On the **Formatting** toolbar (toolbar: A bar with buttons and options that you use to carry out commands. To display a toolbar, use the **Customize** dialog box (point to **Toolbars** on the **View** menu and click **Customize**). To see more buttons, click **Toolbar Options** at the end of the toolbar.), click **Bold** [B].

A definition can also be displayed by clicking it in the topic. Some topics include a Tip that can be clicked to display additional topics.

A.4 Printing a Help Topic

The topic that is currently displayed in the right side of the window is printed by clicking the Print button ( ) in the Help window, which displays the Print dialog box. Selecting Print prints a copy of the topic.

Several topics can be printed at once by selecting a heading or topic in the Contents tab of the navigation pane and then clicking the Print button, which displays the Print Topics dialog box. Selecting Print the selected topic and OK prints only the topic that is displayed in the right side of the window. Selecting Print the selected heading and all subtopics and OK prints all topics under the heading selected in the Contents tab.

A.5 Displaying ScreenTips

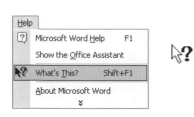

ScreenTips are notes that provide information. A ScreenTip is displayed by selecting What's This (Shift+F1) from the Help menu, which changes the pointer to ⬚?. Pointing to an item on the screen, such as a button on the toolbar, and then clicking displays a short description.

ScreenTips can be displayed in some dialog boxes by clicking the ? in the upper-right corner and then clicking an option in the dialog box:

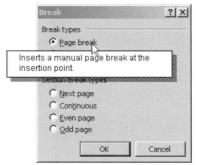

A.6 Where can you go from here?

This appendix discussed ways to use the online help in Microsoft Office. There are other ways to access and search for help topics which can be found by looking for "Help" in the online help. The Microsoft Office web site may also provide answers. Selecting Office on the Web from the Help menu in a Microsoft application displays the Microsoft Office web site in a browser window.

A Guide to Microsoft Office XP Professional

Functions

The following is a partial list of functions that may be used in Excel. In the list of functions that follows:

<value> may be replaced by:
    a single value (such as 10)
    a cell reference (such as C5)
    an expression that evaluates to a single value (such as C5*2)
    a named reference (such as RATE)

<range> may be replaced by:
    a list of cells separated by commas (such as A1, B12, D5)
    a continuous range (such as A1:A10)
    a mixture of both separated by commas (such as A1, B1:B5, C3, C5:C7)
    a named range (such as TAX RATES)

Math and Trigonometric Functions

ABS(<value>) Returns the absolute value of <value>: ABS(10) returns 10, ABS(–10) returns 10.

ACOS(<value>) Returns the arccosine of <value> in radians. <value> must be between –1 and +1.

ASIN(<value>) Returns the arcsine of <value> in radians. <value> must be between –1 and +1.

ATAN(<value>) Returns the arctangent of <value> in radians in the range $-pi/2$ to $pi/2$.

ATAN2(<Xvalue>, <Yvalue>) Returns the arctangent in radians of an angle defined by the coordinates <Xvalue>, <Yvalue>.

COS(<value>) Returns the cosine of <value> where <value> is an angle measured in radians.

DEGREES(<value>) Returns <value> converted from radians to degrees.

EXP(<value>) Returns e (natural logarithim) raised to the <value> power.

INT(<value>) Returns <value> rounded down to the nearest integer: INT(1.9) returns 1, INT(–1.9) returns –2.

LN(<value>) Returns the natural logarithm (base e) of <value>. <value> must be positive.

LOG(<value>, <base>) Returns the logarithm of <value> to the base <base>. <value> must be positive.

LOG10(<value>) Returns the base-10 logarithm of <value>. <value> must be positive.

MOD(<value>, <divisor>) Returns the remainder of <value> divided by <divisor>. <divisor> may not be 0.

PI() Returns the constant 3.14159265358979, (pi), accurate to 15 digits. No argument is used.

RADIANS(<value>) Returns <value> converted from degrees to radians.

RAND() Returns a random number greater than or equal to 0 and less than 1. No argument is used. To generate a number between <low> and <high> use the formula =RAND()*(<high> – <low>) + <low>.

ROUND(<value>, <decimals>) Returns <value> rounded to <decimals> decimal places. When <decimals> is 0, <value> is rounded to the nearest integer.

ROUNDDOWN(<value>, <decimals>) Returns <value> rounded down to <decimals> decimal places. When <decimals> is 0, <value> is rounded to the nearest integer.

ROUNDUP(<value>, <decimals>) Returns <value> rounded up, away from 0 to <decimals> decimal places. When <decimals> is 0, <value> is rounded to the nearest integer.

SIN(<value>) Returns the sine of <value> where <value> is an angle measured in radians.

SQRT(<value>) Returns the square root of <value>. <value> must be positive.

SUM(<range>) Returns the total of the values in <range>.

TAN(<value>) Returns the tangent of <value> where <value> is an angle measured in radians.

Statistical Functions

AVERAGE(<range>) Returns the average of the values in <range>. Cells that are empty or contain text are not included.

COUNT(<range>) Returns the number of cells in <range> that contain numbers, dates, or text representation of numbers.

MAX(<range>) Returns the largest value in <range>. Cells which contains text are not included.

MEDIAN(<range>) Returns the middle number in <range>.

MIN(<range>) Returns the smallest value in <range>. Cells which contains text are not included.

MODE(<range>) Returns the most frequently occuring value in <range>. Cells which are empty or contain text are ignored.

STDEV(<range>) Returns the standard deviation of the values in <range>.

VAR(<range>) Returns the variance of the values in <range>.

Logical Functions

AND(<range>) Returns TRUE if every value in <range> evaluates to TRUE, and FALSE if any value in <range> evaluates to FALSE. If range stores values, 0 represents FALSE, and nonzero values are TRUE.

IF(<condition>, <true value>, <false value>) Returns the <true value> if <condition> is true, <false value> if false. Both <true value> and <false value> may be text.

NOT(<value>) Returns the reverse of <value>. Returns TRUE if <value> is 0, and FALSE if <value> is nonzero: NOT(1+1=3) evaluates to TRUE. <value> must be numeric.

OR(<range>) Returns TRUE if any value in <range> evaluates to TRUE, FALSE if all values in <range> evaluate to FALSE. If range stores values, 0 represents FALSE, and nonzero values are TRUE.

Date/Time Functions

SECOND("<time>") Returns the seconds portion of a time.

MINUTE("<time>") Returns the minutes portion of a time.

HOUR("<time>") Returns the hours portion of a time.

DAY("<date>") Returns the day portion of a date.

MONTH("<date>") Returns the month portion of a date.

YEAR("<date>") Returns the year portion of a date.

DAYS360("<start_date>", "<end_date>") Returns the number of days between <start date> and <end date> based on a 360 day year.

NOW() Returns the current date and time. No argument is used.

TODAY() Returns the current date. No argument is used.

Lookup Functions

CHOOSE(<choice>, <option$_0$>, <option$_1$>, ...) Returns <option$_0$> if <choice> is 0, <option$_1$> if <choice> is 1, and so on. <options> may be text.

HLOOKUP(<value>, <range>, <row>) Locates cell in first row of <range> that contains the largest value less than or equal to <value> and returns the corresponding cell's contents in row <rows>.

VLOOKUP(<value>, <range>, <column>) Locates cell in first column of <range> that contains the largest value less than or equal to <value> and returns the corresponding cell's contents in column <column>.

A Guide to Microsoft Office XP Professional

Financial Functions

In the list of functions that follow:

<rate> is replaced with the interest rate per period

<nper> is replaced with the total number of payment periods

<per> is replaced with the period for which you want to find the interest and must be in the range 1 to nper

<pmt> is replaced with the amount of the periodic payment

<pv> is replaced with the present value

<fv> is replaced with the future value you want to obtain

<type> is the number 1 or 0 and indicates when payments are due: 0 if payments are due at the end of the period and 1 if payments are due at the beginning of the period

FV(<rate>, <nper>, <pmt>, <pv>, <type>) Returns the future value of an investment based on periodic, constant payments and a constant interest rate.

IPMT(<rate>, <per>, <nper>, <pv>, <fv>, <type>) Returns the interest payment for a given period for an investment, based on periodic, constant payments and a constant interest rate.

NPER(<rate>, <pmt>, <pv>, <fv>, <type>) Returns the number of total payment periods required to turn payments into the future value based on periodic, constant payments and a constant interest rate.

PMT(<rate>, <nper>, <pv>, <fv>, <type>) Returns the payment for a loan based on constant payments and a constant interest rate.

PPMT(<rate>, <per>, <nper>, <pv>, <fv>, <type>) Returns the payment on the principal for a given investment based on periodic, constant payments and a constant interest rate.

PV(<rate>, <nper>, <pmt>, <fv>, <type>) Returns the present value of an investment.

RATE(<nper>, <pmt>, <pv>, <fv>, <type>) Returns the interest rate per period of a loan.

Keyboard Shortcuts

The following keyboard shortcuts are grouped by application.

Microsoft Office Shortcuts

Files

Ctrl+N   Creates a new blank document, workbook, database, or presentation
Ctrl+O   Displays the Open dialog box
Ctrl+S   Saves the current document, workbook, database object, or presentation
F12   Displays the Save As dialog box
Ctrl+P   Displays the Print dialog box
Ctrl+W   Closes the current file
Alt+F4   Exits the application

Editing

Ctrl+Z   Reverses an action
Ctrl+Y   Repeats an action (Word and Excel only)
Ctrl+X   Cuts the selected data
Ctrl+C   Copies the selected data
Ctrl+V   Pastes cut or copied data
Ctrl+A   Selects all
Ctrl+F   Displays a dialog box with the Find options

Ctrl+H   Displays a dialog box with the Replace options
Ctrl+G Displays a dialog box with the Go To options (Word and Excel only)
Ctrl+K   Displays a dialog box used for inserting a hyperlink
F7   Starts the spelling checker

Help

F1   Displays the Assistant
Shift+F1   Displays the ⟲? pointer

Outlook Keyboard Shortcuts

Ctrl+Shift+A   Creates a new appointment
Ctrl+Shift+C   Creates a new contact
Ctrl+Shift+L   Creates a new distribution list
Ctrl+Shift+E   Creates a new folder
Ctrl+Shift+J   Creates a new journal entry
Ctrl+Shift+Q   Creates a new meeting request
Ctrl+Shift+M   Creates a new message
Ctrl+Shift+K   Creates a new task

Word Keyboard Shortcuts

View

Ctrl+F2   Print previews the document
Alt+Ctrl+P   Switches to Print Layout view
Alt+Ctrl+O   Switches to Outline view
Alt+Ctrl+N   Switches to Normal view

Window

Ctrl+F5   Restores the document's window
Ctrl+F10   Maximizes the document's window
Alt+F5   Restores the Word window
Alt+F10   Maximizes the Word window
Ctrl+F6 Displays the next open document's window
Ctrl+Shift+F6   Displays the previous open document's window

Selection

F8 (once)   Starts selection
F8 (twice)   Selects a word
F8 (three times)   Selects a sentence
F8 (four times)   Selects a paragraph
F8 (five times)   Selects the entire document
Shift+F8   Reduces selection to previous level
Shift+Arrow key   Selects in direction of arrow
Shift+End   Selects to the end of the line
Shift+Home   Selects to the beginning of the line
Shift+PgDn   Selects one screen down
Shift+PgUp   Selects one screen up
Ctrl+Shift+Right arrow   Selects to the end of a word
Ctrl+Shift+Left arrow   Selects to the beginning of a word
Ctrl+Shift+Down arrow   Selects to the end of the paragraph
Ctrl+Shift+Up arrow   Selects the beginning of the paragraph

Insertion Point Movement

Ctrl+Left arrow   Left one word
Ctrl+Right arrow   Right one word
Ctrl+Up arrow   Up one paragraph
Ctrl+Down arrow   Down one paragraph
Ctrl+PgUp   To the top of the previous page
Ctrl+PgDn   To the top of the next page
Ctrl+Home   To the beginning of the document
Ctrl+End   To the end of the document

Character Formatting

Ctrl+Shift+Plus sign Applies or removes superscript formatting
Ctrl+Equal sign   Applies or removes subscript formatting
Ctrl+B   Applies or removes bold formatting
Ctrl+I   Applies or removes italic formatting
Ctrl+U   Applies or removes underline formatting

Ctrl+Shift+A   Applies or removes all capital letters
Ctrl+Shift+F   Selects the font in the Font list on the toolbar
Ctrl+Shift+P   Selects the size in the Font Size list on the toolbar
Ctrl+D   Displays the Font dialog box with the Font options displayed
Ctrl+Shift+>   Increases the font size
Ctrl+Shift+<   Decreases the font size
Shift+F3   Changes the capitalization of selected text
Ctrl+Spacebar   Removes all character formatting

Paragraph Formatting

Ctrl+1   Single spaces the selected paragraph
Ctrl+2   Double spaces the selected paragraph
Ctrl+E   Centers the selected paragraph
Ctrl+J   Justifies the selected paragraph
Ctrl+L   Left aligns the selected paragraph
Ctrl+R   Right aligns the selected paragraph
Ctrl+M   Indents paragraph from the left
Ctrl+Shift+M   Removes left indented paragraph
Ctrl+T   Creates hanging indent
Ctrl+Shift+T   Removes hanging indent
Ctrl+Q   Removes all paragraph formatting

Editing

Ctrl+Enter   Inserts a manual page break
Alt+Shift+D   Inserts a date stamp
Alt+Shift+T   Inserts a time stamp
Alt+Shift+P   Inserts a page number
Ctrl+Backspace   Deletes one word to the left
Ctrl+Delete   Deletes one word to the right
F7   Starts the Spelling and Grammar Checker
Shift+F7   Starts the Thesaurus

Table

Alt+Home   Moves to the first cell in a row
Alt+End   Moves to the last cell in a row
Alt+PgUp   Moves to the first cell in a column
Alt+PgDn   Moves to the last cell in a column
Ctrl+Tab   Inserts a tab character in a cell
Shift+Enter   Starts a new paragraph in the cell

Style

Ctrl+Shift+N   Applies the Normal style
Alt+Ctrl+1   Applies the Heading 1 style
Alt+Ctrl+2   Applies the Heading 2 style
Alt+Ctrl+3   Applies the Heading 3 style

Outline View

Alt+Shift+Plus sign   Expands text under a heading
Alt+Shift+Minus sign   Collapses text under a heading
Alt+Shift+A Expands or collapses all text or headings
Alt+Shift+1   Displays all heading 1 paragraphs
Alt+Shift+n Displays all headings up to level n

Alt+Shift+Left arrow   Formats a heading one level up
Alt+Shift+Right arrow   Formats a heading one level down

Excel Keyboard Shortcuts

Window

Ctrl+F5   Restores the document's window
Ctrl+F9   Minimizes the document's window
Ctrl+F10   Maximizes the document's window
Ctrl+F6   Displays the next open document's window
Ctrl+Shift+F6   Displays the previous open document's window

Active Cell Movement

Ctrl+End   To the last cell containing data in the worksheet
Ctrl+Home   To cell A1
Home   To the first cell in the current row
Tab   Right one cell in the current row
Shift+Tab   Left one cell in the current row

Selection

F8   Starts selection
Ctrl+A   Selects the entire worksheet
Shift+Arrow key   Selects in direction of arrow
Shift+Spacebar   Selects the current row
Ctrl+Spacebar   Selects the current column

Formatting

Ctrl+Shift+$ Applies Currency format
Ctrl+Shift+%   Applies Percent format
Ctrl+Shift+!   Applies Number format with two decimal places
Ctrl+Shift+~   Applies General number format
Ctrl+Shift+^   Applies Scientific number format
Ctrl+Shift+#   Applies Date format
Ctrl+Shift+@   Applies Time format
Ctrl+B   Applies or removes bold formatting
Ctrl+I   Applies or removes italic formatting
Ctrl+U   Applies or removes underline formatting
Ctrl+9   Hides rows
Ctrl+Shift+(Displays hidden rows
Ctrl+0   Hides the current column
Ctrl+Shift+)   Displays hidden columns
Alt+' (apostrophe)   Displays the Style dialog box
Ctrl+1   Displays the Format Cells dialog box
Shift+F3   Displays the Insert Function dialog box

Editing

F2   Edits the current cell
F11   Creates a column chart
Alt+Enter   Starts a new line in the same cell

Ctrl+Shift+" (quote)   Copies contents of above cell
Ctrl+Shift+: (colon)   Inserts current time into cell
Ctrl+; (semicolon)   Inserts current date into cell
Ctrl+' (apostrophe)   Copies the formula from the cell above into the current cell
Ctrl+` (accent grave)   Alternates between displaying cell values and cell formulas
F4   Changes a cell's referencing methods (absolute or relative)
F9   Recalculate now

Access Keyboard Shortcuts

Window

Ctrl+F6   Cycles between open windows
F11   Brings database window to the front

Insertion Point Movement

Tab   To the next field
Shift+Tab   To the previous field
End   To the last entry in a record
Home   To the first entry in a record

Selection

F8   Starts selection (in Datasheet and Form view)
F8 (once)   Selects current entry (in Datasheet and Form view)
F8 (twice)   Selects field (in Datasheet and Form view)
F8 (three times)   Selects record (in Datasheet and Form view)
Ctrl+PgUp   Selects first field in record (in Datasheet view)
Ctrl+PgDn   Selects last field in record (in Datasheet view)
Ctrl+A   Selects the entire table
Shift+Right arrow   Selects one character to the right
Shift+Left arrow   Selects one character to the left
Shift+Up arrow   Selects to the beginning of a field
Shift+Down arrow   Selects to the end of a field

Editing

F5   Selects current record number in Record Controls
Ctrl+Enter   Starts a new line in the same entry
Ctrl+' (apostrophe)   Copies contents of same field from previous record
Ctrl+Shift+: (colon)   Inserts current time into field
Ctrl+; (semicolon)   Inserts current date into field
Ctrl+Plus sign   Adds a new record
Ctrl+Minus sign   Deletes the current record
F9   Recalculates the fields in a window

PowerPoint Keyboard Shortcuts

Ctrl+M   Inserts a new slide
Ctrl+D   Creates a duplicate of the selected slide
F6   Switch to the next pane (clockwise)
Shift+F6   Switch to the previous pane (counterclockwise)

Slide Show Controls

N, Enter, Page Down, Right arrow, Down arrow, Spacebar   Performs the next animation or advances to the next slide

Page Up, Left arrow, Up arrow, Backspace, P   Performs the previous animation or returns to the previous slide

B, Period   Displays a black screen or returns to the slide show

W, Comma   Displays a white screen or returns to the slide show

S, Plus sign   Stops or restarts an automatic slide show

Esc, Ctrl+Break, Hyphen   Ends a slide show

Both mouse buttons for 2 seconds   Returns to the first slide

Shift+F10, right-click   Displays the shortcut menu

F1   Displays a list of controls

Appendix C
Creating Customized Forms and Reports

Chapters 13 and 15 explained how to create Access relational database forms and reports using the Form Wizard and Report Wizard. This appendix discusses creating and modifying forms and reports in Design view.

C.1 Creating Forms in Design View

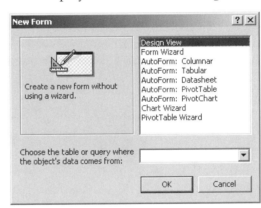

A form is created in Design view by first clicking Forms in the Database window and then clicking the New button (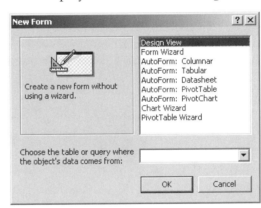) on the Database window toolbar, which displays the New Form dialog box:

Form Layout

A form layout is the arrangement of the fields on the form. When creating customized forms, a form layout should be planned in sketches that place more important and frequently used fields first.

After selecting Design View in the list, a table name must be selected in Choose the table or query where the object's data comes from list. Selecting OK displays a Form window:

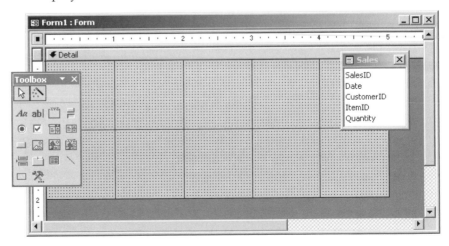

Form Design view has the features:

- a **Toolbox** with controls for placing objects on the form.
- the **Detail section** where objects are placed.
- a **Field list** with fields from the table selected in the New Form dialog box.

adding fields to a form   A field is added to a form by dragging the field name from the field list to the Detail section, which inserts a field name object and a field box object. In the form below, all the fields have been placed on the form:

Note the fields can be arranged in any order. This allows a form to be customized for usability.

adding all fields   All the fields in the Field list can be added at once by first double-clicking the title bar, which selects all the fields in the list, and then dragging the selected fields to the Detail section.

A form is saved by selecting <u>S</u>ave (Ctrl+S) from the <u>F</u>ile menu or clicking the Save button ( ) on the toolbar. The View button ( ) on the toolbar can be used to switch a form between Design view and Form view.

The Form window is closed by clicking the Close button ( ) in the upper-right corner of the window.

C.2 Customizing Forms in Design View

An existing form is displayed in Design view by selecting the form name in the Database window and then clicking the Design button () on the Database window toolbar. Forms created using the Form Wizard can be customized in Design view.

move handle   Clicking a field selects both the field name object and the field box object. Dragging a move handle repositions that object. Note the pointer:

Both objects can be moved together by holding down the Ctrl key and dragging the center of either the field name object or the field box object. Moving objects as a group maintains the current spacing. Multiple objects are selected by holding down the Shift key while clicking the objects to be move. Clicking outside an object removes the selection from all objects.

A Guide to Microsoft Office XP Professional

size handle

Dragging a size handle changes the object size. Note the ⬌ pointer:

Object Sizes

The size of field name and field box objects determine the number of characters displayed not the number of characters stored.

sizing the Detail section

Labels can be added to the form to describe its contents and supply information about fields. A label is added by first selecting the Label control in the Toolbox (Aa), which changes the pointer to ⁺A. Next, clicking the pointer on the form places the insertion point. Typing text and then pressing Enter creates a label. A label can be moved by dragging. A selected label is deleted by pressing the Delete key.

When adding, moving, or deleting fields from a form, it may be necessary to size the Detail section by dragging the black line separating the Detail section from the dark gray area.

Field names, field boxes, and labels are formatted by selecting an object and then applying formatting using buttons on the toolbar. The background color of the form can be changed by clicking an empty portion of the Detail section and then selecting a color from the Fill/Back Color button (🪣▾) on the toolbar.

C.3 Creating Reports in Design View

🗋 New

A report is created in Design view by first clicking Reports in the Database window and then clicking the New button (🗋 New) on the Database window toolbar, which displays the New Report dialog box:

Report Layout

A report's layout is based on the fields it should contain. If fields from different tables are be included in a report, the report should be based on a select query.

New Report

Create a new report without using a wizard.

Design View
Report Wizard
AutoReport: Columnar
AutoReport: Tabular
Chart Wizard
Label Wizard

Choose the table or query where the object's data comes from:

OK   Cancel

After selecting Design View in the list, a table or query name must be selected in Choose the table or query where the object's data comes from list. Selecting OK displays a Report window as shown on the next page:

- a **Toolbox** with controls for placing objects on the report.

- the **Page Header section** for placing information that should appear at the top of every page.

- the **Detail section** for placing the field box objects.

- the **Page Footer section** for placing information that should appear at the bottom of every page.

- a **Field list** with fields from the table or query selected in the New Report dialog box.

adding fields   The steps for adding a field to a report are:

1. Drag the field from the field list to the Detail section. A field name object and field box object are displayed.

2. Select the field name object and then select Cut from the Edit menu.

3. Click the Page Header section and then select Paste from the Edit menu. The field name object is placed in the Page Header section.

4. Drag the objects to align the field name object and field box object so that the field name is directly above the field box.

The steps above can be repeated to add multiple fields to the report. After all the fields have been added, the Detail section should be shortened by dragging the bottom boundary. Objects in a report can be sized just as in Form Design view. For example, the DRF Sales Report in Design view may look similar to:

A report is saved by selecting Save (Ctrl+S) from the File menu or clicking the Save button ( ) on the toolbar. The View button ( ) on the toolbar can be used to switch a form between Design view and Report view.

The Report window is closed by clicking the Close button (☒) in the upper-right corner of the window.

C.4 Customizing Reports in Design View

An existing report is displayed in Design view by selecting the report name in the Database window and then clicking the Design button (Design) on the Database window toolbar. Reports created using the Reports Wizard can be customized in Design view.

A report usually contains a report header with a title and a report footer with summaries. Selecting Report Header/Footer from the View menu displays the Report Header and Report Footer sections. The information in these sections is displayed on the first and last pages of the report, respectively.

The records in a report can be sorted and grouped. Selecting the Sorting and Grouping button ( ) from the toolbar displays a dialog box. A field to base a sort is selected from the top Field/Expression box. A sort order is selected from the top Sort Order box:

Grouping is specified by selecting a field in a Field/Expression box and then selecting Yes in either the Group Header or Group Footer box, which automatically adds a section to the report where the corresponding field box object can be dragged.

C.5 Adding Summaries to a Report

A summary is added to a report by creating a formula in a Text Box object in the Report Footer section. For example, to display the number of records in a Sales report:

1. Select the Text Box control (abl) in the Toolbox.

2. Click the ⁺abl pointer in the Report Footer section, which displays two objects. The left object is for a label, and the right object is for a formula.

3. Select the label object, click again to place the insertion point, and type Sales records.

4. Place the insertion point in the object that will store the formula and type =COUNT([TransID]).

5. Drag the objects until they are properly aligned.

When the report is previewed or printed, Sales records and the total number of sales records are displayed on the last page of the report.

To learn more about customizing reports, exam reports created using the Report Wizard in Design view. For example, in Design view, the June Temperatures report created in Chapter 15 using the Report Wizard looks similar to:

Note the grouping, headers, footers, and summary. Note also the different formats.

Index

S

SAFE 1-18
Safety and Freedom through Encryption Act of 1999 *see* SAFE
sales representative 1-20
Same as Previous button 7-14, 7-15
sans serif fonts 5-4
Save All command 12-2
Save and Close button 2-7, 2-10, 2-13, 3-3, 4-13
Save As command 5-14, 11-4, 14-13
Save As Query button 13-22
Save As Query command 13-22
Save as Web Page command 11-20
Save button
Save button 4-10, 8-6, 12-2, 13-8, 13-19, 14-6, 14-11
Save command 4-4, 4-7, 8-6, 13-8, 12-2, 14-6, 14-11, 17-3
saving
   document 4-7
   event 2-7
   file 12-2
   workbook 8-6
   worksheet 8-4
scanner 1-12
scanning 3-19
schedule 2-2
scheduling an all day event 2-6
Scientific formats 8-12
screen 17-1
screen saver files 3-12
ScreenTip 4-10, 7-11, 7-17, A-1
scripts 3-12
scroll arrow 4-17
scroll bars 4-17, 4-18, 8-2
scroll box 4-17, 4-18
scroll
   document 7-11
   preventing 11-10
   records 13-14
   sheets 10-2
search text 6-4
searching 9-2
second generation computers 1-6
section break 7-12
   continuous 7-12
   deleting 7-13
section headers and footers 7-14
section page numbers 7-15
sections 7-12, 7-18
   creating in a document 7-12
security 3-12
Select All button 8-10
Select All command 5-2
Select All Records command 16-1
select query 14-10
   applying 14-11
   creating 14-9
   deleting 14-13
   modifying 14-13
   saving 14-11

select query *continued*
   sorting results 14-14
   text criteria 14-16
   using a range 14-16
Selected Chart Title command 10-24
Selected Legend command 10-24
selecting
   cells 8-10
   text 5-2
Send a Copy button 7-20
Send button 3-12, 3-21
Send/Receive button 3-12
series 8-23, 10-7
serif fonts 5-4
server 1-13, 1-15
Set Print Area command 11-14
sheet 8-1
   adding 10-2
   copying data between 10-2
   data *see* data
   deleting 10-2
   displaying 10-1
   moving data between 10-2
   order 10-2
      changing 10-2
   printing 10-5
   renaming 10-1
   scroll buttons 10-2
   scrolling 10-2
   tab 8-2
      color 10-1
      right-clicking 10-1
   using multiple 10-1
Shift key 5-2, 8-10
Shockley, William 1-6
short date/time field format 13-3
Show Level list 7-9
Show Table button 14-5, 14-13
Show Table command 14-13
Show the Office Assistant command 4-4, A-1
Show/Hide ¶ button 4-11
signature 3-15
silicon wafers 1-7
single field type 13-2, 13-7
single spacing 5-11
size
   font 5-5
   field 13-2
slice 10-7
slide 17-1, 17-18
   adding 17-6
   adding a chart 17-16
   adding a picture 17-8
   adding footers 17-13
   deleting 17-6
   displaying 17-3
   sketches 17-17
slide buttons 17-3
Slide Design task pane 17-14, 17-18
slide icon 17-3
slide indicator 17-4
Slide Layout task pane 17-6

Slide Master command 17-18
Slide Master View toolbar 17-19
Slide Master 17-18
   Close 17-19
   Title 17-19
Slide Navigator command 17-4
slide order
   changing 17-9
   displaying 17-9
slide pane 17-2
Slide Show button 17-4
Slide Show command 17-3
Slide Show view 17-13, 17-14
Slide Sorter command 17-3
Slide Sorter view 17-3, 17-15
Slide Sorter View button 17-9
slide transition 17-13
Slide Transition command 17-14
Slide Transition task pane 17-14
slide transitions 17-3
Slides option 17-10
Small Booklet Style 3-8
smart menu 5-2
smart tag 4-12, 8-15
   indicator 4-12
Smart Tag Actions button 4-12
Smithsonian 1-4
software 1-9, 1-15
solid line
   creating with table leaders 5-22
Sort Ascending button 11-2, 14-2, 16-5
Sort Ascending command 14-2
Sort box 14-14
Sort command 11-3
Sort Descending button 11-3, 14-2, 16-5
Sort Descending command 14-2
sort order 15-4
sorting
   data 11-2
   key sort column 11-3
   select query results 14-14
   records 14-2
Sorting and Grouping button C5
source 9-3
Source Data command 10-20, 10-22
space mark 4-11
spaces after a period 4-3
speaker 17-1
speaker notes 17-3, 17-20
special characters *see* symbols
   finding 6-5
speech 17-1
Spelling button 8-6
spelling checker 4-8, 17-6
spelling checker 3-11, 8-6
spreadsheet 8-1, 8-2,
   see also workbook, worksheet
SRAM 1-9
standard field format 13-3
Stanford Research Institute 1-15
star topology 1-13, 1-14

U

U.S. Census Bureau 1-3, 1-5
Underline button 5-6, 8-12
underline text 5-6
underlined letter 4-4
Undo Automatic Numbering option
   6-16
Undo button 5-2, 8-4, 9-8, 10-13
Undo command 5-1, 8-4, 9-8, 10-13
Unfreeze Panes command 11-10
Unicode 1-10
units of measure 6-10
UNIVAC 1-5, 1-8
universal machine 1-5
University of California 1-15
University of Pennsylvania 1-4
Update Field button 16-4
Update TOC button 7-12
updating, record 14-3
upstream 1-16
URL 7-17
USENET 1-17
user name 3-9

V

vacuum tubes 1-5
values 8-3, 8-11
vCalendar 3-20
vCard 3-18
vertical bar chart 10-7
View button 2-3, 13-15, 14-1, 14-13
View Show command 17-4
view
   changing 4-17
   Datasheet 13-15, 14-1, 14-10
   Design 13-6, 13-15
   Filter by Form 13-21, 13-23
   Normal 4-16
   Print Layout 4-16
   Calendar 2-4
Virtual 3-18
virus 3-19
   the Love Bug 3-19
virus definitions 3-19
Visual Basic .NET 1-6
visuals 17-1
VLOOKUP
   function 11-8
   table 11-8
   using text 11-12
von Leibniz, Gottfried Wilhelm 1-1
von Neumann, John 1-5

W

WAN 1-12
wavy line, green 4-9
wavy line, red 4-8
Web see WWW
web browser 1-16, 7-17, 11-20
Web Layout view button 4-17

web site 1-16, 7-17
web, saving worksheet for 11-20
Webmaster 1-20
Week button 2-4
Week command 2-4
What's This? Command 6-12
Wide-Area Network see WAN
Width command 8-9
wildcard 14-22
Window menu 12-1
Windows Taskbar 4-1
Windows XP 1-10
Wingdings 5-4
wireless local-area network
   see WLAN
wireless networks 1-14
Word Count command 6-20
word processor 4-1
Word window 4-2, 4-4, 4-9
word wrap 4-3
word, synonym 6-8
words, counting 6-21
Work Week button 2-4
Work Week command 2-4
workbook 8-1, 8-2,
   see also worksheet
   closing 8-6
   copying data between 12-3
   creating from a table 16-6
   embedding 12-15
   linking 12-15
   saving 8-6
worksheet 10-1, see also sheet
Worksheet command 10-2
worksheet 8-1
   data see data
   errors 8-14
   letters 8-2
   numbers 8-2
   e-mailing 11-19
   expanding 9-1
   hyperlink 11-17
   planning 9-1
   previewing 8-6, 8-8
   printing 8-6, 9-10, 11-10, 11-14
   saving as HTML 11-20
   saving for web 11-20
   sketch 9-2
World Wide Web see WWW
worm 3-19
Wozniak, Stephen 1-8, 1-9
wrapping text 4-3
write for space 6-20
write, data 1-6
WWW 1-16, 7-17

X

x-axis labels 10-8
x-axis title 10-8
y-axis title 10-8

Z

Zoom box 4-17
Zoom button 8-6
Zoom command 4-17